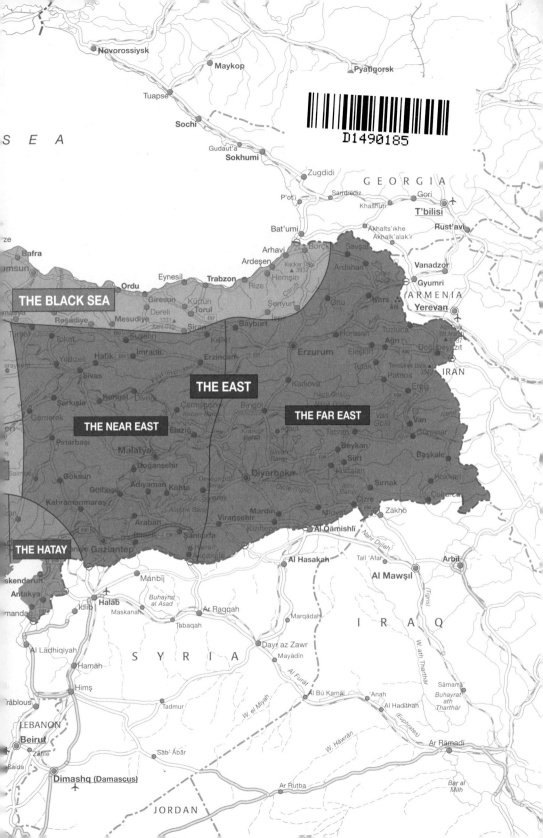

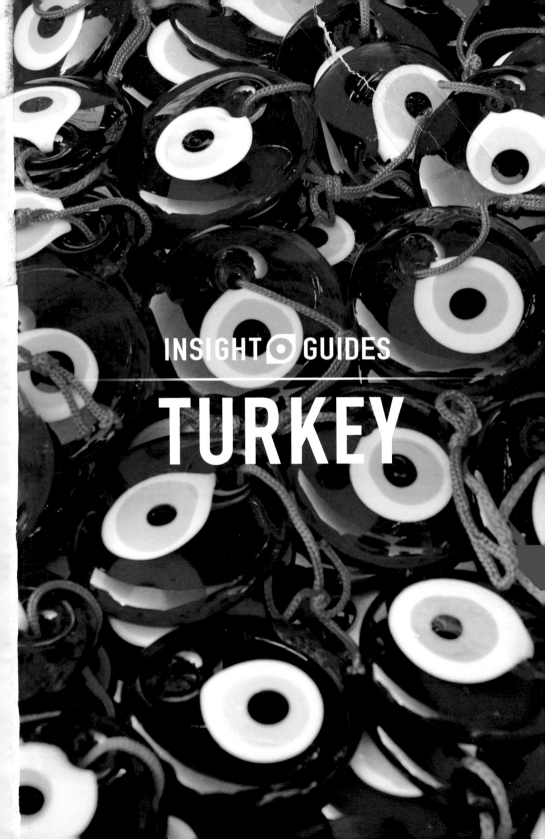

INSIGHT ◉ GUIDES

TURKEY

PLAN & BOOK
YOUR TAILOR-MADE TRIP

BRAZIL   **CHILE**   **ECUADOR**

TAILOR-MADE TRIPS & UNIQUE EXPERIENCES CREATED BY LOCAL TRAVEL EXPERTS AT INSIGHTGUIDES.COM/HOLIDAYS

Insight Guides has been inspiring travellers with high-quality travel content for over 45 years. As well as our popular guidebooks, we now offer the opportunity to book tailor-made private trips completely personalised to your needs and interests. By connecting with one of our local experts, you will directly benefit from their expertise and local know-how, helping you create memories that will last a lifetime.

HOW INSIGHTGUIDES.COM/HOLIDAYS WORKS

STEP 1
Pick your dream destination and submit an enquiry, or modify an existing itinerary if you prefer.

STEP 2
Fill in a short form, sharing details of your travel plans and preferences with a local expert.

STEP 3
Your local expert will create your personalised itinerary, which you can amend until you are completely satisfied.

STEP 4
Book securely online. Pack your bags and enjoy your holiday! Your local expert will be available to answer questions during your trip.

BENEFITS OF PLANNING & BOOKING AT INSIGHTGUIDES.COM/HOLIDAYS

PLANNED BY LOCAL EXPERTS

The Insight Guides local experts are hand-picked, based on their experience in the travel industry and their impeccable standards of customer service.

SAVE TIME & MONEY

When a local expert plans your trip, you save time and money when you book, even during high season. You won't be charged for using a credit card either.

TAILOR-MADE TRIPS

Book with Insight Guides, and you will be in complete control of the planning process, from the initial selections to amending your final itinerary.

BOOK & TRAVEL STRESS-FREE

Enjoy stress-free travel when you use the Insight Guides secure online booking platform. All bookings come with a money-back guarantee.

WHAT OTHER TRAVELLERS THINK ABOUT TRIPS BOOKED AT INSIGHTGUIDES.COM/HOLIDAYS

Trip to Portugal

Every step of the planning process and the trip itself was effortless and exceptional. Our special interests, preferences and requests were accommodated resulting in a trip that exceeded our expectations.

Corinne, USA   ★★★★★

Trip to Vietnam

The organization was superb, the drivers professional, and accommodation quite comfortable. I was well taken care of! My thanks to your colleagues who helped make my trip to Vietnam such a great experience. My only regret is that I couldn't spend more time in the country.

Heather   ★★★★★

DON'T MISS OUT
BOOK NOW AT
INSIGHTGUIDES.COM/HOLIDAYS

CONTENTS

Travel tips

Maps

LEGEND
Insight on
Photo story

THE BEST OF TURKEY:
TOP ATTRACTIONS

△ **Istanbul.** The capital of two great empires has an unrivalled position on straits separating Europe from Asia, superb Byzantine and Ottoman monuments, and some of the best dining and entertainment opportunities in the country. See page 127.

▽ **Pamukkale.** The solidified mineral-rich "waterfalls" of the pale travertine terraces are a cliché of Turkish tourism, but unmissable nonetheless; the extensive remains of Roman Hierapolis up top are an added bonus. See page 221.

▷ **Colossal heads at Nemrut Dağı.** Mountaintop shrine in the middle of nowhere, this monument to the pretensions of an obscure local satrap of the 1st century BC is best viewed at sunrise or sunset. See page 350.

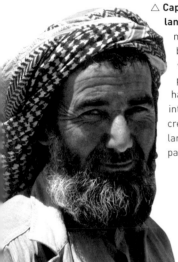

△ **Cappadocian landscapes.** Created millions of years ago by two nearby volcanoes, the tuff-pinnacle badlands have been eroded into bizarre shapes to create a dreamlike landscape. See page 309.

△ **Museum of Anatolian Civilisations, Ankara.** Outstanding collection of artefacts spanning Anatolia's early history, from the Palaeolithic to the Phrygian eras. See page 289.

△ **Ephesus.** The most extensive and best-preserved ancient city in Turkey. See page 212.

▷ **Sumela Monastery.** An ancient Byzantine monastery hidden away in a spectacular forested canyon. See page 331.

△ **Şanlıurfa.** Get a feel of the Middle East in this ancient town in the southeast of the country. One of the most atmospheric places in Turkey, replete with overhanging medieval houses and warren-like bazaars. See page 352.

▽ **Lycian Rock Tombs.** There are literally thousands of them, seemingly no two alike, in the most improbable places along the Turquoise Coast; with their graceful profiles and relief carvings they're irresistibly photogenic. See page 238.

▷ **Ani ruins.** The former capital of Bagratid Armenia, which flourished from the 10th to the 13th centuries, contains several of the finest Armenian churches in this region, amid dramatic scenery. See page 366.

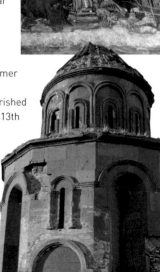

THE BEST OF TURKEY: EDITOR'S CHOICE

The wonderfully preserved Theatre at Aspendos.

BEST ANCIENT MONUMENTS

Trajan Temple, Pergamon. German archaeologists have re-erected columns and architraves in partial atonement for a compatriot's abduction of the nearby Zeus altar reliefs. See page 197.

Library of Celsus, Ephesus. Effectively the logo of the site, this 2nd-century AD endowment with its elaborate façade has been assiduously restored by Austrian excavators. See page 214.

Tetrapylon Gate, Aphrodisias. An astonishing elaborate structure just to mark the intersection of two Roman streets, this cluster of columns supports finely worked pediments. See page 221.

The Theatre, Aspendos. Roman imperial structure in almost as good condition as when new – and accordingly a supremely atmospheric festival venue. See page 260.

Zeus temple, Aizanoi. With standing walls and columns, the most complete of three Zeus temples in Anatolia, a Corinthian affair funded by Emperor Hadrian. See page 300.

Monumental gates, Boğazkale. Massive gates flanked by relief carvings punctuate the incredible 6km (4 miles) of walls enclosing this capital of the once-mighty Hittite empire. See page 306.

Trajan Temple at Pergamon.

BEST EXPERIENCES

"Blue Cruise" along the southwest coast. Discover secluded, pine-shaded coves and islets between Bodrum and Finike on a traditional *gulet*. See page 381.

Hot-air ballooning over Cappadocia. A bird's-eye, early-morning view of the region's volcanic formations. See page 394.

Mevlevî ceremony, Galata Mevlevîhanesi. More atmospheric, and genuine, than the tourist events – the whirling dancers here really are practising dervishes. See page 144.

Taking a Turkish bath. Indulge yourself with the full treatment in a historic hamam. See page 152.

Anamur castle dominates the shoreline.

BEST SOUVENIR PURCHASES

İznik tiles. These quartz-based, intricately glazed products of a revived craft are streets ahead of resort-shop dross, and worth every extra penny. See page 175.

Cezeriye. Forget *lokum* (Turkish delight) with its artificial colours and preservatives; this delectable carrot-and-coconut confection is actually good for you. See page 100.

Sahlep mix. Pure *sahlep* – ground orchid root – is banned for export, so buy *sahlep*-rich mixes for this hot drink sovereign against colds. See page 99.

Leather jackets. For that slightly retro, elegant-gangster look, nothing beats a black or tan, well-cut item available in almost any significant resort. See page 139.

Carpets. Focus of the hard-sell in every resort, but the quintessential Turkish folk art makes a souvenir you'll have decades of enjoyment from. See pages 112 and 404.

Nar ekşisi. Sour pomegranate syrup, a nod to Persian influence in the cuisine, has various uses: in salad dressings, meat marinades, even beer! See page 95.

Gulets at Bodrum.

BEST MEDIEVAL CASTLES

Bozcaada (Tenedos). Huge but now domesticated and fetchingly lit by night; Byzantines, Genoese, Venetians and Turks have successively modified it. See page 186.

St Peter's, Bodrum. Once a main stronghold of the crusading Knights of St John, now well restored and home to several worthwhile museums. See page 225.

Anamur (Mamure Kalesi). Among the most romantically sited castles in Turkey, a huge Armenian-built seaside affair with its toes in the sand. See page 267.

Korykos and Kız Kalesi. Not-quite-twin castles, built by the Byzantines and local Armenian kings: one on land, the other facing it on an islet. See page 271.

İshak Paşa Sarayı, Doğubeyazıt. More fortified pleasure-palace than castle, this engaging pastiche of every conceivable indigenous Anatolian style seems a mirage in this bleak landscape. See page 367.

Hoşap, Hakkâri. Fairytale castle on a crag, the redoubt of a 17th-century Kurdish chieftain. See page 373.

Carpet vendor.

Turkey's southern and western coasts are fringed by long sandy beaches and crystal-clear water.

BEST MOSQUES

Selimiye Camii, Edirne. The masterwork of the great Ottoman imperial architect Sinan, its dome and four minarets dominating the town from its hilltop. See page 160.

Süleymaniye Camii, Istanbul. Another work of Sinan: some connoisseurs claim it as his best, with its dome soaring 47 metres (154ft) from the floor. See page 140.

Yeşil Camii, Bursa. Although never quite finished outside, riotous blue and green Tabriz tiles inside, culminating in the sultan's loge, make this exceptional. See page 173.

Ulu Camii, Birgi. Post-Seljuk, pre-Ottoman oddity that feels almost Andalusian with its interior Roman colonnade, gabled roof and bands of green tilework. See page 207.

Eşrefoğlu Camii, Beyşehir. The apotheosis of all-wood mosques in Turkey, with a veritable forest inside of naturally illuminated carved columns, rafters and galleries. See page 303.

Mahmud Bey Camii, Kasaba. This wooden mosque rivals Eşrefoğlu with its polychrome railings, carved entrance and coffered ceiling. See page 326.

Ulu Camii, Diyarbakır. The first great Seljuk mosque, built in 1091, extensively recycling masonry from earlier pagan and Christian buildings on the site. See page 370.

BEST BEACHES

Kıyıköy, Thrace. Long, amazingly undeveloped sand beaches fed by lazy rivers flank this old Byzantine stronghold on the Black Sea. See page 164.

Aydıncık, Gökçeada. Soft, heaped blonde sand, transparent, flattish waters – and yet a prime windsurfing spot, on this barely developed north Aegean island. See page 167.

Altınkum, Çeşme. Sand backing to dunes, iridescent water, low-key water sports, and a slightly alternative ethos make this chain of small coves a winner. See page 199.

Mesudiye Ova Bükü, Datça peninsula. A stretch of gold-brown sand bookended by two headlands framing the island of Tílos, and washed by surprisingly bracing water, make this a popular boat-trip destination. See page 230.

Patara. The longest (15km/9 miles) continuous beach in Turkey, its thick sand a turtle-nesting ground, with boogie-boarding possible in summer. See page 243.

Çıralı. Long, sand-and-pebble beach that's another turtle destination, but with a superior inland backdrop to Patara's, and calmer, deeper water. See page 249.

Side. Plenty of (commercialised) sand here, with every creature comfort to hand, but it offers the novelty of ancient ruins right on the beach. See page 261.

BEST BITES

For more information on Turkish specialities, see page 93.

Semiz Otu. Literally 'fat weed' – after the succulent lobular leaves of purslane, made into a refreshing dip with yoghurt.

Pide. Turkish 'pizza' – always fresh and piping hot from the oven, cut into bite-sized slices; ideally paired with ayran yoghurt drink.

İçli köfte. Bulgur, nuts, vegetables and ground meat in a spicy crust. A moreish starter.

Mantı. The ultimate comfort food – central Asian mince-stuffed ravioli doused in yoghurt and chilli oil.

Hunkâr beğendi. Rich dish of lamb, aubergine purée and cheese – a good winter choice.

Tavukgöğsu. Boiled and strained chicken meat, semolina starch and milk pudding – a lot tastier than it sounds.

Kazandibi Golden. Crusted backed treat of flour, corn starch, sugar, milk and vanilla.

BEST TRADITIONAL TOWNS AND VILLAGES

Cumalıkızık. Time-warped village of semi-fortified houses near Bursa. See page 174.

Adatepe. Architectural showcase with solid mansions ringed by the same volcanic rocks they're built from. See page 191.

Şirince. This hill village of substantial houses is the coolest place to stay near Ephesus. See page 216.

Muğla. Sprawling hillside old quarter of tiled houses with beaked chimneys and curious doors. See page 231.

Safranbolu. Museum town of elaborate, three-storey, half-timbered mansions that still supports some of the trades that made it prosper. See page 323.

Yörük Köyü. Saranbolu too busy? Then head a short way east to this isolated, smaller version of its neighbour, with dozens of listed mansions. See page 324.

Amasya. Ottoman mansions, Selçuk and Mongol monuments and ancient cliff-tombs, all straddling a river. See page 326.

Mardin. Tawny-stone, Arab-style medieval dwellings, leavened by churches and mosques in a spectacular blufftop setting. See page 367.

BEST HIKES AND TREKS

Trekking in the Kaçkar mountains. They may not be Turkey's highest range, but certainly rank among the most beautiful, and user-friendly. See page 332.

Trekking the Lycian Way. This coastal route, ideal for spring or autumn, notionally takes five weeks to complete, but the wildest, most popular sections are near Fethiye between Kabak and Gavurağili, and between Kaş and Üçağız. See page 243.

Hiking in the Aladağlar. This easterly portion of the Toros Mountains, with jagged karstic peaks bracketed narrow valleys and high passes. Access is initially from Niğde. See page 337.

Trekking the Bolkar Toros. Very fit and self-sufficient trekkers can tackle this southernmost section of the Toros, with rewards of the startlingly blue lakes of Çini and Karagöl. Trailheads at Maden and Darboğaz villages. See page 337.

St Paul's Trail. Follow in the footsteps of the apostle on this long-distance route beginning at ancient Aspendos, using ancient Roman roads on your way up to the Anatolian plateau around Lake Eğirdir. See page 259.

Friday prayers in Süleymaniye Camii.

BEST CHURCHES

Kariye Museum (Chora Church), Istanbul. The finest mosaics and frescoes in Turkey, a late flowering of Byzantine art. See page 140.

Ihlara Vadısı, Cappadocia. The dozen accessible rock-cut churches in this idyllic valley sport wonderfully idiosyncratic frescoes, a primer of early Byzantine iconographic conventions. See page 316.

Tokalı Kilese, Cappadocia. The best-preserved frescoes of the various churches in the Göreme region. See page 312.

Öşk Vank, Georgian valleys. Massive interior columns anticipate European Gothic in the grandest of the local monastic churches. See page 335.

Deyrul Zafaran Monastery, Mardin. Named for its yellowish masonry, this ancient monastery, continuously inhabited since AD 495, was long the seat of the Syrian Orthodox patriarch. See page 368.

Armenian Church of the Holy Cross, Lake Van. The most exquisitely set (on an islet) of Anatolian Armenian churches; restored interior frescoes complement exterior reliefs of biblical scenes. See page 372.

The frescoes inside Tokalı Kilise, Göreme.

Copperware is ubiquitous in bazaars throughout Turkey.

Minarets and skyscrapers in the Levent district, Istanbul.

WELCOME TO TURKEY

There's something for everyone in Turkey. The trouble is that, for centuries, almost everyone has tried to grab a slice.

Statues of local heroes guard the entrance to Gazantiep castle.

The ancient Greeks and Romans knew it as *Asia Minor* – that landmass protruding from Asia into the eastern Mediterranean, defined by the Black Sea on the north, the Aegean to the west and Mesopotamia to the south-east. To the ancient peoples who preceded them, it was simply *Anatolia*; after 1923, under Atatürk, the country became *Türkiye*, the Land of the Turks.

Since prehistory, this sprawling land of mountain ranges, high plateaux and fertile river valleys has divided Orient and Occident. The Persian king Xerxes crossed westwards with his Asian hordes on their way to victory at Thermopylae and defeat at Salamis; Alexander the Great led his Macedonians eastwards to India in pursuit of his great empire, leaving an indelible Hellenistic stamp on Anatolia. The Romans used Asia Minor as a granary and bulwark against their enemies to the east.

Over the next 1,000 years, Anatolia became the nucleus of the Byzantine Empire, with its capital, Constantinople, undoubtedly the most powerful and magnificent city in the world. It was here that early Christianity first took root, only to be replaced by Islam, first introduced by the 7th-century Arabs, and then imposed by the Seljuk and Ottoman Turks, who pushed the frontiers of the Ottoman Empire from the Persian Gulf to the Atlantic, from Cairo to Budapest.

Antique books from the Museum of Turkish and Islamic Arts.

The collapse of the Ottomans in 1918 was followed by the abrupt and ruthless carve-up of the once-formidable empire. Yet under Kemal Atatürk's leadership, the Turks rapidly regained Anatolia and a new republic emerged to take on a very different role in the 20th century.

Following decades of explosive growth and development that transformed much of the country, Turkey's recent political and economic challenges have delivered severe blows to the tourism industry, with the number of foreign visitors dipping to 25 million in 2016. However, Turkey's newest and friendliest invasion appears back in full swing after the record-breaking year of 2018, with some 40 million foreign visitors arriving in search of warm seas, magnificent scenery, echoes of ancient history, fine food and a friendly greeting. *"Hoş geldiniz!"* – Welcome to Turkey.

GEOGRAPHY

Turkey packs a huge variety of landscapes and climatic conditions in a correspondingly large area.

Some foreigners equate Turkey with camel-populated deserts, a misconception perhaps encouraged by the "Turkish and American blend" tag-line on classic Camel cigarette boxes, and the bazaar and mosque in the desert on the back. In fact, pure sand desert is the one environment you *won't* find in the country, which offers almost everything else from subtropical cloud-forest along the eastern Black Sea coast – conditions also ideal for tea plantations and hazelnut groves – to the olive groves of the balmy Aegean Sea.

A mere three percent of Turkey's 783,560 sq km (302,532 sq mile) area – comprising Thrace and part of Istanbul – falls within Europe, though this is home to 10 percent of the population. The other 97 percent occupies the peninsula of Anatolia (*Anadolu* in Turkish), extending over 1,600km (1,000 miles) from the Aegean on the west to the eastern frontiers (though only about half that distance from the northerly Black Sea to the Mediterranean in the south).

Rock formations in the Göreme Valley.

VOLCANOES AND EARTHQUAKES

Geologically, Turkey is a complex jumble produced by the ongoing collision, beginning about 65 million years ago, of the African and Arabian tectonic plates with the Eurasian one. Consequences include volcanoes, numerous hot springs and frequent, destructive seismic activity along the North Anatolian fault, which extends in an arc from the Sea of Marmara to Lake Van. The worst recorded tremor (Richter 8), in December 1939, levelled Erzincan and killed an estimated 33,000 people, though the August 1999 İzmit earthquake (Richter 7.6), with at least 25,000 fatalities and widespread damage, figures more in recent memory. Happier results of primordial volcanic eruptions 30

Turkey's principal volcanic cones – Hasan Dağı, Erciyes Dağı, Süphan Dağı and Ağrı Dağı (5,165 metres/17,216ft, the country's highest point) – are all extinct or deeply dormant.

million years ago are the eerie badlands of Cappadocia, consisting of tuff (compressed volcanic ash) very conducive to excellent wine grapes – and bumper crops of tourists.

ANATOLIA: A NATURAL FORTRESS

The central Anatolian steppes at the heart of Turkey are naturally defended by two mountain systems, which have always iso-lated the interior from the coast climati-cally and culturally. The southerly mountain chain, forested with conifers and rising close to the Mediterranean, is the Taurus (*Toros* in Turkish), an extension of a great karst mass beginning in Dalmatia and continuing through Greece to Turkey. The foothills and coastal plain between Fethiye and Adana exhibit plenty of karstic phenomena: caves, sink-holes, deep canyons and suddenly appearing or disappearing rivers and cascades. Further

View from Tahtalı mountain above Antalya.

Ø TRANSHUMANCE

The ancient practice of transhumance still per-sists in parts of Anatolia, with shepherds migrat-ing with their livestock from winter quarters to highland pastures each summer, just as they always have. The summertime abode for the herd-ers is the *yayla*, ranging from goat-wool yurts in the Taurus to clusters of wood-and-tin shacks in the Kaçkar. Their inhabitants – various ethnic groups along the Black Sea, Yörüks near the Mediterranean – have an almost mystical bond with their *yayla*, and many Black Sea *yayla* natives now living overseas make a point of showing up every summer for reunions and festivities.

north, the Pontic ranges run parallel – and close – to the Black Sea coast, forming the edge of the Eurasian plate. Partly granitic and, especially in the easterly Kaçkar moun-tains, heavily glaciated, the slopes are clothed in broadleaf and mixed forest, particularly on the northern edge. Rivers slicing through both ranges – although fewer in the Taurus – are short and sharp as they drain to the Black Sea and the Mediterranean.

To the west, the Gediz and the Büyük Men-deres (source of English word 'meander') wind more lazily towards the Aegean, water-ing some of the country's most fertile terri-tory, full of cotton, sultanas, figs or peaches. Yet aside from these areas, the deltas of the Yeşilırmak and Kızılırmak (Turkey's longest river) bracketing tobacco-rich Samsun on the Black Sea, Thrace, and the Çukurova of the Şeyhan (near Adana), made famous by nov-elist Yaşar Kemal, there's little flat land any-where in Turkey.

The vast central plateau – with an average elevation of 1,100 metres (3,600ft), divided into discreet *ovas* (basins) – has always been a breadbasket. Many agricultural areas have seen water tables drop precipitously due to drought over recent decades, the tapping of deep fossil reserves and an over-reliance on thirsty crops like corn and sugar beets. Indeed, before well-drilling technology and modern irrigation projects, ova crops were limited to seasonal, rain-dependent wheat, oats and barley, of which Anatolia's biggest ova – the Konya Plain – continues to be the largest pro-ducer in the whole country. Here at least, the situation has been somewhat alleviated since the 2015 inauguration of the 17km "Blue Tun-nel," which diverts water to the Konya Plain from the Bağbaşı Dam (opened 2012) along the Göksu River in the Taurus. The tunnel is part of the Konya Plain Project (KOP), slated for completion in 2020, which aims to irrigate the entire basin's one million hectares of land. Questions remain over the initiative's sustain-ability and environmental impact.

For now, aside from clusters of poplars around farms or willows marking stream beds, much of the interior remains tree-less – largely the result of human (or live-stock) intervention. Reforestation was one of

Atatürk's obsessions, and most forests still belong to the state; many people have landed in jail for surreptitiously cutting down even one tree.

Most tourists head for the coast – well over 8,000km (5,000 miles) of it. The Black Sea is generally pebbly; the Mediterranean either side of Antalya is more reliably sandy, while the Aegean has the most deeply indented and variable shoreline, plus many islands.

Driving through inner Anatolia involves covering huge distances of lonely, dun-coloured landscape between towns, akin to transiting Great Basin states like Nevada or Utah, with the main signs of road-side life being the huge rest-stop complexes, modern descendants of the ancient *kervansarays*. The emptiness is not deceptive; the back country has long been depopulating for various reasons, so that Turkey is now 75 percent urbanised.

THE WILD EAST – AND MIND THE GAP

Close to the Iranian and Armenian borders where the Taurus and Pontic ranges meet in a jumbled topography known formally as the Anti-Taurus, conditions are even harsher. The mean elevation ramps up to nearly 2,000 metres (6,500 ft) and winter snowfall can cut villages off for days; summers are so short that little garden produce matures other than parsley and radishes. Outside of sheltered stream valleys, trees are even scarcer than further west, such that the heating and cooking fuel in many villages is still *tezek* (cow dung patties). It's a hard-scrabble existence, with the only significant rural livelihood derived from sugar beets, hay and livestock.

The lower-lying southeast of the country is dominated by the fan-shaped flood plain of the Euphrates and Tigris (Firat and Dicle in Turkish) rivers, Turkey's very own chunk of Mesopotamia. The region is significantly Kurdish and Arab in both culture and terrain, an undulating plateau sloping down to Syria. The colossally ambitious Southeast Anatolia

Project (*Güneydoğu Anadolu Projesi* or GAP), begun in 1974, aims to straddle both rivers with no fewer than 29 dams; the largest, Atatürk Barajı on the Firat, has made cultivation of a variety of crops possible on what was previously wasteland, while 19 of the dams will generate electric power in a country with scant petroleum reserves. But large agribusiness holdings benefit rather than small farmers (the latter often driven out by rising waters), and the scheme has proven otherwise controversial. Sharp cuts in the

A village in the Pontic mountains.

amounts of cross-border water flows have strained relations with Iraq and Syria, while many major archaeological sites such as Zeugma and Samsat have been submerged before being properly examined. Amidst ongoing international (and local) uproar, the most imminent victim is the ancient town of Hasankeyf on the Tigris, where the Ilısu Dam was completed in 2018 – despite the withdrawal of all international funding for the project in 2009. As of this writing, the filling of the dam remains on hold due to water shortage complaints across the Iraqi border, though Turkish authorities – including Erdoğan himself – appear determined to push the plan forward.

The beautifully preserved
Temple of Zeus at Euromos.

DECISIVE DATES

c.6500–5600 BC
Çatalhöyük, among the oldest agricultural communities, thrives.

c.5600–3000 BC
Fortified towns at Hacılar, Can Hasan and Yumuktepe.

c.3000–2200 BC
Sophisticated Bronze Age metallurgy proven by hoards at Troy and Alacahöyük.

c.2000–1200 BC
Hittites create the first advanced Anatolian civilisation.

c.1230–700 BC
From the Balkans and the Black Sea, the "Sea Peoples" invade; their descendants include the Phrygians.

c.850–590 BC
Urartians flourish around Lake Van; Greeks colonise coasts.

546–499 BC
Persian conquest of Anatolia by Cyrus II and Darius I.

333 BC
Alexander the Great crushes the Persians at Issos.

281 BC
Pergamon becomes an independent kingdom, allying with Rome in 190 BC.

133 BC
King Attalos III leaves Pergamon to Rome; Anatolia becomes a Roman province.

AD 45–58
Paul the Apostle evangelises Asia Minor.

Trojan horse on the Çanakkale waterfront.

AD 325
Council of Nicaea codifies Christian doctrine and condemns heresies.

BYZANTIUM, SELJUKS, CRUSADERS

AD 330
Emperor Constantine establishes capital at Byzantium, henceforth Constantinople, and encourages Christianity.

AD 391–395
Theodosius I prohibits paganism. Upon his death, Constantinople becomes seat of the Eastern, Byzantine empire, with Rome that of the Western, Latin empire.

AD 527–565
Reign of Justinian sees massive building programmes and ephemeral conquests.

637
Arab invasions begin; southeastern Anatolia Islamised. Bulgars, Armenians and Persians soon attack Byzantine borderlands.

726–843
Iconoclasts ban religious images of the human form; many churches are literally defaced.

1071–1243
Seljuk Turks rout Byzantine army at Manzikert; a Turkish-speaking, Islamic kingdom emerges in central Anatolia until defeated by the Mongols. The Byzantines retreat to the Aegean and Black Sea coasts, as well as around Istanbul.

1204
Fourth Crusade occupies Constantinople until 1261.

THE OTTOMANS

1453
The Ottomans, under Mehmet II, conquer Constantinople, and rename it Istanbul.

1512–20
Selim I conquers Mesopotamia and Egypt, styles himself caliph, head of Sunni Islam.

1520–66
Süleyman the Magnificent presides over Ottoman golden age.

1683–1830
Catastrophic defeats end Ottoman expansion; peace treaties favour the Habsburgs and Russians.

1908
Young Turk revolution results in military-parliamentary rule, with the sultan as figurehead.

Accession of Mehmet II in Edirne.

1914–18
Turkey defeated in World War I as a Central power, though Mustafa Kemal leads successful Gallipoli resistance.

THE REPUBLIC

1919–22
War of Independence: Nationalists under Kemal expel all foreign armies.

1923
Sultanate abolished; Turkey becomes a republic, with Kemal as president. Treaty of Lausanne sets borders and stipulates exchange of minorities with Greece.

1923–38
Kemal dictates sweeping reforms, including mandatory surnames.

1950–52
First free elections; Turkey joins NATO.

1960, 1971, 1980
Military factions lead coups after political-economic crises.

1974
Turkey invades Cyprus.

1984
Kurdish separatists (the PKK) begin armed insurrection.

1983–93
Turgut Özal dominates Turkish politics as prime minister and then president.

1999–2000
Catastrophic Marmara earthquake; Turkey becomes candidate for EU membership.

2002
The Islamist AK Partisi (Justice and Development Party) decisively elected.

2007–10
AK re-elected in landslide victory; its candidate, Abdullah Gül, controversially becomes president. Ergenekon military-secularist conspiracy to destabilise country uncovered.

2013–14
June 2013 protests against the building over of Gezi Parkı in Istanbul harshly suppressed but spark nationwide demonstrations against

Map of Istanbul in 1572.

Erdoğan's increasingly autocratic rule. Despite this AKP wins 2014 local elections, and he becomes president.

2015
Turkish efforts against Kurdish fighters in Syria and Islamic State attacks combine to unravel a 2013 ceasefire between government and PKK.

2016
In the wake of a failed coup attempt, President Erdoğan cracks down on suspected conspirators, detaining tens of thousands.

2018
Erdoğan wins more snap elections, securing a five-year term as president.

2019
Erdoğan's ruling AKP loses Istanbul's mayoral election after a campaign season in which the economy takes centre stage. The President demands a re-count and run of the vote, sparking protest and international condemnation.

THE CRADLE OF CIVILISATION

Straddling Europe and Asia, Anatolia was a natural junction between cultures, crucial in the development of civilisation.

Since the earliest times, Anatolia has figured prominently in the history of civilisation. The Euphrates and Tigris rivers, both rising in eastern Anatolia, flow into the heart of the so-called Fertile Crescent extending from the Nile to the Persian Gulf, while ancient Mesopotamia now lies partly in southeastern Turkey. These areas were home to some of the first human settlements on Earth (see box). Somewhat later, the Old Testament refers to local personalities – including the patriarch Abraham, who came from Edessa (now Şanlıurfa), and Noah, whose ark supposedly landed on Mount Ararat.

ANCIENT BEGINNINGS

Human presence in the region ranks among the oldest known on the planet. 400,000-year-old human remains have been discovered in a cave at Yarımburgaz near Istanbul – the oldest yet found outside Africa. The first people to have left any traces other than bones were members of a hunting colony who built a complex of stone circles comprising *stelae* intricately carved with animal figures dated to 9500 BC, at Göbekli Tepe in Mesopotamia. At about the same time, others executed powerful paintings and carvings on cave walls at Belbaşı and Beldibi near Antalya.

Within three millennia, the transition from hunting and gathering to settled communities was mostly complete. Çatalhöyük, south of Konya, cedes to Jericho the honour of being the world's first town, but by 6250 BC it had a population of around 5,000, and was the first place to irrigate crops such as barley, or to domesticate livestock. By 5000 BC, Hacılar (220km/135 miles west of Çatalhöyük) had streets, houses with doors, and exquisite pottery.

Hittite figurine of Sun Goddess Arinna.

⊘ THE FERTILE CRESCENT

The eastern half of the so-called Fertile Crescent, an area corresponding today to southeastern Turkey and northern parts of Iraq, is thought to have nurtured the very first human settlements during the period 10,000–8000 BC. A unique combination of natural advantages apparently encouraged the hunter-gatherers in this region to take up sedentary farming. The first advantage was an abundance of various forms of wild wheat (like emmer and einkorn), easily gathered and stored, and suitable for cultivation. The other decisive factor was the presence of the wild ancestors of modern sheep and goats, both easily domesticated.

THE BRONZE AGE

With the discovery of copper, the pace of change accelerated, reflected in the successive levels of settlement mounds (*höyük* in the Turkish singular) formed by generations of mudbrick houses crumbling on a single spot. The most famous mound is at Troy, originally settled in about 3000 BC. Little has survived from its earliest levels, but this apparently was a sophisticated community with large houses, while sturdy city walls indicate well-developed political and military infrastructure.

Remains of Bronze Age man found at Karataş.

⊘ TREASURE OR TALE?

The Dorak Treasure, supposedly glimpsed briefly (and sketched) by British archaeologist James Mellaart in 1958, was purportedly wrought by the Yortans, neighbours of the Trojans, and had allegedly been dug up around 1920. The detailed drawings, published in the *Illustrated London News*, caused a sensation, since if the hoard – which included gold and silver objects, gem-encrusted jewellery and idols of Africans and a nude goddess – was genuine, Bronze Age history would have to be rewritten. Later investigations, however, suggested strongly that some if not all of the "find" was an elaborate hoax – and no items have ever resurfaced.

We know the Bronze Age Anatolians largely from their pottery – dark, red, or burnished to a metallic sheen. Unlike in contemporary Egypt and Mesopotamia, there were no written records in the Anatolian patchwork of minor kingdoms and city-states. Nevertheless, archaeological sites show continuous occupation, increasing competence in construction and crafts, and growing trade connections.

THE SECOND MILLENNIUM

Late in the third millennium BC, devastating invasions from the northwest destroyed the prosperous Anatolian civilisation. Once the dust had settled, we can identify some of the groups living in Anatolia, although their exact origins remain a mystery. Among them were the Hattis (speakers of a native Anatolian language) and newer arrivals, speaking the Indo-European Luwian language in the north and west, and Hurrian in the south and east. Beyond the Euphrates, the Mitanni kingdom was ruled by an Indo-European aristocracy related to the Hurrians.

A chronicle of the second millennium is made partly possible by discoveries of documents written on clay tablets, seals and stone monuments. Hundreds of clay tablets, detailed records of Assyrian traders in metals and textiles, were discovered in 1925 at Kanesh (modern Kültepe), 21km northeast of Kayseri.

THE HITTITES

Shortly after 2000 BC, the Indo-European Hittites, probably originating from the eastern Caucasus, conquered Hattuşa (modern Boğazkale), ending the Hatti dynasty centred there and at nearby Alacahöyük. As he left, the last Hatti king cursed the city, decreeing that it should be abandoned for ever. Within two centuries, however, Hittite king Labarnas I made it his capital, seat of a powerful empire stretching from the Aegean coast to Mesopotamia.

When the immense ruins of Hattuşa were first unearthed in 1906, they presented a stark puzzle. Memories of the Hittites were limited to the Old Testament reference to "Uriel the Hittite" – and even he came from the much later southern Hittite principalities.

Knowledge of the larger, older Hittite kingdom in the north revived with the discovery of cuneiform and hieroglyphic tablets at Hattuşa. The Sumerian forms could be read at once. It was soon realised that the Hittite language was Indo-European, some words being close to modern English – such as "watar" for water. Hittite culture and religion borrowed heavily from the Hattis, who were assimilated rather than conquered.

From about 1800 to 1200 BC, Hittite rulers presided over a network of client principalities, elaborately administered by a huge caste of scribes. Besides their main cities, Hittite monuments are found at Kemalpaşa and Manisa outside İzmir, at Eflatunpınar west of Konya, and near Adana.

The most important of the new peoples were the Phrygians, who appeared around 800 BC and set up a kingdom covering much of west-central Anatolia. Of Thracian origin, they spoke an Indo-European language written in a modified Phoenician alphabet, still seen on monuments at Midas Şehri (Yazılıkaya). They probably also had archives, but excavations at Midas Şehri and Gordion, west of Ankara – have failed to uncover any, perhaps because they no longer used clay tablets. Much of what we know about the Phrygians comes from the Greeks, who had been settled for some time along the Aegean

Silver drinking vessel, c.1400–1200 BC.

Rock carving in Yazılıkaya depicting god Sharruma and King Tudhaliya, c.1250 BC.

Although their records are lost, rival neighbouring Arzawa, Lukka and Ahhiyawa states seem to have been similar but less powerful, ruled by a warrior class who spoke Luwian, from which the common place name ending -assos may derive.

THE PHRYGIANS

From about 1230 BC onwards, the arrival of the "Sea Peoples" smashed the civilisation of both the Hittites, and the Mycenaeans on the Greek peninsula, so thoroughly that they all but passed out of memory until their rediscovery in modern times. Among the casualties was Troy VII, whose story, eventually told by Homer in the *Iliad* some four centuries later, still stirs the imagination.

coast of Asia Minor and were significantly influenced by Phrygian religion, art and music.

Two Phrygian kings live on in legend – Gordios (who gave his name to the city, and the riddle of the Gordian knot, broken by Alexander) and his successor, Midas of the golden touch. The massive tomb of another Phrygian ruler, excavated in the 1950s and one of many grave mounds at Gordion, yielded impressive bronze and wooden art but surprisingly no golden objects.

Within a century the Phrygians succumbed to Cimmerian raiders and the semi-indigenous Lydians, who established a powerful kingdom based at Sardis (near İzmir), yet much of central Anatolia continued to speak Phrygian until about AD 300.

THE CLASSICAL YEARS

With the arrival of the Greeks, coastal Turkey entered a millennium that produced immense wealth and sophistication.

For over a century (c.670–546 BC), the Lydians dominated the western half of Anatolia. Famous for their plangent music, love of luxury items and invention of coinage, they remained on friendly terms with their Greek neighbours, whose awe at their wealth has survived in the expression "as rich as Croesus" (560–546 BC), last of the Lydian kings.

> Persian rule inhibited, though did not entirely stop, the growth of city-states. Throughout coastal Anatolia, thriving towns possessed municipal institutions and sophisticated public amenities, such as theatres and baths.

PERSIANS VERSUS GREEKS

In 546 BC, Lydia was invaded by Persian king Cyrus II, who captured Croesus and burnt him alive. From their capital at Persepolis (now in western Iran), Cyrus' successors Darius I and Xerxes I expanded their empire westwards to the Aegean. Lydian Sardis became the seat of one of four Persian satraps (client rulers). The Greek coastal cities of Ionia, which had been intellectual centres – Homer is thought to have been born locally in about 700 BC – hated Persian rule, regarding it as repressive.

The Persians were notoriously vindictive. After quelling a five-year (499–494 BC) revolt, they razed Miletus, one of the most splendid of the Ionian cities, while at Xanthos on the Lycian coast, the inhabitants preferred mass suicide to the Persian yoke. Despite this, a few semi-autonmous dynasties emerged, notably the Hecatomnids at Halikarnassos (now Bodrum).

Alexander the Great at the Battle of Issos.

Inland, the situation may have been better. In Cappadocia, where many Persian nobles settled, their culture remained alive for decades after Alexander's victory. Nevertheless, monuments of the period are scarce: the best-known survivals are three stelae from Daskylion in northwest Anatolia, dating from about 400 BC, now displayed in the Istanbul Archaeological Museum.

ALEXANDER THE GREAT AND HELLENISM

Anatolia between 670 BC and AD 300 is distinguished by the steady advance of Classical Graeco-Roman civilisation. The most significant catalyst for change was Alexander the Great, the youthful king of Macedonia, one of history's meteors (see page 281). Only 11 years separate his first setting foot in Anatolia in 334 BC from his death in 323 BC, yet in that time he managed to set up one of the greatest (if shortest-lived) empires ever known. Motivated by a passionate desire to liberate Anatolia from Persian rule, Alexander spread Greek culture and language everywhere his armies marched, first through the coastal city-states founded centuries before by Ionian traders, then spreading inland and eastwards. Even after his death, the empire remained culturally Greek, with its vast territories carved up amongst four of his generals. For a generation after the death of Alexander the Great and the establishment of rival kingdoms by his successors, the history of Anatolia was marked by constant warfare between would-be kings.

Although these powerful players command attention, the abiding political units of the period were the cities, which ran their own affairs while paying lip service and tribute to overlords. Walls and water, as much as the theatre and *bouleuterion* (city-council hall), comprised Hellenistic and Roman culture in Anatolia. Cities had streets and market squares lined with colonnades, high defensive walls with grandiose gates, temples for the gods, baths and gymnasia for hygiene and health, stadiums, theatres and odeons for entertainment.

It was an age of splendid architecture, erected by slaves; even the smaller municipalities were graced by grand columns and carved capitals. The most magnificent monument of all was the Zeus altar at Pergamon (whose superb friezes are now in Berlin's Pergamon museum). Equally worthy of respect are some extraordinary engineering projects, notably aqueducts; the end of the ancient world coincides almost exactly with their destruction by Arab raiders during the 7th century.

This period also saw the gradual disappearance of local languages such as Carian, Pamphylian, Lycian and Phrygian, which survive only as monumental inscriptions. There seems to have been no major literature in these languages to rival that of ancient Greece, and the Anatolian languages faded gradually as first the prosperous classes, and later the peasantry, favoured Greek as a means of communication and for most of their daily purposes. The overall picture is one of slow, voluntary and peaceful assimilation of indigenous peoples.

In southeastern Anatolia, Syria and Palestine, however, Hellenistic culture confronted a written, Semitic language – Aramaic – which it was never

---

The Celts left little mark on Anatolia other than their language – spoken for the next 600 years. According to St Jerome, the Celtic dialect of Ankara could still be understood in northern Gaul late in the 4th century AD.

Roman sarcophagus from the 2nd century in Istanbul's Archaeology Museum.

fully able to absorb or subdue. Cultural and linguistic tension between the Semitic Middle East and Hellenism bedevilled the Roman (and Byzantine) empires and contributed to the later rise of Islam and Arabic.

THE CELTS IN TURKEY

In 279 BC, King Nikomedes I of Bithynia (near present-day Bursa) rashly invited Celtic mercenaries from central Europe into Anatolia for assistance in suppressing a rebellious brother, allowing them to settle in eastern Phrygia on the west bank of the Halys River (today the Kızılırmak). These Celts were kinsmen of the Gauls who colonised what are now France, Britain and Ireland, and called their new home Galatia. A robust, warrior people, they preyed upon the wealthy Hellenistic city-states. Barbaric but valiant, they were immortalised late in the 3rd century BC by the famous "Dying Gaul"

Pergamon's water supply began in the mountains 45km (28 miles) north of the town, running through a triple-pipe system with no fewer than 240,000 sections.

vacuum threatened to destabilise existing trade routes. Pergamon, by now one of the wealthiest, largest states in Anatolia, allied itself with the Romans, but the growth of Latin power was generally unpopular, and it came as a shock when, in 133 BC, Attalos III, the last Pergamene king, bequeathed his kingdom to Rome.

Over the next century, local rulers such as Mithridates VI (r. 110–63 BC), king of Pontus on the Black Sea, tried to stem the Roman advance; in 88 BC, uprisings in various Anatolian cities massacred some 80,000 Roman civilians. Succes-

Carving at the Genoese fortress behind the village of Anadolu Kavaǧi, located at the northern mouth of the Bosphorus near Istanbul.

sculpture; the original bronze sculpture is now lost, but a near-contemporary marble copy resides in Rome's Capitoline Museum.

THE RISE OF THE ROMANS

The troublesome Gauls were checked by Attalos I, king of Pergamon, in 230 BC, but a new and more significant threat was emerging in the shape of the growing political and commercial power of Rome. The turmoil surrounding the rivalry of the Hellenistic Anatolian kingdoms had drawn the Romans to the area. Hard-headed pragmatists, they rarely tried to annexe territory outright unless they had strong economic reasons for it. Anatolia was not only rich with raw materials, but the power

sive Roman military expeditions were organised to defeat Mithridates and consolidate Rome's grip on the province. Mithridates was halted first by Sulla in 84 BC, and much later by Pompey the Great, who forced the cagey old man to flee to the Crimea in 63 BC. Rather than be dragged in chains to Rome, Mithridates tried to poison himself but failed – during his 71 years he had imbibed far too many toxins as antidotes against assassination, and was obliged to have a trusted servant run him through with a sword.

In 47 BC, at the Battle of Zela (modern Zile, near Tokat), Julius Caesar defeated Pharnaces II, son of Mithridates, and uttered the famous boast: *"Veni. Vidi. Vici."* ("I came. I saw. I conquered.") The remaining semi-independent kingdoms of Anatolia were gradually absorbed by the Romans over the next century, and the eastern frontier was pushed back to Armenia and the Euphrates, though the border often fluctuated thereafter, under continued pressure from the Parthians around Lake Van.

THE ROMAN CENTURIES

Roman activity in Anatolia extends from their defeat of the Selucids at the Battle of Magnesia in 190 BC to the division of the empire in AD 395. During these centuries, the Latin Romans, originally pagans and republicans, morphed into Greek-speaking, imperial and Christian Byzantines. Yet they continued to call themselves "*Romaioi*", which is why the Greek Orthodox of Anatolia and Cyprus are still known, in Turkish, as *Rum*.

Roman domination with its *Pax Romana* brought security and prosperity to Anatolian cities, which grew in size and splendour. But it also meant exactions by tax farmers, eager to squeeze all the money they could from the province they had gained at auction; they had no interest in local welfare and inevitably sparked fierce resentment. However, Roman imperial rule also brought many advantages to the less developed interior, where living standards surpassed those of the early 20th century and the population reached about 12 million.

Grave stelae of this period offer a window into its society. Some depict haughty senatorial families; others show simple farming folk. Traces of politics also appear on surviving monuments. Emperors and even certain imperial family members were worshipped as gods, just as earlier the Hellenistic kings had been.

CRISES AND RESPONSES

By the 3rd century AD, the vast Roman empire was increasingly challenged and destabilised by the emerging force of Christianity – consciously opposed to Classical civilisation and its values – while its borders were threatened by barbarian raiders. In AD 258, Gothic tribes poured deep into the heart of Anatolia, ransacking many towns and cities, and kidnapping people as slaves. Simultaneously, the Sassanian Persians, successors to the Parthians, attacked again along the eastern borders, and Emperor Valerian was taken prisoner in AD 259 at Edessa (modern Şanlıurfa) by Persian king Shapur I and, according to most accounts, later executed. The Goths were finally

sent packing by Claudius II, who assumed the honorific Gothicus; a column commemorating the victory still stands at Sarayburnu in Istanbul.

Diocletian (r. AD 284–305) reorganised both the army and system of government and attempted to combat inflation. Copies, chiselled in stone, of his famous edict ordering a price-freeze can be seen throughout Anatolia, most notably at Aphrodisias. However, his newly designated regional capital at Nicomedia (İzmit), from where he unleashed a ferocious persecution of Christians, did not last long in that role.

Emperor Constantine I (AD 280–337).

⊘ EARLY CHRISTIANS IN ANATOLIA

Christianity took root early and widely in Anatolia, thanks to the tireless evangelising of Paul of Tarsus, in AD 45–58. By AD 100, congregations existed in most major cities of the Roman world. The powerhouse of early Christian thought was Antioch (Antakya), the apostle Peter's base before he moved to Rome. It remained one of the four chief bishoprics of the early Church until taken by the Arabs in AD 637. In AD 110, the governor of Bithynia, Pliny the Younger, wrote to Emperor Trajan requesting advice on how to handle the local Christians. This signalled the start of persecutions that lasted for the next 200 years.

IVSTINIAN.

Sixth-century Italian (Ravenna) mosaic of the Byzantine Emperor Justinian I (527–65).

BYZANTIUM

The Byzantine Empire, eastern arm of the once-mighty Roman Empire, was a ferment of religious fervour, artistic splendour, palace intrigue and barbarian invasions.

The late Roman Empire was marked by the struggle for supremacy between paganism and Christianity. The AD 311 Galerius Edict formally ended the persecution of Christians in the empire; the very next year, at the battle of the Milvian bridge, co-emperor Constantine (r. AD 306–37) defeated his rival Maxentius after having a celestial vision of a luminous cross, and thereafter expressed his preference for Christianity – though for reasons of state he was not baptised until he was on his deathbed.

Over the next decade, Constantine defeated and disposed of the two remaining co-emperors, leaving himself as sole ruler. In 322, he decided to leave the traditional hub of power (and pagan worship) at Rome and establish a new, "clean-slate" capital in Asia Minor, by now the wealthier and more civilised part of the empire. He first chose the site of Troy on the Dardanelles, replete with Homeric associations; the walls were nearly complete when he changed his mind (thanks to another nocturnal heavenly visitation) and selected the small port of Byzantium on the Bosphorus instead.

Dedicated in 330 and extravagantly decorated with plundered treasures from all over the classical world, the new capital was renamed Constantinople (it became Istanbul after 1453). The emperor had been working on the project for six years. Astonished courtiers watched as Constantine marked the bounds of the new city way beyond the edge of old Byzantium.

DIFFERENT STRANDS OF CHRISTIANITY

Constantinople became the seat of Christianity, and the venue for numerous acrimonious disputes over the nature of the True Faith (disputes that had been present right from the new religion's earliest days). This set the tone for hundreds of years: for most of its history, the Byzantine Empire was beset

A column capital with cross, at the Basilica of St John, Selçuk.

by theological problems which sapped the energy of emperors and scholars, causing sometimes unbridgeable political and social divisions.

Yet these disputes are often virtually impossible to understand today. What was the fuss about? Basically, the young Church was obliged to thrash out agreed versions of its central dogmas – against the rationalisations of philosophers and diverse cultural and linguistic communities with their own interests to defend. Once Christianity had ceased to be a matter of private conscience but had become the state religion, discipline and homogeneity of belief were seen as essential. Earlier Roman emperors may have thought themselves divine; by contrast, Byzantine rulers were seen as God's vice-regents on earth, with their courts (and ceremonies) reflecting the unseen heavenly one.

The core issue was whether Jesus Christ was

In AD360, Basil of Kayseri (Cappadocia) wrote a set of monastic rules still used by the Greek Orthodox Church. The Rule of St Benedict is based on them.

Eleventh-century fresco of the Last Supper in a Cappadocian church.

God, man, or (as mainstream Orthodoxy held) both at once. At the two extremes were Monophysitism and Arianism. Arius, an Alexandrian priest, believed that Christ was not God but rather a heroic superman. The Monophysites arose as a reaction, stressing the divinity of Christ. Between the two positions, from the 4th to 8th centuries, lay others of every conceivable variation. The semi-Arians said Christ was of similar, but not the same, substance as God. He had the mind of God but a human soul (Apollinarianism) or one will but two natures (Monothelitism), while the Nestorians believed that the Virgin gave birth to Christ, not to God. There were numerous other subvariants, and the controversy became so

acrimonious that no Anatolian bishop was quite sure of anyone's orthodoxy. Accordingly, Constantine convened the first Ecumenical Council at Nicaea (İznik) in 325, which formalised the system of belief still stated in the Nicene Creed, and condemned the various heresies prevalent up to that time (though more were to emerge, necessitating six further doctrinal councils).

Arianism faded away within a few generations of the first council (but never disappeared: Isaac Newton was an Arian). Monophysitism has survived to the present day amongst Syriac and Armenian Christians. All heretics were persecuted by Constantinople, which greatly weakened the empire over time. There is also evidence to suggest that the doctrinal warfare was used as a pretext to persecute the non-Hellenic peoples of the borderlands.

THE ADVANCE OF THE HOLY MEN

The first monasteries appeared in Byzantine territory during the 3rd century; throughout the next century, the monks spearheaded a fierce attack on paganism. Temples were closed, trashed or converted, statues were defaced or thrown out and oracles shut down. Emperor Julian the Apostate (361–3), the great-nephew of Constantine, attempted to turn the clock back by espousing Neoplatonism, but died in 363 fighting the Persians. All subsequent emperors were Christians. The final blow came in 392 when Theodosius I definitively prohibited pagan worship throughout the empire and decreed Christianity as the established religion.

⊘ ICONOCLASM

Byzantium and Islam each influenced the other: in 726, Emperor Leo III banned representations of human beings, provoking a religious crisis. Iconoclasts – mostly native to eastern provinces and exposed to Islamic norms – battled with advocates of images, mostly from the west. In place of icons or figural frescoes, iconoclasts embossed crosses (or abstract designs) on coins, city walls, rural chapels and urban church apses. The Seventh Ecumenical Council of 787 under Empress Irene re-instated icon worship, a move reversed by Emperor Leo V in 813. Only in 843 did the icon-supporters finally triumph, with iconoclasm condemned as heresy.

THE BYZANTINE ASCENDANCE

While the West was wracked by invading Goths, Vandals, Franks and other barbarians culminating in the fall of Rome in 476, the Byzantine Empire thrived, largely unaffected. In Anatolia, the 5th and 6th centuries were periods of tremendous splendour under emperors such as Theodosius I (379–95), Theodosius II (408–50) and Justinian I (527–65). Greek began to replace Latin as the language of the court and administration; the educational system became explicitly Christian. Imperial power grew and municipal traditions waned as senators sought careers as monks or bishops.

Emperor Justinian I has gone down in history as the builder of St Sophia (Aya Sofya) and the codifier of Roman law, but these were only parts of a vast imperial agenda which also aimed to reconquer the western territories lost 60 years earlier to the Germanic chieftains. Justinian's armies secured North Africa and part of Spain relatively easily, but the reconquest of Italy required a long and exhausting war.

To finance all this, Justinian's finance ministers John and Peter squeezed the cities of Anatolia and Greece, weakening what remained of the Classical, urban institutions. The contradiction was felt acutely by contemporaries, such as the historian Procopius, who publicly eulogised Justinian for his ambitious campaigns, while privately lambasting him in his *Secret History* as a devil in human form, married to a prostitute (the empress Theodora), who delighted in humiliating his subjects.

BARBARIAN INVASIONS

The empire came under renewed threat at the end of the 6th century. The Danube frontier was attacked by the Avars, a Central Asian people similar to the Huns, and the Slavs, who both flooded south. Emperor Maurice (582–602) struggled to contain the challenge. In the east, the Sassanid Persians – hereditary foes of the empire – crossed the entire length of Anatolia to reach the Sea of Marmara at Chalcedon (Kadiköy) and seized Byzantine provinces as far away as Egypt. It was Persia's greatest local triumph since they had wiped out the Lydian empire.

Settled life was impossible for the next century. Most cities were destroyed, although Constantinople and Thessalonike survived, and the economic and cultural collapse unprecedented since the long-forgotten invasions which had destroyed the

Hittite Empire 2,000 years earlier. In 622, Angyra (Ankara) was sacked and its population massacred or enslaved. Remarkably, Emperor Heraclius (610–41) was able to expel the Persians by 628, but the

> *Justinian's legacy did not endure. His extravagant projects permanently harmed imperial finances, and soon after he rescued Italy from the Goths, it was overrun by the Lombards.*

Coin commemorating the 10th anniversary of Theodosius I's reign.

effort so exhausted both the Persian and Byzantine empires that neither was able to resist the sudden appearance of a new enemy – the Arab armies pouring north and west out of the desert under the banner of Muhammad and Allah.

ISLAM

The Arab invasions of the 7th century introduced Anatolia to Islam – today it is the religion of the vast majority of the population. To the Byzantines, the Arabs appeared to be wild, primitive tribesmen, a notion quickly overturned when the Byzantine host was routed by the Muslim horsemen under Khalid ibn al-Walid, the "Sword of Islam", at the August 636 Battle of Yarmuk (in present-day Jordan).

In 647, Arab armies entered central Anatolia, taking Caesarea (Kayseri), the great Byzantine frontier defence station, and other cities. Their first great siege of Constantinople began in 673, lasting four years. It was repulsed by the Byzantine fleet, as was the second siege in 717–18, but the Byzantines lost most of their eastern provinces. Their new frontier stretched from east of Selucia (now Silifke) on the south coast, past Caesarea to a point east of Trebizond (now Trabzon) on the Black Sea. Tarsus, Melitene (Malatya) and Theodosiopolis (Erzurum) became Arab garrison

Figures in many frescoes in Cappadocia were targeted by iconoclasts.

towns from which they raided Byzantine territory.

Islam brought a new civilisation, religion, language and script – a radical departure for an area which had been predominantly Greek-speaking since the days of Alexander. In principle, however, Islam tolerated people of other Bible-based religions, provided they accepted inferior status and paid special taxes. Accordingly, Anatolia remained multi-ethnic and multi-religious until the 20th century.

BYZANTINE REVIVAL

The turning point came in 866, when Byzantium had for a decade been effectively ruled by Caesar Bardas on behalf of his weak nephew

Michael III, "the Drunkard". While campaigning against the Arabs, however, Bardas was murdered at the instigation of Emperor Michael's chamberlain, a Thracian peasant called Basil.

Basil, of Armenian descent, had run away from the family farm in Thrace when he was a teenager. He lodged in a Constantinople monastery before getting a job as a stable groom, first in the wealthy household of Theophilitzes, a friend of the emperor, and later, in the palace itself where he doubled as a champion wrestler. He quickly became Michael's favourite (and possibly his part-time lover), found a patron in the wealthy widow Danielis, and was married off to Michael's mistress Eudoxia. After Bardas' assassination, Basil was crowned co-emperor with Michael on 26 May 866.

On 23 September 867, Basil, realising he was falling from favour, murdered Michael III to become the empire's sole ruler. From this sordid beginning emerged Byzantium's most glorious dynasty, the so-called Macedonian. Over the next 200 years, the frontiers were expanded in all directions, with wars fought and won against the Saracens across the Mediterranean, the Egyptian Fatimids, the Abbasids of Baghdad, and the Bulgars to the north.

Basil I was succeeded in 886 by his notional son Leo VI – who may in fact have been the offspring of Michael III and Eudoxia. Less than a century later, the general-emperor Nikeforos II Phokas reconquered Crete and Cyprus from the Saracens before being deposed and murdered at the instigation of his empress, Theophano.

Under the plain-spoken, uncouth but very competent Basil II (alias "Bulgar Slayer", 976–1025), the late Byzantine state reached the apogee of its glory. With the aid of soldiers sent by Vladimir of Kiev (in return for which Basil's sister Anna was given as bride to Vladimir upon his adoption of Christianity), Basil quelled a revolt by two generals before restoring Syria to the empire.

In 1000 he turned to the Balkans to deal with the rebellious Bulgarian tsar, Samuil, who had amassed a large kingdom at Byzantium's expense, comprising much of present-day Greece, Albania, Macedonia (FYROM) and Bulgaria. After 14 years of progressively rolling back the Bulgars, Basil crushed the tsar's army at the Battle of Kleidion, taking 14,000 prisoners. They were blinded and sent back to Samuil's court at Ohrid in groups of 100, each led by one man who only had one eye put out. When Samuil beheld this gruesome spectacle, he suffered a stroke and died within two days. By 1018, his lands were annexed to Byzantium.

Basil II also re-extended the frontiers to Crimea and Bagratid Armenia to the northeast, and in the west, restored much of Italy to the Byzantine sphere. He was preparing a campaign to retake Sicily when he died in 1025, an ascetic, unmarried warrior with no heir.

He more or less finished the dynasty in the same year (1054) which saw the final rupture with the Catholic Church, ostensibly over doctrinal disputes concerning the precedence of the Holy Ghost, but really the result of a turf war over dioceses in southern Italy. This precluded any substantial western aid to isolated Byzantium, while at the same time civilian bureaucrats in the capital feuded with landed generals of the provinces, leaving the frontiers poorly defended by these warlords' personal armies of mercenaries.

Christ with Constantine IX and Zoe, St Sophia.

DECLINE AND FALL

Although Basil had left the empire's finances sound and the army in good morale, in many ways his death signalled the beginning of the end for Byzantium. The Macedonian dynasty deteriorated through mediocre nonentities – beginning with Basil's brother and successor, Constantine VIII, and continuing with the three hapless husbands of the empress Zoe (r. 1028–50), who spent most effort running her own cosmetics laboratory to keep herself in prime condition, but who – by the time she first married – was too old to produce an heir. Having murdered both her first husband and her adopted son, Zoe was in turn outlived by a third spouse, Constantine IX Monomachos.

⊘ EXTREME ASCETICS

Some early Byzantine ascetics sought extraordinary ways to evince their faith (and retreat from overly adulant followers). Respected for their extreme self-denial and assumed closeness to God, they were the celebrities of their time; their fulminating pronouncements were heeded even by emperors. St Simeon Stylites lived atop a pillar near Syrian Aleppo for 37 years (422–459), while Daniel the Stylite (409–493) spent 33 years on a pillar at Anaplous on the Bosphorus, attracting visitors like Emperors Leo I and Zeno. Some Syrian holy men, called "dendrites", preferred to live in trees, and had far less to do with the public.

AN EMPIRE UNDER THREAT

Faced by the onslaught of adversaries from every direction, the Byzantine Empire shrank to a tiny territory around the walls of Constantinople.

Byzantium, the final vestige of the Roman Empire, struggled on for another four centuries, at times regaining ground but ultimately doomed to disintegration. The population decreased steadily, invaders breached the frontiers and foreign powers – Seljuks and Crusaders – played an ever greater role in state affairs. The first hint of trouble came in 1071 when the Byzantines faced a new enemy, the nomadic Turks from Central Asia.

THE EARLY TURKS

Attila the Hun, Genghis Khan and Timur, commanding their hordes (from *ordu* or "army" in Turkish), today evoke images of bloodthirsty horror. However, these figures should be evaluated within the standards of the era – nomads versus settlers, the stirrup versus the plough. In the Central Asian steppes, nomads migrated from one unreliable waterhole to the next, fighting drought and climate extremes. It was only natural that when these poor herdsmen encountered cropland, they pillaged it. From this stock emerged the Turks.

Language alone sets them apart from Indo-European or Semitic peoples. Besides the western Turkish spoken in modern Turkey, millions of Turkic peoples in central Asia, parts of Iran and the Caucasus speak a form of Turkish or related tongues such as Mongolian or Tatar, members of the Ural-Altaic family of languages along with Estonian, Finnish and Hungarian.

Early Turks, as described in the *Epic of Dede Korkut*, first written during the 14th century, were patriarchal but monogamous. When a couple failed to produce children it was accepted as fate; taking a second wife was not an option. Traditionally, the Turks married outside their

Attila the Hun, king of the Hun empire from AD 434–453.

"Turks" first appear in 6th-century AD Chinese annals as T'u-chüeh or Dürkö. The 8th-century AD Orkhon inscriptions of Mongolia, written in runic characters, are the earliest known proto-Turkish texts.

tribe to establish alliances, which partially explains the frequent conflation of Mongols and Turks; Temujin – better known as Genghis Khan – may have been half Mongol and half Turkish.

The Turks, like the Mongols, were renowned horsemen and soldiers. The Abbasid caliphs of Baghdad, once aware of these qualities, recruited (and converted) them as paid warriors or superior slave soldiers. By the early 10th century, most military commanders of the caliphate were Muslim Turks.

THE SELJUKS

Early in the 11th century, the Turkic Seljuk tribe set up a west Asian state with Persian Nishapur as its capital. Recent, enthusiastic converts to Sunni Islam, they were not content with this but, under Tuğrul Bey, proclaimed themselves the rightful heirs to all lands conquered during and immediately after the time of the Prophet Muhammad, in particular the Levant and Egypt. To secure their rear as they concentrated on these goals, Tuğrul parlayed with the Byzantine emperors of Constantinople.

However, the borderlands between Seljuk and Byzantine territory were hardly peaceful. Armenian and Byzantine aristocrats recruited militias from among Turcoman *raiders* (a very motley crew with Shi'ite and pagan beliefs) or Byzantine *akritoi* (an equally varied body of regular and mercenary, Greek and exotic, border guards); both engaged in part-time brigandage, leading Seljuks and Byzantines to accuse each other of bad faith.

By 1064, the Seljuks had conquered Byzantine Armenia and were attacking elsewhere. Emperor Romanos IV Diogenes confronted a Seljuk army commanded by Tuğrul Bey's nephew Alp Arslan near Manzikert, north of Lake Van, in 1071. Although vastly outnumbering the Seljuk (and Kurdish) cavalry, the Byzantine troops – who included unreliable mercenaries; one general, Andronikos Doukas, who hated Romanos; and another, Joseph Tarhaniotes, who simply fled with his men – were completely outmanoeuvred. The Turks melted away when charged, lured the main Byzantine force forward, and showered the depleted Byzantine ranks with arrows before closing in on three sides. Although most imperial soldiers (including the treacherous Andronikos) escaped alive, the captives included Romanos himself.

Alp Arslan detained Romanos courteously for a week, releasing him upon payment of a large ransom, the promise of a Byzantine bride, and promulgation of a treaty which handed southeastern Anatolia to the Seljuks, though allowing the Byzantines to keep lands to the west. But when Romanos returned to Constantinople, he was deposed, then blinded, by new emperor Michael VII Doukas (Andronikos' kinsman). The treaty was a dead letter, and central Anatolia lay open to resumed Turcoman raids.

THE SULTANATE OF RUM

The reign of Alp Arslan's successor, Malik Shah, marked the zenith of the greater Seljuk empire, now based in Isfahan in the heart of present-day Iran. After Malik's death in 1092, Seljuk holdings steadily shrank, while shifting west towards Ana-

The Byzantine monastery at Alahan, one of many Christian institutions to thrive under Seljuk rule.

tolia. The Seljuk Sultanate of Rum, ruled by Kiliç Arslan I from Iconium (Konya), restrained the ungovernable Turcomans, and reached a truce with the Byzantines under Manuel I Komnenos after checking their attempt to retake central Anatolia at the Battle of Myriokephalon in 1176.

With no more Byzantine attacks in the offing, the Sultanate of Rum flourished in the first half of the 13th century, reflected in abundant Seljuk architecture still surviving in modern Turkey. The best examples of such "poetry in stone" can be seen in Erzurum, Divriği, Sivas and Konya. Here the Sufi mystic Jelaleddin Rumi (*Mevlâna*) graced the court of Alâeddin Keykubad I, and initiated the peculiar whirling dervish ceremony.

Turcoman clans scattered to found Anatolian mini-states even before the final Seljuk decline. Their petty emirs remained obscure except for one of their number, Ertuğrul, a warlord with a patch of land granted him by Sultan Alâeddin Keykubad I (see page 47). His son Osman was destined to found what was to become one of the world's mightiest empires – the Ottoman.

THE MONGOL HORDES

The cultural effervescence of the Sultanate of Rum suffered an abrupt, unhappy end at the

THE ARMENIANS

Compared with the *arriviste* Turks and Mongols, the Armenians could claim a long history of settlement in the region. They were first recorded living beside the Urartians during the mid-6th century BC. Herodotus claimed they came from western Anatolia, though recent theories have the Armenians originating from a short distance east; in either case they spoke an Indo-European language, and gradually colonised an area bounded by modern Sivas, the Çoruh valley, Lake Sevan in the Caucasus, Lake Urmia in Persia and the upper Tigris.

The church of St Gregory at Ani in far east Turkey.

hands of Genghis Khan's Mongol hordes, who erupted from the depths of Central Asia to devastate much of the known world before returning nearly as quickly whence they came. Just as they had overwhelmed the Byzantines 170 years before, the now-sedentary Seljuks succumbed to this newest wave of nomad arrivals.

On 26 June 1243, despite Frankish mercenary reinforcements and Byzantine auxiliaries sent by the Kingdom of Trabizond, the Seljuk army was routed at Köse Dağ, near Erzurum. The sultanate limped on until 1307, still producing the occasional blue-tiled public monument, but politically subservient to the Ilkhanid Mongol empire, originally shamanic/Buddhist but finally Muslim, which lasted until 1335.

The Armenian alphabet – still in use – was devised in AD 404 by the scribe Mesrob Mashtots, and inaugurated a period of literary, scholastic and theological ferment.

Around 390 BC, local Persian satrap Orontes I founded a semi-autonomous Armenian dynasty, replaced by the Artaxiads in 190 BC. Artaxiad King Tigranes II "The Great" (ruled 95–55 BC) assisted father-in-law Mithridates VI of Pontus in his struggle against the Romans, while forging an empire from the Caspian to the Mediterranean. In retaliation the Romans invaded, compelling Tigranes to accept vassal status in 66 BC – though Armenia survived as a buffer state between the Roman and Persian realms until the late 4th century. According to one account, Christianity was adopted in AD 301 under King Tiridates III, courtesy of St Gregory the Illuminator, making Armenia the earliest Christian nation, though this title is disputed by Ethiopia.

Armenia's initial flowering ended with formal partition in AD 387 between Persia and Rome, condemnation by the Byzantines for heresy in AD 451, Arab invasions, and the advent of

Engraving of Enrico Dandolo diverting the Fourth Crusade to the Constantinople.

regional princes. One such clan, the Bagratids of the Çoruh valley, became prominent during the 9th century. The Bagratid kingdom, based first at Kars, then Ani, lasted for almost 200 years; imposing monuments from this period still dot the local landscape.

Despite its relative prosperity, the Bagratid kingdom remained something of a pawn between the Abbasid caliphate of Baghdad and Byzantium; the latter foolishly deposed the last Armenian ruler in 1045, allowing the Seljuks to overrun Armenia. Most Armenians fled, remaining faithful to their language and faith, but some princes converted to Islam to continue opposing the Byzantines with the Seljuks.

By the early 1100s, the Bagratids had re-emerged as a mixed Armenian-Georgian dynasty which controlled northern Armenia (and endowed more splendid churches) until the Mongols arrived in 1236. Meanwhile, Armenian refugees in southerly Cilicia had formed an independent kingdom in 1080, which sided with the Latin Crusaders and even the Mongols against Byzantium. One lasting result of the former alliance was the emergence of an Armenian Catholic Church. After the Cilician kingdom collapsed in 1375, the local Armenian population coexisted, often as a minority, with Turks, Kurds and Arabs.

THE CRUSADES

The final threat to Byzantium came from the European Catholic powers. A plea for help from Emperor Alexios I Komnenos in combating the infidel Seljuks, and the desire to redeem the Holy Land from them, saw the First Crusade proclaimed by Pope Urban II in 1095.

Byzantium, less troubled by theological considerations than by the loss of its lands, assisted the First Crusade during 1097–8 and the Second Crusade in 1147–8, but both times Crusader passage through Byzantine territory was marked by widespread destruction. The Catholic Crusaders regarded the "heretical" Orthodox state as little better than the Seljuks. They seized Antioch (briefly), Edessa and eventually Jerusalem, establishing autonomous Latin principalities, rather than returning them to Byzantine authority. Matters deteriorated later in the century, with Sicilian Normans occupying Corfu and looting Salonika (Thessalonike).

Worse followed in 1204, when the Fourth Crusade, goaded by Greek-hating Venetian doge Enrico Dandolo, gave up any pretence of fighting Islam, capturing and sacking Constantinople instead. Count Baldwin of Flanders was crowned head of a new Latin Empire around the Sea of Marmara, while various Latin principalities took root in what is now Greece.

The Byzantine nobility set up provisional kingdoms at Trebizond, Arta and Nicaea; their recovery of Constantinople in 1261 under Michael VIII Palaiologos was essentially a twilight action. The once-powerful empire became a tiny rump state, dependent on the toleration of the Venetians, Genoese and Ottoman Turks, whose territory grew to surround Byzantium over the next two centuries.

THE OTTOMANS

Out of nowhere, the warlike Osmanlı clan supplanted the Seljuks in challenging the Byzantine Empire, forming a dynasty that lasted until 1922.

As the Mongols first invaded Anatolia in the 1220s, an exhausted band of retreating Seljuks led by Sultan Alâeddin Kaykubad I were cornered by a detachment of the barbarians from the east. Just as all hope seemed lost for these Turks, a wall of horsemen appeared on the crest of a nearby hill, pausing, it seemed, just long enough to determine the victor and claim their share of the spoils. The chieftain of the horsemen signalled his men forward, drawing his scimitar as he charged.

But instead of joining the apparent victors, the horsemen spurred their steeds towards the Mongol flank, and carved their way through to the surprised relief of Alâeddin. Grateful for his life, the Seljuk commander asked the leader of the gallant horsemen his name: Ertuğrul, came the answer.

So legend tells of the advent of Ertuğrul Gazi, the Turcoman warlord (see page 44), and his 444 horsemen, and the subsequent founding of the Ottoman Empire courtesy of Ertuğrul's son Osman (born 1258). Even if the accuracy of the account is questionable, Ertuğrul's intervention did help (temporarily) stem the tide of Mongol incursion, and with Alâeddin's blessing he acquired the small fiefdom of Söğüt, near modern Eskişehir in western Anatolia. This would become the base from which the Ottoman Empire spread first across Anatolia into Europe, later growing to encompass most of the Middle East.

BEGINNINGS

At the time they settled in Söğüt, Ertuğrul's tribe had not yet converted to Islam. It is also doubtful that they numbered more than 4,000 souls, including women and children – hardly a force to

The janissary corps.

⊘ DREAMS OF WORLD DOMINATION

While staying at the house of Sheikh Edebali, his spiritual mentor, Osman dreamt that the moon issued from his host's breast before disappearing into his own. Soon a giant tree sprouted from Osman, covering the Caucasus, Atlas, Taurus and Balkan ranges while the Tigris, Euphrates, Danube and Nile watered its roots. In the valleys were towns whose domes and towers were surmounted by the Islamic crescent. The leaves of the tree took the form of swords, and a strong wind sprung up, pointing them all in the direction of Constantinople, which appeared as a fabulous diamond ripe for plucking.

breach the walls of any Byzantine city. But given the chaos resulting from the Mongolian devastation of Anatolia, coupled with internal rifts in the late Byzantine state itself, no dreams were,

The gazi mentality depended on ongoing warfare against the infidel – not least to reward Muslim victors with fresh territory for timars or quasi-feudal land grants.

perhaps, too implausible. As the power vacuum grew, so did the occasion for a new dynasty to impose order, and the Ottoman Turks soon seized this opportunity.

Several factors tilted in their favour. Their fief lay on the march between the Seljuk-Muslim lands of Anatolia and the rump Byzantine state based at Nicaea (İznik). It was a convenient frontier along which to invite *gazis* (warriors for the faith) to expand the realm of Islam – Dar al-Salam (The Abode of Peace) – at the expense of the infidel's Dar al-Harb (The Abode of War).

Sultan Orhan and his court.

⊘ THE JANISSARIES

Murat I elaborated the practice (begun by Orhan) of drafting the most able-bodied sons of Christian subjects (Slavs and Albanians much more than Greeks) into an elite praetorian guard. Isolated from their origins, they owed absolute, personal loyalty to the sultan. Bereft of everything but their own esprit de corps, these *yeniçeris* (janissaries) would eventually become the scourge not only of Europe, but of the Ottoman Empire itself.

The concept of slavery was different in the medieval Islamic and Christian worlds, and an even greater contrast existed between domestic slaves and the servant-warrior janissaries of the Ottomans.

Local confidence in Christianity was at an all-time low, wrecked by doctrinal schisms which made the road to piety confusing and filled with pitfalls. More to the point, on Ottoman lands, taxes amounted to 50 percent of earnings for non-Muslims, while believers paid only a tithe (10 percent). On Christian land, serfs were still bound as feudal labourers to their overlords. Wedged firmly between a rock and a hard place, untold numbers of Byzantine peasants (as well as clergy and soldiers) converted to Islam.

Osman Gazi's forces grew from his father's reputed 444 horsemen to over 4,000 men. In 1301, they came into direct conflict with Constantinople for the first time, near Baphaeon. Although inferior in numbers, the Muslims easily overcame the disorganised forces of Andronikos II Palaiologos.

The defeat of an imperial army by a still-obscure Muslim clan sent shock waves through the recently restored empire. The reverberations (and promise of further booty) brought holy warriors and converts from across Anatolia flocking to join Osman. The next confrontation occurred outside Nicomedia seven years later. Byzantium was routed a second time, and the Ottomans gained effective control of the entire Anatolian hinterland and the remaining Byzantine cities in Asia Minor, chief among which was Bursa.

After a decade-long siege, Bursa's garrison commander finally surrendered in 1326, and he, his forces and most of the city's inhabitants embraced Islam. Osman Gazi had died two years earlier, leaving his son and successor, Orhan, a firm foundation on which to build.

THE EARLY OTTOMAN STATE

The reign of Osman's second son, Orhan I (1324–59), was marked by reorganisation and expansion. He consolidated the proto-Ottoman state around one religion, Islam; Bursa became one large construction site for mosques and religious schools; and Orhan promoted the *ahis*, brotherhoods analogous to the Christian chivalric orders, whose members were ardent in pursuit of both military success and spiritual exercise.

Next, he reorganised the enthusiastic waves of religiously inspired horsemen into discrete military units ranging from shock troops to a regular cavalry and infantry. Finally, Orhan embarked on a multi-pronged expansion programme. He initially conquered or co-opted minor Turcoman emirates to the south before setting his sights on Christian Thrace, crossing the Dardanelles and Sea of Marmara.

His first entry into Europe came, oddly enough, in 1337 at the invitation of the Byzantine pretender, John Kantakouzenos, who enrolled his daughter, Theodora, into Orhan's harem in exchange for aid during the civil war over the imperial succession. When peace was finally agreed through a co-emperorship, with John VI (as he now was) marrying off another of his daughters to the legitimate Byzantine emperor John V Palaiologos, Orhan's role as king-maker (and relative to kings) in Constantinople was firmly established.

By the end of his reign, Orhan had multiplied his territory several times over, mostly through invitations from his rivals and enemies. Yet with the succession of Orhan's son, Murat, this

---

Until the early 17th century, brothers of each new sultan were strangled with a silken cord – in 1595, Sultan Mehmet III had 19 siblings murdered to safeguard his throne.

Portrait of Yavuz Sultan Selim ("the Fierce").

policy of aggrandissement-by-diplomacy was set aside; the Ottomans marched on Europe by force of arms and the call of destiny.

MURAT I

The second half of the 14th century saw the steady expansion of the Ottoman realm, at the expense of both Constantinople and its would-be heirs in the Balkans. Within 18 months of his accession, Murat I (1359–89) controlled all of Thrace, including Adrianople (renamed Edirne), which was to become the Ottomans' third capital.

Murat I understood the importance of developing new administrative policies to cope with his European conquests. Unlike the Christians of Asia Minor, who had long been exposed to

Islam, and were more easily assimilated, the Balkan peoples were tenacious of faith. Neither mass slaughter of these infidels nor forcible conversion were viable options; instead the system of *millets* or subject groups came into existence. Under this system, minority populations – based on religion – were officially recognised, with their leaders held responsible for the communities' taxes, communal and legal affairs.

Yet this recognition came only after surrender. During the campaigns, any captured Christian women instantly became the chattel of the Otto-

first act was to have his younger brother, Yakub, strangled in order to ensure his leadership of the state. This grisly practice of fratricide upon enthronement, justified by

---

Christopher Marlowe's drama, Tamburlaine the Great, contains a scene in which the humiliated Beyazit and Despina are wheeled around Anatolia in a cage, insulted and ridiculed by former subjects.

A bloody version of the battle between the Turks and Crusaders, by Antonio Calza (1653–1725).

man army – eventually resulting in the extremely heterogeneous bloodline of the modern Turk.

KOSOVO AND THE RISE OF BEYAZIT

In 1389, Murat met his end on the battlefield at Kosovo, on the verge of victory over a Serbian-led confederation; he was assassinated by Miloš Obilić, son-in-law of the Serbian leader Stefan Lazar Hrebeljanović, who had accused his relative of treason. Obilić, apparently trying to prove his loyalty with his life, feigned defection and requested an audience with Murat, only to run the 70-year-old ruler through with a dagger as he knelt before him.

Murat's son, Beyazit, was proclaimed sultan immediately upon his father's death. His

creative interpretation of the Qur'an, continued for well over two centuries. Beyazit I next avenged the assassination of his father by massacring all the Serbian notables (including Stefan Lazar) captured during the campaign. Finally, he married Lazar's daughter, Despina, allowing her brother to retain a quasi-independent Serbia, although he was forced to supply troops to the Ottoman sultan and allow Muslim settlement in his fief. The repercussions are still being felt today.

BEYAZIT AND THE LAST CRUSADE

If the Crusades up to 1291 had been inspired by the desire to re-establish the True Faith in distant Jerusalem, the last Crusade was a desperate effort to forestall the infidel Turks from knocking down the door to Europe itself. In the summer of 1396, an "international brigade" of nearly 100,000 knights, drawn from across Christian Europe, assembled in Hungary under King Sigismund. The Crusaders initially found little to test their mettle save the women and children of Niš, whom they massacred although they were Orthodox Christian. After marching down the Danube valley, pillaging en route and capturing two minor fortresses, the rampant army made camp around the town of Nicopolis in modern Bulgaria, hoping to starve the Turkish garrison into submission. At last, Beyazit arrived to relieve the town. While Sigismund urged caution and a thought-out battle plan, certain vainglorious French knights opted for immediate combat. Believing the Ottoman front guard to be their entire formation, they charged on armoured steeds, wreaking havoc on these expendable auxiliaries. They then dismounted and made their way to the crest of the hill, only to find that they had merely dispatched a fraction of an army of over 60,000 highly trained and disciplined archers (including Serbian allies). Some 10,000 knights, hopelessly weighed down and on foot, were slaughtered within hours, with a cowering knot of survivors fording the Danube to safety. Central Europe was left essentially undefended.

Surprisingly, Beyazit did not follow up this victory, returning to Constantinople to resume an intermittent siege of the city, a prize that had eluded his forefathers for over a century. But soon a new and wholly unexpected challenge appeared from the east, in the form of the lame but iron-willed Mongol, Timur, often known as Tamerlane.

TIMUR THE MONGOL

Some historians of the Muslim lands refer to a "Big Foot" in Central Asia, which periodically kicks out its nomadic elements, sending them further afield in search of booty, prosperity and power. At the very moment when the Ottomans were relishing their victory over Christian Europe, Timur's mounted Mongol archers came close to extinguishing them altogether.

The build-up to the Battle of Ankara was chiefly due to Ottoman provocation. Inflated by the success of his European victories, Beyazit seized lands belonging to eastern Anatolian vassals of Timur, then threatened to cuckold the Tatar ruler. With personal honour at stake, Timur had no choice but to march against his fellow Muslim, taking Sivas from Beyazit's son Süleyman in 1401.

Beyazit's foolish pride still knew no bounds. In summer 1402, the two armies closed on the plain northeast of the citadel of Ankara, but Beyazit's forces were exhausted after a long march from the Sea of Marmara in torrid conditions. Timur seized the initiative and

Beyazit taken captive by Timur.

positioned his army between Beyazit's troops and the citadel, which should have been the Ottomans' last defence. Beyazit's doom was assured when the majority of his cavalry deserted to Timur. At the end of the day, the once-invincible janissaries and Ottoman foot soldiers lay dead on the field or were in headlong flight, with Beyazit himself taken captive. Bound in chains, Beyazit was used symbolically as Timur's footstool; the Ottoman was also obliged to see his favourite wife, Despina, serve the Tatar overlord naked at dinner, and then raped before his eyes. Beyazit soon went mad, and after eight months of captivity, died.

The Ottoman domains in Asia Minor barely outlived their erstwhile sovereign: Bursa was soon sacked and Timur's hordes ranged as far as Smyrna (modern İzmir) to uproot the last colony of Crusaders on the Mediterranean coast,

> *The 1453 fall of Constantinople is one of the most significant dates in European history. By disrupting trade from the eastern Mediterranean, and encouraging Byzantine scholars to move west, it is likely to have spurred the Renaissance.*

Portrait of Sultan Mehmet by Gentile Bellini, 1479.

with the skulls of his victims gathered in a pyramid to mark the occasion.

RISING FROM THE RUINS

Beyazit I was survived by four sons who, as Timur's vassals, were unable to practise fratricide until the old Mongol's return to Samarkand in 1403. Then the wars of succession began in earnest; after a decade of chaos, Beyazit's youngest son Mehmet I emerged as the victor. In 1421, his son, Murat II, ascended the throne and oversaw a steady rise in Ottoman fortunes. During his 30-year reign, the Ottomans reoccupied Anatolia, overran most of Greece and turned cannons on the walls of Constantinople for the first time.

But Murat also had a contemplative turn, and in 1444 renounced the throne in favour of his young son Mehmet II, the son of a Serbian princess, in order to retire as a dervish to his palace at Manisa outside İzmir. After two years, however, he was obliged to return to the throne to deal with the situation in the Balkans, where Hungarian King Ladislas and his heir, Hunyadi, in concert with the Wallachian prince Vlad III the Impaler (more familiar as Dracula), were gaining ground against the Ottomans. At the second Battle of Kosovo in 1448, Hunyadi and the Wallachians were crushed by Murat's forces. The only persistent threat thereafter was Albanian renegade Gjergj Kastrioti Skanderberg, who from 1443 until his death in 1468 preserved Albanian independence, which was only extinguished in 1479.

THE FALL OF CONSTANTINOPLE

In 1453, Constantinople had a population of scarcely 40,000, a mere shadow of Constantine's metropolis over 1,000 years earlier. The Byzantine hinterland, which had once stretched from southern Iberia to the Caucasus, had been reduced to a few farms near the city walls. For two centuries the now-minuscule Byzantine "Empire" had been little more than a Turkish dependency, its princesses married into the harems of various sultans in a realpolitik attempt to maintain a fragile, often humiliating, independence. That the city would eventually fall to the Ottomans, especially with distractions like the Mongols now vanished, was a foregone conclusion.

Within months of Murat II's death and the subsequent ascension of his often wayward but talented son, Mehmet, in 1451, the final siege of the imperial city was under way. Mehmet marched his troops within sight of the Byzantine walls before building the castle of Boğaz Kesen ("Throat Cutter"; now known as Rumeli Hisarı) on the upper Bosphorus, equipping it with heavy ordnance never seen before in eastern warfare. Pairing it with the earlier castle of Anadolu Hisarı on the Asian side of the straits, Mehmet had effectively cut off any aid to the threatened city via the Black Sea.

The Ottoman cannons were cast by Urban, a Hungarian renegade who had first offered his services in 1452 to the Byzantines. So impressed was Mehmet with his work that the young sultan made an order for a new cannon twice the size of that mounted at the Bosphorus castle, which had already sunk a Venetian ship attempting to run the blockade. This new "toy" was so heavy that the bridges between Edirne and Constantinople had to be reinforced before the monstrosity could be transported to within firing range of the city walls.

Such fortifications and new armaments contravened existing treaties, but when the last Byzantine emperor, Constantine XI Palaiologos, protested, Mehmet beheaded his envoys. Urban's cannons menaced the walls of Byzantine, and a Turkish fleet – previous attempts to take the city had failed largely through lack of an Ottoman navy – materialised in the Sea of Marmara. The only reinforcements to run the Turkish blockade were 700 Genoese under the command of Giovanni Giustiniani, and nine Venetian merchant-ships (and their crew) at anchor in the Golden Horn, which were transformed into warships. A company of Catalans, some Cretan sailors and numerous Turks under the pretender Orhan also rallied to the emperor's defence.

The siege formally began on 6 April, with Mehmet demanding complete and unconditional surrender. The soon-to-be last Byzantine emperor's reply, in equally formal manner, was that it was Mehmet who had made the decision to break the peace, and that God would favour the righteous. There was to be neither surrender nor mercy.

As Mehmet's cannons and siege machinery battered away at the city's walls, teams of oxen dragged Ottoman boats over the hill behind Pera and down into the Golden Horn, where this fleet opened up another front against the low harbour walls, stretching the limited number of defenders even further. Still the Christians held on, outnumbered seven to one by the Sultan's army of nearly 90,000. Giustiniani and his men performed military miracles by throwing back successive waves of attackers and patching up gaping holes in the walls as soon as they were formed.

On 29 May 1453, Mehmet ordered the final assault, promising his men the traditional three days of plunder and rapine to boost their flagging morale. Ranks of Ottoman soldiers, accompanied by the roar of cannons and the crash of cymbals, stormed the walls, scenting imminent victory. First the shock troops fought and fell back, then regulars, then line after line of the sultan's well-rested janissaries waded through the human debris in their path to test the ultimate resolve of the city's exhausted defenders. Finally, the Genoese commander, Giustiniani, fell mortally wounded, and with him, the whole resistance collapsed. The once-magnificent Byzantine Empire was no more.

Panoramic painting of Sultan Mehmet's conquest of Constantinople in 1453.

As all hope was lost, the last emperor of Constantinople was seen discarding his royal insignia and plunging into onrushing hordes of janissaries; his body was never found.

Mehmet the Conqueror entered the city in imperial style, wearing a majestic turban and riding on a white stallion. The sultan held prayers at Aya Sofya, which was immediately turned into a mosque. Constantinople was soon renamed Istanbul (an elision of the Greek "Stin Poli").

📷 SÜLEYMAN THE MAGNIFICENT

This influential sultan excelled in many roles: as conqueror, statesman, legislator and patron of the arts. This was the golden age of the Ottomans.

The most famous and powerful of the Ottoman rulers, Süleyman inherited the throne at the age of 26 and reigned for 46 years (1520–66). Painted portraits offer varying pictures of him, but memoirs and historical records are more consistent about his appearance. He was "tall, broad-shouldered", had a "long graceful neck... aquiline nose... dark hazel eyes... fair skin, auburn hair, beetling eyebrows... long arms and hands."

The young sultan immediately proved himself to be a man of many parts – and many titles. The Europeans dubbed him "the Magnificent", even during his reign; he preferred the title "Kanuni" (lawgiver). His ground-breaking *Kanun-i Osmani* (Ottoman legal code) reconciled judgements of the nine preceding sultans with each other, and Islamic law, to establish a comprehensive judicial system with a guarantee of equal justice for all and a measure of leniency in the penal code.

As caliph and ruler of Islam's holiest places, Süleyman consolidated Sunni supremacy over the Shia, while his skill as a military strategist more than doubled the size of his empire.

At home, he was a great patron of the arts: architecture, painting, calligraphy, illumination, weaponry, tiles and textiles, woodwork, metalwork and literature all flourished during his reign. He himself was an accomplished goldsmith and a fine poet whose collected works furnished many proverbs.

The all-mighty Süleyman.

Twenty-nine painters (half of them Europeans) worked in the Palace Studio, producing many albums of miniature paintings depicting Ottoman military campaigns and court life.

Süleyman's naval forces totally dominated the Mediterranean, while his armies swept east, northwest and south across three continents.

Süleyman's wife Roxelana.

An Overly Uxorious Ruler

Until Süleyman, Ottoman sultans traditionally did not marry, enjoying instead large and fruitful harems. But this father of eight sons and one daughter fell in love with and married one of his originally Ukrainian concubines, Roxelana, later known as Hürrem. During their 25-year marriage, it is thought that Süleyman remained monogamous.

Hürrem was clever and ambitious, the first of many generations of harem women to involve themselves in palace politics. Five of Süleyman's sons died in infancy or adolescence, but she was determined to keep the succession path clear for her favourite but useless son, Selim.

She persuaded the sultan to order and then witness the execution first of his capable, well-liked heir-apparent by a previous liaison, Mustafa, and then (after strife between Selim and Beyazıt) her son Beyazıt and Beyazıt's four sons. All were strangled with a silken bow as it was illegal to shed royal blood.

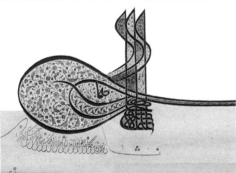

The tughra (official seal signature) of Süleyman the Magnificent.

Süleyman's dagger and gold flask with dragon-head spout, rubies and emeralds, in the Topkapı Palace.

Even the clothes worn by the royal family were works of art, lavishly embroidered with silk, and gold and silver thread.

THE DECLINE AND FALL OF THE OTTOMANS

After the "golden age" under Süleyman the Magnificent, the next 350 years were downhill all the way.

The Ottoman Empire reached its zenith, not only territorially but also in administration and culture during the reign of Sultan Süleyman the Magnificent (r. 1520–66; see page 54). But beginning with his successor Selim II, "the Sot", a slow, steady decline set in. Institutions which had once contributed to imperial glory could not adapt successfully. The sultans themselves, with a few exceptions, were mediocre, and the empire's fate depended increasingly on the competence of his Grand Vizier, essentially a prime minister chosen from amongst the top janissaries.

CORRUPT JANISSARIES AND WARLORDS

Deterioration began with the debasement of the janissary recruitment tradition (see page 48) and the system of land tenure. Both the janissary command and palace management had originally been in the hands of the most promising recruits in the annual *devşirme* or levy, rounded up from among Christian village youths. They were sent to Istanbul, converted to Islam, and put through rigorous training which ensured their absolute loyalty to the sultan. Other boys were settled with Turkish families in the provinces, learning a trade and the Muslim way of life before joining the janissary ranks.

The janissary system eventually became corrupted when free Muslims were allowed to join, marry and pursue an independent trade whilst rarely showing up for military duty. Numbers swelled as sons of existing members rushed to sign up to an easy sinecure, and there were frequent mutinies to exact more money both from the sultan and from commoners. The originally subservient slave corps soon in fact became

A European idea of a janissary execution. Most Western images of the Turks involved violence or sex.

By the 18th century, janissaries had become proverbial for their loucheness and indiscipline – "swears like a drunken janissary" was a favourite late-Ottoman locution.

power-brokers in the capital, and committed the first regicide to taint Ottoman history.

Osman II (1618–22), unhappy with the listless performance of his troops during his unsuccessful Polish campaign, decided to counter janissary domination by forming an Asian and Egyptian conscript army. Upon learning of the scheme, the janissaries revolted, beheaded the Grand Vizier and forced the young sultan to ride on a broken-down nag amid insults, before raping and then strangling him in the dreaded Yedikule (Seven Towers) prison. When the hapless Selim III (1789–1808) attempted a near-identical reform, he too was deposed and murdered.

Meanwhile, land grants to the *sipahis* (regular cavalry) also became hereditary rather than meritocratic, generating a caste of local warlords known as *derebeys* (lords of the valley). Their revolts and depredations devastated Anatolia, beginning a long-standing pattern of rural depopulation.

"INFIDEL" SUPREMACY

For centuries, the Ottomans had grown wealthy by controlling vital trade routes to the east – the Silk Road overland from China, and the sea lanes from India through the Red Sea to the eastern Mediterranean, which in many ways had become a Turkish lake. Indeed, one of the motivations of Christopher Columbus in sailing west was to find a way to China and India which avoided Ottoman fleets. His success in discovering the New World and Vasco da Gama's later voyage around the Cape of Good Hope to India were unmitigated disasters for the Ottomans. Not only did they lose their grip on trade routes to the Orient, but the shiploads of silver and gold flooding into Europe from the New World effectively debased the Ottoman currency.

Additionally, the Europeans' daring voyages gave new importance to naval, geographical and military science – and better ships, captains, navigation and guns meant "infidel" victories. Inexorably, the Europeans took control first of the Atlantic, then the Indian Ocean and finally the Mediterranean. The Ottoman conquest of Cyprus in 1571 and their successful siege (1648–69) of Candia on Crete said far more about Venetian weakness than Ottoman strength. Within months of the fall of Cyprus, a grand coalition of Spain, the Papal states, Genoa and Venice sunk a Turkish fleet at Lepanto in the Gulf of Corinth, ending notions of Ottoman invincibility.

The Islamic astronomical and mathematical heyday of the 8th to the 11th centuries had become a thing of the past, with fundamentalist Islamic jurisprudence inhibiting further intellectual growth. This contrasted sharply with a Europe rapidly emerging from the Middle Ages into the Renaissance. Thinkers, freed from religious dogma, were making huge advances in scientific discovery, philosophical speculation and technology. Even the printing press, already used for 250 years in Europe, was only allowed by the Islamic clergy in 1727.

As the once-formidable empire crumbled from within, formerly cowed rivals were eager to nibble away at the edges. The 1606 Peace of Žitava gave Hungary to the Habsburgs, while the second Ottoman siege of Vienna (1683) – a

Istanbul's *Grand Bazaar in Ottoman times.*

⊙ THE KAFES

After Mehmet III (r. 1595–1603) set a grisly record in the bloodletting which attended each new succession by killing all 19 of his brothers (some still infants), as well as most of his sisters, the attitude towards fratricide changed. Ahmet I (r. 1603–17) initiated a new system: once the oldest male of the dynasty ascended the throne, other heirs-apparent were kept in luxurious captivity in the Kafes (Cage), accompanied only by eunuchs, women and the odd tutor who reported their every move. Many potential sultans became deranged by this treatment; Ibrahim I "the Mad" (r. 1640–8) drowned 280 harem women in a fit of jealousy.

major turning point in East–West relations – failed even more ignominiously than the first one. Russia gained the Crimea and parts of the Black Sea northern shore in the Treaty of Küçük Kaynarca (1774); Napoleon invaded Ottoman Egypt in 1789, although nominal Ottoman control of the region was re-established by 1801. Although the Ottomans remained a force to be reckoned with in their core territory, ejecting the Venetians from their last strongholds on the Greek peninsula in 1715, and checking the Aegean naval invasion of Catherine the Great's

The Sultan Ahmet (Blue) mosque.

⊘ ORIENTALIST FANTASY

By the 1700s, Europe had lost its fear of the "Turk", while increased trade and colonialism created a market among eager collectors. European music, art and literature began to feature orientalist images: in Mozart's opera *Abduction from the Seraglio*; in paintings such as Jean-Baptiste Vanmour's *A Turkish Hunting Party* (1711), *The Death of Sardanapulus* (1827) by Delacroix, Ingres's *The Great Odalisque* (1814) and *The Turkish Bath* (1862); and in romantic literature like Byron's *Childe Harold's Pilgrimage* with its pashas and harems, Coleridge's *Kubla Khan* (1816) and Edward Fitzgerald's *The Rubaiyat of Omar Khayyam* (1859).

favourite Count Orloff in 1770, these were brief retrenchments. Moldavia and Wallachia became autonomous principalities (1829), while Greece emerged as an independent kingdom (1832).

CRIMEA AND CAPITULATIONS

Throughout the 19th century, the empire's balance of trade went haywire as the Industrial Revolution that was transforming Western Europe turned Turkey into a source of cheap raw materials and a market for manufactured European products; domestic commercial concessions granted to the West worsened the situation. Not only were the postal service, urban street cars, electricity generation and railway network managed by foreigners, but legal privileges known as the Capitulations meant that any foreigner who asked for the protection of a foreign consulate could not be tried in an Ottoman court.

The Ottoman economy was further disrupted by the Crimean War (1853–56), fought in an alliance with the British and French against Russia. This bloody war, which began with a dispute over the Holy Land (and, more broadly, about Russian expansionism), was characterised by inept strategy, most famously depicted in Lord Tennyson's *The Charge of the Light Brigade*. It also inspired two English women – Florence Nightingale and Mary Seacole – to establish war hospitals in Istanbul based on modern nursing practice.

Massive borrowing at high interest rates led to state bankruptcy in 1873, and – in a further indication of the way the wind was blowing – the empire came under Western financial supervision with the establishment of the Public Debt Administration in 1881. Despite various attempts at reform during the latter part of the 19th century, territorial losses continued.

REFORM ATTEMPTS

Reform of the Ottoman Empire began in earnest with Sultan Mahmut II (1808–39). In 1826, he replaced the decadent janissary corps with a Western-trained, standing army. After obtaining the support of the Muslim clerics, the sultan asked each janissary battalion to spare 150 men for the new planned force; the janissaries refused and overturned their soup kettles in the traditional signal of revolt. But forces loyal to Mahmut opened fire from the Seraglio, and 4,000 janissaries were killed in their barracks. Thousands more were slaughtered in the streets of Istanbul and in the provinces as a general purge began.

Next the sultan schooled French-speaking bureaucrats who staffed a formal diplomatic corps and civil service. The Tanzimat edict of 1839 established (in principle) orderly tax collection, fair and regular conscription, and equal treatment in law for non-Muslims.

Yet notions of "equality" held little attraction for many Ottomans, and was resisted fiercely by non-Muslims, who until then had been exempt from military service. As prosperous tradesmen and farmers – often under foreign protection – they were loath to interrupt business for the sake of a lengthy period of national service.

FIRST CONSTITUTION AND THE "YOUNG TURKS"

In 1876, the Ottoman Empire adopted its first written constitution, just as one of its most controversial sultans, Abdülhamid II (1876–1909), came to the throne. Meanwhile, the growing pan-Slavic movement in the Balkans culminated in a disastrous 1877–78 war instigated by Russia, which resulted in an autonomous or independent Bulgaria, Romania and Montenegro, while the British annexed Cyprus and the Russians much of northeastern Anatolia. Muslim refugees flooded into western Anatolia as some of the Ottomans' richest hinterland was lost. The crisis prompted Abdülhamid to suspend the new constitution, dissolve parliament and rule autocratically for the next 30 years. The sultan's autocracy (and industrious secret police) inevitably fomented opposition, and a clandestine society, the Committee for Union and Progress (CUP), emerged, intending to restore constitutional rule.

In 1908, in the so-called "Young Turk" Revolution, the CUP-infiltrated army revolted in Selanik (Thessaloníki in Greek), forcing the sultan to schedule elections and reconvene parliament. The following year, after a botched counter-revolution, Abdülhamid II was forced to abdicate in favour of his brother Mehmet V (1909–18). Although at first ostensibly democratic and reformist, the CUP – which had the most deputies in the new parliament – became increasingly militarist and nationalist, almost a foregone conclusion given the traumas of the

Ottoman railways were notoriously circuitous in their routing – not because the German contractors were paid by the kilometre, as myth asserts, but because of a desire to protect them from naval bombardment.

Sultan Abdülhamid II – the first Ottoman ruler to be photographed.

Italian seizure of Tripolitania and the Dodecanese islands (1911–12) and the Balkan Wars (1912–13), which saw most Ottoman possessions in Europe lost to Bulgaria, Serbia and Greece. Only eastern Thrace was saved.

All through Abdülhamid's reign, European powers vied to establish influence on the "sick man of Europe", cajoling and threatening by turns. The most successful suitor was Germany, itself a newly formed nation-state. Military delegations, trade and projects like the Berlin-to-Baghdad and Hejaz railways were used to woo the Ottomans to the imperial German side as Great Power rivalry cranked up in the early years of the new century.

WORLD WAR I

When war broke out in August 1914, the Ottomans hesitated, while the British promptly seized two warships being built, in England, for the Ottoman fleet under public subscription in Turkey. Germany adroitly exploited this by running two warships through an Allied Mediterranean blockade and "donating" them to the Ottomans. With a change of flag but not of crew, the new "Turkish" warships sailed across the Black Sea to launch shells at Russian ports in the Crimea. To the chagrin of many in Istanbul,

Mahmud Şket Paşa, protector of the Ottoman constitution, riding through the streets of Istanbul in 1909.

Ottoman Turkey officially became a Central Power in November.

Still digesting humiliating defeats by the Italians and Balkan alliances, Turkey was scarcely prepared for war. The British ousted the last Ottoman khedive of Egypt in 1914, and the former province became a major base for English activities in the Middle East, including the Arab uprising against Ottoman rule, led in part by T.E. Lawrence. Meanwhile, to the northeast, the forces of tsarist Russia pressed inexorably west as far as Erzurum. The only comfort came from the northwest, when Bulgaria entered the war on the Central side in

"I am not ordering you to attack; I am ordering you to die," Mustafa Kemal lectured his undersupplied troops at Gallipoli. Struck near the heart by shrapnel during the fighting, his life was saved by a pocket watch.

October 1915, which allowed direct rail supply from Austria.

GALLIPOLI

Aside from defeating the British at Mesopotamian Kut, the only successful Ottoman military action during the war was the 8-month defence of the Dardanelles in 1915, where the combined French, British and Australian–New Zealand (ANZAC) forces had landed at Gallipoli. A certain Colonel Mustafa Kemal (later known as Atatürk, see page 87), chief deputy of German commander Liman von Sanders, oversaw a brilliant but brutal defence for the Ottomans, winning a heroic reputation that subsequently served him well when he started building the Republic of Turkey.

ARMENIAN CASUALTIES

On all other fronts disaster followed disaster. The situation in the remote eastern provinces, where many Armenian nationalists sided with tsarist Russia or France on the promise of future independence, was especially critical. By now the CUP had become effectively a military triumvirate run by Cemal Paşa, Talat Paşa and Enver Paşa (who had lost an entire army to intense cold and the Russians). Early in the war (actually, even before) this junta decided that Christian Ottoman subjects constituted a disloyal fifth column and had to be neutralised accordingly. Already in early 1914, nearly half a million Greek Orthodox had been massacred or deported from the Aegean regions in revenge for the ethnic cleansing of Muslims during the Balkan wars.

On 24 April 1915, the CUP authorities ordered the deportation of all Armenian civilians, except those in İzmir and Istanbul, the disarming of all Armenians in the Ottoman army and the dismissal of all Armenian civil servants. Over the next ten months, hundreds of thousands of Armenian civilians were rounded up and marched towards detention camps in Mesopotamia; few made it there, the majority being killed at the outset or falling vic-tim to disease or starvation. The world Armenian community – and many neutral historians – assert that at least a million were killed; Turkish advo-cates hotly dispute the existence of any deliberate extermination, and admit at most 300,000 casual-ties under "wartime conditions" – while pointing to nearly half a million Turkish civilian deaths, many of these at the hands of Armenian militias in eastern Anatolia. The Süryani (Assyrian Christian) communities of southeastern Anatolia, similarly accused of throwing in their lot with the British,

THE END OF THE EMPIRE

When the Ottomans capitulated with the sign-ing of the Mudros Armistice on 30 October 1918, the once-proud empire was but a ghost of its former self. The 1920 Treaty of Sèvres recognised the British occupation of Iraq and Palestine, while Syria (including Lebanon) was ceded to France under the League of Nations' mandate system. Controversially, independent Armenian, Assyrian and Kurdish states were envisioned in the eastern provinces. Not even central Anatolia was sacred, thanks to secret

The Ottoman army had just two victories in World War I – at Gallipoli in 1915, and against the British at Mesopotamian Kut in 1916.

fared little better, often being killed in tandem with local Armenians.

Whatever the truth of these competing asser-tions, Anatolia emerged from a decade (1912–22) of war largely bereft of its entrepreneurial Chris-tian population, which early 20th-century censuses had estimated at well over 2 million. Fighting between the Turks and the fledgling Armenian republic (which had emerged in 1918) only ended with the Treaty of Alexandropol in 1920, which spelled the end of the Armenians' dream of their own independent state. Demilitarised, what was left of independent Armenia was soon overrun by Soviet forces and assimilated into the USSR, until it finally achieved independence in 1991.

wartime agreements made amongst the Allies. Eastern Thrace and much of the Aegean was given to Greece, while Italy and France were assigned "spheres of influence" along the Medi-terranean coast. The Dardanelles, Bosphorus and Constantinople were placed under "inter-national control". After almost six centuries the reign of the Ottomans was over.

It took the crushing ignominy of military defeat, invasion by Greece and one man in the right place and time to foster the emergence of a modern Turkish nation-state from the ashes of empire. The place was a Black Sea port, the time May 1919, and the man Mustafa Kemal, hero of Gallipoli.

THE REPUBLICAN ERA

With the end of World War I and the collapse of the Ottoman Empire, the stage was set for the rise of Atatürk's republic.

Joining the losing side in World War I cost the Ottoman Empire millions of lives and huge chunks of territory. As far as the vanquished Ottoman empire was concerned, the victors dispensed with US President Wilson's Fourteen Points for peace and national self-determination. The Treaty of Sèvres that the sultan's representatives were forced to sign in May 1920 merely implemented secret wartime protocols for the empire's dismemberment.

In late 1918 the British became the main garrison force in Istanbul, still the Ottoman capital, while the Bosphorus and Dardanelles straits, sought for centuries by Russia as a gateway to ice-free seas, were "internationalised" by the terms of the treaty. The Armenians and the Kurds were theoretically granted their own states in eastern Anatolia, as were the Pontian Greeks on the eastern Black Sea coast, but none survived the establishment of the new Turkish republic just four years later. The Kurds, having failed to secure a state, revolted repeatedly in eastern Turkey between 1925 and 1984. The French occupied parts of southeastern Turkey, while the Mediterranean coast between Bodrum and Antalya – opposite the Dodecanese which they had already seized in 1912 – went to the Italians. Meanwhile, the Greeks, ably represented by Eleftherios Venizelos at the Versailles peace conference, were after a bigger prize – a state straddling two continents and reuniting the ancient Ionian colonies with the motherland. Greece was subsequently given eastern Thrace, and, more importantly, the principal Aegean port of Smyrna (İzmir) with its rich hinterland.

This wholesale dismembering of the Ottoman empire left Turkey as a small rump state, perceived by many as a national humiliation.

A contingent of the Turkish army during the War of Independence, 1922.

The obligatory adoption of surnames in 1934 elicited patriotic ones often at odds with reputations – as one wag put it, the laziest chose Çalışkan (Industrious) while those with Armenian grandparents opted for Öztürk (True Turk).

THE WAR OF INDEPENDENCE

The Greek landing at Smyrna on 15 May 1919 goaded latent Turkish patriotism and resentment into action. Four days later Mustafa Kemal, the hero of Gallipoli, arrived at Samsun on the Black Sea coast, ostensibly to supervise the disbanding of patriotic militias which had arose in defiance of the Allies. Once safely away from Istanbul, he renounced his commission and set about converting these militias into a proper nationalist army. Two ideological conferences convened in deepest Anatolia promulgated the so-called National Pact – which demanded an independent Turkey with viable borders, and abolition of foreign privileges. On 23 April 1920, the nationalists formed the first Grand National Assembly in Ankara, following the forcible British closure of the last Ottoman parliament.

The beleaguered nationalist army had to fight a multi-front war against the Armenians, the French, the Italians, and most dangerously the Greeks, whose expeditionary armies had by late 1920 driven deep into Anatolia over French and Italian objections. The only aid came from the new Soviet Union and contributions from Asian Muslims. But during August 1921, the 22-day-long Battle of Sakarya, fought just west of Ankara, turned the tide of the war; the Greeks' failure to capture Ankara doomed their occupation. Impressed by Kemal's leadership (and resenting augmented Greek power), the French and Italians soon came to terms with the nationalists, even supplying them with arms, and withdrew; only the British still supported the Greek adventure.

The Greeks dug in, but exactly a year later Kemal commanded the decisive counterattack at Dumlupınar, west of Afyon. The bulk of the Greek army was annihilated, its commander-in-chief even taken prisoner; the ragged remnants were chased back to İzmir, fleeing in waiting boats. The liberation of İzmir on 9 September 1922 was followed within four days by a hugely destructive fire and massacres of Christians. But another Greek army, supported by British divisions, remained intact in eastern Thrace, and the threat of further war lingered until the 11 October armistice at Mudanya acknowledged the reality of the Greek defeat.

ESTABLISHING THE REPUBLIC

In early 1923, the Allies clumsily sent double invitations for peace talks in Lausanne, Switzerland: one to Sultan Mehmet VI, ruling Istanbul alone, one to the Ankara regime. Infuriated, the latter abolished the monarchy on 1 November 1922. Two weeks later the last sultan ignominiously

boarded the British HMS *Malaya* under cover of darkness, bound for Malta and exile.

Turkey's sole delegate to the Lausanne conference was Atatürk's trusted confidant and general İsmet Paşa (latter İnönü) . By his determined insistence on the National Pact, he succeeded in wearing down such eminent diplomatic adversaries as British Foreign Secretary Lord Curzon. The final treaty, signed 24 July 1923, completely negated Sèvres, endorsed the National Pact – and additionally stipulated the departure of most Muslims from Greece

Site of the 1923 Conference of Lausanne.

and Orthodox Christians from Anatolia, the first regulated ethnic cleansing of the 20th century.

Kemal and his circle now embarked on the harder task of rebuilding a conflict-ravaged country. On 29 October 1923, the Grand National Assembly proclaimed the Republic of Turkey, with Ankara as capital. Its first president, inevitably, was Mustafa Kemal, and its first prime minister İsmet Paşa, leader of the newly founded Republican People's Party (CHP in Turkish) – for the next 57 years, a nursery for aspiring politicians, a medium for authoritarian government, and a laboratory for paternalistic, top-down social engineering.

Kemal and Co. wanted a radically Westernised new state, but existing institutions were unmistakably Eastern. Moreover, ties to the *ummah* (the global Muslim community) were yet far deeper rooted in history than ties to the nascent Turkish nation, with many Turks shunning involvement in politics, industry or urban commerce, considered "infidel" activities unworthy of Ottoman gentlemen. The new regime faced the daunting tasks of creating a national consciousness, absorbing Western civilisation and reinterpreting Islam.

Social reform by fiat was easy; the Kemalists had more mixed results in the economic sphere. With the departure or demise of the

İsmet İnönü, close associate of Atatürk and second president of the Republic.

Christian business class, a new bourgeoisie had to be created from scratch. Investment banks were set up as early as 1925, but the 1929 crash and ensuing global depression discredited capitalism in the eyes of Turkey's elite, who noted the apparent immunity of the Soviet economy from the catastrophe. Newly created state-run enterprises were crucial in an industrialisation modelled on Italian Fascism as well as Communism. Self-sufficiency and import substitution became the order of the day, with heavily subsidised mining, steel, cement, glass, textile and paper works promoted in the first Soviet-style Five-Year Development Plan (1934–9).

AN END TO ISOLATION

Turkish foreign policy until the 1930s was isolationist and (except for a successful campaign to annexe French-held Hatay) non-interventionist. Though the CHP imitated aspects of authoritarian interwar regimes, it frowned on the aggressiveness and race-baiting of Nazism and Fascism. İsmet İnönü's accession as president upon Atatürk's death in late 1938 produced no major changes.

İnönü's main accomplishment was keeping Turkey out of the world war which erupted in 1939. This required not only skilled tightrope walking above the warring sides – using vaguely worded "treaties of friendship" – but an iron hand domestically. Although officially neutral, the country remained on a war footing economically, while supplying chromium ore to both sides, alternately sheltering or expelling Jewish refugees, and crawling with foreign agents of every description. Turkey declared war on Germany only in early 1945, just in time to qualify for UN membership.

Meanwhile, the honeymoon of the 1920s and early 1930s between Turkey and the Soviet Union had reverted to mutual hostility. In 1945, Moscow renewed demands for "international" control of the straits either side of the Sea of Marmara, and for the return of the Kars and Ardahan districts on the Armeno-Georgian frontier, ceded in 1920. Given these threats, the offer in 1946 of American protection was eagerly accepted, a mutual courtship spurred by Turkey's sensing the value of a reliable, anti-Communist sponsor

⊘ DRASTIC REFORMS

In early 1924, the caliphate was abolished, religious courts closed, and members of the Ottoman court exiled. After a Kurdish-Islamist revolt in the east, all dervish orders were proscribed in late 1925 and their *tekkes* (lodges) shut. In 1926, religious law was replaced by a uniform civil code, and the Gregorian calendar introduced. In 1928, Arabic script was replaced by a Latin alphabet, and Arabic or Persian vocabulary dropped in favour of old-Turkish or French words. Fezes and turbans were abolished, but the veiling of women was less easily halted. Women were given the vote in 1934, and encouraged to compete with men professionally.

and America's delight at finding a malleable and strategic Middle Eastern client state. It led directly to Turkey's involvement in the Korean War (1950), admission to NATO (1952) and its controversial recognition of Israel.

FIRST MULTI-PARTY POLITICS

Atatürk's rule had been viewed by many as autocratic from the start. In 1924, leading CHP figures defected to form the opposition Progressive Republican Party (PRP). It lasted barely six months; in February 1925 the Kurd-

farming sector and more open religious observance, a combination which proved popular with an odd cross section of voters ranging from pious rural peasants to the emerging middle

The 1946 visit to Istanbul of the battleship USS Missouri was so providential for the beleaguered Turks that the authorities ordered the municipally run brothels open for free to the sailors.

Celâl Bayar (right) with the Turkish Foreign Minister Tevfik Rűştű Aras (centre) and the Greek Prime Minister Ioannis Metaxas in Athens in 1938.

ish-Islamist revolt in the east took months to suppress and gave Atatürk an excellent pretext to ban the PRP in the interests of unity. In 1926, after a plot to assassinate him was uncovered, many former PRP deputies and surviving CUP members were accused of involvement and hanged. Barring another brief experiment with an opposition party in 1930, the CHP monopolised power until 1950.

In 1946, a group of expelled CHP members, including lawyer-landowner Adnan Menderes and Celâl Bayar, a banker and ex-associate of Atatürk, formed the opposition Democrat Party (DP). Its platform comprised relaxed regulation of private enterprise, support for the neglected

class. By 1950 the DP was in power, with Bayar as president and Menderes as prime minister.

ERRATIC PROGRESS

Copious American economic and military aid under auspices of the Truman Doctrine, in part a reward for apparent democratisation, lent a markedly pro-American tone to DP-era development. In return, Turkey granted the United States extensive military facilities – including bases for nuclear missiles, later dismantled as part of the settlement ending the Cuban crisis.

Domestically, populist incentives to free enterprise led to chaotic expansion. More tractors to farmers boosted production and exports, but massive imports of foreign goods and overly generous rural loans and public spending left the country with a huge trade deficit and national debt leading to repeated currency devaluations.

Three decades after his hanging, Menderes was rehabilitated by solemn reburial in a mausoleum in Istanbul, and the naming of numerous streets and facilities (including İzmir's airport) after him.

Turkish Prime Minister Bülent Ecevit electioneering in Rize, 1979.

Although re-elected in 1954 and 1957, the DP became increasingly repressive, censoring the press, winding up the CHP and instigating anti-Greek pogroms in Istanbul amidst the first Cyprus crisis. Menderes was finally deposed on 27 May 1960 in a widely popular military coup, then convicted and hung by a military tribunal, along with two of his ministers.

For 16 months, Turkey was run by a National Unity Committee which drafted a new, markedly liberal constitution. Free elections resumed, the right to strike was confirmed, and Turkey's first socialist party appeared. Members of the now-banned DP enrolled in the newly formed Justice Party (JP), whose chief

Süleyman Demirel began a political career spanning 37 years. In 1965 and again in 1969, the JP took power with promises of free-market policies and unimpeded foreign investment.

DESCENT INTO CHAOS

The late 1960s saw an explosion of left-wing activism which continued into the next decade, while political polarisation prompted a low-key 1971 military intervention. The 1973 elections forced Bülent Ecevit's CHP into a coalition with Necmettin Erbakan's National Salvation Party – the first appearance on the national stage for political Islam.

Hoping for a clear parliamentary majority after his Cyprus action Ecevit sought early re-election. But far-right forces outflanked him, taking power in April 1975 as a coalition featuring Demirel's Justice Party and Alpaslan Türkeş's neo-Fascist National Action Party (MHP). Thereafter, things degenerated markedly, with the economy hamstrung by shortages, inflation and huge debt, while sectarian and political violence left some 5,000 dead by 1980 and the country on the verge of civil war.

On 12 September, the generals struck again, intent on a more thorough overhaul than in past coups. General Kenan Evren and other military commanders formed the notorious National Security Council, which assumed absolute power. All political parties were shut down and their leaders detained. Tens of thousands of suspected "terrorists" were tried in military courts, with 25 executed for major crimes and massacres, though the radical right and Islamists suffered far less than Marxists, trade unionists, professors and other left-leaning intellectuals. The universities were purged and a new, restrictive constitution promulgated.

FROM ÖZAL TO THE CRASH

General elections were held in November 1983, but with all pre-coup parties and their leaders banned. The surprise, landslide winner among just three parties allowed to campaign was Turgut Özal's ANAP (Motherland Party), a rather broad group encompassing everyone from free-marketers to Islamists. Özal, a Texas-trained engineer, charismatic speaker and adherent of the still-clandestine Nakşibendi dervish order, embodied its inherent contradictions. There was a sudden relaxation of trade restrictions, a provocative influx of foreign luxury goods, and encouragement of large, export-orientated enterprises. Enormous sums were spent on developing tourist infrastructure, and foreign investment was welcomed. Inflation and public budgets soared, as did corruption, but given overall economic growth, opportunities existed.

By 1990, four major opposition parties had emerged – Demirel's DYP, Erdal (son of İsmet) İnönü's SHP, the resurgent CHP and the Democratic Left Party (DSP) headed by Ecevit – which

for mafiosi foreign and domestic. Refah (and Erbakan) were soon proscribed and, in the Turkish way, a successor party – Fazilet (Virtue) – immediately emerged.

Turgut Özal remains a controversial figure – a hero for many as one who opened up the country more than anyone since Menderes, despised by others for his nepotism and toleration of sharp practice.

The former prime minister Turgut Özal, who went on to become president.

soon formed various coalitions to eclipse ANAP. Özal, now president, died in April 1993, succeeded by Demirel, who handed the DYP reins to American-trained economics professor Tansu Çiller. She initially raised hopes as the first female Turkish prime minister, but her leadership proved shambolic, dogged by pervasive corruption, overt gangsterism and coalition infighting.

The immediate beneficiary of this was Necmettin Erbakan's latest Islamist party Refah (Welfare); within a few months he was top dog in an improbable coalition with Çiller, but in June 1997 was nudged out of office by discreet military machinations, having accomplished little other than closing Turkey's 79 casinos (gambling is forbidden for Muslims), a mecca

Ⓒ CYPRUS

In July 1974, Ecevit ordered a military landing in northern Cyprus in response to the overthrow of Cypriot President Makarios and his replacement with an extreme nationalist regime seeking union with Greece, expressly forbidden by 1960 treaties confirming the island's independence. The "Peace Action", as Turks term it, was ostensibly designed to protect the Turkish Cypriot minority, but within a month, despite the new regime's replacement with Makarios allies, Turkey had occupied the northern third of Cyprus, where its forces remain today. Only Turkey recognises the controversial Republic of Northern Cyprus, set up in 1983.

THE KURDISH QUESTION

Denied their own state after 1923, the question of Kurdish independence has been a long-standing problem for the Turkish government, particularly with the formation of the PKK militia in the late 1970s (see pages 82 and 373). In November 1998, Kurdish separatist leader Abdullah Öcalan was finally captured in Kenya and tried (like Menderes) on a remote island in the Sea of Marmara, signalling what appeared the winding down of the PKK insurgency. Many Turks, especially those who had lost relatives

A family camping outside their destroyed family home in the aftermath of the 17th August 1999 earthquake in İzmit.

serving as soldiers, supported his death sentence, but with the eyes of Europe on Turkey, this was commuted to life imprisonment.

Towards the millennium, earthquakes literal and metaphorical rocked the country. In the small hours of 17 August 1999, a Richter 7.4 shock with İzmit as the epicentre crippled the country's industrial heartland. Aside from an estimated 25,000 dead, and the exposure of massive local corruption permitting erection of shoddy blocks of flats, the quake had less predictable but more positive consequences. The military, which looked after its own barracks first rather than aid rescue operations, had its reputation irretrievably tarnished. Greek

rescuers were among the first foreign teams on the scene, and sympathy led to a rapprochement between Turkey and Greece.

In May 2000, President Demirel's attempt to change his permitted term of office from one 7-year to two 5-year spans failed and he was replaced by Turkey's senior judge, Ahmet Necdet Sezer, whose single term was distinguished by his respect for the law and limits to presidential powers.

At the millennium the Turkish economy was again in free fall, with numerous spectacular bank failures and implosion of the currency from late 2000 through early 2001. World Bank economist Kemal Derviş was appointed Minister of Economy with extraordinary powers, stabilising the situation – along with an IMF aid package.

START OF THE ERDOĞAN ERA

By summer 2002, yet another rickety left-right secularist coalition – headed by Ecevit's DSP – was on the rocks, prior to November elections handily won by the AKP (Justice and Development Party). Born out of the ashes of the Refah and Fazilet Parties, the AKP formed the first non-coalition government since 1987 (the only parliamentary opposition was the CHP). Combative leader Recep Tayyip Erdoğan took the role of prime minister and has been the de facto leader of the country since. Although Islamist, the AKP initially proved a competent economic manager, with inflation reduced to single digits and tourism a steady earner despite the Iraq invasion and occasional terror attacks. Deriving support from devout Muslims and townspeople from the Anatolian interior, the party threatened to outflank the "White Turks" (mostly of Balkan descent) comprising the army, academia, civil service, big business and much of the media, who had run the country since 1923.

In 2007, a political crisis erupted when the AKP nominated foreign minister Abdullah Gül as candidate for president (a role previously recruited from the secular establishment). The military posted an online warning, the so-called "e-coup", hinting they might act if Gül was chosen by parliament. Millions of secularists took to the streets in orchestrated rallies against Gül's candidacy and what they saw as creeping Islamisation, yet the AKP's gamble of early parliamentary elections on 22 July paid off with an enhanced majority and a second term, while Gül became president.

The main focuses of AK's second and third terms were the linked Ergenekon and Balyoz conspiracies. Ergenekon is the mythical central-Asian homeland of the Turks, whence they were led west ages ago by a grey wolf (thus Bozkurt, 'grey wolf', an extreme nationalist organisation). Balyoz – 'Sledgehammer' – was supposedly a contingency plan for a new military coup, alleged to have been ready since

verdicts were eventually annulled in 2015, following nearly a decade of legal battling.

Talks of accession to the EU – itself mired in a surmounting debt crisis (see page 78) – stalled in 2007, falling steadily beyond concern thereafter along with the notion of democratic reform. Already by 2010 the country was again largely split in two, the AKP winning the bulk of the interior provinces and the CHP winning most municipal elections along the Aegean and Mediterranean coasts and in Thrace, traditional secularist strongholds. In foreign policy, May

Syrian refugee camp in Antakya, 2012.

2003. Arraigned in late 2008, the first defendants, a huge group of high-ranking generals, lawyers, nationalist politicians, journalists, academics and mafiosi, stood accused of high-profile provocateur assassinations (including the 2007 assassination of prominent Turko-Armenian journalist Hrant Dink) and bombings of secularist institutions to create the impression of an Islamist threat that would justify a military coup. Hailed by some as a finally decisive confrontation with the ever-meddling 'deep state', the trials were dismissed by others as a purge of the former secular establishment. In the light of pronounced procedural irregularities inside and outside court (not least dubious documentary evidence), all 2013

2010 saw a major downturn in diplomatic ties with old ally Israel, when Turkey took strong exception to the Israeli commando storming in international waters of the Turkish-flagged Mavi Marmara, with nine fatalities amongst the Turkish and foreign human rights activists aboard. The ship had been carrying aid supplies towards Gaza, which Israel deems an illegal Palestinian port. Despite an Israeli apology in 2013, relations between the two countries have remained mostly rocky since.

Under AKP foreign minister Ahmet Davutoğlu, Turkey touted a 'zero problems with neighbours' policy, effectively a neo-Ottoman stance to increase Turkey's positive influence in its former territories from North Africa to the Middle East to the Balkans. In 2011, this was put to severe test by the so-called 'Arab Spring' – where many demonstrators saw the Turkish government as a possible role model – and by the Syrian civil war. Thousands of Turkish workers were forced to flee revolutionary Libya, while ties with Assad's Syria, carefully cultivated since 2002, unravelled. Erdoğan's pleas for reform by Assad's regime fell on deaf ears, and by early 2012 the AKP – always more likely to have sympathised with the largely Sunni resistance than the Alawite

country continued to visibly boom, with foreign investment accepted from almost any quarter, including Gaddafi-era Libya, China, Russia and Saudi Arabia. Many towns and cities – and particularly AK-controlled ones – were transformed beyond recognition. Closer examination, however, shows that almost invariably the firms to receive contracts for major infrastructure projects have been staunch AKP financial backers.

The party's obsession with public pietism has threatened to impinge on Turkey's

Gondola ride on the Porsuk River in once-dreary Eskişehir.

'heretics' of the ruling Syrian Ba'ath party – had formally declared for the insurgents, who set up their notional government-in-exile in Istanbul. An unprecedented influx of refugees began to enter Turkey, the majority of them being settled within the ten border provinces though many others heading west to Istanbul.

Despite the spillover of regional turmoil, the AKP was rewarded with another victory in the June 2011 elections, earning nearly 50 percent of the vote. This granted an unprecedented third term in power (though not quite enough of a parliamentary majority to make the unilateral changes to the constitution that Erdoğan desired). A major factor in their continued success was that, put simply, the

tourism sector – beyond the price or unavailability of alcoholic beverages or the unacceptability of public displays of affection. In October 2011, the former church of Aya Sofya in İznik, which had been a museum for the sake of its frescoes and floor mosaics, was converted into a mosque. In July 2013, the same occurred with the Aya Sofya church in Trabzon (both sites, however, now include sections for non-Muslim visitors). Efforts have been ongoing to convert the giant namesake of both monuments in Istanbul, though these have proven unsuccessful in the face of robust opposition – as well as the practical reality that the site remains the country's top tourist draw.

GEZI PARK, SCANDAL AND TROUBLE IN THE SOUTHEAST

A craze for faux-Ottoman kitsch construction – and shopping malls, in particular – sparked the Gezi Part Protests of May/June 2013. One of the city's last public green spaces, just beside Taksim Square, is a park that was to be privatized and built over as a mall. The violent police eviction of a protest sit-in here led to demonstrations and Occupy-type camps, not only in Istanbul but across Turkey for weeks, with casualties of over a dozen and up to 8,000 injured.

ban on demonstrations in the adjacent Taksim Square, it remains a frequent flashpoint for anti-government demonstrations.

In December 2013, the uncovering of a massive bribery scandal threatened to mar the AKP's long-held reputation as the 'clean' option, contrasted against the two brazenly corrupt decades of its predecessors. Police found millions in handy undeclared cash, in one case in a shoebox, at various suspects' residences. Erdoğan's reaction was to impede the work of, or dismiss outright, hundreds of

Trans Pride parade in Istanbul.

Demonstrations were attended by everyone who felt excluded by AK's social vision: LGBT people, Alevîs, anti-AK Islamists, single mothers, football club members, Kurds, environmentalists, anarchists, old hippies, atheists, communists and academics, to name just some groups. They were protesting not just Gezi per se but the ongoing privatization of public space across Turkey without consultation, brutal police tactics, Erdoğan's increasingly autocratic demeanour, the institutionalisation of Sunni Islam, Turkey's participation in the Syrian war and internet/social media censorship. Erdoğan predictably dismissed them all as 'pillagers' (*çapulcular*) and foreign agents. Erdoğan's mall has yet to be built, however, and despite a government

police investigators and prosecutors behind the operation, plus a cabinet reshuffle. Worse was to follow in February 2014, when five recordings (apparently genuine) were posted on YouTube of the PM telling his sons to hide suspicious cash stashes, perversely vindicating Erdoğan's hatred of all social media.

The PM vehemently denied, condemning the charges as a coup attempt and pointing fingers at foreign nations while dismissing thousands of judges and prosecutors and police and tightening the government's hold on the media. The most pointed accusations were cast at the reclusive Islamic preacher and commentator Fethullah Gülen, previously an AKP mentor. The government proposed shutting down all private religious academies affiliated to Gülen's Hizmet movement – its main activity – which mortally offended his many protegés among AKP MPs, the judiciary and the police, a network likened by some to Catholicism's Opus Dei. Eventually, four cabinet ministers were forced to resign before the case was abruptly dropped and the tape evidence ordered destroyed.

Despite the corruption allegations, Erdoğan handily won the Turkish presidency in a direct national vote in 2014, succeeding Abdullah Gül, while Ahmet Davutoğlu became PM. The ceremony was boycotted by opposition CHP, which claimed the elections were carried out unfairly.

In October 2014, national attention turned sharply towards the southeast, where an April 2013 ceasefire between Turkey and the PKK had previously offered hope for an end to the long and bloody Kurdish conflict. However, Kurdish protests were reignited in connection with the much-publicised siege of Kobanî, in which Turkish forces were accused of withholding aid to Kurdish YPG fighters and, purportedly, even faciliting the efforts of the growing Islamic State (IS). On the heels of an emboldening success for the pro-Kurdish People's Democratic Party (HDP) in June 2015, the intensity of the clashes was raised further still by yet another deadly attack, this time in the town of Suruç. As the Turkish military ramped up bombing raids on YPG bases, violent protests flared up across the region, destroying large parts of towns and cities (most notably Diyarbakır). Hundreds were estimated to be killed while hundreds of thousands more displaced, bolstering a tally that was already the world's largest.

Recep Tayyip Erdoğan.

⊘ THE COUP ATTEMPT OF 2016

On July 15th, 2016, a faction of the Turkish military swept in to occupy Taksim Square, two major bridges over the Bosphorus and other key sites in Ankara and Istanbul. Among these was the headquarters of state broadcaster TRT, where the coupists announced that they had seized control of the country in the interest of defending democracy from creeping authoritarianism. Erdoğan appeared on the air waves, calling on his supporters to take to the streets to defend democracy. The major squares of Ankara and Istanbul were filled with government supporters who helped to storm the Bosphorus Bridge (renamed the 15 July Martyrs Bridge). The final coupists surrendered.

Indeed, by late 2015 over two million refugees had arrived from Syria, straining Turkish resources and significantly altering local demographics in the southeast as well as in Istanbul. Roughly a million exited Turkey to the west, sparking heated debates across Europe that culminated in a March 2016 pledge by the EU to pay Turkey €3bn in exchange for its best efforts to clamp down on the flow of migrants. A month after an especially deadly pair of bomb attacks in Ankara left 100 dead, snap elections were called in November 2015: Erdoğan's AKP emerged victorious yet again, regaining a majority in parliament.

In the ensuring months, the ruling party became increasingly mired in internal and diplomatic disputes, most notably over a downed Russian fighter jet and over the German parliament's recognition of the Armenian genocide. Media censorship reached unprecedented levels with the seizure of Turkey's largest daily newspaper, Gulen-linked Zaman. To make things worse, the wave of large-scale suicide attacks rolled on, perpetrated by both Islamists and Kurdish separatists, including a June attack at Ataturk Airport that left 42 dead. Clearing a potential path for an expansion of Erdoğan's presidential powers, PM Davutoğlu resigned in May of 2016.

AN ATTEMPTED COUP AND ITS AFTERMATH

In the early hours of July 15th, yet another violent coup attempt was brought to an end. Erdoğan hailed the incident – in which he narrowly escaped death – as a "gift from God," a chance to consolidate his power and clean up the military. Within a week, upwards of 40,000 people had been detained, including 10,000 soldiers and nearly 3,000 judges. A three-month state of emergency was announced, only to be finally lifted two years later in July 2018 – just after Erdoğan's most recent electoral triumph. Since the early hours of the coup attempt, the government has pointed the finger firmly at the reclusive, self-exiled Fethullah Gulen, insisting that the US return him to face prosecution. Gulen has denied all involvement, and his continued stay in Pennsylvania has been a major thorn in the side of US-Turkey relations. Meanwhile, Erdoğan continues to clamp down on supposed conspirators within Turkey, a circle that has widened to include virtually all of Erdoğan's political foes and critics.

THE CURRENT OUTLOOK

Though narrowly, Erdoğan finally won his long-sought-after referendum in April 2017. Among other things it entailed a transition towards an executive presidency, significantly extending the powers of the office while dissolving the office of the PM. In June 2018, two years on from the attempted coup, Erdoğan called for yet another round of snap elections, securing a successive term in office – one newly imbued with sweeping powers granted by the recent referendum.

Erdoğan and his acolytes have continued to crack down on critical voices at home, jailing them in the thousands under the pretext of terrorism. Abroad, he has aimed to forge closer ties with Russia and Iran while failing to repair those with the US. The latter levied damaging sanctions in response to Turkey's continued strikes against US-backed Kurds in Syria, exacerbating Turkey's mounting financial woes. After a dramatic plunge of the lira over the summer of 2018 the economic crisis has begun to ease slightly along with US sanctions, facilitated by Turkey's release of an American pastor in October 2018.

Indeed, the ramping up of controversial megaprojects in recent years has signaled resilience in the face of a host of unenviable challenges. Among those completed have been high-speed rail corridors, new and

Çamlıca Mosque.

expanded motorways, bridges and tunnels beneath the Bosphorus. A 'wild' (Erdoğan's own adjective) plan to cut a shipping canal (the Kanal İstanbul) from the Black Sea to the Marmara through European Thrace has also been set in motion (due for completion in 2023), while, for himself, Erdoğan erected a giant new presidential palace in Ankara. Istanbul's enormous new Ottoman-style Çamlıca Mosque is the largest the country, while its gargantuan new airport is the largest in the world. Regardless of how long Erdoğan's rule lasts – and of how much longer the blustering rhetoric of religious nationalism will carry the day – the legacy of the AKP is already set in stone.

The trendy restaurants under the Galata Bridge have a fabulous view of the Yeni Camii.

Young girls posing in front of the Sabancı Merkez Mosque.

MODERN TURKS:
A QUEST FOR IDENTITY

With Turkey modernising rapidly, its people are poised between traditional rural values, liberal Islamism and global capitalism.

Ne mutlu Türküm diyene!" (Happy is he who calls himself a Turk!). This famous quotation from a 1927 speech of Atatürk's is still inscribed on monuments country wide. Despite its patriotic sentiment, however, its meaning is ambiguous in a country that has been inhabited for 9,000 years by many tribes and religions, voluntary settlers and refugees, which regards its origins as Asian, its institutions largely Western and its values increasingly Islamic.

Older people steeped in republican ideology will profess vague ethnic kinship to the Turkic nomads who swept into Anatolia early in the last millennium. However, only a few thousand Turks imposed their civilisation and language on a much larger indigenous population. Deeper racial links between modern Turks and Central Asia are more fantastic than factual. Yet the concept lingers stubbornly in the Turkish self-image, a holdover from the time of Atatürk, when the state's founders scrambled to devise a new concept of nationhood which circumvented centuries of Ottoman rule. Only since the 1990s has Turkey acknowledged any value in the kaleidoscope of different ethnicities which have contributed to Anatolian culture.

The older generation.

THE REPUBLICAN REWRITE

After the collapse of the Ottoman Empire, the republic found it expedient to ignore the recent past and look further back for national heroes. During Atatürk's westernising social revolution, when the hat replaced the fez (itself a 19th-century innovation) and a Latin alphabet supplanted Arabic script (deliberately divorcing contemporary Turks from 800 years of Ottoman history), all things Ottoman were reviled as retrograde; any identification with Muslim, much less Greek, culture was simply inadmissible.

Purported Asiatic ancestors, chosen according to transient intellectual trends (some uncomfortably close to Nazi dogma), included briefly the Sumerians and the Hittites, before the short-lived but glamorous Seljuk Turks were declared suitable national role models. The Huns and Mongols got honourable mentions too, which resulted in many boy-children named Selçuk, Attila and Cengiz (as in Genghiz Khan): spectacular PR blunders for a country seemingly oblivious to the last two's bloodcurdling reputation in Europe. At one point the Turkish language was deemed to be the mother-tongue of all others; such crackpot theories remained in school textbooks until the 1970s. All this betrayed a deep-seated insecurity and perhaps doubts that plain old Anatolian Turks – the word had been an Ottoman insult, connoting "rube" or "yokel" – deserved to be in the driver's seat.

SEARCHING FOR A NEW OUTLOOK

A century later, Kemalist civic principles still (ostensibly) guide the republic. Turkey's booming cities, new highways and bridges, vast dams, extensive tourism infrastructure and increasing involvement in the world economy – it is one of the G20 – can be at least partially credited to Atatürk's reforms. Unfortunately, the cult of personality developed after his death and the force-feeding of Kemalism has led to intellectual complacency that finds it easier to repeat clichés than explore changed realities and pose difficult but essential questions. Ideas designed to motivate 10 million Turks in the traumatic wake of World War I defeat are not necessarily appropriate for today's country of 77 million (and counting) inhabitants.

The republic is a diasporic ingathering par excellence, rivalled in this respect only by Israel: the explicit corollary to "Happy is he who calls himself a Turk" has been "A Turk is anyone will-

Farmer in Van, far-east Turkey.

⊘ PERCEPTIONS OF SELF AND OTHERS

Perceptions of Turkey abroad remain central to Turkish self-esteem. The 19th-century image of the Ottoman Empire as the "Sick Man of Europe" produced a palpable national inferiority complex, while humiliation by the victorious World War I Allies further aggravated sensitivities. Even well-intentioned attempts to voice justifiable criticism of Turkey may be met with extreme defensiveness. There is perpetual exasperation at grim portrayals of Turks and Turkey in Western fiction (think *Pascali's Island, The Rage of the Vulture*) and films (*Midnight Express*), while foreign news coverage is often sensational and poorly informed.

ing to call themselves a Turk". This has included people from ex-Yugoslavia, Bulgaria, Romania, the Crimea, Albania, Circassia, Bosnia, Daghestan, Azerbaijan, Georgia and other far-flung locales, making a mockery of any theoretical common racial origin espoused by the more fanatical pan-Turkists.

Until the early 1990s, it was hazardous to admit to having (say) Kurdish, Armenian or Cretan background; more recently it has become positively trendy among younger people looking to define themselves as pieces in a diverse cultural mosaic. But despite this, a law against "denigrating Turkishness" (a catch-all offence) remains in place, and the late journalist Hrant Dink, before his 2007 assassination by ultra-nationalists, attracted prosecution by pro-claiming that he was "a Turkish citizen of Armenian descent" – still an unacceptable concept.

A GLOBALLY AWARE POPULATION

Profound demographic change following both internal and overseas migration (and a certain amount of foreign settlement) have helped change Turkey's view of itself in the world. Over 6 million Turks now live abroad, over 5 million of these in Europe, with up to 4 million in Germany alone. Despite periodic lulls, foreign tourists continue to

styles. This continued under the republic in music as *aranjmanlar*, whether this meant tango à la Turca, Elvis Presley impersonators, or Anatolian rock. There have recently been genuine, creative attempts at syntheses of foreign and Turkish

Seventy percent of Turkey's people live in cities. Of a total population of 83 million, over a quarter are under 15.

Demonstrator wearing an Atatürk mask in Istanbul's Gezı Park.

pour into Turkey, reaching the country's remotest corners; marriage with locals (something almost unknown before the 1960s) is on the rise. Turks travel and study abroad for short periods in ever-increasing numbers, watch imported (if dubbed) series on over 200 TV channels, speak more languages (especially English) and are positively glued to the internet – even if the authorities frequently block sites (like YouTube, Twitter or Wikipedia) deemed to have breached some lingering repressive law, or Erdoğan's sensibilities.

Although some conservatives (with little faith in the robustness of Turkish identity) bleakly warn of wholesale westernisation as a result, it's worth remembering that the late Ottoman Empire was adept at assimilating and adapting foreign

The long-standing alliance with the US has cooled since the 2003 Iraq War, which was opposed by 90 percent of Turks. Numerous diplomatic spats – including the refusal of the US to extradite the suspected instigator of the 2016 coup attempt and US backing of Syrian Kurdish fighters have further widened the rift.

styles, rather than merely imitation, not just in music but also fashion, art installations and film-making, replacing the derivativeness or ideological prescriptiveness of earlier republican efforts.

GROWING PAINS

Unfortunately, this confident new profile masks deep divisions and disruptive factors within modern Turkey. Mid-Noughties economic growth rates of nearly 8 percent annually – now much reduced to about 2 percent – have occurred in one of the most unequal societies on earth. Some industrial magnates are worth billions, but a decent, trained-professional salary is barely 1,000 euros per month. The nationwide minimum monthly wage is supposedly 2,020TL (lately about 338 euros) after taxes and deductions – so pay scales remain dismal. Unemployment remains in double figures, ensuring continued emigration, while unemployment benefits are almost nonexistent. Meanwhile, the cost of many essentials equals that of much of Mediterranean Europe. Accordingly, nightclubs thronged by designer-clad youth and shops bulging with cutting-edge consumer durables can be provocative to some, with petty (and not so petty) crime on the increase.

The class gap remains vast, a chasm of mistrust separating secular urbanites in the west from those still rooted in provincial values even

World Peace Day celebration in Van.

⊘ HAREM SCARUM

Following their conversion to Islam over 1,000 years ago, the Turks also adopted the Muslim practice of secluding women. The area of the house where men entertained guests became the *selamlık*; the part reserved for the women of the household, including daughters and aunts, was the *harem* (forbidden sanctuary). Enough is known about harem life to dismiss as laughable the common stereotype of it as a prison for sex slaves. The harem was, in fact, the domain of the first wife, whose permission was required before a husband could acquire extra wives – something exceptional rather than the rule outside of palace circles, as he would have to support (and pay attention to) all wives equally. Women in upper-crust harems – notably at Topkapı Palace – were trained in the arts and religion, as well as in household management.

Women born into the upper echelons of society never went out except with a chaperone, and a facial covering; shopping was undertaken by slaves. Only shameless, infidel hussies appeared or performed uncovered in public; most of the great female café singers of late Ottoman times were Greek, Jewish or Armenian. This convention persisted well into republican years – Safiye Ayla, Atatürk's favourite performer, felt obliged to sing from behind a curtain at her 1932 'special command' concert for him.

if no longer resident in the provinces. This has meant electoral success for the Islamist AK Party, having governed since 2002 only through pledging to preserve a secular state. The army's watchful eye has precluded any Iran-style fundamentalism, though it is perhaps more defanged than ever of late following the 2016 coup attempt.

Education is another divisive subject. Although tuition for universities and polytechnics is largely free, competitive entrance exams mean mainly young Turks from rich families attend expensive private cramming academies. Recent years have seen a massive expansion of government-supported, religiously-infused Imam Hatip schools. While popular among Muslims for offering a moral education, minorities are significantly less keen. Overall, however, Turkey has made great strides of late in raising graduation rates.

Since the coup attempt of 2016, freedom of expression has become increasingly conditional, with forcible closures of political parties and media outlets and frequent arrests of journalists, writers and intellectuals. At the time of writing, Turkey continues to hold the world's number one position for jailed journalists. In July 2018, following the AKP's most recent electoral success, an end was announced to the country's two-year state of emergency, though the government continues to hound and silence its critics, most often through levying charges of terrorism.

TURKISH WOMEN

Stereotypes die hard. European art and literature have traditionally depicted eastern, Islamic women as docile creatures, clad in all-enveloping garments when not dancing before their master in transparent silks. As a result, some visitors are surprised to find Turkish women in a bar after a day's work at their chosen profession, be it civil servant, hotel staff, lawyer or doctor. How many wives do Turkish men have? One, legally, in this secular state – the Muslim tradition of four is illegal. Do women still wear head coverings? Some do, but this is often an assertion of national identity in defiance of a too-rapid and rather vulgar westernisation rather than a purely religious observation.

Winds of change. The major social upheavals of World War I and the subsequent War of Independence radically affected the status of Turkish women. Many began working in munitions

factories, while wives and daughters of the elite became vocal supporters of the nationalists. Accordingly, female emancipation became one of the cornerstones of the republican reform project. The new civil code adopted in 1926 significantly altered traditional family life. Polygamy and religious marriage were abolished, a minimum age for civil marriage set, while divorce, right to inheritance and child custody became the prerogative of both sexes. Women also gained equality as witnesses in court; previously, under Islamic law, the testimony of two women was equal to a

Lace workers in Sardis.

man's. Moreover, female suffrage applied to local elections in 1930, to parliamentary ones in 1934 – years before some European countries.

Theory and practice. But theory is one thing, practice another: the Islamic ethic concerning female submission to male authority still pervades much of modern Turkish society, particularly in rural areas: many urban Turkish women are appalled to see rural wives toiling in the kitchen after a day's labour in the fields while their husbands occupy the local teahouse. Recent changes to the civil code allow married women to keep their maiden name, work without their husband's permission, be the legal head of a household and get an equal split of communal property upon divorce, but alimony can be difficult to claim, given the vast amount of unregistered income in the country. Better-off Turkish women ensure their name appears on family property deeds; uneducated, sometimes illiterate rural women with scant understanding of their rights don't. Thus many remain in abusive marriages – divorce is still a scandal in religious circles, and often a woman's own family will not take her back if she leaves her husband.

There has been a recent upsurge in so-called "honour killings" – the doing away with young, or not so young, women who have supposedly

A Kurdish woman holds a portrait of a woman who died in an "honour killing".

brought shame on their families through extra-marital relations, refusal of an arranged marriage or merely flirting with someone disapproved of by Papa. The official tally for such incidents of several hundred annually is a gross underestimate.

A matter of class. In remoter villages most women wear some kind of head covering, and moving to towns does not imply shedding such garb. Urban feminism tends to be the preserve of educated, well-off women, who disdain their more traditional sisters living nearby in working-to-lower-middle-class neighbourhoods. There, a spectrum of religious "fashion statements", in the main freely chosen, has emerged. At one extreme are wearers of the full, black abaya "cloak"

(*çarşaf*), while the more moderate "raincoat brigade" favours patterned scarves and loose overcoats in pastel colours. Younger "new Islamic" women may wear bright, fashionable clothes covering the wrists and the ankles, but tight enough to show off their figures, with designer headscarves wrapped around their throats.

ETHNIC MINORITIES IN TURKEY

Since the Stone Age, Anatolia has been home to numerous races, cultures and faiths, many still found here today. Central Asian Turkish blood is a relatively new contribution to the melting pot. The Ottomans did not consider themselves as Turks, and by the 16th century were so intermixed (not least through a harem preference for Circassian or Slavic blonde women) that Asian roots were largely irrelevant. In general, Ottoman society was tolerant of different races and origins, though religion, not ethnicity, was one's mark of identity. But the authorities were not above setting *millets* against each other when it suited them to provoke tensions – for example after Orthodox Patriarch Gregory V was hanged by the sultan in 1821 for failing to quell the Greek revolution, his corpse was given to a group of Jews to desecrate, then thrown into the Bosphorus where a Cretan fisherman rescued it.

From 1984 onwards, the struggle between the Kurdish PKK insurrectionary militia and the state has loomed large in Turkish politics. The Kurds (see below), however, are not the only group whose identity has been suppressed in republican Turkey. Christian minorities such as the Greeks, Armenians and Süriyani often live precariously, regularly condemned by nationalists as detrimental to the nation's security. The Alevîs, a Shi'ite Muslim sect (not an ethnic group; see page 88) who make up almost a quarter of Turkey's population, have also frequently been targeted for physical attack as well as scurrilous calumny. Additionally, the Sunni-dominated Ministry of Religious Affairs gives scant recognition or financial support for Alevî beliefs or social programmes.

THE KURDS

Kurdish origins are obscure, but they have certainly inhabited the region between Syria, Iraq, Iran and eastern Turkey since antiquity. Some consider them descendants of the Medes, who dominated the Lake Van area after the collapse of Urartian civilisation. Others maintain they are the Karduchi encountered in 401 BC by the Greek historian-general Xenophon, who described them as a "freedom-loving mountain people".

Kurds identify themselves by clan, within larger tribes headed by powerful *ağas* or chieftains. The Kurdish language, an Indo-European tongue related to Iranian (not Turkish), has four mutually unintelligible dialects, two of which (Kurmanji and Zaza) are spoken in Turkey. They are also divided by faith – Alevî Kurds are concentrated near Erzincan and Tunceli, while in

the offing, especially if the Turkish state allows cultural rights (including teaching and broadcasting in Kurdish), the development of southeast Turkey that truly benefits locals, and a Kurdish-interests party not continually threatened with closure. See also page 373.

ETHNIC GROUPS OF THE CAUCASUS

The Black Sea coast and mountains are home to several Caucasian groups such as the Laz, who trace their ancestry to ancient Colchis, where Jason and his Argonauts came to steal the

Kurdish children in the poor section of Alibaşa, in Diyarbakir.

the far southeast Sunni dervish orders historically had many Kurdish members. There are at least 15 million Kurds in Turkey, with war and economic migration meaning that over half have left their original homes in eastern Anatolia.

The PKK conflict has to date left around 40,000 dead on all sides, hundreds of thousands of internal Kurdish refugees, and engendered great bitterness amongst Turks. Although the capture of the PKK leader Abdullah Öcalan in 1998 saw a pronounced lull in the war, sporadic clashes have resumed in recent years, most notably in 2015 and 2016 when street battles led to the destruction of large swathes of Kurdish towns and cities. Realistic people on both sides of the issue recognise that an independent Kurdish state is not in

There are around 35 million Kurds worldwide, mostly living in Turkey, Syria, Russia, Azerbaijan, Armenia, Lebanon and Iran in the Middle East, but with a far-flung northern-European diaspora. Their only de facto state is in northern Iraq.

Golden Fleece. Although they converted from Christianity to Islam in the 16th century, they still speak a language related to Mingrelian and Georgian. Current population estimates range between 500,000 and 1.5 million, the majority of them having relocated to the cities of western Turkey in recent decades. The Laz are noted for their energetic style and dry sense of humour, as well as their keen business acumen; especially in the contracting business and the restaurant

> *Returned Almanyalılar (German Turks), resented and envied in equal measure, perform approximately the same function in Turkish society as returned Greek-Americans do in Greece, with their cash remittances and perceived vulgarity.*

Adana resident.

trade, though traditionally they were farmers and sailors. For many years the repeating of jokes at their expense – akin to Pontian jokes in Greece, or west-country sheep-molesting stereotypes in England – was a favourite pastime; the Laz took it in their stride, retorting that other Turks were merely jealous of their success.

The Hemşınlis of the Kaçkar Mountains are an Armenian tribe speaking an archaic dialect of Armenian, who only converted to Islam in the early 1800s. They are famous as pastry cooks across Turkey and somewhat less numerous than the Laz.

There are also perhaps 50,000 Pontian Greek Muslims who converted slightly before the Hemşınlis, and were thus allowed to stay

in republican Turkey. Their language, Rumca, is mutually intelligible with the medieval Greek spoken by the descendants of Orthodox Pontians living in Greece, and there is in fact an annual pastoral festival in the Black Sea mountains where members of the two groups meet and socialise.

THE GREEKS

Greeks have lived in Asia Minor since the early first millennium BC, and although some hate to admit it, many modern Turks have Greek ancestry, given the degree of intermarriage from the 12th century onwards. Under Ottoman rule, the Greek Orthodox church (*Rum Ortodoks* in Turkish) comprised its own *millet*, and (like the Armenians and Jews) had considerable autonomy in running communal affairs. Until the fall of the Ottoman Empire, Greek Orthodox communities (many speaking Turkish as a first language) were scattered across much of Anatolia, while between a quarter and a third of the population of Istanbul were ethnic Greeks. The seat of the Eastern Orthodox Church has been in Istanbul since the 4th century AD, and the spiritual leader of world Orthodoxy, the ecumenical patriarch, still resides in Fener district.

But in accordance with the 1923 Treaty of Lausanne, Greece and Turkey agreed to exchange religious minorities. Nearly 1.3 million Greek Orthodox were compelled to leave Anatolia (many had already done so), and almost 400,000 Muslims were sent from Greece. The only exemptions were the 110,000 Orthodox of Tenedos and İmroz islands and Istanbul. They were allowed to stay as a counter to a near-equal number of Muslims (ethnically Turkish, Pomak or Gypsy) left in western Thrace.

The policy may have seemed expedient at the time, but it caused enormous personal suffering and severe economic dislocation for both nations; many now consider it a major error. After anti-Greek riots in 1955, the Cyprus crisis of 1974 and government confiscatory measures or restrictions on education, there was little hope of a continued vital Greek presence in Turkey; the permanently resident Istanbul community has dropped below 2,000 (plus a smaller number living in İzmir disguised as "Levantines" with Italian nationality).

The dwindling population of native-born Greek Orthodox pose a major threat to the continued existence of the patriarchate, since by Turkish law every ecumenical patriarch must be a Turkish citizen. The Orthodox theological seminary on Halki (Heybeli) in the Princes' Islands, the major training centre for future clergy, has been closed since 1971. So far international pressure to reopen the school has had no effect.

Finally, another class of "Greeks" – Muslim in this case – dwells on the Aegean and Mediterranean coasts, with concentrations around Çanakkale, Ayvalık, Bodrum and Side. Most are from Crete or Lesvós, and nostalgically proud of their roots; despite pressure to assimilate, many can still speak island dialects three generations after the transfer from Greece.

THE SÚRYANIS AND ARABS

The Tür Abdin Plateau, east of Midyat and Mardin in southeast Turkey, was an important centre for Syriac Orthodox Christianity from the 6th century onwards, and in medieval times there were 80 monasteries in the region. Only three

Immigrant Armenian children participate in class.

☉ THE ARMENIANS

At its peak, Armenian territory stretched from northeastern Anatolia to northwestern Persia, with an offshoot Cilician kingdom. This once-powerful empire was overrun by the Persians and Ottomans in the 15th century, although Armenian Apostolics continued to live locally. The Cilician kingdom was the source of Armenian Catholics, while American missionary activity during the 1800s produced a crop of Armenian Protestants.

Armed Armenian revolutionary-nationalist organisations appeared during the 1890s, provoking 1895–96 pogroms which cost 100,000 Armenian lives. Worse came during World War I, when some east Anatolian Armenians sided with the invading Russians. The genocidal massacres of 1915–16 remain a source of immense controversy today, hampering efforts to normalise diplomatic relations between Turkey and the modern republic of Armenia. Promises of independence from the statesmen at the Versailles Peace Treaty came to nothing after the Turks and then, conclusively, the Russians overran the short-lived postwar independent Armenian republic.

Today about 70,000 Armenians remain in Istanbul, where they are still prominent in the arts and small business; the Armenian Apostolic Patriarchate is at Kumkapı in old Istanbul. Perhaps 15,000 Armenians still live in the east, having nominally converted to Islam after 1916; most fear to identify themselves openly.

(Mar Gabriel, seat of the bishop; Mar Yakoub and Deyr-az-Zaferan) still function, along with various churches in Midyat, Mardin and the plateau villages, while just a few hundred Assyrian Christians still live locally. Nationwide there are now around 15,000 Süryanis (as they are called in Turkish), mostly in Istanbul where they have a reputation as superb jewellers. Until the 1970s there were 20,000 in the Tür Abdin alone, but Kurdish extortion and general Muslim bigotry resulted in large-scale emigration, in particular to Sweden and the US. Numbers had already

Erzurum boy.

been substantially reduced during World War I, when approximately 300,000 Süryanis were despatched by the Ottomans, in tandem with the Armenian genocide. The church liturgy is conducted in Syriac, a Semitic language essentially identical to biblical Aramaic but written in its own script.

Ethnic Arabs: There are anywhere from 1.5–2 million ethnic Arabs in Turkey, the vast majority in the far southeast, in and around Mardin, Urfa, Harran and the Hatay province – historically a part of Syria which was controversially annexed to Turkey in 1939. Although many people speak Arabic as a first language, and Syria long agitated for the return of the Hatay, any separatist initiative is going nowhere.

THE JEWISH COMMUNITY

There were already indigenous Jews in Istanbul and Bursa before the Ottoman conquest, but most of today's Jewish community trace their ancestry to 1492, when Sultan Beyazit II gave asylum to 150,000 Sephardic Jews escaping death or conversion after the edict of Queen Isabella and King Ferdinand of Spain. Encouraged by the Ottomans, who valued their skills, the Jews established Turkey's first printing press in 1493, and many famous Ottoman court physicians, financiers and diplomats were Sephardic. But the community stagnated educationally and had declined in influence by the 18th century, to be surpassed socially by the Greeks and Armenians.

Neutral Turkey did not officially grant visas to Jews fleeing Nazi-occupied Europe, though individual diplomats saved hundreds of refugees. But after a discriminatory wartime tax against religious minorities, and the 1955 anti-Greek riots which also targeted Jews, emigration to Israel accelerated. Today the local Jewish community, mostly in Istanbul and İzmir, numbers around 15,000, much depleted since 2002 by an anti-semitic climate under AK governments. Yet roughly twenty synagogues (not all active) still exist in Istanbul, plus eight more in İzmir.

THE ROMA

Turkish-speaking, Muslim Roma live predominantly in Thrace, the Aegean region and around Samsun; as elsewhere in the Balkans, they are generally disadvantaged and scorned by mainstream Turks. The settled Roma of Thrace and the Bergama area are the most well-off. Estimates as to their population vary widely, official sources putting their numbers at 500,000 and non-official sources at up to 5 million.

NOMADS (YÖRÜKS)

Few true nomads remain in Turkey, but there is still seasonal transhumance (see page 22) to *yaylas* (pastoral colonies) in the Taurus Mountains from northwest of Fethiye to northeast of Adana. Thought to be descendants of the Oğuz Turkic tribe, many have preserved the fair complexion and green eyes of their ancestors; a few are actually Turcoman, and Alevî in religion. Mountain trekkers in the Taurus will probably encounter inhabited Yörük *yaylas* during the summer.

ATATÜRK: FATHER OF THE NATION

The founder of modern Turkey still commands adulation from the vast majority of his country, despite the dissonance between his legacy and the aims of the ruling AKP.

Indeed, billboards often portray Erdoğan alongside Atatürk, and bronze statues or busts of the latter still occupy the choicest spot in every Turkish town, a canonical repertoire of photos graces hotel lobbies and official foyers, while ridges overhead feature his pithy quotes, and cut-out silhouettes of the great man pacing about at Gallipoli. His Balkan features and piercing blue eyes bore little resemblance to the purported Central Asian ancestors he identified for Turks; some suggest part-Jewish roots on his father's side, though more scholarly opinion points to a mixed Slavic-Albanian background. Nevertheless, Mustafa Kemal (as he was born) is the focus of one of the most enduring personality cults in modern history, the literal Father (Ata) of the Turkish republic.

Born in 1881, the only surviving son of a customs official and a devout peasant mother in the now-Greek northern Aegean port of Selanik (today Thessaloniki), eight-year-old Mustafa chafed at the conventions of the district religious school, the beginning of his distaste for organised Islam.

Kemal enrolled at the local military academy, before transferring to Harbiye War College in Istanbul, where he was caught up in clandestine publication of a seditious newspaper, and punished by a transfer to Damascus as captain – far away from the locus of power. Even so, in 1906 he set up a revolutionary society there which soon merged with the pan-Ottoman Committee for Union and Progress (CUP) headed eventually by the ill-fated triumvirate of Enver, Cemal and Talat. Unlike them, Mustafa Kemal remained a strict legalist, calling for the separation of the military from politics, and evoking the lasting suspicion of the triumvirate, in particular the jealous Enver.

In 1911, Kemal volunteered for service in Libya against the Italian invasion there; however, the outbreak of the catastrophic Balkan Wars the following year brought him back to Thrace where he helped Enver recapture Edirne, although the latter was given all the credit, and soon contrived to have Kemal dispatched to Sofia as a military attaché. Enver went on to drag Turkey into World War I, after which the entire triumvirate met violent ends. Mustafa Kemal, who had emerged as the only undefeated commander at war's end, was well placed to assume leadership of the struggle to save the heartland of the lost empire – the successor state to be known as "Türkiye", the Land of the Turks. In the two decades before his death in 1938, he led armies to victory in the War of Independence, replaced the sultanate with a republic (serving as its first president) and introduced sweeping secular reforms.

Bust of Mustafa Kemal Atatürk looking out to the Dardanelles.

Today, over 80 years after succumbing to liver cirrhosis, Kemal Atatürk (as he renamed himself when surnames became obligatory) is still revered across Turkey, his writings and speeches a source of often contradictory wisdom. His reputation is protected by the 1982 constitution, with severe penalties for infractions.

Certainly, the officer corps committed to preserving his heritage have no doubts about former cadet number 1238; every year, when Atatürk's number is called out at the roll call of the graduating class of new military cadets, there is but one uniform response: "He is among us."

RELIGION IN TURKEY

Sunni Islam in republican Turkey is flourishing, despite nearly a century of official secularism.

Even though 98 percent of Turks are at least notionally Muslim, the republic of Turkey was until somewhat recently explicitly secular, with religion strictly a matter of private conscience, excluded from public life and policy. However, a pietist Sunni climate has prevailed since the rise of the AKP in 2002. Particularly over its most recent decade, Erdoğan's party has gradually expanded the role of faith within the public sphere, spurring increased polarisation between pious loyalists and the secular opposition.

MUSLIMS

The *ezan* (call to prayer), issuing from speakers on mosque minarets, exhorts the faithful five times a day: dawn, midday, mid-afternoon, sunset and two hours after dark. Yet the interpretation of Islam in Turkey has traditionally been liberal, bearing little resemblance to the strict codes of practice in Iran and Saudi Arabia. By the 1500s, the Ottomans had adopted the Sunni Hanafite school of jurisprudence, which interpreted the Qur'an using analogy and opinion.

Alevîs: Most Turks are Sunni, but there are also 20 million Shi'ite Alevîs spread across the country, who hold more liberal and even left-wing beliefs. These two distinct sects arose after Muhammad's death, during disputes over the succession of a new caliph. The future Sunnis elected Abu Bakr, who governed consensually; the breakaway Shi'ites believed in a hereditary authority, descending directly from Muhammad through his daughter, Fatima, and her husband, Ali, still greatly revered.

Alevîsm in Turkey dates mainly from the campaigns of Shia Shah Ismail of Persia in the early 16th century; although resoundingly defeated at Çaldıran by Sultan Selim I, stragglers from Ismail's army retreated to isolated areas of

The mosque in Safranbolu, on the Black Sea.

⊙ THE SOURCES OF ISLAM

Islam is the newest of the three Abrahamic religions, founded in the 7th century AD when the Prophet Muhammad's divine revelations were conveyed orally and memorised by his followers. They were not written down as the Qur'an until after Muhammad's death, and save for certain recommendations, gave scant direction as to actual practice of the new religion. Accordingly, the *Sunnah* – a collection of anecdotes and sayings *(hadiths)* attributed to Muhammad – became a supplemental basis of much Islamic belief and law. A wide disparity in interpretation of the Qur'an and the *Sunnah* has resulted in today's diversity of Muslim practice.

Anatolia. Separated from mainstream Shi'ite practice, distinctive Alevî traditions emerged; itinerant travelling holy elders (dedes) replaced the traditional clerical hierarchy, for example, and the Qur'anic ban on alcohol was relaxed.

Women have equal status with men, praying together in cemevleri (meeting houses) rather than mosques, a custom which has led to scurrilous allegations of orgies, and the forcible imposition of "proper" mosques on Alevî villages. Their leftist-secularist inclinations also provoke mistrust among fundamentalist Sunnis, which has occasionally resulted in violence.

Sufis: Other Sunni sects include various Sufi orders (tariqats), whose rituals combine elements of pre- and early Christian practice, Buddhism and Neoplatonism. Dancing, music and repetitive chants have all been used in the central practice of zikr (literally, "remembrance of God"). In Ottoman times, the Sufi brotherhoods formed tekkes (lodges), similar to Christian monasteries. Orders were led by şeyhs, and novices (murids) were disciples of a fully fledged dervish; all took vows of poverty, relying on alms.

Atatürk's suppression of the dervish orders (along with the practice of worshipping at the tombs of dervish şeyhs) was never entirely effective, and since the 1970s these have discreetly re-emerged. The most famous, and visible, is the sophisticated, urban-based Mevlevî order, which reveres the mystic poet Mevlâna Celaleddin Rumi of 13th-century Konya, but there also were (and still are) the more conservative Halveti-Cerahi, Kadiri, Rifâi and Nakşibendi sects (the late president Özal was a Nakşibendi adherent).

The Mevlevî ceremony, in which dervishes wearing voluminous robes and conical hats whirl to the pulse of drums and strains of mournful music, was revived in recent decades as a "folkloric manifestation" and tourist attraction, especially at the annual (December) Konya festival commemorating the death of Mevlâna. However, more genuine manifestations take place all year at the Galata Mevlevîhane in Istanbul, where participants actually profess to live as Sufis, rather than treating the whirling as merely a fancy-dress exercise.

Bektaşis: The Bektaşi order, followers of Hacı Bektaş Veli (1209–71), is based at Hacıbektaş, near Kırşehir in central Turkey, where their founder is buried. Like their Alevî affiliates, and indeed all Shi'ite sects, they recognise Ali as the rightful successor to Muhammad; heads of the order are called babas. The Bektaşis absorbed numerous non-Muslim practices, including a version of baptism, and also celebrate the Zoroastrian spring-equinox festival, Nevroz, as Ali's birthday. Their ethical teachings stress the precedence of inner intent and purity over outward observance, and avoidance of inconsistency or ostentation.

RELIGION AND THE OTTOMANS

Islam, and religion generally, played a crucial role in the Ottoman Empire. Islam helped create

Ritual ablutions at Beyazit Mosque, Istanbul.

Muslims espouse five basic practices: the statement of their creed ("There is no God but Allah and Muhammad is his Prophet"), prayer, giving alms, fasting during Ramadan (Ramazan in Turkish), and making a pilgrimage to Mecca.

solidarity among ethnically diverse elements and, through the millet system for Christians and Jews, provided a clear legal structure for subjects of all creeds. The Ottoman sultan became the protector of the entire Islamic world following the Turkish conquest of the holy places Mecca and Medina, and Egypt where the caliph was captured, in 1516.

Under the Ottomans, a corps of Muslim scholars (the *ulema*) pronounced on all religious matters, taught theology, administered mosques and schools, and controlled the courts.

Early Ottoman theologians were influenced by Al-Ghazali (1058–1111), a Persian scholar who, while vehemently attacking ancient Greek philosophy, encouraged empirical observation and experiment. As a result, many Muslims achieved notable results in astronomy, mathematics and medicine, using (for example) scientific methods to fix the position of the *qibla*

Turkish Islamist women rally in support of lifting a ban on headscarves in universities.

(prayer niche in mosques), which had to point towards Mecca.

As the empire slowly declined, progress was stifled through a series of reactionary measures. Under pressure from calligraphers whose livelihood was threatened, printing presses were forbidden until the early 18th century. In 1580, Sultan Murat III closed an observatory in Istanbul on the grounds that the astronomers were "insolent enough to try to pry open the secrets of the universe" – secrets known only to Allah. Meanwhile, across much of Europe the Renaissance was in full swing, and the discoveries it fuelled were soon reflected in technological advances. But even the resulting, repeated battlefield successes of Christian states against the

Ottomans were insufficient to convince a hidebound, arrogant clergy, who saw no need to learn from infidels. It was not until the 19th century that Western innovations were allowed to be widely disseminated within the empire.

ISLAM UNDER THE REPUBLIC

All this changed with the establishment of the Turkish republic; Atatürk's sweeping reforms also meant that the clergy, now effectively paid civil servants, were subordinated to a special Ministry of Religious Affairs (known as Diyanet). Even the *ezan* in Arabic, the sacred language of Islam, was outlawed in 1932 in favour of a Turkish version (until the 1950s Menderes government reinstated it).

The 1980–83 junta, and the Özal government thereafter, encouraged "moderate" religious expression as a bulwark against leftist extremism and Kurdish nationalism. The junta made religious education compulsory in state schools for all primary and secondary pupils, with no parental opt-out allowed as before. There was a huge increase in the number of *Imam Hatip okulları* (private religious secondary schools), first set up under Menderes. Godfather of all this was the Ocak (Hearth) movement, which had emerged in the 1970s, advocating a national identity comprised of pre-Islamic Turkism and Islam.

These measures let various genies out of the bottle – and prompted predictable secularist reaction. The military's tolerance of "Islam Lite" did not extend to its own ranks, where radical Islamists were periodically purged from a force seeing itself as the main guardian of the Kemalist flame. In 1998, obligatory secular primary education was increased from five to eight years, drastically weakening the secondary religious academies by depriving them of influence and tuition money. Many parents were unhappy, as these schools had performed well compared to the woeful state sector and anyway devoted just a few hours weekly to Arabic and Qur'anic study.

The 1990s saw Islamist political parties gain considerable ground, especially in large cities, by addressing issues and providing services apparently beyond secularist capabilities. Such parties (and their leaders) were successively banned for contravening the constitution, but to no avail. Indeed, for most Turks, Islam remains a much sounder source of values and spiritual succour than anything deemed to be imported from the West, and a more indigenous expression of identity than the *de haut en bas* arrogance of the secular elite.

For many of these, the AKP – political Islam's Turkish incarnation for going on two decades – fits the bill thanks largely to its anti-secular, anti-Western and often populist rhetoric. Many others, however, are increasingly unsettled by the party's vigorous pursuit of shaping – as Erdoğan himself has heralded – "pious generations" further expanding Imam Hatip religious

After many years of Islamist attempts, the wearing of headscarves by female civil servants or MPs, and beards by men, was finally permitted in late 2013. Both had already been allowed at universities since 2010. Hitherto, these bans had effectively barred young people of conservative background from a public career, or admittance to university.

St Paul souvenirs.

Prayers in a mosque.

schools, lengthening the scope of compulsory religion classes in public schools, excluding mention of Charles Darwin and his theory from curricula, cracking down on alcohol sales and consumption, condemning the use of contraceptives and overseeing a proliferation of Ottoman-style mosques, among other things. While loyalists praise the AKP's efforts as true to purpose, recent polls suggest that religious convictions have actually slipped in recent years, with Deism and even atheism making gains, particularly among Turkish youth. True to form, Erdoğan has countered such developments by pointing to a Western conspiracy to corrupt Turkish morality. Many others – from across the religious spectrum – point to AKP rule itself.

⊘ EXPERIMENTING WITH RELIGION

Before the advent of Islam, Turkic nomads practised shamanism, presided over by the sky-god Tengri. Eventually some tribes, like the Uighurs, adopted Buddhism, while others became Zoroastrians, Nestorians or Monophysites. The Khazar empire became Jewish from the 8th century until its fall some 300 years later. Only during the 10th century did most Turks convert to Islam, following their encounter with the Arabs. Today almost 250,000 Christian Turks, the Gagauz, still live in parts of the Balkans, Moldova and the Ukraine, while the Karaim, Jewish Karaylar Turks originally from the Crimea, are found in Russia, Lithuania and Poland.

Turkey excels in fresh produce.

FIT FOR A SULTAN'S TABLE

Turkey's wide-ranging terrain and climatic diversity produces a variety of foodstuffs. Together with the palette of herbs and spices, it makes for one of the world's great cuisines.

For 500 years, the Ottoman Empire ruled much of the Balkans and Middle East, and at Istanbul's Topkapı Palace great chefs created a sumptuous cuisine which rivalled the epicurean delights of ancient Rome. They were encouraged by the sheer variety of fish, fowl, meat, fruit and vegetables produced in Turkey, as well as the numerous cultures that have flourished in Anatolia since ancient times – archaeologists have deciphered a Sumerian tablet that turned out to be a cookbook of sorts, containing almost all the items and spices familiar to present-day Turks.

Today, from the Balkans to the Middle East, from the Caucasus to North Africa, virtually all nations share a taste for the savoury kebabs (kebaplar), rice-based pilaus (pilavlar), aubergine or chickpea specialities and tangy white sheep, cow or goat cheese (beyaz peynir) whose preparation became an art form in the Topkapı kitchens and the province of Bolu, where aspiring cooks started out peeling vegetables in one of the numerous culinary schools set up by imperial decree. Even today Bolu remains famous for its chefs.

In early Ottoman times, the riches of the sultan's table owed much to Persian cuisine, notably the Abbasid-dynasty banquets which disappeared after the Mongol destruction of Baghdad. However, the taste for meat charcoal-grilled on a skewer, known as şiş (pronounced "shish") kebab, probably originated as "fast food" on the Central Asian steppes or in the shepherds' pastures of Anatolia, while many vegetable- or pulse-based dishes can be found in different versions across the Middle East. Today, Turkish tastes are more notably Mediterranean and Levant-based than Persian-influenced, and visitors may notice an odd conservatism in the native palate.

The döner kebab is one of Turkey's most famous exports.

Ottoman court poets used food as metaphor in love verses, the vocabulary still surviving in Turkish romantic discourse today. Prestigious titles were granted to master chefs, and palace recipes were guarded with utmost secrecy.

Accordingly, "Ottoman" food is difficult to find, and not every traveller will be lucky enough to come across the best Turkish cuisine. While on the whole tasty, fresh and nutritious, standard resort fare can get monotonous after a few days, since restaurant owners play safe and pitch the known quantities of *döner* and *şiş kebap* to the wary and unadventurous, steering you away from odd local fish and rich *inegöl köfteleri* (cheese-stuffed meatballs) or, God forbid, *koç*

> *From Adana eastwards, chillies – often fiery – enliven the most unlikely ingredients (including cows' udders). Sumak, a tart, reddish purple powder made from the ground berries of Rhus coriaria, is universally dusted on kebabs.*

every taste. Freshness and seasonality are essential when ordering meals – a trip to the local *halk pazarı* (street market) should clue you up as to which ingredients are currently available.

In the more temperate areas of the country, salad-lovers will find a variety of unusual, spicy greens appearing along with the standard, micro-chopped tomato-pepper-onion-and-cucumber mix called *çoban salatası* (shepherd's salad). *Roka* (rocket) is an essential garnish for fish, along with lemon and salt; you may also find spiky *tere* (bitter cress, a member of the mustard family), *nane*

A typical breakfast of bread, olives and tea.

yumurtası (ram's testicles), spit-roasted lamb offal wrapped in gut (*kokoreç*), and *beyin salatası* (raw lamb brains) in favour of pepper steak and hamburgers. To experience the real thing, head for working men's soup kitchens or those restaurants which have earned a reputation for authentic Ottoman or eastern Turkish cuisine.

REGIONAL SPECIALITIES

Most native-born urban dwellers in Istanbul and Ankara have an aversion to highly spiced food and garlic, associating them with the Anatolian-peasant culture they disdain. However, as you move south and east, such middle-class prejudices swiftly disappear, and if you know which regional specialities to ask for, there are surprises to match

(fresh mint), or even *kuzukulağı* (sorrel). Cultivated rather than weedy purslane (*semizotu*) is typically served blended with yoghurt; another common *meze* (appetiser) is sharp, crumbly goat's cheese cured in a goatskin (*tulum peyniri*) served with chopped walnuts.

The Antalya region is famous for its citrus fruits, notably oranges, at their best in December or January, when it is still sunny. The Turkish word for orange, *portakal*, is derived from Portugal, from where the fruit first came to Anatolia in the 16th century, having originated in China. Further east, towards Alanya, locally grown bananas are smaller and tastier than imported varieties, but are being edged out all the same, while avocados are now fairly well established.

The Aegean region is famous for *çöp şiş*, tiny pieces of lamb threaded onto wooden skewers like satay sticks – a popular truck-stop grub. People buy four or six at a time and dip them in a spicy mixture of cumin, oregano and hot pepper, then roll them up in a *yufka* – akin to a flour tortilla – or a *dürüm* (like a chapati). The Antalya regional speciality, *hibeş*, is a starter made of sesame paste, lemon, hot pepper and garlic. Heading east of Alanya, the bread changes from the European loaf to Middle Eastern unleavened *pide*, similar to Indian nan; *pide* is also universally served with soup during Ramadan.

In the far southeast, (Şanlıurfa, Gaziantep and Antakya), the food becomes much spicier. Şanlıurfa is known for its onion-laced *şiş* kebabs (as well as the difficulty of ordering a beer: this is a city of pilgrimage for Muslims) and Antakya for hummous – the chickpea paste with garlic now so familiar in the West. *Nar ekşisi* (sour pomegranate syrup) – used in tomato and onion salads, as well as the basis of meat sauces – owes more to Persian heritage than most Turkish food.

The Black Sea is home to the *hamsi* (anchovy, usually crisp-fried in cornmeal), hazelnuts, dairy products, *muhlama* (a sort of fondue made from cheese, butter and corn flour), and cornbread – elsewhere in Turkey corn is considered food fit only for livestock. In central and eastern Anatolia, *saç kavurma* is an elegant meat-and-vegetable medley stir-fried in a shallow wok (usually at your table) which tastes rather like a Hungarian goulash. This dish has clear links with the outdoor cooking of Central Asia.

THROUGH THE DAY

Breakfasts – especially at the simpler kinds of accommodation – are dominated by *beyaz peynir* (creamy white feta-like cheese) and various kinds of olives, with butter, honey, jam, tomatoes, cucumbers and boiled egg often making an appearance as well. Alternatively, special bakeries serve a variety of *böreks*, filo pastries with cheese or meat fillings.

The staple of lunch-time *lokantas* (from the Italian *locanda*) is *sulu yemek* (literally, "liquid food"), vegetable- and meat-based stews, or *hazır yemek* (ready food), including more involved oven casseroles. Even simpler are the *çorbacıs* (soup kitchens), open long hours while purveying a range of soups from the innocuous

mercimek (lentil) to *paça* (trotters) and *işkembe* (tripe), the latter two favourites of clubbers and hardened drinkers in need of a hangover preventative and small-hours restorative. *İşkembe*, similar to Mexican *meñudo* but without hominy, is preferentially consumed with crushed garlic from a bowl, red pepper flakes and a lashing of vinegar.

Evening meals usually start with a selection of *mezes* which the waiter brings to the table on an enormous platter. This is particularly convenient for foreigners as written descriptions

Traditional chicken casserole.

⊘ DINING OUT

Some of the finest restaurants are attached to upmarket hotels. In various establishments, you might be asked whether you prefer to eat fish or meat – it is not a done thing to mix the two – so that appropriate seating can be chosen. Ideally, fish – whether ocean-going or freshwater – should be eaten beside the sea or under streamside plane trees, while meat dishes are best enjoyed within sight of the *ocakbaşı* or central grill. Along the south and west coasts, eating al fresco is the normal thing to do – indeed the Ottomans introduced the concept of outdoor dining to Europe.

of the dishes often don't do them justice or are eccentrically translated (eg "cigarette pie" for *sigara böreği*, etc). Most are *zeytinyağlılar*, cold vegetable-based dishes cooked in olive oil, or salads of pulses or wild greens (extending to *deniz börülcesi*, glasswort or marsh samphire), but you can opt for hot *mezes* like *arnavut ciğer* ("Albanian-style" sautéed lamb's liver with onions), *mücver* (courgette frittata) or *içli köfte* (bulgur wheat, nuts, vegetables and meat in a spicy crust).

It is also well worth keeping an eye out for less common *meze* delicacies, verging on main courses, such as *çerkez tavuğu* (Circassian chicken) – steamed, boned and puréed breast meat smothered in a sauce of walnuts, breadcrumbs, garlic, oil and lemon.

Dolmalar ("stuffed things") are also popular, and can be made with courgettes, aubergines, peppers, grape leaves, cabbage leaves, tomatoes, mussels or artichokes, filled with a mixture of rice, pine nuts, currants, herbs and spices. They are doused in olive oil and lemon juice and served hot with meat, or cold with yoghurt.

Fish is minutely classified – there are several separate names for the bluefish alone, depending on size/age, from *çinakop* (the smallest) to *sarıkanat* (medium) to *lüfer* (adult), never served more than a day old, and at its prime in the autumn. Fish restaurants are likely to feature starters such as fried *kalamar* (squid); *levrek turşu* (marinated sea bass); *balık köftesi* (hot fish rissoles); or salt-cured fish, either the premium *lakerda* (bonito) or *çiroz* (high mackerel). Main dishes will encompass grilled or fried fish of the season – though with rare exceptions outside of tourist areas, seafood is as expensive in Turkey as anywhere else in the Mediterranean and you're advised to confirm the per-portion or by-weight price in advance.

Top-drawer seafood dishes include *kılıç balığı*, swordfish skewered with peppers and tomatoes; *kalkan*, turbot served with lemon wedges; *buğlama*, fish stew often flavoured with dill, made from any of the larger catch of the day; and *karides güveç*, a clay-pot casserole of shrimp, hot peppers, tomatoes and cheese (vegetarians should note that a similar dish made with mushrooms is often available). All the usual Mediterranean breams, often farmed, are found in Turkey; more distinctive (and cheaper) are Black Sea or Marmara species such as *mezgit* (whitebait) and *istavrit* (horse mackerel), or north Aegean favourites like *sardalya* (sardine) and *papalina* (sprat).

Kebab (*kebap* in Turkish) has figured prominently in local cuisine for over 10 centuries, and its meaning has enlarged to include meats that have been boiled, baked or stewed. Meat is usually cooked with vegetables – for example with *şiş* kebabs, pieces of green pepper, tomato and onion add flavour to the

Fishing on a small scale.

⊘ AŞURE

Aşure is the Turkish version of a devotional dish found across the Balkans. *Aşure günü*, the tenth day of Muharrem, was when Hüseyin, son of the fourth caliph Ali, was slain at the Battle of Karbala, becoming a martyr for Shi'ites and their Turkish adherents, the Alevîs and Bektaşis. Elders of the latter sect break a 10-day fast at the start of Muharrem with a communal meal of *aşure*. A sweet porridge of pulses, grains, raisins, pomegranate seeds and nuts, it also called 'Noah's pudding', after a legend relating how after the first sighting of dry land, Noah commanded that a stew be made of the remaining sorts of food on the Ark.

morsels of meat, or in the *güveç* dishes baked in a clay casserole. Lamb is the meat par excellence in Turkey and is not only grilled but the basis of various baked dishes like *kuzu tandır* where a whole lamb is baked in a brick oven, still sunken into the ground in many villages. Other wonderful kebab dishes, often related to their region of origin, include Adana kebab – ground lamb highly seasoned with red pepper, coriander and cumin, wrapped around a skewer and grilled; or İskender (Bursa) kebab, where luscious slices of *döner*

taste for foreigners. There are strawberries in May, cherries in June, melons in July and August, and apples, pears, pomegranates and grapes in autumn.

Melon and white cheese are enjoyed when lingering with digestifs after a meal. Fancier restaurants may offer figs stuffed with almonds, apricots bursting with cheese and pistachio paste, or candied pumpkin with clotted cream and walnut chunks.

Turkey's various milk-based puddings are also well worth sampling, perhaps the best-

Turkish cheese for sale in the outdoor markets of Eminönü, Istanbul.

Simit are bread rings covered in sesame seeds.

meat are spread over *pide* bread, smothered in yoghurt, hot tomato sauce and butter.

If your main course is a meat dish, it might come accompanied by rice, which can be simply cooked with butter and meat broth or, alternatively, richly seasoned with pine nuts, currants, herbs and liver. Alternatively, it may be accompanied by bulgur wheat, or merely a garnish salad and some slices of *pide*.

DESSERT

In restaurants, dessert usually means a selection of seasonal fruits. Winter is the time for citrus fruit and bananas; in spring, there may be green almonds and plums, often an acquired

known being *muhallebi*, a milk pudding made from rice flour and rosewater, served cold and maybe dusted with pistachio nuts. Other varieties that are not cloyingly sweet include *fırın sütlaç* (rice pudding baked in a clay dish); *keşkül* (vanilla and almond custard); or the incredibly involved *tavuk göğsü*, made with imperceptibly ground or shredded chicken breast. Scraping the bottom of the pan for the burnt bottoms of *tavuk göğsü*, another popular dish emerges: *kazandibi*, served dark side up and sprinkled with nuts and maybe cinnamon. Some or all of these, as well as a kaleidoscope of *helva* – any combination of baked semolina flour, butter, sugar and flavoured water – will be available in better restaurants.

Those with a particularly sweet tooth should seek out a traditional *pastane* (patisserie). In earlier days, before fast-food restaurants and cafés provided an alternative, young courting couples or families would make the *pastane* a Sunday ritual. Hence you'll notice, particularly in larger cities, that "traditional" *pastanes* are often romantically decorated in styles from original Art Nouveau to 1950s milk-bar. Even the names of the desserts themselves – Lady's Navel, Lips of the Beloved and Nightingale's Nests, to name just some – bear wit-

A tasty selection of mezes.

ness to the overblown romance favoured by Turkish suitors.

At *pastanes*, you'll find all the restaurant-type desserts cited above, as well as *lokum* (Turkish Delight – basically solidified sugar with pectin, flavourings and maybe nuts) and the pan-Middle Eastern confections like *baklava* or *kadayif* made from varying proportions of sugar, flour, nuts and butter. A popular elaboration of *kadayif* is the artery-cloggingly rich Arab dessert known as *künefe* – the same sheer filaments poised over soft white cheese and sometimes topped with *dondurma* (traditional, sticky Turkish gelato) for good measure. Speaking of which, *dondurma* still (just) holds its own against inroads being made by the rainbow of

exotic flavours sold by upmarket standard ice-cream parlours like the Mado chain.

Sweets such as *baklava* or *helva*, rather than alcohol, are the customary gift to take when one goes visiting.

TURKISH SNACKS

Perhaps the most delicious snack – almost a full meal in itself – is *pide* or "Turkish pizza", flat and pointed-oval-shaped like the eponymous soup-bread but stuffed with a range of savoury toppings (typically cheese, mince or

> *Most restaurant owners are mystified by the concept of vegetarianism and may tell you a dish is meatless despite being cooked in stock. In cities and fashionable resorts, however, Western health food has become trendy.*

sucuk – sausage) and then cut into bite-sized pieces before being served. The venue, with its wood-burning oven going from mid-morning until nearly midnight, is a *pide salonu*. Pide shouldn't be confused with *lahmacun*, small, round, thin-crust concoctions sold from streetcarts, or *simit* – bread rounds topped with sesame seeds. Out in the countryside, stalls (invariably staffed by women) making and selling *gözleme* are ubiquitous. Resembling a stuffed paratha, *gözleme* come in a wide range of sweet or savoury flavours. In Istanbul and İzmir, itinerant peddlers of *midya dolması* (mussels stuffed with rice, pine nuts and allspice) should be treated with caution: never, ever indulge in the summer months.

Dried fruit, seeds or nuts are eaten at any time or during any social occasion, and the little shops that sell them by weight (typically 100gm a shot) are frequently open late at night. Roasted hazelnuts and unshelled black sunflower seeds are the favourites, with powdery dried chickpeas (*leblebi*) not far behind.

WINE, *RAKI* AND BEER

Vineyards are found mostly in the Aegean region, Cappadocia and Thrace, and wine-making has been practised here since the Neolithic era. But despite this long legacy,

Turks were never great wine-drinkers, and during Ottoman times wineries were run by the Christian minorities. For decades republican Turkey lagged behind other Mediterranean rivals, given persisting Islamic inhibitions and the negative effect of Tekel, the now-defunct state spirits enterprise. Tension persists today as tourism vies with religious scruples. The west and south secularist coasts are generally "wet" while most of the devout interior is "dry". Everywhere, alcohol prices are high as excise taxes combine a sense of virtue with fiscal opportunity. In 2013, several laws were passed to further hamper the industry, among them the banning of all advertisements for alcoholic products.

The quality and availability of wine (şarap) has improved enormously since the 1990s, as private wineries with foreign-trained oenologists come to the fore. Dominating the domestic market are the four largest vintners, Kavaklıdere, Doluca, Kayra and Sevilen, while regional brands worth seeking out include Turasan, Narbağ and Peribacası (Cappadocia), Feyzi Kutman (relying on Thracian grapes), Suvla (Gallipoli), Sevilen (Aegean region) and several on Bozcaada (Tenedos). Red wine is kırmızı, white beyaz, rose roze.

The national aniseed-flavoured aperitif, rakı, originated as a dodge to get around the Qur'an, which only proscribes wine. It's akin to other Mediterranean distilled grape-waste spirits like grappa and ouzo, though a bit stronger at 45–48 percent alcohol. Rakı is dubbed "lion's milk" (aslan sütü) as the anise component turns it cloudy white when it comes in contact with ice or water, and is considered the ideal accompaniment to seafood. Since the state spirits monopoly was wound up, the best of many private distilleries is considered Efe, though Burgaz is much cheaper and nearly as good – with Efe, go for the blue label grade, with Burgaz, the green label. Unfortunately, most restaurants and bars offer only the ex-Tekel Yeni Rakı.

The most popular beers are Efes Pilsen, Carlsberg and Tuborg, all at about 5 percent. Efes also makes a Dark label (6.1 percent) and "Xtra" (7.5 percent), and there's even Gusta (5 percent), a dark, locally brewed wheat beer, possibly a tribute to the taste of Turkish workers returned from Germany.

SOFT DRINKS

Uncarbonated bottled water is offered chilled at restaurants; naturally carbonated mineral water (maden suyu) is also available. Tap water is best avoided – usually heavily chlorinated and foul-tasting – though some places will filter it and serve it free in jugs. In rural areas, many springs are potable – the popular ones may have collection queues.

Freshly squeezed juices are also widespread, especially along the coast, where oranges (portakal) are abundant; also popular are nar suyu

Baklava consists of filo pastry, honey and pistachio nuts.

(pomegranate juice) and karadut suyu (red mulberry juice) – delicious but expensive.

Another excellent summer thirst-quencher (and much the best accompaniment to pide) is ice-cold ayran, a yoghurt, salt and water frappé. Traditionally the best, frothy (yayık or churned) ayran was sold by street vendors, though nowadays you're more likely to get it in sealed bottles.

The most popular winter city drinks are cold boza, mildly fermented and millet-based, and hot milk with cinnamon and sahlep, the latter made from the pulverised tubers of Orchis mascula. Sahlep, commonly offered on ferries and at street stalls, is considered sovereign against colds and (possibly because of the suggestive shape of the orchid tuber) a mild aphrodisiac.

📷 TURKISH CAFÉS

Encounter the authentic character of a
Turkish neighbourhood at one of the
numerous tea or coffee houses.

Turkey is the home of the coffee house. The concept
was introduced to Europe by the Ottomans in the
1600s after Western travellers had admired Istanbul's sociable *kahvehanes* – even if Ottoman authorities intermittently banned them as dens of vice and
potential sedition, and the *ulema* deemed coffee a
stimulant forbidden by the Qur'an.

These days, Turkish cafés range from traditional *çayhanes* (tea houses) or *kahvehanes* (coffee
houses) to contemporary venues indistinguish-
able from Western equivalents. Compared with
the more opulent city centre examples, a typical
rural café (or a backstreet urban one) can seem
desperately unromantic, with spartan decor, dusty
windows, a battered woodstove, and an all-male
clientele attired in flat caps.

At trendier cafés, *nargiles* (hookahs) – once
exclusive to older men – have made a comeback
among the young, though their futures remain
under threat (as is all café trade) by stringent 2009
anti-smoking laws. Now one can officially smoke
tömbeki (compressed tobacco) only outdoors
(though violations abound).

As for Turkish coffee itself, this is prepared by
combining finely ground, roasted robusta beans with
water and sugar in a long-handled, tapering small
pot *(cezve)*. (You'll be asked
if you want your coffee
plain – *sade*; medium
sweet – *şekerli*; or
cloying – *çok şekerli*).
The brew is allowed
to rise twice without
actually boiling, the
esteemed resultant froth
decanted first into little cups,
then the liquid, and the sedi-
ment (never drunk) last.

Turkish coffee.

The best nargile cafés in Istanbul can be found at
Çorlulu Ali Paşa Medresesi, under the Galata Bridge
and at Tophane.

Elders playing cards in a café in Şanlıurfa.

Pouring and serving Turkish tea (çay) at the nargile café Çorlulu Ali Paşa Medresesi, Istanbul.

Teas

Given the higher cost of coffee, the staple of çayhanes is çay (tea): served black and sweet (*never* with milk) in small, tulip-shaped glasses. It's prepared in a double boiler, typically aluminium, known as a çaydanlik or demlik – the tea is steeped in the bottom half, with the resulting brew combined with plain hot water from the top part. You can ask for açık (mild) or demli (strong) tea – if you say nothing it will probably arrive stewed to the point of undrinkability.

Tea is, perhaps surprisingly, a relatively new fashion, promoted during the late 1930s as part of the republican self-sufficiency programme, relying on plantations around Rize in the Black Sea region. Sadly, home-grown tea isn't always of the highest quality, seldom matching the average Indian or Sri Lankan teabag, though patriotic Turks will certainly bridle at this verdict.

There are also several popular herbal teas or tisanes available: adaçay, a kind of sage quite common in the Aegean and west Mediterranean areas; papatya (chamomile) and ıhlamur (linden blossom), the latter two popular for those stricken with colds or flu.

Students hanging out at an Ankara café.

Cafés and restaurants line the streets of former fishing village Kumkapı, an ideal place to savour Turkey's café-culture.

Tea is served in tulip-shaped glasses.

ANATOLIA'S ANCIENT ARTS

Anatolia's historic art is infinitely varied – from squat Hatti fertility figurines to towering Roman temples and sumptuous medieval tilework.

When most people think of Turkish art and architecture, the first thing that springs to mind is probably the southerly Golden Horn skyline which includes Topkapı Palace, Aya Sofya and the nocturnally illuminated minarets of the Blue Mosque. Here is a fairytale vision indeed, but these relics of Byzantine and Ottoman splendour mark only one small segment of Anatolia's dazzling heritage, for the country has been inhabited by many cultures stretching back millennia.

THE FIRST CITY OF ART

Ongoing excavations at Çatalhöyük (see page 303) south of Konya have astonished even the scholars working there. Some 8,000 years ago, Anatolia's bountiful resources nurtured some of the world's first settled communities, allowing them to develop sophisticated religion, art and architecture as well as indulging in personal vanity, evidenced by finds of obsidian mirrors, lead and copper jewellery, terracotta seals, and pots of what may have been body paint. Even more astonishing relics are the houses, reminiscent of the 1,000-year-old Native American cities in New Mexico and Arizona. These seem to have been used first as domestic dwellings and later as shrines, and yielded some of the earliest wall paintings ever found, as well as fascinating ritual relief sculptures. Some paintings show hunting parties and sexual congress and others a ritual "excarnation" of bodies by vultures.

Numerous "Venus of Willendorf"-style figurines found in grain bins and graves imply a matriarchal culture, while the famed "horned bench" may have been a slab for laying out the dead. In other Çatalhöyük house-shrines, there are bulls' skulls covered in clay and ranged up the wall, totem-pole fashion, over which a vaguely humanoid form may be perched. The

Hatti fertility figurine.

Settlements along the coasts during the third millennium BC show that Anatolian metalwork was greatly prized in exchange for semi-precious stones and other luxury items from Greece and Syria.

best finds are now displayed in the Museum of Anatolian Civilisations in Ankara (see page 289).

THE BRONZE AGE

Third-millennium BC Bronze Age finds indicate that the development of metallurgy spurred the rise of many central Anatolian civilisations, such as the Hatti, predecessors of the Hittites. Hoards of gold jewellery and lavish ceremonial objects (such as frequently occurring female double-idols) have been found in graves at heavily for-

> *The most powerful deity in the Hatti-Hittite pantheon was the sun goddess Arinnitti/Wurusemu; her consort Tarhun/Taru, who killed the cosmic dragon Illuyanka, was the god of sky and storms.*

Hittite chimera at the Museum of Anatolian Civilisations, Ankara.

tified and densely packed settlements such as Alacahöyük (see page 306).

Both the aboriginal Hatti and later Hittites (c.2000–1200 BC) knew about astronomy and used the sun disc as a common artistic symbol, together with goddesses, stags, bulls and other animals. Hittite art and architecture is also renowned for its imposing size, epitomised by the fortifications of their capital Hattuşa. Here, gigantic rock-cut reliefs of warrior gods and sphinx-like creatures suggest a powerful, militaristic but also highly organised and humane state without the cruelty depicted in Assyrian reliefs. The late-Hittite summer palace at Karatepe (see page 276) is nearly as impressive, with depictions of royal banqueting scenes, where guests are surrounded by musicians and fanned by servants.

Remains of the Phrygian (c.800–700 BC) capital at Gordion (see page 293) and elsewhere show superb stone tombs, thrones and fortifications, rock carvings imitating wooden gables with niches for movable cult images, and floors of finely crafted pebble or brick mosaic. Grave goods were generally vessels of cast bronze, while art displays a strong geometric symmetry, in finds of kilims and gold embroidery as well as crisply designed painted pottery.

The Urartians, who occupied the area around Lake Van from the 9th century BC, were impressive builders and engineers, leaving behind networks of castles and fortresses, together with superbly crafted rock tombs, cisterns and irrigation channels. Their metalwork, especially large bronze sacrificial cauldrons with human or animal heads, was in international demand even in antiquity. These are noted for their similarity to the best Minoan and Etruscan craftsmanship, with high-crowned bearded gods over curling seawave borders under geometric suns.

THE HELLENIC COAST

Ancient Caria was a large region around the Aegean coast, and while its culture underwent many transformations, it can still be characterised as Hellenic. Bodrum (ancient Halikarnassos) was the most prominent Carian city, whose Persian vassal-ruler Mausolos was committed to the Hellenisation of the region. His own pagoda-like mausoleum (whence the word originates) was considered a wonder of the world, but little remains today (see page 226); the tomb became building material in the 14th century for Bodrum Castle. However, a 4th-century BC tomb discovered during construction work in 1989 is thought to be that of his sister, Princess Ada, who oversaw the completion of the mausoleum; she was found with a crown of gold leaves, silk *peplos* (loose robe) and ornaments intact. The crowned skull was sent to Manchester University's Medical School for facial reconstruction, and the likeness of the result to a bust of Princess Ada discovered at Priene (now in the British Museum) is quite remarkable. Her exquisite jewellery and wine goblet are now displayed in glass cabinets in the Carian Princess Hall of Bodrum's Museum of Underwater Archaeology.

The Lycians, who occupied the wild, mountainous territory between Fethiye and Antalya, were first documented by the Hittites more than 3,000 years ago as an ungovernable, matriarchal people with an idiosyncratic culture and intense love of freedom; on two occasions, faced with conquest by the Persians and Romans respectively, inhabitants of the largest city of Xanthos preferred to immolate themselves rather than live in vassaldom.

Given the small population of pre-Roman Lycia, its cities probably had no more than 5,000 people, and, as most buildings were made of wood, archaeologists have only been able to identify a few structures. The most enduring Lycian artefacts are their distinctive "Gothic" sarcophagi, many highly decorated and graphically detailing the punishment that awaited vandals. Like other ancient peoples, the Lycians worshipped their ancestors and occasionally sought guidance from the dead through oracles.

There are four basic types of Lycian tomb, the most curious – and no doubt oldest – form being the pillar-tomb, where the burial chamber is perched on top of a column; the best examples are at Xanthos (see page 242). These may indicate that the earliest Lycians continued the tradition of their Neolithic ancestors by offering mortal remains to the birds – much as the Indian Parsis still do today. Temple-tombs, such as those built into the cliffs at Kaunos and Fethiye (see pages 232 and 239), are the more sophisticated version of the intriguing "house tombs" like those found at Myra (see page 247) – lovingly rock-cut models of the plain wooden Lycian dwellings, often three storeys high. Finally, there are more conventional sarcophagus-type tombs also used by later cultures.

Xanthos was so intact when the intrepid Sir Charles Fellows (see page 243) got here in 1840 that the majority of the sculptures and inscriptions were filched and now sit in the British Museum. Excavations carried out since the 1950s, however, reveal enough of the city for the imagination to build on. The most curious pillar-tomb is one with plaster-replica reliefs depicting either harpies or sirens carrying away the souls of the dead, and other seated figures receiving gifts or regarding opium poppies.

THE CLASSICAL ERA

The Graeco-Roman period (950 BC–AD 300) is considered by many to be the zenith of ancient

Anatolian art and architecture, especially in the city-states along the Aegean and Mediterranean coasts. The abundance and richness of these classical sites is a major money-spinner for Turkey. An indispensable read for those interested in Greek and Roman architecture is *The Ten Books on Architecture* by Vitruvius, a Roman architect and engineer of the 1st century BC.

The Classical "pediment" or triangular gable structure is an early indicator, typical of Hellenistic, Greek and even Lycian and Lydian rock tombs. Of the three principal column designs, the simple,

The temple-tomb of Amyntas, in Fethiye, is one of the most elaborate of the Lycian rock tombs.

fluted Doric column is considered the earliest; the Ionic column, typified by the scroll-shaped capital, may have developed in the Carian region, while the ornate, foliated Corinthian column (which later included a composite with the Ionian style) was not much used until the Roman era.

This period saw the birth of town planning. The Greeks, who preferred to build their cities on slopes, originated the idea of siting the principal temples and treasuries on an acropolis (low hill to one side of town) while the agora below was primarily a marketplace, but also used for political meetings. The Romans renamed this area the forum, and tended to place their civic buildings and temples nearby.

Greek theatres usually occupied natural cavities on hillsides. They often had temples to Dionysos (patron god of actors) nearby; early

The architecture of the Byzantine church was symbolic; the dome represented heaven with Christ at the centre of the firmament, while apostles and saints lower down the walls reflected a hierarchy.

theatrical performances were religious in nature and only performed during festivals. Jolly Dionysos himself probably originated as an Anatolian god of fertility and wine, possibly related to the Hittite god of agriculture, Telepinu, son of Tarhun. Indeed, Classical culture involved a great deal of mingling with beliefs indigenous to Anatolia.

The Roman era began in 190 BC, concluding in the *Pax Romana* (27 BC–AD180); under the empire, Ephesus became capital of the province of Asia. Roman town planning was similar to that of their Greek predecessors, but displayed

Roman mosaic, Antakya.

⊘ FIRST-CLASS PLUMBING

The homes of the wealthier occupants of Ephesus – the so-called Terrace Houses – offer some of the best-preserved evidence of Roman daily life. The houses were equipped with central heating and hot-water taps, while the walls and floors were adorned with exquisite mosaics and frescoes. However, as is still true in much of the Mediterranean, windows faced an atrium rather than looking out on the town; the life of the rich citizen was considered private and family-oriented. The inward orientation of the courtyard houses emphasised cool dimness and conservation of water; the centre of the roof was open, slanting inwards, and rainwater collected in the *impluvium*, a shallow pool in the atrium, often with a well beneath.

In one house, a grand, two-seater toilet perhaps tells us something about Roman philosophy, though it is open to personal interpretation. The walls are decorated with frescoes of men, perhaps in the agora, near sundials. "Wait for a Convenient Time or Die" is inscribed, cryptically, in Greek on one wall, while on another is emblazoned "Nine to Five".

Especially noteworthy is the way in which tastes have come full-circle since ancient times. Walls were hand-painted with floral motifs, while furniture was of marble-topped wrought iron. The roof, which has been rebuilt to its original design, was made of pine beams with skylights and completely covered in clay tiles.

a penchant for colonnaded streets. The Romans were far more interested in blood sports than high drama; the word "arena" actually comes from the Latin word for sand, strewn about to absorb blood and other effluvia from whatever sport took place in the formerly Greek theatres that had been suitably modified for the purpose.

THE CULT OF ARTEMIS

The Greek and Roman religious pantheon is traditionally headed by Zeus/Jupiter and a host of jealous female consorts, although there is evidence that the older mother goddess Kybele had substantial influence in encouraging the worship of the virgin Artemis at Ephesus, and also had a later effect on Christianity in the form of the Virgin Mary.

The original Temple of Ephesian Artemis was built around 700 BC, but the third version – vintage c.550 BC – became the largest structure in the Greek world, and the first monument constructed entirely of marble. There were 127 columns, the 36 standing in front covered with reliefs, giving the impression of a forest. It was a suitable setting for a nature goddess – the mistress of animals, like her predecessor Kybele – whose original idol, according to legend, fell from the sky as a meteor. Archaeologists suspect the temple's design was influenced by Egyptian, Assyrian and Hittite architecture, and the Marble Lady who dwelt inside was not very Hellenic either, generally depicted flanked by wild beasts and/or sprouting bulbous protuberances which may represent (scholarly opinion differs) breasts, eggs, the testicles of sacrificed bulls – or those of her priests, who obligatorily castrated themselves and dedicated the result to the goddess. Little remains of the temple, but many examples of Artemis and her antecedents can be found in nearby Selçuk's Ephesus Museum.

BYZANTIUM AND THE CRUSADERS

In the 4th century AD, the relocation of the emperor to Constantinople and the state's espousal of Christianity propelled Byzantine architecture away from its Roman origins. Buildings of this era are easily recognisable by square-hewn stonework or two layers of brick-and stone-filled sandwiching rubble that could more readily be curved. Doors and windows are usually constructed as semi-circular arches.

Churches have two basic designs. With a nod to the civic architecture of Rome, the early basilica is basically rectangular, twice as long as it is wide, with two rows of columns dividing it into a central nave and side aisles. By the 6th century, dome construction had been perfected. This required transepts (side arms) to support its bulk, and thus the cruciform church emerged. Ingenious curved surfaces – pendentives and squinches – are the immediate supports of the dome.

Most Byzantine churches were decorated with frescoes or mosaics representing biblical scenes,

Tenth-century Byzantine mosaic depicting the Virgin Mary.

usually presented in cartoon-strip fashion accessible to semi-literate or illiterate parishioners. Some of the finest extant paintings are found in the Cappadocian cave-churches (see page 310), where they have miraculously escaped the depredations of gravity, Islam and the iconoclasts.

The Crusades (11th–13th centuries) wrought vast damage on whatever native architecture they encountered – "pagan", Jewish, Orthodox or Muslim. Temples were pillaged or burnt for lime and masonry stacked horizontally for hastily built fortifications. Coastal Turkey between the Dardanelles and the Hatay remains dotted with numerous Crusader castles, plus a few Genoese examples built in their capacity as allies of Byzantium.

ISLAMIC ART

Seljuk architecture is noted for its delicacy, influenced by Persia, though local Muslims did not baulk at using animal or human reliefs in their stonework. The most characteristic feature of Seljuk mosques is a *mihrab* (prayer niche) over the entrance, looking not unlike an elaborate jelly-mould. The Seljuks also perfected the art of geometric tilework, often formed into Arabic characters or Kufic script, some of the finest examples of which can be seen in Konya (see page 302).

Book from the 16th-century Safavid period at the Museum of Turkish and Islamic Arts in Sultanahmet, Istanbul.

The Ottomans were great lovers of luxury, and their early arts are distinctly oriental in style, including Chinese dragons and the classic yin-yang symbol. Turkish shadow puppets *(Karagöz)* are clearly related to those of Java, and came to Turkey via Ottoman occupation of Egypt in the 16th century. However, Ottoman culture is primarily noted for its stunning architecture, a unique fusion of Asian, Islamic and Byzantine styles, best exemplified by the works of Mimar Sinan (see page 160). Another art form perfected by the Ottomans was miniature painting and calligraphy, notably the elaborate monogram *(tuğra)* used by each sultan, which was even engraved on his silverware and is greatly prized by collectors

today. Amasya was the centre of calligraphic art in the 15th century; one of its masters, Şeyh Hamdullah, was brought to the capital by Sultan Beyazit II – his work can be seen in the Beyazit mosques of both Istanbul and Amasya.

İznik tilework reached its peak late in the 16th century, and there are outstanding examples of İznik tiles in the mosques of Bursa and at the Rüstem Paşa Camii in Istanbul. The craft had essentially vanished by the mid-1700s, and has only recently been revived (see page 175).

The period 1893–1909 produced a flowering of Art Nouveau architecture in Istanbul, most of it the work of resident Italian Raimondo Tommaso d'Aronco. Many fine examples still remain, especially around Beyoğlu, on the Marmara University campus and the Princes' Islands.

UNDER THE REPUBLIC

It's indisputable that Turkey's artistic and architectural treasures date from pre-republican times. Until the 1970s, painting and sculpture, in accordance with Kemalist ideology, were merely derivative of Western movements – including socialist realism.

The less said about contemporary architecture, the better; the London art critic Brian Sewell's curmudgeonly comment in *South From Ephesus* that "no building built during the republic is worth tuppence" is only slightly over the top. The roots of this baleful profile lie in a toxic cocktail of earthquakes, corruption, the tastes of returned German-Turks and developer greed. About the best that can be expected in resort areas is faux-Ottoman *rustique*, as at Akyaka near Marmaris. The trend has, unfortunately, only accelerated under the AK governments, who are enamoured of kitsch re-created Ottoman monuments, typified by Istanbul's enormous Çamlıca Mosque (opened to worshippers in 2018), Turkey's largest.

One of the very few contemporary architects who displayed respect for tradition or the environment was three-time Aga Khan award winner Turgut Cansever (1920–2009), fêted for his Demir Village development and Ertegün mansion in or near Bodrum, and the Turkish Historical Society HQ in Ankara. After three decades battling insensitive urban planners in Istanbul, he too had strong views on the subject, railing against "centralised, technocratic despotism, which clusters human beings in monstrous apartment blocks."

VERNACULAR ARCHITECTURE

Despite the foregoing, attractive traditional dwellings, in a variety of regional styles, are still much in evidence across Turkey.

Notwithstanding repeated fires, extensive destruction in the 1919–22 War of Independence, and the inevitable homogenisation brought by cheap concrete, a good deal of vernacular architecture survives in Turkey. By "vernacular" we mean indigenous building styles, disregarding foreign imports like the Russian terraces of Kars, the Levantine gingerbread townhouses of İzmir's Alsancak district, and Greek neoclassical mansions in Ayvalık or Foça.

Ottoman Istanbul was largely built of wood (with interior plastering), from the terraced houses of the common people to the *yalıs* (grand waterside summer mansions of the aristocracy), over 600 of which still line the Bosphorus. The oldest *yalıs* date from 1699, and although today many are neglected, many others have been restored. Some visitors assume that the weathered bare wood was always on view, but in their heyday both terrace houses and *yalıs* were brightly painted.

Elsewhere in Anatolia, vernacular houses conform to a pattern seen throughout the Balkans, perhaps originally Byzantine. Dwellings are usually two-storeyed, the lower floor stone-built, with few or no windows and iron-reinforced double doors. Once through these, there's a stone-paved courtyard *(hayat)*, with rooms around it used for storage and stabling animals. The upper storey is built with light lath-and-plaster *(bağdadi)*, which allows it to overhang the ground floor, perched on wooden struts. A rectangular overhang is a *şahnişin*, a rounded bay a *cumba*. The upper living quarters have many windows, though these were traditionally fitted with a lattice to protect female virtue (while still allowing ladies of the house to spy on the street). Fireplaces had conical hoods, and wooden ceilings were often elaborately carved; women's and men's quarters were separated as the *haremlik* and *selamlık* respectively. Sleeping arrangements consisted of mattresses laid out on the low benches which typically ran parallel to the outer walls; during the day, the bedding was rolled up and stored away in cupboards underneath. Wash basins were sometimes ingeniously concealed in other cupboards in the walls.

Cumalıkızık, near Bursa, is probably the most complete surviving vernacular village, although Safranbolu, between Ankara and the Black Sea, is on an even grander scale, many of its mansions attaining three storeys, and employing half-timbering to distribute the extra weight. Mudurnu lies about halfway between them both geographically and in style, but also has a timber-and-stone mosque. There are

Houses in Istanbul's Kumkapı neighbourhood.

several of these dating from the 13th and 14th centuries, the stars being the all-wood Mahmud Bey Camii at Kasaba near Kastamonu and the Eşrefoğlu Camii at Beyşehir near Konya, where forests of wooden columns support the roof.

On the Aegean the main attraction is at Muğla, which lovingly preserves 400 18th-century white-plastered houses with outsized beaked chimneys and wooden doors with a smaller central cutout, the *kuzulu kapı*. The southeast of the country features more Arab-influenced, kasbah architecture, as in Urfa's tawny limestone medieval houses with their corbelled *şahnişins*, and Mardin's golden-hued mosques, medreses and mansions, some of which were built by indigenous Christians.

SAZ, JAZZ AND SUFI CHANTS

Turkish music draws on a kaleidoscope of influences from every corner of the old empire – and more recently, the wider world.

Turkey's indigenous music varies from stately Ottoman classical to forms of folk music and devotional or ritual genres such as Mevlevî (see page 89) ritual music. *Sanat* (art) singing and gypsy *fasıl* ensembles are both derived from Ottoman classical music, while *özgün* is a progressive outgrowth of "pure" folk.

Turks have also readily assimilated and adapted foreign styles. Jazz has been fashionable among urban intellectuals since the 1950s – after all, the famous Atlantic record label was founded by two Turkish brothers, Ahmet and Nesuhi Ertegün. Today, Turkish record labels are committed to avant-garde projects, while clubbers enjoy hip-hop, electronica and various Western-Turkish fusion genres.

Such a sound spectrum wasn't always a foregone conclusion. The young republic, besotted with all things Western, applied this to music; the rich heritage of Ottoman classical and devotional music was denied official support and banned from the airwaves in favour of sanitised, Soviet-style folk ensembles and Western classical, the two often bizarrely combined, as in Ahmet Adnan Saygun's tedious *Yunus Emre Oratorio*. Not until the 1970s did these strictures relax.

CLASSICAL, ART AND *FASIL* MUSIC

The classical music of the Ottoman court was considered to be too heterogeneous to serve as a politically correct basis for a new national music. Many of its composers were Crimean, Azeri, Jewish or Christian, and included several sultans; its modes were (and still are) based partly on the Arabic tradition, partly on ancient Greek treatises. Typical instrumentation includes *ud* (fretless, 11-stringed lute), *ney* (end-blown reed flute), *tanbur* (3-stringed

Clarinet player in Istanbul.

long-necked lute), *kanun* (finger-plucked zither) and *def* (frame drum).

A direct outgrowth was *sanat* (art) music, which showcased the voice in suites of vocal improvisations (*şarkı*) interspersed with instrumental interludes; most *şarkı* date from the late 19th century. Standout singers have included Münir Nurettin Selçuk (1901–81), Safiye Ayla (1907–98), Zeki Müren (1931–96) and Bülent Ersöy (1952–).

Fasıl is an even more commercial descendant of Ottoman classical music, disparaged as "belly-dance music" by the uninformed and played disproportionately by Gypsies in nightclubs. To the classical instrumental mix *fasıl* adds *keman* (violin), *darbuka* (goblet drum), and most significantly the low-pitched G-*klarnet*, which leads the ensemble and defines this irresistibly danceable genre. Şükrü Tunar (1907–62) was considered the first great clarinettist; worthy successors include Mustafa Kandırali (1930–), Barbaros Erköse (1936–) and Selim Sesler (1957–2014).

SUFIS AND AŞIKS

Devotional Mevlevî music consists of *âyin*, complex modal compositions dating back to the 1400s, and the influence of Sufi poet Celaleddin Rumi (Mevlâna). *Küdüm* (small kettle drums), *kanun* and *rebab* (a small lap fiddle) provide accompaniment; however, the *ney* is the principal instrument, its tone considered to symbolise the voice of the soul yearning for union with the divine. The best-known contemporary ney-player is Süleyman Ergüner.

Aşık means "the one in love", though Turkish bardic songs concern spiritual or political yearning rather than romantic pursuit. *Aşık*s accompany lyrics by medieval poets such as Yunus Emre and Pir Sultan Abdal on solo *saz* (a simple long-necked wooden lute); most of the bards belong to the Bektaşi and Alevî sects, known for their liberal egalitarianism. Aşık Veysel (1894–1973) was the classic proponent, while Arif Sağ and Feyzullah Çınar have kept the flame burning for younger generations.

ROCK, *ÖZGÜN* AND NEW WAVES

Rock music became popular with students during the 1970s, despite it being frowned on as "corrupting", and politically unsuitable. Guitarist-songwriter Cem Karaca figured in most of the bands of the Anatolian fusion-rock movement which was nearly choked off by the 1980s junta.

In large part fuelled by a spirit of resistance, *Özgün* emerged in the early 1980s, combining rural melodies with guitar- or saz-based harmonies, other acoustic instruments and mellow vocals. Zülfü Livaneli and group Yeni Türkü were the "founders", followed by Grup Yorum, whose protest songs have often landed the band in prison over the decades (most recently, all eleven members were arrested in 2017).

Contemporary musicians have continued to reinvent regional folk styles, notably among them Birol Topaloğlu and Fuat Saka from the eastern Black Sea coast. More recently, Gaye Su Akyol – hailing from the same region – has gained international acclaim for her blend of

classical Turkish tonality and Western indie rock and grunge; as has three-piece Baba Zula for its unique layerings of dub and electronica over an electric saz core.

Jazz fusion projects have included those led by percussionist Okay Temiz, Erkan Oğur on fretless electric guitar, and pianist Ayşe Tütüncü, drawing on folk themes and other influences.

There is a long-standing interest in the folk or popular music of the upper Balkans and Greece, spearheaded by accordion player Muammer Ketencioğlu. Nostalgia for the Balkan homelands

Whirling Mevlevî dervish.

of many contemporary Turks' forebears ensured immense popularity for the soundtracks of the 2007–08 television serial *Elveda Rumeli*, filmed in Macedonia, and indeed for any Balkan melodies with Turkish (or Romany, or Slavic) lyrics.

Popular music has long been dominated by the profilic Sezen Aksu, her career kick-started by collaboration with Armenian-Turkish jazz musicians Onno and Arto Tunç, and subsequently Goran Bregovic; among her prominent disciples are Eurovision contest winner Sertab Erener and former teen idol Tarkan. Largely introduced via migrants in Germany, Turkish hip-hop is also increasingly popular among the youth, while Turkey's own recent migrant influx has brought along with it an infusion of Arab sounds.

HEIRLOOMS OF THE FUTURE

Quality Turkish carpets are among the most beautiful, intricate and luxurious in the world – but buyers need to be discriminating.

An unforgettable part of a Turkish holiday is being pulled off the street by a multilingual carpet dealer and having scores of carpets unrolled before you as you sip tea and listen to the merchant regale you with the origin, meaning and age of each piece.

The Turks claim to have created the knotted-pile carpet, supposedly brought from Central Asia by the Seljuks. When they settled in Anatolia they encountered an already thriving indigenous tradition of flat-weave kilims whose ancestry dates back to Neolithic times.

SEARCHING FOR AUTHENTICITY

Formerly, every village had its own techniques and patterns that made finished carpets as distinctive as fingerprints. These days, however, most weavers use standardised designs and colour schemes tailored to foreign tastes, and the end product often has little bearing on local tradition. This, together with increased population mobility, means that nobody can disentangle the various influences, and many regional styles are in danger of being lost. Some merchants actually beat or intentionally fade their goods to fake "antiquity". Finding a genuinely unique carpet can be hard work.

Quality control and commitment to heritage are two reasons why carpet cooperatives such as the DOBAG Project near Ayvacık have been set up, to re-teach women to use traditional designs and vegetable dyes. The quest for authenticity also explains the heightened interest in the vivid kilims and *sofras* (woven mats) produced in the eastern provinces of Hakkâri and Van. These were little valued until the late 1960s, and so escaped direct marketplace influence until then. Today, they are prized for their bold but simple abstract designs, and their prices have risen steeply.

A contemporary kilim.

CHOOSING A PRIZE

The quality of a carpet or kilim is generally determined by the density of its weave – if you check the backs of most carpets, it is easy to see which are better made from the clarity of the design. High-quality, pure-wool, knotted-pile carpets are the most expensive, while kilims are much cheaper. *Cicims* have embroidered designs stitched into them, while *sumaks*, flat-weave rugs or saddlebags from Azerbaijan, are heavily overstitched with the pattern visible only on top, and are good for heavily used areas. Pure silk carpets cost nearly three times as much and are generally small, delicately coloured and intricately woven, the very finest containing as many as 900 knots per square centimetre.

Colour is as important as the weave. Kilims and carpets using only traditional, earth-toned vegetable dyes are the most prized by collectors – they have a luminous and subtle quality which chemical colours cannot match, and are much kinder on the wool, making the carpet last longer. The limited range of very bright colours obtained from natural dyes also serves to curb village weavers' inclinations for garish colours.

It's quite easy to spot chemical dyes, even the subtler "natural-identical" ones which mimic natural hues. Part a section of the pile with your

they paid for. Try, if possible, to carry it home; arranging shipping yourself will almost certainly mean paying more import duty, as you cannot use your traveller's allowance. It is also surprising how much you can knock off the price by refusing the "free" postage.

You are unlikely to encounter genuine antique carpets in any standard bazaar, but remember that Turkey has very strict laws on the export of antiquities. Any carpet or kilim over 100 years old must be cleared by a museum as exportable, and be accompanied by a certificate.

Carpet for sale in Istanbul's Grand Bazaar.

fingers – if the tint at the bottom is different to the top, it's probably a chemical dye – and has possibly been faded artificially on the surface. Caustic lye or chlorine-bleaching will seriously reduce the carpet's longevity. Moisten a white handkerchief and rub the pile; if any pigment comes off, it's again likely to be synthetic; any bleach odour will be evident.

Ultimately, the best way to choose a carpet is personal taste, so shop around before you buy. For more on Turkish carpet types, see page 114.

GETTING IT HOME

Many shops offer to post your carpet home for you – it's best to demur, as tales abound of travellers finding that what they receive is not what

⊘ BUYER BEWARE

The more pushy carpet-dealers are often young men who have invested their savings in rugs; they rent space in resort areas, then pester the life out of anyone passing, using touts who work on commission. Owner-occupied carpet shops are usually staffed by more laid-back, older men who know a great deal about their stock. But all aim to sell carpets at the highest possible price, and most will tell a potential customer anything plausible, even extending to so-called certificates of authenticity. And don't believe 'this price is only for today' – that's only true if you agree on a price, then refuse to buy (extremely bad manners).

📷 PATTERNS OF LIFE: CARPETS AND KILIMS

Marco Polo, crossing Anatolia in the 13th century, commented on the beauty of Turkey's carpets. Many of today's offerings are equally magnificent.

Bergama carpets, made in and around the eponymous town in northwest Turkey, are comprised entirely of wool

Until the 1900s, most households across the length and breadth of Turkey possessed looms to produce carpets, sacks, saddlebags, cushion covers, infant slings and various household furnishings. The result of this abundance has been the development of an astonishing range of styles, techniques and designs: the mock-Caucasian thick piles of the Çanakkale area; the sumptuous carnation motifs of Milas; the hard-edged geometric patterns of Cappadocia and Denizli; the stylised figurines of Tuckoman rugs near the Persian border; and the wild floral and arabesque designs of Ottoman court carpets, woven at workshops in Istanbul and Bursa. The heirs to the latter tradition today are the finely woven silk-and-wool carpets of Hereke, home to the 19th-century imperial workshops.

Choose from silk Persian rugs, traditional home-woven Anatolian kilims (a woven rather than knotted mat) and prayer rugs.

In the past, thread for the domestic looms was hand-spun from wool, goat hair, cotton or linen; silk was manufactured in the imperial factories in Bursa. Each district had its own specialist dyer. Colours were traditionally obtained from indigenous plants. Madder root produces shades from brick-red to orange, pinks and purple, and was a lucrative export crop as one of the only reliable red dyes until the 1860s. Other important dyes were indigo for blue, saffron for yellow and walnut drupes (also exported) for black and brown.

The earliest known Turkish pile carpets (on display in Istanbul and Konya) are crude but powerful 13th-century Seljuk examples discovered in Konya and Beyşehir; flat-weave kilims have probably been in production locally since the 3rd millennium BC.

Carpets made at the Ildız carpet factory in Milas are hand-woven, with the cleaning and spinning of the wool, and the dying of the yarn, all done by hand.

Bold geometric designs have been an intrinsic part of Turkish art since ancient times.

Louder than Words

Turkish carpet and kilim motifs *(nakıh)* are traditionally handed down from mother to daughter. In accordance with Islamic tradition, animal and human motifs are highly stylised. Among Turkish nomads, the *elibelinde* or arms-akimbo motif represents good luck, while flocks of birds may stand for homesickness. The tree of life is a classic spiritual symbol, though the beech tree is thought to relate specifically to Central Asian shamanist beliefs. An eight-pointed star can represent fate or the Wheel of Life.

Prayer rugs *(namazlık)* frequently show a *mihrab* (prayer niche), to be pointed towards Mecca; a mosque lamp hanging from the arch denotes divine light. Funereal carpets, for graveside worship, may contain images of cypress trees, headstones and blue skies above the *mihrab*, representing paradise.

The pattern of two triangles, tips touching, often represents a girl, and may be used in a "dowry" kilim for luck and light work after marriage. Single triangles may represent talismans worn by nomads.

The carpet inside the Blue Mosque (Sultan Ahmet Camii) in Istanbul.

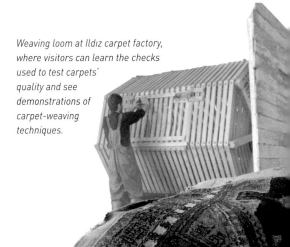

Weaving loom at Ildız carpet factory, where visitors can learn the checks used to test carpets' quality and see demonstrations of carpet-weaving techniques.

Dramatic Sumela Monastery near Trabzon.

The aqueduct at Uzuncaburç.

The Blue Mosque in Istanbul.

The lunar landscape
of Pamukkale.

INTRODUCTION

A detailed guide to the entire country, with principal attractions cross-referenced by number to the maps.

Turkey is simply too huge to treat every sight with the detail it deserves, but we have covered every popular area and most of the more obscure attractions. Some parts of Turkey are so remote that reaching them requires your own transport and/or two full days of over-land travel, though budget domestic airline routes have lately opened up many hitherto inaccessible corners of Anatolia. The far southeast has the least tourist infra-structure in the country and, sadly, for the time being remains mired in Kurdish-related troubles exacerbated by spillover from the Syrian conflict.

Inside Adana's Sabancı Merkez Mosque.

We have divided Turkey into seven regions, each with a short introduc-tion and detailed map. These are then sub-divided into manageable geographical bites. In magnificent, stately Istanbul, the old and new cities face each other across the Golden Horn. Also covered are the Bosphorus and the Princes' Islands. Wrapped around the Sea of Marmara are the small but fascinat-ing regions of Thrace (European Turkey) and Marmara, each in its time hosting the capital of the Ottoman Empire.

Field of opium poppies.

The western and southern coasts are lapped by warm, turquoise-blue waters, with limpid sands or shady pines, luring millions of tourists each summer. The Aegean Coast comprises four areas – the north; İzmir and its hinterland; the south coast, beyond Ephesus; and the tourist havens of Bodrum and Marma-ris. From here, the beautiful Mediterranean Coast runs east for over 1,500km (1,000 miles), through the ancient realms of Lycia (west), Pam-phylia (centre) and Cilicia (east), before turning south into the Hatay.

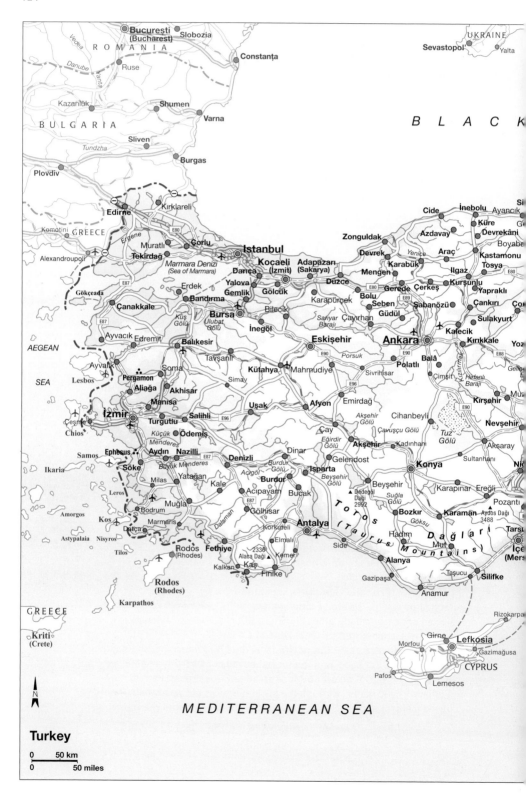

Bucureşti
(Bucharest)   Slobozia

Vedea   R O M A N I A

Danube   Ruse

Ialomiţa   Constanţa

UKRAINE

Sevastopol   Yalta

Kazanlŭk   Shumen

B U L G A R I A   Varna

B L A C K

Sliven

Tundzha   Burgas

Plovdiv

Edirne   Kırklareli

Cide   İnebolu   Ayancık   Si

Si   Gi

Komotini   GREECE   *Ergene*   E80

Küre   Devrekâni

Muratlı   Çorlu   İstanbul   Zonguldak   Azdavay

Boyaba

Alexandroupoli   Tekirdağ   Marmara Denizi   Kocaeli   Adapazarı   Devrek   *Yenice*   Araç   Kastamonu

(Sea of Marmara)   Darıca   (İzmit)   (Sakarya)   Karabük   İlgaz   Tosya   E80

E87   Erdek   Yalova   Düzce   Mengen   E80

Gökçeada   Bandırma   Gemlik   Gölcük   Bolu   Gerede   Çerkeş   Kurşunlu   Yapraklı

Çanakkale   Bursa   Bilecik   Karapürçek   Seben   E89   Şabanözü   Çankırı   Ço

Kuş   Ulubat   *Sarıyar   Çayırhan*   Güdül   Sulakyurt

E87   Gölü   Gölü   İnegöl   *Barajı*

AEGEAN   Ayvacık   Edremit   Balıkesir   Eskişehir   Ankara   Kalecik   Kırıkkale   Yoz

Tavşanlı   E90   E90   Balâ   E88

Ayvalık   Soma   *Porsuk*   Polatlı   *Kızılırmak*   Gelir

SEA   Lesbos   Pergamon   Simav   Kütahya   Mahmudiye   Sivrihisar   Çimşit   *Hirfanlı   Barajı*

Aliağa   Akhisar   Uşak   Afyon   Emirdağ   Kırşehir   Mu

İzmir   Manisa   *Akşehir   Gölü*   Cihanbeyli   E90

Çeşme   Turgutlu   Salihli   E96   Çay   *Çavuşçu Gölü*   *Tuz   Gölü*   Nevşehir

Chios   *Küçük   Menderes*   Ödemiş   Eğirdir   Akşehir   Kadınhanı   Aksaray

Samos   Ephesus   Aydın   Nazilli   E87   Dinar   *Gölü*   Gelendost   Konya   Sultanhanı   Ni

Ikaria   Söke   *Büyük Menderes*   Denizli   *Burdur   Gölü*   Isparta

Milas   Yatağan   Kale   *Acıgöl*   Burdur   *Beyşehir   Gölü*   Beyşehir   Karapınar   Ereğli

Leros   Muğla   Acıpayam   Bucak   ▲ *Dedegöl   Dağı*   *Suğla   Gölü*   Pozantı

Bodrum   E87   2992   Bozkır   Karaman   *Aydos Dağı*   3488

Amorgos   Kos   Marmaris   Gölhisar   *Göksu*   Tarsı

Astypalaia   Nisyros   Daliça   *Dalaman*   Korkuteli   Antalya   Hadim   D a ğ l a r ı   İçe

Tilos   Rodos   Fethiye   2336   Elmalı   M o u n t a i n s)   Mut   (Mers

(Rhodes)   Alaca Dağı ▲   Kemer   Side   Alanya   *Taşucu*   Silifke

Kalkan   Kaş   Finike   Gazipaşa   Anamur

Rodos
(Rhodes)

Karpathos   Rizokarpa

GREECE

Kriti   Girne   Lefkosia
(Crete)   Morfou   Gazimağusa

CYPRUS

Pafos   Lemesos

↑
N

MEDITERRANEAN SEA

Turkey

0 ___ 50 km
0 ___ 50 miles

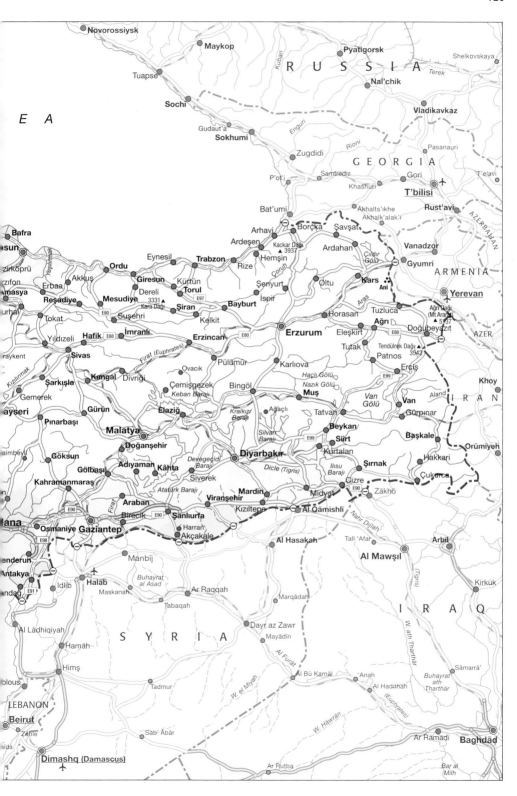

ISTANBUL

Capital in turn to the Roman, Byzantine and Ottoman empires, modern Istanbul is a vibrant city split in two by the continent-dividing Bosphorus strait.

Turkish coffee.

Maybe it's the magic of its famous trio of names – Byzantium, Constantinople and Istanbul – but this is a city which has always brought out the fantasist in visitors. Even today when it is bulging at the seams with an estimated 16 million residents, Istanbul can still seem ineffably romantic. Bounded by sea on three sides, even in the most built-up parts of the city you're never more than a glimpse away from a coruscating stretch of water. Glance up from a narrow alley in the bazaar and, rising imperiously from atop one of the old quarter's seven hill tops, are the graceful domes of an imperial mosque. Even the locals, bound-up in the minutiae of everyday life, occasionally pause to appreciate the aesthetics of their city.

Most visitors to Istanbul concentrate on the Historic Peninsula, the triangle of land at the confluence of the Bosphorus and the Sea of Marmara, separated from Thracian hinterland by the 6km-(3.75 miles-)long, 5th-century Land Walls. Here first the Greeks, then the Romans and finally the Ottomans built their cities. Here it's just about possible to forget about modernity and revel in a dream of ancient splendour.

The Sultan's bath in the Harem section of the Topkapı Palace.

Just a tram and funicular ride away the modern city waits to be discovered on frenetic İstiklal Caddesi, where suddenly the average age of a passer-by slumps to about 25, and virtually every vestige of the ancient past has given way to shops, clubs, restaurants and bars. Sipping a beer alongside Istanbul's gilded youth at a pavement café in trendy Asmalımescit, you could be forgiven for wondering why a question mark should still hang over Turkey's accession to the European Union.

But even that is to see only two faces of the modern city. To find the pious Istanbul where the call to prayer still brings the faithful running five times a day, you need to venture into Fatih, or further afield to Eyüp – areas of town still dotted with reminders of the Byzantine and Ottoman past.

Carpetmakers Street inside the Grand Bazaar.

Halıcılar
Caddesi

ISTANBUL: OLD CITY

The heart of Old Istanbul is Sultanahmet, the area
around the Topkapı Palace, the Aya Sofya and the
Blue Mosque that reeks of past glories.

When people speak today of Old Istanbul they are usually thinking mainly of **Sultanahmet**, the extraordinarily beautiful peninsula overlooking the point where the Sea of Marmara meets the Bosphorus and the Golden Horn. This outstanding location became the natural home to Byzantium, the capital first of the Eastern Roman Empire and then of the Byzantine Empire that evolved out of it, and then, after 1453, to the Ottoman Empire that replaced it. Not surprisingly, it's home not just to some of the most splendid monuments of the Ottomans but also to some of the greatest survivors from Byzantium, with the Ottoman Topkapı Palace and Sultanahmet (Blue) Mosque more or less rubbing shoulders with Byzantine Aya Sofya. Even today it's impossible to dig a hole in Sultanahmet without coming upon evocative traces of the romantic Roman, Byzantine and early Ottoman past.

It's Sultanahmet that accounts for a large part of Istanbul's wonderful skyline of soaring minarets, curvaceous domes and pointy chimney stacks that jut up from the wooded surroundings of Topkapı, although in Byzantine times the city actually extended as far as the battered Land Walls that can be seen on the way in from Atatürk airport. These walls, together with the even more battered Sea Walls that defended the Golden

Horn, also marked the effective limit of the early Ottoman city – so all the other truly great Ottoman monuments such as the Süleymaniye Mosque are enclosed inside them. From the late-Byzantine period the Genoese established a semi-independent trading colony across the Golden Horn in Galata, thus beginning the development of New Istanbul. With the exception of Kadıköy and Üsküdar, most of the Bosphorus settlements were not established until the 17th and 18th centuries. The urban sprawl that has swallowed them all into the maw of

Preparing nargiles for use at the Corlulu Ali Pasha Medresesi in Beyazit.

Tip

Camii is the Turkish for mosque; aya means saint (hagia in Greek, the language of Byzantium), so churches that have been converted to mosques can have more than one name.

modern Greater Istanbul is a product of the latter part of the 20th century.

ORIGINS

According to legend, Istanbul was established by the Megaran leader, Byzas, in the 7th century BC. After consulting the oracle of Delphi in Greece, he was instructed to settle across from the "land of the blind ones". Encountering a community living at Chalcedon on the Asian shore, Byzas concluded that the earlier colonists had, indeed, been deprived of their sight when they overlooked the superb location across the Bosphorus in Europe, and the colony of Byzantium was born on Seraglio Point, where the Sea of Marmara, Bosphorus and Golden Horn meet.

The settlement was largely left in peace until it was captured by Septimius Severus in AD 196 and absorbed into the Roman Empire. Some 130 years later, a heavenly vision inspired Constantine the Great to choose the city as his New Rome (see page 37). Officially founded on 26 November 326, and renamed Constantinople, it was now destined for greatness,

and rapidly filled with the treasures of the ancient world.

CONSTANTINE AND JUSTINIAN'S CITY

The name Constantinople soon conjured up images of wealth beyond the dreams of the petty kings and princes of Europe, whose capital cities ranked as villages in comparison. However, it was Justinian the Great who turned it into a truly world-class city in the 6th century, and by the 9th century the population had reached nearly 1 million. Its main streets were not only paved, but covered, and decorated with columns and fountains.

Precious little remains of the glorious Byzantine city, apart from the shattered remnants of the great walls and the occasional sacred structure, most notably the church of Aya Sofya (Hagia Sophia to the Greeks). Other relics lie around the Hippodrome, west of the Blue Mosque. A surprising number of later Byzantine churches, however, are still dotted about the city, most of them converted into mosques.

The **Imperial Palace of Bucoleon** ❶ (Bukoleon Sarayı) dates back to the reign of Justinian and once towered over the private harbour of the Byzantine emperors on the Sea of Marmara. Traces of it can still be seen by walking down Küçük Ayasofya Caddesi and turning left along Kennedy Caddesi, the shore road. When sacked by Crusaders in 1204, the palace was described as containing 500 interconnected halls and 30 chapels decorated with gold mosaic. All that remains now is a single façade connected to the old sea walls, with three enormous marble-framed windows and the corbels of a vast balcony that must have commanded a spectacular view.

Justinian's palace is thought to have stretched inland to encompass the area around Aya Sofya and the Sultanahmet (Blue) Mosque, and to have extended right up to the vast Yerebatan Sarayı underground cistern. The main

Aya Sofya, converted from church to mosque in the 15th century.

part of the palace accessible to visitors is the **Mosaic Museum** (Mozaik Müzesi; daily 9am–5pm; charge), in an alley off the **Arasta Bazaar** Mon–Sat 9am–7pm), an area of craft and souvenir shops behind the Blue Mosque, which displays a magnificent stretch of the original mosaic floor.

The **Küçük Aya Sofya Camii** (Little Aya Sofya, previously SS Sergius and Bacchus; daily during daylight hours), dating from 527, stands near the Bucoleon Palace southwest of the Blue Mosque, and contains a beautiful two-storey marble colonnade. It was converted into a mosque soon after the conquest of 1453.

THE HIPPODROME

The **Hippodrome** ❷ (At Meydanı; beside the Blue Mosque) was originally laid out by the Roman emperor Septimius Severus, but it was Constantine who established the horserace arena – with a crowd capacity of more than 100,000 – as the public centre of his city. It was here that Justinian's partner, Theodora, the daughter

of a bear-trainer, first appeared on the stage of history as a theatrical performer. In 532 the Hippodrome was the site of the notorious Nika Riots, sparked by a clash between the rival Green and Blue chariot-racing factions that soon morphed into a full-blown insurrection in which the Aya Sofya (Hagia Sophia; see page 133) was destroyed by fire and Justinian almost driven from his throne. When his troops finally entered the Hippodrome, some 30,000 people were slaughtered.

There are three monuments left in the Hippodrome. The Obelisk of Pharaoh Thutmose, more commonly known as the Column of Constantine, was brought by Constantine from Karnak in Egypt. The Serpentine Column (Yılanlı Sütun), which is formed by three intertwined metal snakes, stood originally in the Temple of Apollo at Delphi. Perhaps the most curious of the three monuments, it represents Constantine's eclectic (and not necessarily Christian) decorative tastes. The Knitted Column (Ormetaş), or Column of Constantine VII Porphyrogenitus, was restored in the early 10th

The Obelisk of Pharaoh Thutmose in the Hippodrome.

The Mosaic Museum in Sultanahmet.

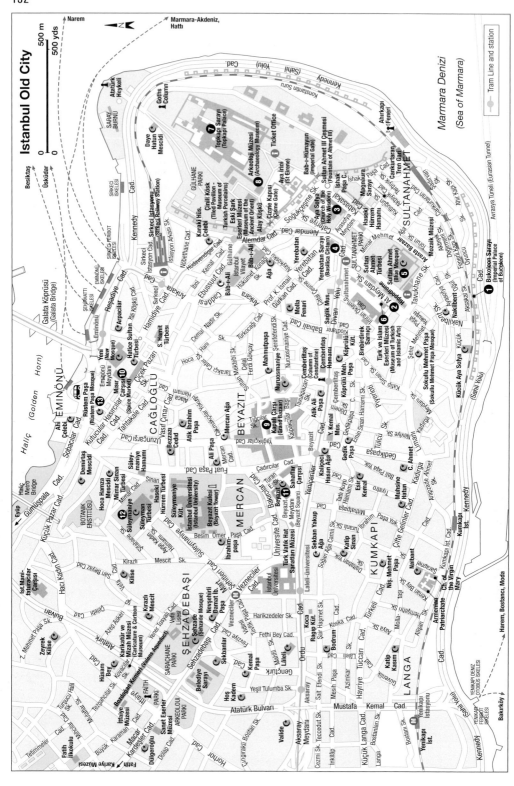

Istanbul Old City

↑ Narem

Marmara-Akdeniz, Hattı

N

500 m
0
500 yds
0

Besiktaş
Üsküdar

Marmara Denizi
(Sea of Marmara)

⊙ Tram Line and station

Haliç
(Golden Horn)

EMİNÖNÜ

CAĞLOĞLU

BEYAZIT

MERCAN

ŞEHZADEBAŞI

FATİH

GÜLHANE
PARKI

SULTANAHMET

KUMKAPI

LANGA

Galata Köprüsü
(Galata Bridge)

SARAY
BURNU

SARAYBURNU

Topkapı Sarayı
(Topkapı Palace) ⑦

Arkeoloji Müzesi
(Archaeology Museum) ⑧

Aya İrini
(St Eirene)

Aya Sofya
(Church of the
Holy Wisdom) ③

Sultan Ahmet
(Blue Mosque) ④

Yerebatan
(Basilica Cistern) ⑤

Kapalı Çarşı
(Grand Bazaar) ⑨

Arasta Bazar ⑥

Harem, Bostancı, Moda

Bakırköy

Kennedy (Sahil) Yolu

century but is thought to be many centuries older. The bronze plates that originally covered it were carted off to Venice along with the four bronze horses now in St Mark's in Venice after the Crusaders sacked the city in 1204.

AYA SOFYA (HAGIA SOPHIA)

At the eastern end of the Hippodrome, across Sultanahmet Park, is magnificent **Aya Sofya** ❸ (www.ayasofyamuzesi. gov.tr; Tue–Sun 9am–7pm, Nov–mid-Apr 9am–5pm; charge), otherwise known by its Greek name, Hagia Sophia or the Church of Holy Wisdom. It's the principal Byzantine building still standing in Istanbul and one of the finest architectural creations in the world, not least because of its stunning and hugely innovative dome. Dedicated in 536 during the reign of Justinian, the church, the third on the site, was the architectural wonder of its day. People have been astounded by its enormous size ever since, even more overwhelming from the inside than the outside.

The first church, built by Constantine's son, Constantinus, burned to the ground in 404, while the second, built by Theodosius in 415, was torched during the Nika Riots of 532. The present structure, whose dome has inspired architectural design for 1,500 years and established the template for Ottoman mosques, was the creation of Anthemius of Tralles and Isidorus of Miletus, who laboured for almost six years before the church was consecrated on 26 December 537; it was reconsecrated 26 years later after repairs following an earthquake that ruined the symmetry of the dome. The dome now stands 56 metres (183ft) high and measures 32 metres (105ft) across. The acres of gold mosaic reflected the light of thousands of candles, which illuminated the building so well that it was used as a lighthouse.

Tradition maintains that the area around the emperor's throne was the official centre of the world. Enter through a double narthex containing some of the old church's original mosaics and proceed into the vast empty acreage of what was once the nave but which is now dominated by four huge cartouches bearing the

Inside Aya Sofya, showing the Sultan's viewing platform.

Detail of the upside-down Medusa head in the Yerebatan Sarayı.

Arabic names of the early caliphs that bear witness to its conversion into the prayer hall in 1453. To the left of the entrance is the "sweating column", where Justinian was said to have cured a migraine by resting his head against the stone, leading to the belief that, when rubbed, each of the pillars in the church could cure a specific disease. The touch of centuries of visitors has resulted in a deep dent, now framed in brass and called the "holy hole".

When Justinian built Aya Sofya, he filled it with decorative mosaics. Later emperors added figurative ones, destroyed by the iconoclasts between 729 and 843 (see page 38). Most of the mosaics in the church today post-date that period, and were preserved after the Muslim conquest of the city (when it became a mosque), thanks to a simple coat of whitewash. They were rediscovered during renovations in the 1930s when Atatürk converted Aya Sofya into a national museum.

After walking round the nave you should ascend to the galleries to view the best of the mosaics. The most

Entering the Blue Mosque.

striking are those on the eastern wall of the south gallery, showing Christ, John the Baptist and the Virgin Mary. In the last bay of the same gallery is an unmissable mosaic of the Empress Zoë and her husband, Constantine IX Monomachus. The latter's head was superimposed over that of Zoë's first husband, Romanus, the stable boy who seduced the 50-year-old spinster before trying to shuffle her off to a nunnery. He failed, and his face – and his life – were removed from all association with the throne for ever. A mosaic depicting Constantine and Justinian giving the city of Istanbul and Aya Sofya to the Virgin and Child can be seen over the exit door.

When you leave Aya Sofya be sure to duck round the corner and pass through the turnstile that leads back into the grounds where you can inspect the beautifully tiled tombs of some of the early Ottoman sultans. The eastern corner of the Aya Sofya complex houses the **Carpet Museum** (Halı Müzesi; Tue–Sun 9am–6pm, Nov–Mar until 4pm; charge) a collection of over 800 fine antique oriental carpets and kilims.

Facing Aya Sofya across the square is the **Haseki Hürrem Hamamı** (www.ayasofyahamami.com; daily 8am–10pm), built in 1556 for Roxelana, wife of Süleyman the Magnificent. In 2010 it was restored to its original function as a Turkish bath.

THE YEREBATAN SARAYI

Diagonally across from Aya Sofya, near the top of Divan Yolu (Imperial Way), is the **Basilica Cistern** ❹ (Yerebatan Sarayı; yerebatan.com; daily Apr–Oct 9am–6.30pm, Nov–Mar 9am–5.30pm; charge), otherwise known as the Sunken Palace. Begun by Constantine but expanded by Justinian in 532 for storing the imperial water supply, it may originally have been accessible from the Imperial Palace complex, but fell into disuse during Ottoman times.

Today, fully restored, its eerily lit underground chamber provides an unusual attraction. The cathedral-like ceiling is supported by 336 columns 9 metres (28ft) high of varying style and origin. The two huge Medusa heads used as pedestals, one upside down and one on its side, were probably poached from pre-Christian ruins. The cistern still contains a metre or so of water, over which bridges have been built to give visitors access. So inspiring is the site that it has been used as a film set and for audiovisual installations during the Istanbul Arts Biennial.

A few blocks down Divan Yolu, on Klodfarer Caddesi, the **Cistern of 1,001 Columns** (Binbirdirek Sarnıcı; www.binbirdirek.com; daily 9am–6pm unless closed for a function; charge) is a second, even older, Byzantine cistern, dating back to Constantine's original 4th-century city. Recently restored and opened to the public, this is another extraordinary building, with 264 columns. It was said to hold enough water to support 360,000 people for 10 days.

Today, it is often used for private weddings and other functions.

THE BLUE MOSQUE

The most famous mosque in the old city is the **Blue Mosque** ❺ (Sultan Ahmet Camii; daily, but closed at prayer times – best visited early in the morning; entrance is free, but donations are appreciated), facing Aya Sofya across Sultanahmet Square, and deriving its architectural style from the earlier church. It has blue stained-glass windows, and exquisite İznik tiles decorate its interior. It was built between 1609 and 1616 by the architect Mehmet Ağa, a student of the great architect Sinan, as a means of showing the world that he had outstripped his master – and the architects of Aya Sofya – and as a tribute to the superiority of Islam. It maintains that symbolism for many Muslims. With around 260 windows, and an associated religious school, hospital, *kervansaray* and soup kitchen (the *külliye* or "complete social centre" in the Islamic sense), the mosque is impressive for its size alone. Its six

The Yerebatan Sarayı is little more than an extravagant cistern.

minarets nearly caused a diplomatic incident as this was as many as the great mosque in Mecca; the sultan had to donate an extra minaret to Mecca to quell the row.

Facing the Blue Mosque across the Hippodrome is the **İbrahim Paşa Sarayı**. This private palace is home to the **Museum of Turkish and Islamic Arts ⑥** (Türk ve Islam Eserleri Müzesi; www.tiem.gov.tr; Tue–Sun Apr–Oct 9am–7pm; Nov–Mar 9am–5pm; charge), one of the best museums in Turkey housed in the finest extant Ottoman residential building in Istanbul. Built in 1524 for one of Süleyman the Magnificent's grand viziers, its quality and location point to a man of great power, who ruled as second in command for 13 years before Roxelana persuaded Süleyman that the man had become too big for his turban and had him strangled. The museum specialises in religious artefacts and antique carpets, with some fragments dating back to the 13th century. Don't miss the ethnographic exhibition in the basement, which traces the rich history of domestic life and dress and contains fascinating reminders of the lost nomadic lifestyle.

TOPKAPI PALACE

Located to the northeast of Aya Sofya is the **Topkapı Palace ⑦** (Topkapı Sarayı Museum; http://topkapisarayi.gov.tr; Wed–Mon Apr–Oct 9am–6.45pm, Nov–Mar 9am–4.45pm; separate charge for the Harem). The complex is considerably smaller than the original, which used to extend down to the Sea of Marmara and include the area covered today by Sirkeci railway station and Gülhane Park, but the grounds are still enormous. You need half a day to appreciate it properly.

The Topkapı was the nerve centre of the extensive Ottoman Empire after Mehmet the Conqueror's greatgrandson, Süleyman the Magnificent, made the decision to make it the seat of the Ottoman Empire and his royal residence. The vast palace provided the setting for many events, both sublime and sordid, for 400 years until the construction of Dolmabahçe Palace further up the Bosphorus in the mid-19th century.

Though reflecting Mehmet II's original plans, the sprawling, eclectic compound overlooking the confluence of the Bosphorus, the Golden Horn and the Sea of Marmara bears no single particular architectural stamp. Every new sultan elaborated on the building according to need, and four major fires wrote off whatever architectural unity might initially have existed. The only original buildings left from the time of Mehmet II are the Treasury building (Raht Hazinesi), which was Süleyman's original palace, the inner and outer walls, and a pavilion known as the **Tiled Kiosk** (Çinili Köşk).

Set just southwest of the palace, the Tiled Kiosk houses the **Tiled Kiosk Museum**, which displays early Seljuk and Ottoman ceramics as well as some exquisite İznik tiles from the

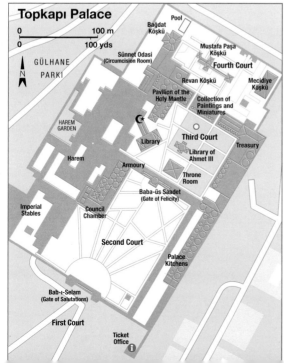

Topkapı Palace

0 ___ 100 m
0 ___ 100 yds

GÜLHANE PARKI

N

Pool
Bağdat Köşkü
Sünnet Odasi (Circumcision Room)
Mustafa Paşa Köşkü
Fourth Court
Revan Köşkü
Mecidiye Köşkü
Pavilion of the Holy Mantle
Collection of Paintings and Miniatures
HAREM GARDEN
Library
Third Court
Treasury
Harem
Library of Ahmet III
Armoury
Throne Room
Baba-üs Saadet (Gate of Felicity)
Imperial Stables
Council Chamber
Second Court
Palace Kitchens
Bab-ı-Selam (Gate of Salutations)
First Court
Ticket Office

17th and 18th centuries. It is part of the **Istanbul Archaeological Museum** complex, a trio of museums facing onto one another just east of Gülhane Park (Tue–Sun Apr–Oct 9am–7pm, Nov–Mar 9am–5pm; single charge for all three). The main building houses the **Archaeology Museum** ❽ (Arkeoloji Müzesi), containing Greek and Roman antiquities and a magnificent sarcophagus erroneously claimed to belong to Alexander the Great. Just to the south is the third museum of the complex: the **Museum of the Ancient Orient** (Eski Şark Eserleri Müzesi), containing Sumerian, Babylonian and Hittite treasures.

The **Istanbul History of Science and Technology Museum in Islam** (Istanbul Islam Bilim ve Teknoloji Tarihi Müzesı; daily Apr–Sept 9am–5pm, Oct–Mar 9am–7pm; charge), set just west of Gülhane Park, is filled with immaculate models of pioneering Muslim inventors.

The main Topkapı Palace complex consists of several distinct areas including the **Outer Palace** (Birun), **Inner Palace** (Enderun) and the **Harem**, each containing courtyards connected by a maze of passageways. At one time more than 50,000 people lived and worked in the palace, a veritable city within a city, with dormitories for guards, craftsmen and gardeners, all wearing their own distinctive garb for easy identification. In addition to discreet neighbouring mosques and baths, the palace even had its own zoo, where lions, elephants, bears and other gifts from foreign rulers were kept.

The main entrance, the **Imperial Gate** (Bab-ı-Hümayun), was erected by Mehmet II in 1478. It leads to the First Courtyard where the janissaries, the praetorian guards of the Ottomans, were once headquartered. Just to the left after the gate is **Hagia Eirene** (Aya Irini; Wed–Mon 9am–4.30pm), one of the oldest Byzantine churches in Istanbul. Originally dedicated in 360, it was completely rebuilt in 537, and briefly functioned as the cathedral of Constantinople until Aya Sofya was completed later the same year. Never converted

⊙ Tip

It is best to visit the Topkapı Palace early, since it gets extremely crowded in the peak tourist season.

Harem women of the Topkapı Palace, c.1870.

⊙ LIFE IN THE HAREM

Daily life in the Harem must have been a chaos of wailing babies, competitive mothers and harassed servants. The only men allowed in were the various princes, black eunuchs (colour-coded by job for easy identification) and, in emergencies, the so-called Zülüflü Baltacılar ("Tressed Halberdiers"), who wore exaggeratedly high collars to screen their prying eyes. As the empire decayed, the complex became more and more overcrowded; by the mid-1800s, there were over 800 odalisques in the Harem – virtual slaves living in often squalid conditions.

Yet despite its oppressive reputation, real romance could also flourish in the Harem. The 17th-century Sultan Abdülhamid I wrote a love letter to one of his paramours proving that political status is no match for the arrows of passion: "My Rühhah, your Hamid is yours to dispose of. The Lord Creator of the Universe is the Creator of all beings, and would never torment a man for a single fault. I am your bound slave, beat me or kill me if you wish. I surrender myself utterly to you. Please come tonight I beg of you. I swear you will be the cause of my illness, perhaps even of my death. I beg you, wiping the soles of your feet with my face and eyes. I swear to God Almighty, I can no longer control myself."

Traditional figurines for sale in the Grand Bazaar.

The Ottoman Empire's imperial seal at the Topkapı Palace.

into a mosque, the breathtaking church served as an armoury and is now used as an occasional venue for visual arts events and concerts.

Near the ticket office and the shop, the second gate, built by Süleyman the Magnificent in 1524, is known as the **Gate of Salutations** (Bab-ı-Selam). This is the proper entrance to the palace. The courtyard beyond was renowned for its cypress trees, fountains, peacocks and gazelles designed to create an impression of calm and tranquillity. On the right are the domes and chimneys of the palace's huge kitchens. Next to the Divan (council) chamber opposite the kitchens are the Clock Museum and the excellent Armoury, complete with sultans' swords, maces and other weapons.

The **Gate of Felicity** (Bab-üs Saadet) leads to the **Throne Room** and the **Treasury**, home to the Ottomans' almost obscene accumulation of jewels and precious metals. Security is tight for the staggering display of opulence, which includes bejewelled daggers, ivory book covers, huge slabs of emerald and the 86-carat Spoonmaker's Diamond, among the twenty largest in the world. Also in this courtyard, and always busy with visitors from the Islamic world, are the rooms containing relics of the Prophet, including his robe, beard and a tooth. Opposite, more rooms contain a sumptuous display of imperial robes.

THE HAREM

Of all the parts of the palace, it is the Harem (Wed–Mon Apr–Oct 9am–6.45pm, Nov–Mar 9am–4.45pm; charge) in the Second Courtyard that most inflames visitors' imaginations, fuelled by images of odalisques and slaves reclining on divans waiting for the sultan's pleasure. There were over 300 rooms (roughly 20 are open today), but half were cramped cubicles for the lesser eunuchs, servants and concubines. Rooms increase in size and opulence as you approach the chambers of the favourite concubines and four legal wives. Thanks to the legacy of Roxelana, chief wife of Süleyman the Magnificent, the Valide Sultan ("mother of the sultan") became effective queen of the domain and could exert great influence – her apartment was second only to the sultan's voluptuously ornate private rooms.

Even in its most decadent days, the Harem was hardly the den of unfettered sex and iniquity conjured up by many – there was too much competition. Sex with the sultan could hardly be a spontaneous affair – according to records left by one legal wife, he simply requested the Chief Black Eunuch to inform the girl he had chosen, after which she was bathed, perfumed, dressed and sent a gift. Unless she was especially favoured, he then presented himself at her chamber, (only a very few ever entered the sultan's rooms), where the date and time were recorded. If she became pregnant, that, too, was recorded; if the birth resulted in a boy, she acquired the elevated status of *Haseki Sultan*. Some sultans were known to be uninterested

in and even hostile towards women, and a preference for boys was not unknown. Osman II even wore spiked shoes in the Harem so that the grating sound would warn the women to get out of his way.

For the first 150 years of Ottoman rule, the brothers of each new sultan were strangled with a silken cord – in 1595 Sultan Mehmet III had 19 siblings murdered to forestall later power struggles. This could lead to difficulties later if no heir was forthcoming, and later Ottomans rethought the strategy. The Fourth Courtyard contains the **Gilded Cage** (Veliaht Dairesi – actually just another suite of rooms), where, in an effort to cut down on such rampant fratricide, the siblings of the heir apparent were kept safely out of the way in indulged isolation, awaiting the possibility of power. Such conditions were not ideally suited to producing great leadership, however, and are often considered to have contributed to the fall of the empire. Deli Ibrahim (Ibrahim the Mad) suffered from extreme paranoia after 22 years in debauched isolation – his reign is primarily remembered for the 280 concubines he ordered to be drowned in the Bosphorus upon hearing rumours of a Harem plot.

THE GRAND BAZAAR

Heading west towards the city walls, **Divan Yolu**, once the avenue of state trodden by viziers and pashas (high officials of the Ottoman Empire), is now lined with tourist shops, travel agencies and uninspired restaurants, while tramlines occupy the street. Several blocks west, Divan Yolu changes its name to Yeniçeriler Çaddesi (Avenue of the Janissaries) and arrives at Beyazit Square and the entrance to the **Grand Bazaar ❾** (Kapalı Çarşı), a favourite tourist haunt, the size of a city street block, where everything from carpets to leather jackets, antiques, silver, icons and gold is haggled over. Competition keeps prices reasonable, but shop around before you commit to heavy bargaining. Don't

expect to pick up some rare and dusty item for peanuts; the bazaar is a high-rent area, and traders are sharp.

Another popular bazaar, close to the ferry docks at Eminönü, is the Egyptian **Spice Market ❿** (Mısır Çarşısı). There are few things on sale here that you can't get more cheaply elsewhere, but it provides a good range of herbal products, Turkish Delight and cold meats, as well as the eponymous spices. More interesting is the medieval warren of old craftsmen, coppersmiths and woodworkers behind and to the right of the bazaar, home also to the delightful Rüstem Paşa Camii.

Just west of the Grand Bazaar is Beyazit Square, which opens onto the main campus of Istanbul University. The **Beyazit Camii ⓫**, clearly inspired by the domes of Byzantine Aya Sofya, was the earliest of the classical Ottoman religious buildings that soon came to dominate the Islamic world, replacing the traditional open courtyard structures favoured by the Arabs.

The spire at the centre of the University is the **Beyazit Kulesi**. Originally

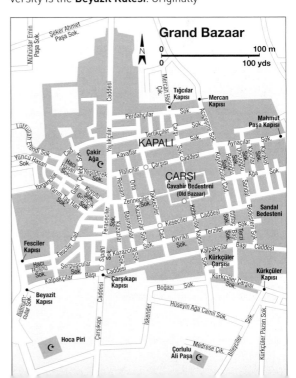

⊙ **Tip**

Take the tram that hogs Divan Yolu to reach the Eminönü waterfront, the Galata Bridge, Beyoğlu (New Town) and the Dolmabahçe Palace.

built of wood and used as a fire tower, it burned in one of the periodic infernos that have plagued the city since earliest times, and was replaced by the present stone structure in 1828.

Beyond the university is the towering splendour of the **Sülemaniye Mosque** ⑫ (Süleymaniye Camii), or, built by Mimar Sinan for the great man himself. It is the second-largest mosque in the city, and one of the finest in the world. Construction began in 1550. Inside, the mosque is almost square, measuring 58 by 57 metres (190 by 186ft); the diameter of the dome is 27 metres (88ft) and its height 47 metres (154ft). Less ornate than most imperial mosques, the structure invites you to find a corner in which to meditate. It was comprehensively restored in 2010.

In the peaceful back garden, through a forest of ornate tombstones including those of two other sultans, are the tombs of Süleyman the Magnificent and Roxelana. Süleyman's tomb is octagonal and covered with İznik tiles, while his wife's is smaller, with a cylindrical base recessed from the corners of the building.

The **Atık Ali Paşa Camii** (Yeniçeriler Çaddesı, Beyazit), one of the oldest in the city, is worth seeking out.

Especially beautiful, however, is the small **Rüstem Paşa Camii** ⑬, on Kutucular Caddesi, Eminönü, not far from Galata Bridge. Yet another Sinan-designed structure, it was commissioned in 1561 by the grand vizier Rüstem Paşa, husband of Süleyman the Magnificent's favourite daughter, Mihrimah, and is notable for its superb İznik tile work.

WEST TO THE FATIH DISTRICT

Away from Sultanahmet the tourists quickly melt away, and Fatih, like most of the rest of the old city, is very much traditional Turkey where women still wear headscarves and men obey the call to prayer.

Around five kilometres (3 miles) west of the heart of the old city around the Aya Sofya is the **Kariye Museum** (Kariye Müzesi; Chora Church; http://kariye.muze.gov.tr; Thu-Tue Apr-Oct 9am-7pm, Nov-Mar 9am-4.30pm; charge). Take a taxi or the tram to the Pazartekke stop, from where it is a fascinating twenty-minute walk north along the line of the Land Walls. Chora is Greek for "in the country", reflecting the fact that the church was originally built beyond the city walls in the 6th century. In the 12th century it was glorified with extensions and decorations under the patronage of Theodoros Metokhitos. In the years between 1453 and 1948 when it served as a mosque, its mosaics and frescoes, – the finest to survive in all Byzantium – were whitewashed over. Today it is a museum, the walls restored to relate the stories of Christianity according to Greek Orthodoxy.

Close to the Chora Church is **Edirnekapı**, one of the gates in the Land Walls that date back in part to the 5th century, although they were much patched up and added to in the ensuing centuries until Sultan Mehmet the Conqueror finally crashed through

Musical instruments and gold, carpets and antiques – all can be purchased at the Grand Bazaar.

them in 1453 to take control of the city. Worth seeking out on the line of the very impressive Land Walls, and easily reached from the Topkapı stop on the tram, is the **Panorama 1453 History Museum** (Panorama 1453 Tarihi Müzesi; panoramikmuze.com; daily Apr–Oct 9am–7pm, Nov–Mar 9am–5pm; charge). The interior of this domed museum is painted with a dramatic yet plausible 360 degree panorama of the Ottoman assault on the walls in 1453. Walk south down the line of walls for Yedikule (Mon–Sat 9am–6pm; charge), a mighty Ottoman fortress boasting seven towers and incorporating the famous Byzantine-era Golden Gate of Constantinople in its structure.

Also in Fatih is the **Molla Zeyrek Camii** (formerly the Church of the Pantokrator), built around 1120 and the largest Byzantine church in the city after Aya Sofya and the Kariye Müzesi. You may also want to examine the **Aqueduct of Valens**, a huge structure dating back to 375 and straddling busy Atatürk Bulvarı that was once an important component in the complex system that brought water into the city from as far away as Thrace.

EYÜP

On the upper reaches of the Golden Horn, **Eyüp** is one of Turkey's most holy sites. In fact, after Mecca, Medina and Jerusalem, **Eyüp Camii** (daily except at prayer times) vies with Damascus and Karbala for the honour of being the fourth most important place of pilgrimage in the Islamic world. "The Süleymaniye is glorious, Sultanahmet is beautiful, but it is the Eyüp Mosque which is holy" so the saying goes, and, indeed, the conservative religious nature of Eyüp will be instantly apparent from the number of women wearing chador-like black robes. Visitors are advised to dress modestly, behave respectfully and refrain from taking photographs, especially of the women. Avoid Eyüp on Fridays, the main day of prayer.

The mosque was built in the 15th century under Mehmet the Conqueror on the spot where Eyüb Al-Ansari, an elderly companion of the Prophet Muhammad, fell during the first Arab siege of Constantinople in the 670s. His tomb is said to have been discovered here shortly after Mehmet the Conqueror's successful siege of eight centuries later, however, there is evidence that the Greeks themselves frequented the tomb in order to pray for rain in times of drought. At weekends, newlyweds attend the mosque after their legal, secular wedding to be blessed by the imam, the bride often wearing a stylish white wedding dress with a white satin scarf covering her hair.

From here, take the cable car or walk up through the cemetery, its old Ottoman tombs topped with stone turbans, to reach the much-touted **Pierre Loti Café**, made famous by a Turcophile French author (real name Julien Viaud) in the 1800s. From here there is a fabulous view over the Golden Horn. Sip tea from a glass in this most conservative of settings.

İznik tiles in the Rüstem Paşa Camii.

⊘ THE GOLDEN HORN

The Golden Horn is a flooded river valley, once the private playground of the sultans and a favourite picnic venue until the 1950s, when it became a stinking, heavily polluted backwater. In recent years, however, the water has been cleaned up and promenades laid along both sides, attracting back the local picnickers who flock here over summer weekends.

There are several stories about how the Golden Horn got its name, which appears to be of Greek origin. Was it because of the golden glow cast on the water by the setting sun? Or because gold coins were tossed into it in 1453 by panicking Byzantines? Or because of its shape? Whatever the truth may be, the Turks call it more prosaically the Haliç meaning simply "bay".

The southern shore is more inviting, with a pleasantly landscaped waterfront running from beside the Atatürk Bridge and passing close to the **Greek Orthodox Patriarchate**, the **Church of St Stephen of the Bulgars** and the **Ahrida Synagogue**, showing the once-rich religious mix of the city in just a short distance. On the opposite shore at Hasköy, the **Rahmi M Koç Museum** (Hasköy Caddesi; rmk-museum.org.tr; daily 10am–5pm, Sat–Sun 10am–6pm; charge), housed in an old iron foundry, is a fascinating private collection of everything involving science, technology and transport – great for kids.

ISTANBUL: THE NEW CITY AND THE BOSPHORUS

"New Istanbul" is a jazzy mix of Ottoman alleys, Art Nouveau mansions and steel-and-glass skyscrapers. To the east, dividing Europe and Asia, the Bosphorus is lined with handsome summer houses and attractive fishing harbours.

⊙ Main attractions
Galata Bridge
Galata Tower
Istiklal Caddesi
Asmalı Mescit
Taksim Square
Dolmabahçe Sarayı
Cruising the Bosphorus
Princes' Islands

Maps on pages 143, 148 ⊙

It is perhaps misleading to describe the area loosely termed **Beyoğlu** – the area north of the Golden Horn, which stretches from the 14th-century Galata Tower to the swinging nightclub district of Taksim – as the "new" city (as any Turk would think of it). Most of the genteel architecture is more than a century old, and its history, predominantly one of foreign settlement, dates from the Middle Ages. Most intriguingly, it was the designated European Quarter during early Ottoman times, earning a reputation for both culture and debauchery, which attracted many curious Muslims and off-duty janissary soldiers. Later, the area was settled by other minorities welcomed by the Ottomans, and the ensuing cultural cosmopolitanism has survived to the present day through the impact of Greek, Jewish, Armenian, Italian, Russian and other settlers, whether merchants, natives or refugees. Today it is still the part of town most popular with expat foreigners, who continue a long-established tradition of making homes here.

The original Greek name for the area was Pera, meaning "beyond" or "across" (from the old city). By the 17th century it had become synonymous with taverns and bawdy licentiousness. According to the Turkish traveller Evliya Çelebi, there were "200 taverns and wine houses where the Infidels divert themselves with music and drinking". Prostitution, both male and female, was (and still more or less is) overlooked by the authorities.

From the 17th century onwards the Western powers built their embassies here, imprinting a European stamp on the neighbourhood. Many of these mansions are now used as consulates, although the Americans have long since retreated to a more easily fortified location up the Bosphorus in İstiniye.

CULTURAL CAPITAL

Despite the fact that the city was dethroned in 1923, when Ankara was

Taksim Square, the heart of modern Istanbul.

declared the capital of the new Republic of Turkey, Istanbul has remained the undisputed commercial and cultural hub of the nation. This is where most major businesses maintain their head offices, where all new trends in art, literature, music and film begin, and where most of the money is made and kept.

All this has caused something of a conflict within the social fabric of the city, as poor rural migrants – frequently from the troubled east – pour into Istanbul looking for employment, only to find themselves treated as second-class citizens. Today, the area of Galata around the bridge is a mix of traditional shops, especially plumbers, merchants and hardware shops run by conservative Muslims, as well as trendy cafés, restaurants and galleries.

Heading uphill from the waterfront things become less workaday, with the streets around the landmark Galata Tower attracting hordes of tourists. Higher up, around Tünel, where the underground funicular railway ends near trendy **Asmalı Mescit**, the emphasis is decidedly on nightlife.

GALATA BRIDGE TO GALATA TOWER

One of the most famous city landmarks is the **Galata Bridge ❶** (Galata Köprüsü) that connects Eminönü with Karaköy, thus linking the old city to the new. The fifth bridge on the site seems so crucial to getting around today that it's hard to believe there was no permanent crossing point here until the 19th century. Today it is permanent home to a colony of fishermen who pay little heed to the tram rattling to and fro behind their backs. The current model opened in 1994. From the next bridge just to the west – the Haliç Metro Köprüsü – was completed in 2014, offering wonderful views east over the Golden Horn from its pedestrian walkways.

Karaköy, one of Istanbul's up-and-coming neighbourhoods, has in recent years seen a flourishing of cafés, galleries and boutiques. Home to a small, lively fish market, at its southern edge is the busy ferry terminal linking Kadıköy and Haydarpaşa. It's also where the cruise ships dock to disgorge thousands of tourists into the old city.

Anchovies for sale at the daily fish market in Karaköy.

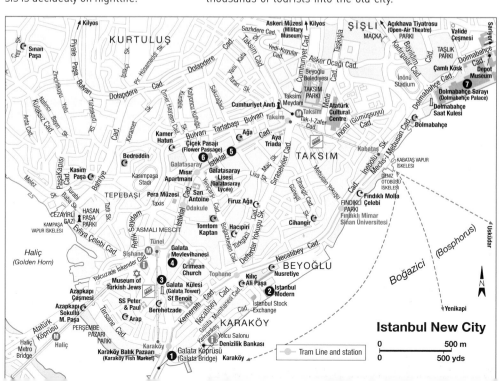

Istanbul New City

| Tram Line and station |

0   500 m
0   500 yds

Simit vendors are ubiquitous in Istanbul.

The Galata Tower looks down on a Beyoğlu street.

Originally a Customs warehouse further east along the pier at Karaköy, **Istanbul Modern ❷** (Meclisi Mebusan Caddesi Liman Sahası; www.istanbulmodern.org; Tue–Sun 10am–6pm, Thu until 8pm; opens 11am Sun; charge) houses contemporary Turkish paintings, sculpture, photography, video and sound installations. It also has regular touring exhibitions, an art-house cinema and a chic café-bar with superb views. At the time of writing, the museum has been temporarily moved up the hill to Beyoğlu (Meşrutiyet Cad 99) while the Karaköy building is renovated, so be sure to check the website for the latest.

From Karaköy most people ascend to Galata and Tepebaşı using the Tünel, a short funicular railway operating since 1875 which terminates at the southern end of bustling İstiklal Caddesi. Mid-way between Karaköy Tünel and the Galata Tower is **SALT Galata** (Bankalar Caddesi 11; www.saltonline.org; Tue–Sat noon–8pm, Sun noon–6pm; free) a hip contemporary arts centre housed in the late 19th-century building formerly occupied by the Ottoman Imperial Bank. In the

original bank vaults is the **Ottoman Bank Museum** (www.obmuze.com), which gives an intriguing insight into the bank's business and the largely Greek and Armenian minorities who worked here.

Galata Tower ❸ (Galata Kulesi; off Yüksekkaldırım Caddesi; daily 9am–7pm; charge) was built as a watchtower in 1348 by Genoese settlers who had been granted free trade and semi-independent status following the Latin occupation. Take an elevator to the top for a sweeping view of the city, though be warned that it can be uncomfortably crowded around sunset. To enjoy the views a bit longer, head to the 8th-floor café. More cafés ring the square at the bottom of the tower, which is a popular meeting place. From here **Galipdede Caddesi** winds uphill past a concentration of music shops interspersed with small cafés, boutiques and hostels to reach the upper station of the Tünel funicular.

Beyoğlu and Galata are also home to several functioning Christian churches, including liberal Anglican, Dutch Reform and Roman Catholic establishments. There are also several synagogues in Galata, evidence of a dwindling, mainly Sephardic Jewish community, who were first welcomed into the city in 1492 when fleeing the Inquisition. The best place to find out more is the The Quincentennial Foundation Museum of Turkish Jews (Büyük Hendek Cad 39; www.muze500. com; Mon–Thu 10am–4pm, Fri until 1pm, Sun until 2pm; charge), housed in an attractive neoclassical former synagogue a minute's walk from the Tünel station in Karaköy.

Nor are Muslim minorities left out: the public are able to visit the **Galata Mevlevihanesi ❹** (Galip Dede Cad 15; Tue–Sun 9am–4.30pm; charge), a dervish centre that is officially a museum. Although their beliefs are derived from those of the Konya dervishes (see page 303), the Galata dervishes follow a separate Dede (master) and are decidedly New Age, being the first to allow women to participate in the dance ceremony.

Performances of their whirling trance-dance form of worship take place every fortnight or so in summer, with dates and times posted outside the building. They also perform regularly in the run-up to the Mevlevî Festival in mid-December.

MOVING UPTOWN

The Tünel funicular from Karaköy deposits you at the southwestern end of **İstiklâl Caddesi ❺**, the main street through the New Town, running from Tünel to Taksim Square, which is primarily dedicated to shopping, entertainment and culture. Just over 1.6km (1 mile) long, it is serviced by an atmospheric old tram which trundles along the pedestrianised street. There are more cinemas here than in any other part of the city (films are shown in their original languages with Turkish films tending to rule the roost these days), as well as many small art galleries. Housed in the handsome old Hotel Bristol, the **Pera Museum** (Meşrutiyet Caddesi 41; Tue–Sat 10am–7pm, Sun noon–6pm; charge) has first-rate 19th-century Turkish portraits, paintings and

porcelain. It also hosts temporary exhibitions by leading international artists.

Nearby is one of the more famous landmarks of old Beyoğlu. The wonderful, century-old hotel made famous by Agatha Christie, the **Pera Palaş Oteli** was built to accommodate passengers from the Orient Express. Its lobbies are cluttered with 19th-century furniture and its plush corridors redolent with intrigue. Room 101, where Atatürk stayed, has been set aside as a museum (daily 10–11am, 3–4pm; free) displaying a handful of his personal effects.

In recent years the **Asmalı Mescit** district, a veritable warren of alleyways leading west off İstiklâl Caddesi to the north of Tünel, has become particularly fashionable, with all sorts of restaurants and art galleries opening in the narrow pedestrian streets.

The nightlife zone continues through the lively *meyhanes* (boozy, cheap restaurants) of **Çiçek Pasajı ❻** (Flower Passage) and **Nevizade Sokak** to Taksim, where many of the "alternative" (gay, transsexual, rave, techno and new jazz) nightclubs are found. In these often

The restored historic tram runs along İstiklâl Caddesi from Taksim to Tünel.

◉ Fact

The name Taksim refers to the 18th-century stone reservoir that once stood on the site of Taksim Square and a division (tasksim) in the water mains, an important part of the city's water system.

decrepit-looking streets are some of the best (and cheapest) small restaurants in town: on the menus Russian and Armenian specialities rub up against classic Turkish fare and the general sense of internationalism that defines the cultural heart of Istanbul. Nevizade Sokak, which runs off the same fish and vegetable market as the more famous Çiçek Pasajı, and where Gypsy musicians and hawkers still stroll the tables, offers more of the original flavour of the district – though it is somewhat rowdier. Get there early on summer evenings or seats may be hard to find.

TAKSIM AND BEYOND

At the far end of İstiklal Caddesi, Taksim is the high-rise heartland of modern Istanbul. In the middle of the giant concrete expanse of Taksim Square is the **Cumhuriyet Anıtı** (Republic Monument), created in 1928 by Italian sculptor Pietro Canonica, depicting Atatürk among the founders of modern Turkey. **Gezi Park**, a small patch of green just north of the square, was the scene of heavy-handed policing in the spring of 2013, crushing anti-government protests that erupted after the announcement of Erdoğan's yet-unfulfilled plans to replace the small park with a barracks and shopping mall.

The area around the Hilton Hotel and Harbiye, just to the north of Taksim, is a centre for business and entertainment, with many of the city's cultural events held in venues such as the **Cemal Reşit Rey Concert Hall**, the **Lütfi Kırdar Convention and Exhibition Centre** and the **Açık Hava Tiyatrosu** (Open-Air Theatre).

The **Askeri Müzesi** (Military Museum; www.askerimuze.tsk.tr; Wed–Sun 9am–5pm; charge) has an interesting collection of weaponry, elaborate costumes and some impressive embroidered tents from Ottoman military campaigns. In summer, the Ottoman Mehter Military Band dresses up in janissary finery for concerts between 3pm and 4pm daily.

Harbiye leads to Vali Konağı Caddesi in **Nişantaşı**, a glitzy shopping area. Adjoining Teşvikiye and Maçka are also home to some of the city's best small art galleries and boutiques. North of here are the upmarket residential neighbourhoods of **Etiler** and **Levent**, full of the sort of trendy-cum-pricey restaurants and malls favoured by the see-and-be-seen crowd.

THE DOLMABAHÇE PALACE

The wonderfully over-the-top **Dolmabahçe Sarayı** ❼ (Dolmabahçe Palace (Tue–Sun Oct–Feb 9am–4pm, Mar–Sept 9am–4pm; guided tours only; charge) was the 19th-century vision of Sultan Abdülmecid, its vainglorious excess fuelled by his desire to upstage his European rivals. It represents everything that is jarring about Istanbul aesthetics, with tons of gold being wasted on over-elaborate decoration that bankrupted the state, although there are also some stunning carpets and objets d'art on display. Atatürk died here, his simple room a stark contrast to the general impression of overwhelming kitsch. A janissary

Café life near İstiklâl Caddesi.

band performs here on Tuesday afternoons in summer.

Abdülmecid died shortly after the palace's completion; his successor and brother, Abdülaziz, was apparently so disgusted with the building that he built his own palace, the **Beylerbeyi**, on the opposite shore (see page 151).

THE BOSPHORUS

According to legend, the Bosphorus ("Ford of the Cow") gained its name when Zeus, playing away from home as usual, had an affair with the beautiful nymph Io. Jealous Hera sent a swarm of gnats to irritate Io, whom Zeus transformed into a heifer who ran to the channel and swam to the other side.

Since Greek times, the deep, 32km (20-mile) strait linking East and West has been one of the most strategically significant waterways in the world, witnessing the passage of Jason's Argonauts and the arrival of the first Greek settlers of Byzantium. Because of its unique strategic value, the 1936 Montreux Convention declared the Bosphorus an international waterway, and Turkey can only police vessels flying a Turkish flag. In 1936, around 150 ships passed through the straits; today that number is over 80,000 and growing, mainly due to the huge export demand for Russian, Central Asian and Caucasian oil. Understandably, with the channel sometimes no more than 800 metres (0.5 mile) across, there are real safety fears, and control of the Bosphorus has become a political hot potato. There are some extremely controversial plans, first announced in 2011, to bypass the Bosphorus by building a new waterway, Kanal İstanbul, linking the Black Sea to the Sea of Marmara west of the city, scheduled to be completed to coincide with the Turkish Republic's 100th anniversary in 2023.

SUMMER RETREAT

In the late Ottoman period, the Bosphorus shore was occupied by villages and summer residences for aristocrats and wealthy citizens attracted by the cool breezes, forests and opportunities to row their brightly painted *caïques* (traditional wooden boats). The pashas built themselves airy stone palaces, while other privileged members of Istanbul society erected beautifully carved wooden mansions called *yalı*. Some are still standing, though many more have fallen victim to fire, storms or errant ships.

These days, the European and Asian shores north of Beşiktaş and Üsküdar are part of the rapidly expanding suburbs, even if the less developed Asian shore still retains its plane trees with Byzantine roots (or so the coastal teahouse owners will tell you). Both shorelines are desirable places to live, dotted with seafood restaurants and expensive modern dwellings. By far the best way to admire them is on a Bosphorus cruise.

CRUISING THE BOSPHORUS

Relatively inexpensive municipality-run round trips leave from the main ferry dock at Eminönü close to the southern end of the Galata Bridge. There are three sailings daily in summer and

No expense was spared in the construction of the ornate Dolmabahçe Palace.

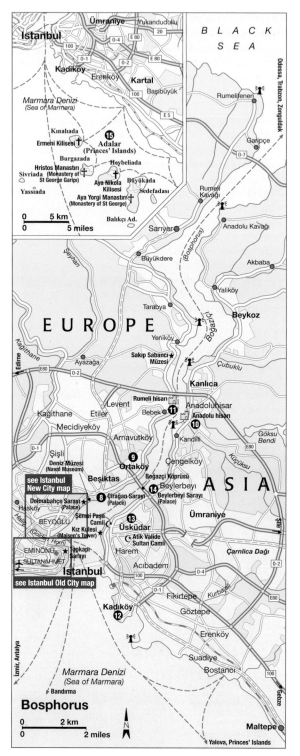

one in winter, starting around 10.30am (check times and latest information at www.sehirhatlari.com.tr), taking two hours each way, with a 2.5 hour stop for lunch in Anadolu Kavağı on the Asian side near the Black Sea. A number of private companies also run Bosphorus cruises, such as Plan Tours (tel: 0212-234 7777; www.plantours.com), which offers dinner cruises (see page 379). Both Sehir Hatlari (http://en.sehirhatlari.istanbul/en) and Turyol (www.turyol.com) also have frequent 1.5 hour-long Bosphorus crusies up to the second Bosphorus suspension bridge and back to Eminönü.

The circular tour first passes out of the mouth of the Golden Horn, with the Topkapı and Seraglio Point to your right. Midstream is **Kız Kulesi** (Maiden's Tower; see page 151), a Greek watchtower rebuilt as a lighthouse in the 12th century and completely remodelled several times since, while the **Dolmabahçe Sarayı**, in all its over-the-top Baroque glory, is on your left.

Next up along the European waterfront is the **Çirağan Sarayı ❽**, also built by Abdülaziz. Burned to a shell in the 1920s, it has been restored as the luxury Çirağan Hotel Kempinski complex. Behind it, on the slopes leading uphill, is the attractive **Yıldız Park**, once part of the sultan's private estate but now favoured by courting couples and wedding parties. Near the Beşiktaş ferry dock stands the **Deniz Müzesi** or Naval Museum (http://denizmuzesi.dzkk.tsk.tr; Tue–Sun 9am–5pm; charge), which displays some of the elaborate *caïques* used by the sultans to move between their waterfront palaces.

The first bridge, formally called the **Bosphorus Bridge**, was officially renamed the 15 July Martyrs Bridge following the 2016 coup attempt (during which the bridge was blocked). When it was built in 1973, its 1,074m (3,525ft) span made it one of the world's longest single-span suspension bridges. Beneath it to the west spreads the once modest village of **Ortaköy ❾**, having ceded its waterfront to a succession of trendy galleries, gift shops and ambitious bars and restaurants as well as a pricey Sunday crafts market. On the Asian shore near the bridge is the **Beylerbeyi Sarayı** (see page 151).

Arnavutköy (Albanian Village) is known for its wooden mansions in Art Nouveau style, refurbished and selling at astonishing prices. Further north, wealthy **Bebek**, the former home of distinguished 19th-century Turkish poet Tevfik Fikret, houses the **Aşiyan Museum** (Aşiyan Yokuşu; Tue–Sun 9am–4pm; free) and a long strip of waterfront restaurants, bars and cafés.

To the north, Asian **Anadolu Hisarı ⑩** (Anatolian Castle) and European **Rumeli Hisarı ⑪** (European Castle) straddle the straights. The latter **castle** (Thu–Tue 9am–7pm; charge) was built in 1452 when Sultan Mehmet used the two fortifications to choke off aid to beleaguered Constantinople during the final siege of the city. The semi-ruined amphitheatre within the castle is still used for occasional concerts. Just south of Rumeli Hisarı the quirky, early 20th-century

red-brick Perili Köşkü (Haunted mansion) houses the Borusan Contemporary (www.borusancontemporary.com; Sat and Sun only 10am–7pm; charge), a state-of-the-art contemporary arts gallery.

Completed in 1988, the next suspension bridge to the north is even longer than the first, spanning 1,090m (3,580ft). Beyond it is the village of Emirgan, home to the magnificent **Sakıp Sabancı Müzesi** (www.sakipsabancimuzesi.org; Tue–Sun 10am–6pm, Wed until 10pm; charge), displaying fine and decorative art and calligraphy; several rooms are kept as they were when the Sabancı family lived here. Check the venues temporary art exhibitions, in the past these have included luminaries such as Picasso, Dali and Anish Kapoor.

At Sarıyer, two fine old mansions house the **Sadberk Hanım Museum** (www.sadberkhanimmuzesi.org.tr; Thu–Tue 10am–5pm; charge), with evocative displays of archaeological finds from across Anatolia, dating from the Neolithic to the Byzantine period, and 19th-century life.

At the far end of the Bosphorus, Anadolu Kavagi's **Genoese castle**

⊙ **Tip**

Make sure to visit Emirgan Park in April when the Tulip Festival is in full swing and the grounds are a fantastic riot of colour.

Crossing the Bosphorus, from Üsküdar to Beşiktaş.

(daily 8am–sunset; free) has great views out towards the Black Sea, and the 45-minute walk (round-trip) will give you an appetite to eat at one of the many waterfront fish restaurants.

On the return journey the ferry also stops in **Kanlıca** which is famous for its delicious yoghurt, served with sugar.

THE ASIAN SIDE

If you don't want to take a full Bosphorus cruise it's perfectly easy to get a taste of things by hopping on a ferry at Eminönü and heading across to the Asian side of Istanbul at **Kadıköy ⑫**.

Kadıköy, a lively modern suburb, lacks any big historic monuments, but it does offer a delightful market area whose narrow cobbled streets are always packed with local shoppers.

This part of the city was originally founded as Chalcedon by Megaran settlers, although there is nothing left to remind visitors of that today. Instead you can admire a few 19th-century churches that recall Istanbul's lost Greek and Armenian populations, or hop on an elderly tram to trundle up to Moda where

it's possible to have lunch in what was once a pretty little ferry terminal at the end of a causeway.

ÜSKÜDAR

An alternative destination accessible by ferry from Eminönü, or the Eurasia tunnel opened in late 2016, is **Üsküdar ⑬**, a far more conservative Asian suburb adorned with many magnificent mosques, including Turkey's largest, the enormous Çamlıca Camii, visible from afar on a hilltop to the east. Opened to worshippers in 2018, it was ostensibly built to reflect Erdoğan's legacy. Disembarking from the ferry you'll first encounter the **İskele Camii** (also called the Mihrimah Sultan Mosque), which originally stood right on the waterfront. Facing it is a fine 18th-century fountain.

More old mosques can be taken in on a walk along the waterfront towards Kadıköy. This route will take you past the the 16th-century **Şemsi Paşa Camii**, and then out along a stretch of the shore that has been given a promenade. This is **Salacak**, from where you can catch a ferry for the short hop out to **Kız Kulesi**

Travelling by horse-drawn carriage around Büyükada, one of the Princes' Islands.

(www.kizkulesi.com.tr; daily 9am–7pm; charge), the Maiden's Tower, a prominent and much photographed landmark tower that has served all sorts of functions over the years but now is essentially a café-cum-restaurant with views.

If you journey inland from the shore at Salacak you should be able to find the 15th-century **Rum Mehmet Paşa Camii**, which looks rather like a Byzantine church from the outside, and the imposing 18th-century Ayazma Camii, named after a sacred spring in the grounds. Finally, if you head straight inland and keep walking uphill you'll come to the **Atik Valide Sultan Camii**, regarded as one of the architect Sinan's finest works.

Heading north from Üsküdar beyond the first Bosphorus bridge is the 19th-century **Beylerbeyi Sarayı** ⑭ (Tue–Wed and Fri–Sun Apr–Oct 9am–5pm, Nov–Mar 9am–4pm; charge), built by Sultan Abdülaziz (who ignored the fact that there was no money left in the till) after he had taken a dislike to the Dolmabahçe Palace recently built by his father, Abdülmecit. The lavishly furnished summer palace will still strike many visitors as excessive, although its smaller size and relative lack of visitors make it seem more bearable. Abdülaziz is thought to have conducted an affair with the Emperor Napoleon's wife Eugenie here.

THE PRINCES' ISLANDS

At the height of summer, when temperatures are soaring and the traffic is oppressive you may feel the need to escape to one of the city's favourite retreats, the **Princes' Islands** ⑮. Accessibly situated in the Sea of Marmara, the nearest of them is only 14 kilometres (9 miles) from the ferry port, but just far enough to escape the heat and fumes. There are actually nine Princes' Islands but only four of them are regularly inhabited: Kınalıada, Burgazada, Heybeliada and Büyükada.

Ferries stop at each island in turn, and in theory you could just about

squeeze in a lightning visit to them all in the same day. However, what makes the islands so special is their slow, relaxing pace. Although there are now quite a few administrative vehicles on Büyükada, for the most part these islands are still blissfully traffic-free; you walk, cycle or get about them in the horse-drawn carriages that can be hired on all except Kınalıada.

Büyükada ("Big Island") is the last stop on the ferry run and by far the most popular destination with visitors if only because it offers the greatest choice of places to eat and drink, as well as the chance to climb uphill to St George's Monastery (Princes' Islands) **Aya Yorgi**, an atmospheric cluster of chapels with memorable views. It's also well worth taking a stroll along **Çankaya Caddesi** to appreciate the beautiful 19th-century wooden houses in a multitude of different designs and their colourful gardens.

The second-largest island, Heybeliada, is relatively quiet, home to a Naval Academy and a defunct Orthodox Seminary.

> ⊙ **Tip**
>
> Ferries to the Princes' Islands leave from Kabataş, just south of Dolmabahçe Palace. The inexpensive two-hour trip to the car-free island of Büyükada makes a great day out from the city.

The fortress of Rumeli Hisarı.

📷 A TRIP TO THE TURKISH BATH

The soapy pleasures of a trip to the hamam are revitalising, and an authentic Turkish experience.

As a spectator sport, nothing surpasses a trip to a Turkish bath, or hamam. Be sure to visit one during your stay. Many people are put off the idea because they don't know what to expect (or what to do). Don't worry. The rules are simple, based on those of the old Roman baths or the Scandinavian sauna, and the locals will soon steer you straight. The sexes are usually segregated either in different baths or by different hours. Nudity is not the norm, so wear underpants beneath the tea-towel-like *peştamal* (sarong) that you will be given. In the better baths you will also be given a towel and wooden clogs *(takunya)*, although in more rural areas it's best to bring your own towel.

Change out of your clothes in the reception area *(camekân)*. From there, you move through to a cool side room where you can wash down before entering the central hot steam room *(hararet)*. In the old baths, this is often a spectacular domed space at the centre of which is a large marble slab *(göbektaşı)*. The surrounding walls are lined with basins which you fill with water to the required temperature before scooping it over yourself very carefully so as not to get any soap in the basin *(hurna)*. Then lie down on the slab and receive an energetic face, foot and/or full-body massage, or a scrub down with a camel-hair glove *(kese)*.

Most five-star hotels feature luxurious, modern hamams, but some of the more basic traditional bathhouses are well worth a visit for the atmosphere. Istanbul in particular has a number of superbly preserved Ottoman bathhouses, worth visiting as much for the architecture as for the wash and scrub.

Sarongs (peştamals) are the traditional attire worn in hamams; they are usually made from cotton and thinly woven to ensure they dry quickly.

You can choose to either wash yourself or opt for a massage.

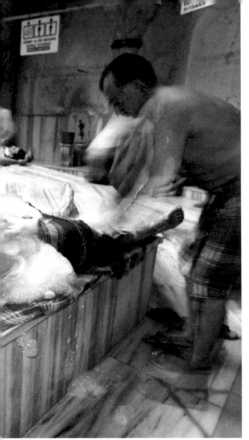

Receiving a vigorous full-body massage whilst lying on the central heated marble slab, known as a göbektaşi, in the hot steam room. A kese is used to exfoliate the skin.

Inside Istanbul's Çemberlitaş Hamam, one of the city's most prominent bathhouses and probably the most popular hamam.

Hamams remain sociable places. Before home plumbing, baths were a communal activity that could last the entire day as families bathed and talked.

The Traditional Hamam

Today Turkish baths are largely places that people visit for fun, but there was a time before modern plumbing reached most houses when a visit to the baths was more of a necessity. In those days the baths played an important role in social life. In them mothers would quite literally size up potential brides for their sons, and before their weddings women would often resort to the baths for a party. Frequently they would come to the hamam for much of the day, bringing with them their children (including pre-pubescent boys) and enough food to keep them going. In the baths women would henna their hair and wax their bodies; men would gather to exchange news and just to enjoy themselves.

Many museums in Turkey preserve relics of the days when wealthy hamam-goers routinely showed up for their bath wearing clogs inlaid with mother-of-pearl and clutching a little metal "bag" in which could be found delicate combs and towels embroidered with silver and gold thread.

Peştamals ready for use.

Ancient and modern – the view across Bergama from the ruins of Pergamon acropolis.

THRACE AND MARMARA

Northwestern Turkey is the meeting point of Europe and Asia, with European Thrace and Asian Marmara wrapped around the eponymous sea.

A replica of the wooden horse of Troy.

Thrace and the south Marmara coast attract numerous visitors annually. History fans find a land of ghosts – from the warriors at ancient Troy who clashed for the sake of a pretty face to the many thousands who died in the horrific battles at Gallipoli. Although the area is close to Istanbul, it differs substantially in character from that great city.

Thrace (Trakya) forms the tiny northwestern part of Turkey-in-Europe, occupying about a quarter of the ancient region of Thrace. Rolling, forested hills, tracts of fertile sunflower fields or vineyards, and stream valleys – stretching from the Marmara to the Black seas – are bisected by the old D100 road and E80 motorway, successors to the Roman Via Egnatia, and Turkey's main road links with Europe.

To the southwest, Thrace ends at the Aegean and the Dardanelles, that strategic strait between the Sea of Marmara and the Aegean that featured so prominently during World War I. Its principal city, Edirne, which replaced Bursa as the Ottoman capital, stands near the borders with Greece and Bulgaria. Thracian beaches are few and mostly uninspiring – except for Kıyıköy, Erikli and the glorious ones on Gökçeada (İmroz) island.

Fishermen at Lake İznik.

The southern Marmara displays great physical variety. Verdant hills around İznik hint little at the great, snow-capped mountain overshadowing Bursa. Despite runaway development, its old quarters and important monuments – and showcase suburb village of Cumalıkızık – never fail to charm. West of Bursa lie two lakes – Uluabat Gölü, where an appealing village sits amidst ancient Apollonia, and Küş Gölü, hosting an important bird sanctuary. Back on the coast, offshore islands in the Sea of Marmara are mostly the preserve of the working classes from Istanbul at weekends. Bustling Çanakkale, on the south Dardanelles shore, marks the gateway to the Aegean – and to Troy, the most famous local ancient site, where Schliemann's spirit still broods over the plundered hill.

THRACE

The last remnant of European Turkey, prosperous Thrace lends a geographical basis to the country's bid to join the EU.

According to the philosopher Xenophanes (c.570–475 BC), the ancient Thracians were a blue-eyed, red-haired people matching the images of their gods. Herodotus reckoned they would have been invincible, if only they could have united, while later Thracians maintained this martial reputation. Before the turbulent 20th century, the population was extremely mixed, with Greek or Bulgarian Orthodox, plus settled Roma, everywhere, and Armenian and Jewish communities in the towns. Under the republic Thrace became home to Slavic Muslim refugees, particularly from Macedonia and Bulgaria, who have brought a more worldly outlook with them.

Despite venerable religious monuments, Thrace is a secularist stronghold, with a higher standard of living than Anatolia's. The main earners here are tobacco, rakı, sunflowers for their oil and assorted root crops. Tourism, except at a few beach resorts and the Gallipoli battlefields, is insignificant.

EDIRNE

Modern **Edirne** ❶ (estimated pop. 142,000) straddles the main land route linking Turkey with southeastern Europe. There has been a settlement at this strategic junction of the Meriç, Arda and Tunca rivers since the ancient Thracian town of Uskudama.

Sunflowers, grown for their oil, are Thrace's major crop.

An important Roman garrison which manufactured shields and weapons, it was renamed Hadrianopolis in honour of Emperor Hadrian's visit in AD 125. Under Diocletian (245–305), it became capital of one of the four provinces of Thrace. It was sacked three times by the Bulgars between 814 and 1002, and occupied thrice during the 12th century by Crusaders before falling to the Ottomans in 1361. Now renamed Edirne, the growing city served as the empire's capital from 1413 to 1458. Süleyman the Magnificent (1520–66) was one of

Main attractions
Edirne: Selimiye Camii
Edirne: Kaleiçi houses
Kıyıköy
Gallipoli cemeteries
Gökçeada: hill villages
Gökçeada: Aydıncık beach

Maps on pages 162, 160

several emperors who liked to hunt in the local countryside, returning to Constantinople only when the croaking of the unconquerable marsh frogs made sleep impossible.

By the early 19th century, Edirne had become a provincial backwater, with almost half of its population consisting of Bulgarians, Armenians, Greeks or Jews. However, such multicultural tranquility did not last. Edirne was occupied briefly by the Russians in 1829 and 1878, and by the Bulgarians – who called it Odrin – in 1913. Recaptured by Turkey the same year, it was taken by the Greeks in 1920 and held by them until 1922; Turkish sovereignty was only confirmed in 1923.

Today, Edirne is a university town with a leading medical school, youthful population and busy cafés, though the pious atmosphere created by numerous venerable mosques means that licensed restaurants are scarce. Thanks to its location near the E80, Turkey's main motorway to Europe, Edirne has also become a major business centre, although conventional tourist facilities are meagre if growing slowly.

SELIMIYE CAMII

The magnificent **Selimiye Camii** Ⓐ dominates Edirne from its hilltop position. Considered by many to represent the pinnacle of Ottoman architecture, it was built between 1569 and 1574 for Sultan Selim II by master architect Sinan, who was 80 years old when he accepted the commission. The enormous *külliye* (mosque complex), comprising the mosque itself, an *arasta* and a *medrese*, looms above the Dilaver Bey Parkı. The *arasta* (shopping arcade whose rents maintain the mosque), where souvenirs and religious objects are sold, is the work of Sinan's pupil, Davut Ağa.

Sinan's design of the Selimiye comprises 18 small domes, which lead the eye to a great central cupola framed by four slender, 71-metre (232ft) -high minarets. Red Edirne sandstone has been used extensively and effectively for decoration, particularly over the arches in the courtyard. Inside, one is awed by the extraordinary sense of space and

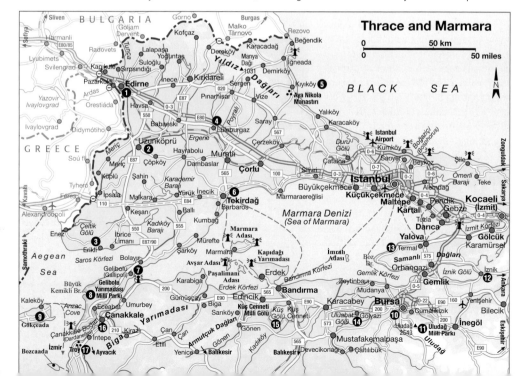

light conveyed by the great floating dome (31.28 metres/103ft in diameter and 44 metres/144ft above the floor), supported by eight giant, stately pillars arranged in a circle. The mosque's rectangular plan is cunningly masked by the arrangement of the side galleries – those on the lower floor open to the outside while the upper floor opens inwards. The lower part of the *mihrab* and the sultan's *loge* (balcony) are clad in fine İznik tiles, and there is a beautifully carved marble *mimber* (pulpit).

The courtyarded *medrese* behind the mosque is now the **Türk-İslam Eserleri Müzesi** (Museum of Turkish and Islamic Arts; Tue–Sun Apr–Sept 9am–7pm, Oct–Mar 9am–5.30pm; charge). Its collection includes an embroidered satin tent used by Ottoman viziers, embroidery, weapons, glass, photographs and records of oil-wrestling matches. The nearby **Edirne Müzesi** (Edirne Museum; Tue–Sun Apr–Sept 9am–7pm, Oct–Mar 9am–5.30pm; charge) has items, some of which are labelled in English, from ancient Aenos at the mouth of the Meriç, as well as Hadrianopolis.

There is also an ethnographic section with the emphasis on village carpet-weaving and colourful bridal costumes.

THE CITY CENTRE

The restored **Eski Camii** in the city centre was constructed between 1403 and 1414. Modelled on Bursa's Ulu Cami, it is a square building divided into nine domed sections. Its upkeep was paid for by revenues from the **Bedesten**, built in 1418 to store and sell valuable goods; according to the 17th-century chronicler Evliya Çelebi, 60 nightwatchmen guarded its treasures. Nearby stand two more of Sinan's buildings, the *kervansaray* built for Grand Vizier Rüstem Paşa (now a hotel) and the **Semiz Ali Paşa Çarsısı** (market). Shop here for Edirne's novelty soap *(meyve sabunu)*, shaped like fruit and vegetables; other local specialities, catering for the sweet of tooth, are *badem ezmesi* (marzipan) and *deva-i-misk* (a type of *helva*).

Just north of the Bedesten, the **Üç Şerefeli Camii** (the Mosque of the Three Balconied Minarets, built 1438–47) marked a stylistic innovation

The vaulted ceiling of Edirne's restored Eski Camii mosque.

Sinan's masterpiece, the Selimiye Camii.

⊙ SINAN, ARCHITECTURAL GENIUS

Mimar Sinan (1489–1588), the greatest Ottoman architect, influenced religious and civic architecture during his lifetime and long after his death. Born probably to Armenian parents near Kayseri, he was recruited in 1512 as a janissary under the *devşirme* system and rose rapidly through the ranks. His ability as a military engineer, along with the knowledge gained from viewing so many monuments – Christian and Islamic – on his extensive travels across the empire, eventually brought him to the attention of Sultan Süleyman the Magnificent, whose grand vizier appointed him chief imperial architect in 1539 – a position Sinan retained under two subsequent sultans.

Over five decades Sinan's output was prodigious, amounting to nearly 400 constructions across the Balkans and Middle East. In addition to minor works like aqueducts and fountains, he was involved in the design and construction of 35 palaces, 84 mosques, 46 hamams, 22 tombs, 12 *kervansarays*, 17 *imarets* (soup kitchens) and 57 *medreses*. In his lengthy memoirs, the *Tezkeret-ül-Bünyan*, he classed pre-1550 commissions like the Şehzade Camii in the capital as apprentice works, but the Süleymaniye Camii, also in Istanbul, as the fruit of maturity, and the Selimiye Camii in Edirne as his masterpiece. He was buried in a simple tomb he had designed for himself in the gardens of the Süleymaniye mosque.

in early Ottoman architecture. For the first time a massive central dome was placed over a rectangular floor plan, a concept that the architect evidently found difficult to realise – the dome is supported by massive pillars with awkward wedge-shaped areas filled by small, turret-like domes at the sides. Yet although patently experimental, the interior breathes strength and reassurance, while the exterior has beautiful decorative details in the mellow local red sandstone. The courtyard, festooned with arcades of pillars, was the first built for a mosque by the Ottomans, while the three minarets, each decorated in a different stone pattern, were the tallest in Edirne until the construction of the Selimiye Mosque. Each of the balconies is approached by separate staircases within the same minaret, an engineering miracle.

Opposite stands the **Sokollu Mehmet Paşa Hamamı** (daily 8.30am–11pm for men, 9am–5pm for women; charge), also built by Sinan and still a functioning traditional bath, with a fine dome and plasterwork. Near the hamam stands

the Makedonya Kulesi, the last remaining tower of the **Roman-Byzantine fortifications**. The rest of the walls were pulled down after the Ottomans had expanded deep into Europe. Today, the partly restored tower overlooks an excavated patch of Roman Hadrianopolis.

Across busy Talat Paşa Caddesi to the south lies the compact, grid-plan **Kaleiçi** quarter. This is the oldest part of town, with many ornate Belle Epoque wooden town houses built by the now-vanished Jewish and Bulgarian communities. At its southeastern end stands the bright yellow Büyük Sinagogu (Grand Synagogue; Tue–Sun 9am–5pm), which now functions as a museum.

BEYOND THE CENTRE

On a hillock a short distance east of the Edirne Museum is the **Muradiye Camii G** (only open at prayer times), built by pious sultan Murat II between 1426 and 1435 as a *zaviye* (monastery) for the Mevlevî dervishes. Later the dervishes moved into a *tekke* (lodge) in the garden, and the main building was converted into a mosque. Sadly its once-glorious interior

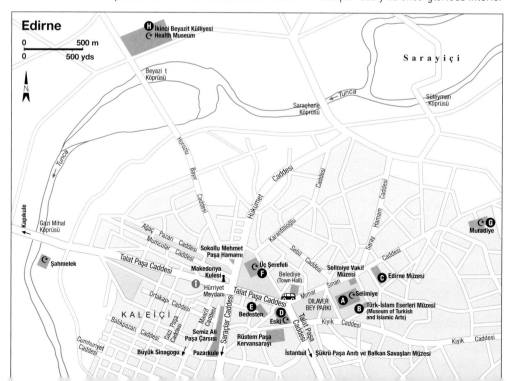

was wrecked when many of its İznik tiles were stolen in 2002, but enough remain to make a detour worthwhile.

A 20-minute walk (or short drive) northwest of town into the countryside, over bridges, dykes and islands of the Tunca, brings you to the **İkinci Beyazit Külliyesi Health Museum**  (daily 9am–5.30pm; charge). The largest such charitable foundation in the Islamic world, it was built in 1484–88 by Beyazit II; it comprises a mosque, insane asylum, hospital, *imaret*, pharmacy, hamam, travellers' hostel, storerooms and kitchens. Here, Lady Mary Wortley Montagu, wife of the British ambassador to the Ottomans, took the bold step in 1716 of having her children inoculated against smallpox, a practice unknown in most of Europe until decades later.

At the southwest corner of the complex, the asylum's domed, hexagonal, white stone treatment room is surrounded by alcoves where patients would rest and be soothed by the sound of running water or music. Today, there are wax figures of patients being treated, medical instruments

and copies of some lurid 15th-century pictures of operations in progress.

You may walk back to the city on paths or lanes running parallel to the complicated system of dykes that protect Edirne from floods, while inspecting the half-dozen graceful Ottoman **bridges** over the Tunca. The Meriç, further south, has only one bridge, the huge but elegant **Mecidiye**, erected 1842–47 and now essentially the municipal logo.

On the highest hill, southeast of the centre, the **Şükrü Paşa Anıtı ve Balkan Savaşları Müzesi** (Tue–Sun 9am–5pm; free) is a memorial-museum dedicated to the Bulgarian siege of Edirne during the 1912–13 Balkan War, built around the tomb of the Ottoman defence commander Şükrü Paşa.

THE REST OF THRACE

Uzunköprü ②, 64km (40 miles) south of Edirne along Highway 550 (E-87), gets its name from a 1,400-metre (4,600ft) -long bridge, with 174 arches, at the north of the town, built during the reign of Murat II. Like Edirne's smaller Ottoman bridges, it is far too narrow for contemporary

Detail from a 4th-century Roman family tombstone in Edirne.

The mosque in the Beyazit Külliyesi complex.

traffic; an ugly but necessary modern replacement has been built 2km (1.5 miles) east. Beyond Keşan, a quiet side road off the 550 leads to Edirne's designated beach resort on the Aegean, **Erikli** ❸. Its buildings, as so often, are nondescript but the sand – almost 2km (1 mile) of it – is anything but. Nearby, beachless İbrice Limanı hosts several scuba schools taking advantage of good diving conditions in the gulf.

Due east of Edirne on a relatively minor, bucolic road, **Kırklareli** is, perhaps surprisingly, the current capital of Thrace, rather than larger Edirne. Saránda Ekklisíes (40 Churches) to its former Greek inhabitants, Lozengrad (Vineyard-ville) to its departed Bulgarians, it epitomised the ethnic stew of pre-Republican Thrace. Today its main attraction is a Roma festival held in early May, while beyond beckons an official border crossing to Malko Tărnovo in Bulgaria. In **Lüleburgaz** ❹, the **Sokollu Mehmet Paşa Külliyesi**, built by Sinan in 1549–69, comprises a mosque, hamam, *medrese* (religious school), *türbe* (tomb) and market. Bosnian Sokollu Mehmet,

A fishmonger in Erikili.

a product of the *devşirme* system (see page 56), began funding the project while governor of Rumeli but finished it serving as grand vizier.

Equidistant from both **Kırklareli** and **Lüleburgaz** on the sparsely populated Thracian Black Sea coast lies **Kıyıköy** ❺, the ancient Medea. It is flanked by two rivers which carry sand down to magnificent beaches, among the best in Turkey. The fortified old town has considerable charm, as do surviving half-timbered fishermen's houses, but it's no secret, and can be packed with *İstanbullus* in season. Carved into a hillside less than a kilometre southwest of town is the Aya Nikola Manastırı (St. Nicholas Monastery; open access), its chapel, cistern and monks' cells dating back to the 6th century.

Tekirdağ ❻ (medieval Rodosto, ancient Byzanthe) is the main bright spot of the Thracian Marmara shore, a major port famous for its rakı-distilling industry, eponymous meatballs, ferry services across the Marmara, and the unexpected, well-signposted **Rákóczi Müzesi** (Rákóczi Museum; Tue–Sun 9am–noon, 1–5pm; charge). Since 1932, the museum has been installed in the house where Transylvanian Hungarian Prince Ferenc II Rákóczi (1676–1735) spent his last years after leading a futile revolt against the Habsburgs from 1703– 11. The building, owned and restored by the Hungarian government, rather overshadows the paltry exhibits.

Southwest of Tekirdağ extends Thrace's major vineyard and winemaking region, though a potentially scenic coastal road is rough and impossible to find without local navigators. Instead, follow the D110 (E-84) highway west, then turn off along Highway 555 to Şarköy, typical of the resorts pitched towards locals here.

THE GELIBOLU (GALLIPOLI) PENINSULA

Bolayır marks the narrowest point of the Gelibolu Peninsula; here one can see both the Saros Gulf and the Dardanelles.

Otherwise it's only remarkable for two tombs: one of Süleyman, favourite son of Sultan Orhan I, who died in a hunting accident nearby, and the other of Namık Kemal (1840–88), prominent Ottoman essayist and poet. There are more sturdy tombs in **Gelibolu** ➐, whose attractive old harbour is flanked by fish restaurants and the lone surviving tower of the Byzantine fortifications. The tower is now the small Piri Reis Müzesi (Tue, Wed, Fri–Sun 9am–5pm; charge), dedicated to the 16th-century Turkish admiral and cartographer.

Despite the shared name, the town is not really a practical base for visiting the tragic World War I Gallipoli battlefields, still another 50km (30 miles) distant. Poignantly, this is one of the most beautiful regions of Turkey. Once shell-blasted and treeless, the peninsula now supports fertile farmland or pine forests with rich flora and fauna, making up the **Gallipoli National Historic Park** ➑ (Gelibolu Yarımadası Tarihi Milli Parkı). Moderate temperatures even in summer and a lack of heavy traffic makes it uniquely suitable for touring by mountain bike.

GALLIPOLI BATTLEFIELDS

It takes a full day to visit the major battlefields, cemeteries and memorials, with a packed lunch advisable as restaurants are almost non-existent. The Allied cemeteries and memorials date from the early 1920s, mostly designed by Scottish architect Sir John Burnet to replace makeshift graveyards of 1915. A useful introduction – and first stop for standard tours – is the Çanakkale Destanı Tanıtım Merkezi (Epic Promotion Centre; tel: 0286-810 0050; Wed–Mon 8.40am–3.30pm; charge). A kilometre (0.6 miles) east of the ferry port of Kabatepe, the museum features archival photos, maps, touching letters home, weapons, uniforms, mess-kits and personal effects.

9 km (5.5 miles) southeast of the museum is Eceabat, where hourly ferries link Çanakkale. There are wonderful views across the straights from its well-restored castle (Tue–Sun 9am–5.30pm; charge), originally built by Mehmet II shortly before the siege of Constantinople – to keep the Papal Navy from aiding the Byzantines.

Oil wrestlers struggle for a slippery hold.

☉ OIL WRESTLING

Turkish Yağlı Güreş (oil wrestling) is a traditional summer sport. According to legend, it began as a means to keep Ottoman soldiers trim. Competitions began in 1361, when Süleyman, son of Sultan Orhan I, invited 40 champions to wrestle while returning from a battle. By dawn the next day, the last two had died of exhaustion, but where each hero fell a spring gushed from the ground. To this day the festival is held at Kırkpınar ("40 Springs"), just outside Edirne, and the basics of the sport have remained the same. Most modern wrestlers are village boys with some regional success, dreaming of fame and riches.

Each year, about 1,000 wrestlers, covered with olive oil and clad only in leather breeches, compete at Kırkpınar in several categories classed by height, not weight, from toddler to full-sized. Betting is brisk, a listless performance booed, and no quarter is given by the *pehlivans* (wrestlers). Referees only monitor illegal holds and announce the winner after a wrestler's shoulder is forced to the ground or a contestant collapses. Matches last 30 to 40 minutes on average depending on size category, with 10 to 15 minutes of "overtime" allowed to break draws. After each relay of matches, victorious competitors pair off again until only one – the *başpehlivan* (champion) – remains standing.

Organised, half-day tours visit only the most convenient memorials around Kabatepe; equally interesting sites at the far south end of the peninsula are only accessible independently or with a custom tour.

The most famous sites are nearby at the Lone Pine Cemetery and **Anzac Cove**, where Australian and New Zealand troops lie, and **Çonkbayırı**, site of particularly desperate encounters, dramatised in Peter Weir's 1981 film *Gallipoli*. Also in this area, one of numerous Turkish memorials assiduously marked since 2002, is the cemetery of the 57th Ottoman regiment, many of whose poorly armed members were ordered to their deaths by Mustafa Kemal to buy time for reinforcements to arrive.

The Anglo-French landings were well south, either side of Cape Helles, the Turkish equivalent of Land's End; here loom the huge British memorial obelisk near the cape, the French monument and cemetery at Morto (Corpse) Bay, and the colossal Abide, or cenotaph, for all the Turkish dead.

A cement monument at Arıburnu Cove bears Atatürk's 1934 message of reconciliation:

There is no difference between the Johnnies and the Mehmets to us,

Where they lie side by side here in this country of ours,

You, the mothers who sent their sons from faraway countries, wipe away your tears;

Your sons are now lying in our bosom and are in peace.

After having lost their lives on this land,

They have become our sons as well.

Every year on 25 April, ANZAC Day, a solemn 5.30am ceremony at adjacent Anzac Cove is attended by dignitaries of the two antipodean nations – and up to 10,000 others. They commemorate the Allied campaign undertaken to knock Ottoman Turkey out of the war by storming Istanbul, after attempts in late 1914 and early 1915 to force the Dardanelles by sea had failed owing to comprehensive Turkish mining. An amphibious assault on several points along the peninsula, commencing at dawn on 25 April 1915, quickly went awry: Anglo-French landings near Cape Helles were almost annihilated and ANZAC forces came ashore at the wrong beach. Under heavy Ottoman fire, they nonetheless advanced inland over two days towards Çonkbayır, where one Mustafa Kemal, later Atatürk, commanded the Turkish lines and miraculously escaped death on several occasions. On 27 April, he launched a silent, pre-dawn bayonet charge which stopped the ANZACs. Thereafter, except for an abortive British landing at Cape Suvla in the north, the battle settled into stationary trench warfare, until in November the Allies threw in the towel, and finished evacuating Gallipoli by 6 January 1916.

GÖKÇEADA

Gökçeada ❾ (formerly İmroz or Imvros), northwest of the entrance to the Dardanelles, is linked by six daily ferries from Kabatepe and one from Çanakkale

Gallipoli exhibit in Eceabat, the nearest town to the battlefields.

(bound for the port town of Kuzu Limanı). Taken by Greece during the Balkan Wars, the island reverted to Turkish control in 1923, although the 7,000 local Orthodox Greeks were more or less left in peace for 40 years thereafter. However, when the Cyprus conflict flared up in 1964, Turkey turned up the pressure through land expropriation, heavy garrisoning, the closure of all Greek schools, restrictions on grazing and fishing, and Muslim settlement from the mainland. This had the desired result: only a few hundred ethnic Greeks remain.

Since the post-1999 thaw in Greco-Turkish relations, this diaspora has returned seasonally to renovate abandoned houses and attend some of the many churches – a point of honour given that Ecumenical Patriarch Vartholomeos (the highest official in the Orthodox Christian Church) was born here in 1940. Still, the older generation remains wary, dependent as they are on governmental good will, and resentful that they can't leave property to their children who don't qualify for Turkish citizenship.

Gökçeada is now awakening to its potential to attract tourists, thanks to rugged volcanic landscapes, characterful villages and excellent south-coast beaches. Summer visitors comprise a few Romanians and Bulgarians, but mostly thousands of returning Greeks and their descendants, plus cosmopolitan Turks who enjoy their company, especially at the 14–16 August Orthodox *panayır* (Festival of the Virgin).

Most facilities are in the northwest, around the functional inland capital of **Merkez** (Panayiá), its fishing port of **Kaleköy** (Kástro), with crumbled castle overhead, and **Eski Bademli** (Glykí). Still very Greek in feel are the remoter villages of **Zeytinli** (Ágii Theodóri), with its many sweetshops, and **Tepeköy** (Agrídia), venue for the *panayır*. The largest village and former capital was **Dereköy** (Skhinoúdi) in the west, its 1,900 houses now mostly abandoned. **Aydıncık** in the far southeast is one of the best beaches in the Turkish Aegean, with windsurf schools; **Lazkoyu** (Agía Káli) and **Gizli Liman** further west have few or no amenities but are even more scenic.

Small Greek Orthodox church in Gökçeada.

MARMARA

This green and fertile region south of the Sea of Marmara features prominently in legends, from Karagöz shadow plays to the siege of Troy.

Main attractions
Bursa: Muradiye complex
Bursa: Yeşil complex
Cumalıkızık
İznik tiles
Yalova: Termal
Troy

Maps on pages 160, 169

In classical times the area south of the Sea of Marmara (the ancient Propontis) was divided between Bithynia and Mysia. According to Herodotus, the Bithynians were a fierce, warlike people who originally came from Thrace. After Alexander the Great expelled the Persians from Asia Minor, the Bithynians formed an independent kingdom based at Nicomedia (modern İzmit). According to Homer, the Mysians were allies of the Trojans, but Mysia's location and extent were unclear, and there is no record of a Mysian kingdom. Before the Romans made it part of the Province of Asia in 133 BC, Mysia had been ruled by the Lydian, Persian and Pergamene kings.

BURSA

The historic city of **Bursa** ⑩ is dominated by the great bulk of 2,554-metre (8,377ft) **Uludağ**. Until the 1980s Turks spoke of "Yeşil" Bursa ("Green" Bursa) because of the city's sylvan setting. Since then, concrete underpasses, overpasses and new high-rise structures have transformed its symmetry and skyline, while new quarters straggle interminably along the E90 through-road. Some lament that Yeşil Bursa has become "Çimento Bursa". Fortunately, the historic Ottoman quarters remain relatively unscathed.

According to the ancient Greek geographer Strabo, Bursa was founded by the Bithynian King Prusias I Kholos "the Lame" (reigned 228–182 BC), who gave his name – altered to the Hellenistic "Prousa" – to the city. Legend has it that Carthaginian general Hannibal helped him choose the site.

In 74 BC, Bithynia was willed to Rome by its last ruler, the ineffectual Nicomedes IV Philopator. Prousa prospered under Roman and early Byzantine rule, but suffered greatly from the 7th- and 8th-century Arab raids and fell to the Seljuks in 1075. Subsequently, it was fought over by the Crusaders,

Studying the Qur'an in a Bursa mosque.

Byzantines and Turks until, in 1326, it was conquered by Gazi Orhan I, whom the 13th-century Moroccan traveller, Ibn Battuta, described as "the greatest of the Turkmen kings, and the richest in wealth, lands and military forces."

Bursa was the first true Ottoman capital, and its rulers lavished money and care on it. Orhan issued his first coins here in 1327 and set up a bazaar with a *bedesten* in 1340. Apart from recent development, the present form of the city still follows Ottoman lines, with the central areas surrounding the mosques and religious foundations built by the first six Ottoman sultans. Today, with over 2 million inhabitants (many of them from Artvin province or of Balkan Muslim descent), Bursa is the fourth-largest city in Turkey, with the same civic pride felt by its first Turkish citizens in the 14th century. True, its industrial prosperity has rendered large swathes of it rather unsightly; nevertheless, its old quarters present an unrivalled display of early Ottoman architecture, including nearly a dozen mosques and tomb complexes.

ÇEKIRGE

The elegant suburb of **Çekirge** Ⓐ, 4km (2.5 miles) west of the city centre, is the best place to stay if you're driving.

The **Eski Kaplıca**, erected on the site of Roman and Byzantine baths, and the **Yeni Kaplıca**, built in 1552 by grand vizier Rüstem Paşa, are two of Bursa's many historic mineral baths. Mineral water, rich in iron, sodium, sulphur, calcium, bicarbonate and magnesium, used to gush in abundance from the mountainside at temperatures ranging from 54–84°C (129–151°F). For reasons either geological or climatic, the flow was sharply curtailed during 2009–11, but fortunately has resumed since.

You may be able to catch a shadow puppet play at the **Karagöz Evi** (Karagöz Theatre and Museum; museum open Tue–Sun 9.30am–5.30pm; performances Thu & Fri 11am & 2pm, Sat noon) at Çekirge Caddesi 3. Further information is available from the Karagöz Antique Shop (see margin). Shadow-puppet plays probably came with the Turks from Central Asia. A popular form of entertainment in Ottoman

⊙ Fact

Bursa's traditional shadow puppets are made from camel hide, oiled to become translucent, then painted. Şinasi Çelikkol's Karagöz Antique Shop in the bazaar at Eski Aynalı Çarsı 12 (tel: 0224-221 8727, www.karagozshop.net) has an interesting range of puppets for sale and organises performances.

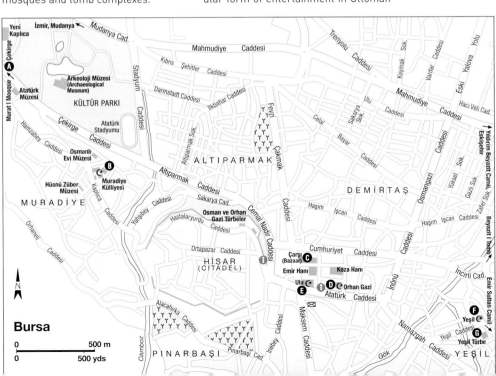

Bursa

society, they were often performed in coffee houses. The stories feature Karagöz (Black Eye) and his stooge Hacivat in a series of comic, often rather bawdy, routines. The two characters were originally based on workmen who laboured on the construction of the Orhan Gazi Camii. Their antics so amused the other workers that they held up work on the building of the mosque and, as a result, were executed on the orders of the angry Sultan Orhan.

TOMB AND MOSQUE OF MURAT I

Also in Çekirge is the **Mosque of Murat I**, built between 1366 and 1386. Murat, known as Hudâvendigâr ("Creator of the World"), spent most of his reign at war (thus the long delay in the mosque's completion). The tomb of the warrior-sultan, murdered in the hour of Ottoman victory at the 1389 Battle of Kosovo, lies across the road in a lovingly tended garden, his sarcophagus resting between eight columns which support the dome.

The mosque is based on the usual inverted T-plan, but has unusual features which are sometimes attributed to its possible design by a Christian architect. On the ground floor was a *zaviye* (dervish lodging), upstairs a *medrese*. Some suggest that this was for teaching "orthodox" Islam, and that its position above the dervish quarters symbolises victory over heterodox mysticism. Today only the lower floor is open to visitors.

Heading towards the old city, you reach the **Kültür Parkı** (Çekirge Caddesi; always open; charge when admission booths staffed), with pleasant gardens, a small boating lake, and a few expensive restaurants and nightclubs. Inside the park, the **Arkeoloji Müzesi** (Archaeological Museum; Tue-Sun 8am-noon, 1-5pm; charge) has an interesting collection, in particular intricately worked metal ornaments from all over Anatolia.

MURADIYE AND HISAR

Just south of Çekirge Caddesi, the **Muradiye Külliyesi** ❸ (daily 7am-7pm; no charge but you may want to tip the *bekçi* – warden) was built between 1424 and 1426. It comprises a mosque, an *imaret* and a *medrese*; the tombs of Murat II (ruled 1421-51) plus various other members of Ottoman royalty were added incrementally over the next century. Above the portico of the mosque, brick patterns highlighted in azure tiling depict the heavenly spheres, while thunderbolts in blue glazed tiles are set into the marble to the right of the entrance. The T-shaped interior plan, with *eyvans* (alcoves) flanking the main domed space, is typical of early Ottoman mosques, based on Seljuk prototypes.

In the lovely gardens are 12 tombs of various styles, open in rotation. Murat's austere tomb lies under a dome raised on Roman columns. Like all the early Ottoman sultans, Murat was a renowned fighter on the battlefield, but, as recorded by Edward Gibbon, "He seldom engaged in war till he

⊙ THE STORY OF SILK

The ancient Chinese first realised that the small caterpillars infesting the leaves of the white mulberry tree spun themselves a cocoon, whose single gossamer thread, hundreds of metres long, could be used to produce a fabric of filmy lightness and incredible strength. For about 3,000 years they jealously guarded the secret and monopolised the market.

Byzantine Emperor Justinian I (AD 527–65) recruited two Persian monks to smuggle silkworms hidden in bamboo canes from China to Constantinople. Silk production became a state monopoly, based in Bursa. The Ottomans similarly encouraged local production, producing magnificent fabrics and carpets. Among the 2,500 items on display in the wardrobe section of the Topkapı Palace are many superb silk brocade and velvet garments, made in Bursa.

The silk industry had collapsed by the 1800s, outcompeted by French and Italian enterprises, but state intervention has since revitalised it. However, villagers seem increasingly reluctant to raise the troublesome silkworms – which must be kept in temperature-controlled, dark lofts – so merchants are complaining that they cannot buy enough silk, even at the annual cocoon auctions. Whether the home-grown trade will last in the face of cheap imports (once again, from China) is questionable.

was justified by a previous and adequate provocation. In the observance of treaties his word was inviolate and sacred." Attracted to the mystical life, he opted to abdicate temporarily to be a dervish, and eschewing pomp and circumstance, he asked to be buried under the open occulus of the dome, so that the rain and moonlight might bathe his grave.

Deeper in the garden, past beds of flowering shrubs under the cypresses, is the tomb of Cem Sultan, one of Ottoman history's more tragic figures. After Mehmet II's death in 1481, intrigues prevented Cem, the sultan's favourite son, from reaching Istanbul before his brother Beyazit II, who proclaimed himself sultan. The two fought briefly, then Cem fled abroad to seek refuge with various Christian powers, who used him as a pawn to extract protection money from Beyazit . He died in Naples on 25 February 1495, probably poisoned by Pope Alexander VI at Beyazit's behest. A man of action, culture and poems redolent of the pain of exile, had Cem ascended the throne Ottoman history might have been very

different. Now he rests in a tomb full of blue tiles below and extravagant painted calligraphy above. Nearby, Süleyman the Magnificent's regrettably murdered first-born son, Şehzade Mustafa, lies in a tomb lined with İznik tiles depicting hyacinths, tulips and blossoming shrubs.

Muradiye is in one of Bursa's older quarters. A couple of streets south from the *külliye*, the **Hüsnü Züber Müzesi** (closed temporarily for restoration; charge) occupies a well-refurbished Ottoman mansion dating from 1836. The collection comprises various carved wooden implements, some made by the late Hüsnü himself, though the building is the main attraction. Across the park to the north of the *külliye* is the **Ottoman House Museum** (Osmanlı Evi Müzesi; Mon–Sat 8am–7pm), in a restored 17th-century house.

From here, continue along Kaplıca Caddesi, across the Cılımboz Deresi, to the other old residential quarter of **Hisar** (Citadel), still enclosed in fortifications. At the northeast edge, with fine views, stand the **Osman ve Orhan**

Mescit (small mosque) in the courtyard of Koza Hanı in the old silk market, Bursa.

The minarets of Ulu Camii in Bursa.

Gazi Türbeler (Mon–Sat 8am–7.30pm), tombs of the first Ottoman leaders, indifferently restored in 1868. Below to the northwest, beyond stepped parkland, begins Sakarya Caddesi, now home to most of the rather tame nightlife in this devout, alcohol-scarce city.

THE BAZAAR AREA

The **Çarşı** Ⓒ (Bazaar), founded by Gazi Orhan in the 14th century but substantially extended by subsequent sultans, is still the commercial centre of Bursa, crowded with locals inspecting wares laid out in the narrow alleys lined with small shops. The gleaming modern Zafer Plaza pyramid-mall sits to the west. At the bazaar's northwest corner, the **Bedesten**, built by Sultan Beyazit I but completely restored in 1960 after a fire, still sells precious goods like jewellery and gold brocade, its impregnable doors locked each night. As so often in the Ottoman system, some of its revenues helped support the nearby Orhan Gazi Camii and Ulu Camii.

Just off the bustling market lanes stand several *hans* (shop-halls) built around quiet courtyards often shaded by trees, cooled by fountains and provided with a teahouse. Orhan built the **Emir Hanı**, the earliest example of the rural *kervansaray* adapted to the requirements of urban commerce. Much altered since, its rooms could be used as shops, storage areas or dwellings. The rather grand two-storeyed **Koza Hanı** has a tiny octagonal *mescit* (small mosque) in the courtyard where the annual summer silk-cocoon auction is now but a shadow of its former self. But dazzlingly coloured silk wares still adorn the counters of the surrounding shops.

Just uphill stands the much-restored **Orhan Gazi Camii** Ⓓ (Orhan Gazi Mosque), established in 1339. A massive five-bayed porch adorned with Byzantine columns fronts the T-shaped main building, the first of several such in Bursa. The two main domed chambers are flanked by *eyvans* with smaller cupolas, where apparently *ahis* (members of an apprentice guild and religious brotherhood) stayed and worshipped. Orhan himself ruled for 33 years and, as the son-in-law of

Silks galore inside Koza Hanı.

Byzantine Emperor John VI Kantakouzenos, became intricately involved
in the civil wars attending the final
Byzantine decline.

BURSA'S GREAT MOSQUES

The massive bulk of the **Ulu Camii E**
(Great Mosque), built by Yıldırım Beyazit
I (reigned 1389–1403), dominates the
bazaar from the southwest. Before battling a Crusader army at Macedonian
Nicopolis in 1396 he supposedly promised that, if victorious, he would build 20
mosques – a vow interpreted afterwards
as one mosque with 20 domes arranged
in five rows and upheld by massive pillars. Beneath the higher, central dome,
once open to the sky, is the şadırvan
(ablutions fountain). The rough-hewn
walls of warm-toned, limestone from
Uludağ just uphill are pierced at inter-
vals by windows, while doors on three
sides are surrounded by carved marble
portals. The door on the north side was
apocryphally modified by Timur when he
occupied Bursa in 1402.

From here, walk east, then southeast, across one of Bursa's two mountain streams – the Gök Dere – until
reaching the **Yeşil Camii F** (Green
Mosque), begun in 1419 by Çelebi
Mehmet I (reigned 1413–21) and still the
most spectacular of the city's imperial
mosques, despite never being finished
and severe 19th-century earthquake
damage. Its name comes from the tur-
quoise-green tiles which once covered
the roof and the tops of the minarets,
and still persists (along with delicate
carving) around the windows. Inside,
the eye is overwhelmed by the richness
of the decoration. Circles, stars and
geometric motifs on turquoise, green,
white and blue tiles explore all possible
permutations in a composition which is
both harmonious and complex. By the
beautifully decorated *mihrab*, a Persian
inscription credits the work to master
craftsmen from Tabriz.

The Yeşil Camii, like others in Bursa,
is another *zaviye*-type mosque with a

şadırvan in the middle of the central
hall, flanked by two *eyvans*. Doors also
open off the central space to rooms
with elaborate stucco shelving and fireplaces, thought to be *tabhanes* (dervish
hostels). Immediately to the right and
left of the entrance, narrow stairs lead
to the richly decorated sultan's *loge*
(balcony), overlooking the prayer hall.
You will need the *bekçi*'s (warden's)
consent to see this.

Across the road, past various view-
cafés competing for your custom,
Mehmet I's **Yeşil Türbe G** (Green
Tomb; daily 9am–1pm, 2–6pm) is
among the loveliest buildings in
Bursa. Walk slowly around the tomb
to enjoy the extraordinary turquoise
of the plain tiles, now replaced when
necessary with new İznik material,
and the richness of the patterned
tiled lunettes over the seven windows. Apart from the elaborately
decorated *mihrab*, the interior features plain Tabriz tiles on which are
set lozenges of patterned tiles. The
empty sarcophagus of the sultan –
the body is actually well below ground

*A traditional Bursa
house, now used as
an antique shop.*

Waterfall on Uludağ.

level, in accordance with Islamic law – is flanked by those of his family.

Slightly to the right of Yeşil Türbe, set among the cypresses of a large cemetery, is the **Emir Sultan Camii**. Rebuilt after 1804 in the kitsch-Baroque style popular at that time, it was originally erected around 1400 by Emir Sultan, a Bokharan dervish and counsellor of both Beyazit I and Murat I.

The Yıldırım Bayezid Külliyesi (**complex of Beyazit I**; closed until late 2020 for restoration works) lies on an outcrop a short walk to the north beyond a quiet residential neighbourhood. Built between 1390 and 1395, it consisted originally of a mosque, *imaret*, two *medreses*, a hospital, palace and Beyazit's *türbe*. Today only the mosque, tomb and one *medrese* remain. Beyazit's body was brought back to Bursa after his unhappy captivity and death at Akşehir, as a prisoner of Timur. Reviled by subsequent sultans for his defeat (Murat IV visited Bursa expressly to kick the tomb), Beyazit rests under a plain sarcophagus.

The interior of the Yeşil Türbe (Green Tomb).

AROUND BURSA

Just south of Bursa, at an altitude of 1,900–2,500 metres (6,235–8,200ft), the richly forested **Uludağ Milli Parkı**  ("Big Mountain" National Park) has long claimed to be Turkey's premier ski resort, packed from December to April.

In late spring and summer, the mountain attracts people more interested in natural history, offering long walks by tumbling brooks and across slopes carpeted with wild flowers to several glacial tarns near the summit, actually outside park boundaries. The 9km (5.5 miles) cable car, opened in 2014, has provided a big boost to the hotels and restaurants that abound near both the Sarıalan picnic area (the line's third station) and the summit station, Kurbağa Kaya (1,870m; 6,140ft).

Some 17km (11 miles) from the city centre, in the eastern foothills of Uludağ, **Cumalıkızık** is a picture-perfect Ottoman village which entered (inter)national consciousness by serving for five years as a location for a Turkish TV serial. Low-key tourism has not been long in following, with at least two of the delightful old houses restored as inns – reservations at weekends are essential.

İZNIK (NIKAIA, NICAEA)

The small lakeside town of **İznik** ⑫ (formerly Nikaia or Nicaea) lies 80km (50 miles) northeast of Bursa. It was founded in 316 BC by Antigonos I Monopthalmos (the One-Eyed), one of Alexander's successors. It was seized 15 years later by rival general Lysimakhos and renamed Nikaia after his deceased wife. The city prospered under Roman rule; Pliny the Younger, governor of Bithynia (AD 111–13), lived here and rebuilt the theatre and gymnasium.

The town has played an instrumental role in the history of Christianity. In AD 325, Nikaia was the venue for the First Ecumenical Council, which condemned the Arian heresy and formulated the Nicene Creed still used by most Christian denominations. The Iconoclastic controversy (whether Christians should continue to revere icons) was settled by the Seventh Ecumenical Council, held in the Basilica of St Sophia in 787.

The city was held briefly by the Seljuks after 1081, and was the capital of the Byzantine Laskarid dynasty during the Crusader occupation of Constantinople in the 13th century. Nikaia was taken for the Ottomans by Orhan I in 1331 and soon renamed İznik. Skilled craftsmen brought here from Tabriz in Iran by Yavuz (the Fierce) Selim I (reigned 1512–20) consolidated an existing ceramic industry which made İznik tiles famous. Those used to adorn the classical Ottoman mosques were all produced here; technique had declined before production moved to Kütahya late in the 17th century.

İZNIK SIGHTS

İznik merits a visit just for its beautiful lakeside situation, though sadly nearby beaches are not first-rate. However, there are several restaurants and hotels overlooking the water.

The city's ancient double walls and two of the seven original gates are intact, while in the former **Aya Sofya Basilica** – which hosted the coronation of four Byzantine emperors – a few

Detail of an İznik tile in the Topkapı Palace in Istanbul.

⊘ İZNIK TILE MANUFACTURE

Since 1993, the İznik Vafkı (İznik Foundation) has led efforts to revive traditional tile-manufacturing techniques; there are now many workshops in town. Innovative designs, beyond Ottoman floral cross sections, include depictions of the region's fruit and olive trees, or *kadırgas* (galleons), all extremely popular motifs. Most kilns work primarily to order for domestic customers, and usually stock only a few specimens of any design – casual drop-ins hoping to decorate an entire kitchen or bathroom may be disappointed.

The toughest, highest-quality (and priciest) tiles are not ceramic-based but made from locally quarried quartz. This is finely ground up, reconstituted to 85 percent purity and formed into "biscuits". These are sanded, underglazed and left to air-dry for a week, then fired at over 900°C (1,620°F) for 17 hours. Next, designs are stencilled on, painstakingly painted in (usually by women) using metal-oxide pigments mimicking semi-precious stone colours, a top glaze applied, and the tile popped back in the kiln for four days. The temperature of final firing determines whether the glaze emerges glossy, half-glossy or matte. Quartz-rich tiles are porous to air, have excellent acoustic qualities (hence their use in mosques), modulate light reflections and make excellent insulators, as they contract slightly in winter and expand in summer.

surviving remnants of the old church can be seen. Among these are the mosaic pavement of Justinian's original 6th-century church and a faded 7th-century fresco of Christ, John the Baptist and the Virgin. Though the building was converted into a mosque in 2011, the relevant sections remain open to tourists, who are encouraged to be mindful of worshippers.

Just east of here are a number of old mosques, including **Hacı Özbek Camii**, built in 1333 – the earliest Ottoman mosque in Turkey which can be dated accurately. Further along is the **Yeşil Camii** (Green Mosque), built between 1378 and 1392 by Candarlı Kara Halil Paşa, with particularly harmonious proportions. Sadly, the original tiles on the minaret disappeared long ago and have been replaced by inferior substitutes from Kütahya.

İznik's **Arkeoloji Müzesi** (Archaeological Museum; closed for restoration until 2020) is housed in the three-domed Nilüfer Hatun İmareti, named after the wife of Orhan I, a beautiful and distinguished Greek noblewoman

entrusted with the affairs of state during the bey's military campaigns. The grounds remain accessible, containing some fine marble statuary.

Just offshore to the southwest of the ancient city lies another site of interest, discovered in 2014: a sunken 4th-century basilica dedicated to St. Neophytos, a teenager killed by the Romans. Archaeologists have posited that it was here that Nikaia's historic First Ecumenical Council took place. In 2018, plans were announced to build an underwater archaeology museum (set to open by the end of 2019) on the spot, allowing visitors to view the remains from above, as well as to suit up with scuba gear to dive to the ruins.

YALOVA, TERMAL, MUDANYA AND ZEYTINBAĞI

Yalova, Bursa's main port on the southern shore of the Gulf of İzmit, is served by regular car-ferries from Istanbul. More appealing is the spa of **Termal** ⑬, 12km (7 miles) inland in a forested area, popular with Arab and Turkish holidaymakers. There are several good hotels, while the hot pool of the Kurşunlu Banyo (www.yalovatermal.net; daily 7.30am–10.30pm; charge) is a testing 60°C (140°F) at source. The thermal springs were popular with the Romans and Byzantines; interest in them revived during the Belle Epoque.

Mudanya, though much closer to Bursa, is its less busy port (see margin). The rocky coastline just west is unremarkable except for **Zeytinbağı** (Trilye in Ottoman times), a formerly Greek-inhabited port with a Byzantine church (now a mosque), old mansions and some seafood restaurants.

THE MYSIAN LAKES

West of Bursa, the two great lakes of ancient Mysia appeal in different ways. **Uluabat Gölü** ⑭ is still often called by its old name Apollyon, after ancient Apollonia, whose masonry has been seamlessly interwoven with the

The exquisite Yeşil Camii (Green Mosque) in İznik.

charming village of **Gölyazı**, accessible by local bus from Bursa, 38km (24 miles) away. There's a morning fish auction, storks' nests, a few half-timbered houses and lake fish to eat at the single restaurant. **Küş Gölü** ⑮, about 72km (45 miles) further west, hosts the **Küş Cenneti Milli Parkı** (Bird Paradise National Park; daily 9am–6pm; charge), one of the largest wildlife sanctuaries in western Anatolia. From the observation tower you can see up to 246 species of birds, both resident and migratory – the best seasons are spring and autumn.

ÇANAKKALE

Because of the location it is likely that there were settlements here before recorded history, as control of the Dardanelles brought wealth and power. The Persian King Xerxes I built his bridge of boats across these straits' narrowest part in 480 BC to land 200,000 troops in Thrace, but his planned conquest of Greece ended in defeat at Salamis and Plataea. Ever since, the Dardanelles have remained a crucial control point between the European and Asian continents, as well as between the Aegean and the Sea of Marmara and the Black Sea beyond.

Çanakkale ⑯ is several hours by car or bus from Istanbul, with most long-distance buses using the ferry link with Eceabat – though the local airport receives frequent, popular flights from Ankara and Istanbul. The town became an active trading and transit point between Asia and Europe after Sultan Mehmet II built fortresses here on each shore in 1452, to begin his stranglehold on Constantinople. Although the town may not have entirely reclaimed the status it enjoyed in the 19th century, when it was a cosmopolitan mini-Smyrna home to scores of consulates and customs houses, Çanakkale has improved considerably since the 1990s. The compact old quarter with its houses built by the vanished Christian and Jewish communities has been refurbished, and there is an attractive seaside promenade. Visitors to Troy and Gallipoli frequently base themselves here.

Quayside restaurants serve fresh (if pricey) seafood. Enjoy a glass of tea

The harbour at Çanakkale.

or a beer in one of the cafés while you savour the bustling activity of the port and its never-ending parade of large freighters, fishing boats and car-ferries. Just north of the quay rises the massive wooden horse that was used in the 2004 film, *Troy*. To the south stands the Ottoman fortress, which houses one section of the **Naval Museum** (http://canakkalemuze.dzkk.tsk.tr; Tues–Sun 9.30am–noon, 1.30–5pm; charge), the other sitting across the cannon-lined park to the north (same hours and ticket). A short walk to the east of here is the **City Museum** (Çanakkale Kent Müzesi; 9am–5pm), offering a recent historical overview of the town.

Çanakkale's collection of ancient artefacts are housed in the Arkeoloji Müzesi (Archaeology Museum; Tue–Sun 9am–5pm; charge), set 1.5km (1 mile) to the south along the road to Troy. Most of the collection consists of brass implements, glazed pottery, gold and jewellery, unfired clay lamps and Hellenistic figurines from the nearby Bozcaada and Dardanos tumuli, while some of the museum's former star attractions have been moved south to fill the Troy Museum.

TROY

The name **Troy** ⑰ conjures up visions of the star-crossed lovers Helen and Paris, of Greek and Trojan heroes, of betrayal and revenge, of cunning and deceit, of a huge wooden horse, of the destruction of a great city and of blind Homer who immortalised it all in two epic poems, the *Iliad* and *Odyssey*. Did Helen and Paris, Agamemnon and Klytemnestra, Achilles and Odysseus ever exist? Was there really a siege of Troy? Are Homer's epics at all historical?

Whether you regard Homer as just an early minstrel and itinerant entertainer, or as the source of history's most profound legends, the adventures of his characters have become an integral part of world literary heritage, and their fates have enthralled and moved countless generations.

A LITTLE HISTORY

In 333 BC, Alexander the Great came to Troy where he made a propitiatory sacrifice to the spirit of Priam (king of Troy during the Trojan War, according to Greek mythology) and received a gold crown from a citizen of Sigeion (where, it was believed, the Greeks had beached their ships). He also exchanged his weapons and armour for some kept in the Temple of Athena – thought to date from the time of the Trojan War. He then anointed his body with oil and ran naked to the mound where Achilles was supposedly buried. His lover, Hephaestion, did the same at the purported tomb of Achilles' companion, Patroklos.

Troy was destroyed during the Mithridatic War of about 82 BC and rebuilt by Julius Caesar. It received special honours from several emperors as the birthplace of Aeneas, legendary founder of ancient Rome. When Emperor Julian the Apostate (AD 361–63) visited Ilion, as Troy was then known, he was greeted by the

Ceramic Trojan horses souvenirs, Çanakkale.

local bishop, Pegasios, who offered to show him the sights of the ancient city. Julian was astonished to find a fire smouldering on an altar at the so-called temple of Hector and the statue of the hero covered in oil. The bishop explained: "Is it not natural that they [the people of Ilion] should worship a brave man who was their own citizen, just as we worship our martyrs?"

Because of the growing importance of nearby Alexandria Troas, the city soon began to decline, something accelerated by the silting of its harbour. Khristodoulos of Imbros relates how Sultan Mehmet II "inspected the ruins... [was] shown the tombs of Achilles, Hector and Ajax [and said] 'It is to me that Allah has given to avenge this city and its people... Indeed it was the Greeks who before devastated this city, and it is their descendants who after so many years have paid me the debt which their boundless pride had contracted... towards us, the peoples of Asia.'"

The early 17th-century Scottish traveller William Lithgow was not particularly impressed by Troy in 1610: "Well I wot, I saw infinite old Sepulchers, but for their particular names, and nomination of them, I suspend, neither could I beleeve my Interpreter, sith it is more then three thousand and odde yeares agoe, that Troy was destroyed.'"

In a May 1810 letter to Henry Drury, Lord Byron seemed preoccupied with rather more earthy matters: "The only vestige of Troy, or her destroyers, are the barrows supposed to contain carcasses of Achilles, Antilochus, Ajax, etc.; – but Mt Ida is still in high feather, though the Shepherds are now-a-days not much like Ganymede."

SCHLIEMANN'S GREAT DISCOVERY

From 1871 to 1873, self-made millionaire and amateur archaeologist Heinrich Schliemann excavated at Troy using the *Iliad* (and preliminary digs by the Briton Frank Calvert) as his guide, while academics laughed at the mad German who was squandering his wealth so foolishly. But Schliemann found treasure, starting with a necklace, then gold cups, copper daggers, axes, lance-heads and cauldrons, silver vases and two extraordinary golden diadems worn, he judged, by royalty. In fact he had not found Homer's Troy: this collection came from the remains of a prehistoric Bronze Age civilisation a millennium earlier.

ONGOING CONTROVERSY

Subsequent investigations by other archaeologists revealed more than nine separate levels of occupation at Hisarlık tumulus. Professor Carl Blegen, leader of the 1932–38 University of Cincinnati expedition, believed that Troy VII was Priam's city, and that it was destroyed in about 1260 BC; in the 1950s, Professor Moses Finley countered that there was no evidence of a hostile Mycenaean expedition to Troy. The late archaeologist George Bean also maintained there were no finds from Hisarlık to connect Troy's destruction with a Greek invasion,

Remains of the odeon at Troy.

and that the paltry remains of Troy VII bore little resemblance to the fine city described by Homer. But then during the 1990s the late Manfred Korfmann discovered traces of distant perimeter fortifications that indicated a town far larger than just the citadel ruins – and just possibly resistance to a siege during the 13th century BC.

In late 2009, Dr Oliver Dickinson elegantly summarised the sceptics' arguments against a historical 10-year campaign: no documented prior interaction between Greeks and Hittites at Wilusa, the latter's name for Troy; striking inaccuracies in the Homeric Catalogue of Ships compared to the real attributes of Greek city-states of the era; pervasive anachronisms in Homeric description of Mycenaean religion, palace architecture and weaponry, making the *Iliad* and *Odyssey* a vintage-700 BC pastiche of Bronze and Iron Age customs.

THE SITE AND MUSEUM

A modern wooden horse at Troy can be climbed.

Another point of controversy is the on-site replica of the Trojan horse at the entrance to the site (not to be confused with the more striking one on Çanakkale's waterfront). Many visitors find it ridiculously out of place; for others it is a pleasantly frivolous attraction at an otherwise visually dull site. Others are reminded of the moment when the stunned defenders realised that they had been duped and that their city was doomed. As in the literary original, the reconstruction is entered from underneath, and you can look out over the ruined city and the Troad plain to see with modern eyes what Homer could only imagine.

The site itself (daily Apr–Sept 9am–7.30pm, Oct–Mar 8am–5pm; charge) has relatively little to show for its illustrious pedigree, though multiple explanatory panels placed along a circular touring path help make sense of the place. Begin your tour at the massive tower in the great wall of Troy VI. Continue through the east gate, passing the carefully constructed houses of Troy VI, to the more careless constructions of Troy VII. From the summit you look over the plain to Homer's "wine-dark sea", and can see Schliemann's great north–south trench. Northwest of the paved ramp, against the wall of Troy II, he found his hoard of treasure.

Facing the tiny village of Tevfikiye, a kilometre (0.6 miles) east of the site, is the modern, four-storey **Troy Museum** (www.troya2018.com; daily Apr–Sept 9am–7.30pm, Oct–Mar 8am–5pm; charge), opened in 2018. Many of its 2000 artefacts emerged from the Alexandria Troas site, while others come from Assos, Tenedos and Apollo Smintheion. Among the star items here is a collection of gold jewellery – part of it repatriated in 2012 after years in the Penn Museum of Philadelphia – and two sarcophagi: the late Archaic "Polyxena", in perfect condition with a procession on one side and the sacrifice (in grisly detail) of Priam's daughter on the other, plus the fourth-century BC "Altıkulaç", more battered but with a finely detailed boar hunt and combat scene.

🔍 TREASURE-SEEKERS

As elsewhere in the region, Western archaeologists have plundered Turkey's priceless heritage by liberally interpreting official permissions to dig.

In 1829, a seven-year-old German boy, Heinrich Schliemann, received a Christmas gift, Ludwig Jerrer's *Illustrated History of the World*. It contained a striking engraving of Aeneas fleeing from burning Troy bearing his father Ankhises on his shoulders and leading his son Askanios by the hand. Deeply impressed, the precocious child pestered his father with questions, deciding there and then that one day he would find Homeric Troy.

The well-travelled adult Schliemann amassed a fortune trading in gold, indigo and gunpowder in California and Russia, while learning 13 modern languages besides German. In 1868, finally ready to realise his childhood dream, he visited sites in Greece and Turkey, producing a book, *Ithaca, the Peloponnese and Troy*, which named the mound of Hisarlık as the site of Troy. Classical scholars, who dismissed the *Iliad* and the *Odyssey* as merely poetic myths, ignored him.

In 1871, Schliemann began to dig a huge trench through the 32-metre (105ft)-high mound, convinced that Homeric Troy lay at the lowest level. In 1873 he found the ruins of a fortified city and a cache of gold, copper and silver objects, as well as precious jewellery, which he called "Priam's Treasure". In fact, his discoveries were much older, being the remains of a Bronze Age town from 2400 BC. He made three more excavations at the site before his death in 1890.

Schliemann has been criticised for the cavalier way he treated Hisarlık mound, but there was then no canon of established practice for him to follow. His determined publicising of his finds, both at Troy and Mycenae, helped stir the public imagination, and he is now regarded as one of the fathers of modern archaeology.

His illegal removal of the treasure is harder to excuse, and indeed the Ottoman government banished him from the site until 1876. His wife briefly wore some of the jewellery before presenting it to the German nation in 1881. Since then, the cache has had a chequered history. Stolen from Berlin by the Red Army in 1945, it reappeared in Moscow in 1993 and is now the subject of a legal dispute involving Turkey, Germany and Russia. Return of the artefacts to Germany is ostensibly prevented by a 1998 Russian law which established the controversial principle of legalizing the Red Army's looting from Germany as compensation for the plundering of Soviet cultural treasures by the invading Wehrmacht.

Schliemann is the most famous of them. Motivated by a desire "to lay bare the wonders of Lycia" – and enrich collections in the West – Sir Charles Fellows rediscovered 13 ancient cities. With the sultan's permission, he shipped 78 cases of Lycian sculpture and architectural fragments to England in 1840, removing a further 27 cases of artefacts from Xanthos two years later. Every piece was charted, assessed for damage and numbered first. Thomas Newton, took a statue of Demeter and a carved lion from Knidos, plus some colossal seated figures from the Sacred Way at Didyma. Fellows' and Newton's spoils grace the British Museum's galleries.

All three treasure-hunters must be censured for their arrogant rape of Turkey's patrimony, but Schliemann did have permission to dig, if not remove the finds, and the others were also given permission by the sultan.

Heinrich Schliemann, obsessed by a dream, helped create modern archaeology.

The magnificent limestone cascades at Pamukkale are Turkey's most dazzling natural wonder.

THE AEGEAN COAST

Turkey's west coast is a heady mix of ancient ruins, sandy beaches and beautiful scenery.

The Aegean coast marks the western edge of Asia Minor, an alias of the Anatolian peninsula which has figured so prominently in history. But where ancient armies once marched and clashed, now only gentle winds off the azure-hued Aegean caress the ruins of the past. Even seasoned travellers will be impressed by the alluring oak- or pine-tufted scenery and culturally significant sites.

Between Troy and İzmir, the main archaeological destination of ancient Pergamon requires almost a full day to see its scattered attractions, while smaller Assos is just as incomparably situated. Despite a relatively short tourist season for the north Aegean, beaches – most notably on Bozcaada (Tenedos) island, at Sarımsaklı near Greek-built Ayvalık, and along the Çeşme peninsula – are in ample supply. Conveniently, most major sights are located near the coastal highway.

Keeping a close eye on fish in harbour shallows.

İzmir is a massive city, uncharacteristic of the Aegean coast but convenient for journeys inland to Ottoman Manisa and ancient Sardis. The resort of Kuşadası is a more likely seaside base, where one can enjoy hedonistic nights while devoting the day to sightseeing. Priene, Milet (Miletus) and Didyma are only short trips away, though at least half a day is needed for Efes (Ephesus), by far the most-visited local site. The nearest towns to Ephesus are monument-studded Selçuk and the architectural preserve of Şirince. Also inland, but still in the Aegean region, beckon the commercialised but unmissable travertine terraces of Pamukkale, and the comparatively unvisited charms of Aphrodisias.

Marmaris harbour.

South of the eerie lake of Bafa, ringed by unsung ancient sites, the coast becomes more convoluted in bays and peninsulas either side of Bodrum, the premier southwest Aegean resort. Between here and more recent upstart Marmaris yawns the little-frequented Gulf of Gökova, one of many venues for the *Mavi Tur* (Blue Cruise) out of either port.

THE NORTH AEGEAN COAST

Troy may be more famous, but nearby Assos and Pergamon are of greater interest, while the northern Aegean coast itself is sufficient to charm any visitor.

Main attractions
Bozcaada
Assos acropolis
Adatepe
Ayvalık
Cunda
Pergamon acropolis
Altınkum beaches
Alaçatı

Maps on pages
188, 195

Astonishingly, there are still parts of the north Aegean coast that have not been overrun by tourists (mostly Turkish hereabouts). Head only a short distance from the few resorts and it is still possible to see many traditional aspects of rural Turkish life, with shepherds and their flocks blocking the road, farmers working their fields and a ruggedly beautiful landscape of mostly volcanic origin.

BOZCAADA (TENEDOS)

The small island of **Bozcaada** ❶, barely 7 nautical miles from the mainland and visible from Troy, is where – according to Homer who knew it as **Tenedos** – the Greek fleet moored while canny Odysseus and his men hid inside the wooden horse, waiting to surprise the Trojans. Even more than neighbouring Gökçeada (İmroz), it has been "discovered" with a vengeance since the 1990s, mostly by Istanbul yuppies, and can be quite overrun in midsummer. Access is by sea-bus from Çanakkale – mostly timed to coincide with flights to and from Istanbul or Ankara – or conventional car-ferry from **Geyikli İskelesi**, about 60km (37 miles) southwest of Çanakkale.

During spring and autumn Tenedos – the name still used, unofficially – is a fairly tranquil place, which trades on its assets of a single, architecturally homogeneous port guarded by a huge castle, a half-dozen south-coast beaches and an equal number of wineries. The **castle** (daily 10am–8pm; charge), originally Byzantine, has subsequently been modified by every occupier. Partially restored, it offers fine views from the ramparts as well as a smattering of amphorae, tombstones and rusted cannon. The town, with some exquisite old mansions along its cobbled streets, was once 80 percent Greek Orthodox but now, after the same sort of measures exercised on İmroz, only a handful remain in

The amphitheatre at ancient Assos.

their old quarter, huddled beneath the nicely restored belfry of the church. Around the corner, a privately-run **museum** (late Apr–Oct 10am–7pm; charge) offers a closer look at the town's unique, multicultural history with thousands of old family photos as well as wartime letters and soldiers' uniforms. In a Homeric echo, there is still a fishing fleet at anchor, but that's deceptive – much of the seafood at the quayside restaurants is frozen and unseasonal, and an undemanding clientele means that listless cooking and rip-offs are not uncommon.

In season a few minibuses scoot around the island, or you can rent scooters and mountain bikes to reach the excellent, sandy beaches. The most developed one is **Ayazma**, its name recalling the sacred spring (now run dry) of the disused monastery just inland. **Sulubahçe**, just west, is even sandier but without facilities, while **Habbele** – beyond the rocks further west – has a single snack bar. East of Ayazma, **Beylik**, "**Aqvaryum**" **Bay** and **Tuzburnu** cove all have their partisans, but no amenities.

ASSOS (BEHRAMKALE)

Ancient **Assos** ❷, about 85km (53 miles) south of Çanakkale, commands the straits separating Anatolia from the Greek island of Lésvos. To get there, turn right off the main E87/550 highway at the picturesque small town of **Ayvacık**, set in rolling farmland a few kilometres from the coast. In late April, the annual *panayır*, derived from an ancient pagan festival, is an unusual week-long celebration of food, livestock-trading and music which brings together the area's people, most of them settled nomads. Ayvacık is also the main centre for the DOBAG carpet-weaving project, with guaranteed natural dyes (see page 114) – though note that the results are not generally sold locally.

From Ayvacık – an equally good road heads west from Küçükkuyu, along the coast – a narrow road threads over hills covered in olive and oak trees. After crossing a splendid 14th-century Ottoman bridge, with views toward

Local crafts in Assos' modern village.

The picturesque harbour at Behramkale.

⊘ BOZCAADA WINES

A favourable climate and volcanic soil mean that Bozcaada wines have always been famous. Traditional grape varieties found nowhere else (except İmroz) are the white Vasilaki and Çavuş, and the red Karalahna, Kuntra (Kundúra in Greek) and Karasakız. The white grapes are extremely sweet, so are fermented to almost 13 percent alcohol to get a palatable result. Local red wines are rather tannic owing to the practice of leaving the entire grape in the fermentation vats. There are currently six vintners on the island, of which Talay, Corvus and Çamlıbağ – the most esteemed – run well-signposted tasting boutiques in the old Greek quarter. The Talay place even has a wine bar upstairs, with cheese and charcuterie platters accompanying wine by the glass.

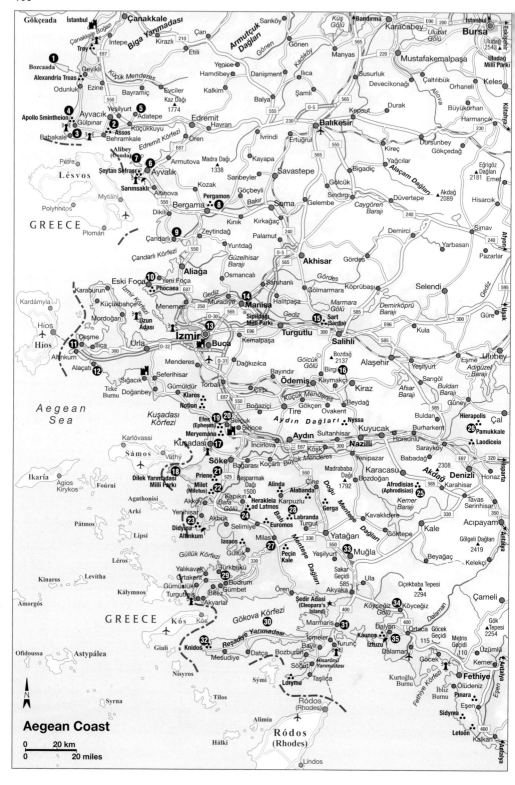

Aegean Coast

0   20 km

0   20 miles

the ancient acropolis, one fork in the route ends at the edge of upper **Behramkale village**. The typical basalt-built houses – protected from modern adulterations by law – line increasingly narrow streets hairpinning past small shops and eateries on the way to the acropolis. Just below it, a 14th-century mosque has been converted from a Byzantine church, hence a cross and Greek inscription above the door.

The main road continues sharply downhill, past ancient walls and tumbled sarcophagi of the necropolis, to Behramkale's little **harbour**. Like its uphill neighbour, it was largely inhabited by Greek-Orthodox before 1923. Both became fashionable with Turkish artists, actors and academics well before Bozcaada, and the same caveats apply – show up midweek, or during May and September, and you should be able to secure prime accommodation at a reasonable price. You can swim at lower Behramkale's narrow ribbon of seashore fringing the stone buildings here (most of them abandoned acorn warehouses converted to hotels), but

the closest proper (pebble) beach, **Kadırga**, is 4km (2.5 miles) east, ringed by a dozen or so hotels.

ASSOS ACROPOLIS

The Hellenistic walls of ancient Assos are nearly 3km (2 miles) long, enclosing the modern village, and their intact patches stand to a height of 14 metres (46ft). The Byzantine circuit is far more compact, enclosing only the remnants of the **Temple of Athena** (daily Apr–Sept 8.30am–7.30pm, Oct–Mar 8.30am–5.30pm; charge), built in about 530 BC at the top of a near-vertical drop of 240 metres (750ft), and dedicated to the goddess of both war and handicrafts. The temple was first excavated by the young Francis H. Bacon of the Antiquarian Society of Boston in 1881, and a few Doric columns re-erected by another American dig almost a century later. In a previous restoration attempt, cement was ill-advisedly used, though, thankfully, such was fully replaced by masonry from the original quarry in 2011. Yet the setting, not the paltry remains, is the thing: visit near dawn or

Restored columns of the Temple of Athena, Assos.

The 14th-century Ottoman bridge on the approach to Behramkale village.

Wild flowers grow amongst the Pergamon ruins.

sunset for the most impressive panorama from the temple platform, taking in the Edremit Gulf to the east and Lésvos island (Midili to the Turks) floating opposite in the Aegean, just 6 nautical miles away.

It was from Lésvos that colonists came to found Assos in about 950 BC. The city reached its zenith during the 4th century BC when ruled by Hermeias, an eunuch disciple of Plato; Hermeias attempted to devise the ideal city-state as described by Plato in his famous work *The Republic*. From 348 to 345 BC Aristotle – who ended up marrying Hermeias' niece – and botanist Theophrastos both lived in Assos as Hermeias' guests, carrying out important early work in the natural sciences. St Paul also passed through en route to Lésvos during his third evangelical journey (c.55 AD).

BABAKALE, SMINTHEION AND ALEXANDRIA TROAS

West of Behramkale, a good road threads high above the Aegean, still opposite Lésvos, through more stone

villages. End of the line, 34km (21 miles) from Assos, is sleepy **Babakale** ❸, at the westernmost point of Asia Minor. A working fishing port flanked by olive groves and a yacht marina that is as big as the town, Babakale offers some of the most dramatic sunsets in the Aegean, best enjoyed from its well-restored 18th-century castle (daily 8am–sunset; charge) – among the last such structures the Ottomans built). Nearby are a medieval mosque and a few carved fountains.

Some 9km (5.5 miles) inland stands the shrine of **Apollo Smintheion** ❹, between **Gülpınar village** and the ancient city, Khryse (or Chryse). The partially restored temple, just beyond the parking lot of the site (daily Apr–Sept 8am–8pm, Oct–Mar 8am–5pm; charge) – honours one of the more bizarre avatars of Apollo, as Destroyer of Mice. The mythical original colonists here, Teukros and Skamandros of Crete, had their weaponry eaten by mice, and remembered an old sage who had advised them to settle where attacked by the "sons of earth". This

⊙ THE PERGAMENE DYNASTY

Although Pergamon had existed since the 8th century BC, it became prominent only under Lysimakhos, one of Alexander the Great's successor-generals. His eunuch-steward Philetaeros inherited the town and its treasure after betraying Lysimakhos to the Seleucids in 281 BC. Philetaeros exercised considerable influence well beyond Pergamon before bequeathing it all in 263 BC to his nephew Eumenes I, first of the Pergamene dynasty.

This dynasty established a kingdom which grew to encompass much of western Anatolia, and was responsible for the many public buildings that made Pergamon such a glittering city. Eumenes' nephew Attalos I saved the region from marauding Gauls, while Eumenes II (ruled 197–159 BC) allied himself with the Romans. He built the theatre, Zeus temple and the library, which rivalled Alexandria's. Parchment was invented after the jealous Egyptians stopped supplying papyrus.

In 133 BC, Attalos III left the kingdom to the Romans, who accepted it as a toehold from which to expand into most of Anatolia. Except in 88 BC, when the city's Roman citizens were slaughtered during the Mithridatic wars, it prospered under both republican and imperial rule. Its most famous native was the physician Galen (AD 129–202), whose theories remained influential in Western medicine until the 16th century.

they assumed to mean the rodents, and thus founded Khryse here. The town itself is also being excavated and restored, with a square reservoir, arcaded baths and part of the Sacred Way from nearby Alexandria Troas uncovered thus far.

Khryse is rich in Homeric significance, as the place where Agamemnon abducted Khryseis, the resident priestess of Apollo. Her father Khryses the priest appealed for help to Apollo, who duly inflicted a plague on the Greeks, lifted only when the girl was returned to her father. Agamemnon then demanded Briseis, the mistress of Achilles, as compensation, leading to a feud between the two warriors that permeates the entire *Iliad*. Beside the temple is a one-room museum (same ticket and hours), containing damaged pediment reliefs that show many of these scenes.

From here, the coast road follows the course of the ancient Sacred Way 34km (21 miles) to **Alexandria Troas**, founded by Antigonos I, a general of Alexander the Great, in 300 BC. For years a half-buried jumble of ancient masonry, it's now being properly excavated. Revealed so far are 8km (5 miles) of city wall, a shop-lined avenue, an odeion, a nymphaeum, an unidentified agora temple and a sizable baths complex, where a single arch has been constructed. There's no admission charge (yet) though the warden may give you a tour (in Turkish only).

THE GULF OF EDREMIT: ADATEPE TO ÖREN

The easterly access road for Assos meets the main highway again at Küçükuyu, a small fishing port and olive-oil pressing centre that's the gateway to **Adatepe** ❺, 4km (2.5 miles) northeast in the forested foothills of Kazdağı, the ancient Mt Ida, where Zeus and Hera were believed to have observed the fighting at Troy. An 800-metre (0.5 mile) path climbs through the pines from the outskirts of town to the understated Zeus Altar (open access). Though only a few slabs of stone remain, the views over the gulf of Edremit. Like Cumalıkızık near Bursa,

> **⊘ Tip**
>
> The sheltered waters around Ayvalık, famous for their coral, submerged archaeological artefacts and sea caves, provide ample opportunities for scuba diving. Several dive operators run trips from the south quay.

Sunset dinner, Ayvalık.

Ottoman Greek House in Old Ayvalık.

Girls parade on Youth & Sport Day, also known as the Commemoration of Atatürk Day, in Bergama.

Adatepe has sprung to fame through appearance in a Turkish TV serial, and its imposing stone mansions, of a piece with the volcanic boulders lying around, are statutorily protected. Yeşilyurt, a similar distance northwest of Küçükuyu, has a more free-wheeling building code, to the detriment of its yellow-masonry houses, though it does have a fine, late medieval mosque.

From Küçükuyu to the county town of Edremit, the gulf coast here presents a dreary sequence of holiday villa developments for urban Turks, interspersed with the area's remaining olive groves. The only relief comes beyond Edremit at the more human-scale resort of **Ören**, with its long sandy beach facing west, and ample accommodation.

AYVALIK

A side road leads west from the E87/550 highway, through an undistinguished, modern suburb like most others in Aegean Turkey, before suddenly entering the distinctive older core of **Ayvalık** ❻. With its many small, secluded harbours, the region

has been settled since ancient times, but the town visible today dates from the early 18th century, when it was established, as Kydonies, by Ottoman Greeks. As of 1790, the place was conceded many privileges by Grand Vizier Cezayırlı Hasan Paşa, who, while serving as Ottoman admiral, had been rescued in 1771 by the Greeks of Ayvalık after a calamitous defeat by the Russian navy. The numerous Greek-built mansions, olive mills and over a dozen churches all date from this heyday, which made the town the second most elegant and prosperous on the Aegean coast after Smyrna (İzmir). This period ended with the exchange of populations, when local Orthodox Christians were replaced largely by Muslims from Crete and Lésvos (Midili) island opposite. Their older generations still understand – and speak – Greek.

Ayvalık lives increasingly on tourist revenue and second-home sales rather than olive-based products, though the clientele is largely Turkish, and from Istanbul, owing partly to substantial distance from the nearest international

airport. The picturesque south quay, with its fishing and excursion-boat fleet, overlooks an almost completely landlocked bay separated from the open sea by two dozen wooded islands.

The old quarter just inland has meandering lanes lined by handsome Greek **mansions** and less imposing dwellings. The maze-like street plan threading the entire town was supposedly devised to assist smugglers eluding the authorities. Equally apocryphal – or equally true – is the story that many of Ayvalık's better-off families came into their riches without much effort after the population exchanges. The departing Greeks, convinced that they would eventually return, hid gold and jewellery in the walls or under the floorboards, where it was discovered by the new occupants.

Almost all of the town's Greek Orthodox **churches** have been converted into mosques, while preserving their original features – thus juxtaposed belfries and minarets are an essential part of the Ayvalık skyline, best enjoyed (along with the spectacle of tiled roofs) from one of the hillier neighbourhoods. The main landmark churches are Ágios Ioánnis, now called the Saatli Camii after its clocktower, and Ágios Geórgios, lately the Çınarlı Camii. Unconverted Taksiyarhis, another beautifully restored old church up the slope, is now a museum (daily Apr–Sept 9am–7pm Oct–Mar 8.30am–5.30pm; charge), while Faneromeni, restored in 2018 and famed for its *ayazma* (sacred spring), lies to the south near the fish market.

SARIMSAKLI AND CUNDA

The closest proper beach to Ayvalık is at **Sarımsaklı**, 8km (5 miles) south, one of the longest sandy strands along the north Aegean coast, with all the usual water sports offered. The somewhat downmarket resort just inland, with its standard-issue accommodation, eateries and bars, is considerably less inspiring. From the link road between

Ayvalık and the Sarımsaklı resort strip, a narrower road leads up to the highest point in the Ayvalık area, **Şeytan Sofrasi** (the Devil's Table). This affords a spectacular view north over Ayvalık Bay and pine-covered islets, and west towards Lésvos (Midili). It's the place to be at sunset, but preferably out of peak season. During summer or at *bayram* times evening bus tours converge here, and access becomes impossible.

The largest of the area's islets, clearly visible opposite Ayvalık, is **Cunda ⑦**, known officially as **Alibey Adasi** and to its departed Greeks as Moskhonísi. Although now connected to the mainland by a causeway (and bus service), the half-hourly boat journey from Ayvalık quayside is more pleasant. The old town – built to a sloping grid plan, unlike labyrinthine Ayvalık – rewards a wander on foot. Sleepier than its neighbour but restored to a greater extent, Cunda is a favourite target for well-heeled, vehemently secular city Turks keen on owning an Aegean second home. They can be found thronging the main quay

⊙ Tip

Drivers or cyclists should take the old, direct road from Ayvalık to Bergama, via the Kozak plateau – it's no slower and more enjoyable than the main highway. The magnificent stone-pine forests seen en route are the source of the famous local pine nuts *(çam fıstığı)*. Buy these in Ayvalık, not for inflated prices in Bergama.

Fisherman at Ayvalık's south quay.

with its cafés and seafood tavernas, the latter featuring fried *papalina* (sprat).

At the heart of the architecturally protected town stands the privately-restored Taksiyarhis cathedral (not to be confused with Ayvalık's church of the same name), worn down over the years by earthquakes and re-opened since 2014 as a museum (www.rmk-museum.org.tr/taksiyarhis; Tue–Sun Apr–Sept 10am–7pm, Oct–Mar 10am–5pm). Cunda has plenty of secluded swimming bays and an old monastery reachable only by sea – boat tours operate from Cunda's quay.

MODERN BERGAMA, ANCIENT PERGAMON

Beyond Ayvalık, the main highway leads southeast through the territory of ancient Aeolia, veering inland away from the minor resort of Dikili past productive farmland – and some geothermal installations near extinct volcanic cones. On the quieter side roads, horse carts still trundle along, and there is a noticeable Roma presence. One of these roads leads, along

the valley of the Bakır Çayı (the ancient Kaikos River), past the Maltepe tumulus, to the market town of **Bergama**. The centre is busy and characterful, worth a walk if you have the energy after the adjacent ruins.

Towering 300 metres (1,000ft) above town, the ruins of **Pergamon** ❽ command an extraordinary 360-degree view. One can understand how this great Hellenistic city dominated the entire region, as a centre of culture, commerce, rhetoric and medicine to rival other centres of Mediterranean Hellenism such as Ephesus, Alexandria and Antioch.

Allow several hours to visit the ruins. There are two main areas – the Asklepion and the Acropolis (open daily Apr–Set 8am–7pm, Oct–Mar 8.30am–5.30pm; separate charges) – as well as some minor sites within Bergama town itself. Visitors without their own transport will probably opt for the cable-car ride up to the car park and main ticket booth of the Acropolis. The Bergama terminus of the 8-person *teleferik* is on Akropol Caddesi, about 600m

Kızıl Avlu.

northeast of the Red Basilica (Kızıl Avlu). Its 2011 inauguration has rather reduced the market for taxi transfers up to the site, or jointly to the Asklepion – bargain strenuously.

THE ASKLEPION AND THE MUSEUM

The ruins of the **Asklepion** are about 2km (1.5 miles) gently uphill to the west of central Bergama and just about feasible to walk to, if the day is not too hot. Initially dedicated to Asklepios, god of healing, this was not your average medical clinic but the first complete health spa in history.

The process went something like this: a tired, overwrought Greek or Roman businessman, politician or military leader would arrive at the Asklepion to be greeted by attendants. He was then led down the colonnaded Sacred Way (a busy bazaar of merchants and advisers) before choosing from a variety of treatments or sensuous experiences designed to eliminate stress. Prospective patients would have their dreams analysed (2,000 years before Freud), browse through good books in the library, go for a dip in the sacred healing springs, and then round it all off with a visit to the 3,500-capacity theatre, for an exciting production of a play by Sophocles and some socialising with friends. In theory the process could take as little as a few hours, but one usually spent days or even weeks here relaxing and recuperating from the strains of Graeco-Roman life.

The 2nd-century AD **Temple of Asklepios**, easily recognisable due to its circular shape, is worth a closer look, if only to appreciate the fine skill of the stonemasons who created it. It was designed as a miniature of Rome's Pantheon, and archaeologists have since found an underground tunnel that brought in water from a nearby spring. Just southwest of this, downhill, is the circular, rather more intact **Temple of Telesphoros**, son of Asklepios. As part of the healing ritual patients slept in both temples, perchance to have Asklepios appear to them in a dream, with his advice to be analysed

Headless statue at the Temple of Trajan.

The colonnaded Sacred Way (Via Tecta), part of the Asklepion ruins.

later. A fine Ionic colonnade fronts the somewhat over-restored theatre.

Back in Bergama, stop at the small but satisfying **Pergamon Müzesi** (Tue–Sun 8.30am–5.30pm; charge), on the main street near the tourist office. This is one of the earliest museums to collect artefacts from Pergamon and its surroundings; unfortunately the best exhibits are in Berlin, so the museum has to content itself with a model of the impressive Temple of Zeus. Still, there are many vivid statues evincing a pioneering naturalistic technique in depicting anatomy, which later influenced Renaissance sculpture. There's also a large figurine of Aphrodite, found at the Roman spa and asklepion **Allianoi**, 19km (12 miles) to the east. Allianoi had barely been excavated before the Yortanlı irrigation dam was built, threatening it with submersion. Despite international protests, the site was inundated early in 2011.

KIZIL AVLU (RED BASILICA) AND OLD TOWN

Pergamon's spectacular theatre.

Approaching the Bergama Çayı (the ancient Selinos stream), you come upon an imposing ruin straddling the river, the **Kızıl Avlu** (Red Basilica; daily Apr–Sept 8am–7pm, Oct–Mar 8.30am–6.30pm; charge), renovated in 2018. Dating from the 2nd century AD, it was originally a vast temple to the Egyptian gods Serapis, Harpokrates and Isis. Two underground tunnels carried river water beneath the building's foundations. Pergamon was one of the Seven Churches of the Apocalypse addressed by St John the Divine, who cited it in Revelation 2:13 as "where the throne of Satan is", perhaps a reference to the Egyptian cult; later, the Kızıl Avlu was converted into a much smaller basilica by the Byzantines. Originally, the red-brick building was covered in marble, but this has long since vanished and nowadays only the floor paving retains any marble finish.

There are some interesting antique and carpet shops opposite the Red Basilica, but too many coach tours have had their effect on prices of the merchandise, which itself is a mixture of genuine antiques, old pots and pans and the odd fake.

Just uphill is the fascinating old town, its hillside lane-houses part Greek-inhabited before 1923. The **Ulu Camii** was commissioned by Sultan Beyazit I in 1398–99. The bazaar in the flatlands offers brightly painted shopfronts over-loaded with perilously heaped goods – goatskins, cheeses, fruit, honey, yoghurt and pine nuts – as well as some basic, unlicensed restaurants.

THE ACROPOLIS

For the energetic, there is a path up to the fabled Acropolis from Bergama, though it's probably best to use it down-hill on your return. Most people will arrive by cable-car or private car to the car park and ticket booth at the top. As you pass the scant remains of a monu-mental gate, you enter one of the great-est centres of Hellenistic civilisation, excavated between 1878 and 1886 by Carl Humann, a railway engineer employed by the Ottoman government. He had been alerted to the existence of the forgotten site by some locals who sold him a piece of mosaic from the **Temple of Zeus**. Its **altar**, of which only the stepped base – underneath two flourishing stone pines – remains, was largely whisked away to Berlin, where its magnificent reliefs, highlighting a battle between titans and gods, are now the main attraction in the city's Pergamon Museum.

On the next terrace up lie the equally sparse foundations of the **Temple of Athena Polias Nikephoros**, the oldest temple in Pergamon. Built in the Doric style at the end of the 4th century BC, it was dedicated to the city's patron god-dess Athena "who brings victory". The north stoa of the temple abutted the famous library, once filled with over 200,000 volumes collected by Eumenes II and Attalos II. According to Plutarch, all of these were later presented to Cleopatra by Mark Antony to replace damaged portions of Alexandria's library, where they were ultimately lost.

Still further uphill looms the mas-sive, much-photographed **Temple of Trajan**, dedicated to the deified Roman emperor Trajan, and completed during the reign of Hadrian. German archae-ologists have re-erected many of its Corinthian columns, plus most of the stoa which surrounds it on three sides.

Over the precipice from the two tem-ples plunge 80 rows of seats for the incomparably set theatre. The most steeply inclined in the ancient world, it still managed to hold 10,000 specta-tors (and is still used during the annual Bergama Festival). At the very bottom, a long terrace gave access from the upper agora, leading past the orches-tra to a small Temple of Dionysus, god of drama, to one side. Pacing the orchestra area, perhaps imagining long-vanished performances, one can make out the holes for stakes sup-porting temporary scenery – because of the topography and presence of the temple, there was no permanent stage. Standing here, you can confirm the superb acoustics of the theatre: an actor (or tourist) speaking in a normal voice can be heard clearly even at the 80th row of seating.

The Temple of Trajan, on the Acropolis.

Çeşme statue of Kaplan Giray, who was Khan of Qirim three times.

From the upper agora, where Carl Humann's grave lies, an ancient street paved in andesite cobbles descends to the **Temple of Demeter** and the remains of a massive **Gymnasium**. This was divided into three sections for different age groups: the lowest level for small boys, the middle terrace for adolescents, and the highest, most elaborate complex for young men. This was flanked by two **baths** – whose marble washbasins are still discernible – and contained an ephebeion hall, where training and initiation ceremonies would be held. By Hellenistic times, the ancient Athenian notion of a two-year course of study aimed at forming "sound bodies and sound minds" through military drills and studies in tactics had evolved into a well-rounded curriculum. This in turn formed the basis of modern secondary and university education from the medieval era to the early 20th century.

Eski Foça manages to retain some elements of its traditional character.

Below the gymnasium and lower agora is the **South Gate**, erected by Eumenes II, the main (and very well defended) entrance to the city in ancient times. The perimeter walls nearby show clear evidence of Ottoman restorations, when rubble and bricks held together by mortar were used instead of the mortarless tight fit of Hellenistic masonry.

ÇANDARLI AND FOÇA

From Bergama a short journey leads southwest to **Çandarlı** ❾, 35km (23 miles) southwest on the coast. This (usually) sleepy place occupies a small peninsula jutting into the bay, coming alive in summers and weekends with Turkish families on holiday. Çandarlı is built on the site of ancient Pitane, but there is precious little to see of that ancient Aeolian city other than old masonry copiously recycled into the multi-towered 14th-century **Genoese fortress** (closed to the public), restored in the 1990s. The little port-resort is blessed with two sandy beaches: a south-facing one east of the peninsula with its handful of surviving old Ottoman houses, and the more popular one looking west to the Karaburun peninsula and Foça.

Continuing around Çandarlı Bay (Çandarlı Körfezi) past the industrial port of **Aliağa**, remarkable only for its ship-breaking facility and massive petrochemical complex – among the first set up in Turkey, under Menderes. A few kilometres beyond Aliağa, a turn-off west leads to the contrasting resorts of Yeni Foça and Eski Foça, with startling seascapes en route. First encountered is **Yeni Foça**, with its core of old Greek houses, an exposed beach, and a dominant ethos of second homes pitched at people from Manisa and İzmir. An intriguing target in the hills above, 8km (5 miles) away, is the relatively unspoilt village of **Kozbeyli**, with a much-esteemed spring (potable water is a problem locally), a characterful café noted for its *dibek kahvesi* (coffee ground in a giant mortar and pestle) and more old houses.

Most guidebooks, if they mention Foça at all, refer to **Eski Foça** ❿, the site of ancient Phocaea on the western end of the peninsula, founded by Ionian

colonists early in the first millennium BC. Herodotus lauded the Phokaeans as "the pioneer navigators of the Greeks... who showed their countrymen the way to the Adriatic, Tyrrhenia and the Spanish peninsula as far as Tartessos." To achieve these naval feats, the Phokaeans solved the problem of sailing heavily laden boats in shallow waters by designing a new flat-bottomed vessel. They were the founders of many colonies in the Sea of Marmara, the Black Sea and the Mediterranean, including the French city of Marseilles.

The fortress of **Beşkapılar** (originally Byzantine-Genoese; closed to the public outside public events), and two historic mosques, sit on a promontory dividing the two bays; ruins of the ancient town are sparse and difficult to find. Along the busier, more attractive north harbour, called **Küçükdeniz**, stands a line of charming Ottoman-Greek houses, many now restored as accommodation and fish restaurants. Beaches, many of which charge an entrance fee, are found on the 25km (15-mile) stretch of road between here and Yeni Foça.

"Phokaea" is related to the ancient Greek for "seal", a name perhaps elicited by the suggestive contours of the islets seen just offshore (as at Ayvalık, daily boat excursions visit them) – or perhaps the animal itself, which features on the (pardon the pun) municipal seal. There are still said to be at least a few dozen Mediterranean monk seals resident locally, their numbers happily on the rise in recent years; a local research foundation monitors and supposedly protects them.

ÇEŞME AND ALAÇATI

Less than an hour's drive west of İzmir on the motorway, or 80km (50 miles) along the more leisurely old road, **Çeşme** ⓫ is an inevitably popular but still attractive family resort at the tip of the second westernmost peninsula in Turkey. Besides land links to İzmir,

there are year-round ferries to the Greek island of Híos.

The pace of life has quickened here since the opening of a posh new yacht marina at the south end of the bay, but you can still enjoy its well-preserved Ottoman domestic architecture, a hamam, and a restored 14th-century Genoese **castle** (Mon–Sat 8.30am–5pm), which contains a small museum of finds from nearby Erythrae. It also hosts events throughout the late June/early July İzmir Festival. Remoter attractions include the thermal spas at the busier resort of **Ilıca**, 6km (3.5 miles) east, and the superb sandy coves at **Altınkum**, 9km (5.5 miles) south.

A similar distance southeast is **Alaçatı** ⓬, contrastingly upmarket and trendy with the chattering classes of İzmir. Here, a trickle of restored boutique hotels and trendy bistros has become a wave, with prices at – or over – Greek or Istanbul levels. Alaçatı has its own beach 4km (2.5 miles) south, though it can't compare to Altınkum unless you're windsurfing or kite-surfing, for which conditions are perfect.

Windsurfing at Alaçatı.

İzmir's waterfront livens up at dusk.

İZMİR, MANISA AND SARDIS

İzmir enjoys a stunning position at the head of a long gulf; Manisa's setting is also its salient point, while modern times have left ancient Sardis relatively untouched.

Turkey's second-largest port and third-largest city, **İzmir ⑬** (ancient Smyrna), is also one of the country's major industrial and commercial centres. For overseas travellers, it was long a base for excursions to the renowned archaeological sites to the north (Pergamon), east (Sardis) and south (Ephesus), though this role is waning.

ANCIENT SMYRNA

İzmir experienced centuries of attack by successive occupying armies – all lured by her crucial geographical location and mild winters. The tiny Neolithic settlement at Tepekule (today Bayraklı, northeast of the centre) grew in size and importance after Ionian colonists arrived during the 9th century BC and turned it into a prosperous settlement. After a period of decline, Alexander the Great moved the acropolis late in the 4th century BC to Mount Pagos; it was soon named Smyrna, possibly after the Amazon queen Samornia.

Roman rule from the 1st century BC oversaw an era of peace and prosperity and the addition of many grand civic buildings, of which little now remains. The city, with a population of 100,000, thrived as the harbour of its rival Ephesus silted up. Smyrna was one of the Seven Churches of the Apocalypse, and its octogenarian bishop, Polycarp, was martyred in AD 156 for refusing to deny his faith.

The clock tower in İzmir.

Arab seaborne raids of the 7th century AD marked the start of many vicissitudes. Seljuk Turks briefly captured the city in 1077, soon to be ousted in turn by the Byzantines, the Genoese, the crusading Knights of Rhodes, Timur's Mongol hordes and minor Turkish emirs before falling finally to the Ottomans in 1415. Under Ottoman administration, the city – now called İzmir – became predominantly Christian, the majority being Greek Orthodox, with some Armenian and Levantine Catholics. There were also sizeable Jewish and Muslim

Main attractions
Pounda district, İzmir
Etnografya Müzesi, İzmir
Sultan Camii, Manisa
Marble Court, Sardis
Artemis Temple, Sardis
Birgi: Çakırağa Konağı &
Ulu Camii

**Maps on pages
188, 203**

◉ Tip

The easiest – and safest – way to get up to the Kadifekale is by bus No. 33 from the Konak bus terminal (buy tickets first from the small booth at the bus stop). Walking down from Kadifekale after dark, through a rough neighbourhood, is expressly not recommended.

Spices for sale.

minorities. A wealthy entrepot on the Silk Road with a cosmopolitan lifestyle, it was dubbed, disparagingly, *gavur* (infidel) İzmir.

İZMIR TODAY

In contrast to its past, İzmir now attracts less privileged Turks from all over Anatolia searching for work. The city thus presents familiar modern Turkish problems – an oversubscribed infrastructure (partly relieved by motorways, a tramway and an expanding metro system which also serves the airport) and sprawling, illegally built shantytown suburbs to the east. Still, the revitalised centre feels cosmopolitan and lively, and locals (aside from a few street hustlers) are laid-back. The city is arguably at its best during the annual İzmir Festival, when music and theatre performances grace both its streets and its modern concert halls, while also expanding beyond to make the most of the region's wealth of historical backdrops.

The imposing fortress of **Kadifekale** ❹ on flat-topped Mount Pagos rises majestically behind the

city and offers unparalleled vistas in all directions. The grounds of the "Velvet Castle" contain a wonderful mixture of people: picnickers, well-dressed citizens out for a stroll, and young romantics gazing into each other's eyes over tea in one of the gently shaded outdoor cafés. Just inside the main gate, climb up the steps leading to the top of the wall for views encompassing the Çeşme peninsula to the west, Karşıyaka across the bay, and the mountains shielding Manisa on the northeast side.

SHOPPING THEN AND NOW

Smyrna's ancient marketplace lies just a short distance east of the modern bazaar, via a network of narrow streets. The **Agora** ❸ (daily Apr–Oct 8am–7pm, Nov–Mar 8.30am–5.30pm; charge) dates back to late Hellenistic times, but today the relatively small clearing contains colonnades around a central esplanade, built during the reign of Marcus Aurelius late in the 2nd century AD.

On leaving the Agora, turn right along Gazi Osman Paşa Bulvarı; after about 100 metres/yards, take one of the small

◉ THE GREAT FIRE OF SMYRNA

After World War I, Greek troops were authorised by the Allies to land at Smyrna, doing so on 15 May 1919. In their eyes this was a prelude to carving out an expanded Greece straddling two continents, but within four years their imperialist venture had collapsed ignominiously. The routed Greek army poured into Smyrna early in September 1922, to be evacuated by their own fleet on 8 September. The victorious Turkish forces entered the city the next day (a date widely commemorated here), and after pillaging and massacres of Christians in revenge for similar Greek actions, set fires in the Armenian quarter on 13 September, apparently waiting for favourable winds to blow the flames away from the Muslim quarters. Within two days 70 percent of the city had burnt to the ground, with thousands incinerated alive; the only non-Muslim district which escaped destruction was Pounda (today called Alsancak). *Gavur İzmir*, as probably intended, was no more. A quarter of a million desperate refugees huddled at the quayside, trying to avoid the blaze, while anchored American, French, British and Italian vessels refused to let them on board until the third day of the inferno. This scenario, disputed by republican Turkish apologists (though not terribly strenuously), is supported by numerous eyewitness accounts, most notably of American consul George Horton and various missionary educators.

streets on the left into **Kemeraltı C**, (Covered Bazaar) the city's old bazaar. Although it cannot compare to the one in Istanbul in terms of variety and interest of stock (except for leather goods and hubble-bubble pipes), it does possess character and atmosphere – and often a few pickpockets. The only explicitly touristy part is the **Kızlarağası Hanı**, a reconstructed Ottoman market, now housing craft workshops, souvenir stalls and courtyard cafés.

You finally emerge from the crowded maze of bazaar lanes onto waterfront **Konak Meydanı D**, with its distinctive clock tower, donated by Sultan Abdülhamid II in 1901, and a charming **mosque** of 1748, ornately decorated with Kütahya tiles. Now fully pedestrianised, Konak is bordered to the south and west by Kent Tarihi Park, which extends over the busy road to the ferry terminal.

İzmir's best museums lie just south of Konak in the Bahribab Parkı (sometimes called the Turgutreis Parkı), a few minutes' walk away. The **Arkeoloji Müzesi E** (Archaeological Museum; www.izmirmuzesi.gov.tr; Apr–Oct 8am–7pm, Nov–Mar 8.30am–5.30pm; charge) has a varied and interesting collection of Roman monumental art downstairs, while the other floors are devoted to Greek art from Archaic to Hellenistic times. The neighbouring **Etnografya Müzesi F** (Ethnographic Museum; same hours as above) has a wider appeal with its reconstructed Ottoman pharmacy, a bridal chamber and circumcision room. The museum also covers the manufacture of the blue beads that serve as an antidote to the evil eye, and features exhibits on camel-wrestling and rope-making.

Around sunset, take a leisurely stroll along the palm tree-lined **Kordon** (promenade) **G**, joining hundreds of locals for a bayside stroll to the north of Cumhuriyet Meydanı or south of the Konak Pier shopping centre. On summer evenings the *imbat*, the cooling offshore breeze of İzmir, is best enjoyed seated at one of the many cafés lining the *kordon*.

MANISA

From İzmir, the scenic but high-speed Highway 565 winds over forested

Tile detail on the Konak mosque, İzmir.

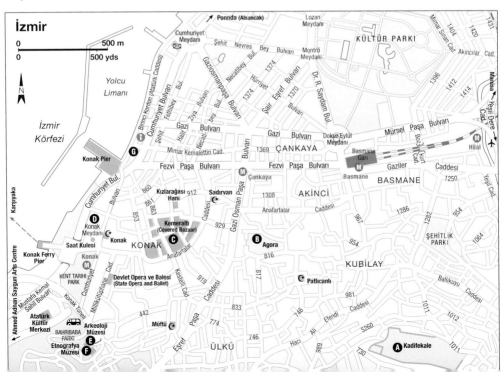

mountains to the Gediz valley, famous for its sultana grapes. One of these mountains was the ancient Mt Sypilos, which influenced Manisa's earlier name, Magnesia ad Sypilum. Arrayed impressively at the foot of **Spil Dağı**, as the sculpted crags are now called, modern **Manisa** ⑭ is an unexpectedly interesting city, held by every power in the area since its legendary founding by warriors returning from the Trojan War.

Alexander the Great liberated the place from the Persians in 334 BC, while a Roman and Pergamene force routed Seleucid armies here in 190 BC, setting the stage for Roman and Byzantine prosperity. Manisa finally fell to the Turkish emir Saruhan in 1313. Under the Ottomans it was a favourite training ground for crown princes, sent here to serve as local governors. Most of what you see today was rebuilt after Manisa was destroyed by Greek forces during their retreat in 1922; supposedly only a few hundred buildings were left standing. Although relatively few tourists come here, there is enough of interest to spend half a day or longer here.

Republic Square in Manisa.

A handful of well-signposted Ottoman monuments in the centre constitute most of the interest. The **Sultan Camii** with its calligraphy-daubed portico is the oldest (1522), the focus of a *külliye* whose buildings still survive. Just uphill stands the **Muradiye Camii**, one of the last (1583–5) works of master architect Sinan, commissioned by Sultan Murat II. Built to a by then old-fashioned T-plan, it contains a fine carved *minber* (pulpit) and İznik tiles. The *medrese* next door now houses the **Archaeological Museum** (Tue–Sun Apr–Sept 9am–7pm, Oct–Mar 8am–5pm; charge), which has a fountain and mosaics from the synagogue at ancient Sart (Sardis).

In a park just north of the Muradiye Camii, a statue of a bearded, water-pouring figure honours "**Tarzan**", real name Ahmet Bedevi (1899–1963). A celebrated local eccentric (though born in Mesopotamia) who lived as a half-clad dervish in the nearby mountains, he planted trees and exhorted others to follow his environmentalist example.

Walking downhill to the west, at the base of the originally Byzantine

Sandıkkale citadel, you will reach the famed **Crying Rock** (*Ağlayan Kaya* in Turkish**) of Niobe**, part of Spil Dağı Milli Parkı (Spil Mountain National Park). This is allegedly the petrified remains of Niobe, the arrogant daughter of local king Tantalos (from whom we get the word "tantalise"), who derided the nymph Leto for her mere two offspring while boasting of her own 14 beautiful children. These were slain forthwith by Leto's children, Artemis and Apollo, after which the unfortunate Niobe begged Zeus to petrify her and end her pain. Alas, the bereaved mother continued to weep perpetually, the very stone wet from her tears. Unhappily, the tale is more evocative than the site itself, merely a weather-worn outcrop which indeed exudes rivulets for some time after a rain.

SART (SARDIS)

Ancient **Sardis ⑮**, 85km (53 miles) east of İzmir, and 65km (40 miles) from Manisa, was occupied from at least 1300 BC onwards, growing into a major Roman and Byzantine city. Along the way, it was capital of the Lydians who, according to Herodotus, had the curious customs of permitting women to choose their husbands, and condoning the prostitution of young girls to allow them to earn their dowries. The Lydians also claimed to have invented all of the pastimes that were common to them and the Greeks, including dice and knucklebones.

An 8th century BC king, Kandaules, allowed one of his bodyguards to glimpse his beautiful wife naked; discovering this, the queen gave Gyges, the bodyguard, the option of death or of murdering Kandaules and becoming king in his stead – which Gyges did. Gyges was the ancestor of Kroïsos (aka Croesus, who ruled 560–546 BC), last of the Lydian kings, who interpreted an ambiguous Delphic oracle to mean that he would be victorious in battle against Persian King Cyrus – which Kroïsos wasn't, causing the end of his empire.

The invention of coinage has been ascribed to Alyattes, father of Kroïsos. At first coins were made of electrum, an alloy of gold and silver, without inscriptions and bearing only a lion's head – symbol of the Lydian dynasty

The reconstructed Marble Court at Sardis.

founded by Gyges. Kroïsos introduced coins of pure gold and silver.

The expression "rich as Croesus" comes from the fact that the Paktolos stream, which still flows by Sardis, washed down gold flecks from Mt Tmolos (today Bozdağ), to be caught in sheep fleece. The presence of this wealth was attributed by Ovid to Midas's "golden touch"; eager to be rid of what had become a curse, Midas bathed in the Paktolos on the instructions of the gods, the gold passing from his body into the stream.

THE RUINS

Bozdağ still looms above the fertile plain of the Gediz Cayı (ancient Hermos River). At its feet lies the **Temple of Artemis** (daily Apr–Sept 8am–7pm, Oct–Nov 8am–5pm; charge), whose massive scale – about 45 x 100 metres (150 x 320ft) – rivals the other three great Ionian temples at Ephesus, Samos and Didyma. Construction began around 550 BC, but it was destroyed in the Ionian revolt; Alexander the Great paid for reconstruction. Today only 15 columns remain erect, just two at full height, but the setting against a backdrop of wooded hills is magnificent. The altar was built at the west end of the temple, perhaps to avoid it being overshadowed by the slopes above.

Much further up these slopes to the east is the **Acropolis**, considered impregnable. Apocryphally, one of the soldiers of Persian Emperor Cyrus saw a defender drop his helmet over the walls and climb down to retrieve it. Using this route, Persian commandos were able to break through, defeating the Lydians in about 546 BC.

The ascent to the Acropolis takes 45 minutes and requires sturdy walking shoes, but the fantastic view from the peak justifies the effort. Some 10km (6 miles) north across the Gediz plain is the Lydian **Royal Cemetery**, now called Bin Tepe or "Thousand Mounds" after its tumuli. Just beyond Bin Tepe lies **Marmara Gölü**, Lake Gygaea of antiquity, which attracted early Bronze Age settlement. All these local landmarks appear in Greek and Latin literature. In the *Iliad*, Homer sang of the Gygaean lake, "snowy" Mount Tmolos and the "eddying"

Vineyards pattern the landscape around Sardis.

Hermos. In Ovid's *Metamorphoses*, a personified Tmolos judged the musical competition between Apollo and Pan.

Downhill from the Temple of Artemis and just across the old highway stands another fascinating complex of buildings (same hours; included in temple charge), many of them covered due to ongoing excavations. The **Marble Court** is a grandiose entrance to a partially-restored Roman gymnasium and baths complex, dating to the early 3rd century AD and carefully reconstructed. Its column capitals are decorated with carved heads of gods and satyrs, including the memorable "Laughing Faun", a masterpiece whose mischievous smile and features show Greek influences. The remains of the largest known ancient **synagogue** lie southeast of the Marble Court. A marble table with eagles on the legs occupied the altar end, apparently in defiance of Judaism's ban on human and animal representation in temples. The wall-mounted mosaics are replicas of those in Manisa's Archaeological Museum, but extensive floor mosaics were left *in situ*.

ON BOZDAĞ

The nearest accommodation and food for visitors with transport lies south, up the forested mountain. First stop could be **Bozdağ village**, with famous spring water, a few rustic *pansiyons*, outdoor restaurants and, surprisingly, a ski resort overhead at 2,150 metres (7,050ft). A little further is the reedy lake of **Gölcük**, a favourite beauty spot when the lowlands bake in summer heat, with hotels, cafés and restaurants which sometimes serve catfish *(yayın)*.

The local surprise, on the southern flanks of Bozdağ, is the village of **Birgi** (ancient Pyrgion) **16** , its surviving half-timbered houses culminating in the delightful **Çakırağa Konağı** (Tue–Sun 8.30am–5.30pm; charge), the restored 18th-century mansion of a local worthy, with carved wood panelling and extensive murals. Across the ravine stands the 14th-century **Ulu Camii** (Great Mosque), with a beautifully tiled *mihrap* (niche), an exquisitely carved *minber* (pulpit), and ancient columns upholding a pitched wooden roof.

Temple of Artemis, Sardis.

TURKISH FESTIVALS

Turkey offers a vibrant spectrum of cultural festivals: of music, the arts, film, folklore and some quirky rural observances.

The Turkish festival year is packed with interest for the visitor. Events organised by the Istanbul Foundation for Culture and the Arts are the best known overseas. April kicks off with the International Film Festival, followed by the Classical Music Festival (June), where top international soloists perform in historical venues like Aya Irini church; it precedes the three-week July Jazz Festival, encompassing rock as well as jazz groups. Odd-numbered years see the International Istanbul Biennial (Sept–Nov), with art installations scattered at historic venues across the city, while even years see the Design Biennial (same months). Acts are profiled on www.iksv.org, but tickets are bought through www.biletix.com.

Coastal resorts and archaeological sites get their fair share of entertainment – ancient theatres and medieval castles make supremely atmospheric venues for catching a spot of Turkish or Western music, ballet, dance or opera, most notably in Izmir and Ephesus (May–July), Aspendos (June–July) and Bodrum (September). Previously known as the Altın Portakal (Golden Orange), the Antalya Film Festival (October) inevitably uses more prosaic facilities, but features some of the best in new local and overseas cinema.

Among religious festivals of most interest to visitors, the Hacıbektaş commemoration (late August) in the namesake village, attended by Bektaşis and Alevîs, is a more genuine manifestation than Konya's overexposed Mevlâna festival (mid-Dec).

Squelchy combat is the theme of the Kırkpınar Oil-Wrestling competition at Edirne (July). Beastly rather than human antagonists meet, somewhat bizarrely, at Aydın province's camel-wrestling contests (Dec–Jan), and at Artvin's Kafkasör bullfights (late June–early July).

Henna tattoos feature at traditional festivals.

A fire-eater performs during the Islamic holy month of Ramadan. Ramadan involves fasting, but is also a time for celebration and spectacles.

Camel wrestling involves two males wrestling after an in-heat female is led past them.

Girls don traditional clothing.

The Gypsy Spring Festival

The Roma of Thrace have for centuries observed the spring-to-summer transition festival, called Kakava locally but Hıdırellez – or Ederlezi, as in the song made famous by Goran Bregović – everywhere in the Balkans. Hıdırellez is a corruption of Hizir and Ilyas, two prophets in the Shi'ite/Bektaşi tradition, conveniently syncretised with the major Balkan Orthodox saint George (6 May in the old Julian calendar). Accordingly celebrations are held from the evening of 5 May into the next day. The main events are at Kırklareli and especially Edirne's Sarayiçi district, where a bonfire is lit at dusk on 5 May, with crowds singing all around it and a communal meal served. When the pyre attains sufficient size, young Roma men leap over it, a practice thought to bring luck and health for the coming year. At dawn the next day, young girls proceed down to the Tunca in their mother's bridal gowns, accompanied by *zurnas* (shawms) and *davuls* (deep-toned drums), and bathe in the river, sometimes leaving the gowns in the water to be retrieved by others, again for good fortune.

...e entry at the Antalya Sand Sculpture Festival.

...ung women wear traditional dress and dance during ...uth and Sport Day (Atatürk's birthday), an annual ...tional holiday in May.

Turkish oil wrestlers rely on strength and endurance more than clever moves in this national sport. Tournaments take place throughout the country, with Edirne hosting the annual championships in summer.

Swimming amongst the ancient columns in the Thermal Baths at Pamukkale.

THE SOUTHERN AEGEAN

It's not hard to see why the Southern Aegean region is at the forefront of Turkey's booming tourist industry: some of the country's best beaches, with virtually guaranteed sunshine, are complemented by dramatic ancient ruins.

Kuşadası **⑰**, "Bird Island", faces a superb gulf partly closed off by the Greek island of Samos. Until the 1970s, it was a sleepy place, consisting of little more than a hillside quarter with old, tile-roofed houses and the partly walled medieval Kale district in the flatlands. Since then Kuşadası and satellite municipalities have grown into a conurbation of over 100,000; it's the major gateway to Ephesus (Efes) for cruise-ship patrons, who disembark here much to the delight of carpet, leather and knick-knack shop proprietors. Commission-hungry tour guides ensure maximum time for their charges inside the tatty bazaar here, and minimum time at the ruins themselves. The place's main virtues are serviceable beaches, well-developed nightlife, a large stock of accommodation and good connections for those relying on public transport.

Diminutive **Güvercin Adası** (Pigeon Island), connected to the mainland by a causeway, is dominated by its renovated old castle (daily 8am–11pm). Fortified by the Genoese, the castle walls border well-kept gardens and teahouses, while just inside is displayed the 15-metre skeleton of a fin whale. Beaches near town get fairly crowded in summer; the best, emptiest and most remote is broad, sometimes surf-pummelled **Pamucak**, 15km (9.5 miles) to the north.

Popular Güvercin Adası (Pigeon Island).

DILEK NATIONAL PARK

For a complete antithesis to the Kuşadası scene, head for the **Dilek Yarımadası-Büyük Menderes Deltası Millî Parkı ⑱** (Dilek Peninsula-Büyük Menderes Delta National Park; daily summer 8am–6.30pm, last exit 7pm, earlier closure spring/autumn; closed winter; charge), 28km (17 miles) south of Kuşadası. Although much loved by Turks on summer weekends, it remains one of the most pristine environments on the Turkish Aegean, partly thanks to the fact that the tip of

Main attractions
Ephesus ruins
Ephesus museum, Selçuk
Ancient Priene
Apollo temple, Didyma
Frescoed monasteries, Mt
  Latmos
Pamukkale travertines
Zeus sanctuary, Labranda

Maps on pages 188, 212

the peninsula – its twin summits comprising the ancient Mt Mykale – is an off-limits military zone.

Beyond the ticket gate, a paved road extends 10km (6 miles) past four beaches: **İçmeler, Aydınlık, Kavaklıburun** and the prettiest, fine-pebble **Karasu**. Some beaches have (expensive) snack bars – locals bring their own picnics. Between Aydınlık and Kavaklı Burnu, a walkers-only track signposted as "**Kanyon**" forges 15km (9.5 miles) south and inland, over the summit ridge, to Eski Doğanbey village. It takes about four to five hours to hike. A trailhead placard details the lush flora and fauna on the mountain. The forest cover includes wild chestnut, arbutus and *Pinus brutia*, as well as eighteen plant species endemic to Turkey. The local fauna extends to the rare white-tailed eagle, jackals, badgers and wild boar, who often appear at the beach parking lots to raid the rubbish bins.

Eski Doğanbey, the Ottoman Greek village of Domatça on the south slope, has been restored beautifully by urban trendies but has few short-term

facilities other than a seasonal park-information centre and a café.

EPHESUS (EFES)

Unmatched by any other Mediterranean archaeological site aside from Pompeii, **Ephesus** ⑲ (Efes in Turkish) appeals to visitors ranging from serious scholars to those with a more casual interest.

Strabo, Pausanias and Athenaios all relate the same colourful foundation legend for Ephesus. Androklos, son of Kodros, king of Athens, had been advised by an oracle to establish a city at the spot indicated by a fish and a boar. Arriving here late in the 11th century BC, Androklos and company found some locals frying fish by the seaside; one fish jumped out of the frying pan, scattering live coals and setting alight a thicket in which a boar was hiding. The boar rushed out and was killed by Androklos, thus fulfilling the prophesy. The new city was founded at the northern foot of Mount Pion, with worship of the Athenians' goddess Artemis syncretised easily with the indigenous Anatolian Kybele.

By the 6th century BC, Ephesus had prospered despite lacking any military or political power, thus attracting the attentions of Lydian King Kroïsos in 560 BC. The Ephesians stretched a rope around the nearby Temple of Artemis and retreated behind it, believing the goddess would protect them. Kroïsos and his army, perhaps amused by the townspeoples' naïveté, treated the captured city leniently. The **Archaic Artemis temple** was still under construction, so to please the Ephesians and the goddess, Kroïsos presented the temple with a set of carved column capitals, one of which had his name inscribed on it. These relics are now in London's British Museum.

In 356 BC – tradition states it was the night of Alexander the Great's birth – the temple was set on fire by one Herostratos, who wanted to be remembered for posterity, a goal he achieved

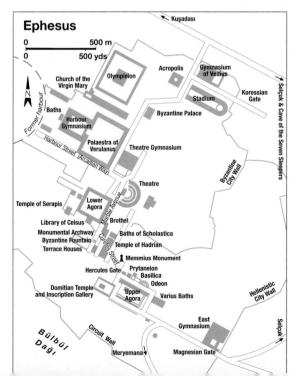

Ephesus

0   500 m
0   500 yds

Kuşadası

Church of the Virgin Mary
Olympieion
Acropolis
Gymnasium of Vedius
Koressian Gate
Selçuk & Cave of the Seven Sleepers
Stadium
Baths
Harbour Gymnasium
Byzantine Palace
Former Harbour
Palaestra of Verulanus
Theatre Gymnasium
Harbour Street (Arcadian Way)
Byzantine City Wall
Theatre
Temple of Serapis
Lower Agora
Marble Avenue
Library of Celsus
Brothel
Monumental Archway
Baths of Scholastica
Byzantine Fountain
Temple of Hadrian
Terrace Houses
Curetes Street
Memmius Monument
Hercules Gate
Prytaneion
Basilica
Odeon
Domitian Temple and Inscription Gallery
Upper Agora
Varius Baths
Hellenistic City Wall
East Gymnasium
Selçuk
Bülbül Dağı
Circuit Wall
Meryemana
Magnesian Gate

– his act has inspired a 1939 Sartre short story and a 2001 Armenian film by Ruben Kochar.

WONDER OF THE WORLD

The Ephesians at once began building an even finer structure which, when completed, ranked as one of the Seven Wonders of the World. Work was still in progress when Alexander arrived in 334 BC. He was so impressed that he offered to fund completion, but the offer was politely refused on the grounds that one god should not make a dedication to another. Today, a lone Ionian column looms amid a few foundation blocks, often submerged in a small marsh beside the Selçuk–Ephesus road – a pitiful reminder of what was once a glorious structure.

Ephesus reached its zenith during the Roman imperial era, when Augustus declared it the capital of the province of Asia in place of Pergamon. An inscription from Ephesus at this time calls itself "the first and greatest metropolis of Asia", and indeed it was. The permanent residence of the Roman governor, it had a maximum population of 250,000, and acted as the commercial hub of the Aegean; the only threat to its prosperity was the constant silting up of the harbour by the Kaistros River, today the Küçük Menderes. Despite many inspired or misguided attempts to deepen the channel or divert the river, Ephesus now lies 5km (3 miles) from the sea.

St Paul arrived in AD 51, and within two years gained enough followers to establish a church here. A backlash against the new religion, described in Acts 19:23–19:40, was spurred by secular rather than sacred interests. Demetrius, head of the union of silversmiths who had a lucrative business selling statuettes of Diana (the Roman version of Artemis), was incensed by Paul's proselytising, and arranged a rally of thousands in the theatre shouting, "Great is Diana of the Ephesians!" St Paul wanted to face down the crowd but was restrained from doing so by his companions Gaios and Aristarhos, departing shortly thereafter for Macedonia. Yet Christianity spread quickly in Ephesus and eventually supplanted the pagan goddess's cult.

THE RUINS

Most of the surviving ruins of Ephesus belong to the Roman imperial period. An exception is the **Circuit Wall**, built by Lysimakhos and an outstanding example of Hellenistic fortification. It has largely disappeared at lower elevations, but stands nearly intact along the crest of **Bülbül Dağı** (Nightingale Mountain, the ancient Mt Koressos) to the south of the city. Anyone energetic enough to climb up will find gates and towers of high-quality workmanship.

The northerly access road first passes the **Gymnasium of Vedius**, a 2nd-century gift to the city from that wealthy citizen. In typical Roman fashion, the building combined a gymnasium and baths. The adjacent Hellenistic **Stadium** was restored during Nero's reign (AD 54–68). Further

Turkey has a long bee-keeping tradition, and remains a significant producer today. Local honey is usually included in a Turkish breakfast.

Sarcophagus at Ephesus, most of whose ruins date from the Roman imperial period.

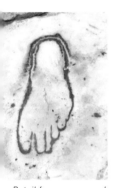

Detail from a supposed brothel advertisement on a wall at Ephesus.

Statue of Scholastica at the entrance to her baths.

along the road (just past the parking lot) stands the **Church of the Virgin Mary**, built in the 2nd century as a warehouse and converted to a basilica in the 4th century AD – the first known church dedicated to the Virgin.

The city's most impressive thoroughfare, the **Harbour Street** (or Arcadian Way) linking the old port and the theatre, is named after Byzantine Emperor Arcadius, who remodelled it in AD 395–408. About 500 metres (1,600ft) long and 11 metres (36ft) wide, both sides of the streets were covered with porticoes giving onto shops. Excavations unearthed an inscription indicating that the colonnaded street was lit at night by 50 lamps, at a time when only Rome and Antioch shared this distinction.

Beside this street, the imposing 2nd-century **Harbour Baths** form one of the largest structures in Ephesus, with a 30-metre (100ft)-long elliptical pool and 11-metre (36ft)-high marble columns supporting a vaulted brick roof. Next door, the **Harbour Gymnasium** has a colonnaded courtyard, paved with mosaic.

The restored **Theatre**, originally constructed during the reign of Lysimakhos into the slopes of Mount Pion (today Panayır Dağı), was large enough to hold 24,000 people and is still used for the annual May festival. From the top seats there is still a splendid view. Its excellent acoustics were further enhanced in ancient times by the judicious placing of clay or bronze sounding vessels. Below the theatre stands the more sympathetically restored **Library of Celsus**, its façade effectively the logo of the city, like a grandiose film set left behind after the shooting of a Roman spectacular. It was actually built in AD 110–17 by Gaius Julius Aquila for his father Gaius Julius Celsus, still entombed under the west wall, but destroyed by invading Goths in AD 262. Behind it, and the lower agora, lies the **Temple of Serapis**, which had eight massive columns with Corinthian capitals that individually weighed 57 tons, although apparently the structure was never completed.

At the library, the road bends and becomes **Curetes Street**, which extends up to the Magnesian **Gate**. At the beginning of the street on the left stand the **Baths of Scholastica**, built in the 1st century AD and reconstructed early in the 5th century by the lady whose headless statue can be seen in the entrance hall. The originally three-storeyed building was very popular, as both rich and poor could use the complex of heated rooms and pools free of charge, although only the rich could afford the time to linger for hours, gossiping while being massaged by their servants.

Next door, a peristyle house identified as the Brothel because of an inscription found in the adjacent latrines, has some delightful mosaics and traces of frescoes. An overly endowed clay Priapus found in the well is now in the Ephesus Museum.

The fascinating **Temple of Hadrian**, begun in AD 118, has four Corinthian columns supporting an arch with a bust of Tyche, the patron goddess of the city, in

the centre. The plaster cast on the site of the original frieze (now in the Museum) has three 3rd-century panels depicting gods and goddesses, including Artemis Ephesia, and a 4th-century addition of the Byzantine emperor Theodosios and his family – remarkable when one considers Theodosios's vehement opposition to paganism. On the opposite side of Curetes, the **Terrace Houses** (daily 8am–4.30/6.30pm; separate charge) offer a compelling portrait of everyday life with their mosaics, murals and under-floor heating systems.

SELÇUK

The small town of **Selçuk** ⓴, some 23km (14 miles) northeast of Kuşadası, owes its importance to its proximity to Ephesus, and to its Ephesus Museum. From the museum, near the central junction and minibus station, allow a 30-minute walk to Ephesus, though during summer even this short journey can be exhausting. Taxis and minibuses, however, are plentiful. There are also various decent restaurants in Selçuk, any of them preferable to those immediately outside the entrance to Ephesus itself. Given that the town also has attractive accommodation to suit most budgets, plus a few lively bars, it makes a viable overnight base, especially for backpackers and independent travellers. Parking rental cars is also much easier than in Kuşadası.

The **Ephesus Museum** (daily 8.30am–5.30pm, until 6.30pm in summer; charge) has an exceptional, well-displayed collection, though labelling could be more elaborate. Floor mosaics and a fresco of Socrates from one of the Ephesian terrace houses, cult statuettes, coins and other relics all create a vivid impression of ancient life. Other famous exhibits include a bronze statuette of Eros on a dolphin, two complete marble statues of Artemis – flanked by beasts and adorned with enigmatic bulbous protuberances, and a headless Priapus, balancing a tray of fruit (symbolising fertility) on his pride and joy.

The **Basilica of St John** (daily 8am–5pm, closes 7pm summer; charge) lies just south of the Byzantine fortress on the hill of Ayasoluk. St John

The Library of Celsus, part of the Ephesus ruins.

The marble statue of Artemis is a highlight of the Ephesus Museum.

supposedly lived the last years of his life locally; after his death in about AD 100, a shrine arose over his grave. Emperor Justinian erected a monumental basilica here in the 6th century, which endured until destroyed by Tamerlane's Mongols in around 1402. During the 1960s, what was once one of the largest Byzantine churches was partly restored by a Christian foundation based in Ohio. The presumed tomb of the evangelist lies at the altar end of the central nave, under a simple slab. The now-vanished dome was supported by partly re-erected marble and brick pillars, between which stand blue-veined marble columns bearing the monograms of Emperor Justinian and his wife, Theodora. The baptistry just to the north, with its cruciform plunge-pool, dates from the 5th century.

At the foot of the hill stands the elegant, late 14th-century **İsa Bey Camii** (usually open, except at prayer times), built in a transition between Selçuk and Ottoman styles. There are recycled Roman columns in the vast courtyard, with more inside upholding the gabled

The İsa Bey Camii, Selçuk.

roof and dome with its original tile-work in the squinches.

MERYEMANA, ŞIRINCE AND MAGNESIA AD MEANDRUM

According to one tradition, the Virgin Mary came to Ephesus with St John and lived here from AD 37 until her death in AD 48. Her purported house, **Meryemana** (www.meryemana.info; daily Apr–Oct 8am–6pm, Nov–Mar 8am–5pm; charge), was discovered in 1891 by Lazarist priests from Smyrna acting on a dream of Catherine Emmerich, a simple German nun who never left her convent. Situated 8km (5 miles) south of Selçuk, it is now a papally endorsed focus of pilgrimage, and merits a visit if only for the wooded paths and mountain streams. The Byzantine building, just possibly with 1st-century AD foundations, has been converted to a chapel and is also a popular outing for Muslims, who venerate Mary by tying votive rags onto a specially provided trellis. Daily Christian Masses are conducted here.

Şirince, a formerly Greek village only 8km (5 miles) east of Selçuk,

makes a delightful destination after visiting Ephesus, though it too is well established on the tour-bus circuit. There is nothing ancient here, just fresh air, traditional houses, two churches (one restored) and a relaxing atmosphere. Known as Kirkince to its Ottoman Greek founders, the village was resettled by Muslims from Macedonia after 1923, who brought their Islamically dubious habit of wine-making with them – though sadly, idiosyncratic basement brews have been replaced by the uniformly dull product of the local cooperative.

Much quieter and off the beaten path is ancient **Magnesia ad Meandrum** (Magnesia on the Maeander; daily 8.30am–5pm), 25km (16 miles) southeast of Selçuk. There are only scant remains of the ruined Temple of Artemis, partly submerged in winter months, though excavations are ongoing, having unearthed six large and intact Greek statues here in 2018. It's worth the walk southwest to the old theatre and stadium, carved into the hillsides at the feet of Mount Thorax.

PRIENE

The ancient Ionian city of **Priene** ㉑ (daily Tue–Sun 8.30am–5pm, until 7pm in summer; charge) is easily reached by a short, scenic drive from either Kuşadası or Selçuk, via the cotton-processing town of Söke; en route pines and olive groves alternate with occasional fields of ripening cotton bolls.

Priene has a spectacular location, on a natural terrace partway up Mount Mykale, its outriders presiding majestically over the ruins. Once an active port established at about the same time as Ephesus, the town had to be moved during the 4th century BC to outpace silt deposition by the River Maeander (today the Büyük Menderes, whose oxbows, lagoons and delta sprawl below the site). Hellenistic Priene was laid out in a grid pattern devised by city planner Hippodamos of Miletus in about 450 BC, and never much tampered with by the Romans, who favoured nearby Miletus.

Entry today is via the northeast gate (the more complete **southeast gate** can be used to exit). One of the first structures encountered is the exquisitely

The Temple of Hadrian.

preserved, three-sided **Bouleuterion** (Council Hall). Immediately uphill is the horseshoe-shaped **Theatre**, with front-row thrones for city dignitaries and a Roman stage building.

But Priene's most striking monument is the **Temple of Athena Polias**, designed by Pytheos, who also planned the Mausoleum of Halikarnassos, and wrote an architectural manual still consulted in Roman times. During the 1960s, five of the original 30 Ionic columns were re-erected; the rest still lie about like so many sausage-slices.

MILETUS (MILET)

There was a Bronze Age settlement here long before the semi-mythical, 10th-century BC foundation of the city Miletus by Neleos, another son of King Kodros. However, the present ruins of **Miletus ㉒** (daily Apr–Sept 8.30am–5pm, Oct–Mar 8.30am–7pm; charge) date from after its second foundation, since the original city was destroyed by the Persians in 494 BC. Like Priene, the new town was planned according to Hippodamian principles. Ephesus may

enjoy greater fame today, but Miletus was the most important city of the Ionian League. Its enterprising spirit and favourable position on a promontory jutting out into the Gulf of Latmos made it not only the wealthiest emporium of its time but also an intellectual centre.

The finest surviving building here is the 2nd-century AD **Theatre**, seating 15,000 people and surmounted by a Byzantine **castle**. There is some intricate relief work on the stage building – including angelic beings duelling with beasts – and huge vaulted passages underneath the seating tiers.

Most of the city buildings to the east are badly ruined. The most interesting, though standing to barely half its original height, is a 2nd-century AD **Nymphaeum**, fed by a vanished aqueduct which distributed water to the entire city. Another recipient of the water was the **Baths of Faustina**, built in about AD 150 in honour of the extravagant wife of Marcus Aurelius. Inside are two interesting spouts which fed the cold plunge pool – one in the shape of the personified river-god Maeander, the other in the form of a lion.

Five of Priene's Athena temple columns have been re-erected.

A short distance away stands the beautiful **İlyas Bey Camii**, built in 1404 by one of the Menteşe emirs, who ruled this part of Anatolia before the Ottomans consolidated their power, to celebrate his return after being held hostage in the Mongol court. The minaret collapsed in a 1958 earthquake, but the great banded-brick dome, delicate carved stone filigree at the entrance and finely worked *mihrab* make it a masterpiece. It was once part of a complex comprising a baths and *medrese*, both of which have been partly restored and fitted with wooden canopies.

Just past the mosque on the road to Didyma is the Miletus Museum (daily Apr–Sept 8.30am–4pm, Oct–Mar 8.30am–6.30pm; charge), housing local finds from Miletus, Priene and the Sacred Way that once linked the sanctuary in Didyma.

DIDYMA

The most impressive single monument in the south Aegean is the **Temple of Apollo at Didyma** ㉓ daily 8am–5.30pm in winter, 8.30am–7pm in summer; charge). There has been an oracle-shrine – but never a town – on this site since the Bronze Age; Ionian settlers merely imposed their cult of Apollo in the 8th century BC. This early phase in Didyma's history ended with the sacking of the Archaic temple by the Persians in 494 BC. When Alexander the Great arrived, the oracle proclaimed him the son of Zeus, which pleased him so much that he retrieved the cult statue of Apollo from Persia and ordered the building of a new super-temple. Work continued for five centuries, and while it was never actually finished, with only three of the 72 completed Ionic columns still standing, the remains rarely fail to impress, especially towards sunset when you are likely to arrive after a day's touring. Mascots of the site are the two Medusa heads, one with furrowed brow and tight ringlets, mounted just below the ticket booth.

Didyma today stands marooned amidst the mushrooming development of modern **Didim**, which spreads north of **Altınkum** ("Golden Sand") – Turkey's answer to England's Blackpool, with its curious combination of both Turkish and foreign working-class patronage. Beyond

Bursting cotton buds drift like snow across the arid summer landscape.

The not-so-lucky columns.

Herakleia tombs by Lake Bafa.

Herakleia, viewed from the lake.

the main beach, ringed with bars and restaurants, precious little of the coast remains unblocked by development. Another stretch of sand lies just north of Didyma at Mavişehir cove, the ancient Panormos, where seagoing supplicants disembarked to approach the oracle along a sacred way.

LAKE BAFA AND HERAKLEIA AD LATMOS

Certainly one of the oddest places in the Aegean region, **Bafa Gölü** (Lake Bafa) was once an inlet of the Aegean but became cut off by the capricious River Maeander (Büyük Menderes). Its warm, often weedy waters vary from almost fresh to brackish depending on recent rainfall and incursions of seawater up the convoluted channel system of the Menderes. On the northeast shore, **Herakleia ad Latmos** ㉔, one of the most romantic sites in Anatolia (unenclosed; charge during daylight hours), falls within ancient Caria (Karya in Turkish) and more specifically the modern village of Kapıkırı. This is easiest approached by a well-marked 9km (6-mile) -long side

road branching north off the main Söke–Milas highway at the town of Bafa.

The serrated volcanic crest of **Mount Latmos**, some 1,500 metres (4,921ft) high, inspired its Turkish name Beşparmak (Five Fingers). A bastion of this wild, formidable mountain curves down to **Kapıkırı**, while the walls of ancient Herakleia with their gates, towers and parapets run up the ridge. The city ruins are scattered engagingly across the village, and include the square **Athena temple**, the absidal **Sanctuary of Endymion**, a Byzantine **island-castle**, and **tombs**, some with their lids ajar as they were left by early grave-robbers. To really capture the spirit of the place it's best – preferably in spring or autumn when temperatures are more moderate – to either take boat trips on the lake or hike up the mountain. Numerous islets in the lake were a popular refuge in Byzantine times. Kapıkırı *pansiyon* staff are happy to oblige with arrangements or guiding.

West of the village, **İkize** Adası sports another castle and a church, while further beyond, **Menet Adası** is similarly

endowed, and faces a white-sand beach where boat trips make a swimming stop. Inland, the most popular targets are the **Yediler monastery** and the **Stylos hermit-cave**, both adorned with fine frescoes from the 11th to the 13th centuries. Deeper into the mountain are more paintings, in this case prehistoric pictographs; several days are needed to properly explore the area.

APHRODISIAS (AFRODISIAS)

Named after the goddess Aphrodite, successor to the more ancient fertility deities Nin and Ishtar, ancient **Aphrodisias** ㉕ (Afrodisias in Turkish), whose site was occupied since about 2,800 BC, had grown from a cult centre to a proper city by late Hellenistic times. However, devastated by earthquakes during late antiquity and abandoned by the survivors after Arab raids, the once-splendid city was largely forgotten until, in 1961, the late Professor Kenan Erim of New York University began excavations. These revealed an unparalleled cache of sculpture carved from locally quarried marble. Statuary produced here met the needs for effigies across most of the Roman world, from Spain to the Danube, and despite this far-flung dispersal the local **museum** (daily Apr–Sept 8am–7pm, Oct–Mar 8am–5pm; one charge for site and museum) is crammed full of examples.

A loop-trail from the museum forecourt tours the city's highlights, all from the Roman imperial era. The well-preserved **Theatre** had its orchestra and stage converted into an arena for bloody spectacles during the 2nd century. East, beyond the colonnades of the agora, the **Baths of Hadrian** retain their floor tiles, but ironically little is left of the Temple of Aphrodite, the city's patroness, owing to Byzantine interventions. A short detour north from the loop leads to the 30,000-seat **Stadium**, one of the finest in the world, and the venue for quadrennial festivals of sport, music and drama. Finally, the most striking structure is the restored **Tetrapylon**, a monumental columned gateway whose pediments feature elaborate reliefs.

PAMUKKALE, HIERAPOLIS AND LAODICEIA

Magical **Pamukkale** ㉖ (daily Apr–Sept 8am–9pm, Oct–Mar 8.30am–5pm; charge during daylight hours), the "Cotton Castle", lies 19km (12 miles) north of Denizli, off the main highway from Aydin. It's actually a solidified cascade of travertine, formed by calcium bicarbonate-laden hot springs just uphill that have left stalactite-festooned terraces and scallop-shaped pools as they drain over the escarpment here and cool. Over the years considerable damage was done by bluff-top hotels (now demolished) siphoning off the flow of water, and too many tourists walking on the travertines, but now – in keeping with Pamukkale's status as a Unesco World Heritage Site – access to the terraces is highly restricted. Only a few pools remain open, though bathing is better done up above in the **Antique Pool** (same hours; charge), formerly an ancient sacred pool.

○ **Tip**

Aphrodisias' site and museum are 49km (30 miles) southeast of Nazilli, turning south off the main Aydin–Denizli highway after passing the town of Kuyucak. If you don't have transport, consider taking a tour from Pamukkale, as there is no direct transport to the site. Shuttles run from Kuyucak to Karacasu, and from there to the ruins. The nearest accommodation and lunch restaurant are in Geyre village, adjacent to the ruins.

Village women in Kapıkırı.

Ildız carpet farm at Milas, where kilims and wool and silk carpets are produced.

Pamukkale has been created by mineral-rich hot springs.

It's exhilarating to paddle through what feels like 36°C (65°F) soda water while gazing at submerged ancient column fragments.

On the plateau above the terraces lie the splendid ruins of ancient **Hierapolis** (same admission policy as travertines), founded by Eumenes II of Pergamon as a spa town. Levelled by earthquakes in AD 17 and 60, it was rapidly rebuilt under Roman patronage, attaining its zenith during the 2nd and 3rd centuries. The **Theatre** is vast, and the stage building with its intricate friezes has been reconsolidated by Italian excavators. Below the theatre yawns the **Plutonium**, a small grotto sacred to the god of the underworld, where you can hear gushing water and the hissing of poisonous gas. A grill guards the cave-mouth now, but in antiquity the eunuch priests of Kybele could apparently enter without ill effect. Nearby, a primary **Roman avenue** bisects the city from the south to north gates, exiting the latter to a **triple arch** built by Domitian. Beyond this is the vast **necropolis**, its most elaborate tomb that of Flavius Zeuxis. At the western edge of the site, within the large Roman bath complex, is the worthwhile Archeological Museum (Tue–Sun Apr–Sept 8.30am–7pm, Oct–Mar 8.30am–4.45pm; charge), housing statues and sarcophagi gathered from across the region.

If staying at Pamukkale, don't miss the opportunity to visit **Laodiceia** (signposted as "Laodikya"), 3km (2 miles) south. According to ancient sources the city was founded by the Seleucids, though intensive ongoing excavations have revealed its origins to stretch as far back as the 6th millennium BC. **Laodiceia** prospered in Roman times before disappearing from history upon the Seljuk conquest. Considered an up-and-coming site of the region, the site (Apr–Sept 8am–7pm, Oct–Mar 8am–5pm; charge) features Anatolia's largest stadium, two huge theatres, a paved, colonnaded street, a nymphaeum and four bath complexes.

MILAS, LABRANDA AND EUROMOS

Milas ㉗ is a satisfying county town with a noted Tuesday market; the region is

famous for its fine fabrics, coarse goat-hair shoulder-bags, and earth-toned carpets with geometric patterns.

Milas also has fine examples of Ottoman domestic architecture, often with ornate chimneys, and several interesting mosques including the **Ulu Camii**, built by the Menteşe emirs in 1370. Some 400metres/yds north of this stands the Roman **Baltalı Kapı** (Gate-with-Axe), so called after the double-headed axe carved into the north-facing keystone. The town's most spectacular monument, though, is the **Gümüşkesen**, a Roman tomb 800metres/yds west of the centre; with its Corinthian colonnade supporting a pyramidal roof, it's thought to be a mini-replica of the Halikarnassos Mausoleum (see page 226).

Some 15km (9 miles) north of Milas by paved road (albeit one progressively narrowing and abused by lorries from an open-cast mine), the Zeus sanctuary at **Labranda** (daily Apr–Oct 9am–7pm, Nov–Mar 8am–5pm; charge) has the loveliest setting of any ruin in Caria, on spring-fed terraces at 600m (2,000 ft) elevation, with sweeping views over the Milas plain. The god was venerated here at least from the 7th century BC, though most of the ruins one can see now were erected 300 years later. Around the Zeus temple on the highest terrace are two partly intact **androns** (banqueting halls), a **priestly residence** and a **fountain-house**. Monumental steps link these with two **propylaea** (porticoes) and a **Byzantine church** converted from a Roman baths. Despite the salubrious climate and secure water supply, there was never much of a town at this isolated spot, finally abandoned when the Seljuks swept across Anatolia.

Some 13km (8 miles) outside Milas on the road to Lake Bafa, the magnificent **Temple of Zeus** at ancient **Euromos** (daily Apr–Oct 8.30am–7pm, Nov–Mar 8.30am–5pm; charge) is one of the three best-preserved in Asia Minor. Endowed by Roman emperor Hadrian but never finished, its 16 Corinthian columns are visible fleetingly from the highway but more dramatic up close.

The impressive theatre at Hierapolis.

Bodrum's Castle of St Peter boasts a spectacular setting.

BODRUM AND MARMARIS

Either resort is a good starting point for a journey along the Carian coast, with its venerable history and spectacular scenery, varying from sandy beaches to fjord-like inlets.

Situated on a peninsula opposite the Greek island of Kos, **Bodrum**  is one of the most popular resorts in Turkey. As Halikarnassos, this was the birthplace of Herodotus (c.485–425 BC), known to some as the "Father of History" but to others as the "Father of Lies" because of his fanciful travel accounts.

BOATS AND PARTIES

Until the 1960s, Bodrum was just a pretty Aegean port earning a subsistence living from sponge-diving. Today it is one of Turkey's principal yachting centres and also a linchpin in the booming "Blue Voyage" trade. The marina (west) quay is lined with excursion boats and their touts; one-day outings all follow similar itineraries. These typically involve stops at grotto hot-springs on the margin of Kara Ada, visible from Bodrum; the "Akvaryum" at Ada Boğazı, a snorkelling venue now, alas, quite devoid of fish; and a final stop to swim, perhaps at Kargı Beach where camels may be ridden.

Bodrum's striking, whitewashed, cubist-style houses, now protected by preservation orders, crowd narrow central lanes, and are draped with cascades of bougainvillea and other subtropical vegetation. They form a sharp contrast to the main local hedonistic scene of fine dining, shopping and some of the liveliest nightlife in Turkey.

Fun in the water at Gümbet beach.

Despite the town's assiduously cultivated reputation for offering all things to all visitors, and some hotels staying open year-round, the tourist season remains stuck in the usual Aegean June-to-September groove.

BODRUM CASTLE

The towers and battlements of the **Castle of St Peter** (daily 9am–4.30pm, summer until 6.30pm; charge) dominate the town from its strategic promontory dividing the harbour in two. It was built by the crusading Knights of St John, who

⊙ **Main attractions**
Castle of St Peter
Bodrum nightlife
Gümüşlük, Bodrum peninsula
Millennial çinar tree, Bayir
Mesudiye, Ova Bükü beach
Muğla, Ottoman houses
Sultaniye hot springs, Köyceğiz lake

📍 **Map on page 188**

plundered the Mausoleum for ready-cut masonry, still visible in the castle walls. The knights arrived in 1402 and continued to work on their castle throughout the 15th century, finally completing it in 1522, but were forced to abandon the fortress shortly afterwards, when Ottoman sultan Süleyman the Magnificent captured Rhodes.

Today, the castle is entered from the west; stairs and gates embellished with coats of arms lead to the lower and upper courtyards with their various towers and special exhibits. Coloured arrows indicate suggested routes, and you can get onto the ramparts for fine views of the town and harbour. The **Museum of Underwater Archaeology** (www.bodrum-museum.com; **Tue–Sun 9am–4.30pm; charge**) is distributed over several buildings here. The chapel houses a brilliantly reconstructed 7th-century Byzantine wreck, discovered nearby at Yassıada; elsewhere, Mycenaean, Roman and early Islamic glassware is displayed. There's more of the same in the **Glass Wreck Hall**, perhaps the most interesting gallery, featuring

a flat-bottomed Fatimid-Byzantine freighter sunk in 1025 at Serçe Limanı near Marmaris, and meticulously restored by archaeologists. Besides its cargo of coloured-glass fragments, the crew's personal effects are exhibited.

The **Uluburun Wreck Hall** in the upper courtyard contains a rich trove of Bronze Age objects, including the world's oldest-known shipwreck, which sank in the 14th century BC off Kaş. Treasures recovered from the cargo include gold jewellery, daggers, ivory, and a two-panel "book" formerly containing wax and the scarab-seal of Egyptian queen Nefertiti.

The **Carian Princess Hall** beside the French Tower contains the remains and effects of a local 4th-century BC noblewoman, found in a miraculously unlooted local tomb in 1989. The richness of the finds – a golden diadem, drinking cup, and jewellery – lends some credence to the possible identification of the lady as Ada, last queen of Caria, brought back from exile by Alexander the Great in 334 BC. A team of British forensic specialists has reconstructed her facial profile from the skull.

Children may enjoy a visit to the **English Tower**, packed with armour and with trophies of war adorning the medieval-themed cafeteria. Another potential kids' hit is the Knights' dungeons below the **Gatineau Tower**, where taped groans and mannequins attempt to evoke the horrors which transpired here. The inscription above the door declares *Inde Deus Abest* ("Here God does not exist") – even more chilling when you realise that it was put there by monks.

MAUSOLEUM OF HALIKARNASSOS

To the northwest of the castle lies the Mausoleum of Halikarnassos (Tue–Sun summer 9am–7pm, winter 8am–5pm; charge). It was one of the ancient Seven Wonders of the World, consecrated to the memory of ambitious Mausolos, Persian-appointed satrap (king) of Halikarnassos

⊙ BOHEMIAN BODRUM

Long before it became a conventional resort, Bodrum welcomed the bohemian and the eccentric. The earliest such habitué was Cevat Şakir Kabaağaçli (1890–1973), the "Fisherman of Halikarnassos", exiled here in 1925 on a three-year term for sedition. He remained in Bodrum voluntarily for much of the rest of his life, penning short stories and novels, while pioneering the concept of the "Blue Voyage" by disappearing for weeks at a time on a primitive sponge-diver's boat, as related in a 1993 biopic, *The Blue Exile*.

Ahmet and Nesui Ertegün were the sons of the 1935–46 Turkish ambassador to the US, caught the jazz bug there, and stayed. They established Atlantic Records, the label that signed (among others) Charles Mingus, Otis Redding, Aretha Franklin, Led Zeppelin, Ray Charles, John Coltrane and the MJQ – thus largely explaining the popularity of jazz, soul, rock and blues amongst Turkey's chattering classes. Both Ertegüns have passed away now, but for years Ahmet's villa in Bodrum was a hub of summer social life.

Perhaps the most outrageous resident, from 1970 until his death in 1996, was Zeki Müren, among the most accomplished Turkish *sanat* (classical art) singers and a flamboyant transvestite – though he mostly appeared out of drag at his favourite local bar. Zeki's villa, number 11 of the street named after him, contains a small museum of career memorabilia.

during the mid-4th century BC. The mausoleum was commissioned by his sister/widow, Artemesia the Younger, resulting in a monument topped with a pyramidal roof and a chariot with effigies of Mausolos and herself in triumph. Precious little remains above ground today, after pilferage by the Knights of St John, and removal of the chariot and friezes to the British Museum between 1846 and 1857.

BODRUM PENINSULA

Bodrum town itself, despite its easterly bay being named Kumbahçe ("Sand Garden"), does not offer prime swimming – for better beaches, and sometimes for a more tranquil stay, head out onto the peninsula. Its villages are all easily accessible by bus or (sometimes) boat services, but be warned that, while the town has some zoning controls, the peninsula has relatively few.

Gümbet, 3km (2 miles) west, is effectively a suburb of Bodrum, with a long, if gritty, beach and a youthful, hard-drinking, largely British clientele. **Bitez**, the next bay west some 10km (6 miles) from town, attracts an older crowd. It offers a windsurfing school and mooring for yachts, but a less good beach.

Ortakent, straddling the main highway west of Bodrum, has an old towerhouse dating from 1601 and access, through mandarin orchards, to the longest beach in the area, **Yahşi Sahil**.

At Gürece, leave the main road to follow the narrower one looping around the far southwest shore of the peninsula. The first cove, **Kargı**, alias "Camel Beach" after the beasts ridden here, is a popular target for boat trips, but Bağla cove further on is monopolised by a holiday village. There's better public access to the excellent beach at **Karaincir**, while **Akyarlar** just beyond has a real village feel, with a mosque and mostly Turkish patronage at the various fish tavernas overlooking the picturesque fishing port.

Rounding the wind-buffeted lighthouse cape of **Hüseyin Burnu**, you'll find a few undeveloped but gently sloping sandy beaches that are ideal for wind- and kitesurfing – thanks to the wind channel between here and the facing Greek islet of Psérimos. Most of the coast between here and **Turgutreis** has

Bodrum's Museum of Underwater Archaeology.

Clubbers get foamed at Bodrum's Halikarnossos nightclub.

Peacocks wander the courtyards of Bodrum's Castle of St Peter.

been taken over by development, most of it unashamedly downmarket, all-inclusive complexes, though the town's open-air market is well attended. By contrast, **Gümüşlük** presents an intriguing combination of the posh and the Turkish-bohemian, partly because the ubiquity of ancient Myndos (upon which Gümüşlük is sited) means that villa development is strictly controlled and the shore is vehicle-free. Yachts anchor and swimmers snorkel above submerged archaeological remains, while above ground you can spot ancient walls and towers. The southerly beach is only average, but the little port on the north is an enchanting (if expensive) venue for dining literally on the water.

In the northwest corner of the peninsula, **Yalıkavak** was one of the last working sponge-fishing villages, but now middle-of-the-road tourism predominates. The beach is unspectacular, though the hillside scenery – dotted with 300-year-old windmills – is appealing when not blanketed in housing projects. Further east on the road circling back to Bodrum, **Gündoğan** (formerly Farilya) is

a resort aimed at middle-class Turks, while **Türkbükü** (or Göltürkbükü) fancies itself the St Tropez of Turkey. Decidedly upmarket hotels, pitched to well-heeled Turks, line the approach road and ostentatious motor-cruisers anchor in the sheltered bay here.

THE BLUE VOYAGE

Bodrum is one of the acknowledged termini for the classic **Mavi Yolculuk** (Blue Voyage) between here and Marmaris, via the unspoilt, pine-fringed **Gökova Körfezi** ③ and other inlets between the Datça and Hisarönü peninsulas. The Gökova Gulf is a strictly protected natural area, and coastal settlements are scarce. On the north shore your boat might call at the little bays of Mazıköy, Çökertme with its fish tavernas and sheltered beach, or Akbük, where wetlands and excellent mooring sandwich a coarse-pebble beach. On the south shore, popular overnight anchorages include İngiliz Limanı (English Harbour), so named after a British naval vessel that sheltered here from pursuing German craft during World War II; Karacasöğüt; and Sedir

Adası (alias Cleopatra Island), allegedly a trysting place of Mark Antony and his Egyptian bride.

Many agencies in both Bodrum and Marmaris act as representatives for crewed and skippered *gulets*, the traditional Blue Voyage wooden schooner. Late spring and autumn are the most pleasant, and reasonably priced, seasons.

If you'd rather arrange it all before departure, especially as a yacht flotilla, two reputable, unusual booking agencies in Britain are SCIC (tel: 0629-063 180; www.scicsailing.eu), a handful of Bodrum-based *gulets* which actually travel under sail power rather than (as is usual on such craft) with merely decorative rigging, and Day Dreams (tel: 01884-840 786; www.daydreams-travel. com), a larger fleet of *gulets* or schooners welcoming singles and couples.

MARMARIS AND ITS PENINSULA

Marmaris ㉛ is reached along a 27km (17-mile) road off the main highway between Muğla and Fethiye, formerly an old eucalyptus-flanked avenue, but long since superseded by a four-lane divided expressway. An apocryphal tale relates that the town's name derives from an episode when Süleyman the Magnificent disparaged the state of the fortress here by exclaiming *"Mimarı as"* (Hang the architect). Lord Nelson was more impressed by the area's potential when he used the large bay to prepare his fleet before attacking (and defeating) Napoleon's navy at Egyptian Aboukir in 1798.

The near-perfect natural harbour and splendid setting ringed by pine-clad hills elicit admiration, and Marmaris – with its Netsel marina, among the largest in Turkey – unsurprisingly vies with Bodrum as a starting point for cruising. The town itself has little of interest beyond the tiny ex-Greek old quarter at the base of the small, restored **castle** (daily Apr–Sept 8.30am–7pm, Tue–Sun Oct–Mar 8.30am–5pm; charge), its rooms housing various finds from the peninsula and its ramparts offering panoramic views of the marina. Marmaris is principally a downmarket resort for both Turks and foreigners,

Panoramic view of Marmaris and its harbour.

Marmaris market.

with an abundance of English comfort food, beer-swilling bars and raucous clubs. Development creeps down the west flank of the bay to successively calmer satellite resorts – each with a decent sandy beach and water sports on offer – at **İçmeler** (9km/5.5 miles away) and **Turunç**, 12km (7.5 miles) further along a steep, winding road. By far the best beach, and least developed setting (thanks in part to the walls of ancient Amos just above on the headland) is at the next cove, **Kumlubükü**, the end of the line for the east-coast road.

Beyond here, the road – notionally paved but steep, narrow and potholed – forges into the interior of the convoluted, forested **Hisarönü** (or Loryma) peninsula. Here, overland travel is excruciatingly slow, the only really top-standard highways being one from near Turunç to Söğüt, and another from Hisarönü, off the Marmaris-Datça route, to Bozburun. This is truly boat (or walking) country, with marinas or decent anchorages – and shipyards where wooden *gulets* are still built in the traditional manner – at west-coast,

beachless **Orhaniye, Selimiye** and **Bozburun**. Bozburun, well used now to yacht flotillas and their denizens, might seem like the end of the world, but persevere to arrive at **Söğüt**. This is an unspoilt village with an inland quarter and a delightful shore *mahalle* (quarter) looking to Greek island Sými, with fishing boats pulled up on the pebble beach.

Once past Söğüt and the poorer nearby village of Taşlıca, the onward dirt track winds through the mysterious remains of ancient Keresse to end at **Serçe** Limanı, a magnificently protected inlet with a simple taverna and lots of yachts. Pleasure boats also drop anchor at the deep fjord of ancient Loryma, near the tip of the peninsula, where pines have long since yielded to Mediterranean scrub.

Inland attractions are limited to a small seasonal **waterfall** near Orhaniye, and the village of **Bayır**, whose glories are a huge *çınar* (plane tree), said to be 2,000 years old, in the main square, and a nearby souvenir stall whose tightly juxtaposed displays recall a Salvador Dalí installation: mannequins in beekeepers' suits, tubular beehives made of mud, dangling gourds, soft-toy donkeys and sheep, plus towels imprinted with the visages of Atatürk or assorted Shi'ite, Alevî or Bektaşi martyrs and bards.

THE REŞADIYE PENINSULA

A different highway, similar to a rollercoaster but of decent width, leads west from Marmaris 69km (43 miles) to **Datça**, a humdrum market-and-realestate town whose resort function is owed largely to decent yacht anchorage. The final approach is through a fertile agricultural landscape, and the shoreline *mahalle*, draped over promontories separating two rather scrappy beaches, has some appeal, but there's more 3km (2 miles) inland at **Eski Datça**. A stone-built village tastefully restored by urban artists, the local geezers still feel comfortable holding forth in the central *çay bahcesi*.

Beyond Datça lies truly the last frontier of Aegean tourism (and real estate), albeit one that is steadily being tamed since the onward highway was paved. The scenery becomes ever more dramatic, with defiles and forested crags, prior to the turning down to **Mesudiye** and its idyllic **Ova Bükü** beach, amply supplied with food and lodging. A paved coastal corniche road continues to bigger and busier **Palamutbükü**, which since the 1990s has grown to be a major resort for Turks – and has prepared a small port to attract yachts or excursion boats from Datça. You return to the main highway through what must be one of the largest almond groves in the world; everywhere here the almond is king, and given the nuts' high global price, the orchards are probably safe from developers.

Ancient **Knidos** ㉜ (daily Apr–Sept 8am–7pm, Oct–Mar 8am–5pm; charge) occupies Tekir Burun at the end of the peninsula. With its two harbours astride one of the main Aegean shipping lanes – at least one always suitable for mooring in this permanently windy place – you can see why the city was moved here during the mid-4th century BC, from its prior location near modern Datça. The site, covering both a mainland district and an island (now joined to the mainland but off-limits), has been sporadically excavated, but there is little to see other than a fine Hellenistic **theatre** and a Byzantine **basilica** with extensive floor mosaics. All but vanished is the Temple of Aphrodite, which housed a famous **cult statue** of the goddess created by the Greek sculptor Praxiteles (390–330 BC), who supposedly used the famously beautiful Athenian courtesan Phyrne as a model. Through sacred prostitution, the love-cult brought Knidos almost as much income as harbour fees. Byzantine zealots predictably destroyed the Aphrodite, but copies and fragments still exist. The statue base and temple site were located in July 1969 by the splendidly appropriately named American heiress and amateur archaeologist, Iris Cornelia Love.

MUĞLA

Some 54km (34 miles) north of Marmaris, the provincial capital of **Muğla** ㉝ stands out for several reasons. Its

The sandy beaches and watersports on offer at Marmaris and its peninsula increase the area's appeal to families.

The harbour at Datça.

centre is exceedingly well run, orderly and leafy, with attractive modern architecture offsetting its famous old hillside quarter of hundreds of strictly protected **Ottoman houses**. Some of these are Greek-built, dating from the 18th and 19th centuries. Two well-preserved medieval *kervansarays* have found a new lease of life: the **Konakaltı Hanı** is now an art gallery, while the **Yağcılar Hanı** contains souvenir shops and tea stalls.

KÖYCEĞIZ AND DALYAN

Continuing eastwards 40km (25 miles) from the Marmaris junction on Highway 400, the first place of any consequence is **Köyceğiz 🔼**, a sleepy, pleasant market town on the eponymous lake, once an arm of the sea, like Bafa Gölü (Lake Gölü). Relatively few foreigners stay, but there are decent hotels (at Turkish, not overseas, prices) and restaurants along the lakefront promenade. Boat tours are offered from here to Kaunos and the local hot springs.

A short way south is the riverside resort town of **Dalyan**. The name means

"fish weir", after the system of barriers among the reeds which catch sea bass, caught as they head for the sea after breeding in Köyceğiz Lake. Upstream towards the lake are the open-air **Ilıca mud-baths**, whose gloriously messy contents (which reach 40°C/104°F) are said to address a host of ailments; on the lake's south shore, at **Sultaniye**, stands a more conventional round **hot springs** pool under an Ottoman dome (same temperature; daily 8am–11pm; charge). The resort itself, totally given over to foreign tastes, does have a unique riverside setting, with little boats constantly putt-putting up and down past reed-beds.

Daily boat tours, or a road 15km (9.5 miles) long, both head for remote **İztuzu Beach** (charge), 3.5km (2.2 miles) of hard-packed, gently shelving sand where giant loggerhead turtles come to lay their eggs during summer. Development of the beach is accordingly limited, and access forbidden at night.

KAUNOS

For over a millennium, under Persians, Greeks, Romans and Byzantines, ancient **Kaunos** (daily Apr–Sept 8am–7pm, Oct–Mar 8am–6pm; charge) was one of the leading towns of Caria, despite always being considered an unhealthy place due to malarial mosquitoes. It was probably abandoned, however, due to silting up of its harbour – the ancient port is now a bird-haunted, reedy lake.

Parts of the site, on the west bank of the Dalyan Çayı, are clearly visible from the resort in the form of clustered Lycian-style **cliff tombs**, one incomplete one showing clearly the method of construction – from the top down. Ongoing excavations are exposing progressively more of the hillside city; revealed thus far are a Hellenistic theatre with a nymphaeum outside, Roman baths, a Byzantine basilica, a Doric temple with a colonnade, and below this a fountain-house.

View of the Kaunos cliff tombs from the Dalyan river.

Internal population movement, water shortages, a decline in traditional crafts, and full-saturation coastline development – the negative face of Turkey's tourist industry.

Bodrum and its peninsula make a useful case study for the effects of tourism on coastal Turkey. Officially about 36,000 people live in the town, but during July and August the population of the entire peninsula can swell almost tenfold on any given day, packed into an area of roughly 120 sq km (46 sq miles). The nearby Bodrum-Milas International Airport receives up to 5 million annual arrivals, including from Britain on charter, easyJet and jet2 airlines. But unlike at Dalaman or Antalya airports, the majority of these arrivals are still Turkish, not foreign, many of whom are residential tourists occupying second homes in the phalanxes of villas which carpet every sea view hillside and greatly outnumber hotel accommodation. There's never been much of a public coastal access ethic in Turkey, and numerous formerly deserted beaches have had the way to them blocked by private developments.

END OF THE OLD WAYS

The world economic crisis has only slowed, not stopped, construction projects, and both short-term tourism and real-estate development have accelerated the demise of traditional local livelihoods. Sponge-diving ceased in the 1960s, while more recently mandarin and olive groves are either cut down or neglected. Mandarins in particular need ample water, which has never been abundant locally as the numerous surviving *gümbets* (domed Ottoman rainwater cisterns) testify. Existing and proposed golf courses will only increase pressure on water resources. Unless water is piped in from the mountains of the interior, or desalinisation plants set up, the sea will eventually invade local aquifers which are limited to the few small coastal plains, rendering the aquifers useless.

The needs of residential tourists have also warped local commerce: the main roads across the peninsula – continually disrupted by widening works to relieve perennial congestion, or chewed up by construction lorries – are lined by huge shopping malls comprising supermarkets, plant nurseries, builders' merchants, indoor or garden furniture retailers, and bath/kitchen outfitters. Traditional crafts and workshops are gone, or their products – like reed matting – imported from elsewhere in Turkey.

NEW JOBS AND ROLES

Job opportunities at Bodrum's seaside resorts, as everywhere on the Aegean and Mediterranean coasts, have acted as powerful magnets for internal migration from eastern Turkey, either seasonal (those staffing hotels, shops and restaurants) or permanent, as entire families relocate to set up businesses. This has resulted in momentous social changes in what were historically closed communities, little changed since the 1923 population exchanges deposited Greek-speaking Muslims, expelled from Crete, here.

One also sees plenty of the stereotypical encounters between Turks (usually men) and foreigners (usually women), and the resulting mixed marriages, visible in the tourist trade as restaurant or shop partnerships.

Tourists mimic a tin of sardines on the beach at Bodrum's easterly Kumbahçe bay.

Pretty Alanya harbour.

Carved masks in Myra.

THE MEDITERRANEAN COAST

Precipitous gorges, ancient cities, Crusader castles and gentle turquoise seas make this area a holiday paradise.

The beach at Kemer.

The Turks call their patch of the Mediterranean the *Akdeniz* (White Sea); others, familiar with the hue of its translucent waters, prefer the tag "Turquoise Coast", at least for the western portion.

Since the mid-1980s, this area has become a major sun-and-sea destination, via international airports at Dalaman and Antalya, with mega-resorts either side of Antalya. Former fishing villages have metamorphosed into villa-laced boomtowns, archaeological sites like Side have discos around the temple walls and golf courses proliferate. Fortunately, you can still find plenty of enchantment away from the mass-market resorts, though for how much longer is a moot point.

We have divided this coast into four sections, based roughly on ancient regions. Lycia, in the west, is the most beautiful, with mountains plunging steeply to a shore of cave-riddled cliffs and secluded coves. Resorts here range from the backpacker haven at Olympos to upmarket, ex-Greek Kalkan and Kaş, via mass-market Ölüdeniz.

Pamphylia is bracketed by the sophisticated city of Antalya on the west and castellated Alanya on the east. Much in between is fertile, scenically humdrum plain, with long, golden beaches and fabulous archaeological sites like Perge, Aspendos and Side to compensate.

Dolls made out of pumpkins make typical gifts from Alanya.

Western Cilicia (essentially Alanya to Adana) features rugged coast up to Silifke, with some of the most hotly contested real estate lying beyond, now humming with industrial and agricultural enterprise. The coast bends south into the Hatay, around biblical Antioch (Antakya), the last province to be joined to the republic. The Hatay spent nearly two centuries as a Crusader principality, while today it has more cultural (and linguistic) affinities with Syria.

LYCIA

Enchanting Lycia – largely cut off from the interior of Anatolia until the 1980s – has always been home to proud, independent people. The Lycians have traditionally looked to the sea for trade and cultural cues.

Maps on pages
238, 244

The independent-minded Lycians, probably an indigenous, pre-Hittite people (and not settlers from Crete, as Herodotus claimed), occupied the "bulge" between present-day Fethiye and Antalya from around 1400 BC. They had their own language, still to be seen on inscriptions, but are best known for their spectacular tombs.

From the 6th century BC onwards, at least 20 cities in this region banded together in a loose federation, in which each city voted according to its importance. Between 547 and 540 BC, however, Cyrus II conquered western Anatolia; Persian rule was briefly interrupted when Kimon's Athenians appeared in 454 BC and enrolled the Lycians in the Delian League. The Hellenistic era began when Alexander the Great re-expelled the Persians in 333 BC as the cities of Lycia surrendered one by one, some with positive glee. Shortly afterwards, under Ptolemaic rule, the Lycian Federation was reformed, although the native Lycian language died out over the next century, to be replaced by Greek.

In 197 BC Antiokhos III of Syria ejected the Ptolemies; he in turn was defeated by Rome in 189 BC. Awarded to Rhodes, the Lycians rebelled and, within 20 years, the Roman Senate granted the troublesome cities

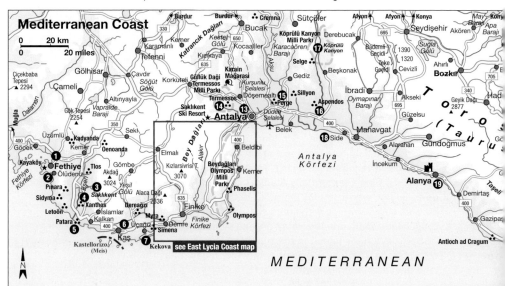

autonomy under a renewed federation. After the Battle of Philippi in 42 BC, victor Mark Antony awarded the territory its freedom, leaving it the only part of Asia Minor not under Roman domination. A century later, Emperor Vespasian (AD 69–79) brought the joint province of Lycia and Pamphylia back under direct Roman control.

Though Lycia became immensely wealthy during the 1st to 3rd centuries, a disastrous earthquake in 241 signalled decline, and after the Arab raids of the 7th and 8th centuries it remained a remote, backward area. Under Ottoman rule the highlands became the realm of *yörük* nomads, whilst the few coastal settlements were inhabited by Greek Orthodox colonists from the islands opposite. Only in the early 1980s was Lycia's spectacular shoreline connected to the rest of the country by proper roads. Now, even the tiny villages have been discovered by outsiders.

FETHIYE AND KADYANDA

At the western edge of Lycia, **Fethiye** ❶ is a growing port and market town tucked between a broad, islet-speckled bay and the foothills of Baba Dağı (the ancient Mount Antikragos). There has been settlement here since the Lycians founded Telmessos, about 2,500 years ago. Byzantine Makri was renamed in 1934 to honour Fethi Bey, a pioneering World War I Ottoman pilot who crashed to his death in Syria. Most of Fethiye – flattened by earthquakes in 1856 and 1957 – is modern, while the Knights of St John extensively quarried antiquities to reinforce the Byzantine castle overhead (open access), so little remains of the ancient city except for some temple-type tombs in the cliff looming above. Best of these is the grandiose **Tomb of Amyntas** (up the steps from Kaya Caddesi; daily 8am–sunset; charge), so identified from a 4th-century BC inscription. The over-restored **Theatre** behind the **tourist office** (İskele Meydanı 1, opposite the main harbour; tel: 0252-614 1527) has been partially excavated, while the worthwhile **museum** (off Atatürk Caddesi; daily June-Sept 8am-7pm, Oct-May 8am-5pm) contains finds from local archaeological sites, including Kaunos and Tlos.

Despite much of the old bazaar having been converted into attractive shops, restaurants and clubs, and a pedestrianised promenade along the working harbour, Fethiye is now more

Choosing henna tattoo designs at Fethiye.

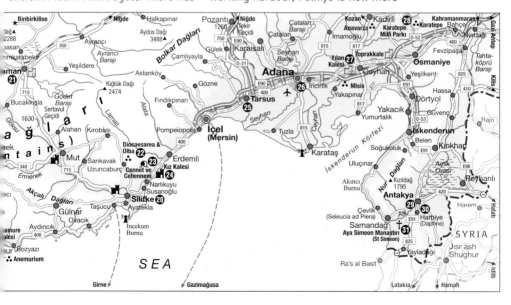

of a shopping centre for nearby resorts rather than a tourist destination in itself. Except for backpackers waiting to board a budget "Blue Cruise", relatively few visitors stay overnight, and the town is increasingly a focus of the area's burgeoning second-home trade.

For more cultural stimulation, head north 21km (13 miles) into the hills, beyond sleepy Üzümlü village, to ancient **Kadyanda** (open access but charge if guard present). Of a similar age to Telmessos, the ruins – which include a **necropolis**, fortifications, a long narrow **stadium** with seats, and a **theatre** – nestle in dense conifer forest, with a self-guiding loop path to take you around the highlights. You can either drive here or trek the old, marked path between the village and the site (90 minutes).

ÖLÜDENIZ AND KAYAKÖY

Fethiye itself has no beaches; the nearest is at **Çalış**, 4km (2.5 miles), a mosquito-friendly, déclassé resort slowly being converted to holiday homes. The area's premier beach, featuring on every second tourist-office poster of Turkey,

Exploring the gorge at Saklıkent.

lies across the peninsula at **Ölüdeniz ❷**, the "Dead Sea", 25km (15 miles) away.

Until the late 1980s, this was one of the Mediterranean's most beautiful hideaways, a cobalt lagoon encircled by platinum sand, with Aleppo pines leaning over the water. But the overlanders' obligatory halt of yore has since become a standard mass-market resort. The entire valley behind less scenic, adjacent **Belceğiz** beach is crammed to capacity with restaurants and hotels, most of the latter dominated by package companies. The environs of the lagoon are a national reserve (dawn to dusk; charge for pedestrians and vehicles), though the narrow spit of land between the lagoon and the open sea is host to either parked cars or sun-loungers. Although Belceğiz promenade is attractively pedestrianised, the crowds may drive one to the undeveloped forest-service beach of **Kıdrak**, or the picturesque beach cove of "Butterfly Valley", an old hippie hideaway served by water-buses.

The eerie ghost town of **Kayaköy** (formerly Levissi; Apr–Oct 8.30am–6.30pm; Nov–Mar 8.30am–5pm; charge) makes

a fascinating excursion, easily reached off the main road between Fethiye and Ölüdeniz, or directly up from Fethiye, starting from the street at the foot of the rock tombs. Kaya was home to about 3,500 Greek Orthodox until the population exchange of 1923. The Macedonian Muslims who arrived to take their place considered the land poor in comparison to what they had left behind, and soon drifted away; thus most of the nearly 600 houses (and three large churches) here – the largest such abandoned town in Asia Minor – stand empty and ruined. Plans to convert them to a holiday village have been thwarted by a strict preservation order, and descendants of the original Greek deportees still return on pilgrimage in significant numbers.

MINOR LYCIAN CITIES – AND SAKLIKENT

Heading east from Fethiye along Highway 400, turn off briefly along Highway 350 towards Korkuteli after 22km (13 miles), and follow signs to ancient **Tlos** (daily 8.30am–dusk; charge). The place was already known to the Hittites during the 14th century BC, and the castle here was inhabited until the 1800s. A tomb at Tlos was found intact with its treasure in late 2005. Ongoing excavations have revealed an early Christian cemetery on the grounds of the evocative **Yedi Kapı baths** with its seven-windowed apse overlooking the valley. The Roman **theatre**, with 34 rows of seats backed against the flanks of Akdağ, has some wonderful stone reliefs amongst the tumbled masonry of the stage building.

Nearby **Saklıkent** ❸ (dawn–dusk; charge), 44km (26 miles) southeast of Fethiye, is a popular retreat from scorching coastal temperatures. This cool, dark gorge emerging from the foothills of Akdağ, about 300 metres (1,000ft) high and 18km (11 miles) long, is impassable to all but the technically equipped after about 2km (1 mile) in (and that's heading downhill, abseiling the many sheer drops). For the rest of us, a boardwalk leads about 150 metres/yds into the gorge to where the Ulupınar springs boil up.

Besides Tlos, other Lycian cities, mostly unexcavated, are tucked away

> **⊙ Fact**
>
> In 1984, French archaeologists found inscriptions spelling out the dress code for visitors to the Letoön. Anyone entering the sanctuary had to wear plain garments and simple shoes. Jewellery, elaborate hairstyles and broad-brimmed hats were banned, as were all weapons.

Ölüdeniz beach.

up side valleys off the main, fertile floodplain of the Esen Çay. **Pınara** (open access; charge when guard present), 47km (29 miles) southeast of Fethiye, was a 4th-century BC colony of Xanthos which then became a prominent member of the Lycian Federation in its own right. Upon leaving Highway 400, fork left after 3km (2 miles), before reaching Minare village, for the final dirt-track approach to the site. The earliest town is built at the top of a sheer cliff honeycombed with Lycian tombs, of which the most interesting is the "**Royal Tomb**" near the ticket booth, with clear reliefs of urban scenes on its porch. The heart of the city, just above, is today jumbled masonry amongst pines, though the **theatre** across the valley is well preserved.

About 12km (7 miles) southwest of the Pınara turning, the scattered remains of **Sidyma** (open access) co-exist with the modern village of Dodurga, much of which has been built with ancient masonry. The main points of interest lie just east, where many free-standing **tombs** of the necropolis,

Pony trekking through Patara's dunes.

square and gabled rather than rotundly "Gothic" as elsewhere, sport marvellous reliefs.

THE LETOÖN

Coming from Sidyma on the old highway, watch for a sign reading "Kumluova, Karadere, Letoön 10" pointing down the correct side road to the compact but more rewarding ruins of the **Letoön** sanctuary (daily Apr–Sept 9am–7pm, Oct–Mar 8am–5pm; charge). Here are three adjacent **temples** dedicated to Leto (a titaness loved by Zeus) and her children, Apollo and Artemis, together the presiding deities of Lycia. French archaeologists have partially reconstructed **Leto's shrine** with stone from the original quarry. Beyond the temples lies a **nymphaeum**, permanently submerged by the high local water-table, and home to frogs, terrapins and ducks. A well-preserved Hellenistic **theatre** has 16 relief masks above the northeast face of the vaulted entrance passage.

XANTHOS

Xanthos ❹, located 1km (0.75 mile) from Highway 400, above the town of Kınık (daily Apr–Sept 8.30am–7.30pm, Oct–Mar 8.30am–5.30pm; charge), was the leading town of Lycia, known for pride so fierce that twice its inhabitants preferred mass suicide rather than surrender to a numerically superior foe. The first time was in 540 BC, when the Persian general Harpagos besieged the acropolis; rather than submit, the men of Xanthos made a funeral pyre with their women, children, slaves and belongings and set it alight. "Then, having sworn to do or die, they marched out to meet the enemy and were killed to a man" said Herodotus – except for eight who were away at the time.

In 42 BC, two years after the murder of Julius Caesar, Brutus besieged Xanthos, but again its citizens chose self-immolation, so that he gained control of an empty city, aside from 150 prisoners taken alive. Following

Mark Antony's victory over Brutus, he rebuilt Xanthos, which became the capital of Roman Lycia.

The site was virtually intact when British explorer Sir Charles Fellows arrived here in 1838. He returned four years later in HMS *Beacon*, whose sailors spent two months carting away the monuments for exhibition in the Lycian Room at the British Museum.

Today, two tombs in front of the theatre, and an inscribed "obelisk" (in fact also a tomb) have become the trademarks of the site. The so-called **Harpy Tomb** takes its name from an early attribution of the reliefs around the top chamber (a plaster cast of the original in London) depicting winged women. They are now thought to be sirens, carrying away the souls of the dead to the Isles of the Blessed. The other is a regular sarcophagus of the 3rd century BC; a relief on the side, now removed, was three centuries older and had apparently been reused.

The **obelisk** stands at the corner of the Roman agora. Mainly inscribed in Lycian, with a few lines of Greek which have allowed tentative deciphering, it recounts the life and times of an unnamed local 5th-century BC hero, cited as the brother of Prince Keriga. East, beyond the "late" (Byzantine) agora, are the remains of a **Byzantine basilica**, which contains superb mosaics in abstract patterns.

PATARA

Patara ⑤ was another powerful Lycian city. Today it is better known for its 12km (7.5-mile) white-sand beach, the longest in Turkey, often with a considerable summer surf. This giant sandpit is as popular with breeding turtles as it is with lounging tourists, and the swamp behind the dunes is a vast archaeological site – thus it is all strictly protected, with most tourist facilities confined to the village of Gelemiş.

To reach Patara (ruins and beach daily Apr–Oct 9am–7pm, Nov–Apr

8am–5pm; charge, ticket valid for one week), follow the signs off Highway 400 9km (5.5 miles) west of Kalkan, or a similar distance from Xanthos; the site begins 5.5km (3.5 miles) from the main road. Patara was supposedly the winter home of the sun god, Apollo, and had an oracle as famous as the one in Delphi. The town was also the birthplace of St Nicholas, better known today as Santa Claus (see page 246). Before the harbour silted up in the Middle Ages, Patara was a prosperous port; now, its ruins are scattered over a vast area of field, dunes or swamp, much of it cleared of vegetation.

At the official entrance stands a triple **monumental arch** (1st century AD), which doubled as part of an aqueduct. Further in, there is a **baths** complex similar to the one at Tlos, and a large paved area, perhaps an **agora**, with many columns re-erected by the excavators. Towards the beach stand the heavily-restored **bouleuterion**, where the Lycian Federation apparently met, and the intact **theatre** (2nd century BC), its stage building partly reconstructed.

⊘ Tip

Five kilometres (3 miles) before Kumluca, where Highway 400 swings northward, continue east along the coastal road for another 20km (12.5 miles) to reach a scenic stretch of the Lycian Way, from Karaöz down to the French-built lighthouse at Gelidonya Burnu, with the Beş Adalar (Five Islands) as a backdrop. From the trailhead beyond Karaöz, it's an hour's round-trip walk to the cape.

The Harpy Tomb at Xanthos.

From the top, there is an excellent view of the other monuments and of the coastline. A boardwalk leads from a car park to the beach, which has a good-value municipally run snack bar employing local people.

FORMER GREEK PORTS

In the decades before the 1923 population exchanges, the base of the Lycian "bulge" was inhabited mainly by Greek traders and fishermen, whose attractive ports still bear traces of those times. Harbourside mosques have been converted from Greek churches by little more than the addition of minarets.

Kalkan has become one of the most sought-after havens in Turkey, its original core of Ottoman-Greek houses overhanging steep, narrow alleys long since swamped by mushrooming suburbs of villas. Nearly half the local population is foreign (and largely British). Sadly, the bohemian ethos and boutique *pansiyons* of the 1980s are largely gone, as second-home ownership has outstripped short-stay tourism; prices and tastes in boutiques, restaurants and bars are pitched at north European wallets and prejudices.

The town's pebble beach is just west of the marina, and the seas around Kalkan are ideal for diving. As with many karstic shorelines, submarine freshwater seeps are common, especially around sea-caves, making the surface much colder than deeper waters.

If it all gets too much at sea level, head 8km (5 miles) inland and uphill to **İslamlar,** which is still known by its Ottoman-Greek name Bodamya (Rivers). Streams, greenery and coolness abound here, as well as a handful of trout-farm restaurants.

A dramatic cliff-hugging route east from Kalkan covers the 27km (17 miles) to Kaş. The main features en route are photogenic, coarse-sand **Kaputaş beach**, 6km (3.5 miles) along, and the nearby **Mavi Mağara**, the second largest sea-cave in the Mediterranean, with Blue Grotto effects inside – bargain hard in Kalkan for a boat-trip there.

Kaş ❻ (107km/64 miles southeast of Fethiye; 181km/109 miles southwest of Antalya) is a more broad-spectrum, congenial resort than Kalkan, still partly retaining its old identity as a county town. Most recent development has scaled the steep hillside behind, or out along the trailing Çukurbağ peninsula to the southwest. Kaş has retained some style at just-affordable prices (partly because of a substantial Turkish clientele), with excellent restaurants, cafés, bars, designer clothing outlets and upmarket boutiques. But as at Kalkan, there are no significant in-town beaches – hotels with swimming pools are much in demand.

Ancient **Antiphellos**, the predecessor of Kaş, began to develop in Hellenistic times and by the Roman period was the region's leading port. Surviving structures include a restored Hellenistic **theatre (open access)**, with the Mediterranean as an astounding backdrop, less than 2km (1 mile) west of town on Necip Bey Caddesi; nearby

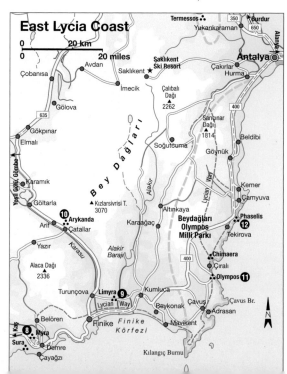

East Lycia Coast

0   20 km
0   20 miles

stands a unique, square Doric tomb, the **Kesme Mezar**. Some neglected, rock-cut **Lycian tombs** can be seen on the cliff-face to the east, while the double-decker **Lion Tomb** stands at the top of Doğruyol Caddesi, a lively pedestrianised street lined with souvenir shops.

The very attractive island of **Meis** (Kastellorizo), immediately opposite Kaş, is the easternmost of the Greek islands, and links between the two places remain strong, as the islanders have always shopped in Kaş whatever the state of relations between Turkey and Greece. Now that both are official ports of entry for their respective countries, crossing or staying overnight is easy – a fast ferry makes the trip twice daily in season.

KEKOVA

The most popular domestic boat trip out of Kaş is to **Kekova inlet** ❼. Alternatively, you can hire a boat in **Üçağız**, 38km (24 miles) east of Kaş; to drive there, turn off Highway 400 after 18km (11 miles). Since the 1980s, tiny Üçağız

has awoken to tourism, most recently through serving as an important halt on the Lycian Way. A day out on the water with a visit to Kekova Island provides an idyllic combination of sunshine, swimming and historic ruins.

Along the margins of Kekova Island facing the mainland lie the submerged remains of a **sunken city** (called Batık Şehir), destroyed in Byzantine times by a vicious earthquake. To protect submarine artefacts, it is strictly forbidden to snorkel or even swim here; your best view underwater will be with a sea-kayaking expedition, organised by adventure agencies in Kaş. At the southwest tip of the island, called Tersane, you're allowed ashore near the almost-vanished remains of a Byzantine apse.

At the east edge of Üçağız is the Lycian necropolis of **Teimiussa**, its "Gothic" chest-type tombs spread out along the shore. Further around the coast, accessible by a longish walk or a more pleasant kayak-paddle or tour-boat-ride, is **Kale** village (ancient Simena). It sits below the crenellated

Souvenirs depicting St Nicholas are sold in Demre.

The rocky coast near Kaş.

One of the carved masks at the ruins of Myra, presumed to be from the frieze belonging to its theatre.

Myra's theatre sits below the cliff containing the carved tombs.

ramparts of a Crusader **castle** (daily 8.30am–sunset; charge), within which is a small Greek theatre, seating 200 people. Kale makes for an idyllic stay, though waterside restaurants – mostly having cut deals with boat tours – are undistinguished. A lone Lycian sarcophagus standing in shallow water nearby lures visitors to pose beside it for photographs.

DEMRE AND MYRA

Demre is a resolutely modern town, marooned in an ugly sea of tomato-growing greenhouses – one of the least attractive, and airless, spots in Lycia, but there are some local attractions which justify it as a day-trip destination.

In the town centre, the **Noel Baba Kilisesi** (Church of St Nicholas; daily Apr–Oct 9am–7pm, Nov–Mar 8am–5pm; charge) is a much-modified Byzantine church on the site where St Nicholas was bishop during the 4th century AD. The church was originally built in the 6th century over his tomb, extended by Constantine IX in 1043 and

again by the Russians in 1862, prior to being recently covered with a hideous protective canopy by Turkish archaeologists. St Nicholas's purported sarcophagus is clearly an earlier pagan affair intended for a couple, and in any case his remains have not been here since 1087, when a band of devout pirates carried them off to Bari, Italy, where the Basilica of San Nicola was built to receive them. A commemorative Mass is held in Demre annually on 6 December, the saint's feast day, although the town tends to be swamped by Russian pilgrims throughout the year.

About 4km (2.5 miles) west of central Demre are the ruins of the ancient Lycian harbour of **Andriake** (daily Apr–Oct 9am–7pm, Nov–Mar 8am–5pm; charge), once an important centre for the production of royal purple dye. Ongoing excavations have revealed a Byzantine church, a synagogue, an agora, a bathhouse and a vast 2nd-century AD Roman granary, built by Hadrian as a central supply depot for the entire empire. The

⊘ SANTA CLAUS

St Nicholas was born in Patara in about AD 270, later becoming bishop of Demre, where he died in 346. He was a leading member of the Church and a delegate to the Council of Nicaea in 325, known both for his immense kindness and the miracles he performed in his lifetime. The link with Father Christmas stems perhaps from two legends: that he cast three bags of gold coins into the home of a merchant who had hit hard times, enabling his daughters to marry, and that he restored to life three boys who had been cut up by a local butcher. The first of these stories is also said to be the origin of the three gold balls that are still used today as the sign of a pawnbroker. Eventually, this busy saint became patron of Greece, Russia, prisoners, thieves, students, sailors, travellers, unmarried girls, merchants, pawnbrokers and children.

The Dutch, who corrupted his name to Sinterklaas (from which came Santa Claus), began to celebrate by filling the children's clogs with presents on the eve (5 December) of his feast. In America, this custom was soon attached to Christmas, and the shoe became a stocking. The jolly man in red with a white beard was the 20th-century invention of the Coca-Cola company – one of their most enduring advertising campaigns.

structure now houses a fine **museum** filled with regional finds. Just to the west, the small marina of **Cayağzı** (or rather its keen boatmen) pitches itself as an alternative departure point for Kekova, featuring a smattering of cafés and restaurants overlooking the water. The beach here, however, is easily bested by that of nearby Sülüklü, reached by a separate road heading west from the museum.

Myra ❽ (daily Apr–Oct 8.30am– 7.30pm, Nov–Mar 8.30am–5.30pm; charge), 2km (1.25 miles) north of the town centre, was founded in the 5th century BC. It grew into one of the most important cities in the Lycian League, and later into a Christian bishopric, visited by, among others, St Paul. Unlike most Lycian cities, it survived in some form until the 1300s.

Myra has some of the finest Lycian cliff-tombs (closed), many with "log-cabin" features carved into the rock – presumably reflecting domestic architecture of the period. The carvings are mostly in poor repair, but the overall effect of this stacked architecture of death is dramatic. The Roman-era city below the cliff is dominated by a large theatre, whose seating and access tunnels are intact, but part of its stage building has collapsed. However, many relief carvings and inscriptions are still visible, in particular a macabre set of comedy and tragedy masks, presumably from the frieze. Visit as early as possible in the day to catch the morning sunlight on the cliff – and avoid enormous coached-in crowds.

INTO THE MOUNTAINS

Finike (ancient Phoenike) is now a somewhat nondescript port, the usual terminus for *gulet* cruises east from Fethiye, but mostly a market town for local citrus and tomato growers. In history, it figures mainly as the site of the "**Battle of the Masts**" in 655, the first major naval victory of the Muslim Arabs over the Byzantines. Finike also

marks the start of Highway 635, one of the few roads to cross the Taurus Mountains into inland Lycia, offering a spectacularly beautiful excursion, taking in ancient Limyra and Arykanda en route to Elmalı.

After 5km (3 miles) along the 635, **Limyra** ❾ (open access) will be signed a kilometre (0.6 miles) off the road to the right. This was the 4th-century BC capital of Pericles, ruler of a section of Lycia. His tomb, the **Heroön**, topped the highest point of the most extensive necropolis in Lycia; its elaborate carvings are now in Antalya Museum. It is a steep 40-minute climb up, but the views are astounding. Less energetic visitors may content themselves with the freestanding 4th-century BC **Tomb of Xatabura** near the theatre, with reliefs of a funeral banquet and the judgement of the deceased. Regrettably, long after sporadic Austrian excavations, the site is now neglected and poorly labelled.

Return to the main road for a further 28km (18 miles) to the mountain hamlet of Arif and the stunning ruins of

⊘ Tip

Despite easy access from the highway, Arykanda – certainly among the most picturesque of ancient Lycian cities – remains among the least visited. When visiting during the off-season you're likely to have the ruins all to yourself.

Inside Noel Baba Kilisesi in Demre.

Take the cable car from the resort of Kemer to ascend 2,365 metres (7,757 ft) to Tahtalı mountain's summit.

Olympos' beach is part of the Beydağlari Olympos National Park.

Arykanda  (daily Apr–Sept 8.30am–7.30pm, Oct–Mar 8.30am–5.30pm; charge), whose setting has justifiably been compared to Delphi in Greece, overlooking as it does a deep valley between two high mountain ranges. Just above the tiny car park, a **basilica** has fine mosaic floors, including a medallion with two birds. Nearby is an impressive **baths** complex standing 10 metres (33ft) high at the façade, with windows over two storeys and a plunge-pool still visible inside. Uphill from here, one of several "**monumental tombs**" was adapted as a church early in the Christian era. Heading back west across the ravine which divides the site, you'll find the Roman imperial **agora** with its clumsily restored **odeon**, plus an impressive **theatre**, attractive **stadium** and sizable **villa** nearby.

The main road continues north, past seasonal **Avlan Gölü**, over fertile agricultural upland devoted to apples, potatoes and sugar beets, to the market town of **Elmalı**, at the foot of 2,459-metre (8,068ft) Elmalı Dağ. The town has an externally tiled 17th-century mosque and a few dilapidated but once-elegant timber-framed Ottoman mansions, but is mostly the location for a choice in onward itinerary.

Heading southwest towards Kaş also takes you through **Gömbe**, which makes a better lunch-stop (or overnight base) than Elmalı. This is also the turn-off point for expeditions west to scenic, limpid **Yeşil Göl** (Green Lake), the only such body of water in the Akdağ massif. It's best visited in spring just after snowmelt, for the vivid wildflower displays. You'll need local directions and preferably a 4WD vehicle to get within a short walk of Yeşil Göl.

Going west instead from Elmalı towards Fethiye, the minor road northwest, then west, is very scenic and passable to all cars, except in winter when the Göğübeli pass is snowed up. After about an hour's drive, just before meeting Highway 350, you'll pass the side turning to İncealiler, "gateway" village to the extensive remains of ancient **Oenoanda**, one of the last founded (2nd century BC) and highest (1,400 metres/4,600ft) Lycian towns. Despite the willingness of foreign teams, no full-scale excavation has yet been allowed, though several hundred stone fragments recovered from the site – inscriptions by Diogenes outlining the philosophy of Epicurus – have drawn significant scholarly attention in recent years. The 45-minute path-walk up from İncealiler will give you a taste of what visiting Lycian ruins was like 30 years ago. Peeking out amongst the pines on the ridge are necropolis tombs, a massive **aqueduct**, an equally massive Hellenistic **city wall** with towers and windows, and jumbled civic buildings flanking the presumed **agora** inside. You're unlikely to meet another living soul except for the odd hunter, browsing goat or red squirrel.

THE OLYMPIC COAST

East from Finike, the first place on the coast (besides Gelidonya Burnu) likely to prompt a stop is **Adrasan**, the beach "suburb" of Çavuş village, where a river lazily meets the sea at a long, sand-and-pebble beach overlooked by pyramidal Musa Dağı. It's popular amongst Brits and Turks, with a scuba-dive outfitter and boat trips along the rugged coast to the otherwise inaccessible cove of Ceneviz Limanı and to the island of Suluada.

From Adrasan, it's an easy drive north 16km (10 miles) along a secondary road to ancient **Olympos** ⓫ (daily Apr–Sept 8.30am–7.30pm, Oct–Mar 8.30am–5.30pm; charge), with the final landward approach through one of the largest backpackers' hang-outs in Turkey, a succession of wood-built "**treehouses**" – at their busiest before or after Gallipoli's ANZAC Day. Stream and valley exit to the sea through the ruins, most of them unlabelled and overgrown in tropical profusion, but the determined can find a monumental Roman **portal**, an arcaded **warehouse**, a Byzantine **aqueduct** and various tombs. The far end, guarded by Byzantine-Genoese fortifications, marks the start of an excellent, long sand-and-pebble beach.

Drivers will need to retrace their steps and access this beach by a different road descending from Highway 400 to **Çıralı**, the burgeoning if still somewhat "alternative" resort. Being part of the **Beydağları Olympos Milli Parkı**, threaded along its entire length by the Lycian Way, and also a sea-turtle hatching ground, means that development here is (theoretically) limited and must be set well back from the beach. The only local cultural diversion is the **Chimaera** (Yanartaş; open access but charge), a 20-minute walk slightly uphill from Çıralı's 100-plus *pansiyons*. The Chimaera is a cluster of unquenchable flames which have burnt since antiquity, when it was the heart of a sanctuary to Hephaestos (Vulcan), god of fire. The flares – fed by a unique mix of gases issuing through tiny fissures – are best seen at dusk.

Phaselis ⓬ (daily 8am–7pm; charge) is the most accessible Lycian site, some 33km (21 miles) north of Çıralı, just off Highway 400. Set on a wooded peninsula between three bays, all used as harbours in antiquity and now serving as beaches, it's predictably popular with both bus- and boat-tours. Founded in the 7th century BC by Rhodian colonists, the city had a reputation for unscrupulousness and sycophancy; Emperor Hadrian's visit here in AD 129 prompted the construction of a massive gate at the big-beach end of the main **paved avenue** through the city's heart.

Aside from Phaselis, there is little of interest between Çıralı and Antalya along the increasingly broad and busy Highway 400. The one sizeable port, Kemer, long ago lost any intrinsic charm to overbuilding, and neither will the all-inclusive resorts at Tekirova, Çamyuva, Göynük and Beldibi appeal to casual passers-by.

○ **Tip**

Bring a picnic (as well as beach gear) to Phaselis as snack-caravans here are inconveniently placed and expensive.

Chimaera flames.

📷 PLANTS AND WILDLIFE

Populated by both European and Asian species, the mountains, plateaux and coastal regions of Turkey are home to a rich variety of plant and animal life.

Turkey's flora and fauna draws on two continents – Anatolia lies at the western limit of many Asian plant and animal species, while familiar European species are much in evidence across the country. Most of the natural forest cover disappeared centuries ago, but rich stands of woodland survive in certain mountain areas: this varies from the evergreen species (mostly Aleppo pine) which covers Mediterranean- and Aegean-facing foothills to the dense broadleaf forest of the wetter Black Sea mountains. The austere interior is transformed in May and June when the landscape is carpeted in a beautiful array of wild flowers.

All the Eurasian land-mammal families are amply represented, from bats and various rodents on up to mountain goats, brown bear and grey wolf. European species such as wild boar and weasels co-exist with more exotic wildlife such as jackals, the caracal (Persian lynx), and even a few leopards in the more remote parts of the Taurus mountains. The Asiatic lion became extinct in Turkey in the late 19th century (the only wild population is now in India).

The Mediterranean and Aegean support rich marine life, particularly in areas close to nutrient-bearing river mouths. Dolphins are still often spotted, while sea turtles lay eggs on less developed Mediterranean beaches.

Conservation efforts include over 70 national parks and reserves, and the activities of organisations like the Doğal Hayatı Koruma Derneği (the local affiliate of WWF). Forests are strictly protected but wildfires are a problem in many areas.

A bee orchid (Ophrys lutea ssp. galilaea)

Sea turtle swimming near the Aydıncık coast in far-eastern Turkey. Turkey claims around 20 nesting beaches of the globally threatened sea turtle Caretta Caretta.

A mouflon, a species of mountain sheep relatively widespread in the east of the country, with a smaller population in the central Taurus Mountains in southern Turkey.

Dalmatian pelicans in the Gediz estuary; their numbers have swelled in recent decades.

Bird-Haunted Wetlands

Turkey's numerous wetlands act as permanent avian habitats, or vital rest-stops and breeding grounds for birds migrating during spring or autumn between east Africa or the Middle East, and the Balkans. Such environments consist of coastal river deltas, or swamps and lake margins of the interior; many are threatened by illegal construction or reclamation for agricultural use. One safe locale is Kuş Cenneti (Bird Paradise) at Manyas Gölü near Bursa, where up to 3 million migrators alight in a good year. Over 270 species have been recorded, including pelicans, storks, herons, spoonbills and spotted eagles. Another, well inland just southeast of Erciyes Dağı, is the Sultansazlığı, a 2,000-hectare (5,000 acre) complex of saline lake and freshwater marsh and reedbed which boasts a similarly broad profile of bird residents. The advent of irrigation here proved initially a disaster, though upgrades to the system have seen the water table rise to previous levels again. Equal to either is the Aegean-coast bird sanctuary at Çiğli-Sasallı near İzmir, comprising saltpans in the former delta of the Gediz River, which hosts kestrels, plovers, terns, stilts and avocets. On the Mediterranean, the deltas of the Göksu and Tarsus streams are home to black francolin, Smyrna kingfisher and Audouin's gull.

'ild poppies, as here at Pergamon, bring a vivid splash of :olour to the Anatolian countryside in late spring.

'ild echinops (globe thistle, a common garden plant in 'urope) on the Anatolian plateau.

As in much of Europe, white storks are thought to bring good fortune; their huge nests atop telegraph poles or chimneys are a feature of many Turkish villages.

The Roman amphitheatre at Aspendos.

PAMPHYLIA

Less proud and more pragmatic than Lycia, Pamphylia was happy to cooperate with Alexander and the Romans, assuring itself a good share of the conquerors' largesse.

The broad and fertile Pamphylian Plain, bound by the blue waters of the Mediterranean to the south and the sculpted limestone peaks of the Taurus range to the west and north, possesses a rare natural beauty. This fertile region flourished in the Graeco-Roman period, and the wealthy cities which once blossomed along this coast are now a wonderfully preserved collection of ruins for the visitor to explore. The region is booming as the sea, sun and sand tourism capital of Turkey, with over 12 million tourists passing annually through Antalya airport, the country's busiest outside of Istanbul. The downside, as ever, is overdevelopment, with much of the shoreline between Antalya and Alanya now lined with lookalike hotels, apartments and golf-courses.

ANTALYA

The hub of Turkey's Mediterranean coast is **Antalya** ⑬ (ancient Attaleia). Turkey's fastest-growing city, its population has swelled from around 30,000 in the 1950s to over a million today. Although much of the city is now a jumble of high-rise apartment blocks, offices and hotels, its location – overlooking the startlingly blue waters of the Gulf of Antalya to the saw-tooth line of the misty purple Taurus Mountains – remains stunning. The central walled old quarter is ranged prettily around a tiny harbour at the foot of the

Antalya's Konyaaltı beach.

cliffs, and the city has several lovely park areas, bringing welcome relief in the long, hot summers. It's even possible to swim and sunbathe right in the heart of the city. Despite its rapid development, the places of interest to a visitor are all very central, and it makes a great base to see the surrounding sights, amongst the finest in the country.

Antalya was founded in 158 BC by King Attalus II of Pergamon and bequeathed to Rome in 133 BC. Although badly battered by the Arab invasions of the 7th century, it remained

Main attractions

Antalya Archaeological Museum
Termessos ruins and national park
Ancient Perge
The Roman theatre at Aspendos
Trekking on St Paul's Trail
The old town of Side

Maps on pages 238, 254

The Saat Kulesi (Clock Tower) marks the entrance to Kaleiçi, Antalya's old quarter.

in Byzantine hands until the Seljuks arrived in 1206, and was a regular staging post for Crusaders on their way to the Holy Land. In the 1390s, control was handed to the Ottomans and remained with them until the area was occupied by Italy in 1919. Three years later, it was returned to Turkey.

KALEIÇI, THE OLD TOWN

The heart of Antalya is the beautifully restored walled old quarter known as **Kaleiçi A** (inside the castle). The harbour here is filled with wooden leisure craft which ferry tourists out along the foot of the pocked-limestone cliffs on which the city stands, while the alleyways radiating out from the water's edge are lined with alfresco seafood restaurants and cafés along with a veritable swarm of souvenir shops, pensions and boutique hotels. Walking around the old town on a balmy summer's evening is a delight, with bougainvillea spreading in a riot of purple over the stone and timber fronts of Ottoman-era town houses, and the scent of jasmine sweet in the air. Be

warned, though: everyone wants to sell you something, whether it's a boat tour or a carpet, a glass of freshly squeezed orange juice or a meerschaum pipe, so come prepared with your thickest skin.

Before plunging into the mayhem of the old walled city, pause for a moment beside the equine **Atatürk Heykeli B** (Monument) in Cumhuriyet Square. The bronze statue itself is impressive but, more importantly, it offers the best vantage point in the city. Just to the left, the fortified **Saat Kulesi** (Clock Tower) at Kalekapısı, built in 1244 as an integral part of the city's defences, marks the entrance to the old town. Beside it is the 18th-century **Mehmet Paşa Camii**, with its typically Ottoman dome and slender, cylindrical minarets. Opposite, to the north across the tram track, is a bustling bazaar, mainly given over to fake designer clothing and football shirts, though part of it is devoted, more traditionally, to gold.

Just west of the Mehmet Paşa Camii is the **Yivli Minare C** (Fluted Minaret). Antalya's most photographed building, it provides a magnificent foreground

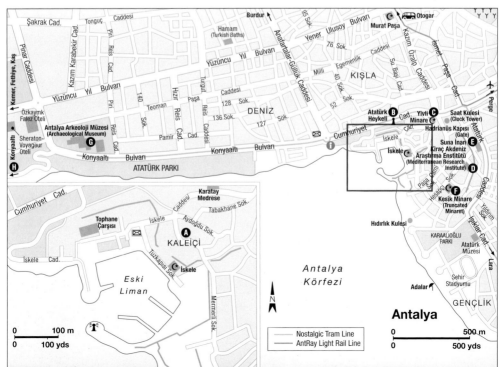

for the panorama across the bay to the mountains, especially at sunset. It's also the symbol of Antalya and its oldest Seljuk monument, dating from the reign of Sultan Alâeddin Keykubat I (1219–38). Exquisite turquoise-and-blue tiles are set into the 8-metre (26ft)-high minaret, while the pool in front is of marble. Close by is a simple and elegant 14th-century octagonal *türbe* (tomb), made of fine white masonry in the tradition of Central Asian Turks. The large whitewashed building to the side was formerly a dervish convent. Carry on down the hill and you reach the elaborately carved entrance of the **Karatay Medrese**, a religious school built by a Seljuk vizier in 1250. Right on the harbour front and housed in a 19th century Greek warehouse is the Oyuncak Müzesi (Toy Museum; Tue–Sun 9am–6pm; charge). Inside are myriad retro-favourites, including tin-toys and Barbie dolls.

Within the maze of alleys overhung by wooden-frame houses, best reached from Atatürk Caddesi, two Ottoman mansions and the Greek church of Agios Georgios have been turned

into the **Suna-İnan Kiraç Akdeniz Araştırma Enstitütü D** (Mediterranean Research Institute; Kocatepe Sok 25; http://akmed.ku.edu.tr; Thu–Tue 9am–6pm; charge). The Greek church houses a permanent exhibition of Çanakkale pottery, while the building in front of it is a loving re-creation of a 19th-century Ottoman house, with a series of rooms decked out in period style, complete with lifelike mannequins. Directly opposite across the narrow street, the other courtyard house is home to a fine collection of books and documents detailing the rich archaeology and history of the region.

A few blocks further north is **Hadrian's Gate E** (known as Üçkapılar to Turks), a stately triple-arched structure of white marble, built in honour of the emperor's visit in AD 130. Step through it to re-enter the modern world of **Atatürk Caddesi**, a palm-tree-lined street enlivened by the ringing bell of the passing period tram and a constantly changing series of clothes shops, restaurants and cafés. Head south down Atatürk Caddesi to **Karaalioğlu Parkı**, atop the

The fortified harbour at Kaleiçi.

⊙ Tip

It's possible to swim right in the centre of big city Antalya, useful to know if you're staying in the pretty old town of Kaleiçi. Just head to Karaalioğlu Park for the Adalar Beach Club, which features a decked wooden area at the foot of the cliff. Mermerli is below the Mermerli Restaurant in Kaleiçi, and boasts a small sandy beach. Both have moderate admission charges.

cliffs to the east of the harbour, a peaceful shady park ideal for sitting out the heat of the day.

On the clifftops above the harbour stand the old city walls and ramparts built by the Greeks and restored by the Romans and Seljuks. Here, just outside the park and back in Kaleiçi, is the 13.5-metre (44ft) **Hıdırlık Kulesi**. The sombre lower square section is believed to have been a Hellenic tomb, while the tower itself was built by the Romans in the 2nd century AD, possibly as a lighthouse, and adapted by the Seljuks for defence. From here a marble-clad street leads back into the old town to the **Kesik Minare ⑤**, where a truncated minaret is all that remains of a 13th-century mosque that was struck by lightning in 1851. Originally a 5th-century church dedicated to the Virgin Mary, it was constructed using 2nd- and 3rd-century spoils.

THE ARCHAEOLOGICAL MUSEUM

The **Antalya Arkeoloji Müzesi ⑤** (Archaeological Museum; 8.30am–5.30pm; charge) is one of the finest in Turkey. It is located 2km (1.5 miles) west of the town centre, and easily reached from the Old Town by the period tram.

Most of the finds come from the surrounding area, spanning several millennia of prehistory from the Karain Caves, Bronze-Age jewellery and toys from Elmalı, and exquisite Classical statuary from Perge and Aspendos, beautifully displayed in the Perge Gallery. The Hall of the Gods displays statues of the Greek gods, Emperors Hadrian and Septimius Severus and their empresses, while the Sarcophagus Gallery contains – among plentiful stone sarcophagi – the elaborate Sarcophagus of Hercules, returned to Turkey in 2017 after a half-century sojourn in Switzerland, as well as the tomb of a much-loved dog, Stephanos. Other exhibits include part of a stunning mosaic collection from Xanthos depicting the infant Achilles being dangled by his mother into the River Styx. A display of icons includes the familiar portrait of St Nicholas and a box which once contained his "relics". Facing it is a superb collection of 6th-century church silver, part of

Sarcophagus from the ancient city of Perge at Antalya's Archaeological Museum.

which was looted and ended up in Dumbarton Oaks Museum, Washington. There is also a broad-based ethnographic collection with displays on Turkish lifestyle, dress, musical instruments and carpets.

KONYAALTI BEACH

To the west of the city is the pebbly 3km (2-mile) -long **Konyaaltı Beach Ⓗ**, providing Antalya with an attractive seafront, with several of its finest hotels and a number of good restaurants. Beach Park, at the eastern end of the beach, is a dedicated leisure area with bars, nightclubs, restaurants and cafés in abundance. On the cliff top above is Antalya Aquarium (daily 10am–8pm; charge), which claims to be the world's longest tunnel aquarium. Opposite, in the grounds of the **AKM Culture Park**, is a very popular water park, equipped with various water slides and rides. Also here is the **Cam Pyramit** (Glass Pyramid), a concert venue, and, next to it, the **AKM Cultural Centre** which hosts, amongst other events, Antalya's annual Altın Portakal (Golden Orange) international film festival.

Many of Antalya's mass-market hotels march in serried ranks along the cliff tops of **Lara**. This area, stretching for about 15km (9 miles) east of the city, has become an entire suburb of monolithic hotels and holiday apartments. Many have steep staircases down the cliff to private swimming platforms. Beyond the cliffs is Lara beach, a moderately attractive public bathing strip which, unlike Konyaaltı, boasts a beach which is both sandy and shelves gently into the sea.

NORTH AND EAST OF THE CITY

Tucked away in the lofty mountains northeast of Antalya is a small ski resort, **Saklıkent** (Hidden City), which – in a good season – offers reasonable skiing from early January through to the end of March. It takes around an hour and half to drive to 50km (30 miles) from the city centre, more or less at sea level, to an altitude of 1,800 metres (5,900ft).

The ancients had a taste for inland vistas, and the plateau behind Antalya, a separate ancient kingdom known as Pisidia, is as studded with ruins as the

Turkish lokum, also known as Turkish Delight, can be found in flavours other than the original rosewater, such as chocolate, almond, orange, pistachio and walnut.

The dramatic setting of the Termessos theatre.

Antalya is home to several quarries. These onyx vases and dishes for sale at Perge make typical gifts from the region.

White-water rafting in Köprülü Kanyon.

shores of the Mediterranean. One of the most remarkable of these inland sites is **Termessos** (daily Apr–Oct 8.30am–7.30pm, Nov–Mar 8am–5pm; charge), set in the beautiful **Güllük Dağı Termessos National Park** (same hours as site; separate charge) high in the mountains 37km (22 miles) northeast of Antalya. It is accessed off the D-350 to Korkuteli. The car park is about 9km (5.5 miles) along a forest road; there is then a steep 2km (1.5-mile) walk to the site. There are no refreshments, so you'll need to bring your own.

The hilltop location and formidable defensive walls of this Pisidian city so daunted Alexander the Great in 333 BC that he abandoned his siege, torched the local olive groves and slunk away.

The origin of Termessos is uncertain, but the founders, who called themselves the Solymians, are identified with the Pisidians who occupied the lake district around Burdur and Eğirdir further north. They called their city the "Eagle's Nest" with good reason. It is perched between summits at about 900 metres (3,000ft), and the views to the coast and across the mountains are magnificent. The ruins are also fascinating. The superb theatre, the most dramatically situated in Turkey, is the high point of any visit to the site, staring across a narrow canyon to rugged Güllük Dağı (Rose Mountain). Other remains include an agora, a gymnasium, an odeon and five enormous water cisterns carved into the rock. Dozens of stone sarcophagi climb the hillside to the fire-watch tower above. On the way back down to the car park don't miss the tombs, some displaying mock-temple relief-carved façades, cut from the cliff face.

The caves of **Karain Mağarası** (daily 8.30am–5pm; charge) are 27km (16 miles) northwest of Antalya, off the D-650 to Burdur, about 6km (4 miles) from the main road. Finds from these remarkable caves go back to the Palaeolithic (Old Stone Age), some 30,000 years ago. People are thought to have lived here for nearly 20,000 years, and excavation has yielded tools, axes and other crude implements, the skull of a Neanderthal child, and the bones of an ancient elephant, hippopotamus and bear. Most are on display in Antalya and Ankara, but there is a small on-site museum.

The limestone country around Antalya is riddled with waterfalls, of which the most famous are the **Düden Şelalesi**, two separate cascades on a powerful underground river. The Upper Falls, which have carved out a pretty gorge 14km (9 miles) northeast of town, are a popular local picnic spot. Much more spectacular, albeit backed by drab ranks of high-rise blocks, are the 20-metre (65ft) -high Lower Düden Falls, which crash over the cliff into the sea in the Antalya suburb of Lara. They are best seen from one of the many boat trips leaving from Antalya harbour.

The **Kurşunlu Şelalesi**, about 23km (14 miles) east of Antalya (7km/4.5 miles off the main road), are even more popular because of their proximity to Perge and Aspendos. The unusual green-coloured water is surrounded

by walkways, picnic tables, a children's playground and souvenir stalls.

PERGE AND SILLYON

The most impressive ruins on the Pamphylian coast are at **Perge** ⓫ (daily Apr–Oct 9am–7pm, Nov–Mar 8am–5pm; charge), some 15km (9 miles) east of Antalya along the D-400 (also easily reached by the AntRay light rail line from the city centre). Known to the Hittites as far back as 1300 BC, the city was a successful trading centre, which kept itself alive and healthy through pragmatism – it had no defensive walls until fortified by the Seleucids in the 2nd century BC. Alexander the Great was welcomed in, and used the city as a base throughout his Anatolian campaigns. Perge finally declined during the Byzantine era when the river silted up, stranding the port 12km (7 miles) from the sea.

The red **Hellenistic Gate** towers still stand close to their original height, but most of "modern" Perge – the stadium, bathhouses, 14,000-seat theatre (on which extensive restoration works were launched in 2018) and colonnaded street – belongs to the period of *Pax Romana*. The resplendent **agora** dates from the 4th century AD. The **stadium** (234 metres/775ft long and 34 metres/110ft wide, with seating for 12,000) is one of the best-preserved of the ancient world. Of its 30 outward-facing chambers, 20 were used as shops; several wall inscriptions reveal the names of their proprietors as well as their trade.

The magnificent finds from this ancient city on display in the Antalya Archaeological Museum include numerous sarcophagi along with colossal statues of gods and emperors. One name that crops up frequently on the bases of statues is that of a woman, Plancia Magna. She was the daughter of the governor and a priestess of Artemis, goddess of the moon and patron of the city, in the 2nd century AD. Her legacy contributed approximately 20 statues to the city; her tomb, or what remains of it, is situated just outside one of the city gates.

To reach **Sillyon** (open access; guide recommended), turn left off the D-400 7km (4 miles) east of Perge and follow the road for 8km (5 miles) before

⊙ Fact

Perge was where St Paul set off on his first proselytising journey in AD 46, heading north from the prosperous city to cross the formidable barrier of the Taurus Mountains en route to Antioch in Pisidia, high on the Anatolian plateau.

⊙ ST PAUL'S TRAIL

The St Paul's Trail is a superb, way-marked long-distance walking route inspired by the 1st-century AD missionary travels of St Paul. Starting in either Perge or nearby Aspendos, spectacular Graeco-Roman sites set on the rich Pamphylian Plain, twin paths snake their way over the southern spurs of the mighty Taurus Mountains before joining at the remote, peak-ringed ancient city of Adada. Now a single path, the route forges north through pine forest, along gorges and over high mountain passes to the beautiful blue expanse of Lake Eğirdir, Turkey's largest fresh-water lake. Curling around the mountainous western shore of the lake, the route finally strikes across the rolling Anatolian plateau to Antioch in Pisidia, where St Paul first preached to the gentiles.

Düden Şelalesi (Düden Falls).

> ⏻ Tip

The ancient theatre at Aspendos hosts an annual opera and ballet festival (usually the first three weeks in September), with a prestigious mix of Turkish and foreign companies. Tickets are reasonably priced, performances on balmy evenings spectacular.

climbing the steep unmarked track to the site. The flat-topped acropolis was once the site of a city as old and rich as Perge (but never conquered by Alexander). Beware of tumbling into one of the hidden cisterns when exploring. Sadly, its ruins were badly damaged during a series of landslides in 1969, and today it is usually ignored in favour of its more spectacular neighbours.

ASPENDOS

Some 45km (25 miles) east of Antalya and 5km (3 miles) off the main road, imposing **Aspendos** ⑯ (daily Apr–Oct 9am–7pm, Nov–Mar 8am–5pm; charge) is graced by one of the finest surviving Roman **theatres** in the world. Built during the reign of Emperor Marcus Aurelius (AD161–80) and seating 15,000 people, the elaborate structure is almost intact, the exception being part of the upper cornice. It is still used for concerts today (see margin). Its architect was Xeno, a local lad whose formula for creating perfect acoustics remains something of a mystery – a coin dropped from the orchestra pit

can be heard distinctly from the galleries. The Seljuks used the theatre as a *kervansaray* in the 13th century; on Atatürk's suggestion it was later used for oil wrestling. For 1,800 years it has withstood earthquakes, the ravages of war, the weather and the march of time.

Behind the theatre lie the ruins of the acropolis, agora, nymphaeum, and what is one of the best surviving examples of an aqueduct from the Roman world. The annals inform us that the river was navigable as far as Aspendos and the city was used as a naval base, improbable though this seems today, as the site is 12km (8 miles) from the sea. It certainly prospered from trading luxury goods, a tradition kept up by local shopkeepers today.

The fast-growing, purpose-built coastal resort of **Belek** is only a stone's throw from Antalya airport. It has a wonderful white-sand beach, currently shared by a burgeoning line of seriously upmarket resort hotels and some rather beleaguered turtles, while inland is a growing sea of cheap apartment blocks and largely anonymous "all-inclusive"

Camel rides are available on Side's eastern beaches.

hotels catering to their mass-market clientele. There is also an ever-increasing number of golf courses.

KÖPRÜLÜ KANYON

A short distance beyond Aspendos, a tarmac road cuts off the main coastal highway and leads up to the beautiful, cool, green **Köprülü Kanyon** ⑰, a high mountain gorge sliced by the tumbling milky turquoise Köprülü Çayı (Eurymedon River). The river has become very popular for white-water rafting, with literally thousands of people a day riding the (by rafting standards fairly tame) bubbling torrent. The journey to **Beşkonak** village, reached after 43km (26 miles), is more life-threatening than the rafting because of the numerous tourist coaches speeding recklessly along the narrow, winding road. The plethora of waterside restaurants at Beşkonak exists largely to feed the white-water rafting hordes. Beyond the town, a dramatic Roman bridge spans the canyon.

A paved road leads a further 14km (9 miles) up from the canyon across a high plateau, its soft volcanic rock carved and twisted into columns ("fairy chimneys" redolent of those in Cappadocia) by the wind, to the village of **Altınkaya** (Zerk) and the ruins of ancient **Selge** (open access). Very little remains aside from the magnificent Greek-style theatre with a backdrop of snowcapped peaks. The stadium has been turned into a terraced field for one of the local families. The Roman road, forum, Byzantine basilica and twin temples to Artemis and Zeus are more imagination than fact. Locals will often offer to guide you to the few remains of the ancient town's reliefs and statues, hidden in rock slides and undergrowth.

SIDE: OLD CROWDS AND NEW

Although founded as long ago as the 7th century BC, the atmospheric town of **Side** ⑱ has undergone its most startling transformation since the 1970s, when it was a sleepy fishing village. Many of today's *pansiyon* and restaurant owners were yesterday's fishermen who have lost interest in the humble hook and line. Blessed

Bars and shops in Side.

with good beaches either side of the peninsula on which it stands, evocative Roman and Byzantine ruins and a charming old town, tourism has become big business here. Yet despite the plethora of hotels, restaurants, discos, bars and carpet, designer clothing and jewellery shops, Side retains its charm as a living open-air museum in a spectacular setting.

Side (meaning "pomegranate" in Anatolian) is no stranger to crowds. With a population of some 60,000 in the Hellenistic era, it was the largest, richest port on the south coast, with an unsavoury reputation. Rampant piracy flourished, with prisoners sold as slaves in the town agora then sent to the island of Delos, a notorious depot for human merchandise in antiquity. Alexander the Great's biographer Arrian recorded that when his master captured the city in 333 BC, its people spoke a tongue unknown to the invaders – in fact it remains undeciphered to this day. Ancient Side declined in the 7th century under relentless Arab attacks, and

was finally abandoned in 1150 after earthquakes, too, had taken their toll.

The incoming road follows the line of the original ancient street, and is lined with the ruins of Roman shops. On the left, in front of the massive bulk of the theatre, are the extensive remains of the **agora**; beyond it is a mass of dunes backing an attractive beach. The 20,000-seat **Theatre** (daily 8am–7.30pm; charge) is one of the most impressive Roman structures in Turkey, and is now home to an annual music, opera and ballet festival held each September.

Across the road from the agora and theatre, the old **Roman Baths** now house the town **museum** (daily Apr–Oct 9am–7pm, Nov–Mar 8am–5pm; charge), displaying finds from local excavations, including many fine, albeit headless, statues; St Paul was so convincing as a speaker that the newly converted Christians rushed out and, in a fit of wild overenthusiasm, decapitated their former pagan deities. In fact, Side served as a bishopric in the Byzantine period, and many of the monuments lying in such profusion around the village are relics of the early Christian era.

Running the gauntlet of importuning restaurateurs and souvenir shop salesmen, make your way through the pretty old town to the twin **Temples of Apollo and Athena**. There's little remaining bar a few re-erected columns topped by Corinthian capitals and a section of pediment, but its setting (especially at sunset) on the rocky headland is dramatic.

Neighbouring **Manavgat** is a bustling business and farming community. Monday is market day and a good opportunity to buy the local crafts, old coins or rugs found among the fruit, vegetables and squawking chickens. The only other reason to visit the town is for an excursion by boat up the river to the pleasant, if unspectacular, **Manavgat Şelalesi** (Manavgat Falls).

The Red Tower's battlements provide a fine view of Alanya's harbour.

Boats leave from Side or – better value and quicker – from the quay beside the main bridge in town. Natural vegetation forms a tropical curtain over the Manavgat River.

A few kilometres on, a yellow sign points up a scenic road to **Alarahan**, a well-preserved and atmospheric Seljuk *kervansaray* on the banks of the Alara River, constructed in 1231 by Sultan Alâeddin Keykubat I. On a rocky crag above sits **Alara Castle**, its fortress wall running crazily along the summit, a long tunnel leading down through the mountain to the river.

ALANYA

Ever-expanding **Alanya** ⓳, 110km (70 miles) east of similarly named Antalya, sprawls along two broad bays as one of Turkey's most popular resorts. The city centre is sliced emphatically in two by a magnificent 250-metre (800ft) -high rocky promontory jutting out into the Mediterranean. On the summit, nearly 7km (4 miles) of ancient curtain walls with 150 bastions wind around three towers, forming the most spectacular and effective fortress on the Turkish coast. There are dizzying views of the sea on three sides, and the orchard-covered foothills of the Taurus behind. Alanya's winter climate is particularly mild, its setting superb, beaches extensive and location – just a couple of hours' drive from busy Antalya airport – very convenient, so it's no surprise that it has a huge population of foreign second-homers from northern Europe.

Although the exact foundation date of Alanya is unknown, the city traces its history back to Hellenistic times, when it was named Coracesium, with the Romans, Byzantines, Armenians, Seljuks and Ottomans all taking their turn at power. Pirate chieftain Diototus Tryphon built his fortress on the peak in the 2nd century BC. The Roman general Pompey fought a notable sea battle against the pirates off Alanya in 67 BC. Later, Mark Antony presented the land to Cleopatra, who made good use of its fine timber, both to rebuild her fleet, and for export.

Late afternoon shadows at Side's Temples of Apollo and Athena.

⏣ HIGH DRAMA

In the 6th century BC, the ancient Greeks began to create a series of religious dance and music dramas in honour of Dionysus (the god of wine, revelry and inspiration). In 534 BC, the first public drama competition, the City Dionysia, was held in Athens. It was won by a masked actor/writer called Thespis, who played all the characters, supported by a large chorus. The performance space was originally a dusty circle (the orchestra) in front of the altar. This was transformed by the mid-4th century BC by the addition of seating into a theatre ("place of spectacles").

The festival developed until three playwrights each had to produce three linked tragedies (for example, the Oresteia by Aeschylus) and a satire, to be performed on the same day, sponsored by a wealthy citizen, a *choregon*. The first Classical play to survive, *The Persians*, also by Aeschylus (who added a second actor), was performed in 472 BC. At much the same time, a winter festival, the Lenea, was dedicated to comedy, much of it broad political satire. Sophocles added a third actor, and by the time of Euripides' plays (from around 430 BC), characters (for example, Medea) were much more psychologically rounded, the chorus more background comment than crucial to the plot. Very few complete plays survive.

Damlataş Cave, whose weeping rocks are reputed to cure human ills.

As the Byzantine Empire declined, the south coast was poorly defended, and various Armenian dynasties took advantage of the weakness. By the 10th century the town had fallen into obscurity, but remained a difficult place to capture as the Seljuks found out in 1221 when they laid siege to its formidable fortress. Legend has it that Sultan Alâeddin Keykubat I, at his wit's end, gambled on a last desperate bid. He conscripted into his army hundreds of wild goats. Tying a lighted candle to each of their horns, he shepherded his new recruits ahead of his army up the cliffs. The credulous enemy, upon seeing the apparent strength of the invaders, surrendered at once and were exiled to Konya – but not before Keykubat had married the daughter of the ousted leader. Keykubat renamed the city *Alaiye* ("city of Ala") in his own honour. It was captured, in due course, by the Ottomans in 1471.

Today, the markedly different contributions of the Romans, Byzantines and Seljuks to the fortress are clearly discernible. The **İç Kale** (daily,

Ruined Byzantine church in the Alanya fortress.

Apr–Oct 9am–7pm, Nov–Mar 8.30am–5pm; charge), or inner fortress, was built at the behest of Alâeddin Keykubat I in 1226. Inside is a domed Byzantine church (6th century) dedicated to St George, a flight of red-brick stairs said to have been used by Cleopatra when she descended to the sea to bathe, store rooms and numerous cisterns – the largest of which could hold 120,000 tons of water – a hefty advantage during protracted sieges. Just outside the wall, the *bedesten* (inn), restored and operating as a hotel, lies within an attractive tangle of ruinous stone houses, vines and fruit trees.

The road to the castle is a steep 5km (3-mile) climb, and a taxi or *dolmuş* to the top is a wise investment. Alternatively, a cable car – opened in 2017 – now whisks you up from Cleopatra Beach to the west, offering wonderful views down the coast. It's well worth taking the walk downhill, through carob and fig trees and scented jasmine, with stunning views of the harbour to the east. There are regular teahouses and drinks stands en route.

Just west of the fortress at sea level, next to the tourist office, is the **Damlataş Mağarasıı** (daily 6am–10am for patients, 10am–7pm for the public; charge) or "Weeping Cave", an exquisite grotto with curtains of dripping stalactites and stalagmites. Its unique atmosphere is said to be capable of curing respiratory ailments, especially asthma: 90–100 percent humidity, a constant temperature of 22–23°C (71–73°F), high levels of carbon dioxide and natural ionisation. People come from all over Turkey for this cure, for which a doctor's certificate is required: four hours per day for 21 days. Knots of bescarved women while away the hours as they knit, sew and crochet their way to a clearer respiratory system in this warm, damp enclave. For those interested, doctors in Alanya will examine you and write the necessary

report. Note that asthma treatment here is not recommended if you suffer from heart problems. Significantly larger and less crowded than Damlataş – while claiming a similarly beneficial environment for asthmatics – is **Dim Cave** (daily 9am–6.30pm; charge), discovered in 1986 and set 12km (7.5 miles) east of town in the direction of Tosmur.

Just round the corner from Damlataş, the modern, compact **Alanya Archaeological Museum** (Arkeoloji Müzesi; İsmet Hilmi Balcı Caddesi; daily May–Sept 8am–7pm, Tue–Sun Oct–Apr 8am–5pm; charge) where carefully selected exhibits include a well-preserved bronze statue of Hercules, dating back to the 2nd century AD.

Directly east of the citadel is the city harbour, heavily fortified by Sultan Alâeddin Keykubat I. Chief among the defences was the 35-metre (115ft) octagonal **Kızıl Kule** (Red Tower), designed in 1227 by a Syrian architect, which is now home to a small **Ethnographic Museum** (Tue–Sun 9am–7pm;

charge). There are fine views from the battlements. Round the point, at the harbour entrance, is another tower, the **Tophane Kule** (Arsenal Tower), used as a cannon foundry by the Ottomans. Between the two is the **Tersane** (open access; best seen from the water), a series of five huge open workshops which were the centrepiece of the Seljuks' naval dockyard, also built in 1227.

Today, the harbour is humming with activity, lined by pavement cafés, with fishing and tourist boats jostling for space along the quays. Alanya's coast is marked by a series of grottoes, and boat trips can be arranged to any or all – Pirate's Cave, Lovers' Grotto, one where phosphorescent pebbles shine up from the sea bed; or to the "wishing gate", an enormous natural hole in the rocks. It is said that barren women who go through this gate will gain the ability to conceive.

Each side of Alanya boasts good, if somewhat grey, sandy beaches backed by a host of hotels; the eastern part of the town sports a wider selection.

○ **Tip**

Most travel agencies in Antalya, Side and Alanya offer day-long rafting trips on the Köprülü river, including transport and meals, as do the hotels along the coast.

Alanya's western beach, with the fortress dominating the hill above.

CILICIA

Turkey's "Pirate Coast" road twists its way across towering cliffs and down to tiny coves, a dramatic landscape carpeted with pine forests and dotted with Hellenistic, Roman and Byzantine ruins.

The flat and increasingly built-up farmland between Alanya and **Gazipaşa** does little to prepare you for the 200km (125 miles) of fabulous coastal scenery ahead. Pine forests and mud-plastered houses cling precariously to the cliffs, terraced banana plantations step resolutely down into the sea, and tiny coves jostle for space. The views on this beautiful stretch of the Mediterranean are superb, especially as the terrain is far too rugged to allow much tourist development. Beyond Silifke, however, the summer high-rise retreats of prosperous Turks begin to dominate the plains approaching the industrialised port of Mersin. Diversions inland pierce the ever-present barrier of the formidable Taurus Mountains, home of the semi-nomadic *Yörük* pastoralists, to give an insight into timeless rural Turkey.

EAST TO ANAMUR

Some 20km (12 miles) east of Gazipaşa it's worth taking a short 2km (1.5-mile) detour to the cliff-edge Hellenistic site of **Antiochia ad Cragum**. It's so difficult to access that you can easily understand why the pirates, for which this coast was notorious in antiquity, were able to fend off the Romans for so long.

Anamur, 130km (80 miles) east of Alanya and several kilometres inland, has no particular claim to fame. Its seaside suburb of İskele, 5km (3 miles) south, is a pleasant small resort with several good basic hotels and fish restaurants along a white-sand beach known for its turtles. Here you can find **Anamur's** small **museum** (Anamur Müzesi; Adnan Menderes Caddesi; tel: 0324-814 1677; Tue–Sun Apr–Sept 8am–5.30pm, Oct–Mar 8am–4.30pm; charge), showcasing finds from the Hellenistic, Roman and Byzantine eras as well as carpets woven by nomads from the nearby Taurus Mountains.

The breathtaking coastal road from Alanya to Gazipaşa.

About 5km (3 miles) west of town, on the southernmost tip of Asia Minor, slumber the ruins of ancient **Anemurium**, meaning "windy cape" (tel: 0324-237 1900; daily Apr–Sept 8am–6.30pm, Oct–Mar 8am–4.30pm; charge). Founded by the Hittites in about 1200 BC, the city became a great trading centre and Byzantine bishopric, thriving until a devastating earthquake in AD 580, followed by Arab invasions. The well-preserved ruins of the town, mainly dating from its 3rd-century heyday, are dominated by the cemetery, a vast sprawl of some 350 domed tombs. The setting and the ruins themselves are intensely atmospheric, despite the fact that they adjoin a swimming beach and picnic area.

Five km (3 miles) east of Anamur town, on the D-400, magnificent **Mamure Kalesi** (Anamur Castle; closed until late 2020 for extensive restoration works) stands romantically with one foot in the sea. The first fortress here was built in the 3rd century AD, but it has had many other incarnations: as a 10th-century pirates' lair, and as the property of 11th- to 12th-century kings of Armenia. The surviving castle was built in 1226 by the great Seljuk Sultan Alâeddin Keykubat I; the mosque and rooms overlooking the sea from the upper battlements were added by Karamanoğlu ruler Mahmut Bey (1300–8). In the late 14th century, it became a mainland toehold for the crusading Lusignan kings of Cyprus, until it was seized by the Ottomans in 1469.

THE GÖKSU DELTA

Ascending and descending in a series of hairpin turns, passing several more aesthetically pleasing but anonymous castles, the coastal road finally hits the Göksu delta near **Taşucu**, one of the two ferry embarkation points (the other is Mersin) for the Turkish Republic of Northern Cyprus. The sole operator, Akgünler Denizcilik, runs four ferries weekly. Taşucu itself is a bustling ferry port with several hotels and *pansiyons* on the waterfront to the east of town.

About 5km (3 miles) further on, at **Ayatekla** (daily, Apr–Sept 9am–7pm, Nov–Mar 8.30am–5.30pm; charge) just left of the highway, a ruined Byzantine

Anemurium's ghostly city of the dead guards the southern point of Anatolia.

Anamur's perfect medieval castle.

☉ Tip

Those tackling the coast road east from Alanya to Silifke should set out early in the morning. The road is long and hazardous because of the number of sharp bends and the heavy goods traffic. If travelling by bus, book a seat on the right to make the best of the superlative views.

Şalgam, a fermented carrot drink, is very popular throughout Southern Turkey.

basilica towers above the underground hermitage of St Thecla, one of St Paul's first converts. On hearing Paul preach the virtues of chastity in Iconium (Konya), she promptly renounced her betrothal; on a later visit to the Apostle in prison, she too was arrested and sentenced to be burnt at the stake and tied naked to a pyre in the arena. A divinely inspired deluge doused the flames. Wild beasts were brought in to devour her, but "there was about her a cloud, so that neither the beasts did touch her, nor was she seen to be naked", according to Acts of Paul and Thecla, written in the 2nd century by an unknown Asian presbyter.

SILIFKE

Like all coastal cities in Turkey, **Silifke** ⑳ has ancient roots, but precious little remains of ancient Seleucia ad Calycadnum, which was one of nine sister cities founded by Seleukos I Nikator in the 3rd century BC after he had gained control of Syria following the death of Alexander the Great.

The town is dominated by a vast hilltop **castle** (currently in the midst of restoration works), a twenty-minute walk from the centre. Built originally by the Byzantines but heavily altered by the Armenians and Crusaders, it was captured by the Turks in the late 13th century. From the ramparts there is a superb view, with all the town's other monuments laid out like a map at your feet. Directly below are the Roman necropolis, aqueduct and a vast Byzantine cistern carved from the bedrock. The **stone bridge** over the Göksu River also has ancient origins (it was first built by Vespasian in AD 78), while the riverside park surrounds an unexcavated *höyük* or *tel* (archaeological mound), first fortified by the Assyrians in the 8th century BC. On the right of İnönü Bulvarı stands a single column of the 2nd- or 3rd-century AD **Temple of Zeus**; no sign has yet been found of the city's famous oracle of Apollo Sarpedonios. The **Ulu Camii** is of Seljuk origin, and while no trace of decoration remains, the *mihrab* and the entrance are original. A kilometre to the east on Taşucu Caddesi, the main Antalya road, is the town's pleasant little **museum**

☉ THE PIRATE COAST

In antiquity, the rocky, inaccessible coast of Cilicia made the region an ideal hideaway for pirates preying on ships plying the lucrative trade route between Syria and the Aegean. Incredibly powerful and well organised, the pirates were initially tolerated by the Romans, as they provided the slaves needed to work their plantations in Italy. The pirates became too bold for their own good, however, when kidnapping prominent Romans for ransom including, in 75 BC, Julius Caesar himself. Even more seriously, they were seen to be threatening the crucial grain supply from Egypt to Rome. In 67 BC the Roman general, Pompey the Great, was given extraordinary powers to quash the sea-borne menace, and used a mix of threats, diplomacy and pardons to induce their surrender.

(Tue–Sun 8am–5pm; charge), with a remarkable hoard of Seleucian coins.

THE ROAD NORTH

Silifke marks the real end of the tourist coast. From here on, the landscape flattens into dreary coastal plains and industrial wastelands, although towns such as ancient Tarsus are not lacking in atmosphere. Many choose to take the breathtaking D-715 road northwest over the mountains to Konya (see page 302) and Cappadocia (see page 309), one of the most captivating places in Turkey.

The early stages of this mountain road follow the turbulent path of the Göksu River. The Third Crusade came to an abrupt end some 16km (10 miles) north of Silifke, when Holy Roman Emperor Frederick Barbarossa drowned while bathing on his way to Jerusalem in 1190; a **memorial** marks the spot. He was a long way from home, and in order to preserve his body until he could be taken to Antioch for burial on Christian land, he was stored in a barrel of vinegar. He was later taken back to Germany.

Upstream is the town of **Mut**, worth visiting, with a 14th-century mosque, the Lal Ağa Camii, a fortress and two domed tombs. About 20km (12 miles) north of town, the beautiful 5th-century **monastery** at Alahan (daily, 8am–7pm; charge) teeters on the edge of the wild Göksu gorge, with traces of fresco still visible in its baptistery and churches.

The road now rises over the Sertavul pass, where migrating birds of prey including short-toed eagles, honey buzzards and Levant sparrowhawks congregate in spring and autumn. Another 70km (45 miles) from Alahan, **Karaman** ㉑ was a powerful autonomous emirate from 1277–1467, so famous that early travellers referred to the entire coast as Karamania. Three fine religious schools, the Hatuniye Medresesi, the İbrahim Bey İmareti and the Ak Tekke; a mosque, the Yunus Emre Camii; and a ruined castle are all that remain of a glorious past, while the small museum also contains finds from Canhasan, about 13km (8 miles) northeast of town, a settlement dating back to the 6th millennium BC.

The spectacular view from Alahan monastery.

Bananas grow in profusion along this stretch of coast, which is also a land of strawberries, thick-skinned oranges and yoghurt.

Gazing into the pit of Hell, one of the Corycian Caves.

About 30km (19 miles) north, a turning to the left leads to a mountain rising sheer above the plain. On its northern flank is the village of **Maden Şehir** and the once majestic Byzantine **Binbirkilise** ("A Thousand and One Churches"). For two periods, from the 5th–6th and 9th–14th centuries, the area was almost as packed with monasteries and painted churches as Cappadocia. There are some ruins, but most have sadly been pillaged for building by the local farmers.

Much closer to Silifke, another slew of ancient sites lies directly to the north. Tucked high in the Taurus Mountains, beside the remote upland village of **Uzuncaburç**, 30km (19 miles) north of town, the ancient city of **Dioceasarea ㉒** (daily 8am–sunset; charge) suns itself in past glories. Founded by the Hittites, this is a superb conglomeration of Hellenistic, Roman and Byzantine ruins.

The **Temple of Zeus**, built in 295 BC by Seleukos I Nikator (321–280 BC), is one of the oldest such sanctuaries in Asia Minor. During the 2nd century BC, its priests evolved into a powerful dynasty of priest-kings, the Teukrides, who ruled the surrounding town with a rod of iron right through the Roman era. Thirty columns remain standing today, four still with their capitals, the earliest Corinthian capitals in Asia Minor. It was converted to a church in Byzantine times, when the sanctuary was destroyed and walls and new doors were inserted between the columns. Nearby are a five-storey tower (late 3rd century BC), a pair of monumental gates, the northernmost of them featuring a trio of richly ornamented arches, a theatre and five columns of the **Temple of Tyche** (Fortune), each made of a single piece of granite nearly 6 metres (20ft) high, brought from Egypt in the 1st century AD.

Three kilometres (2 miles) to the east is ancient **Olba**, worth the walk for its picturesque aqueduct and ancient cemetery, an eerie valley of rock-cut tombs.

Roughly half-way between Sifilke and **Uzuncaburç**, a dirt road winds 8km (5 miles) east of İmamlı via the tiny settlement of Pasli to the imposing **Mezgit Kale**, also known as the **Mausoleum of the Fearless King**. On the side wall of the monument – one of the largest temple-tombs in Cilicia – juts the sculptured metre-long phallus of Priapus, god of fertility. Legend recounts that he was the illegitimate son of Zeus and Aphrodite, and that Hera, jealous wife of Zeus, deformed the child, giving him a phallus equal to his height. He was abandoned out of shame by his mother near the Dardanelles, and was brought by shepherds to ancient Lampsakos (Lapseki).

WONDERFUL WILDLIFE

South of Silifke is the **Göksu Delta**, part of which has been designated a nature reserve. A wide range of waterbirds inhabits the marshes and reeds. Purple gallinule and black francolin survive the predations of hunters in very limited numbers, and the beaches are home to gulls and, in the summer egg-laying season, turtles. Migrating raptors

gather here to feed before resuming their journey across the Mediterranean to Africa. Information about the birds is available from the ÖCKK (Environment Ministry) agency, near the Ayatekla site, tel: 0324-713 0888.

Some 20 kilometres (12 miles) east of Silifke, **Narlıkuyu**, translated as "Well of the Pomegranate", is a pleasant cove lined with seafood restaurants. It is also home to the remains of a famous **Roman bathhouse** (Tue–Sun Apr–Sept 8am–7pm, Oct–Mar 8am–5pm; charge) with a dusty 4th-century AD mosaic floor representing the Three Graces. The spring water was claimed by the ancients to enhance grey matter.

HEAVEN AND HELL

Three kilometres (2 miles) north and inland of Narlıkuyu lies the **Corycian Caves** (daily Apr–Sept 8am–7pm, Oct–Mar 8am–5pm; charge). Better known as **Cennet ve Cehennem** ㉓ (Heaven and Hell), they were formed by underground chemical erosion. Like all the best natural phenomena, they are considered sacred by pagans, Christians and Muslims alike. Heaven (Cennet Deresi) is larger than Hell, with 452 stairs leading down to a Byzantine chapel, dedicated to the Virgin Mary. This, in turn, blocks the entrance to a cave-gorge with an underground river, thought by some to be the Styx. The cave at the far end was home to an oracle. Just north is the gloomy pit of Hell ("Cehennem"), happily inaccessible without climbing equipment as the sides are concave. It was here that Zeus imprisoned Typhon, the many-headed, fire-breathing monster serpent, father of Cerberus, guard dog of Hell.

On both sides of the highway heading east towards Mersin are regimented rows of oranges and lemons, crops of Roman and Byzantine ruins, the last scattered arches of giant Roman aqueducts and an increasingly cluttered forest of high-rise blocks, corrugated iron and billboards.

TWIN CASTLES

Five kilometres (3 miles) east of **Narlıkuyu** stand famous twin medieval castles. On terra firma, 13th-century **Korykos Castle** reuses materials from a city first mentioned by Herodotus in the 5th century BC. On an offshore island, across a 200-metre (650ft) channel, is its sister, **Kız Kalesi** ㉔ (the Maiden's Castle), which was a refuge for pirates before it was fortified by Byzantine admiral Eugenios, in 1104, as a link in the empire's border defences during the Crusades. It was later appropriated by the Armenians, Turks and, in 1482, the Ottomans (both castles are open daily Apr–Sept 9am–8pm, Oct–Mar 8am–7pm; charge). You need to negotiate with a local boatman if you want to get across the water.

The town of Kız Kalesi is a fast-growing resort, mainly frequented by Turkish tourists, and is best appreciated in early summer. From here until Adana, the coast is lined with holiday apartments, villas and beach-side restaurants, making it hard to see the waves from the busy road.

The Goksu River tumbles south through the Taurus Mountains before disgorging into the Mediterranean.

Fact

Adana is famous throughout Turkey for its eponymous kebab, a spicy mincemeat sausage skewered and cooked over charcoal. Locals wash it down with *şalgam*, a red-coloured and fiery concoction based on fermented carrots and turnip.

MERSIN AND TARSUS

Mersin (İçel) is a pleasant enough city but offers little to detain the visitor. Four boats leave weekly for Cyprus, and inter-city buses are frequent. A big, largely modern metropolis with a population of around 1.8 million, the best parts are along the waterfront, where there are broad boulevards, shady parks and a decent supply of restaurants. The modern **Archaeological Museum** (Adnan Menderes Bulvari 54; daily 9am–5pm; charge) houses over 1400 artefacts, covering the broad sweep of Cilician history – including finds from Yumuktepe and Soli. Immediately beside it stands the **Naval Museum** (Tue–Sun 9am–5pm; charge), while to the east, set just behind the broad coastal promenade is the **Atatürk House Museum** (Mon–Sat 9am–4.30pm) a 19th-century villa where the Turkish founder resided on state visits. The city is also known for its joviality, especially around the permanent market area, perhaps due to the number of sailors who frequent the town.

Traders have descended on Tarsus since the pass through the northern mountains was engineered.

Sandwiched between the industrial giants, 25km (16 miles) east of Mersin, **Tarsus** ㉕ boasts a resplendent history stretching back to at least 3000 BC. Though the ravages of war and time have destroyed most vestiges of the past, it is one of the oldest continuously inhabited cities in the world, the ancient city lying 15–20 metres (50–65ft) below the modern one.

When the engineers of ancient Tarsus cut a pass through the northern mountains to the **Cilician Gates**, they created one of the most significant mountain routes of all time; traders and troops have poured through the narrow gorge ever since, including the armies of Xerxes, Alexander the Great and the Crusaders, the latter dubbing the fearful, haunted pass the "Gates of Judas." On the back of the trade route grew and flourished one of the richest and most powerful cities of the ancient world. In 41 BC, at the behest of Mark Antony, Cleopatra arrived by barge, dressed as the goddess Aphrodite and subsequently winning the love of the victorious general. A few decades later, a local Jewish tentmaker named Saul experienced a blinding revelation on the road to Damascus and was transformed into St Paul, the most famous of Christian evangelists.

St Paul's Well, with its curative water (tested every day for purity) supposedly stands on the site of his family home in the old town. It probably has nothing to do with the Apostle, and was named by the Byzantines or the Crusaders, both of whom had a vested interest in liberally applying biblical names to relics and places of minor pilgrimage. **Cleopatra's Gate** (also known as the Gate of the Bitch) certainly had nothing to do with the Egyptian queen. On the other hand, both the well and gate are Roman, while parts of a colonnaded **Roman road** have been uncovered in the bazaar, surrounded by narrow alleys and crumbling Ottoman houses. More modern generations are

represented by two mosques, the **Eski Camii** (Old Mosque), converted from a 12th-century church that was likely in honor of St. Paul, and the **Makam Camii** opposite, where a 2007 excavation uncovered a tomb believed by the faithful to be the tomb of the biblical prophet Daniel. Nearby is the Kubat Paşa Medresesi, built in 1570. Two kilometres north of here, a collection of attractive cafés surrounds the **Şelale**, a wonderfully cooling waterfall/park area on the edge of town.

ADANA

A further 40km (25 miles) east, **Adana** ㉖ has grown rich on heavy industry, cotton and citrus. This is the fifth-largest city in Turkey (after Istanbul, Ankara, İzmir and Bursa), with a population of roughly 2 million and the only commercial airport in the region (until the Çukurova Regional Airport is completed). It is an extraordinary enclave of Mercedes cars and designer boutiques, its hotels and restaurants almost entirely dedicated to business travellers.

Few people outside Turkey know of the city's most awe-inspiring sight – the **Sabancı Merkez Camii** (Central Mosque), an enormous, beautiful new mosque whose white marble reflection sparkles in the Şeyhan River next to an impressive Roman bridge. Opened in 1999, it is a shade bigger than the mosque it is modelled on, Istanbul's Sultanahmet (Blue) Mosque, boasting six minarets and a 51-metre (167ft) dome. Inside, it is embellished with elaborate tiles and gold leaf and can hold 30,000 worshippers. Nearby, the city's beautiful 16th-century **Ulu Camii**, with its black-and-white stripes and octagonal minaret, has been dwarfed.

There are few sights besides the new mosque. A kilometre east of the new mosque is a well-designed but tiny **Ethnography Museum** housed in a Byzantine church (İnönü Caddesi; Tue–Sun 9am–5pm), while another

0.25 kilometres further is the **Archaeological Museum** (Tue–Sun 9am–5pm; charge), housed in a converted factory. There are some fine exhibits here, including Classical and Hittite statuary and some Urartian artefacts.

One of the city's most eminent sons is novelist Yaşar Kemal, whose pen drips with the ochres and reds of the surrounding Çukurova Plain and the plight of the seasonal cotton-pickers who used to descend on it from the Taurus Mountains backing the city (now most of them are Kurds from the eastern fringes of Turkey). His most popular work, *Ince Mehmet* (Mehmet My Hawk), has been translated into a dozen languages and, along with Orhan Pamuk, he is Turkey's most celebrated author. The leftist film-maker Yılmaz Güney also used the city and the surrounding villages as the backdrop for his works on social dislocation and poverty.

About 25km (16 miles) east of Adana, the enormous **US İncirlik Air Base** was used in the Gulf Wars as well during the more recent campaign against the Islamic State.

> ⊙ **Fact**
>
> Adana is one of the hottest places in Turkey; although temperatures rarely exceed 40°C (104°F), the high humidity makes the heat far more oppressive than in the interior.

Adana's dazzling Sabancı Merkez Camii.

THE HATAY

The civil war in bordering Syria, which began in 2011, has had a marked effect on the Hatay, with legal cross-border trade drying to a trickle and refugees from the war-torn state housed in a series of camps. In compensation, the region also offers some of the best food in Turkey and some wonderful archaeological sites.

⊙ Main attractions
Yılan Kalesi
Karatepe
Antakya
Antakya Archaeological
  Museum
Harbiye

⊙ Map on page 238

Due east of Adana is a tangle of dual carriageways and motorways carrying traffic to and from Europe and the Middle East. South of this motorway lies the isolated province of Hatay, a finger of Turkish territory pushing down into the northern Levant. The topography hereabouts is dominated by the fertile Cilician Plain (Çukurova), bound to the north by the foothills of the mighty Taurus range, guarding the approaches to the central Anatolian plateau beyond, and to the southeast by the equally impressive Amanus mountains. Between the Amanus and the eastern shores of the Mediterranean are the lower Ziyaret and Nur ranges, between which runs the fertile Asi (Orontes) river valley.

In antiquity the region benefited from its strategic location as a Mediterranean terminus of trade routes from Central Asia, Persia and Mesopotamia, allowing the development of one of the Graeco-Roman world's wealthiest cities, Antioch (modern Antakya).

CASTLES ON THE PLAIN

Today the broad alluvial flats of the well-irrigated Çukurova are devoted to cotton and other cash crops, tended seasonally by thousands of migrant farm workers housed in shabby tent cities. Many castles still dot the region, most built during the Crusades or under Armenian rule.

Yılan Kalesi ㉗ ("Snake Castle"; daily 8am–7pm) dominates the plain from its perch above the Ceyhan River. The access road is good, but the climb up to the castle is difficult. Probably built by Armenian king Leo III (ruled 1270–89), the fortress walls and battlements still stand proud, bolstered by extensive restoration works in 2014. The origin of its name is obscure; some say the castle had to be abandoned because of snakes, but a more compelling explanation ascribes it to an apocryphal

Highly perched Yılan Kalesi.

"king of the Snakes", an evil half-man, half-snake who terrorised the region and was eventually overcome and killed in Tarsus while attempting to kidnap the daughter of the king.

From Aysehoca, about 30km north (17 miles) along the D-817, a road runs a few kilometres east to the Graeco-Roman city of **Anavarza** (Dilekkaya). Much like a giant Lego set, earthquakes have left rubble strewn across the site, which includes a stadium, theatre, baths, triumphal arch, tombs and mosaics, as well as a heavily fortified Armenian citadel. Ongoing excavations have unveiled what is believed to be the first two-lane road in the ancient world – a small portion of it is currently being restored.

A further 23km north along the D-817 spreads the farming village of **Kozan**, greatly diminished from its former glories as capital of Cilician Armenia. An unmarked road in the middle of town leads steeply up the hill to the west, turning through a series of outer walls to the gate of the striking **castle** (daily 8am–7pm), built by Leo II (1187–1219).

The main walls, ringed by 44 towers, form a saddle linking the twin summits of the long, narrow hill. The capture of the castle and King Leo VI, by Egyptian Mamelukes in 1374, marked the end of the southern Armenian kingdom.

TOPRAKKALE TO KARATEPE

Osmaniye, 92km (57 miles) east of Adana, is a nondescript town noted for the ultra-Turkish nationalism of its inhabitants. En route you will pass close to the massive, crumbling black fortress of **Toprakkale** (daily Apr–Sept 10am–7pm, Oct–Mar 8am–5pm), surrounded on all sides by a motorway junction, demonstrating graphically its crucial position at the crossroads of international trade and invasion routes. Built by the Byzantine emperor Nikephoros II Phokas (AD 963–9), the fortress was used as a base for his successful campaign against the Arabs who had held Antioch since the beginning of the 7th century. Later taken over by the Knights of St John, who remodelled it on Krak des Chevaliers (in Syria), it was eventually abandoned in 1337.

☉ Tip

To make the most of Karatepe, stock up with supplies in Osmaniye and take a picnic with you to enjoy in a designated area not far from the site's entrance. It's pleasantly cool in the wooded hills and views to the lower Taurus are wonderful.

Daphne's signature dish, trout.

☉ CULINARY DELIGHTS

The food in the Hatay is distinctively Arab, unsurprisingly given the history of this Turkish province. Look out for hummus, a rarity elsewhere in Turkey, here dripping in melted butter and often topped by creamy pine nuts. Another delicious pulse-based puree is *bakla*, made from broad beans, garlic, olive oil, parsley, cumin and tahini (sesame) paste. Best of the dips, though, is *muhamarra*, a hot, spicy mixture of bread crumbs, ground walnut, tomato paste and hot pepper. Unusual main courses include *Ispanak Borani*, a stew of spinach, finely-sliced meat, chickpeas and yoghurt, and *köfte* (meatballs) stuffed with cheese and walnuts. *Künefe* is a delicious oven-baked dessert of spun wheat, cheese and syrup, and *kabak tatlısı* a mouth-watering candied pumpkin dish best served with a dollop of cream.

Human remains on display in the Archaeological Museum, Antakya.

About forty kilometres (25 miles) north of Osmaniye, **Karatepe** – dating back to the 8th century BC – (Tue–Sun 8am–noon, 1–5pm; charge) served both as a castle and summer palace for a neo-Hittite king, Asatiwatas. Today, the ruins stand on a U-shaped rock outcrop in an attractive forest overlooking a reservoir on the upper Ceyhan River. A 1km (2/3-mile) circular path loops through the woods between the fort's two main gates, which stand *in situ* protected by tin roofs. Karatepe's chief claim to fame is as the place where Hittite hieroglyphic writing was first deciphered, by comparing it with matching inscriptions in Phoenician script. These hieroglyphs document the building of the city, praising the peace and prosperity of the kingdom, and heaping divine retribution on anyone who dares disturb the gate. Other reliefs consist of wonderfully crude relief carvings, including spear-toting soldiers with hoofed feet, several grinning lions and a superb statue of the Hittite storm god Tarhun/Taru astride a pair of bulls.

Antakya's bazaar.

There is a small open-air **museum** at the entrance to Karatepe, with signboards interpreting the site. One of the chief archaeologists involved with the excavation – and its major champion – was Halet Çambel, a formidable Turkish academic. Having fenced for Turkey in the 1936 Olympic Games, she went on to spend some 45 years working on this unique site.

SOUTH TO ANTAKYA

From Osmaniye, the route south heads across the plains of **Issos**, past a turning to the Sokullu Mehmet Paşa *kervansaray*, *medrese* (religious school) and mosque complex. Directly opposite a Crusader castle, the buildings are superbly lined with coloured marbles and include a marble bathhouse. Local legend claims that it was here that Jonah was cast from the belly of the whale. More certainly, blood soaks the peaceful soil, for this is where Alexander and his army of 35,000 met and defeated Persian emperor Darius and an army of over 100,000 in 333 BC, changing the course of world history.

Alexander's triumph is marked by the town he founded and named after himself immediately after the battle, **İskenderun**. Most of the modern city was built during the French Mandate, and has a pleasant, Levantine feel with a fine promenade, good fish restaurants and a small but well-arranged maritime museum (Tue–Sun 10am–6pm). There are also a scattering of still-functioning 19th-century churches which reflect the Hatay's multicultural, multifaith heritage – Armenian, Greek Orthodox and Catholic. Unfortunately, modern İskenderun is an industrial city and port, and pollution can be a problem.

To the south, en route to Antakya, is a mountain pass known in antiquity as the Syrian Gates, now the **Belen Pass**. The location is much prized by birdwatchers in spring and autumn as it stands astride one of the world's most important migration routes.

To the south, the scenery softens and flows into green rolling hills watered by the Orontes River until the end of the valley pushes against the first outcroppings of the Lesser Lebanon Mountains. Here stands **Antakya** ㉙ the biblical Antioch, once amongst the most important cities in the ancient world.

ANTAKYA: THE PAST

Following Alexander's death, one of his lesser generals, Seleukos I Nikator, established himself as the satrap (governor) of Babylon. During the internecine wars that soon flared between the rival Macedonian generals, Seleukos traded most of his territory in India for 500 war elephants, which won the day against the forces of Antigonus ("the One-Eyed") at the Battle of Ipsos in western Anatolia in 301 BC and established himself as a Mediterranean power. In 300 BC he built his capital across the trade route at Antioch-on-the-Orontes.

Initially conceived of as a *polis*, or city, of some 5,300 male citizens – close enough to the ideal number of Hellenic home-owners advocated by Plato – Antioch soon swelled to a population of nearly half a million, becoming the pre-eminent centre of Hellenic civilisation in the region. The Seleucids lavished attention on their city, building theatres, baths, gymnasia, a stadium that hosted a revived Olympic Games, and other public buildings, all connected by colonnaded streets.

The Seleucids were, in due course, chased out of Asia Minor by the Romans after several disasters and defeats, starting with the Battle of Magnesia when their famed war elephants stampeded and destroyed their own troops. They next became embroiled in the unsuccessful revolt of the Maccabees in Palestine and a series of destabilising wars in the east with the Parthians, and in the west with Egypt. They were finally conquered in 83 BC by Armenian King Tigranes, son-in-law of the redoubtable scourge of Rome, Mithridates the Great. Within 20 years, Roman legions had taken possession of Antioch, which became the capital of the newly formed province of Syria.

Relief sculptures at Karatepe.

The Poseidon mosaic in Antakya Archaeological Museum.

⊙ Fact

It was supposedly in Daphne that Hera, Athene and Aphrodite asked Paris of Troy to judge their beauty competition. Hera promised to make him Lord of All Asia, Athene to make him invincible in battle. He chose Aphrodite, who promised him the most beautiful woman in the world, the already married Helen – which led to the Trojan War.

Antioch became a much sought-after prize, changing hands on numerous occasions over the centuries. During the Byzantine period, it was sacked with cyclical regularity by the Persians. An earthquake in the 5th century killed 250,000 people, and it finally fell to the Muslim Arabs in AD 638. Reconquered by Byzantium in 969, it fell again to the Muslims in 1084, and, after a long siege in 1097, became capital of one of the four Crusader states in the Middle East. When the Mameluke leader Baybars captured the city in 1268, he slaughtered 16,000 soldiers, hustling a further 100,000 off to slave markets in Cairo.

ANTAKYA: THE PRESENT

Today, the material remains of Antioch's former glory are few and far between. Yet the city has an intense atmosphere that seeps through the narrow alleys of the bazaar and around the minarets, making it one of the most charming and entertaining urban centres in Turkey. The closure of the border with Syria following the outbreak of

civil war there in 2011 has, however, affected the atmosphere in the town and surroundings, not least because of the refugee influx and disruption of cross-border trade.

The city is divided neatly in two by the Orontes River; to the west are the wide boulevards and Art Deco buildings of the French colony (1918–38), to the east the narrow, noisy old Arab town.

The **Hatay Archaeological Museum**, 3km (2 miles) east of the centre, is home to a world-class collection of some 50 Roman mosaics (Atatürk Caddesi; daily Apr–Oct 9am–7pm, Nov–Mar 9am–5pm; charge), rivalled in Turkey only by that in Gaziantep (see page 357). Most of them, carefully removed from Roman villas in nearby Daphne, date from the 2nd and 3rd centuries, and seem to leap off the walls. Here is a life-size "Oceanus and Thetis", with the creatures of the deep clustered around them; there the "Happy Hunchback", dancing in glee with erect penis; here again the "Drunken Dionysos" swaying towards the next winery, aided by a small satyr.

Across the river, the edges of the old town, now one huge bazaar, are marked by minarets. Just across from the concrete **Rana Köprüsü** is the **Ulu Camii** (Great Mosque); up the hill, on Kurtuluş Caddesi, is the **Habib Neccar Camii**, formerly a Byzantine church. Also tucked away in the old quarter are a tiny synagogue much visited by Israeli tourists, and a Catholic church which doubles as a pension for the devout. There's also a fine 19th-century Greek Orthodox church containing some pretty Russian icons and Bibles. The Bibles are in Arabic, the language spoken by the Greek Orthodox here (along with many other Antakya natives).

During the period of Roman rule, Antioch had a large Jewish community and became a crucial staging post in the history of early Christianity. St Peter lived here from AD 47–54,

St Peter's Cave, the world's first official Christian church.

frequently joined by the much travelled Paul of Tarsus and St Barnabas. As a result, the city became the seat of the powerful Patriarchate of Asia, a rival Christian centre to Constantinople – chiefly notorious for its heretical scholars. The tiny cave church of **Sen Piyer Kilisesi** (St Peter's Cave; Tue–Sun 8.30am–noon, 1.30–5pm; charge), 2km (1.5 miles) off Kurtuluş Caddesi and northeast of the city centre, is generally regarded as the first Christian church. It was here that the saints gave their new religion a name, "Christianity" (Acts 11:26). The ornate façade was built by the Crusaders. Beyond the church, the mountain road winds 15km (9 miles) to the ruined **Citadel** (3rd century BC–10th century AD).

DAPHNE (HARBIYE)

Some 8km (5 miles) south of Antakya on the road to Syria are the remains of the **Grove of Daphne**, known locally as **Harbiye** ㉚, a favourite place for picnics and recreation for some 3,000 years. Harbiye is, according to Greek mythology, where the nymph Daphne was turned into a laurel bush to escape the unwanted attentions of Apollo. Apollo wove himself a wreath from the leaves, the origin of the laurel of victory.

The Seleucids built a massive temple and oracle complex dedicated to Apollo in the valley, serviced by very real "nymphs" whose duties included delighting the self-deified royal family who claimed descent from the Sun God. Antony and Cleopatra were married here by Egyptian ritual in 40 BC, while the surrounding hills became a wealthy summer resort whose treasure trove of villas produced most of the mosaics now in the Hatay Archaeological Museum.

In AD 362 the last non-Christian ruler of the Byzantine Empire, Julian the Apostate, visited Antioch. Not realising how out of step with the times he was, he ordered the removal of the bones of a martyred Christian bishop from the oracle of Apollo, thus incurring the wrath of the local Christian populace. Despite Julian's apostasy, even in licentious Antioch the pagan age was over.

Tip

The approach to St Simeon's Monastery is difficult. Head west from Antakya taking the Samandağ road (D-420). After 22km (13.5 miles), look for a yellow sign and turn left. From here, a rough gravel road loops up the mountain, for about 8km (5 miles).

Buzzing Antakya.

Today, its ancient buildings vanished, Daphne has been largely overtaken by suburban sprawl, though a small wooded park has preserved an attractive pocket of shaded, babbling streams and waterfalls, making it a popular retreat from the city in summer months. Refreshment stands and restaurants – serving trout – skirt the water.

PILLAR DWELLERS

The early Church attracted many extremists, including a growing number of ascetic monks and other spiritual acrobats who expressed their devotion to God by a complete and utter abnegation of the world.

The most famous of these anchorites was St Simeon the Elder, who devoted his life to sitting atop an increasingly high pillar, while pilgrims flocked to watch him rail against such human frailties as the desire for a good meal and a clean pair of sheets. Local priests even started marketing the saint's waste to the pious for a fee, with the promise that their contributions

The view over to Syria from St Simeon's Monastery.

helped ensure them a place in heaven. "Simony" was thus launched as a Christian concept.

Following Simeon the Elder's death in AD459, a younger Simeon was so inspired that he, too, embraced the holy life. In AD521, at the age of seven, he climbed his own column on a windy promontory of **Samandağ** (Simeon's Mountain). Over the next 25 years, as he fasted, prayed and preached, and the columns grew in height – culminating in a 13-metre (43ft) stone pillar – a thriving monastery grew around his feet. Pilgrims and meditative monks liked nothing more than to see the pious miracle of the young boy sitting atop his pillar in all weathers. An earthquake brought the entire complex into its present state of ruins. Today, **Aya Simeon Manastırı ③** (St Simeon's Monastery; open access) is remote and little visited, well suited to meditations on the relative freedom of thought in our own time.

SELEUCIA AD PIERA

Back down the mountain, turn left for the coast and **Samandağ**, a supposed resort town suffering from waste-strewn beaches and a sea polluted by chemical waste from İskenderun. About 5km (3 miles) north, beyond a parking lot on the east of the village of **Çevlik** ("The Little Cave") – built in and around Antioch's ancient port of **Seleucia ad Piera** – lie the old city's most impressive remnants (daily Apr–Sept 8.30am–7pm, Oct–Mar 8.30am–5pm; charge). No small feat of engineering, the **Titus-Vespasianus Tüneli** is a huge canal, up to 30 metres (98ft) deep, gouged from the rock during the reign of the Roman emperors Vespasian and Titus (AD69–81) in a vain attempt to prevent mountain streams from silting up the port. A trail leads a few minutes south of here to the tombs of Beşikli Cave, resting place of Roman notables, its smooth-worn columns, arches and niches carved out of the side of a cliff.

ALEXANDER

Catalyst for the spread of Greek culture, Alexander the Great was one of the most successful military campaigners of all time.

Born in 356 BC, Alexander was the son of Philip II of Macedonia and Olympias (daughter of King Neoptolemus of Epirus). Brought up in court, he had the best of tutors, including none other than the great philosopher Aristotle, who taught him science, philosophy and medicine, and filled the young prince's head with the glories of Greek civilisation and a burning desire to liberate ancient Anatolia from the Persians.

Winning his first battle at the tender age of 15, Alexander was a firm favourite of the Macedonian army by the time his father was assassinated in 336 BC. His succession to the throne, at the age of only 20, was assured. Philip had already planned the invasion of Asia; Alexander paused only to tighten his grip on the Greek heartland before heading east, landing in Anatolia in 334 BC, at the head of an army of about 30,000 foot soldiers and over 5,000 cavalry.

It took a little under two years for him to drive the Persians from Anatolian soil, culminating in the decisive Battle of Issos. Unsatisfied, he pressed on, to take Egypt, Palestine and Syria, then Persia itself. He had added Afghanistan, modern Pakistan and northern India before his troops mutinied and forced him to turn back in 327 BC.

Alexander was undoubtedly a superb general, with brilliant strategic insight – and tremendous luck. He was courageous, always to be found in the thick of the action, and enormously charismatic, inspiring total devotion, at least until he pushed them too far and his homesick troops refused to go any further. He was also manipulative and pragmatic, using any means at his disposal to win, from military conquest to marriage. He was adopted by the sister of the satrap in Halikarnassos (Bodrum); while in Egypt, he sacrificed to the god, Apis. In 327 BC, he married Roxana, the daughter of the Bactrian chief Oxyartes (he later took Emperor Darius' daughter, Stateira, as his second wife). He founded some 70 new cities and was the catalyst for the great wave of Hellenisation that swept Central Europe and the Near East.

Yet he was also a Boys' Own adventurer who was far more interested in conquering new lands than ruling the ones he had. In Macedonia, he dreamed of being Greek; once in Anatolia, he coveted Persia. Having conquered Persia, he dressed in Eastern robes and demanded to be treated as a deity (one of the few occasions when his men refused his wishes). He drained Macedonia of money and manpower so thoroughly that it never recovered, and simply left local governors in place as he passed. He hated to be crossed, executing those he felt to have betrayed him, including several of his closest friends and advisers. He destroyed Thebes on a whim and torched the Persian royal palace in a drunken rage.

On 13 June 323 Alexander died, at the age of only 32. Evidence emerging in 2014 suggests that the ruler may have been poisoned after drinking wine spiked with a toxic plant extract. He had reigned for 12 years and eight months. Without his force of personality, his empire was doomed, but it is unlikely to have survived much longer, even had he remained alive; it was too big and too unwieldy, and its emperor was a warrior, not a statesman.

Alexander's sarcophagus.

The ruins of a main street at Sagalassos.

Coming home to a 'fairy chimney' near Zelva, Cappadocia.

CENTRAL ANATOLIA

The rolling steppes of inland Anatolia are home to strangely beautiful landscapes and reminders of long-lost civilisations.

Ankara's Copper Alley close-up.

It was amid the flat, fertile steppes and gentle rolling hills of the vast central Anatolian landscape that mankind, some 10,000 years ago, is believed to have first abandoned hunting and gathering for agriculture, the momentous development that led on to the domestication of animals and the development of settlements and trade. Some of mankind's earliest settlements are found in the region. Dating back to around 6000 BC, Çatalhöyük, south of Konya, is one of the world's oldest towns. Some way north, Boğazkale was the capital of the Hittite Empire which flourished from about 1800 BC.

It has been a battleground on and off ever since, witness to campaigns by Persians, Greeks, Romans, Arabs, Seljuk Turks and Mongols amongst others. The region served as a granary to both the Roman and Byzantine empires. The capture of the plains by the Turks in the 11th century deprived the Byzantine Empire of its agricultural wealth and helped speed its downfall. Even today, the region produces most of Turkey's wheat, barley and oats: it was the abundance of naturally occurring varieties of these crops which spurred the early development of agriculture here in the first place.

Exhibit in the Museum of Anatolian Civilisations, Ankara.

Today, travellers to the region pay homage to Atatürk, buried in state in the country's bustling modern capital, Ankara, and visit the superb Museum of Anatolian Civilisations, covering 10,000 years of history. They visit Konya to admire the religious monuments associated with the world-famous whirling dervishes. They gasp at the remains of the great Hittite settlements. Above all, they flock to Cappadocia, to delight in its extraordinary landscape of conical fairy chimneys, underground cities, anthill-like monasteries and rock-cut churches.

ANKARA

A vibrant city of more than 5 million people, Ankara is home to the Museum of Anatolian Civilisations, showcasing artefacts from the most important archaeological sites across the country.

◉ Main attractions
Ulus Meydanı
Ankara Kalesi
Museum of Anatolian
   Civilisations
Alâeddin Camii
Copper Alley
Atatürk Mausoleum

Map on page 288

In 1923, Atatürk chose Ankara to be the new capital of Turkey for several reasons; not only was it central geographically, but it was free of associations with the despised Ottomans. Despite being little more than a dusty, land-locked backwater at the time it became the new capital. Ankara had a distinguished past. It was a flourishing trade and administrative centre in Roman times and is said to have been the place where King Midas, of the golden touch, was born; more certainly, in around AD 400 the city became the summer capital of the Roman emperors, who moved their administration here – at an altitude of 850 metres (2,790 ft) – to escape the baking summer heat of the coast.

Today, hilly Ankara is a residential rather than a touristic city, with its own rather subtle charms. With a population of over 5 million, the city has changed out of all recognition since its rebirth as the capital of the Turkish Republic and today is a place where you can eat out in style, go to a club, visit art galleries or explore an assortment of antiques shops, although it will never be able to match the glamour or interest levels of Istanbul.

CENTRE OF A REVOLUTION

Start your sightseeing in **Ulus Meydanı Ⓐ**, where the enormous equestrian statue of Kemal Atatürk forms part of Turkey's history. Its inscription is written in Ottoman (Arabic) script, since the monument predates Turkey's 1928 adoption of the Latin alphabet. Across the road to the west is the building which housed the first Grand National Assembly, from where Atatürk masterminded his three-year war against the Greeks and the Western powers backing them. This is now home to the **Museum of the War of Independence** (Kürtülüs Savası Müzesi; Cumhuriyet Bulvarı 14, Ulus; tel: 312-311 0473; Tue–Sun Apr–Sept 8.45am–7pm, Oct–Mar 8.45–5pm;

Old and new buildings juxtaposed in Ankara.

charge), while just to the west stands the second venue of the **Grand National Assembly** (Büyük Millet Meclisi), now the **Republic Museum** (Cumhuriyet Müzesi; www.cumhuriyetmuzesi.gov.tr; Tue–Sun 9am–noon, 1–5pm; charge).

From the Atatürk statue, head north along Çankırı Caddesi. About 50 metres/yards along, turn right to reach the **Jülyanüs Sütunu** (Julian's Column), erected in about AD 360, probably in honour of Emperor Julian the Apostate and one of the few surviving Roman columns in Anatolia. Just beyond it is the **Vilayet Binası** (Governorate of Ankara).

A minute's walk northeast of here stands the **Hacı Bayram Camii**, built beside the Temple of Augustus. This is one of the oldest mosques in the city, dating back to the 15th century. Inside is the 15th-century tomb of Hacı Bayram Veli, head of a dervish order that continues to help the poor and needy.

The **Augustus Tapınağı** Ⓑ (Temple of Augustus) was built by the Phrygians and co-opted for the Roman emperor. His Byzantine descendants later turned it into a Christian church. Near the entrance a long Roman inscription, written in Latin and Greek, relates Augustus' deeds. It remains one of our most important sources of knowledge about the emperor and his times.

Back on Çankırı Caddesi, head north and turn left to reach the **Roma Hamamları** Ⓒ (Roman Baths; daily Apr–Sept 8.30am–7pm, Oct–Mar 8.30am–5pm; charge), consisting mainly of foundations, although pillars, tombstones and other remnants of the Roman city are also displayed here in an open museum. The dated Armenian inscriptions on some of the tombstones show that they were reused in the 19th century.

Walk up Hisarparkı Caddesi towards the citadel. Looking down to your left you can admire the fragmentary foundations of a small **amphitheatre**, which has unfortunately remained in a state of neglect since its discovery in 1984.

THE CITADEL

Between AD 622, when it was taken by the Persians, and AD 838, when it was conquered by the Arabs, Ankara was under constant threat from invaders. Its defenders numbered only a fraction of the population of the earlier city, and rather than quarry new stone, they reused older material to strengthen their walls. Until 1915, the open ground between the inner and outer walls was the Armenian quarter, and several hundred of their descendants still live in the city.

The western walls of **Ankara Kalesi** Ⓓ (Hisarparkı Caddesi; daily 8.30am–5.30pm) are the most spectacular, with a line of triangular towers jutting out from the main structure, rather like the prows of a line of ships. Step through the main gate and turn left onto a winding path leading through narrow streets where the houses have hardly changed in the last hundred years. This route takes you to the innermost point of the castle.

The **walls**, built in the mid-7th century, did not always prove effective. In

Remains from the Roman Baths.

Window-shopping in Ankara.

288

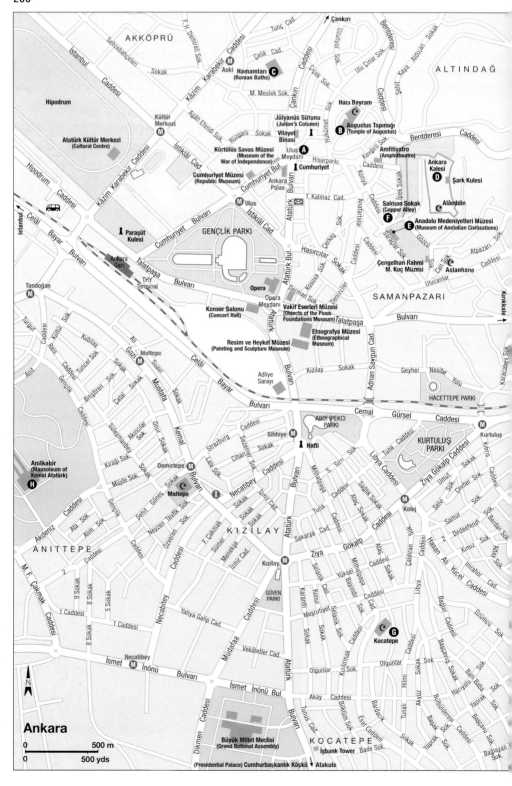

Ankara

0   500 m

0   500 yds

AD 838, the Arabs, under Caliph Muta-sim, sacked the city and killed or took prisoner its entire population. About 10 years later, the Emperor Michael III restored the walls.

Walk through the winding streets down to the south gate of the inner walls and, a few metres above the road, you will see the remains of a large **tower** which was probably the residence of the Byzantine governor. To the right is the **Alâeddin Camii**, a charming little mosque adorned with Classical columns; it is one of the earliest Muslim buildings in the city. Look carefully and you will also see a number of Byzantine crosses above the windows. These were intended as charms against hostile Islamic invaders from the south and east.

In Ottoman times, the Muslim population lived inside the walls and the non-Muslims, the bulk of the city's merchants, around the perimeter. Their houses, with painted plaster walls and elaborate woodwork, one or two of them dating back to the 18th century, are typical of those found in the older cities all across Turkey. Nowadays they are usually divided up and inhabited by several families. Hundreds of those in and around the Ankara citadel have been restored to their past splendour and turned into gift shops, coffee houses and restaurants with stunning views over the city.

Carry on to the south gate in the outer walls to reach a square in front of the 19th-century **clock tower**. Across the road, the **Cengelhan Rahmi M Koç Museum** (www.rmk-museum.org.tr; Tue–Fri 10am–5pm, Sat–Sun 10am–7pm; charge), housed in a *kervansaray* built in 1522, houses exhibits on everything from transport to medicine collected from around the world. Next door, the Erimtan Archeology and Arts Museum (Tue–Sun 10am–5pm; charge), opened in 2015, contains roughly 2,000 mostly Roman and Byzantine ceramics, glass-works, coins and jewellery.

THE MUSEUM OF ANATOLIAN CIVILISATIONS

Downhill from the castle entrance and immediately west of the Erimtan Museum lies Ankara's premier attraction, the **Museum of Anatolian Civilisations ❺** (Anadolu Medeniyetleri Müzesi; Kadife Sokak; tel: 312-324 3160; Tue–Sun Apr–Oct 8.30am–7pm, Nov–Mar 8.30am–5.30pm; charge). Housed in a former *han* (a covered market with workshops) built by Grand Vizier Mahmut Paşa, this is one of Turkey's finest museums, renovated and reorganised to a high standard in 2013. Exhibits are labelled in English. It focuses on the pre-Classical civilisations of Anatolia, and contains artefacts from various digs around the country. The displays begin with the Palaeolithic, take in Neolithic Çatalhöyük, the Assyrian trading colony of Küllepe and pre-Hittite Alacahöyük, before progressing to Phrygian and Roman sites. There are also special collections from the Hittite and Urartian eras. The contents of the Great Tumulus at Gordion include some fine Phrygian woodcarvings still in astonishingly good condition after 2,700

⊘ Tip

If you are staying in Ankara for a few days and use the Metro to get into the centre of town, buy a block of tickets (available in quantities of 2–10) which can be used on buses as well.

Sultanhan monument with Luwian hiero-glyphics at the Museum of Anatolian Civilisations.

years. Particular things to look out for include Neolithic frescoes from Çatalhöyük, vast Hittite stone sculptures, and the emblems of the Bronze Age reindeer gods found in Alacahöyük. Allow two or three hours to do it all justice.

COPPER ALLEY

If you turn left from the castle entrance you will come to a recently restored street which might seem more at home in a small Anatolian town than in the country's capital. Many of the shops here sell wool and goatskins, a reminder that "Angora" – the old form of the city's name – was a world-famous wool centre.

Continue downhill to reach the 12th-century Seljuk **Aslanhane Camii**, whose brick minaret still retains traces of the blue ceramics that once covered it. Inside, the mosque, built upon the foundations of a Roman temple, features an elaborately carved wooden roof, held up by a forest of wooden pillars. At the top of each column is a reused Classical capital, some of which came from the lost temple. To the left,

facing downhill, a stone doorway with a lion beside it leads into an old dervish *tekke*, a medieval lodge whose Roman stonework suggests that it was also built onto a Roman structure.

The side streets in this part of town are full of craftsmen's shops, catering to the needs of an agricultural population coming in from the villages. Turn into **Salman Sokak**, to the right of the Aslanhane Mosque, and you are in one of Ankara's most famous shopping attractions. **Copper Alley ⑤** (as Salman Sokak is known among Ankara's foreign residents, even though *salman* means "straw") is exactly what its name suggests. You can find brand-new copper here, but old pewter plates and copper jugs (lined with tin if they are to be used rather than as ornaments), candlesticks, clocks, antiques and curios of all sorts are also on display. In the past, ancient coins and other valuable objects would be in some of these shops, but these days, most of the "ancient objects" on sale are fakes. If you want something genuine, try a 19th-century plate with a Greek, Ottoman or Armenian inscription.

ANKARA'S OTHER ATTRACTIONS

As befits a capital city, Ankara has a plenitude of museums worth visiting. Just south of the towering Melike Hatun Mosque, completed in 2017, is the **Foundations Museum** (Vakıf Eserleri Müzesi; Tue–Sun 9am–5pm; free), which displays some of the magnificent old carpets from mosques around the country. For Turkish handicrafts and costumes, head a couple blocks south to the **Ethnographical Museum** (Etnografya Müzesi; Opera Meydanı; www.etnografyamuzesi.gov.tr; daily Apr–Sept 8.30am–7pm, Oct–Mar 8.30am–5pm; charge). Next door is the **Painting and Sculpture Museum** (Resim ve Heykel Müzesi; Opera Meydanı; Tue–Sun 9am–noon, 1–5pm; charge), which exhibits the work of most of the best known 19th- and 20th-century Turkish artists.

Ankara's famous Copper Alley.

To the west beyond Atatürk Bulvarı is the **State Concert Hall** (Konser Salonu), which regularly stages Presidential Symphony Orchestra concerts. A short walk south of here and set in an old railway warehouse, **Cer Modern** (www.cermodern.org; Tue–Sun 10am–8pm; charge) hosts the city's most impressive contemporary arts collection, doubling as an occasional concert venue. Other theatres include the state opera, two state theatres, and a whole host of smaller private theatres, many of them near the Ankara Sanat Tiyatrosu, just off İzmir Caddesi near the Atatürk Bulvarı at **Kızılay**.

KOCATEPE MOSQUE

One of the most impressive sites in the city is the **Kocatepe Camii ⓖ**, on the hill southeast of Kızılay. Ankara's largest mosque, the shrine combines the appearance of 16th-century Islamic architecture and 20th-century technology. A replica of Istanbul's Blue Mosque, with four minarets instead of six, it took 20 years to build and opened to the public in the early 1980s. To enter, take the staircases up to the white marble courtyard. In a modern twist, there is a multistorey car park and shopping mall underneath it.

Many government ministries are bunched together south of Kızılay, on either side of Atatürk Bulvarı, the main street running north–south through Ankara. Further south, on the right-hand side of the same road, are the buildings of Turkey's parliament – the **Büyük Millet Meclisi** (Grand National Assembly).

Most of the foreign embassies are located along Atatürk Bulvarı and Cinnah Caddesi, which continues uphill to Çankaya and is crowned by the presidential palace, **Cumhurbaşkanlık Köşkü**. In the well-laid-out grounds is a *köşk (pavilion)* which was **Atatürk's residence** (Tue–Fri 9.30am–5pm, Sat & Sun 1–5pm). Also here is **Atakule** (10am–10pm, until 3am if restaurant is open), a 125-metre (413ft) tower with a shopping centre and revolving restaurant on the top floor, one of Ankara's best-known landmarks.

All travellers to Ankara should visit the **Anıtkabir ⓗ**, the **Mausoleum of Kemal Atatürk** (Anıt Caddesi, Tandoğan; tel: 312-231 7975; daily Feb–Apr 9am–4.30pm, May–Oct 9am–5pm, Nov–Jan 9am–4pm). The monument is located around 1.5km (0.9 miles) southwest of Gençlik Parkı and well-away from most of the other attractions. Despite this, official visitors never miss this national treasure, as protocol requires that they pay their respects to the founder of modern Turkey here.

The mausoleum is partly designed to imitate Hittite and ancient Anatolian architecture. Each province of Turkey contributed stone to the main hall which contains Atatürk's tomb. His body, however, is not kept in the stone catafalque, but is buried in a chamber beneath it. Within the complex, the **Anıtkabir Museum** (same hours) contains books from Atatürk's library, his uniforms and even some of his visiting cards. Vehicles used by the great man are parked outside.

Witness the changing of the guard at the Mausoleum of Kemal Atatürk, Ankara.

Kocatepe Camii, Ankara's largest mosque.

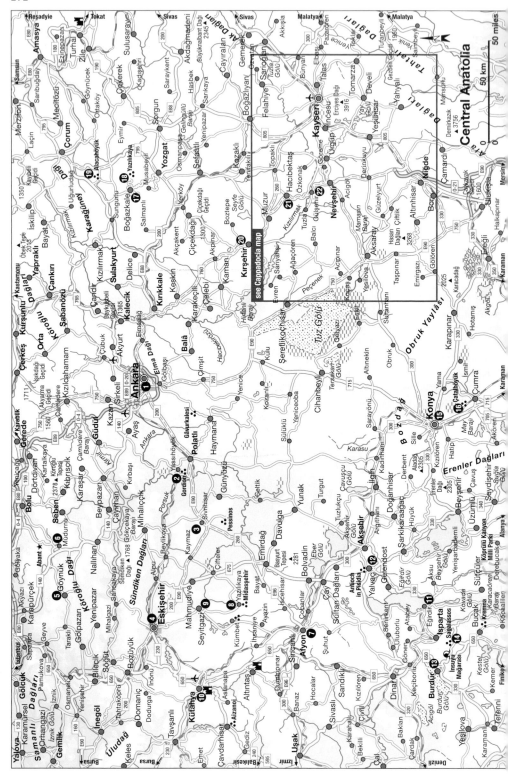

Central Anatolia

see Cappadocia map

50 miles

50 km

NORTHWEST ANATOLIA

The population may be sparse and much of the landscape may consist of bare hillsides with hardly a tree to be seen, yet this was once the heartland of the formidable kingdom of ancient Phrygia.

Three roads lead from Ankara towards the Sea of Marmara and Istanbul. The first follows the D-90 via Eskişehir; the second a remote ramble through the mountains to Beypazarı, Nallıhan and Göynük; the third along the main highway almost due north through the Köroglu Dagları to the Black Sea region.

DUE WEST FROM ANKARA

In a famous corruption trial in ancient Rome, the orator Cicero – who was defending a sticky-fingered Roman governor of Phrygia – managed to ridicule the prosecution witnesses by describing them as "ignorant Phrygians who had never seen a tree in their lives". Cicero's rather cruel joke comes to mind as you take the E-90 highway out of **Ankara ❶** through Polatlı and due west to Eskişehir. This is one of the great roads of history: Alexander the Great, the Crusaders and most of the great armies of the Byzantine and Ottoman empires have travelled along it at some time.

About an hour out of Ankara, the town of **Polatlı** is chiefly notable for having been the furthest point reached by the Greek invaders of Anatolia in 1921. The high tidemark of the Greek invasion is, quite literally,

marked in concrete on the hill to the north of town. Today, Polatlı is the headquarters of an army tank brigade. It also makes the perfect base for visiting Gordion.

MYTHS AND LEGENDS

About 10km (6 miles) northwest of Polatlı, at Yassıhöyük, lie the ruins of **Gordion ❷** (daily 8am–5pm, Tue–Sun in winter; charge), capital of Phrygia during the reign of the fabled King Gordius and his golden son, Midas, in about 800 BC. It remained

⊙ Main attractions
Gordion
Sivrihisar
Eskişehir
Beypazarı
Kızılcahamam
Mudurnu

Map on page 292

Donkeys are still used as working animals in the smaller villages.

a moderately important city into Classical times, though it was later eclipsed by Ankara. There are no romantic classical remains here, however, and there is a lack of shade, which can pose a problem if you visit in summer.

The most impressive features today are the huge burial tumuli of the Phrygian kings, excavated in the 1950s. The tomb of Gordius is an astonishing 50 metres (164ft) high and 300 metres (985ft) across. When first excavated, what was then believed to be the tomb of Midas was filled with a vast variety of objects, although, disappointingly, nothing golden. A tunnel has been constructed to enable visitors to walk into the centre of the mound, where they can inspect a burial chamber built out of huge cedar trunks which the centuries have turned to stone.

The actual remains of the king and the objects buried with him can now be viewed in Ankara's Museum of Anatolian Civilisations (see page 289). In the museum (daily same hours and charge for museum and

Midas' tomb) across the road you can also see the world's earliest mosaic, made out of black-and-white pebbles, while further along the road the walls of the Phrygian capital have been dug out from within the mound that eventually swamped the city.

Sivrihisar ❸ lies about 40km (25 miles) further down the road, which forks at this point: the northern fork runs due west to Eskişehir, while the E-96 branches south for Afyon, and eventually the south and west coasts. Backed by dramatically craggy rocks, the town's focal point is its restored 13th-century **Ulu Camii** (Great Mosque), full of soaring wooden columns – many of them capped with old Roman masonry. Nearby are a couple of Ottoman mosques and a large, poorly restored 19th-century Armenian church. Many of the fine old Ottoman houses are currently being restored. It's an easy excursion to the village of **Nasrettin Hoca**, the pretty, rural birthplace of Nasreddin Hodja (see box), a 13th-century "wise fool" whose image crops up all over.

☉ NASREDDIN HODJA

A philosopher and humourist, Nasreddin Hodja (1208–85) lived in northwest Anatolia when the region was under siege by Mongol invaders. He studied in the religious schools at Sivrihisar and Akşehir, a city 200km (130 miles) southwest of Ankara, and later died in Akşehir, where he is buried. Turkey's most famous folk hero, Nasreddin Hodja figures in jokes throughout the Middle East. His stories, many of which end with a moral twist or clever epigram, are particularly popular among the Turkic peoples. Set in private homes, marketplaces, bazaars, streets, courts and mosques, they describe the minutiae of everyday life, and his subtle jokes and tales exemplify the common sense of the Anatolian people without patronising them.

Ruined walls at Gordion, ancient Phrygia's capital.

About 15km (9 miles) south of Sivrihisar, at **Ballıhisar**, are the Roman ruins of **Pessinos** (Apr–Sept 8am–7pm, Oct–Mar 8am–5pm), one of the three great centres of Roman Galatia – the region settled by the Celts ("Gauls"). Pessinos was situated in the middle of the Phrygian plain, and historians believe that it was abandoned for the relative safety of Sivrihisar during the age of invasions which began after AD 600.

In 1967, archaeologists uncovered a temple dedicated to Cybele, the Roman equivalent of the Anatolian mother goddess, Kubaba. Fragments of various Roman buildings are scattered across an extensive area around the stream running through the present-day village, although the ruins are by no means as dramatic as those to be found elsewhere.

OTTOMAN HEARTLAND

Eskişehir ❹, the Roman and Byzantine Dorylaeum, lies about another hour's drive west of Sivrihisar. Its name means "Old City" in Turkish, and authorities have been hard at work restoring the old Ottoman houses of its Odunpazarı quarter in order to recover some sense of that past. To the west of here, the **ETI Archaeological Museum** (ETİ Arkeoloji Müzesi; Atatürk Bulvarı; tel: 222-230 1371; daily 8am–5pm; charge) displays more than 2,000 artefacts spanning from Neolothic to Ottoman times, including superb mosaics and statuettes from the Roman period. The **Meerschaum Museum** (Tue–Sun 9am–5pm; charge), in the old town, contains a collection of local meerschaum pipes; modern versions are sold nearby. Just north is the City Museum (Tue–Sun 10am–5pm), consisting of wax displays and an impressive contemporary glasswork collection. Next door, the strikingly designed Odunpazarı Art Museum, is set to open in 2019.

Today, the city is a regional industrial powerhouse, hosting the state railways factory for diesel engine locomotives, a big university and Turkey's largest air-force base, with F-16 jet

The rooftops and minarets of Eskişehir.

⊙ Tip

Head for Beypazarı on a Sunday to witness the lively market where women sell everything from colourful fabrics to carrot-flavoured *helva*.

fighters constantly flying over the city and countryside on military manoeuvres. Visitors will notice many local people with East Asian features. They are the descendants of Crimean Tatars who settled in this part of the country after the Turkish-Russian War of 1878.

A little way west is **Inönü**, the scene of two decisive battles in Turkey's War of Independence against the invading Greeks after World War I. Directly north is the Sakarya valley and the rolling landscape from which the Ottoman Empire burst onto the world stage. The small town of **Söğüt** has the distinction of being the birthplace of the world-famous Ottoman dynasty which ruled Turkey, the Balkans and much of the Middle East until the early 20th century. The first of the great war leaders and father of Sultan Osman I was a frontier warrior named Ertuğrul Gazi who ruled a minor fiefdom in Söğüt in the late 13th century. His **tomb** can be visited (daily 8.30am–5.30pm). Outside, the area is decorated with the busts of the greatest rulers of all 17 Turkic states.

To the east, across the river and due north of Eskişehir, the village of **Mihalgazi** was home to a Byzantine Greek warrior chief called Mihal Gazi (also Köse Mihal) who joined forces with Osman and helped him in his meteoric rise to power. Neglected and forlorn, his grave lies in a grassy meadow to the south of the village. It is a reminder of how the first Ottoman ruler made the transition from village raider to self-styled sultan in a single generation – and how easily his allies were forgotten in the heady rush to power.

Keep heading northwest from Söğüt and you come to **Bilecik**, where Osman's wife and his father-in-law, Edibali, lie buried. A few crumbling fragments of wall mark the site of the Byzantine castle which was captured by one of the very first Ottoman armies.

NORTHWEST FROM ANKARA

This route is definitely the back road from Ankara, leading through remote hills to a succession of small hill and mountain towns – **Beypazarı**, **Göynük**, **Taraklı** and **Murdurnu** – so little disturbed by time that they have managed to preserve much of their 19th-century appearance intact.

Under the guidance of a go-ahead local mayor, Beypazarı has carved out a niche for itself as a lovely little Ottoman town with a lively market within easy day-trip reach of Ankara. **Göynük** ❺ deserves to be better known than it is. The approach road is a lonely winding track through the mountains. Once there, you can visit the **Tomb of Akşemsettin**, tutor to Mehmet the Conqueror and the first to issue the call to prayer from Aya Sofya after the fall of Constantinople in 1453. It is lavishly maintained with gifts from the Muslim world. Visit on a Monday morning to witness the colourful local market to which women from surrounding villages bring butter and cheese for sale.

Abant hotel and lake in deep winter.

At the far end of the mountain road, just before you reach Bilecik, are **Taraklı** and **Gölpazarı**, at its centre a most unusual early Ottoman caravansarai. Like Beypazarı and Göynük, Taraklı is full of wonderful old Ottoman houses that go largely unseen by foreigners.

THE ANKARA–ISTANBUL HIGHWAY

The main route from Ankara to Istanbul begins heading north along the E-89 before shooting west via the E-80, part of the Trans-European Motorway (TEM). The E-89 is one of the most scenic routes in the country, running past sometimes gloriously wooded and mountainous countryside.

Another northward route from Ankara follows the D-750 to **Kızılcahamam**, with its hills and woods, and is a favourite picnic and resort spot, famous for its mineral waters, Turkish bath and hot springs. This is also a favourite area for wild-boar hunting. Turn off the highway to reach the town of **Çerkeş**. On your way north to the Black Sea region, with its steep, wooded valleys, you pass the seldom visited towns of **Tosya** and **Osmancık**, the majestic **İlgaz Mountains**, with their small ski resort.

Alternatively, exit to the south soon after the E-89 becomes the E-80 to reach Dörtdivan and continue onwards to **Kartalkaya**, a small winter-sports resort with a handful of ski-lifts and hotels. There is little reason to stop in **Bolu**, a nondescript Anatolian town, but about 32km (20 miles) west, tucked away in the woods, is the spa-and-hotel complex of **Abant**, on the shores of a jade-coloured crater lake. Nearby **Mudurnu** ❻ has a delightful market, a wonderful old hamam, the ruins of a Byzantine fort and many magnificent, if crumbling, Ottoman mansions. Continue a kilometre (0.6 miles) south to glimpse the bizarre housing development that has stirred public outcry in recent years for jarring with the local aesthetic: some 700 identical chateau-style villas placed on the market in 2019, aimed firmly at a Gulf Arab market.

The mountain town of Göynük.

SOUTHWEST ANATOLIA

Lakes and mountains, poppies and pottery, the birthplace of Mevlâna is a little-visited region rewarding for the adventurous traveller to explore.

◉ Main attractions
Phrygian Valley
Eğirdir Gölü
Sagalassos
Konya
Mevlana Tekkesi (Konya)
Çatalhöyük

Map on page 292 ◉

Turkey's vast size means that most travellers rarely venture into Southwest Anatolia – a great shame since the Eğirdir region boasts some fabulous lake and mountain scenery. In October when the trees take on autumnal hues this is one of the most beautiful places in Turkey and nearby Sagalassos is one of the best-excavated and dramatically situated ancient sites in Turkey. The most-visited town here is Konya, birthplace of the revered Mevlâna and the whirling dervishes, but Kütahya, further north, also receives a number of

visitors keen to admire the produce of its ceramics industry.

AFYON, OPIUM CENTRE

In the lush green area around **Afyon** (or Afyonkarahisar) ❼, southwest of Ankara, the farmers grow May-flowering poppies for their opium. The name Afyon even means "opium" in Turkish, and this is the centre of the country's legal opium industry, with a state-run factory which refines opium for the pharmaceutical industry. This is also one of the main production centres for Turkish marble which is excavated, cut and polished here, and then used to make flooring, gravestones and work surfaces.

The centre of Afyon is dominated by a distinctive black outcrop. There is thought to have been a Hittite stronghold here, and the high rock was also used as a refuge by the Byzantines during their wars against the Arabs. The climb up some 700 steps to **Afyon Castle** (open access) is not for the faint-hearted, but the town below has many beautiful 19th-century Ottoman houses and several fine mosques, including the 13th-century Seljuk **Ulu Camii** (Great Mosque) whose roof is supported by a sea of wooden columns. Also worth a look are the **Kuyulu Mescit** (Mosque of the Well), with a

Afyon's legal opium harvest colours the summer landscape purple and white.

tiled minaret, and the 14th-century **Kubbeli Mescit**. (A *mescit* is a small, simple mosque.) The **Archaeological Museum** (Kurtuluş Caddesi; Tue–Sun 8.30am–noon, 1.30–5.30pm; charge) houses relics of the Hittite, Phrygian and Lydian periods found locally.

THE PHRYGIAN VALLEY

A series of villages that once made up the heart of the ancient Phrygian kingdom of King Midas lies north of Afyon in the **Frig Vadisi** (Phrygian Valley). Allow at least two days to explore the valley properly, and don't forget to pack a picnic as the scenery en route is wonderful. **Ayazin** offers rock-cut churches similar to those of Göreme in Cappadocia, while **Kümbet** has a Phrygian tomb from the Roman period with lions carved on it.

Most splendid of all the monuments, however, are those at **Yazılıkaya** ❽ (Midasşehir; daily 9am–5pm), where the flat landscape suddenly gives way to hills and woods, providing the once-great Phrygian city of Metropolis with a hilltop landscape worthy of an Italian Renaissance painting. The most striking sight here is the giant **Midas Monument** (c. 6th century BC) with a curious and undeciphered inscription in the Phrygian alphabet. It probably contained a shrine to Cybele (also known as Mida and, according to Greek legend, the mother of King Midas). On the north slope the Hittite reliefs show that the site has a history stretching back at least 1,000 years before Midas.

About 30km (19 miles) north of Yazılıkaya, a superb Bektaşi *tekke* (dervish monastery) crowns the hill to the south of the town of **Seyitgazi** ❾. In some ways, it is even more spectacular – and certainly larger – than the headquarters of the Bektaşi organisation at Hacıbektaş (see page 307).

Seyitgazi is named after a legendary Arab warrior who died in the siege of Afyon in AD 740, during the Arab-Byzantine Wars. The story relates how a Byzantine princess fell in love with him, and seeing some soldiers creeping in his direction, dropped a stone to signal the danger. Alas, it fell on his head and killed him. His tomb, which is about three times the length of a normal man, can be visited. Beside it a smaller one is said to be that of the princess.

KÜTAHYA: CERAMIC CAPITAL

Kütahya ❿ is an attractive town, with rambling old streets and a citadel ringed by a Byzantine fortress. From the 17th century onwards, Kütahya became the home of the best faïence and pottery in the land, its tiles used on countless mosques, its jugs and bowls found in every upmarket home. The craft has now been revived and there is an interesting small **Tile Museum** (Gediz Caddesi; Tue–Sun 9am–5pm; charge) in a former soup kitchen behind the 15th-century **Ulu Camii** (Great Mosque), one of several fine mosques.

Nearby, housed in a theological school, is the small **archaeological museum** (Tue–Sun 8am–noon, 1–5pm; charge). The **Kossuth Evi**

Ceramic plates made in Kütahya can be found for sale throughout the country.

Rock-cut church in the Phrygian Valley.

Towering walls still ring the lakeside city of Eğirdir.

The amphitheatre at Sagalassos.

(Tue–Sun 8am–noon, 1–5pm; charge), a fine Ottoman mansion belonging to a Hungarian revolutionary, which is preserved as it was in the mid-19th century, is also worth a visit.

Some 27km (15 miles) to the southwest is **Çavdarhisar** and the site of ancient **Aizanoi** (Apr–Sept 8.45am–7pm, Oct–Mar 8.45am–5.30pm; charge), with a fine temple dedicated to Zeus. In antiquity, the city claimed to have been the birthplace of the father of the gods. Seldom visited, this is the best-preserved of Anatolia's Zeus temples and well worth the effort of getting here. There is a huge vaulted chamber beneath.

THE LAKE DISTRICT

South of Afyon is a green and attractive region commonly known as Turkey's "Lake District". There are at least seven significant lakes, the area is well known for its birdlife and the beautiful marked walking route, St Paul's Trail (see page 259), weaves through this mountainous land to its terminus at Yalvaç.

Isparta is chiefly famous for rose oil (attar of roses), an essential ingredient in perfume. The town had a large Greek population until 1924, and a few ruined churches can still be found in the backstreets. A twenty-minute drive away is the town of **Eğirdir** ⑪ at the southern tip of beautiful **Eğirdir Gölü**, the largest freshwater lake in Turkey. The town was founded by the Hittites and became a regular stop on the King's Way, an important trade route between Ephesus and Babylon in the 5th century BC. Two small islands are joined to the town by a causeway, and the further of them, **Yeşilada**, has several attractive *pansiyons* whose owners can usually arrange boat trips on the lake. The ruins of an old **Seljuk fort** (open access) stand on the mainland near the 15th-century **Ulu Camii** (Great Mosque) and the Dündar *medrese* (religious school), which has a beautifully decorated portal but is now used as a shopping centre. Behind the town rises 1,733 metre (5,685ft) high Sivri Dağ, an impressive peak with grand views down over the town, island and lake, and behind to the snowy heights of Davraz (2,637 metres; 8,651ft), with a small but decent ski-resort nestling at the foot of the main ridge.

The drive up the more attractive eastern side of the lake leads to **Yalvaç** ⑫, the ancient Antioch in Pisidia and much visited by Christian pilgrims because of its associations with St Paul. According to the New Testament, it was here that Paul gave his first recorded sermon. This was so successful that the Gentiles pleaded with him to repeat it the following Saturday and the synagogue was packed. The Jews, out of envy, drove Paul from the city.

Antioch in Pisidia (daily Apr–Sept 9am–7pm, Oct–Mar 8am–5pm; charge), founded between 301 and 280 BC on the site of a Phrygian settlement by Seleukos Nikator, later became a Roman colony for veteran soldiers. Today the most significant remains on the site are of a

temple to Augustus, which was once surrounded by a semicircular colonnaded arcade. Huge baths, a nymphaeum, the aqueduct and an early synagogue (later a church) are also visible. The small **museum** (Tue–Sun 8am–5pm; charge) in Yalvaç houses relics from the site and the nearby temple to the god Men.

You may wish to continue on from here along the country road which loops back round the top of the lake and heads southwest to **Keçiborlu** via **Senirkent**. Continue west from there, and the road to Denizli and Pamukkale, with its famous travertines, passes **Dinar**, a town levelled by an earthquake in 1995, and **Acıgöl**, a large, sterile salt lake. Alternatively, head south, down the scrubby shore of the vast saline expanse of **Burdur Gölü**, to the town of Burdur.

Burdur ⑬ itself is dull, but it does have a 14th-century **Ulu Camii** (Great Mosque) and a small **museum** (Gazi Caddesi; daily Apr–Sept 9am–7pm, Oct–Mar 8.30am–5.30pm; charge) which contains finds from Kremna and

Sagalassos (see below), and Hacılar, a site dating back to c. 6000 BC.

About 10km (6 miles) south of the town, signposted left off the main road, is the well-lit **İnsuyu Mağarası** (daily 8.30am–6pm; charge), with 600 metres (190ft) of tunnels, dramatic displays of stalactites and, until recently, nine underground lakes. Unfortunately, a proliferation of wells in the valley above has almost dried up the lakes completely.

ANCIENT PISIDIA

Some 25km (16 miles) east of Burdur, off the D-685 to Isparta, follow signs through the village of Ağlasun to find the ruins of **Sagalassos** ⑭ (www. tursaga.com; daily Apr–Sept 7.30am–6pm, Oct–Mar 7.30am–7pm; charge), which was the second city of Pisidia after Antioch and is currently under excavation and reconstruction. Set 1,500 metres (4,920ft) above sea level on the slopes of craggy Mount Akdağ, it is potentially one of the most complete ancient cities in Asia Minor – its superb 9,000-seat theatre

The wonderfully reconstructed nymphaeum at Sagalassos.

Lake Eğirdir.

Dervishes still whirl, for Allah and the tourists.

Mevlâna's tomb, Konya.

remains just as an earthquake left it. The ancient city includes a theatre, an odeon, a library complete with mosaic floor, and a lower agora with two nymphaea and an excavated baths complex. The upper agora boasts a *bouleuterion* (circular debating chamber), a 12-metre (40ft) monumental column, a painstakingly restored arch dedicated to Emperor Claudius and, perhaps most impressive of all, the Antonine Nymphaeum, complete with water running through it.

The majority of the remains date back to the Roman imperial period but the city was noteworthy much earlier, famously falling to Alexander the Great in 333 BC. Partly reconstructed finds are gathered in the museum in Burdur. Superb computer reconstruction drawings illustrate the major vistas and explain the site and well-constructed walkways are in place to help visitors explore the ruins. The work is a technical masterpiece, and includes investigation of local land-use, road and water systems and plant and animal life in early historical times.

If you keep heading south towards Antalya, you'll reach **Bucak**, the access point for the ruins of **Kremna** (daily Apr–Sept 8.30am–5.30pm, Oct–Mar 8.30am–7pm), about 13 miles (8 miles) away. The approach road winds attractively along a pine-clad valley to a spectacular clifftop city overlooking the Aksu Çayı. A massive earthwork used by the Romans to reach the height of the walls when they were besieging the town is still visible today, but many of the buildings have been badly damaged. The walls of the bathhouse, however, stand to their full height and house some fine inscribed statue bases.

KONYA

The road south from Ankara to Konya forks off from the Mersin–Adana road (E-90) after about 100km (62 miles) of rather dull scenery. To the west of the road is the vast salt lake known as **Tuz Gölü**, a favourite spot for goose-hunters (note that the lake is more accessible from the road to Aksaray).

Konya ⓯ (Ikonium) was the capital of the Seljuk Empire between 1071 and 1308, and remains a centre of Sufic teaching and a pilgrimage destination for devout Sunni Muslims. Visited by St Paul several times around AD 50, it has become an industrial centre in the last few decades and is now ringed with bleak concrete suburbs which wall in the Seljuk monuments at its heart. The citizens are renowned for their piety – alcohol is not sold in stores or restaurants, even though one of Turkey's biggest malt factories is, ironically, located here. Konya has been a stronghold for Islamic parties since the start of the Republican era.

In the city centre is the **Alâeddin Tepesi** (Aladdin's Hill), which has been built up by successive settlement over the centuries. On the top are the last remaining walls of the **Sultani Sarayı** (Palace of the Seljuk

Sultans; currently being restored) and the 12th- and 13th-century **Alâeddin Camii**, once home to some of the oldest carpets in the world (they're mostly in the Museum of Turkish and Islamic Arts in Istanbul now). Of the other major Seljuk monuments in town, the **Karatay Medrese**, an Islamic school built in 1251, is now a **Ceramics and Tile Museum** (Hastane Caddesi; Tue–Sun 9am–5pm; charge) housing, among other things, tiles depicting distinctly oriental-looking Seljuk princesses. The **Archaeological Museum** (Sahibiata Caddesi; Tue–Sun 9am–5pm; charge) has some impressive ancient sarcophagi and some of the finds from nearby Çatalhöyük, although the finest have been carted off to Ankara.

HOME OF THE DERVISHES

Every visitor to Konya wants to see the lovely turquoise-domed **Mevlâna Museum** (Kışla Caddesi; daily Apr–Sept 9am–7pm, Oct–Mar 9am–5pm; charge), the home of the whirling dervishes (see box). At the heart of the complex is the tomb of Mevlâna ("Our Master") Celaleddin Rumi, the founder of the order. Dervish beliefs also appealed to the large Christian population of Anatolia and helped bridge the gap between them and their Seljuk rulers. Mevlâna preached tolerance, forgiveness and enlightenment, and his poetry, even in translated versions, is moving and inspirational.

The **Mevlâna Festival of the Whirling Dervishes** is held in a specially designed stadium every December, and the piety of most of the audience makes it clear that the *sema* (whirling ceremony) has not lost its religious significance. Performances for tourists are given daily in summer (check locally for details).

AROUND KONYA

About 10km (6 miles) outside Konya is the former Greek village of **Sille**, with the remains of the Church of St Michael and a spring dated to 1732. **Çatalhöyük**  (daily 9am–5pm; charge), about 35km (22 miles) southeast of Konya, is among the most significant Neolithic sites in the country. From about 6250–5400 BC, this was a prosperous town of some 5,000 people. Rich and poor lived crammed together in houses which ran directly into one another with no streets between them. The only way to gain entry was by climbing through the roofs. It is the first place in the world whose residents are known to have used irrigation and kept domesticated animals. They wove textiles, used simple carpets and traded in luxury goods, notably obsidian, a mineral used for axes, daggers and mirrors. Most striking of all were their shrines, adorned with statuettes and paintings depicting bulls and fertility rites.

The wooden roof of the magnificent **Eşrefoğlu Camii** at Beyşehir, 77km (48 miles) west of Konya, is supported by cedar columns. Dating from 1299, it is the largest and best-preserved mosque of its kind in the country.

A turret of turquoise tiles is the showy high point of Konya's Mevlâna Tekkesi.

⊘ THE WHIRLING DERVISHES

There was a time when visitors to Turkey could only hope to see the famous whirling dervishes going through their paces in mid-December when they were permitted to perform in Konya. These days, however, it would be hard to visit the country and not come across whirling dervishes of varying degrees of authenticity.

The dervish order was originally founded by Celaleddin Rumi (1207–73), better known in the West as Mevlâna, who was born in what is now Afghanistan but travelled to Konya with his family. Once there, he developed his philosophy of all-enveloping tolerance, at odds in many ways with the modern-day city that houses his shrine. It was Mevlâna's vision that gave rise to the idea that, by rotating their bodies over a prolonged period of time, individuals could be brought closer to Allah, and it was during his lifetime that the costume associated with the dervishes, in which white robes represent shrouds and tall conical caps tombstones, evolved. In 1925 Atatürk abolished all the dervish orders as a potential threat to his secular state, and it is only in recent years that they have started to flourish again. While in Konya you should certainly visit the site of Mevlâna's tomb, but it's also well worth attending a proper *sema* (dervish ceremony) if you get the opportunity.

EAST OF ANKARA

The journey east of Ankara takes travellers through the Anatolian countryside to spectacular ruins of ancient civilisations and the rock churches of Cappadocia.

To the northeast of Ankara is a largely flat area mainly visited by travellers en route to the eastern end of the Black Sea who are keen to explore the World Heritage listed Hittite sites around Boğazkale. The road south to the rock-cut wonders of Cappadocia also kicks off from east of Ankara.

THE ROAD EAST

About 30km (19 miles) east of Ankara, a road known as the "Nato Highway" forks left, leading to the small ski resort of **Elmadağ**.

Kalecik, 80km (50 miles) northeast of Ankara, has a Roman castle with medieval additions and an Ottoman bridge over the Kızılırmak River. Further north along the same road the main sight in **Çankırı** is the **Taş Mescit**, a domed 13th-century mental hospital built by the Seljuk Turks, where music therapy helped people adapt to the stress caused by marauding raiders. The town's **Ulu Camii** (Grand Mosque) was built in 1558 by Süleyman the Magnificent, and rebuilt after an earthquake in 1936.

HITTITE CAPITAL

Anyone staying in Ankara should consider a visit to the ancient Hittite capital, **Hattuşa** ⓱ (daily Apr–Sept 8am–7pm, Oct–Mar 8am–5pm; charge). The ruins stretch out beside the town of Boğazkale, about 200km (124 miles) east of the

capital along the E-88 highway towards Çorum. You can also approach from the south, climbing a minor road through wild mountains, from Yozgat.

At the height of its prosperity in about 1400 BC, the city was the capital of an empire which stretched south to Cyprus and west to the Aegean. Its massive size and majestic setting are unrivalled. Though the higher slopes are now largely bare, it is not difficult to people them in the mind's eye with homes, warriors, priests, clerks, saddlers, cobblers and slaves. The sight is made more evocative

Map on page 292

Main attractions
Boazkale
Alacahöyük
Kirşehir
Hacıbektaş Karşi Kilisesi
(Church of St John, Gulşehir)

Poppies add colour to the landscape.

A craftsman recreates an ancient art at Yazılıkaya. Reproduction of ancient figurines and other artefacts are on sale at many of the country's museums.

The Lion Gate, Boğazkale.

by the knowledge that, not long after 1200 BC, the city was stormed and burned, and never recovered its former greatness.

The site is best explored by car, as the distances can take their toll under a burning summer sun. Begin on the ramparts, looking down at the **King's Gate** and **Lion Gate**. A section of the stonework is kept clear of rubble and weeds, so that it is possible to see the great stone ramparts more or less as they looked in Hittite times. Further proof of the formidable nature of Hittite architecture is provided by the **Yerkapı**, a 70-metre (229ft) tunnel under the walls.

Lower down, on an outcrop of the hill overlooking the valley, the **Büyükkale** (Citadel) was the site of the Imperial Palace, and it is here that the majority of the 3,350 clay tablets from the emperors' archives were found. Thanks to them, this great, vanished civilisation, virtually unknown 100 years ago, now has a detailed written history. Lower down are the foundations of the **Büyük Mabet** (Great Temple), which, in its day, may have been the largest building in the world, dedicated to the weather god, Hatti, and the sun goddess, Arinna. In 1986, archaeologists unearthed a bronze tablet engraved with the terms of a treaty here. This and most other artefacts from the site have been taken to Ankara, though the collection at Boğazkale's small **museum** (Tue–Sun Apr–Sept 8am–7pm, Oct–Mar 8am–5pm; charge) is worth checking out, not least for its pair of sphinxes – one of them returned from Berlin's Pergamon Museum in 2011.

TEMPLE TO 1,000 GODS

The religious heart of the Hittite kingdom lay slightly over 2km (1.5 miles) northeast of Boğazkale, in the rock shrine of **Yazılıkaya** ⑱ (same hours and ticket as Hattuşa). What survives today dates largely from 1275–1220 BC, when it was enlarged by the Hittite emperors. There are two main galleries carved from the rock, their walls covered by reliefs of deities wearing tall, conical caps. Many of the gods' names are not Hittite at all, but Hurrian or Hatti, showing how the culture and religion of the Hittite warrior aristocracy absorbed the beliefs and traditions of the indigenous people they had conquered.

ALACAHÖYÜK

A 20-minute drive further along the road will take you to the third great Hittite centre in the area, **Alacahöyük** ⑲ (Tue–Sun 8am–noon, 1.30–5.30pm; charge). Many of the most famous ancient Anatolian emblems, including the deer and the sun disk which have become symbols of modern Turkey, were discovered here during excavations in the 1930s. Alacahöyük is less picturesque than its neighbours, but one can clearly make out the ground plan of the Hittite and pre-Hittite buildings. The **Sphinx Gate** is the most impressive sight; the other reliefs have been replaced with replicas, the originals now on display in the Museum of Anatolian Civilisations in Ankara. The small on-site museum is mostly filled with ceramics.

OTHER SIGHTS IN THE AREA

Although the Hittite cities are undoubtedly the main drawcards, there are other places nearby that are also worth a quick look. In the tidy town of **Çorum** – to the northeast of Alacahöyük – is another surprising archaeological museum (daily Apr–Sept 9am–7pm, Oct–Mar 8am–5pm; charge) as well as the fine 13th-century **Ulu Camii**, built by the Seljuk Sultan Alâeddin Keykubat.

South of Boğazkale, **Yozgat** was founded by the Çapanoğlu dynasty, a Turkic clan that was influential in the region in the 17th century. It is dominated by the grand **Çapanoğlu Mustafa Paşa Camii**, built in 1779.

Kırşehir ⑳, southwest of Yozgat on the road to Cappadocia, stands on the site of the Byzantine city of Justianopolis Mokyssos. There are two reasons to break your journey here. The first is the **shrine of Ahi Evran** (1171–1261), a mystic whose cult has been compared to that of the Masons because of its association with the crafts guilds. Far more beautiful is the **Cacabey Camii** and *medrese*, built in the 13th century as an observatory and later converted into a mosque. Kırşehir also has a small **museum** (daily 8am–5pm) which contains some items said to have belonged to Ahi Evran. However, the area's most impressive museum lies 50km (31 miles) along the road northwest to Ankara: the **Kaman Kalehöyük Archeology Museum** (www.kalehoyukarkeolojimuzesi.gov.tr; daily 8–5pm; charge), set in a beautifully landscaped garden with interactive displays and finds from the adjacent (and ongoing) excavation site.

The road south from Kırşehir continues towards Cappadocia, passing through **Hacıbektaş** ㉑ which is named after **Hacı Bektaş Veli**, the founder of the Bektaşi order of dervishes who served as chaplains to the janissaries, the storm-troopers of the Ottoman Empire. The Bektaşis were a free-thinking, tolerant community and it is well worth visiting their shrine (Tue–Sun 8am–5pm; charge) where you will usually find local women praying. The small museum contains fine examples of calligraphy. Rooms in the lodge tell their own story: the communal eating hall, with its great cauldrons still hanging by the fireplace, and the meeting room used by the "fathers" of the order, rather like a Western chapterhouse.

Further south is **Gülşehir** ㉒, which sits on the banks of the Kızılırmak, Turkey's longest river. The town centre is dominated by the huge Karavezir Camii, paid for by the "Black Vizier" Seyyit Mehmetpaşa Silahtar (1735–81). Gülşehir is one of the northern gateways to Cappadocia, and of more interest is the stunning rock-cut **Karşı Kilisesi** (Church of St John; daily 8am–5pm; charge), on the southern outskirts, which dates back to 1214. Its frescoes were uncovered in 1995. The one of the Last Judgement is noteworthy as this image is not often seen in Cappadocian churches.

Continuing south to Nevşehir and Cappadocia you will pass the **Açık Sarayı** (Open Palace; daily 8am–5pm), actually a monastic centre with at least three separate rock-cut communal buildings.

⊙ **Fact**

A craftsman recreates an ancient art at Yazılıkaya. Reproductions of ancient figurines and other artefacts are on sale at many of the country's museums.

Kiss of Judas mosaic in Karşı Kilisesi, Gülşehir.

The magical landscape of Cappadocia with its otherworldly rock formations.

CAPPADOCIA

Cappadocia is famed for its eerie lunar landscape, astounding underground cities and spectacular rock-cut churches, their walls decorated with vivid Byzantine frescoes.

The French traveller Paul Lucas was the first Western European to leave an account of a visit to Cappadocia in 1706, but the area remained largely unknown to the outside world for two further centuries until Père Guillaume de Jerphanion stumbled on the rock churches of Cappadocia almost by chance during a journey across Anatolia in 1907. Like Lucas, he was stunned by what he saw: "Our eyes were astounded. I remember those valleys in the searingly brilliant light, running through the most fantastic of all landscapes," he wrote. A 10th-century history tells us that local inhabitants were called troglodytes "because they go under the ground in holes, clefts, and labyrinths, like dens and burrows". Paul Lucas himself understood that he was looking at a man-made landscape and thought he saw pyramids being used as houses, and weird statues of monks and the Virgin Mary.

Even now, when the valleys around the town of Ürgüp are relatively easy to reach (the flight from Istanbul to Kayseri takes an hour, with another hour by transfer bus to the hotels), Cappadocia can seem like a lost world to the arriving traveller. It took the 20th century – and perhaps the invention of photography – to make people really appreciate this extraordinary region.

The best way to see Cappadocia is on a hot-air balloon.

What we call "Cappadocia" today is only a small part of the Hellenistic kingdom and subsequent Roman province which bore the same name. The original province stretched for hundreds of kilometres further east and west. The name is older still. The region is first mentioned in a monument bearing the trilingual epitaph of the Persian King Darius as *Katpatuka* (the "Land of Beautiful Horses"). Several of the fathers of the early Church lived locally, but none of them ever made reference to their unusual surroundings.

Main attractions
Uçhisar
Göreme
Rock Churches
Hot-air Balloon Rides
Zelve
Kaymaklı underground city
Ihlara Vadisi valley

Map on page 310

ANCIENT UPHEAVALS

The geological explanation for the Cappadocian landscape is relatively straightforward. The whole region is dominated by **Erciyes Dağı** ❶ (ancient Mount Argaeus), the third-highest mountain in Anatolia, at 3,917 metres (12,851ft). Millions of years ago, Erciyes erupted, smothering the surrounding area with a torrent of lava extending hundreds of kilometres. This lava then cooled and solidified, before floods, rain and wind did their work, creating deep valleys and fissures in the lava rock, while the slopes were carved into outlandish cones and columns.

Though the white dust from the rocks looks like sand, it is actually much more fertile than the soil of the surrounding central Anatolian steppes. Trees, vines and vegetables grow with ease, a fact which meant that there were always plenty of farmers here. The first of them quickly discovered that the stone of the rock valleys is as magical as it looks, for it is soft until cut into and brought in contact with the air, making it a perfect medium for carving entire buildings out of the rock.

Generations of local people have utilised these unique conditions to hollow out innumerable chambers in the rocks over an area of several hundred square kilometres. Some provided homes for the farmers, others acted as dovecotes or stables. Many were used as chapels, cells and refectories for monks and hermits. And today, people still live in the cave houses, which are wonderfully cool in summer and warm(ish) in winter.

The result is a fairytale landscape, a child's delight, where it's easy to believe that dwarves, elves, fairies and other supernatural beings have just stepped round the corner, or perhaps vanished through a little doorway in the rock.

THREE THOUSAND ROCK CHURCHES

Many visitors only make a brief excursion to the cones and rock churches of Göreme, and spend an hour or two in **Zelve** or **Ihlara**. That's a pity, because Cappadocia is best explored

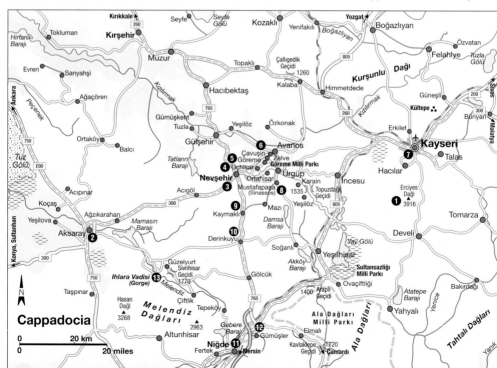

Cappadocia

in a leisurely fashion on foot, by car or on a bicycle. Local firms also hire out horses for trekking expeditions. There are an estimated 3,000 rock churches in the triangle between Kayseri, Niğde and Aksaray; and new caves, "underground cities" and even churches are still discovered from time to time.

The main roads from Ankara and Konya meet at **Aksaray ❷**, which was founded by King Archaelais of Cappadocia. The town contains many Islamic monuments, including the 15th-century **Ulu Camii** (Great Mosque) and the 13th-century **Eğri (Crooked) Minaret**, Turkey's answer to the Leaning Tower of Pisa. The star attraction at the **archaeological museum** (daily 8.30am–noon, 1–5pm; charge), opened in 2014 just west of town, is its collection of mummified cats and children.

The main transport and business hub for the area is the uninspiring town of **Nevşehir ❸**, which has a fine mosque complex, a craggy, Seljuk-era citadel (closed for restoration works) and a small museum (Tue–Sun 8am–5pm; charge). Directly beneath the citadel stretches what will surely become the town's prime attraction as soon as it opens to visitors (2019): a massive underground city, complete with its own beautifully-frescoed church. Accidentally discovered in 2013, the site has been estimated to extend 113 metres (371ft) under the surface, significantly deeper than the well-known complex beneath Derinkuyu.

Uçhisar ❹, 7km (4 miles) east of Nevşehir, is famed for its immense fist-shaped tower of volcanic tufa, honeycombed with chambers. This **citadel** (daily 8am–sunset; charge), the highest point in Cappadocia, offers a spectacular view over what was once a typical Anatolian village below, and also takes in the unworldly rock formations in the Göreme valley. There are several good hotels and restaurants in town.

Many people choose to base themselves in **Ürgüp**, a charming small town known for its boutique hotels,

restaurants and locally produced wine. The town is the richest in the Nevşehir region. It is also handily central to the most fascinating area of Cappadocia.

Nearby is **Ortahisar**, with another towering rock apartment block (daily 8am–sunset; charge) and a smattering of small hotels in a village which still retains much of its local atmosphere.

GÖREME AND ITS CHURCHES

The village of **Göreme ❺** hunkers down amid the fairy chimneys and, with its excellent facilities and laidback atmosphere, has long been one of the most popular places to stay in Cappadocia. Many townspeople still live in cave-dwellings, and it can be very pleasant to walk among their extraordinary houses, and perhaps meet some modern troglodytes. Many *pansiyons* feature cave rooms or fairy chimneys and prices are very reasonable.

Two km (1.5 miles) from Göreme village, on the Ürgüp road, over 30 of the finest churches in Cappadocia are clustered together in the **Göreme Open-Air Museum** (daily Apr–Oct 8am–7pm,

> **⊙ Tip**
>
> Guided expeditions on horseback are organised by Moonlight Horse Ranch in Göreme, while hot-air balloon tours are available from companies in Göreme, Ürgüp, Uçhisar and Çavuşin.

Uçhisar and its myriad chambers.

Nov–Mar 8am–5pm; charge, with additional charge for Dark Church). Almost all date from the 9th–11th centuries.

The **Church of St Barbara** is decorated with red symbols and figurines, including Christ enthroned, and St Barbara, the patron saint of soldiers. Next door is the main dome of the stunningly restored **Elmalı Kilise** (Church with the Apple). Also nearby is the **Yılanlı Kilise** (Church with the Snake), its walls covered with depictions of St George killing the dragon (or serpent) and other strange creatures (St George was the patron saint of Cappadocia; see box). Look also for St Onophrius, an ascetic who dwelt naked except or a long beard in the wilderness, allowing mosquitos to feast on him in repentance for swatting one of their number. Emperor Constantine and his mother Helena are pictured holding the True Cross which Helena supposedly discovered in Jerusalem.

The **Karanlık Kilise** (Dark Church), originally part of a larger monastery, has some of the finest Byzantine wall paintings, including a painting showing the betrayal of Christ by Judas. Another

shows the Transfiguration, with Christ between Moses and Elias on Mount Tabor. Across the road from the main gate, and thus easily missed, the **Tokalı Kilise** (Church with the Buckle) has a glorious profusion of well-preserved murals on deep-blue backgrounds, including the *Annunciation*, the *Agony in the Garden* and the *Journey to Bethlehem*.

If you arrive to find Göreme's Open-Air Museum crowded with coach parties, head instead to the frescoed **El Nazar Kilisesi** (Church of the Evil Eye; 8am–sunset; charge), signposted off the road to the museum, just past the Tourist Hotel.

The **Kılıçlar Vadisi** (the Valley of the Swords), running north opposite the Open-Air Museum, gets its name from the pointed rock formations resembling sabres. The **Kılıçlar Kilise** (Church of the Swords), about 400 metres (440yds) beyond Tokalı, is the biggest ecclesiastical complex in the region. More rock-hewn churches lie scattered to the north in the Red (Kızılçukur) and Rose (Güllüdere) Valleys, some of them featuring frescoes.

Ancient paintings survive in the churches of Göreme, such as at Karanlık Kilise.

ÇAVUŞIN AND ZELVE

Çavuşin ❻, 3km (2 miles) to the north of Göreme town, resembles a gigantic caved-in ant hill. Nearby is a ghost town whose inhabitants were moved down the hill after a rockfall in the 1960s. The **Church of Çavuşin** (daily 8am–5pm), accessible by a metal ladder, has strip narrative frescoes painted in bright green, pink, orange and dove-blue. Among the vivid portraits are a picture of Melias the Magister, a Byzantine-Armenian general who died as a prisoner of the Arabs in Baghdad in 974, and a Byzantine emperor riding a white horse, identified as John Tzimiskes (968–72) who is thought to have visited the area.

A ghost town, cave-houses and churches (few with frescoes) can also be found in and around **Zelve Open-Air Museum** (daily Apr–Oct 8am–7pm, Nov–Mar 8am–5pm; charge), consisting of three rugged valleys east of Çavuşin. It is a great place for rock climbing and has a vast underground **monastery**, which requires serious physical exertion to explore.

Not everything in Cappadocia is Byzantine. **Avanos**, on the northern bank of the Kızılırmak River, north of Zelve, is famed for its pottery, thanks to the rich red clay found along the river banks. The town has scores of shops selling local ware; some of them will let you try your own hand at throwing a pot.

EAST TO KAYSERI

Drive east along the Kayseri road from Ürgüp until you see a sign on the right for the Church of St Theodore, then keep going for about 10km (6 miles) along a village road through the unspoilt village of **Karain**. Further on, the outstanding **Church of St Theodore** (daily 8am–5pm) is located in the village of **Yeşilöz**, previously known as Tagar. It has a central dome and unique 11th-century frescoes, plus you can climb up into a gallery to look down on the nave.

Situated on a vast plain facing Mount Erciyes, **Kayseri ❼** is one of the oldest cities in Anatolia. It served as the capital of the Graeco-Roman province of Cappadocia from 380 BC to AD 17, was

Chairlift at the Erciyes ski resort near Kayseri.

Moreau's painting St George and the Dragon.

⊘ SAINT GEORGE

Patron saint of Cappadocia – and, of course, England – Saint George was a Roman Christian soldier in the service of Emperor Diocletian. He is thought to have been born into a noble family in the Levant, while his father (also a Christian) hailed from Cappadocia. He was martyred in AD 303 after Diocletian attempted, unsuccessfully, to force him to renounce his Christianity. The early Christians soon came to venerate him as a saint.

The legend of St George and the dragon is believed to have originated at the time of the Crusades, some eight centuries after his death, and the earliest known account has been traced to Cappadocia. In all likelihood, it is a case of a much earlier pagan legend being appropriated or otherwise mixed up with the story of the Christian martyr.

⊙ Tip

Try to avoid visiting Cappadocia in July and August when the heat can be oppressive. May, June and September are much nicer.

conquered by Roman Emperor Tiberius, renamed Caesarea, and remained part of the Roman-Byzantine Empire until 1071, when it came under the control of the Seljuk Turks. Today, it is an industrial city, but does boast numerous 13th-century Islamic monuments, such as the **Hunat Hatun Camii**, the mosque built by the wife of the Seljuk Sultan Alâeddin Keykubat which contains her elaborately carved tomb just inside the main entrance. The tomb's emblem is the Döner Kümbet, which was built in 1276 and contains the tomb of Alâeddin Keykubat's daughter, Şah Cihan Sultan. Nearby, the city's **castle** (closed for restoration), which dates back to Roman times, is slated to become a cultural centre. There is also a small **Archaeological Museum** (Gültepe Mah. Kışla Caddesi; Tue–Sun 9am–noon, 1–5.30pm; charge) and, housed in a beautifully restored *medrese*, the **Selcuk Museum** (Tue–Sun June–Sept 9am–7pm, Oct–May 9am–5pm; charge), opened 2014.

Twenty-two kilometres (14 miles) northeast of the city near Bünyan are

The skies of Cappadocia are dotted with hot-air balloons.

the remains of **Kültepe** (daily Apr–Sept 8am–7pm, Oct–Mar 8am–5pm), a 19th-century BC Assyrian and Hittite trade centre.

MUSTAFAPAŞA: TOWN OF PAINTINGS

Largely Greek towns like **Mustafapaşa** ❽ (Sinasos), southwest of Kayseri, never really recovered from the blow they received with the collapse of the Ottoman Empire and the population exchange of 1923, which forced Muslims living in Greece to move to Turkey and Greek Christians living in Turkey to move to Greece. The huge Church of Sts Constantine and Helena in the town centre is a reminder of just how prominent the Greek community was at the end of the 19th century.

Every house has its own stone-sculptured balcony and windows. Inside many of them are late 19th-century frescoes, some with the eyes scratched out by the pious Muslim farmers who inherited the houses in the 1920s. Some of these pictures really stand out in terms of how

distinctive they are from Islamic art. For example, upstairs in the Old Greek House Restaurant there is a startlingly un-Islamic image of a young woman on a swing. If you walk out into the valley beyond Mustafapaşa you will find a few Göreme-style rock-cut churches, most of them badly defaced with graffiti.

A little further south, the beautiful 25km (16-mile) -long **Soğanlı valley** features numerous 9th- to 13th-century churches, along with several Roman rock tombs. The **Kubeli Kilise**, the most unusual of its churches, is built on the top of a pockmarked rock pinnacle and has a rock-cut dome that makes it look like an Armenian church; the **Karabaş Kilisesi**, on the left-hand side of the valley, has lovely – but poorly protected – medieval frescoes.

UNDERGROUND CITIES: KAYMAKLI AND DERINKUYU

No one knows how many underground cities exist in Cappadocia, and more are still being discovered. By far the most notable such discovery of recent years was that of the expansive city found directly beneath Nevşehir, which, as of this writing, has yet to open to visitors. Some of the tunnels were probably in use as early as the Bronze Age, and Hittite seals show that they took refuge here. Many were used from time to time by Christians from Kayseri and elsewhere as they fled from invading Arab and Turkic hordes. As many as 30,000 people could hide in these deep, catacomb-like structures for perhaps three months at a time.

The underground city of **Kaymaklı** ➒ (daily Apr–Oct 8am–7pm, Nov–Mar 8am–5pm; charge), located on the road to Niğde, 20km (12.5 miles) south of Nevşehir, has eight floors. Tunnels have been found connecting the site with the even deeper **Derinkuyu** ➓ ("Deep Well" in Turkish; daily Apr–Oct 8am–7pm, Nov–Mar 8am–5pm; charge), 10km (6 miles) to the south. A complex web of settlements including stables, wine presses, kitchens and wells, Derinkuyu has 13 floors, reaching a depth of 85 metres (279ft). Each chamber has been illuminated.

Painted door in Mustafapaşa.

Derinkuyu, underground city.

Byzantine frescoes inside Eski Gümüşler Monastery.

SOUTHERN CAPPADOCIA

The city of **Niğde** ⓫ came to the fore after the 10th-century Arab invasions had destroyed its less easily defended neighbours. It has several 13th- and 14th-century Islamic shrines and monuments, including the **Alâeddin Camii**, built in 1203, with a *bedesten* or covered market below it. The **Akmedrese**, a Seljuk theological school, serves as a museum (Tue–Sun 8am–6pm; charge).

One of the finest local churches for Byzantine frescoes is the monastery at **Eski Gümüşler** (daily Apr–Sept 8am–7pm, Oct–Mar 8.30am–5.30pm; charge) in the village of **Gümüşler** ⓬, 8km (5 miles) northeast of Niğde. Restored by British archaeologists in the 1960s, the monastery church has a completely preserved courtyard (the only one to survive in its entirety). A room upstairs springs a surprise: a smoky wall covered with non-religious pictures of animals and birds. Outside, a winepress and baths have been discovered.

South of Niğde, the uplands of central Anatolia are separated from the southern coast by the magnificent Taurus Mountains. After the town of **Ulukışla**, the road climbs until it reaches the famous **Gülek Boğazı** (Cilician Gates), a high pass in the mountains which was, for centuries, the only way between the Anatolian plateau and Çukorova (Cilicia). Commercial caravans and invading armies alike had to scale its treacherous heights to reach Tarsus or Adana and the Mediterranean in the south, or to bring goods to the cities of central and eastern Anatolia. Most travellers today take a modern expressway, the Adana road.

ROCK CHURCHES OF IHLARA VADISI

To the west of Niğde, over a hundred churches have been hewn into the walls of the gorgeous 10km (6-mile)-long, 80-metre (262ft) -wide **Ihlara Vadisi** ⓭ (Apr–Sept 8am–7pm, Oct–Mar 8am–5pm; charge). The sheer-sided valley, which encloses the Melendiz River, features a wonderful walk along a well-maintained path. Most of the churches in this area were built in the 11th century and around a dozen may be entered. These include the **Ağaçaltı Kilisesi** (Church under the Tree), with 10th- and 13th-century frescoes, one of them showing Daniel in the lion's den; and the **Yılanlı Kilise** (Church of the Serpents), whose frescoes depict the entombment of Mary the Egyptian with St Zosimus and a lion. The **Purenli Seki Kilisesi** (Church with the Terraces) contains a chamber tomb, separated by pillared arcades, and frescoes. The **Eğritas Kilisesi** (Church with the Crooked Stone) is one of the valley's most important churches, with several distinguished frescoes, most unfortunately badly damaged. The **Kırk Damaltı Kilisesi** (Church of St George) was re-endowed by a Greek nobleman who served the Seljuk Sultan Mesut II at Konya and wore a turban (as the frescoes show) in the last decade of the 13th century.

Cappadocian locals.

HOLY UNDERGROUND

Dig deep and you never know what you may find beneath Cappadocia.

In the early medieval period there were several thousand churches and monasteries in Cappadocia, along with numerous cave-houses and complex underground cities. But who built them all? The history books don't tell us, but there are clues in the fabric of the surviving cave-houses, the remains of tombs and the extraordinary paintings on the walls.

THE FIRST CHRISTIAN MONASTERIES

People have inhabited these underground warrens since the Neolithic era, but the soul of the region was forged from the twin powers of religion and repression. From the 3rd century AD, Cappadocia was a series of small, independent states, ruled by priest-kings. Its isolation attracted many early hermits and other holy men, seeking remote corners of the known world where they could serve their god through uninterrupted fasting, prayer and celibacy. Although they became known as monks – literally *monachos* ("solitary ones") – followers inevitably gathered around them and so, in due course, the first Christian monasteries were born. In AD 360, St Basil of Caesarea laid down a set of rules for these emerging communities. These edicts are still in force in the Greek Orthodox Church, and helped form the basis of the Rule of St Benedict in the West.

Far from withdrawing from life, many early monks saw themselves as the spearhead of the Christian movement. Graffiti crosses scrawled on many Classical temples date back to the monks' attempts to "disinfect" the great buildings of paganism. At the same time, the monks began to carve an extraordinary series of churches and chapels from the soft Cappadocian rock, basing their architecture on established Byzantine practice, complete with capitals and columns.

MUSLIM RULE

Throughout the Roman era (from AD 18) Cappadocia was also a sanctuary for Christians escaping persecution. The Arab invasions of the 7th–9th centuries again saw the area serve as a refuge, with many thousands fleeing for the hills and burrows to escape the relentless march of Islam.

Eventual Arab rule could have spelled the end of the monasteries, but Islam proved more open to religious freedom than Christianity, and Cappadocia flourished in relative safety and stability. Over time, however, the influence of the new religion began to be felt as early "puritans" combined Old Testament prohibitions against idols with the Islamic taboo on human representation. From 726–843, the iconoclasts savagely attacked the frescoes and mosaics; few pre-iconoclast paintings survived the onslaught.

Cappadocia's last great Christian flowering was from the 9th–11th centuries, as the monasteries were redecorated and the land spawned a warrior aristocracy of Byzantine frontiersmen struggling to fend off the Arabs.

The Battle of Manzikert (1071) eventually established Turkish control of this part of Anatolia. The Byzantine landowners were able to survive for another couple of centuries, but by the 14th century the region was firmly under Muslim rule. Only a few small monasteries struggled on in remote corners of the region. Its golden age was over.

The local rock is perfect for carving buildings.

Tea farmers selling their produce in Rize.

The Black Sea Coast near Zonguldak.

THE BLACK SEA COAST

Turkey's northern strip is defined by its mountainous isolation, unpredictable weather and a fierce independence.

Trabzon locals.

Isolated by a chain of high green mountains, the Black Sea region is unlike anywhere else in the country. It is described in ancient Greek accounts – notably the legendary adventures of Jason and his Argonauts – as a terrifying place full of danger; sea-caves leading to Hades, brutal Amazons, and numerous hostile tribes. Medea, the betrayed lover of Jason in Euripides' tragic account, may have been a Laz princess from the far eastern Black Sea, where the kingdom of Colchis and the Golden Fleece were located.

Underwater archaeological excavations suggest that the biblical account of the Great Flood could have a factual basis, and remains of human settlements more than 7,000 years old are being studied. The sea itself was once a freshwater lake, until, some time in the sixth millennium BC, rising levels of the Mediterranean breached a rock barrier at the Bosphorus, rapidly enlarging the lake and rendering it salty.

Black Sea coast landscapes.

The geography, idiosyncratic music and dance, and linguistic quirks of the region give it a singular identity, one that is enhanced by its inhabitants: the Laz, with their aquiline profiles and fair colouring, are concentrated in the vicinity of Pazar, Ardeşen, Fındıklı, Arhavi and Hopa. In the Hemşin valleys of the Kaçkar range, locals still speak a dialect of Armenian, while near Çaykara and Of people speak a form of Greek, yet boast the highest proportion of mosques and religious schools in Turkey. The Giresun highlands were settled by Alevî Turkic tribes in the 13th century; there are more Alevîs in the Fatsa and Bolaman regions. Georgian is still spoken in a few valleys northeast of Artvin.

With 1,250km (780 miles) of coastline, one may still find small beaches and unspoilt fishing villages west of Sinop, but the four-lane highway between Samsun and Hopa is an eyesore – the traveller anticipating visions of the "shimmering towers of Trebizond" may be in for a shock. Turn inland, however, and winding roads lead to green, wet hillsides, ancient castles and churches, fairytale forests and characterful villages.

The Black Sea coast near Sinop.

THE BLACK SEA

Much of the Black Sea coast suffers from an overdose of development, but for those with time and transport there is still magic to be found.

Black Sea beach resorts begin just outside Istanbul, but there are long stretches worth avoiding. Şile is popular with weekending city-dwellers, but horribly crowded, with an often treacherous sea, while **Akçakoca** was badly hit by the 1999 earthquake, though like Şile it offers a Genoese castle and long, sandy beach. Slightly inland from here lies the **Yedigöller Milli Parkı** (Seven Lakes National Reserve), a chain of interconnecting semi-natural ponds at their best during vivid displays of autumnal foliage.

SAFRANBOLU AND YÖRÜK KÖYÜ

The first unmissable stop is **Safranbolu ❶**, some 400km (250 miles) east of Istanbul, where some of the grandest Ottoman mansions in Turkey have been beautifully restored, many as affordable *pansiyons*. Local houses, claimed to number 800, are especially elaborate as Safranbolu prospered as a vital link on a trade route linking Istanbul and Sinop for many years. The town was, and still is, famous for its leather, copper and iron craftsmanship; as its name suggests, Safranbolu is also noted for saffron, some of which finds its way into locally produced *lokum* and *helva*.

The old **Çarşı** quarter (alias Eski Safranbolu) is where interest resides.

Every area has a festival to celebrate the start of summer.

On arrival, visit the tourist office – off the main square on Arasta Sokak – for a selection of brochures and maps, then head for the nearby **Arasta**, now a bazaar full of tourist-pitched crafts and antiques. A few alleys east, the courtyarded **Cinci Hanı**, a 17th-century *kervansaray* is worth a look even if you're not staying at the hotel now installed in its premises. Beyond this stands the **Kaymakamlar Evi Müzesi** (daily 9am–5.30pm; charge) the best restored and most interesting of three such mansions here. Continue up the

Main attractions
Safranbolu
Amasra
Amasya
Hagia Sophia/Aya Sofya, Trabzon
Sumela monastery
Georgian churches
Trekking in the Kaçkar

Map on page 324

⊙ Tip

Predictably, the most spectacular places in the region are the hardest to reach. Public transport is very limited both on the inland village routes and on the gorgeous coastal road from Sinop to Amasra. Plan seriously, and either hire a sturdy vehicle, go with a tour group, or take stout hiking boots and allow plenty of time.

street to the park occupying Hidirlik Hill, offering magnificent views across town. Back on the square, the 17th-century **Cinci Hamamı** (daily 8am–10pm) has been beautifully refurbished, with separate male and female sections.

If Safranbolu proves too commercialised for your tastes, there is another "museum village", **Yörük Köyü**, some 18km (11miles) further east, with 150 or so listed houses, one of which, the **Sipahioğlu Konağı** (daily 9am–sunset; charge), is open to visitors, as is the nearby communal *çamaşırhane* (laundry), now an art gallery. Yörük Köyü was largely inhabited by adherents of the Bektaşi sect, and if you look closely in the laundry you'll see evidence of their doctrines in the 12-sided washing platform (symbolising the 12 imams).

THE COASTAL ROUTE

Beyond Safranbolu, there are two possible routes. The first heads north through Bartın to coastal **Amasra** ❷ (91km/56 miles), a stunning old town draped over two fortified promontories with surviving Byzantine walls. It seems more north Aegean than Pontic, with sweeping sea views and a maze of cobbled paths through the

outer citadel of Boztepe, a Byzantine fortress adapted by the Genoese during the 14th century. Inside are two Byzantine churches, one converted into a mosque, the other used until 1923. Around the bay to the south, the **museum** (Tue–Sun 9am–5pm), renovated in 2017, has a surprising collection of Roman statuary, including fragments that washed ashore nearby during a storm in 2018.

The winding coast east of Amasra rewards the determined, self-propelled traveller with dramatic scenery and occasional timber, shale-roofed dwellings on the point of collapse. Minibus links are limited and driving conditions along sheer drops to a crashing sea challenging, though the road surface has been improved. If you have time, the best way to see this stretch of coast is by bicycle. **Kurucaşile**, still famed for its boat builders, would be the first conceivable overnight stop for cyclists; **Cide** has more accommodation and a long, pebbly beach. Riverside **İnebolu** is much the liveliest place en route to Sinop, with a few remaining Ottoman houses in the centre (mostly unrestored) and good-standard hotels on the shore.

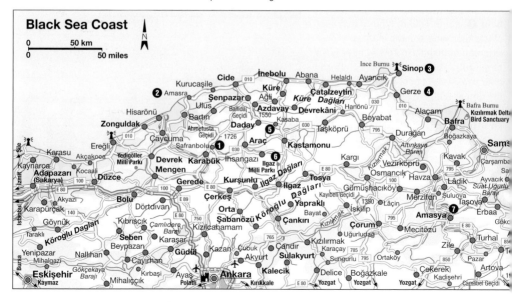

Sinop ❸, 150km (90 miles) from Amasra on a jutting peninsula, has the best natural harbour along this coast, and accordingly (along with Amasra) was settled by colonists from Aegean Miletus during the 7th century BC. A competing legend asserts it was founded by the Amazon queen Sinope, who managed to brush off the ever-amorous Zeus by getting him to grant her one wish: eternal virginity. There are in any case numerous ancient sites in the region (including, apparently, antediluvian settlements on the Black Sea floor). Finds from the more accessible sites are displayed in the **museum** (Tue–Sun 9am–5pm; charge), which incorporates foundations of a 2nd-century BC Temple of Serapis. On the same street are a ruined 7th-century church, the **Balat Kilisesi** (closed for ongoing excavation work), and several Seljuk and Ottoman monuments, including the 13th-century **Alâeddin Camii** and its accompanying **Alaiye Medresesi**, with a carved marble portal.

Most impressive of all are the enormous **city walls**, parts of which stand to a height of 25 metres (80ft). These were of little help, however, on 30 November 1853, when a Russian fleet destroyed a heavily outgunned Turkish squadron anchored here, in one of the opening engagements of the Crimean War.

The best excursions from Sinop are to **Karakum** (Black Sand) beach, 3km (2 miles) east of town, or to the pretty harbour village of **Gerze** ❹, some 40km (24 miles) distant, set back from the pitiless roar of the motorway. It retains some old houses, while a few waterside hotels make it an alternative base to Sinop. The best are those situated along the point, where from your balcony you can watch the fishermen unload the day's catch.

A little further on, you'll cross the **delta of the Kızılırmak**, a labyrinth of marsh, reedbed and dunes up to 12 metres (about 40ft). Protected within **Kızılırmak Delta Bird Sanctuary** since 2016, it hosts some 356 migratory bird species. All this contrasts markedly with the urban sprawl of **Samsun**, home to nearly one million people. The epicentre of the Turkish tobacco trade, it has little of interest to travellers. However, the **Archaeology and Ethnography Museum** – set to re-open in 2019 at its new location by the north end of the harbour – is worthwhile, with outstanding mosaics from a local Roman villa and elegant

Outside the Sultan Beyazit Camii, Amasya.

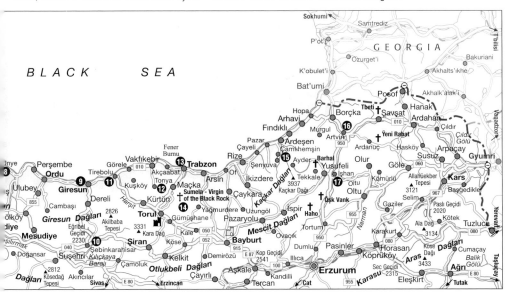

2nd-century BC gold jewellery. Otherwise the city is a place to skip.

THE INLAND ROUTE

If you take the inland route eastwards from Safranbolu, your first stop should be **Kastamonu**, the feudal stronghold of the Komneni clan, who founded a Byzantine dynasty in 1081 which lasted a century. There are also a number of Seljuk and Ottoman monuments, the pick of which is the **Nasrullah Kadi Camii**, from 1509. Some 15km (9 miles) northwest, in the village of **Kasaba** ❺, stands one of the finest mosques in Turkey – the carved wooden **Mahmud Bey Camii**, an intricate structure built in 1366 and retaining almost all its original features. Head south from Kastamonu for 40km (25 miles) and you reach the **Ilgaz National Park** ❻ (Ilgaz Milli Parkı), with dense mixed forest and a small but very scenic ski resort popular with Anakarans. You can continue southeast through the pretty Ottoman villages of **Tosya** and **Osmancık** – or northeast via the sheer cliffs of Sahinkaya **Kanyonu**, the second-deepest canyon in the world, towering above Altınkaya Barajı – to Amasya, one of the most stunningly set towns in all of Turkey.

Amasya ❼ was the first capital of the ancient Pontic kings until they moved to Sinop in 120 BC. Overlooking the Yeşilırmak River, old Ottoman houses cluster around numerous Islamic monuments, while at night floodlights search the cliffs below the citadel for well-preserved cave tombs of the Pontic kings. It was here that the great geographer and historian Strabo was born in 64 BC. Later it became an important Seljuk centre, before being taken by the Ilkhanid Mongols after 1259.

There are two impressive Seljuk mosques – the **Burmalı Minare Camii** (Mosque of the Twisted Minaret) and the **Gök Medrese/Camii**; a 16th-century *bedesten* in the bazaar, between Ziya Paşa Bulvari and Atatürk Caddesi – as well as the **Burmahane Medresesi**, built by the Ilkhanids in 1308 as a lunatic asylum. Across from the Sultan Beyazit Camii, on

Traditional pre-prayer abdest ablutions in Amasya.

⊙ THE HEMŞINLIS

The Hemşinlis are an obscure Caucasian tribe who speak a dialect of Armenian. Ruy González de Clavijo, Castilian envoy to the court of Timur in Samarkand, characterised them in a 1405 account as nominally Christian brigands who demanded a toll for the right of passage through their mountains. They converted to Islam during the early 1800s, but no mosques appeared in the region until a century later. The women, in their brightly coloured scarves (worn as turbans) and patterned pullovers, are unmistakable. The Hemşinli diaspora is huge, extending to Europe as well as major Turkish cities, where they are known for their skills as confectioners and pastry chefs. Most return here in summer to maintain *yayla* traditions or run *pansiyons*.

Atatürk Caddesi, the **Amasya Museum** (Amasya Müzesi; Apr–Sept Tue–Sun 8.30am–7pm, Oct–Mar 8am–5pm; charge) contains a varied collection of artefacts from the different civilisations that have ruled the city, including carved wooden doors, a Hittite idol, astronomical instruments and Mongol mummies. The riverside **Hazeranlar Konağı** (Tue–Sun 8.30am–noon, 1–4.45pm; charge) is a restored Ottoman mansion from 1865, carefully refurbished with period furnishings.

Several of the 18 **rock-cut tombs** on the north bank of the river can be visited (daily dawn–dusk; charge); two of them are interconnected by a laboriously hewn tunnel. Variously used by Pontians, Romans, Seljuks and Ottomans, there isn't a great deal left of the structure, nor of the Pontic palace underneath the later accretions, but the view is mind-boggling.

EAST OF SAMSUN

The ghastly four-lane Highway 10 carries heavy lorry traffic east from Samsun towards the border with Georgia, but off the beaten track inland, there are still some lovely, wild places to explore.

Ünye ❽ (Byzantine Oinaion) has a good beach – **Uzunkum** – just west, and ample tourist facilities, as well as a pleasant town centre, retaining traces of its past in its restored Ottoman homes and important medieval port. The main local site is the **Çaleoğlu fortress** (open access) just 5km (3 miles) inland, with masonry from the Pontic to Byzantine periods.

Further along the coast some 50km (30 miles), a temple to the Argonauts' leader once stood at the tip of **Cape Yason** (Cape Jason); a medieval church marks the spot. **Ordu**, 35km (22 miles) further, is unremarkable other than for a derelict Greek cathedral by the sea and the side road to the beach-encircled crater-lake above **Cambaşı Yaylası**, 64km (40 miles) south.

Giresun ❾ was the ancient Kerasos, from which "cherry" is derived. The fruit was introduced to the West from here by the Roman gourmet-soldier Lucullus in 69 BC. Today the main attraction is offshore around **Giresun Adası**, one of the largest islets on the Turkish Black Sea coast, which hosts part of the late-May Aksu Festival. This is based on a far more ancient pagan observance, with fertility and banishing-misfortune rites still persisting amongst the "cultural events".

For those with a historical bent and their own vehicle, the scenic 106km (66-mile) trip over the **Eğribel Geçidi** to Şebinkarahisar is highly recommended. En route, a right turn at Kümber leads to **Tamdere**, a friendly place to base yourself if planning a day hike to the glacier lake at **Karagöl**, just below the snowy, 3,107-metre (10,193ft) peak of the eponymous mountain range.

Beyond the pass, **Şebinkarahisar** ❿ sits high on a bluff overlooking the Kelkit valley. This was Pompey's Colonia, established after the Mithridatic Wars in

Amasya.

Hemşinli women wear colourful headscarves.

63 BC, although there was a settlement here long before. Byzantine Emperor Justinian's imposing ruined fortress still perches atop a huge basalt rock dominating the town. The area became part of the Ottoman Empire in 1471, when the now-restored **Fatih Camii** was built.

There are also remains of earlier mosques, several Greek churches in nearby villages and – most impressively – the cave-**Monastery of Meryemana** (daily Apr–Sept 8am–5pm, Oct–Mar 8am–6pm), 7km (4 miles) east across the valley in Kayadibi village, which dates from the 5th century AD but was rededicated to St Philip by the Armenians much more recently. Roughly 400 steps lead up the vertiginous cliff, rewarding you with a breathtaking view from the somewhat overrestored site – previously in near ruin due to earthquakes and political turmoil (including a desperate four-week battle between local Armenians and the Ottoman forces who came to deport them in June 1915).

Much of the Black Sea coast is steep and rocky.

Tirebolu ⑪ (formerly Tripolis) occupies a crescent-shaped bay bracketed by two headlands, 41km (25 miles) east of Giresun; the eastern promontory is home to a 14th-century Genoese fortress. This has been a substantial port since antiquity, largely on account of the silver mined in the hinterland; these days the main local product is the **hazelnut** (*fındık* in Turkish), of which Turkey is the world's biggest producer. During summer you'll see broad expanses of them everywhere, still unhusked, spread out to dry.

Görele marks the turn-off to **Kuşköy** (Bird Village), 28km (17 miles) inland, so named because its inhabitants are famed for long-distance communication by means of an archaic "whistle language"; an annual July festival, and currently a Unesco-funded film project, celebrate it. From Vakfıkebir, it's 20km (12 miles) inland to **Tonya** ⑫, inhabited by Greek-speaking Muslims possibly descended from the most fiercely independent of Pontic tribes. Until the 1980s junta put a lid on matters by severely controlling civilian access to firearms, Tonya was notorious for its bloody vendettas. In the

⊘ QUIRKS OF THE BLACK SEA

The Black Sea displays certain peculiarities, a consequence of its uninterrupted connection with the Mediterranean via the Bosphorus, Sea of Marmara and the Dardanelles since the last ice ages ended. Relatively fresh water (18 parts salinity per thousand as against 30–40 parts for proper oceans) occupies its first few fathoms, constantly replenished by the many rivers feeding the Black Sea. The surplus exits via the Bosphorus as a surface current, while a deeper countercurrent of much saltier, denser water from the Aegean heads up into the Black Sea. The result is that layers of less dense, less salty, usually cooler water occupy the top 100 metres (330ft) or so, above the bulk of the sea which forms a sludge of warmer, heavier brine. Since the lighter top layers, supporting abundant marine life, are unable to penetrate the lower depths for mixing and oxygenation, almost 90 percent of the Black Sea's volume is an anoxic, sulphurous wasteland. Dead organisms drift towards the bottom; bacteria oxidizing this organic detritus consume what little oxygen is available, while other bacteria have evolved to use sulphate for metabolising this debris, generating highly toxic hydrogen sulphide. For archaeologists, a major bonanza has resulted, since ancient ships and other artefacts which lie in the deep zone are found exceptionally well preserved owing to the absence of oxidation.

local graveyard, bullets are carved on headstones to represent the number of people the deceased had killed before catching a bullet of his own.

More positively, Tonya is one of several villages to participate in the annual **Kadırga Yayla Festival** (third weekend in July), held at the common boundary point of Tonya, Torul, Görele and Maçka territories and thought to have begun as a peace negotiation after centuries of conflict over grazing lands.

TALL TALES OF TREBIZOND

Trebizond – today **Trabzon** ⑬ – has had a bewitching reputation for close to two millennia, famed for its wealth, its gold-plated palace and cathedral domes, and its sporadic independence. Founded as a Greek colony during the 8th century BC, Trebizond was to reach its cultural zenith when Alexios I Komnenos and his Georgian supporters took control here in 1204 after the Fourth Crusade's invasion of Constantinople. Their local mini-empire lasted 257 years, in part because Mongol raids forced the Silk Road to divert through the city, encouraging a flourishing trade with the Genoese and Venetians, who were surprised to find this outpost of civilisation in such outlandish territory.

Native son and distinguished church scholar Basilios Bessarion (later turned Catholic churchman) carried memories of its magnificence to Italian exile, not long before Trebizond became the last Byzantine outpost seized by the Ottomans. He described just part of the Komneni's "golden palace" as "a long building of great beauty, its foundation being all of white stone, and its roof decorated with gold and other colours, painted flowers and stars, emitting beams of light as if it were heaven itself". Rose Macaulay's famed 1956 *The Towers of Trebizond* perpetuated this image of a fairytale city of sybaritic splendour, its towers "shimmering on a far horizon in luminous enchantment" – although the novel was mainly a penetrating satire on both Turkish and English mores.

In reality, the days of Trabzon's seaborne glory all but disappeared in the late 1800s with the completion of the

Trabzon is the closest large Turkish city to Georgia and Russia, and there are hints of Russian influence in the local architecture.

The modern towers of Trabzon.

Ankara–Erzurum railway, and onward roads into Iran. Russia occupied the city from April 1916 to early 1918, after which an attempt by local Greeks to base their "Republic of Pontus" here ended in defeat and the 1923 exchange of populations. The **Atatürk Köşkü** (daily Apr–Oct 8am–5pm, Nov–Mar 8am–7pm; charge) is the confiscated mansion of the republic's would-be president.

Trabzon's harbour area and city centre are not glamorous anymore; no shimmering towers define the horizon, and Byzantine remains are largely unheralded, with the only hint of past exoticism being a large community of resident Russians. Indeed, trade with Georgia and the Russian Federation supports much of the population of nearly half a million. Tourism is not assiduously promoted, and salubrious lodging is scarce, overpriced and often full of tour groups.

Little remains of the grandiose **city walls** or central citadel (**Ortahisar**) around the site of the Byzantine palace, perched at the west edge of the tableland (*trapezous* in ancient Greek)

which was the original point of settlement. The **Ortahisar Camii** was originally the 13th- to 14th-century cathedral of Panagia Khrysokephalos (Golden-Headed, perhaps after its then-plated dome); today its glorious frescoes and floor mosaics have been whitewashed and cemented over in accord with Islamic sensibilities – Trabzon is generally a very conservative, devout place. The nearby church of **St Eugenios** (the Yeni Cuma Camii since 1461) is similarly plain. Recently restored and opened to the public, the unconverted 9th-century **St Anne church** (Küçük Ayvasil; daily 8.30am–4.30pm) is the city's oldest, its faint traces of frescoes worth a look.

Slightly further east, along or just off pedestrianised Uzun Sokak, stand occasional surviving Greek-built mansions; one of the most sumptuous, on Zeytinlik Caddesi, is now the **Trabzon Museum** (Trabzon Müzesi; temporarily closed for renovation), its star exhibit is a life-sized bronze statue of Hermes.

The monastic church of **Hagia Sophia** (Aya Sofya; daily 9am–5pm;

The cloud-shrouded Monastery of Sumela.

charge) sits romantically 3km (2 miles) west of the city centre on a bluff overlooking the sea. Erected on the orders of local emperor Manuel I Komnenos between 1238 and 1263, it has miraculously retained its vivid and expressive contemporary frescoes, restored by David Talbot Rice in 1957–64, depicting scenes from the life of Christ and the Old Testament. Converted into a mosque after the Ottoman conquest of the city in 1461, it became a museum in 1964. Following a legal dispute settled in 2013, the building was taken out of the hands of the country's Ministry of Tourism and Culture, handed over to the (state) religious authorities and became a working mosque once again. Though still a functioning mosque today, with white screens protecting the faithful from a number of wall paintings, it remains open to visitors.

The only other local "must" is the Armenian monastic church of **Kaymaklı**, 6km (4 miles) southeast on Boztepe hill. Restoration of its frescoes has been underway since 2014, among them surprisingly sophisticated 17th-century wall paintings of the Last Judgement which survived the 20th century through the church's use as a barn.

A MONASTERY TO REMEMBER

The **Monastery of Sumela**, or the **Virgin of the Black Rock** , ranks as one of the Black Sea's biggest attractions. Situated 44km (27 miles) south of Trabzon, it perches dramatically halfway up a sheer palisade that towers above the densely forested Altındere. Legend relates how it was built by two monks from Athens in AD 385, guided by a vision of the Virgin, but it was more likely to have been commissioned by early Byzantine emperors to help convert the pagan natives to Christianity, like several other local monasteries which have essentially vanished. Sumela's heyday, like that of Trebizond, came through patronage by the local Komneni dynasty, which promulgated an edict exempting it from all taxes. Selim the Grim upheld these rights, and other Ottoman sultans even made pilgrimages – such was the place's prestige – but this all ended when the

🔍 TREKKING IN THE KAÇKAR

The wild Kaçkar mountains offer some of the best hiking in Turkey, with magnificent scenery, challenging climbs and *yayla* communities

The glaciated Kaçkar mountains are the highest (3,932m/12,190ft) and most spectacular of the various massifs in Turkey's eastern Black Sea region. The name is derived from the Armenian *khatchkar* (votive relief cross). Its non-porous granite has resulted in hundreds of midnight-blue lakes and burbling streams. Wildflower displays are second to none. Best of all is the opportunity to sample life at the various *yaylas* (pastoral communities), inhabited to varying degrees from late June to early September.

As a barrier range rising steeply from the damp Black Sea coast, the Kaçkar's northwest slopes attract copious mist and rain. This means main passes must be conquered before midday, when cloud typically boils up to obscure everything. The southeast-facing flanks, draining towards the Çoruh River, have more reliable, clearer weather.

The most popular trekking season is summer, but these are the mistiest and most crowded months

Hiking in the Kaçkar mountains near Yukarı Kavron.

– popular wilderness campsites, particularly Dilberdüzü in the heart of the range, overflow at this time. May and June have the most spectacular floral displays (and long days), but most passes are still snowed up (requiring ice axe and crampons), and most *yaylas* are yet to be inhabited for the year. September and early October are also fine, with the least mist, though many *yaylas* will be empty.

There are several classic trailhead villages or *yaylas* on either side of the Kaçkar, all with rustic accommodation and varying levels of supplies, mule hire and guiding services available. On the Çoruh flank, provisions can be purchased in Yusufeli, from where minibuses ply southwest to Tekkale or north to Barhal, Hevek (officially Yaylalar) and Meretet (Olgunlar). Most local place names are of Hemşinli or Georgian derivation, often disguised by clumsy Turkification. On the north side, the highest market town is Çamlıhemşin, departure point for public transport further up to the *yaylas* of Çat and Elevit, or the full-blown resort of Ayder.

Given the complex local topography, with many subsidiary ridges off the main watershed, there are numerous possible itineraries. One of the less frequented routes is the northerly trail, which extends from Barhal up towards the Altıparmak ridge via the Satibe meadows, before angling over to the Önbolat valley and tackling the Kırmızı pass; the pass leads to Avusor *yayla*, linked by dirt road to Ayder (allow two days). In contrast, the classic traverse from Meretet to Dilberdüzü (the main base camp for Kaçkar summit), and then on via ice-filled Deniz Gölü and the Kavron pass, is heavily subscribed. From this pass, there's a choice of looping back to Meretet via Yukarı Kavron *yayla*, the Çaymakçur pass and flower-spangled Düpeduz, or carrying on west to Elevit and the end of a dirt road up from Çat (both two to three days). For the less committed, low-altitude, one-day walks link Çamlıhemşin and Ayder via Pokut and Hazındak *yaylas*, or Ayder with Hazındak, Samistal and the lower Kavron *yayla* – where minibuses whisk you the 13km (8 miles) back to Ayder.

Indispensable for any independent hiking is Kate Clow's *The Kaçkar* guide and map (www.trekkinginturkey.com).

monks departed, together with other local Orthodox, in 1923.

The present buildings probably date from the 12th century and contain many subsequent layers of frescoes, the best being from the 14th and 15th centuries; most have been well restored since 1996, and cover improbable surfaces of the cave-church. Further restoration works have been underway since 2015 (due for completion in May 2019), though in the meantime it's still well worth admiring from a distance.

BEYOND TRABZON

Beyond the turning for Sumela at Maçka, travel up-valley on the E97 towards the **Zigana pass**, straddling the old caravan route towards Erzurum and Persia; it was here that Xenophon's Ten Thousand first glimpsed the sea in 399 BC, on their way back from Mesopotamia. Today only the twisty old road goes over the pass (2,025 metres/6,643ft); a new road just west uses a tunnel.

East of Trabzon along the coast, there is little specific to see at Of (pronounced "oaf") or Çaykara just inland, both bastions of Islamic piety. Çaykara, however, is the gateway to the alpine landscape around **Uzungöl** (Long Lake); with plenty of quality accommodation it makes a feasible alternative to Trabzon.

East of the concreted-over "tea capitals" of **Rize** and **Çayeli**, **Pazar** marks the beginning of the traditional **Laz homeland**. Watch out for men carrying hawks on their wrists; hawking is a traditional Laz sport.

Shortly past Pazar lies the turning inland to the **Hemşin valleys**, the usual northern gateway to the Kaçkar mountains. **Çamlıhemşin** ⑮, built beside the roaring Fırtına (Storm) River, is the region's main market town and minibus connection point; central Türkü Tourism (www.turkutour.com) is a highly recommended trekking outfitter. Both upstream and downstream you'll notice many magnificent stone-arch bridges, some dating from the 17th century. Probably the best example is the **Taş Kemer**, which spans the Fırtına at **Şenyuva**, where some impressive traditional farmsteads nestle at the end of motorised pulleys transferring supplies across the stream.

On the road up from Şenyuva, single-towered **Zilkale** has a mysterious history. Some claim it dates from the 6th century, but it was more likely built by the Trapezuntine Komneni or a local warlord – for who knows what purpose, given the obscure location. It is, unsurprisingly, reputed to be haunted after dark by its former garrison and their horses. The pavement ends at **Çat**, with another delicately arched bridge and the last conventional accommodation to be found before more primitive *yaylas* – and then true wilderness – take over.

A different, wider road from Çamlıhemşin leads 17km (11 miles) up to the (very) hot-springs resort of **Ayder**, another popular jump-off point for the Kaçkar mountains, with comfortable accommodation.

Layers of frescoes cover the interior of the Monastery of Sumela.

Yusufeli lies on the bank of the turbulent Çoruh river, between Ishan and Tekkale.

Tortum Lake.

ARTVIN: "LITTLE GEORGIA"

The Artvin region is still quintessentially Caucasian and offers some of the most impressive 9th- to 11th-century church architecture in the world, legacy of a flourishing of Georgian medieval culture between Tortum, Artvin and Ardahan. Georgians have inhabited southern Caucasia, including these valleys, since antiquity. The king of Georgia adopted Christianity shortly after his Armenian counterpart, but unlike the Armenians the Georgians never broke with the Eastern Orthodox Church, and managed to maintain de facto independence in the face of Roman, Byzantine and Arab incursions.

Early in the 9th century, a branch of the Armeno-Georgian Bagratid dynasty gained footholds as far south as Ani, and ultimately unified various Georgian principalities into a kingdom in 1008, under Bagrat III. At its peak, under Queen Tamar (r. 1184–1213), Georgia extended almost as far west as Bayburt, ruled from Tbilisi by the world's longest-lasting sovereign dynasty until Russian occupation in 1811. From the late 800s,

the valleys south of Artvin were home to some of the finest fresco-painters, stonemasons and architects of the age, resulting in a vast number of fortresses and monastic churches, many of which still survive in village centres or isolated valleys. This golden age came to an end with Persian and Mongol raids of the mid-13th century.

THE CHURCHES

Artvin ⑯ itself has nothing to recommend except its annual Kafkasör Festival – which lately has also featured wrestlers, musicians and vendors from both Turkey and Georgia – plus (relative) proximity to many Georgian churches. Nonetheless, the surroundings are beautiful, with the fertile land clothed in verdant forests and fruit orchards.

Getting around the nearby valleys with their marvellous Georgian churches is considerably difficult without your own transport. There are few tour agents and infrequent *dolmuşes* to the villages by the churches.

The five most impressive churches lie south of Artvin, in the valleys of the Çoruh and Tortum rivers. İşhan ⑰ (Ishkhani in Georgian; interior closed for restoration until mid-2019) is the first, involving a 6km (4-mile) climb from the main road to the village, with its huge, mind-blowing church. Work was begun during the 8th century and only completed 300 years later; the dome rests on four massive columns, while delicate stone carvings adorn the outer walls.

A nearby turning west off the main road leads to Yusufeli, and thence to either Tekkale or Barhal; outside of these villages, close to the southern flanks of the Kaçkar are almost identical, gabled domeless churches, erected during the late 10th-century tenure of David Magistros, Prince of Oltu. **Dörtkilise (Otkhta Eklesia) church** (open access), 6km (4 miles) outside Tekkale village, has eight columns supporting the barrelled ceiling and a choir occupying the west end; the arcaded, derelict

building just northeast was the refectory of this former monastic complex.

The church at **Barhal** (Parkhali), 20 minutes' walk outside the village, essentially Dörtkilise's twin except somewhat smaller, is in better condition owing to the fact that it has long functioned as a mosque; admission is easiest at Friday prayers, or try asking at the school for the keys.

Back on the main highway south, just past Tortum Lake, a turning west leads 7km (4.5 miles) west to Camlıyamaç village with its massive **Öşkvank (Oskhi)** church, another endowment of David Magistros, which again owes a good state of preservation to its long use as a mosque. Currently being restored (with completion slated for 2020), the structure contains a very Gothic colonnade, with no two columns alike, and surviving fresco fragments. Some 9km (5.5 miles) past the lake's southern end, David's first project, the church of **Haho** (Khakhuli) in Bağbaşı, was once the most celebrated of Georgian monasteries, and is still among the best preserved, having served as the local mosque since the 17th century. The dome is topped with a conical roof of varicoloured tiles; inside the gallery flanking the church on the south are high-quality reliefs (including the whale devouring Jonah) and frescoes of Apostles and angels in the apse.

Due east of Artvin, more fine churches in the valley of the Berta River are reached from the road to Şavşat. First up is crumbling 10th-century **Dolishane** in Hamamlı village, with fine reliefs on the south façade; next, half-ruined **Porta** (Khantza) monastery, in Pırnallı village; finally, **Tbeti** stands 11km (7 miles) north of Şavşat at Cevizli village, much battered by treasure-hunters but still with extensive relief work on its apse and south transept, was originally a monastery where the great medieval Georgian epic poet, Shota Rustaveli (1172–1216) supposedly studied for a period.

A detour takes you some 10km (6 miles) south to the trailhead of Cehennem Deresi Kanyonu (Hell's Creek Canyon), touted as Turkey's largest canyon. In a bid to attract more visitors, planning is underway for an 80m (263 ft) glass bridge to span the abyss.

Children in Yusufeli. Georgians have inhabited the Artvin region's valleys since ancient times.

The exquisite stone-arch bridge at Çamlıhemşin.

⊘ DAM CATASTROPHES

Fast-growing Turkey's insatiable thirst for more energy has led to massive dam and hydro-electric projects in the lush wet mountains behind the Black Sea, particularly the Çoruh River Development Plan. The dam near Yusufeli, is the second largest in the project and is set to be completed in 2020. This will eventually be Turkey's tallest, standing at 270m (885ft). There are 15 dams involved in the project, opposition to which has garnered much support at both local and international levels. As a result of these actions, various species of endemic plants and animals are becoming under threat. The dams have already hurt white-water rafting outfits. They have also disrupted transport circulating in the region.

📷 THE GREAT OUTDOORS

There's an abundance of exciting outdoor activities on offer in Turkey, both along the coasts and in the mountains of the interior.

With its often dramatic topography, relatively reliable weather conditions and temperate seas, it's hardly surprising that Turkey is becoming an adventure and outdoor sports mecca. Along the Mediterranean and Aegean coasts, **windsurfing** and **kitesurfing** are big draws wherever sea breezes and onshore landforms combine to produce ideal conditions, particularly around Bodrum, at Alaçatı near Çeşme, and Aydıncık beach on Gökçeada. All the major southwest coast resorts have well-equipped **yacht marinas**, with the convoluted shoreline between Bodrum and Finike especially rewarding. **Scuba diving** is most worthwhile out of Bodrum, Kalkan, Kaş and Adrasan; expect to see corals, rock formations and submerged wrecks rather than huge shoals of fish. The cooler northern Aegean has good diving at Ayvalık and the Saroz gulf.

Inland, **canyoning** – in the toes of lofty Akdağ – is a refreshing way to spend a summer's day, as is **whitewater rafting** along the Dalaman Çayı near Dalyan, the Köprülü Canyon near Antalya, and the Göksu above Silifke (see page 335).

You can get airborne on a **paraglider** above Ölüdeniz and Kaş, or more passively (and expensively) in a **hot-air balloon** over Cappadocia – champagne breakfast usually included. The harsh winters in the Anatolian mountains bring reliable snowfall, although beyond the long-established Uludağ (near Bursa), Turkey's **ski resorts** are little-known to foreigners, including the more remote Palandöken (near Erzurum) and Tekir Yaylası on Mt Erciyes (Cappadocia).

Mountain biking in Cappadocia.

Paragliding over Ölüdeniz.

Hot-air ballooning is a great way to see the Cappadocian landscape. The best flying conditions are April to October.

Outdoor adventure companies lead treks along the long-distance trails as well as into the mountains.

Mountaineering and Hiking

Turkey's rugged interior offers excellent mountain trekking – though you must be resourceful and self-sufficient, as topographic maps are scarce and there's no refuge network as in Europe. The most popular mountains are the glaciated Kaçkar (summit 3,972 metres/13,031ft), inland from the Black Sea. A different experience is provided by the limestone Aladağlar (3,756 metres/12,322ft) and Bolkar Toros (3,585 metres/11,761ft), near Niğde. Given an improvement in the security situation, the spectacular Cilo-Sat range of Hakkâri, culminating in 4,136-metre (13,569ft) Mount Reşko, may become viable once again.

Fortunately Turkey has a new-found wealth of marked walking trails (see www.cultureroutesinturkey.com). Southwestern coastal Turkey has three marked, regularly maintained, long-distance trails: the Lycian Way between Ölüdeniz and Antalya, the St Paul Trail – purporting to follow in the proselytising footsteps of the Apostle – linking Perge with the Eğirdir region, and the 800km (497 miles) CarianTrail (www.cariantrail.com), which snakes along the Bodrum and Datça peninsulas and takes in a wealth of ancient sites. All three have guide booklets with GPS-compatible maps and a developing network of village lodging and meal provision. Other routes include the Evliya Çelebi Way and Phrygian Way in northwest Turkey and Abraham's Path in the southeast.

laçatı, near Çeşme, often has perfect conditions for windsurfing.

White-water rafting down the Çoruh river.

Hiking between Göreme and Çavuşin in Cappadocia's Rose Valley.

337

The road to Nemrut Dağı from Khata.

THE EAST

Few tourists visit the beautiful but troubled plains
of the "Fertile Crescent" and the remote plateaux
and mountains of the Far East.

Ovacık inhabitant.

Eastern Turkey's vast expanse is made up of two distinct
regions, the Near East and the Far East. The former is
dominated by the River Euphrates, home to a series of giant
hydroelectric dams and irrigation canals that have turned
the barren flatlands into an agricultural powerhouse. Its
crowning historic glory is the 2,000-year-old funerary sanctuary of King Antiochus atop the 2,150-metre (7,050ft) Nemrut Dağı, though the amazing temple complex at Göbekli
Tepe, dating back 12,000 years, runs it a close second.
Gaziantep, dominated by an imposing citadel, is a booming regional hub famed for pistachio nuts – and its state-
of-the-art museum houses an incredible collection of
Roman mosaics. Further east, ancient Şanlıurfa, the
city of prophets, claims to be the birthplace of Abraham
and boasts one of the country's most colourful bazaars.

Heading into the far eastern region is Turkey's most
overtly Kurdish city, Diyarbakır, famous for its 6km
(3.5-mile) -long medieval walls. Mardin, overlooking
the Mesopotamian plain, boasts a remarkable collection of honey-hued stone houses, mosques and Syrian
Orthodox churches.

Further east and north the altitude increases, and
sheep and cattle are grazed by nomadic tribesmen in
the shadow of lofty mountains, snow-streaked even
in summer. Here the average elevation rises above
2,000 metres (6,560ft), culminating in the 5,137-metre
(16,853ft) Mount Ararat in the northeast. Pick of the sights in this remote
area is the romantically ruined city of Ani, blessed with a stunning collection of Armenian churches and monasteries, and beautiful Lake Van
where the church of the Holy Cross is set on a tiny offshore islet.

Eastern Turkey is an immensely rewarding place to travel despite
the long distances and, outside of the major centres, lack of creature
comforts. Unfortunately, a recent history of bombings, kidnappings
and violent demonstrations will keep most visitors away. It is vital to
take advice before travelling, particularly around Diyarbakır and the
Syrian and Iraqi borders.

*Snow-capped Mount Ararat
dominates the northeastern plateau.*

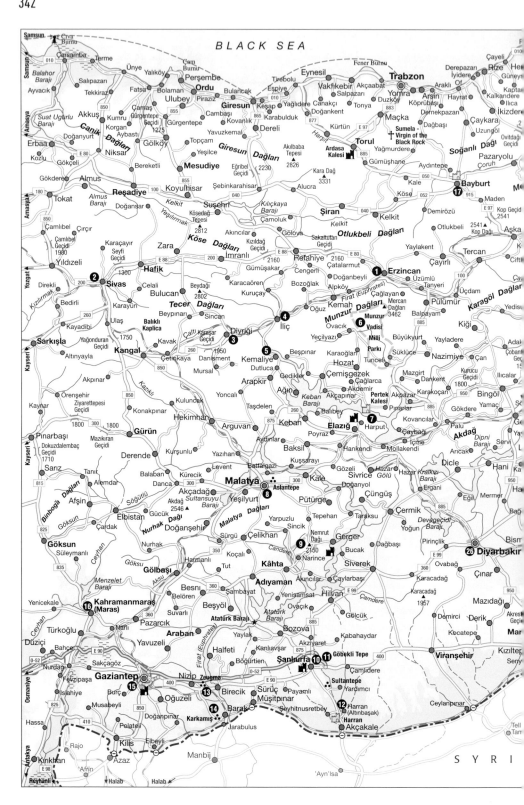

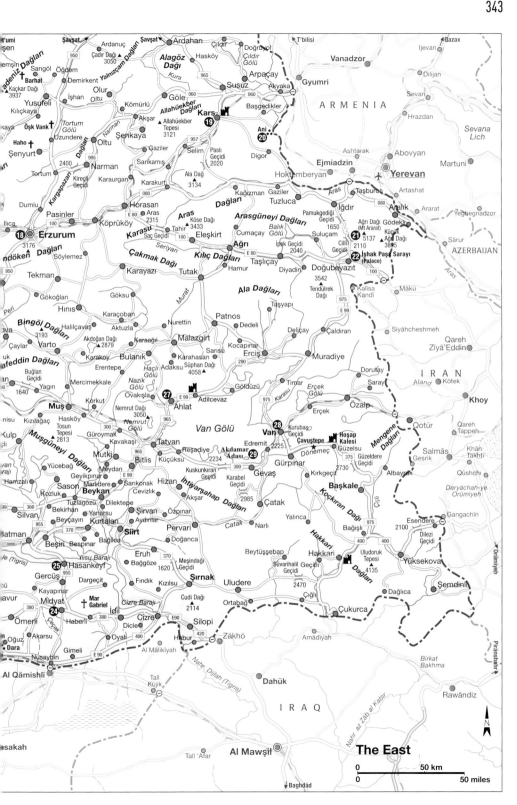

The East

0   50 km

0   50 miles

THE NEAR EAST

This vast, little-known tract of southeast Turkey has some fabulous scenery, from burning plains to towering mountains, and traces of some of the world's oldest civilisations.

Map on page 342

The central Anatolian plateau extends for many bleak and lonely kilometres east of Ankara. Patchy wheatfields alternate with bald hills that centuries of soil erosion have fashioned into eerie sculptures. Brown and ochre predominate, except when the brief glory of May covers the land with grass and wild flowers. This austere landscape is enlivened in patches by plunging gorges and snow-streaked mountain tops. To the south, plateau and mountain give way to the scorched plains of Mesopotamia, newly brought to life by the waters of the massive Atatürk dam.

REGIONAL CAPITAL AND SIGHTS EN ROUTE

Erzincan ❶, some 680km/423 miles, or 9 hours by bus, east of Ankara, is the largest centre in the region, a modern-looking city which was entirely rebuilt after the devastating earthquakes of 1939 and 1992. Beyond it, to the north, the road leads over remote mountain passes to the Black Sea coast. To the south, the wild canyon of the Upper Euphrates gradually emerges into the high plateau of the northeast – the Roman province of Armenia Major.

En route between Ankara (or Kayseri) and Erzincan, **Sivas ❷** (known as Sebastia to Rome and Byzantium) deserves a stop for its thriving crafts bazaar and its magnificent clutch of Seljuk architecture: the 12th-century **Ulu Camii** and the four theological and medical colleges of **Gök**, **Çifte Minareli**, **Şifahiye** and **Bürüciye Medrese**. These all have elaborately decorative 13th-century foundations, built by the Seljuk and Mongol governors. Look for the decorative animals, including pigs, an artistic adaptation from Armenian design that would have been anathema to most iconoclastic Muslims.

Some 15km (10 miles) east of Kangal, famed for a gigantic breed of

Divriği's Ulu Camii, a Unesco World Heritage Site.

sheepdog named after the town, is **Balıklı Kaplıca** (hot springs), renowned for its varieties of skin-eating fish, said to relieve psoriasis. The sleepy iron-mining town of **Divriği ❸** to the east houses perhaps the most significant work of pre-Ottoman Turkish architecture in Turkey, and certainly calls for a detour. The mosque and hospital complex of the **Ulu Camii** (under restoration until 2020) was founded in 1228–9 by the Mengücük dynasty, which ruled the area as vassals to the Seljuks. The main portal is outrageously ornate, a riot of highly un-Islamic relief-carved birds and animals. The complex is perhaps the least well known of Turkey's Unesco World Heritage Sites.

ILIÇ AND KEMALIYE

From Divriği the railway line heads east to **İliç ❹**. The closest thing Turkey has to a classic one-horse town, İliç was founded solely to service the freight and passenger trains that run through it, with a combined teahouse and shelter. The town can only be reached with great contrivance by road – it's far better reached by rail (there are a couple of trains each day for the one-hour ride to Divriği). İliç attracts canoe and raft enthusiasts, who shoot the rapids of the Upper Euphrates here before gliding downstream towards the Keban Dam.

From either İliç or Divriği, it's possible to head down to **Kemaliye ❺**, a quaint little town on the west bank of the Euphrates at the spot where the river starts to fill the valley behind the Keban Dam. Formerly known by its Armenian name of Egin, the town was renamed **Kemaliye** (after Mustafa Kemal Atatürk) in 1922 to commemorate its role in the Turkish War of Independence.

Kemaliye provides an abrupt architectural change from the surrounding traditional Muslim settlements. It is clear that the Anatolian Christians of the 19th century not only enjoyed a much higher standard of living than most of their contemporaries, but that an eye for outward appearance and private ease was a primary concern. Many of their fine houses have been restored, some with delicately

Detail on the north door of Divriği's Ulu Camii.

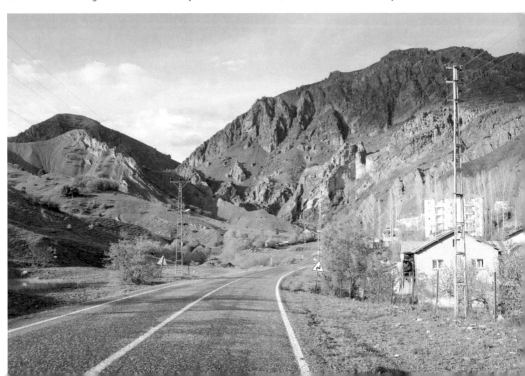

The road to Erzincan.

Catch a ferry from Elaziğ on the south shore of Lake Keban to visit Ovacık and Tunceli on the north shore.

Ovacık street.

carved shutters and balconies overlooking attractive gardens. The town is becoming something of a centre for Turkish outdoor enthusiasts with rafting, hiking up to the surrounding *yaylas* (summer pastures), mountain-biking possibilities and tours up the spectacularly rugged **Karanlık Kanyon** (Dark Canyon).

This central area, formerly dependent on snowfall and rain for dryland farming, has become a major source of grain for Turkey since the completion in 1975 of the gargantuan **Keban Barajı**, a dam at the confluence of the Euphrates and Murat rivers as they churn deep and white out of the mountains of the central Anatolian plateau.

TUNCELI PROVINCE: A TROUBLED PAST

Due east, Tunceli province, along the north shore of **Keban Barajı** (Keban Dam), is one of the least developed, most problematic yet indisputably beautiful areas of Turkey. The towering Munzur mountain range, with an average height of over 2,500 metres

(8,000ft), is the source of many small white-water streams that eventually merge with either the Euphrates or its major tributary, the Murat. The majority of the region's inhabitants are Kurdish by ethnicity and Alevî by religion and, as a result, they fit uneasily into the Sunni-majority, Turkish nationalist orientated state.

Formerly known as Dersim, Tunceli was the site of a dramatic uprising in 1937, when local inhabitants, under the leadership of Kurdish Alevi tribal leader Seyyid Riza, revolted against the central government, blowing up bridges and blocking passes into the Alpine valleys. Reinforcements were shuttled down the newly constructed railway to the east, and the Turkish air force dive-bombed those rebel strongholds beyond the reach of the ground forces, killing thousands and forcibly uprooting thousands more. Half a century later, in the early 1990s, Turkish forces launched a scorched earth campaign in the area in response to its infiltration by PKK rebels, leading ultimately to another round of forced migrations to different parts of the country.

Reinforcing the sense of beleaguerment felt by many locals, the government has appeared determined in more recent years to follow through with its plans to build several additional dams along the Munzur Valley. Were the plans to be executed they would force further evacuations, submerge sacred Alevi sites and massively disrupt the area's rich wildlife. Fortunately, the plans – for now – were scuttled by a 2018 Ankara court decision.

TUNCELI TODAY

The Tunceli region remains relatively underdeveloped, and its remote, jagged mountains, honeycombed with caves, provide cover for separatist groups who clash sporadically with the Turkish security forces. If you

wish to explore the region, expect the occasional roadblock, where your papers will be examined by security forces, and you may be quizzed about why you are here.

Elazığ, on the south shore of Lake Keban, is a natural jumping-off point. A ferry station some 16km (10 miles) north of town provides transport across the lake, past **Pertek Kalesi**, which once dominated the valley floor of the Murat River from a high knoll. These days the castle – built by the Mengücük dynasty – much restored in Ottoman times stands on an island halfway across the reservoir. In recent years its walls appear to have been somewhat overrestored, and plans are in place to launch a boat service to the island, set to feature restaurants and cafés.

OVACIK AND THE MUNZUR VALLEY NATIONAL PARK

Ovacık ("the little valley") is a pretty mountain town of some 6,000 souls, and makes a good base for exploring the natural wonders of the beautiful **Munzur Valley National Park** . The park is dominated by high mountains, snow-streaked well into summer, and the clear, bubbling waters of the Munzur Çayı. The security situation hereabouts is far more stable than it was, and it should be possible to explore the surrounding high pastures, natural springs, valleys and caves – but make sure you take local advice before setting out.

TUNCELI TOWN

The clear, white waters of the Munzur Çayı slowly darken as the silt of scores of mountain streams flush into it, creating a frothing brown river as one proceeds down the mountain towards **Tunceli**. The town, however, has precious little to recommend it – although there are several cheap hotels and an array of rooftop restaurants, enlivened by the relaxed attitude of the local Alevi population towards alcohol. Continue east, either by way of the Pülümür pass to Erzincan and Erzurum, or through Bingöl and Muş to the waters of Lake Van.

Local resident, Ovacık.

Keban Dam.

Malatya is famous for its apricots.

Cobblers in Malatya.

THE EUPHRATES REGION

Back on the southern shore of Lake Keban, **Elazığ** was established in the mid-19th century by, and named Elâzîz after, Sultan Abdulaziz. The distortion in the original name occurred by design in the early years of the republic when many of Turkey's place names were changed to fit better with Atatürk's new nationalism. Like many of the towns and cities of central and eastern Anatolia, Elazığ – although pleasant enough – is primarily a military barracks and there is little here to detain the average tourist.

The history of **Harput** ❼, a few kilometres up the road on the lakeshore, neatly sums up the whole complex, contradictory and often violent history of east-central Anatolia. The restored **citadel** (Wed, Fri–Sun 10am–noon, 1–5pm; charge), founded by the Hurrians in the 2nd millennium BC, was conquered successively by every army that passed from east to west or north to south, including the Urartians, Hittites, Egyptians, Achaemenids, Macedonians, Parthians, Armenians, Romans, Sassanians, Byzantines, Arabs, Seljuk, Artuk and Akkoyunlu and various other sundry Turks. Until the upheavals of World War I, its population was largely Armenian and the town boasted a huge American missionary college, depicted in a black and white period photograph in Harput's tiny museum.

Today, the most significant buildings in the town are the **Ulu Camii** (Great Mosque), with its wildly off-balance brick minaret clinging on for grim death, the austere **Tomb of Arab Baba**, a local holy man, and the paltry remains of the churches abandoned by the Armenians during World War I. Pressed against the eastern edge of the castle hides the diminutive **Meryem Ana Kilisesi** (Virgin Mary Church), converted from a pagan temple in 179 AD and reopened for worshippers in 1999.

MALATYA

Malatya ❽ is a prosperous town famed throughout Turkey for its apricots, which are grown and dried (often on the flat roofs of the area's traditional houses) and brought in from the

surrounding villages for shipment throughout the country and abroad. Malatya's other major claim to fame is as the home town of Atatürk's chief lieutenant, İsmet İnönü. The figure of Turkey's second president surveys the town square from a bronze horse, one of the few places where this honour has been bestowed on someone other than Atatürk. Malatya's **Archaeology Museum** (Tue–Sun 8am–4.45pm; charge), on Fuzili Caddesi, has a small but significant Hittite collection, mainly finds from the nearby settlement mound of Aslantepe.

Aslantepe itself (Tue–Sun 8am–5pm; charge) lies about 4km (2.5 miles) north of town, a substantial mound attractively set amongst stands of apricot trees. The site has been well-laid out with walkways and interpreted for visitors with informative signboards giving information about the various settlements that existed here over the ages. Thorough excavations have uncovered a vast mudbrick palace complex dating back to 4000 BC with wall paintings from 3200 BC,

and there is some fine replica Hittite statuary lining the approaches. In late Roman times, the settlement moved 8km (5 miles) north to **Battalgazi (formerly Eski Malatya)**, which still has a smattering of Byzantine and Seljuk remains, including 6th-century city walls, a 17th-century *kervansaray* and the heavily-restored **Silahtar Mustafa Paşa Hanı**, now often used as a wedding venue. Pick of the remains, though, is the 13th-century Seljuk **Ulu Camii**, noted for its beautiful blue-glazed tilework.

The major reason visitors come to Malatya, however, is because it makes a pleasant base for the trip up Mt Nemrut Dağı (see below).

NEMRUT DAĞI

Commagene, a tiny buffer state on the Upper Euphrates, pinched between the fleet cavalry of ancient Parthia and the inexorable legions of Rome, was a historical aberration. It flourished for the briefest instant during the Roman civil wars which pitted the tyrannicides, Brutus and Cassius, against

Malatya is ideal as a base for those wishing to ascend Nemrut Dağı – and for those with a sweet tooth, as the area's farmers produce huge harvests of cherries and apricots.

Trekking up Nemrut Dağı.

⊘ VISITING NEMRUT DAĞI

The spectacular mountain-top funerary sanctuary of Antiochus I is, for most people, the literal and metaphorical high of a visit to southeast Turkey. Its very remoteness, however, means that an overnight stay somewhere in the vicinity of the site is obligatory. The usual approach to Nemrut is from the south, from either Gaziantep or Şanlıurfa (both 3- to 4-hour drives). There is comfortable accommodation to be found in either hot, nondescript Kâhta or, better, up in the mountains at the village of Karadut. From either of these bases you can drive to the summit area yourself (around an hour), or join one of the locally arranged minibus excursions.

Approaching Nemrut from the north, the best base is Malatya. Minibus excursions are organised from the central tourist office. The 3-hour drive into the mountains is lovely and the trips are organised to reach the summit in time for sunset. Accommodation and meals are provided at a simple pension on the mountain, and you have the chance to visit the sanctuary again for sunrise before departing to Malatya.

The major disadvantage of the Malatya approach is that you do not get to see the lesser, but still worthwhile, sites of Karakuş, the Cendere Roman bridge and Arsameia. Also bear in mind that the road, and the statues, are often snow-bound from early November until late March.

The headless eagle flanks one end of the line of ancient god statues at the funerary sanctuary, Nemrut Dağı.

Decapitated but still awesome, giant stone gods haunt the terraces of Nemrut Dağı.

the fragile coalition of Mark Antony and Octavian, only to be crushed and absorbed into the Roman Empire, disappearing from history as Christianity took hold.

Unlike other forgotten states of late antiquity, though, Commagene sealed its place in history thanks to the incredible stone carvings created by its uniquely self-obsessed ruler, Antiochus I, as his own final resting place. Thousands of visitors make the trek to see these fabulous remains atop towering Nemrut Dağı.

The genealogy of the house of Commagene is obscure, but it is thought to have started out as a lesser line of the Seleucids of Antioch, who established themselves in the foothills of the Upper Euphrates following the rout of the Seleucids at the Battle of Magnesia in 190 BC. They styled themselves as the twin of the Achaemenians of old Iran on the male side, and the descendants of Alexander the Great on the other – the perfect cultural synthesis of East and West, as sought by Alexander himself.

With the decline of the Seleucids and the rise of Rome during the late Republican era, Commagene seems to have been involved with periodic anti-Roman uprisings along the eastern marches, usually associated with the nascent power of Parthia in Iran. Following the Roman defeat of the Pontic king Mithridates the Great in 63 BC, Antiochus I of Commagene was confirmed in power by Pompey, either as a token of trust for Commagenean support against Mithridates, or, more probably, as a gesture of realpolitik to help secure the distant marches on the Parthian frontier. Whatever the motive, the arrangement did not have the desired effect, and a mere eight years later, in 53 BC, the Romans suffered their most humiliating defeat when Crassus and his legions were destroyed at Carrhae, literally on the doorstep of Commagene.

After a long struggle to maintain its precarious independence between the Rock of Rome and the Hard Place of Parthia, Commagene was finally absorbed into the newly established Roman province of Syria during the reign of Nero. Little remained to mark the position of the country's capital, Samosata (Samsat; about 50km/30 miles south of Kâhta), and what there was has now been drowned by the Atatürk Dam. Commagene might have disappeared altogether from history, but for the massive tumulus on Nemrut Dağı. Built by Antiochus for his own glory and honour, it is a fabulous pile of stones and statuary to rival the greatest efforts of the self-deifying, pyramid-building Egyptian pharaohs.

THE SUMMIT

The centrepiece of any tour of Anatolia is a climb to the summit of the 2,150-metre (7,053ft) **Nemrut Dağı**  (Mount Nemrut; daily dawn–dusk; charge) where the statues of the gods of antiquity lie scattered. The route from the south passes a variety of other ruins, including the beautifully preserved Cendere Roman bridge and the citadel of Eski Kâhta (Old Kâhta). Allow at least a day for the excursion. Visitors usually either arrive for sunrise, when the statues on the east terrace are lit by the first red rays of dawn, or for sunset, when the matching statuary on the west terrace is illuminated, equally dramatically, by the setting sun.

A paved road leads up to a car park/café area, from where it's a stiff 20-minute walk up to the summit sanctuary itself. The altitude catches your breath here, and some prefer to let a donkey do the hard work for them. Although quite steep, there is now a well-paved path leading up around the tumulus and down to the car park by a different route.

The first glimpse of the east terrace is truly astounding. For here, atop the highest peak in the region and backed by the mighty tumulus mound (made up of hundreds of thousands of fragments of rock produced when the statues were being carved), is a row of massive headless statues.

In front of them, lined up by archaeologists to match the correct body, are the heads themselves, each around 2 metres (6.5ft) high. From left to right they are Antiochus I, Tyche (Goddess of Fortune), Zeus, Apollo and Hercules. Behind the heads is the stepped platform of a great altar, now used by weary visitors to rest after their climb. In ancient times this was a place where ritual sacrifices were carried out at certain important times of the year in honour of the deified Antiochus and his "fellow" gods – witnessed by adoring subjects who had walked many kilometres to get here. The gods were flanked at either end by monumental statues of a lion and an eagle, the heads of which have also toppled.

Round on the west terrace was a near identical row of deified-ruler, gods and noble beasts. Whether due to vagaries in the amount of exposure or the rock they were hewed from, the fallen heads on the west terrace are much less weathered than those on the east, but they have not been lined up with their bodies.

⊙ Tip

Although the sunrise/ sunset experience on Nemrut Dağı is well worthwhile, particularly for keen photographers, it's just as rewarding visiting in the daytime, when there are fewer people and the temperature more comfortable – sunrise especially can be freezing: take some warm and windproof clothes.

The view from atop Mt Nemrut.

A stone lion sits next to a headless eagle at the summit of Nemrut Dağı. Both creatures were viewed as noble.

Şanlıurfa, city of the prophets.

A path loops back down to the car park/café area from the west terrace, affording stunning views of the mountains to the north and, looking back, to the remarkable tumulus of one of history's most enigmatic rulers.

ESKI KÂHTA

Provided you made a sufficiently early ascent of Nemrut Dağı, the first stop on the way back to Kâhta and the plains is usually **Eski Kâhta** (open access), known in antiquity as Arsameia, the summer capital of Commagene.

There's a fine relief stele of Apollo/Mithridates pointing the way to the ridge-top sanctuary, which once boasted the funerary-sanctuary of Antiochus' father, Mithridates I. En route to the ridge, which is well-marked, are two tunnels leading to an underground cave clearly used in Mithraic rites, when novices would enter the underworld to worship the goddess Cybele, fasting and praying for several days before re-emerging, enlightened, to the rising sun. Both tunnels are blocked by iron grilles for

safety reasons, but above the second is a remarkable relief-carved slab, the equal of anything atop Mount Nemrut itself. Incredibly well preserved, the stele shows a deified Antiochus shaking hands with a club-carrying Hercules. Just above the tunnel entrance is a Greek inscription said to be the longest in Anatolia.

Also close at hand is the **Yeni Kale** (New Citadel), whose crenellated parapets were built by Mamelukes during the time of the Crusades. Though the castle has long been closed for restoration, you can ask the groundsman to let you in. Further along the road to Kâhta is the 90-metre (300ft) single-span **Cendere Bridge** over the Kâhta Çayı – once known as the Nymphaium River and one of the major tributaries of the Euphrates – a Roman structure built during the period of Septimius Severus (AD193–211), with three of its four original columns still standing. Nearer still to Kâhta is the **Karakuş** (blackbird in Turkish) tumulus, surrounded by three sets of carved pillars originally topped with relief carvings and statues, said to be the burial site of the Commagene royal women.

Midway between Nemrut Dağı and Şanlıurfa is the massive Atatürk Barajı, well-worth the 20-minute detour from the main road to view.

ŞANLIURFA

About 75km (50 miles) south of the giant reservoir lies the venerable old town of **Şanlıurfa** . According to Islamic tradition, it is the birthplace of the revered prophet Abraham, before his migration to Canaan (now Palestine).

It was known to the Greeks as Orrhoe or Osrhoe; Seleukos I Nikator, of Antioch fame, first established the capital of his eastern Hellenistic realm here, populating it with Macedonian veterans who preferred to call it Edessa, after their native province. Şanlıurfa remained an important garrison town into Roman times, and was

one of the first centres of the early Church (although it was given over to the monophysite heresy). It was also in Edessa that the great scientific works of late antiquity were translated, with commentaries, into Syriac/Aramaic, whence they made their way into Arabic after the Muslim conquest, only to find their way back to the West following the reconquest of the city by the Byzantines and then the Crusaders. Under Baldwin I, the city was the first of several Crusader states in the Middle East.

Edessa was sacked by the Zengi dynasty during the Muslim "Reconquest" of the Holy Land in 1144; all its men were put to the sword and all the women were sold into slavery. In the 13th century, following the standard Mongol rape of the Middle East, ancient Edessa disappeared from history, re-emerging only after World War I. Thanks for its survival as part of Turkey should go to the local population, who resisted French attempts to include it in Greater Syria. In recognition of this feat, the honorific Şanlı ("great" or "glorious") was added to the old name, Urfa.

Today, Şanlıurfa is a surprising mix of the old and new, with Arab, Kurdish and Turkish peasants in for a day's shopping from the countryside haggling in the traditional bazaar, while young technocrats and engineers bustle between offices and shops lining the modern downtown area. A city of 800,000, its rapid growth has been partly attributable to the building of the Atatürk Dam.

Şanlıurfa traffic lights.

THE SIGHTS

According to Muslim legend, King Nimrod had Abraham launched from a catapult in the city's citadel, to fall into a pile of burning wood. Happily, God intervened and turned the fire to water and the faggots to fish. The **Pools of Abraham** (Balıklı Göl in Turkish; open 24hrs; free), as they are known today, are the jewel in Urfa's tourist crown. Ringed by a couple of Ottoman-era mosque complexes, they are an oasis of cool in the pleasantly landscaped park that unfurls in a swathe

Hercules and Antiochus at Nemrut Dağı.

⊙ Tip

To visit Göbekli Tepe, head out of Şanlıurfa on the Mardin road. After 10km (6 miles) there is a sign on the left to Örencik village and Göbekli Tepe. When you reach Örencik (after 9km/5.5 miles), turn right and follow a track for 2km (1.25 miles) to the gate. A taxi from Şanlıurfa should be around €25.

of unexpected greenery at the foot of the city's impressive **citadel** (daily Apr–Sept 8am–7pm, Oct–Mar 8am–5pm; charge), topped by a couple of massive Corinthian columns (according to local lore the "arms" of Nimrod's catapult) as well as fortifications.

At the foot of the citadel is the mosque complex surrounding the **İbrahim Halilullah Dergâhı** (daily 8am–5.30pm), centred around the so-called "Cave of Abraham". Muslim pilgrims line up to enter the cool depths of the cave and, once inside, throw coins into a small pool, and make a wish (usually they are women hoping to become pregnant).

A little to the north of the castle and pools is the massive two-part complex of the Şanlıurfa **Archaeology and Mosaic Museum** (Tue–Sun 8am–5.30pm; charge), opened in 2014. The first section houses a collection of Edessan mosaics recently discovered at Haleplibahçe, immediately to the east, while further along the tree-lined path to the north is the three-storey archaeological section, its

Irrigation construction on the plains around Şanlıurfa.

displays spanning the breadth of the city's enviable heritage. As well as the usual Greek and Roman finds, there's a remarkable statue of a man, found near the Pools of Abraham. Dating back at least 11,000 years, it has some claim to be the world's oldest statue. Several incredible animal figures discovered at the nearby Neolithic site of Göbekli Tepe are on display here.

The streets of old Şanlıurfa, with their overhanging medieval houses and warren-like bazaars, are a great attraction. Many have been restored and turned into boutique hotels and venues for the city's famous "Sira Geceleri" (traditional music evenings, invariably accompanied by food).

Urfa's central **bazaar**, the *kapalı çarşısı*, is perhaps the very best in Turkey, selling everything from local tobacco to hot-pepper flakes and gold jewellery to Arab-style chequered-headscarves. The bazaar's Ottoman-period **Gümrük Han** (Customs House) boasts rows of tiny workshops looking onto a shady central courtyard packed with tea-sipping locals. The **Ulu Camii**

⊙ THE GAP: AN AMBITIOUS PLAN

The **Southeastern Anatolia Project** (or GAP) is Turkey's most ambitious economic undertaking, consisting of a network of 29 dams, 19 hydroelectric plants and hundreds of kilometres of irrigation tunnels and canals in the Euphrates-Tigris basin. It began in 1974 with the aim of transforming this neglected southeastern region into a breadbasket for the Middle East. The centrepiece is the 84 million cubic-metre (3,000 million cubic ft) rock-and earth-filled **Atatürk Barajı**, the fourth-largest dam in the world, at 80 metres (250ft) high, 800 metres (2,500ft) wide at the base and 20 metres (65ft) wide at the top. It was completed in 1992.

The twin 26km (16-mile long), 1.8km (1-mile) wide **Şanlıurfa Tunnels** and distribution canals which feed off the giant reservoir now irrigate over 1.7 million hectares (4.2 million acres) of plains and the massive investment appears to have paid off, with cotton now grown in abundance in the region, and pistachios and olives as major cash crops. The impressive scale of the engineering is well worth a look and has become a popular tourist sight among Turks – indeed, coach tours of the region aimed at the middle classes of Ankara, Istanbul, İzmir and other western Turkish cities are now generally known as GAP tours. Meanwhile, Syria and Iraq, downstream, are less than impressed at the thought that their water could be "turned off" at any time, and have complained bitterly about reduced flow.

is more Arabic than Turkish in style, its rectangular ground plan and pitched roof giving it a quite different appearance from the standard "dome on a square" Ottoman-style mosque. The Ulu Camii is thought to have been built on the site of the Byzantine-era Church of St Stephen.

GÖBEKLI TEPE

Antiochus I of Nemrut fame was not the first person to build a cult monument on a mountain top in this part of the world. In fact, he was beaten to it by some 9,000 years by the hunter-gatherers who roamed the hills and valleys north of Şanlıurfa just after the last ice age. The significance of **Göbekli Tepe ⓫** (daily Apr–Sept 8am–7pm, Oct–Mar 8am–5pm; charge) is potentially huge, for here appears to be proof that mankind was able to produce great works of art and monumental structures before settling down into sedentary farming communities. The hilltop here, itself well over 800 metres (2,600ft) above sea level, is surmounted by an artificial mound some 15 metres (50ft) high. Within this mound a German archaeological team have uncovered a series of chambers, complete with stone benches. The focal point of the chambers, though, are the beautifully crafted, T-shaped monoliths, several metres high and clearly intended to represent people. Most are decorated with relief-carved boars, snakes, lions, and other, largely predatory, wild creatures. It seems that this hilltop site had great religious significance to the hunter-gatherers who made it, as no evidence of human occupation has, as yet, been unearthed. Its age dwarfs that of, say, Stonehenge, and ongoing excavations may well produce more surprises.

HARRAN

South of Şanlıurfa towards the Syrian border, the landscape once more flattens into the Mesopotamian plain.

Thanks to the waters of the GAP project, the barren landscape is now green with cotton and other crops. The many humps punctuating the horizon are ancient settlement mounds, proof indeed that Mesopotamia was once the cradle of mankind.

Further down the dirt road lies ruined **Sümürtar**, a large mound with a labyrinth of passages and underground chambers used by the Sabians, worshippers of the sun, moon and planets, whose culture and religion managed to survive the onslaught of Christianity and Islam until the 11th century. Today, some poorer villagers have been using the chambers as donkey stables.

Back towards the main road is the village of **Harran ⓬** itself, built in and around the ruins of a mighty walled city whose origins date back to the 4th millennium. The Assyrians were here, and worshipped the moon-god Sin. Next came the planet-worshipping Sabians, who only gave up their faith at the point of the sword of Islam. This was also where the Roman statesman Crassus was defeated by the

The old part of Şanlıurfa mixes restored medieval houses with warren-like alleyways.

The number of bald ibis, a protected species for which Birecik is famous, has started to grow.

Parthians, with the legion standards captured and brought back in triumph to Ctesiphon to the undying shame of the Romans; Crassus himself reportedly died by having liquid gold poured into his mouth. Later, Julian the Apostate worshipped the moon here on the way to his fateful encounter with Shapur I further east. And Harran was the last stronghold of the Sabians, their tradition finally killed by the arrival of the fanatic Crusaders.

Harran today is famous for its strange beehive-style, mud-rendered dwellings, which until quite recently were inhabited. Now most are used for storage or animal shelter, though a couple of complexes have been done up as cafés (very welcoming, Harran literally bakes in the summer months). So thorough a job did the invading Mongols do in the 13th century that there's little left of old Harran except rubble, though it's worth exploring the massive inner citadel in the southeast of the site (a possible location of the Sin temple) and the massive Ulu Camii to the north,

Local children at Harran castle.

easily recognised by its distinctive square minaret.

WEST TO GAZIANTEP

Returning to Şanlıurfa, the road heads west to **Birecik**. Now little more than a truck-stop on the Euphrates, the town's main claim to fame, as indicated by a kitsch statue visible from the road, is the endangered bald ibis. A breeding station has been set up here in an attempt to save these exotic birds.

Viewed from the west bank of the river in the late afternoon, Birecik is most photogenic, with the lazy waters of the Tigris rolling past in the foreground, and the white limestone cliff around which the town is built glowing enticingly in the soft light.

A few kilometres beyond Birecik is ancient **Zeugma** ⑬. Founded at a strategic crossing point of the Euphrates by one of Alexander the Great's generals, it was traditionally an important jumping-off point for Roman adventures in the East, including Mark Antony's disastrous campaign against the Parthians in 36 BC. Part of the GAP project, the Birecik hydroelectric dam made international news in summer 2000, when the remains of several rich Roman mansion houses were discovered here just as the dam was about to be filled. Decorated with elegant mosaics and frescoes, an international rescue effort saved as much as possible from the well-appointed merchants' houses in a mere 10 days. Gaziantep's Zeugma Mosaic Museum now houses the majority of these remarkable finds. Some parts of the ancient city were situated above the current water level, and a couple of luxury villas terraced into the hillside, those of Danae and Dionysus, have been carefully excavated and preserved under an elaborate metal canopy. The site (daily Apr–Oct 8am–6.30pm, Nov–Mar 9am–5pm; charge) is 7km (4 miles) north of the village of Dutlu.

To the west, the area's rolling hills, covered with ripening wheat in early summer, are cut by the tributaries of the Euphrates, flowing southward to the desert flats of Syria and Iraq. In many ways the river marks the point at which Asia really starts – ancient Mesopotamia, the Land between the Two Rivers, where civilisation as we know it began.

KARKAMIŞ

Some 25km (15 miles) south of Nizip, on the Turkish/Syrian frontier, is one of the most important sites in the area, **Karkamış** ⑭. This once powerful and wealthy Hittite city was excavated by Leonard Woolley (ably assisted by a certain T.E. Lawrence) between 1912 and 1915. As well as uncovering some superb remains – the best of which are now in Ankara's Museum of Anatolian Civilisations and the Şanlıurfa Archaeology and Mosaic Museum – Woolley and Lawrence became involved in assorted disputes with the Germans, who were supervising construction of a section of the grandiose Berlin–Baghdad railway which runs at the foot of the mound housing the ancient city. After being off-limits for many years, excavations were resumed in 2011 after being cleared of mines, continuing even as fighting raged just beyond the border, protected by a blast wall. However, the site is unlikely to welcome visitors until the conflict is over.

GAZIANTEP

Gaziantep ⑮, with a fast growing population of around 1.6 million, was a city traditionally associated with copper-beating and mother-of-pearl inlay work. More recently, it has transformed into a city of factories spinning and weaving the raw cotton brought in from fields irrigated by GAP, and processing the industrial quantities of pistachio nuts harvested in the surrounding area.

As well as being the region's business capital, Gaziantep is busily transforming itself into its cultural and tourism centre. It is well placed to do this, with a history stretching back several millennia and a central old quarter blessed with legions of traditional honey-hued houses (many now turned into boutique hotels), an impressive castle, bustling bazaar and many old mosques. Despite its modernity, the city has a distinctive Middle-Eastern atmosphere, and boasts some of Turkey's most distinctive and delicious food – notably *baklava*.

Like its sister city Kahramanmaraş, Antep (as most continue to call it) enjoys an honorific "Gazi" ("Fighter for the Faith") bestowed upon it by Atatürk in recognition of the Alamo-like stand the inhabitants put up against French and Senegalese forces at the end of World War I.

The jewel in Gaziantep's crown is the remarkable **Zeugma Mosaic Museum** (Tue–Sun Apr–Oct 9am–6.30pm, Nov–Mar 9am–4.30pm; charge), which houses a collection of mosaics as

The exotic southeast: camels and the distinctive mud dwellings of Harran.

Local heroes guard the entrance to Gaziantep kale (castle).

impressive as any found anywhere in the Roman world. Some are displayed wall-mounted, others as they would have been *in situ*, in the reconstructed peristyle courtyards of villas, surrounded by pillars and backed by frescoes. The mosaics, frescoes and other finds, notably a superb bronze statue of Hermes, were all salvaged from the Hellenistic/Roman city of Zeugma. The state-of-the-art museum, well-lit and labelled, is arguably the best place in the world to see Roman mosaics. The city's **Archaeological Museum** (Tue–Sun 9am–5pm; charge), which used to house the mosaics now in the Zeugma Mosaic Museum, is still worth seeing for its wealth of other finds from this archaeologically rich region.

The partially man-made mound on which the city's massive **kale** (castle; daily Apr–Oct 9am–7pm, Nov–Mar 8am–5pm; charge) stands has provided finds dating back to the 4th millennium, though the castle itself is largely Mameluke. The views over the town from the castle, especially of the old bazaar quarter at its feet, are

wonderful, and within the walls are the remains of an Ottoman-era hamam (bathhouse) and a couple of 19th-century Russian-made cannon. The castle itself has been much restored, and so have many of the great trading halls and workshops *(hans)* and Syrian-style mosques in the bazaar quarter. Below and west of the kale the **Medusa Museum** (daily 8am–5pm; charge), housed in a fine stone house built around a courtyard, has a superb private collection of small finds dating from the Neolithic to the Islamic periods. These include toy Hittite-era chariots and oodles of gold jewellery. Just north of the kale is the **Emine Göğüş Culinary Museum** (Tue–Sun 8.30am–5.30pm; charge). Here visitors can find out about the history and traditions of Gaziantep's distinctive cuisine, regarded as Turkey's best.

Separated from the bazaar area by the modern city centre is another old quarter, which prior to the Turkish War of Independence was home to the city's sizeable Christian and Jewish minorities. Here beat-up wooden doors

Gaziantep's bazaar.

facing neglected streets open onto beautiful courtyard gardens, replete with orange, plum and pomegranate trees, and tinkling fountains. One of the finest 19th-century mansions houses the excellent **Hasan Süzer Ethnography Museum** (Hanifioğlu Sok.; Tue–Sun 8.30am–5.30pm; charge). On the hill above the museum is a fine black and white domed building. Now the Kurutluş Camii, it was once the Armenian **Church of the Virgin Mary**, dated 1892.

KAHRAMANMARAŞ

The D-400 (E-90) slices west from Gaziantep to Adana and the Mediterranean coast, while the smaller D-835 leads northwest through Arcadian scenery of small neat farms and babbling brooks to **Kahramanmaraş ⑯**.

Formerly known as Maraş, the city of 500,000 acquired the honorific "Kahraman" ("heroic") due to the large number of casualties it suffered during the Turkish War of Independence. Historically an important outpost guarding the second major pass over the Taurus Mountains, it has been sacked by passing invaders, which may account for the singular dearth of antique buildings in and around the town. The exceptions are the 15th-century **Ulu Camii** (Great Mosque), the **Taş Medrese** and the inevitable **citadel**, within which is the **archaeological museum** (Tue–Sun Apr–Sept 8am–7pm, Oct–Mar 8am–5pm; charge), with its collection of Hittite reliefs. On a hill 2 kilometres (1.2 miles) west of here towers the Ottoman-style, 32-dome **Abdulhamid Han Camii**. Completed in 2011, it's among the largest mosques in the country, easily seen from anywhere in the city – perhaps most spectacularly when lit up at night.

Today, aside from the pretty mountain scenery in the region, Kahramanmaraş is known primarily for the best ice cream in Turkey – a combination of cold sugar and cream with a peculiar elasticity and longevity; vendors throughout the country are obliged to wear traditional Maraş costumes in accordance with some unwritten law.

Gaziantep's much-restored castle.

📷 PROPHETS AND PREACHERS

From Noah's perch on Mount Ararat to Abraham's birthplace, Anatolia is steeped in the legends and history of the Bible and early Christianity.

Many sites mentioned in the Old Testament are located in eastern or central Anatolia. Indeed, many scholars believe that the Garden of Eden was between the Tigris and Euphrates (ancient Meso-potamia) in southeast Turkey, though all efforts to find it have failed.

The permanently snowcapped Mount Ararat (Büyük Ağrı Dağı), the biblical resting ground of Noah's Ark, is on Turkey's border with Armenia. Muslim tradition believes that the Ark came to rest on the slopes of the vast Mount Cudi, in Siirt province, about 350km (220 miles) further southwest, near the Iraqi border.

According to Genesis, Abraham and his family lived in Harran, about 50km (30 miles) south of Şanlıurfa. This is also where Abraham took Sarah, where Jacob hid when Esau threatened to kill him, where Rebecca drew water for Abraham's servant, and where Jacob rolled off the stone lid to water Laban's sheep.

Turkey's many New Testament sites tend to be in the western portion of Roman Anatolia. Among them are Antioch (Antakya) , Seleucia ad Pieria (Çevlik), Ico-nium (Konya), Tarsus – the birthplace of St Paul – and Myra (Demre), where St Nicholas served as a bishop in the 4th century. The so-called Seven Churches of Revelation were actually sites of early Christian communities. They are Smyrna (İzmir), Pergamon (Bergama), Thyatira (Akhisar), Sardis, Philadelphia (Alaşehir), Laodicea, near the city of Denizli, and, of course, the great city of Ephesus.

In AD 325, Church leaders meeting in Nicaea (Iznik) hammered out the Nicene Creed – the basic tenets of Christian belief.

Abraham, father of the Jewish nation, spent his childhood in Şanlıurfa. His tomb lies in Birket Ibrahim Mosque.

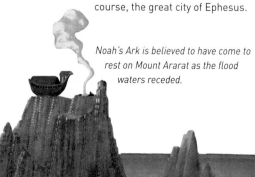

Noah's Ark is believed to have come to rest on Mount Ararat as the flood waters receded.

Early depiction of the Apostle Paul.

The Road to Damascus

St Paul was probably the greatest of the early Christian missionaries and theologians. Born in Tarsus around AD 10, he was a Jew with Roman citizenship, a tentmaker by profession and a zealot by nature. He spent his early years as a rabbi and Pharisee, promoting the persecution of Christians.

After a revelation (some say a blinding vision of Jesus) while on the road to Damascus, all his zeal went into proselytising and converting both Jews and Gentiles to Christianity. He never actually met Jesus.

He then crisscrossed Anatolia and the Eastern Mediterranean. His many writings (letters to the Romans, Corinthians, Galatians, Philippians, Thessalonians, Philemon, and possibly also to the Ephesians and Colossians) are the earliest extant Christian texts.

The concept originated with Christ, but it was Paul who laid down the rules of the Church. In AD 58, he was arrested, and sent to Rome, imprisoned and eventually martyred.

St Paul's Church in Tarsus, one of the oldest continuously inhabited cities in the world, and the birthplace of St Paul.

St Peter lived in Antioch (Antakya) for many years. It was here that followers of Jesus first gathered secretly in a cave church.

As fiery as modern Bible Belt evangelists, St Paul drew huge crowds when he preached in Ephesus' theatre.

THE FAR EAST

There is little trace of Europe to be found in this vast, distant swathe of land, bordered by Syria, Iraq, Iran, Armenia and Georgia. Turkey's Far East is foreign even to many of its countrymen.

Turkey's Far East feels quite different to the rest of the country, which is hardly surprising given that the bulk of the population here is ethnically Kurdish, a people with their own distinctive language and culture. In the Ottoman era, Kurdish chieftains pursued a fiercely independent existence in Anatolia's highest and most remote region, and even today many Kurds resist assimilation into mainstream Turkish society.

The region is best accessed by road either via Trabzon and Gümüşhane in the Black Sea region, or via Şanlıurfa close to the Syrian border. This chapter is split into two – the Northeast and the Southeast – to reflect both routes; they meet at Lake Van. Alternatively, there are good air links from Istanbul and Ankara to Erzurum, Van and Diyarbakır.

THE NORTHEAST

Somewhere between the old Silk Road cities of Gümüşhane and Bayburt the traveller crosses the geographical boundary between the Black Sea and the plateau, as well as the ancient historical boundary between the Pontic-Greek and Armenian cultural zones. Today the region is almost exclusively Muslim, sometimes fiercely so; places selling alcohol in conservative cities such as Erzurum are few and far between, and women draped in all-enveloping chadors

are not an unusual sight. The Christian Armenians, deported during World War I, have left behind little but their beautiful churches, and today's population is a mix of Turks and Kurds.

The main route into the high plateau climbs steeply from Trabzon to the Zigana Pass, which marks the watershed of the Black Sea mountain chain, before dropping to **Gümüşhane**, once famed for the silver mines which give it its name. Just outside the prettily set but nondescript modern town are the scant but atmospheric remains of the

Main attractions
Ani
Mount Ararat
İshak Paşa Sarayı
Mardin
Hasankeyf
Van Kalesi (Rock of Van)
Church of the Holy Cross – Akdamar Adası

Map on page 342

Detail on the Yakutiye Medrese, Erzurum.

◎ Fact

Turkey's three highest peaks are all in the Far East region. Ağrı Dağı (Mt Ararat) soars to 5,137 metres (16,853ft), Mt Reşko near Hakkâri to 4,135 metres (13,566ft), and Süphan on the north shore of Lake Van is a creditable 4,058 metres (13,313ft). Ararat and Süphan are both volcanic peaks, Reşko glacially alpine.

town's Ottoman era. To the southwest **Bayburt** , the provincial capital, is dominated by a stupendous restored fortress (open access), first built by Justinian, rebuilt by the Bagratids, fortified by a Turkish lord in the 13th century, and destroyed by the Russian army in 1828. A mysterious 1km- (0.6 mile) stretch of ancient tunnels lie 17 km (11 miles) northwest of Bayburt, directly beneath the village of **Aydıntepe** (daily 9am–5pm; charge). The purpose of the tunnels, discovered in 1988, is assumed to have been as a shelter for persecuted Christians, though ongoing excavations have yet to reach certainty.

Heading south of Bayburt, the road climbs to the bleak grandeur of the **Kop Geçidi**, a pass which commands a stunning panorama, before dropping down to the most important city on Turkey's northeastern plateau, Erzurum.

THE HIGH PLATEAU

Higher than the central Anatolian basin by about 1,000 metres (3,000ft), the northeastern plateau is broken up by a series of mountain ranges,

Çifte Minareli Medrese.

culminating finally in the volcanic peak of Mount Ararat. Snow buries all for a good half of the year, cutting off many villages from the rest of the world. In spring, these high pastures are an orgy of grass and wild flowers grazed on by huge herds of sheep and cattle.

Historically, the plateau provided a natural route between Asia Minor and the Orient. It was here that the ancient east–west trade route crossed into the Roman-Byzantine world; caravans carrying silk and other oriental riches made their way from China across Central Asia and Persia into Anatolia. From Erzurum, they continued westward to Sebastea and Caesarea, or crossed the Zigana pass to Trebizond (Trabzon).

This accessibility proved to be a mixed blessing, as wave after wave of invaders also broke into Anatolia through the northeast, leaving ruin and desolation in their wake. Between 1828 and 1918, the region was the scene of four wars between the Ottoman Empire and Russia, in each of which the Tsarist armies succeeded in breaching Turkish defences as far as Erzurum. In the war of 1878, Russia occupied – and held until 1919 – the provinces of Artvin and Kars as far as Sarıkamış.

ERZURUM

Ancient Theodosiopolis, named after Emperor Theodosius I ("the Great") who fortified it in the 4th century, **Erzurum** ⑱ is a sombre, austere city, whose outward aura is somehow reflected in the faces of its inhabitants. It's one of the coldest places in Turkey, home to the country's best ski resorts, which in a good season boast 3 metres (10ft) plus of crisp powder snow from December through to March. In summers, the resorts – huddled at the foot of the **Palandöken Dağları** range, which reaches 3,176 metres (10,420 ft) and dominates the city to the south – offer alternative accommodation and ambience to conservative Erzurum. The main resort lies just south of the city while the newer resort of Konaklı is set about 20km (12 miles) southwest of the centre.

A number of historical monuments have managed to survive a history of constant warfare and serious earthquakes. There are three *kümbets* (domed tombs), of which one is the oldest historical building in town, ascribed to Emir Saltuk, the feudal lord whose dynasty dominated the area for a century after the Turkish conquest. The **Ulu Camii** (Great Mosque) was built in 1179 by his grandson, while the small mosque and minaret atop the heavily restored **castle** (set to open in 2019) just to the north is also attributed to the Saltuk beys. The town's architectural masterpiece, the **Çifte Minareli Medrese** (Twin Minaret Seminary; daily 8am–6pm) was built, like its counterpart in Sivas, under the reign of the Seljuks. The Mongols, in their turn, built the **Yakutiye Medrese** (daily Apr–Sept 8am–7pm, Oct–Mar 9am–6.45pm; charge) in 1310, naming it after the local governor of Ogeday, a grandson of Genghis Khan who held court in Tabriz. The Ottomans then rebuilt and resettled the city, contributing the graceful **Lala Mustafa Paşa Camii** in 1563.

Beyond Horasan, some 85km (53 miles) east of Erzurum, the road forks, the left branch heading northeast to Sarıkamış and Kars, eventually linking up with Artvin, in the Black Sea region. The other heads due east to Doğubeyazıt and Ararat, with a turn-off running south to Van.

THE ROAD TO KARS

About 150km (90 miles) northeast of Erzurum, **Sarıkamış**, huddled into the surrounding cold, dark taiga of giant pines home to wolves and bears and endless rows of old Russian barracks, reminds the visitor that he or she has entered what used to be an outpost of the Tsarist Empire. There's a ski resort here to rival that at Erzurum, though the runs are generally easier, curving down through gentle pine forest rather than the bleak, treeless mountains of Palandöken.

Kars  has a 19th-century grid layout, unique in Turkey, that, along with the dusty, once-graceful buildings of the city centre, owes its existence to the Russians during their final, 41-year-long occupation after 1877. Following decades of neglect, Kars is beginning to tidy itself up, and a few of the graceful Russian town houses have been converted into boutique hotels and trendy cafés.

The old city, which served as capital to the Bagratids (see page 45) in the 10th century, is now a slum clinging to the hillside across the Kars stream. It is dominated by a crumbling **fortress** (open access) of the usual Urartian-Byzantine-Armenian-Turkish-Mongolian-Russian pedigree, worth a visit mainly for its panoramic views of the town and the plateau beyond.

Just below lies the town's other major historical sight, the Armenian **Cathedral of the Holy Apostles** at its foot, built in AD 937. Today a mosque (Kümbet Camii), its relatively crude form serves as a taster for much greater glories at nearby Ani. There's also a small **museum** on

Kars is known throughout Turkey for its dairy products, and particularly its cheese.

Austere Erzurum.

the eastern edge of town (Tue–Sun 8.30am–12.30pm, 1.30–5pm; charge), with an interesting ethnography section and some artefacts from Kars' Armenian and Russian past.

ANI: ABANDONED CITY

The ruined city of **Ani** ⑳ (daily Apr–Sept 8am–7pm, Oct–Mar 8am–5pm; charge) lies around 45km (28 miles) southeast of Kars. With a spectacular setting on an exposed bluff separated from neighbouring Armenia by a dramatic gorge, it is one of Turkey's most impressive sites.

A town existed in the pre-Christian era, before the Gamsaragan dynasty of Armenian lords held it for several hundred years. In AD 961, it became capital of the powerful Bagratids and from then until the mid-11th century was one of the most important cities in the Near East, with a population in excess of 100,000. Well defended by mighty circuit walls, the city blossomed, and dozens of beautifully decorated churches were built. Ani subsequently fell to the Byzantines

in 1045 and the Seljuk Turks in 1064. It was later reoccupied by the Armenians, until it finally fell to the Mongols in the 13th century. Shaken by the depredations of Tamerlane, it was terminally abandoned following an earthquake in the 14th century.

Allow at least half a day to make the most of Ani, plus an hour each way for the drive from/to Kars. Entry to the city is through impressive **Aslan Kapısı** (Lion Gate), from where a signed path meanders its way from church to church. Most obvious is the **Church of the Redeemer**, striking because only half of its bulk survives, the rest having fallen victim to a lightning bolt. Clinging to a cliff face above the Arpa Çayı is the exquisite **Church of St Gregory** and its lovely frescoes. Back on the bluff is the monumental but austere **Ani Cathedral**. There are several more worthwhile churches to see, all built from the local red sandstone, as well as the **Menüçehir Camii**, the sole mosque. Note that the border is sensitive and you should not point your camera towards Armenia – it upsets the *jandarma* (rural police force).

EAST TO ARARAT

The main road to Iran from Erzurum follows the line of the ancient caravan route and carries regular convoys of intercontinental trucks heading for Iran, Afghanistan and beyond.

Approaching **Doğubeyazıt**, the towering 5,137-metre (16,853ft) volcanic peak of **Ağrı Dağı** ㉑ (Mount Ararat) hovers into view. Its relative elevation over the surrounding plain – over 4,000 metres (13,000ft) in the north – makes it one of the sheerest profiles in the world. On a typical hazy day, the base of the mountain blends into the blue sky, leaving the enormous white cap of snow hovering eerily in space. The search for the remains of Noah's Ark has been underway ever since the French nobleman Pitton de Tournefort first scaled the mountain in 1707.

Kars corn seller.

ISHAK PAŞA SARAYI

Nearby, a few kilometres above the scruffy town of Doğubeyazit, the exotic **İshak Paşa Sarayı** ㉒ Tue–Sun 8am– 7pm; charge) was built in the 18th century. A delightful architectural mishmash of Georgian, Armenian and Seljuk styles, its lavishly relief-carved walls, domes and minarets make it an orientalist's dream. Although surprisingly built with Mount Ararat hidden by a ridge, its situation is spectacular, with grand views down across the plain this Kurdish chieftain's fortified-palace complex once controlled. Its decaying charm has been marred, especially for photographers, by the controversial addition of a protective, ultra-modern steel and glass canopy.

THE SOUTHEAST

The southeastern corner of Turkey is a fascinating and physically very diverse region in which Turks, Kurds and Arabs coexist, sometimes uneasily. With a few isolated exceptions, such as the vineyard-covered hills of the Tör Abdin plateau, the landscape is austere. The biblical Euphrates and Tigris rivers cut their way through bare, rocky mountains and desert-like plain, and temperatures in the lowlands soar to well over 40°C (104°F) for weeks on end in summer. By way of contrast, the high plateaux and valleys of the mountain ranges around Lake Van are snow-bound six months of the year, and the transhumant pastoralists who are the back bone of the local economy are confined to their winter villages.

Access can be difficult to this troubled part of the country. Heading due east across the plain from **Şanlıurfa** (see page 352), below Mardin and Midyat close to the Syrian border, the long and dangerous E-90 highway is much used by tankers en route to and from Iraq. Meanwhile, the road north and east from Diyarbakır to Iran becomes increasingly hazardous as it enters the high mountains around Lake Van.

MARDIN

Perched majestically on a bluff above the chequerboard expanse of the Mesopotamian plain, **Mardin** ㉓ is the most beautiful and visitor-friendly town in southeast Turkey. It is just a few kilometres north of the Syrian border, with the land hereabouts the closest Turkey gets to a true desert: be prepared for summer temperatures in excess of 40°C (104°F). It is also the launching point for visits to the ancient Roman outpost of **Dara**.

Sometimes known as the "White City" because of the pale stone its beautiful old houses are made from, once-scruffy Mardin has been rejuvenated in recent years and is now the focal point of tourism in the region. Its mixed Kurdish, Turkish, Arab and Syrian Orthodox (*Suriyani* in Turkish) population bears testament to its chequered past. A centre for the Syrian Orthodox Christians since the 5th century, its much-depleted Christian population still worships at some of the town's remaining churches, notably the 6th-century **Church of the Forty Martyrs** (Kırklar Kilise). The most important

⊘ Fact

In 2010 evangelical archaeologists from China and Turkey claimed to have found a 20-metre (65ft) wooden structure, made of planks fastened by tenon-joints, embedded in glacier ice high on the slopes of Mount Ararat. Sceptics claim an elaborate hoax by local Kurdish guides, who make a good living from ark-hunters.

The ruined city of Ani.

building in Mardin, though, is Islamic. The 14th-century **Sultan Isa Medresesi** (daily 9am–6pm; free) is a religious seminary of great beauty with a magnificently carved portal. Its elegant twin fluted domes and the slender minaret of **Ulu Camii**, further down the hill, are the most photographed of dozens of other significant Islamic structures dotted throughout the narrow backstreets, many of them renovated with EU grants. The Arabs conquered Mardin in the 7th century, and it became "capital" of a local fiefdom, that of the Artukids, between the 12th and 14th centuries. The **Mardin Museum** (Tue–Sun 8.30am–5pm) exhibits a small selection of finds dating back to the Assyrian era, housed in a delightful 19th-century mansion. More interesting is the **Sakip Sabancı City Museum** (tel: 482-212 9396; Tue–Sun 9am–5.30pm; charge) at the eastern end of the old town centre. Opened in 2009 in a late-19th century barracks, it tells the cultural and ethnographic history of the city in a series of photographs, signboards and audio-visual displays.

DARA

Still mostly hidden beneath the ground some 30km (19 miles) southeast of Mardin lie the ancient ruins of Dara (Tue–Sun 8.30am–6.30pm; free), just beside the modern town of Oğuz. Most of what remains is the work of Emperor Anastasius I in the early 5th century, and it was outside the 4km (2.5 mile) stretch of walls that Byzantine forces routed the Sassanids in 530 AD during the Battle of Dara. Control of the outpost switched hands repeatedly through the decades, its 573 fall to the Persians said to have driven Emperor Justinian II insane. Abandoned in the wake of the Arab conquest, the city has risen quickly to become one of the region's top attractions since excavations were begun in 2008.

Only a small portion of the site is currently open to visitors. The most impressive parts thus far uncovered are the cavernous cisterns and aqueducts and the elaborate rock-cut tombs, etched into the face of a cliff. Excavations have also revealed a graveyard, church, cemetery, warehouse and colonnaded street, while bodies' bones found in the cisterns have been linked to the Armenian genocide.

DEYRUL ZAFARAN AND THE TÖR ABDIN

The **Deyrul Zafaran Monastery** (Safran Manastırı; daily 8.30am–noon, 1–4.30pm; charge), 6km (4 miles) southeast of the town, was founded in AD 495 on the remains of a temple to the sun. Once the seat of the Syrian Orthodox Patriarchate, the monastery includes a church with beautiful relief frieze-work, a wooden throne and litters once used to carry Church dignitaries.

Deyrul Zafaran is the showpiece of the Syrian Orthodox Church in the region, but its spiritual centre is the isolated monastery of **Mor Gabriel** (daily 9am–11.30am, 1–4.30pm; free guided tour), a large, walled monastery complex set amidst the rolling hills of the Tör Abdin ("Mountain of the Servants of God") some

Işak Paşa Sarayı boasts a variety of architectural styles.

20km (12 miles) southeast of the town of Midyat. There are several more Syrian Orthodox churches in old **Midyat** ㉔ (65km/40 miles east of Mardin), their bell towers clearly visible from the main road in the centre of the town. The old town, built on the slopes of a low hill, is crowned by a gorgeous mansion house, former home of a prosperous Syrian Orthodox merchant family.

The once-sizeable Syrian Orthodox community of Mardin and the Tör Abdin was drastically reduced in the upheavals of World War I, and again in the war between the Turkish security forces and the separatist PKK (Kurdish Workers' Party) in the 1980s and 90s. Now only a few thousand remain.

HASANKEYF

The old town of **Hasankeyf** ㉕, a one-hour drive north of Midyat, has for years been threatened by the massive İlisu dam project. The Turkish government seems intent on pushing the project through, despite the fact that Hasankeyf has been placed on the list of 100 most threatened heritage sites in the world. Construction was completed in 2018, though as of this writing the dam has yet to be filled due to water shortage complaints across the border. It appears inevitable, however, that this once-great medieval city, perched atop a dramatic cliff frowning down on a lazy curve of the green Tigris below, will soon be drowned. In preparation, its exquisite tomb of Zeynel el-Abdin, complete with an onion-shaped dome gleaming with turquoise tiles, was moved in 2017 from its old position on the north bank to higher ground a few kilometres to the northeast.

DIYARBAKIR

Diyarbakır ㉖, some 90km (56 miles) north of Mardin and set on the Tigris, is one of the most vibrant, if troubled, cities in Turkey. It is famed for its massive black basalt walls, second only to the Great Wall of China in size, and gigantic watermelons fed on a mixture of water from the Tigris and fertiliser made from pigeon guano. It is also notorious elsewhere in Turkey for the sometimes militant Kurdish nationalism of its inhabitants, and violent demonstrations break out here periodically. Most recently, fighting in early 2016 left dozens killed and much of the old city damaged. Keep informed of the latest happenings and be wary of pickpockets and stone-throwing kids in the back alleys and on the walls.

The city was annexed by Rome in AD 297, and became a vital part of the line of defence between the Roman and Parthian/Sassanian empires of Persia. Ceded to the Persians after Julian the Apostate's ill-fated campaign down the Euphrates in AD 362, Diyarbakir was conquered once again by the Byzantines and held until the walls were breached by Muslim armies in AD 639. It was later taken by the Ummayad and Abbasid Arabs, Marwani Kurds, Seljuks, White Sheep Turcomans and Safavid Persians, before finally falling to the Ottomans in 1515. Most of the mosques, *medreses* and houses of interest date from the Ottoman period.

Tip

To hear a church service in a language closely related to that used by Christ, visit Mardin's Church of the Forty Martyrs (Kirklar Kilise) on a Sunday morning.

The majority of Diyarbakir's inhabitants are Kurdish.

Inside the Syrian Orthodox Church of the Virgin Mary, Diyarbakır.

Diyarbakir's mosques are typically built from alternating bands of white limestone and black basalt.

A quarter Christian Armenian or Syrian until 1915, Diyarbakır is now Turkey's pre-eminently Kurdish city. Save for the military, civil servants, a few Arabs, and the last surviving Syrian Orthodox families, the population of the city is overwhelmingly Kurdish.

The most distinctive of the town's 22 older mosques is the **Ulu Camii** (Grand Mosque), about halfway down İzzet Paşa Caddesi, Diyarbakır's main drag, between the Harput and Mardin gates. The oldest place of Muslim worship in Anatolia, this was originally the Church of St Thomas. Similar in design to the much grander Umayyad Mosque in Damascus (a city which Diyarbakır closely resembles), the Ulu Cami is built, like its counterpart in Şanlıurfa, on the courtyard plan of Arabian mosques. Nearby is the **Nebi Camii**, built in 1530. It, like many of Diyarbakir's mosques, mansions and *caravanserais* is attractively built from alternating bands of white limestone and black basalt.

At the end of the street to the west is the **İç Kale** (citadel), reopened in 2017 after restoration and complete with the renovated shell of the early Byzantine

Church of St George. Much of the interior, which until 2008 was a Turkish military base, has been renovated and redeveloped for tourism, including the well-stocked and newly relocated **archaeological museum** (Tue–Sun 8am–5pm; charge). Just outside the citadel is the restored Artukid Hazreti Süleyman Cami, built in 1155.

The **Kasım Padişah Camii**, better known as the Four-Legged Minaret Mosque, one of many 16th-century structures in town, has a peculiar minaret, standing in the middle of a crowded thoroughfare. Local legend has it that wishes come true to those who pass under it seven times. Down a winding and child-clogged street from here is the 19th-century Armenian church of **Surp Giargos** (St George), beautifully restored and used for occasional services by Turkey's surviving Armenian community. Just before it is an older church, the **Keldani Kilisesi**, still used by the handful of Chaldean Christians left in Diyarbakır. Most vibrant of the city's remaining churches, though, is that of the **Virgin Mary**, a beautiful Syrian Orthodox church dating back to the 3rd century AD. It has been lovingly restored by the Süriyani diaspora, and is used by the remaining Syrian Orthodox population of just five families.

THE CITY WALLS

Stretching for some 5km (3 miles) around the old city, and once possessing 82 defensive towers, the great basalt walls of Diyarbakır were first built during the reign of Constantine but have been restored repeatedly since. They are still in remarkably good shape in spite of repeated battering by sundry armies throughout history and feature inscriptions and geometric and animal designs.

The main north entrance to the old town is the **Harput Gate**, once known as the **Bab-al-Arman** (Gate of the Armenians). Upon entering, a road leads west along the walls to the **Urfa Gate**, and

beyond that, the **Ulu Beden**, from where there is access to the top of the walls through passages which, unhappily, double as public toilets. The ramparts have been restored, but still lack a guard rail so take care. It's now possible to walk as far as the southern **Mardin Gate**, with great views of the Tigris River meandering below. The slums which once clung like limpets to the inside of the walls have now been cleared and replaced by green parkland.

From Diyarbakır, the main road northeast towards Van through Silvan, just beyond which to the north rose the Batman Dam, and at its feet the massive 6th-century stone arch **Malabadi Bridge**. The road east continues to **Bitlis**, a chaotic town famed for its tobacco, ranged along a river gorge and dominated by a mighty **castle** (currently under restoration) built on an imposing outcrop by one of Alexander's generals.

LAKE VAN

Turkey's largest inland body of water, **Van Gölü** (Lake Van) stands some 1,650 metres (5,500ft) above sea level. Flushed with the run-off from innumerable small streams in the surrounding mountains, it has no visible outlet save for evaporation, which accounts for the lake's high salinity.

At the western head of the lake is **Tatvan**, a dull town but a useful base for excursions along the north shore. The most interesting of these is **Ahlat** ㉗ (open access), a half-hour drive away. Here is a cemetery to die for, where hundreds of beautifully inscribed Seljuk tombstones stand sentinel on a forlorn plain above the lake. Dotted around them are some superb *kümbets*, polygonal tombs with conical roofs built to house deceased Seljuk, Turcoman and Mongol chieftains. Between Tatvan and Ahlat a summer-only road leads north, through a tiny ski-resort towards the lesser **Nemrut Dağı**, a volcanic mountain sporting a spectacular triple crater lake.

Also north of Lake Van is **Süphan Dağı**, a mountain popular with climbers. Beyond that, the attractive village of **Adilcevaz** is tucked away in a green valley spilling down to the lake shore. Above it are the scant remains of an Armenian church and the Urartian citadel of **Kefkalesi** (open access).

VAN: AN ANCIENT CITY

On the lake's eastern shore, **Van** ㉘ is essentially a modern city, laid out on a grid plan between a towering volcanic peak and the lake. It has a long history, however, and was the capital of the Urartian empire in the 8th century BC. The Urartians' major foe, the Assyrians, attacked Van many times between the 9th and 7th centuries BC. In 590 BC it was conquered by the Medes, and later became a part of the Seleucid Empire.

The town and its environs developed a distinctively Armenian character over the following centuries despite succumbing successively to the Persians, Romans, Arabs, Byzantines and, following the battle of Manzikert in 1071, the Muslim Turks. What happened

The Urartian castle at Lake Van, one of the world's oldest surviving fortresses.

Lake Van.

to the old town during World War I remains highly controversial. Armenians claim the Turks butchered the innocent Christian inhabitants of the town, the Turks counter that Van was destroyed by the invading Russians, aided and abetted by treacherous Armenians. Whatever the truth, the town was totally levelled and the new city built a couple of kilometres away.

The region was struck by a devastating earthquake in the autumn of 2011, and many buildings in Van city and the surrounding settlements had to be rebuilt. The city is a pleasant enough base to explore the surrounding area, with plenty of hotels, reasonable restaurants and more than a few bars.

Old Van is to be found between the new Van and the lake, in a melancholic but beautiful expanse of meadow and swamp. Today, all that remains are the minaret of the **Ulu Camii**, scattered fragments of the town wall, a couple of badly damaged Armenian churches and, by the south wall, a pair of attractive, restored Ottoman-era mosques. Of more interest is the famous Rock of Van,

The Armenian Church of the Holy Cross, Akdamar island.

Van Kalesi (daily Apr–Sept 8am–7pm, Oct–Mar 8am–5pm; charge), overlooking the ruins of Old Van, topped by crumbling mud-brick battlements and riddled with the tombs of Urartian notables. Sections of wall and the Ottoman mosque atop the citadel rock have been rebuilt, and the result is rather jarring. Of most interest is the **King Argishti** (786–762 BC) **tomb**, hollowed out of the southern cliff face and accessed via a set of well-worn steps guarded by rickety railings. Also carved into this cliff, and only visible from the old town below, is a massive trilingual inscription dedicated to King Xerxes of Persia. Take care when exploring the citadel, as drops are sheer and there are few safety rails.

AKDAMAR ISLAND

The primary reason for any visit to Van is a trip to the superbly restored 10th-century **Armenian Church of the Holy Cross** (daily 8.30am–6.30pm; charge) on **Akdamar Adası** ㉙, an island reached by a 5km (3-mile) boat ride from a point along the lake shore just past the town of **Gevaş**, some 40km (24 miles) southwest of Van.

With the entire edifice of the Byzantine state about to collapse before the Turkish onslaught, and with only his kingdom standing between the warrior hordes and the soft underbelly of central Anatolia, the Armenian king, Gagik Atsruni, had the church and its palace complex built as a retreat. The church is in the standard Armenian style, with a conical dome atop four axes, with the most impressive feature being the ornate relief-work on the façade, depicting the Old Testament: a veritable zoo of animals and birds rings the roof, door and walls. A major restoration project, completed in 2011, has transformed the church and island, making a visit even more special than in previous years.

The island setting is a delight, its cliffs ringing with the cries of Armenian gulls, almond trees a sea of blossom in spring, and the towering peaks south of the lake reflected in azure waters. There are a few swimming places where you can take a dip in the sodium-rich waters.

HAKKÂRI PROVINCE

Just south of Van, a turn-off leads south to Hakkâri, Turkey's remotest corner. It is also, along with Tunceli (see page 346), the country's most problematic province, squeezed between Iraqi and Iranian Kurdistan, with considerable separatist sentiments of its own. Travel in the area is safe on major highways, but potentially dangerous on country roads and in the mountains. The security forces check papers at roadblocks in the mountains here, and view visitors leaving the main roads and sights with suspicion. Clashes between the Turkish military and Kurdish separatists still occur, so avoid venturing too far off the beaten track.

The first site of interest, 28km (17 miles) south of Van, is **Çavuştepe** (daily Apr–Sept 8am–7pm, Oct–Mar 8am–5pm; charge), a Urartian citadel perched dramatically on a mountain spur. The quality of the stonework here is breathtaking, as is the remarkable inscription carved into the temple doorway. Next up is the dramatic **Hoşap Kalesi** (officially closed for restoration; you can ask the groundsman to let you in), built by the Kurdish despot Sarı Süleyman ("the Blond") in 1643.

The road south leads to **Hakkâri**, through the spectacular gorge of the Zab River. The 4-hour journey from Van here is a scenic joy, but Hakkâri is itself both dull and problematic. Anti-state feelings run high in this economically deprived mountain town, and the proximity to the Iraq border to the south means there is a heavy presence of armed forces at all times. The mountains, though, are glorious, if you can access them, and the Nestorian patriarchal church of **Koçhanes**, 20km (12.5 miles) to the north, is worth visiting. The road winding west of Hakkâri connects the similarly bland border town of Cizre – almost entirely rebuilt after the destruction of the 2015–16 fighting between government and pro-Kurdish forces – before continuing to Midyat and Mardin.

Bitlis elders.

⊘ PKK AND KURDISH SEPARATISM

Estimates of civilians and combatants killed since the Kurdish Workers' Party (PKK) launched a campaign for Kurdish independence in 1984 range between 40,000 and 80,000, while around 3,000 villages have been depopulated. Four million people – mainly Kurds – are refugees. Restrictions on movement continue to affect local Kurds, who in many regions cannot access the high pastures to graze their animals. Many Turkish soldiers have died in PKK attacks, sometimes launched from across the border in Northern Iraq, and this has led to a rise in anti-Kurdish, nationalist Turkish feeling. Following the breakdown of a cease-fire in 2015, thousands were killed. Tensions rose further in the wake of the failed coup attempt of July 2016, as Turkish forces ramped up attacks both within and beyond Turkish borders. Though the group was largely responsible for the ousting of ISIL, Turkey has always considered it a mere extension of the PKK. Intent on driving the YPG back from Turkey's borders, Erdoğan welcomed Donald Trump's December 2018 announcement to withdraw US troops from Syria, though as of this writing, the details remain unclear.

For now, the conflict continues to appear intractable, despite that PKK leader Abdullah Ocalan – captured in 1999 – has called for a resumption of the failed peace talks. Though the targeting of foreigners is extremely rare, travellers in the region are advised to stay vigilant and informed.

The view to Heraklia from
a Byzantine church.

TURKEY

TRANSPORT

GETTING THERE

By Air

Flight time to Istanbul from London is around 3.5 hours, from New York about 9 hours.

Many international airlines have regular direct or connecting flights from major European cities to İstanbul's Sabiha Gökçen Airport (on the Asian side of the city) and to the new Istanbul Airport (European side). As of this writing, the latter – officially inaugurated in October 2018 – only services a handful of flights for Turkish Airlines. Until the airport's complete roll-out (expected by the end of 2019) the old Atatürk International remains in service. There additional direct international flights to İzmir and – very rarely – Ankara. From North America, Turkish Airlines (THY) offers direct flights from New York, Chicago, Los Angeles, Washington, DC, and San Francisco. From the UK, the scheduled full-service direct carriers to Istanbul are THY, Pegasus Airlines, or British Airways (BA).

Among no-frills airlines, Pegasus offers by far the most links to the UK with Istanbul's Sabiha Gökçen Airport, located on the Asian side, as well as Istanbul Atatürk (until the new airport fully opens), while easyJet serves İzmir. Various international carriers, either no-frills or charter, also fly direct from the UK and Ireland to the international airports at Bodrum, Antalya and Dalaman.

Reaching any other Turkish city, in particular Adana, Kars, Kayseri, Trabzon or Van, will involve a connection through Istanbul – often somewhat easier (and possibly cheaper) done with THY. For domestic flights, see box.

Travel to and from the airport

Whichever airport you fly in to, the easiest option to get from the airport into the nearest town is by taxi, of which there is never a shortage. Specimen fares to popular destinations are often posted at taxi ranks, though in practice taxi meter readings can end up slightly higher. The fare will be registered on the meter and should come to under US$20 from most airports (closer to US$30 from Istanbul's new airport). Although cab drivers may not be that good at finding their way around, if you know the name of your hotel, and the area it is in, you will get there.

Hotels can arrange transfers, but this can be much more expensive. It can sometimes be the only option on the coast, however, where some hotels are a couple of hours' drive from the nearest airport.

Major cities also have airport buses, often timed to coincide with the arrival or departure of scheduled flights.

Istanbul From Atatürk **Airport**, the easiest and cheapest way of getting into Istanbul is on a combination of the metro and tramway (change at Zeytinburnu or Aksaray) which will take you to the heart of Sultanahmet in approximately 50 minutes. You'll need to buy two *jetons* (tokens) at the outset. Convenient public transport links have been promised for whenever the new **Istanbul Airport** is fully open (expected late 2019). From **Sabiha Gökçen Airport**, situated out in the Asian suburbs near Pendik, there is a half-hourly shuttle bus (HAVABUS; roughly 1hr 30min) into Taksim; Alternatively take the E10 bus to Kadıköy, where ferries cross the Bosphorus to Eminönü or Karaköy – although this is not recommended for people with heavy baggage.

The city centres of **İzmir** and **Antalya** are also served by metro service from their respective airports.

When leaving Turkey, allow plenty of time for checking in, especially in the high season. Long queues can build up both for the security checks and for check-in and passport formalities.

By Sea

There are no longer any international ferry services from Italy to Turkey, and little hope of their being re-instated. But car and/or passenger ferries sail between the

✈ Airlines

Airlines flying between Turkey, Britain and North America

British Airways: www.ba.com
Delta Airlines: www.delta.com
EasyJet: www.easyjet.com
Jet2: www.jet2.com
Pegasus Airlines: www.flypgs.com
Thomas Cook: www.flythomascook.com
TUI: www.tui.co.uk
Turkish Airlines (THY): www.thy.com

Domestic airlines in Turkey

Turkish Airlines (THY): www.thy.com, national call centre 444 0849
Anadolujet: www.anadolujet.com, national call centre 444 2538
Atlasglobal: www.atlasglb.com, national call centre 0850 222 0000
Onur Air: www.onurair.com.tr, national call centre 0850 210 6687
Pegasus Airlines: www.flypgs.com, national call centre 0888 228 1212
Sun Express: www.sunexpress.com/tr, national call centre 444 0797

Turkish ports of Ayvalık, Çeşme (near İzmir), Kuşadası, Bodrum, Marmaris and Kaş, and the respective Greek islands of Lésvos, Híos, Sámos, Kos, Rhodes and Kastellórizo. Services, provided by either Turkish and Greek boats, run at least once daily between mid-April and mid-October, and sporadically (typically once or twice weekly) in winter. One useful information source (with booking capability) is www.feribot.net.

By Rail

Arriving in Turkey by train from Western Europe is an enjoyable experience if you have sufficient time to make the trip. It's a minimum three-day, three-night journey from Britain, with a typical itinerary being London–Paris–Munich/Vienna–Budapest–Bucharest–Istanbul. Note that there are no longer any cross-border services from Greece. Inter-rail and Eurail passes are valid in Turkey, but are unlikely to save you much money.

An excellent source of information is the website www.seat61.com, which has every possible routing to Turkey, and links for ticket purchases for the various legs of the journey (it's not possible to buy a single return ticket from the UK, which anyway will cost around £500 for second-class standard travel).

Trains from Europe arrive at Sirkeci Station in Eminönü, in the heart of old Constantinople. The station is linked by high-speed train tunnel under the Bosphorus (the Marmaray) to Üsküdar suburb on the Asian side of Istanbul. The restoration and expansion of the venerable Haydarpaşa Station, right on the Asian shore, are due for completion by the end of 2019, from which time it will serve high-speed trains to the Anatolian interior. Until then, these continue to depart from Pendik station, 24km (15 miles) to the east and linked by metro line 4.

For rail information in Istanbul: tel: 0212-520 6575 (Sirkeci; European lines); tel: 0216-348 8020 (Haydarpaşa; Asian lines).

By Bus/Coach

Long-distance coach services operate from major European cities, especially in Germany and Austria, as well as from the Middle East,

Russia and central Asian states. Coaches arrive at the Esenler Otogarı (also called Büyük Istanbul Otogarı), Bayrampaşa, northwest of Istanbul; tel: 0212-658 0505/1010. There are buses and a metro from there to the centre of the city. For details, see City Transport box.

By Car

It is possible to drive to Turkey via Bulgaria or Greece, or via Italy, with a ferry to Igoumenítsa in Greece. EU money has seen the completion of the Egnatia Odos expressway across northern Greece from Igoumenítsa to the Kípi/İpsala border crossing into Turkey, and also vastly improved motorways across Bulgaria to the border town of Svilengrad.

At the point of entry you will need to show the car's registration documents and your driving licence. Your car details will be stamped into your passport, allowing you to drive it for six months in Turkey duty-free. You will also be issued with a certificate which you should keep with you at all times. You must leave the country with the vehicle; should you write your car off during your stay, you will need a special police report certifying that it has not been sold in Turkey.

Documents
In addition to a valid driving licence, you will need the vehicle's log book and proof of ownership (and a power of attorney as proof of permission if you are driving someone else's vehicle), a Green Card (from your insurance company) and insurance (check you are covered for the Asian side of the country and for breakdown). Drivers may use their national licence with a Turkish translation for up to three months, but are advised to obtain an IDP (International Driving Permit).

GETTING AROUND

Domestic Air Travel

There is a good network of reasonably priced domestic flights serviced by Turkish Airlines (THY), Pegasus, Onur Air, Anadolujet, Sun Express and Atlasglobal (see box for contact details). You need to be

flexible about timing if booking at short notice on a popular connection at a busy season (for example, to the Aegean and Mediterranean airports over a public holiday). Early-morning and evening flights between Ankara and Istanbul also fill up quickly. Though you can still book and pay at a walk-in travel agent, all airlines (and the best fares) are increasingly web-based.

Istanbul is linked by direct flights to the following cities from both Sabiha Gökçen and the new Istanbul Airport (or, until the latter is fully functional, from Atatürk Airport): Adana, Ankara, Antakya, Antalya, Bodrum, Dalaman, Denizli, Diyarbakır, Edremit, Erzurum, Gaziantep, İzmir, Kars, Kayseri, Konya, Malatya, Mardin, Nevşehir, Samsun, Şanlıurfa, Sivas, Trabzon and Van. Note that this list tends to expand or contract annually, as new routes are added and unprofitable destinations are dropped. Security is strict and you will be asked to point out your baggage from a pile on the runway before it is transferred to the plane.

By Bus

Turkey has excellent bus services, both inter- and intra-city. Although this is still the preferred method of long-distance travel for many locals, since it is cheap, reliable and generally comfortable, an increasing number of visitors opt to fly between the main centres to avoid a long overnight journey. If you prefer to stick with buses, however, you can leave Ankara at 10pm and be at the south coast by 8am the following morning. Likewise you can also reach Cappadocia from Istanbul on an overnight bus.

Competition between companies is intense; the best – Ulusoy, Varan and Metro – are more expensive and have comfortable, modern buses with proper air conditioning and free refreshments, as well as the traditional libations of cloying lemon cologne. Increasingly, onboard videos are being replaced with television programmes regardless of the fact that the satellite systems come and go, rendering transmission unreliable.

Tickets are easy to obtain; when you approach the ticket offices (which are often next door to one another), touts may pressure you to travel with their company, so choose with care. Places are reserved, and unaccompanied women will usually not be seated next to a man they do not know. Smoking is never allowed on board.

There is no comprehensive national or local timetable, so you have to work out the best route and departure time for yourself. Most routes are operated by several different companies.

Long-distance bus stations

Most long-distance buses depart from the main bus station (otogar) in each town, nowadays often on the outskirts, and there will be ticket offices there and in the city/town centre. There will usually be a minibus service (servis araçı) to take you from out-of-town bus terminals to the centre, or (more likely) vice versa. Most long-haul journeys take place at night.

Istanbul has two main bus stations: at **Esenler** (Bayrampasa, 10km/6 miles northwest of the city), and **Harem** (on the Asian side). The former geographical separation of destinations from each has more or less dissolved, with most buses stopping at both. Coming from central Anatolia, alight at Harem and take a ferry to your likely destination on the European side – far quicker than continuing to Esenler.

By Train

The three largest cities (İstanbul, Ankara and Izmir), and many places between and beyond, are connected by Turkish State Railways (TCDD), but the network is limited to the interior – there is no coastal railway on either the Aegean or

⊘ Major Inter-city Bus Companies

Kamil Koç: (Istanbul, western and southern destinations, and Ankara)
www.kamilkoc.com.tr
National call centre: 444 0562
Metro
www.metroturizm.com.tr
National call centre: 0850 222 3455
Pamukkale: (Istanbul, western and southern destinations, and Ankara)
www.pamukkaleturizm.com.tr

National call centre: 0850 333 3535
Ulusoy: (Istanbul, Ankara, Black Sea region, İzmir and the Aegean, Antalya and the Mediterranean)
http://secure.ulusoy.com.tr
National call centre: 0850 811 1888
Varan: (Istanbul, Ankara, İzmir and southern destinations)
www.suhaturizm.com.tr
National call centre: 0850 250 3838

Mediterranean shores. Therefore, for travel in much of the country, a bus is the only option.

Ordinary rail fares are, however, cheaper than buses – with 20 percent discount for return journeys – and comfortable, especially in first class, though non-express services will be noticeably slower.

The best connections are between Istanbul, Ankara and İzmir (the latter involving a ferry crossing of the Sea of Marmara to Bandırma). Turkey has introduced high-speed trains (Yüksek Hızlı Tren) on select routes, in particular Istanbul–Ankara, Istanbul–Konya, Ankara–Konya, Eskişehir–Konya and Ankara–Eskişehir. Future expansions include Ankara–Sivas (2019) and Ankara–İzmir (2020).

Purchase tickets and reserve seats or sleepers up to 15 days in advance, preferably from the station at which your journey will begin. You should in theory be able to book a ticket to and from anywhere in Turkey in Istanbul, Ankara or İzmir, but it can sometimes prove difficult, especially now with so many closures to permit

high-speed track works. Sleepers get booked up, especially over public holidays. Choose between a küşetli (pull-down couchette-style compartment with six sharing, pillows provided but no bedding); ortülü küşetli (four bunks, bedding provided); or yataklı (first class, with two or three beds, linen included).

The following trips may also be of interest:

The Doğu Express to Kars, which departs from Ankara daily, taking around 24 hours to wind its way across Anatolia via Kayseri and Erzurum to the far eastern border region.

The Vangölü Express departs twice weekly from Ankara to the far southeast, ending in Tatvan on Lake Van and passing through Elazığ en route – handy for Nemrut Dağı. Total journey time is just over 24 hours.

Reservations and Enquiries

In theory, the **Turkish State Railways'** website (www.tcdd.gov.tr) has an English-language booking option, but we defy you to make it work. If you insist, the rail buff's site www.seat61.com has a guide to attempting this. Most people just go to the station in person, scan placards and confirm schedules with staff. Phones are rarely answered, and if so by monolingual staff. It can be well worth paying the small commission asked and having train tickets issued by major Turkish travel agents, especially those in and around Sultanahmet in Istanbul.

City Transport

For up-to-date information on public transport in Istanbul, see www.iett.istanbul.

Istanbul was the original destination for the world's most famous train.

Istanbul buses

City buses are largely run by Istanbul municipality and have the letters IETT on the side. Although you can still pay at the front of some buses with cash or *jetons* (tokens), most are now geared to electronic ticketing and locals pay using an *İstanbulkart* swipe card. You pay 10TL for an İstanbulkart (including 4TL of credit) and then load as much additional fare value as you want onto it, and it can be used on almost all forms of local transport. When boarding a bus, press it against the meter at the front. More than one person can use the same İstanbulkart (press it against the meter for each traveller). Your journey is discounted 33 percent compared to a cash or *jeton* fare. If you need to top-up your credit, look for machines labelled *Elektronik billet ve dolum cihazı*. Fixed-price daily and weekly cards are also available.

Bus fares are cheap but journeys can be slow, and it is advisable not to travel during rush hours as, predictably, it gets extremely crowded.

There are also private *dolmuş* (minibuses), usually yellow, which tend to be faster. On these you pay your fare to the driver or his assistant, the amount dependent on your destination. Look for a big 'D' sign a kerbside for authorised pick-up points.

All buses have a board in the front window and at the side listing the main destinations on the route. There are maps of the network at bus-stop shelters.

Metro and Tram

Ankara, Istanbul and İzmir all have efficient, well-integrated and rapidly expanding metro systems. Istanbul's is as much overground light railway as underground metro, with it's first line (M1) running from the old Atatürk airport via the Esenler otogar to Aksaray and the Yenikapı Transit Centre. From here, the Marmaray runs links Sirkeci before passing beneath the Bosphorus to link Üsküdar and further stations the Asian side. Also from Yenikapı, the M2 line runs north over the Golden Horn to Hacıosman via Haliç, Şişhane and Taksim. Particularly useful for visitors is the overground tram beginning at Bağcılar, passing close to the Aksaray metro station and then the main tourist centres

☉ Dolmuş

An economical method of travelling around a city or to a neighbouring town is by *dolmuş* (literally "full", sharing the same root as the Turkish word for the country's stuffed vegetables). A kind of shared taxi, usually a minibus, the *dolmuş* travels along a fixed route for a fixed fare, paid to the driver. At the start of the route, it may not set off until it is full, which can entail a wait, although this is increasingly rare.

of Sultanahmet and Eminönü before crossing the Galata Bridge to Kabataş. The cheapest and most convenient way to pay is with an İstanbulkart; otherwise you can buy tokens from adjacent booths.

A "nostalgic" tram runs up İstiklâl Caddesi between Tünel and Taksim every 20 minutes, while the tiny Tünel funicular – one of the oldest in the world – saves commuters the steep walk up from the Karaköy ferry docks.

Taxis

Taxis *(taksi)* are bright yellow, reasonably priced and plentiful. In the cities and big towns it is often unnecessary to look for one; they will find you, signalling availability by slowing to a crawl alongside you or hooting. You should check the meter is switched on; it almost invariably will be, but it is still worth checking.

İstanbul now has one flat rate, with meters starting at 4TL and

Sultanahmet tram, İstanbul.

rising at 2.5TL per kilometre (10TL minimum fare); elsewhere the tariff doubles between midnight and 6am.

There are inevitably a few drivers who do their best to augment the fare by driving round in circles or simply saying that the meter is broken; try and check roughly how much it should be before getting in. Most, however, will try their hardest to help you, even if they speak little or no English.

It helps to have your destination written down in case of difficulties in comprehension, and also because your driver may also be new to the area. State the area location first, eg, Sultanahmet, and go into detail later. When your driver gets close to his destination, he will ask for directions. If crossing the Bosphorus in Istanbul, the bridge toll will be added to your fare.

Most taxis operate independently around a local base, which may be no more than a phone nailed to a telegraph pole. There are few radio-controlled networks. Hotels and restaurants will always be able to find you a taxi.

Fixed prices can be negotiated for long distances or sightseeing tours with waiting time built in.

Water Transport

Dardanelles ferries

Until completion of the record-breaking Çanakkale 1915 Bridge (expected 2022), the only way to cross the Dardanelles is via a pair of car-and-passenger ferries: Çanakkale to Kilitbahir (cheaper, shorter) or Ecebat, and from Lapseki

to modern Gelibolu. Departures are frequent and consistent – at Gelibolu and Eceabat, around the clock.

Sea of Marmara ferries

Around the Sea of Marmara, car ferries and sea-buses cross between Pendik on the northern shore, well east of Istanbul, and Yalova on the southeastern shore, and between Yenikapı (near Aksaray) to Bursa, Yalova and Bandırma, the latter being the railhead for İzmir and the northwest Aegean. There are also more informal services, usually April–October only, from Tekirdağ to Erdek or Bandırma on the southern shore of the Sea of Marmara – drivers may find this saves lots of time (if not much money) compared to the arduous land journey around the shoreline.

Timetables for Istanbul-based services can be found at any of the sea-bus or ferry terminals in İstanbul, or online at www.ido.com.tr, including a usable English option.

Istanbul boat services

Divided by the Bosphorus and the Golden Horn, Istanbul has a busy network of large steamers, small water-buses that operate like dolmuşes, sea-buses (catamarans) and water-taxis. Crossing the water is an essential part of a visit to the city.

From the main jetties at Eminönü, Karaköy, Kabataş and Beşiktaş on the European side, you can catch public ferries (Şehir Hatları, www. sehirhatlari.istanbul) to Kadıköy or Üsküdar on the Asian side; buy a jeton at the gişe and drop it in the

İstiklâl Caddesi, Istanbul.

slot at the entrance to the jetty (iskele), or use your İstanbulkart. Each jetty serves one destination which is prominently signposted.

The privately operated dolmuş water-buses, called "motors", cross at certain points, notably between Üsküdar and Beşkitaş, mopping up commuter traffic at rush hour, and running until 1am when the publicly owned ferries have closed. Again, you pay by jeton or use your İstanbulkart. A ferry service also leaves from near the northern end of the Galata Bridge to go up the Golden Horn to Eyüp. There are also scheduled (as opposed to cruise) ferries up the Bosphorus, which depart from west Eminönü – timetables are skewed to favour commuters, however.

Frequent ferries and sea-buses leave the Kabataş ferry port (last stop on the T1 tram line) for the Princes' Islands or Adalar, off the Asian shore in the Sea of Marmara. The full journey takes 45min (sea-buses) to 90min (conventional ferry) and stops at all the islands before terminating at Büyükada, the largest island.

There are also small private ferries, run by Dentur Avrasya or the TurYol cooperative, crossing to the Asian side (and in summer, to the islands) from Eminönü, Beşiktaş, Kabataş or Karaköy; buy tickets at their waterside kiosks.

Free timetables covering the İstanbul water-transport system are available at the ticket offices; the timetables alter in mid-June and again in mid-September.

A **water-taxi** service allows groups of people to summon water transport in exactly the same way as a normal taxi although prices are not cheap unless shared by a large group (tel: 0850-333 8294). There

Private Cruise Boats

The following companies offer luxury cruises for small groups:
Hatsail Tourism & Yachting
Tel: 0212-241 6250
www.hatsail.com
Bosphorus motor-cruises from various European-side moorings for groups or executive meetings with lunch/dinner and cocktails; also yacht cruises on the Aegean and Mediterranean seas.

Blue Guide
Marmaris
Tel: 0252-417 1128
www.blueguide.com
One-week gulet sailing holidays out of Bodrum into the Gökova Gulf, and out of Marmaris to Fethiye. Both private charter and so-called cabin charter, ideal for single travellers or couples.

are more than 30 designated jetties along both sides of the Bosphorus, and on the Princes' Islands.

Bosphorus cruises

A **Bosphorus cruise** (www.sehirhatlari. istanbul) can be a lovely way to view the elegant waterside mansions or yalıs lining the banks of this strait separating Europe from Asia. **Public ferries** leave twice daily in summer and once daily in winter from the Eminönü jetty and go all the way to Anadolu Kavağı, where you can stop for lunch before the return journey. If you want a shorter trip, try one of the more frequent **TurYol private boats** (www.turyol.com.tr; around 1.5 hrs), from the same docks.

Driving in Turkey

Driving in Turkey can be alarming for newcomers. However, if you keep calm and drive cautiously you will be perfectly safe. The condition of main roads is usually reasonable (and improving all the time), although on secondary roads you should avoid driving at night if at all possible.

Road conditions

The road network is extensive, with modern toll motorways in the western half of the country either completed or under construction. You cannot pay the frequent tolls on these (or the big bridges) with cash – your car needs to have an electronic transponder attached to participate in the Hızlı Geçiş Sistemi (High Speed Passage System, HGS). Discuss setting up your own payment account at the outset with your car-hire company so that you are not landed with outrageous 'service charges' for them paying tolls on your behalf. If you arrive with your own car, get a transponder and set up an HGS account at any post office.

An Istanbul ferry boat.

Otherwise, there are numerous dual carriageways, and many three-lane roads where the central lane is used for overtaking. Smaller roads are not well lit, nor well enough signposted, and hazards include trucks and tractors with no (or maybe one) light illuminated, horses and carts, disabled vehicles with no warning triangles (look out for piles of rocks instead), more piles of rocks from landslides, flocks of sheep or goats, ambling cattle and near-invisible cyclists or pedestrians. Few of the mountain roads have crash barriers or other protection and most have narrow hard shoulders. On these secondary roads, always allow ample time for road journeys – at an average speed of no more than 60kmph (37mph).

Surfaces are reasonable, but the overall engineering of the road can be poor, making them excessively dangerous in wet weather and leading to unexpected potholes. Roadworks are a constant problem, especially in the east – and dual carriage-way traffic can go from four to two lanes with little or no warning.

Many vehicles on the road are buses and trucks, and many of the lorries (referred to in Turkish as *tır*, the acronym for Transports Internationaux Routiers) are elderly, overloaded and underpowered (and often charging down the middle of the road, coming at *you*). When empty, however, they can barrel along at surprising speeds. There are more on the road at night – another reason not to drive after dark.

Road marking and signposting is reasonable on the new motorways, but elsewhere lane-lines are faded and junction signposting can be deficient when not downright perverse. Archaeological sites and other points of interest (some decidedly specialist) are assiduously marked by brown signs with white lettering, or yellow placards with black lettering.

Rules of the road

Drive on the right and, unless it is signed otherwise, give way to traffic joining from your right, even on a roundabout or multiple junction where you might think you had right of way.

At motorway junctions, be prepared for traffic coming from unexpected directions, and do not expect to be able to get back on to the motorway easily if you make a mistake. Some dual carriageways have very broad hard shoulders, alarmingly used by locals in the wrong direction, to avoid long drives to the nearest junction.

Traffic lights A flashing yellow arrow means you may turn right with care even if the main light is red.

Safety Everyone is supposed to wear a seat belt, and to carry a warning triangle and a first-aid kit. Almost no one does. You will usually see a small cairn of rocks, or similar, in the road to

warn of a breakdown, but only at the last minute as they are usually placed very close to the vehicle in question.

Drink driving Blood-alcohol limits are in line with European countries – 50mg alcohol per 100ml of blood – so just two beers will put you over the limit.

Traffic police operate control points on the access roads to many cities. You should always carry your driving licence, passport, the car's log book, insurance certificate, pollution compliance and roadworthiness certificates, and vehicle registration, as you may be asked for any or all of them. Make sure rental cars have all of these in the glove box before setting out. They may also run seat-belt checks, breath tests and speed traps, and check for faulty vehicles.

Traffic offences are punishable by stiff fines of 200–400TL (with a "discount" for payment within 10 days); take the ticket to a designated bank to pay – the days of the cop trousering the fine and supposedly issuing a receipt appear to be over.

Driving etiquette

Although Turkey has much the same highway code as other countries, the population does not always obey it. As a result, the country suffers a much higher rate of road-traffic

☉ Blue Cruises by Gulet

A "Blue Cruise" *(Mavi Yolculuk)* is a delightful way to visit the coastal sights of the southwestern shores of Turkey – sailing on a traditional wooden schooner, or *gulet*, at a leisurely place, stopping to swim or sightsee at places of interest on the way. This can be the best way to visit ancient sites, many of which were originally only accessible by sea.

The boats are fully crewed, and usually very comfortable, with every need catered for. You can either book as a group, taking over a whole boat (they vary in size and number of berths); or individually, in which case you will not be able to choose your travelling companions. Some tour companies offer holiday tours

with knowledgeable guides on board.

Cruises start from many different ports, large and small, on the south Aegean and Lycian coasts; you can more or less choose where you would like to begin, depending on your arrival point.

July and August are the most expensive months and very popular, but it can be too hot, especially for ruin-tramping on shore. Spring is quieter, but the sea can be cold. Aficionados enjoy September or even October, when the crowds have gone but the sea is still warm.

"Blue Cruises" are bookable locally, or through specialist overseas adventure travel agents. See also page 394.

accidents per number of vehicles than the UK. Things are gradually improving as the roads get better and more people take proper driving tests, but the golden rule must always be to drive defensively.

Expect the unexpected: sudden stops, reversing, heedless pulling out. Some driver signals mean the exact opposite of their UK or US equivalent. Flashed headlights by an oncoming vehicle on a narrow road or bridge means "I am coming through", not "please go first"; however, on a broader road, it usually means "beware, police checkpoint ahead".

There is a lot of hooting, mostly to warn that you are being passed, or (from behind) to hurry you up. A loud hoot means keep out of the way; two short pips on the hooter sometimes means "thanks".

Do not expect traffic to stop to let you out of a side turning; you have to push in. Do not expect people to use their indicators, or their handbrakes on a hill. Cars in front of you on a steep hill will almost always roll back, so leave room. Do expect overtaking on all sides, last-minute lane changes on motorways, cutting in, and people driving very close to you.

Breakdowns

If you break down in your own car, your insurance documents should tell you what to do. British motoring associations have reciprocal agreements with the Turkish Touring and Automobile Association, TTOK; the American AAA does not; other nationalities should check the position before travelling. For hire cars, always check the spare tire and tool kit beforehand, and get instructions as to what to do in event of a breakdown; "unauthorised" repairs may not be reimbursed. Workshops are always found at the edge of provincial towns, in clusters called sanayis. Tyre punctures in particular (a common incident) are dealt with at a lastıkçı workshop.

Petrol

Fuel is generally among the most expensive in the world, though since 2018 the lira's devaluation has taken away some of the sting. The western two-thirds of Turkey are well supplied with petrol stations, many open 24 hours, some

of which are good places to stop for a meal and a rest as they are well equipped and have clean toilet facilities. The further east you go, the more infrequent the stations become, and you would be wise not to let your tank run low.

Petrol (benzin) is available in several grades. Lead-free petrol (kurşunsuz) is sold at most petrol stations in the more developed parts of the country, but can be hard to come by in the more remote rural areas. Diesel (mazot) is available everywhere, but beware of bargain-priced diesel, which is likely to be exceptionally dirty.

In most of the country it is possible to pay by credit card.

Parking

Take heed of no-parking signs, especially those with a pictograph of a tow truck in action. Although the fines for parking illegally are small compared to those in northern Europe, retrieving a car that has been towed away is extremely time-consuming – the pound is often on the far side of town.

On-street parking areas (look for an otopark sign) are manned by watchmen who will approach as you park, and either give you a receipt or place a ticket on your windscreen. Charges vary, but are not exorbitant – around 3TL for two hours in central Istanbul. In some places on the southwest coast it's a flat-rate of about 5TL.There are also some multistorey car parks (a katlı otopark), a few on-street meters and pay-and-display ticket machines, and valet parking at the smartest hotels and restaurants.

Car hire

To hire a car you must be over 21, and need to have held a licence for a year. You will also need a credit card for the damages deposit. Outlets exist in most cities and tourist areas, or you can book in advance through multinational chains or consolidator/aggregator websites.

Car hire in Turkey varies wildly in price depending on how and where you hire. Walk-in rack rates for the smallest, entry-level cars are typically €40–50 equivalent per day, though you'd be foolish to hire on spec when online pre-booking rates will be about half that, especially for longer periods (see below

⊘ Speed Limits

Urban areas
50kph (30mph)
Open roads
90kph (55mph) for cars
80kph (50mph) for vans
70kph (40mph) if towing a trailer or caravan
Motorways
120kph (70mph) for cars

for a list of useful companies). Only at the very beginning or tail end of the season are locally quoted rates likely to be advantageous. Generally, Antalya, Dalaman, Bodrum, Fethiye and (sometimes) İzmir airport are the least expensive places to rent from; İstanbul, Marmaris, Kuşadası and anywhere in the east are the most expensive.

VAT (sales tax), basic insurance and collision-damage waiver (CDW) should be included in the price, but the waiver excess (the amount you are liable for before the excess takes effect) is not. If you rent for more than 2 weeks a year, then it's well worth taking out annual insurance for this rather than buying it (expensively) from the rental company; www.insurance4carhire.com is a recommended company selling such policies to US- and UK-based drivers.

Hiring through an international company or a nationwide local chain like Almira may allow you to return the car to a different point for no extra charge.

If you pre-book through a consolidator, it is vital to ring the local affiliate company a day beforehand to check that all rental details have registered correctly. Tales abound of the wrong-category car being set aside, or the car allocated to the wrong location, or specified extras (like child seats) not being provided, unless this is corrected in advance.

Motorcycles, scooters and bicycles can all be hired in coastal resorts.

Car Hire Consolidator/Aggregator Websites

In the UK:
www.comparecarrentals.co.uk
www.auto-europe.co.uk (also in US at auto-europe.com)
www.rentalcars.com
www.travelsupermarket.com
www.holidayautos.co.uk

A

Admission Charges

Almost all museums and archaeological sites in Turkey have admission charges, which vary from 5TL for minor attractions to a whopping 60TL for premier sites like Topkapı Palace or Ephesus. Museum passes (www.muze.gov.tr/museumpass) offer good savings. In Istanbul you can get a 5-day pass, a smart choice if you plan to visit a half-dozen of the first-rank museums, palaces and churches. The 15-day nation-wide pass covers some 300 museums across the country. These and several regional passes are available from the ticketing counters of each participating museum. Some remote sites have a single warden who may (in broken English) give a private tour of the site, for which an additional tip is expected.

Addresses

Addresses can seem idiosyncratic to Western eyes; in rural areas, there will be no street names, but the district (*mahalle*) of a particular village is important. Five-digit postcodes are assigned to distinguish the hundreds of identically named villages in different regions.

Street names precede the number; if the address is on a minor alley, this will usually be included after the main thoroughfare it adjoins. When two numbers are separated by a right-hand slash, the first is the building number, the second the flat or office number. Standard abbreviations, which we use in this guide, include "Cad" for *Cadde(si)* (avenue or main street), "Bul" for *Bulvarı* (boulevard), "Meyd" for *Meydan(ı)* (square),

"Sok" for *Sokak/Sokağı* (alley) and "PK" for *Posta Kutu* (Post Box). Other useful terms are *kat* (floor), *zemin kat* (ground floor), *asma* (mezzanine), *han(ı)* (office block), *mahalle* (district or neighbourhood) and *çıkmaz(ı)* (blind alley). *Karşısı* means "opposite to", as in *PTT karşısı*. So if you're given an address as follows – Atatürk Caddesi, Zindan Çıkmazı, Aydın Apartmanı 28/2, Ulupınar, 44582 Maziköy – this means Flat 2 of a named apartment block at no. 28 of the Zindan cul-de-sac, off Atatürk Caddesi, in the Ulupınar *mahalle* of the larger Maziköy postal district.

B

Budgeting for Your Trip

Turkey is no longer the bargain-basement destination it was in the 1970s and 1980s – rates in the south and west coastal resorts, or Istanbul, are comparable to anywhere in the European Mediterranean, though costs in the far east are significantly lower. If you insist on trying to replicate the Hippie Trail experience, staying in Lycian "treehouses" or the few remaining hostels, travelling only by bus and train (especially overnight to save on accommodation), eating in the simplest *lokantas* and avoiding wine or *rakı*, you could just get by on £25/$40 equivalent per day as one of a couple. Staying in modest hotels, having the occasional fish meal and signing on for local excursions or adventure activities will see the daily average budget rise to £60/$100 per person. For a really comfortable existence, encompassing a share of car rental (and the horrendous fuel

costs that entails) while booking into multi-star hotels, count on at least £100/$160 per day per head.

Business Travellers

Visitors on business will often be guests of a Turkish company, and the visit will be governed by the rules of hospitality. You can expect to be whisked from place to place by chauffeured car and thoroughly entertained after hours.

The top hotels in the main cities are geared to business travellers and will be able to provide meeting rooms, office and conference facilities, and reception staff with a reasonably high proficiency in English.

C

Children

Aside from waterparks in or near many coastal resorts, Turkey has few obvious facilities for children, but Turks adore babies and children, and will be delighted you have brought yours along, making a huge fuss over them.

City streets, most especially in Istanbul, are far from buggy-friendly, however; high kerbstones and steep and uneven surfaces make prams almost impossible to push. Buses are often crowded and their entrances are high and awkward. Bring a rucksack-style baby-carrier or papoose; you will quickly realise why most Turkish babies are simply carried in their parents' arms.

Discounts

Normally you pay for children over seven years old on public transport, but you may not pay at all for under-12s at museums. It often seems to be at the whim of the attendant. Hotels offer anything from a third to 50 percent off both room rates and set-meal charges.

Accommodation

Hotels will almost always put up extra beds if there is space in your room. Most places have family rooms, sometimes for as many as six, and even *pansiyons* may have small apartments/suites with a mini kitchen included at no extra cost. You'll need to ask in advance if you need a cot.

Food

There are plenty of Turkish dishes that Western children will find acceptable without having to resort to fast food, although pizzas, burgers and chips can be found easily enough.

Restaurants rarely offer meals specifically for children, but they will do their best to find something for them to eat, even if you can't see anything obvious on the menu. If you would like something plain, ask for *çok sade*, very plain, or *acısız*, not peppery hot. *Çocuklar için* means "for the children".

Dishes children may like include grilled *köfte* (meatballs) and any grilled meat, lamb or chicken *şiş kebabs*; grilled steak or chicken (*tavuk* or *piliç ızgara*); all kinds of Turkish bread; *sade pilav* (rice); and *pide* (Turkish pizza) – except perhaps for the spicy *sucuklu* kind. Chips are *patates tava*, or in resorts – *çips*!

For dessert, Turkish rice pudding (*sütlaç*) is excellent, or you can always ask for a plate of sliced fresh fruit (fruit should always be peeled, to be on the safe side), or *dondurma*, as good as Italian gelato and just as adored by kids.

Babies

Breast-feeding mothers need not feel shy, but as Turks are modest in public, you should be discreet. Wear something loose, or use a large scarf or beach wrap to screen yourself and your baby – this is what rural Turkish women do, and it will come in useful to protect you from hot sun.

Ready-made babyfood can only be found in Western-style supermarkets, which are thin on the ground outside of larger cities, and formula is expensive, so you may prefer to bring your own supplies.

Restaurants will be happy to heat milk for you.

What to bring

You will need plenty of good sunblock (minimum 30 SPF), hats, and loose, light clothes for children in summer. July and August are uncomfortably hot in southern resorts for children unused to such heat and it can be difficult to get them to sleep.

In case of tummy upsets, bring prepacked sachets of rehydration salts such as Dioralyte. Disposable nappies and other baby gear such as Johnson's toiletries are easily found in supermarkets, if expensive for imported brands.

Sightseeing

Little in Turkey is specifically devised with children in mind, but there is a handful of purpose-built attractions. Holiday villages notionally geared to families may still have only minimal play equipment. Foreign travel companies, such as Mark Warner and Club Mediterranée, tend to have good facilities as part of their all-inclusive packages, with childcare for younger children and entertainment for older ones.

Depending on their age and interests, children should enjoy some sightseeing. Palaces can be difficult, as you may have to join a guided tour (even if your children like that sort of thing, the guide's English may be difficult to understand), but scrambling around ancient ruins is usually good fun. In the cities, if you get desperate, you can always head for one of the shopping malls where you will find a children's play area, clean lavatories and fast food.

Istanbul

Take a ferry: one of the best things to do with children in Istanbul is to travel anywhere in the city by water, since there is so much to see.

Topkapı Palace is usually a hit with children. There is plenty of space for them to run around; the Harem can be claustrophobic, although older children might be fascinated. The carriages, costumes, miniature paintings and fabulous treasury are all of interest to children.

The Archaeological Museum has a children's section (although captions are in Turkish), and a mock-up of the Trojan Horse to climb on.

The Rahmi Koç Industrial Museum, Hasköy, is a museum of transport and industrial technology, brilliantly converted from an anchor-and-chain factory. There are a number of working models of steam locomotives, engines and mechanical toys with buttons to press to make them work.

Yerebatan Cistern, Sultanahmet. Fantastic, enormous, atmospheric underground water tank from the Byzantine era. Children can run around on the wooden walkways among the gigantic marble pillars. There are also fish to spot swimming in the water.

Askeri Müzesi (Military Museum), Harbiye. Children may like the sultans' campaign tents on display here, and the ferocious and beautifully decorated curved daggers. The museum is also the venue for performances by the Mehter, the re-created janissary band (summer daily between 3pm and 4pm).

Rumeli Hisarı. The castle at Rumeli Hisarı, a little way up the Bosphorus, is a good place for a scramble around, although caution is advised as there are steep drops and no safety rails.

Cappadocia

With its incredible lunar landscape, underground cities to explore, and hundreds of caves and rock-cut churches, plus the possibility of pony trekking and seeing pottery made in Avanos, Cappadocia is packed with interest for children.

The coast

Sand, swimming pools, sea and water sports are all obvious attractions for kids of all ages. Ancient cities are usually good value as there are plenty of things to climb on, space to run around and, if the parents have done some homework, some cracking stories about what went on there.

Bodrum

The castle of St Peter, home to the Museum of Underwater Archaeology in Bodrum, is a terrific place for kids. It is full of the mysteries of pirates, Crusaders, naval battles and shipwrecks, and even a restored torture chamber.

Climate

Three main climatic zones exist: **The Aegean and Mediterranean regions**. These have a typically

CLIMATE CHARTS

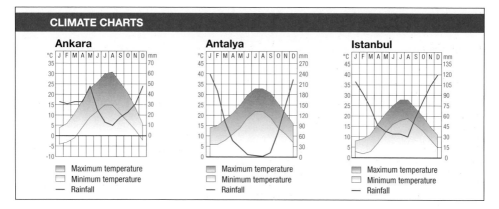

Ankara — Maximum temperature / Minimum temperature / Rainfall

Antalya — Maximum temperature / Minimum temperature / Rainfall

Istanbul — Maximum temperature / Minimum temperature / Rainfall

Mediterranean climate with hot summers and mild winters, with temperatures rising the further south you go.

The Black Sea region and the Marmara zone (which includes Istanbul), which has warm summers, mild winters and relatively high rainfall year-round; Istanbul is drier than points further east.

The central and eastern Anatolian regions (including Ankara), which have hot, dry summers – furnace-like in the southeast, but less hot at higher altitudes. Winters are very cold on the high plateaux.

When to Visit, What to Wear and What to Bring

Clothes Your needs will vary greatly according to the part of Turkey you will be visiting and the time of year. In the height of summer, light, cotton clothing for the Marmara, Aegean and Mediterranean areas is essential, including a long loose cotton shirt to cover your arms and shoulders against the sun, a hat and a high-factor sunscreen, especially if you intend to visit archaeological sites where there can be little or no shade.

For the Black Sea region you may need a light sweater in the evening, a light waterproof garment and water-resistant footwear. Humidity is high. At altitude in central and eastern Anatolia, summer evenings can also be cool.

Footwear Comfortable, sturdy shoes are essential for tramping over historical and archaeological sites. Even the pavements on city streets can be uneven or cobbled. Repairs (at a *kunduracı*) are cheap, locally produced orthopaedic sandals somewhat less so (from 50TL for those made from synthetic materials, suitable for the beach, up to 150TL for all- or mostly-leather versions).

Wet-weather gear Although Turkey is often regarded as hot all year round, winter travellers will soon discover that it has as much rain, snow and ice as many areas of Europe; parts of the country are at high altitude and experience very severe winters. Especially in the Black Sea region, tough water-resistant footwear and a raincoat or jacket will prove invaluable.

Insect repellent Mosquitoes (non-malarial except in the far southeast) can be a severe annoyance especially along the coast in summer, so bring a good repellent. Incense coils, or plug-in electric antibug devices that you use with a tablet, are available locally, as are mosquito nets in the more thoughtful accommodation.

Tampons can be difficult to track down, though you will normally find Western brands of sanitary towels. It makes sense to bring your own.

Crime and Safety

Turkey has an enviably low crime record. This reflects Turkish society: restricted access to guns, low incidence of drug use, respect for law and order, and, most important of all, close-knit communities and enduring family ties. Foreigners and tourists are regarded as guests, so are very well treated; in normal circumstances you can expect the police to be polite and helpful.

Tourist areas are regularly patrolled by special *Turizm* or Foreigners' Police, who should do their best to help you and should speak some French, English, German or Arabic.

Inevitably, there is still some crime, especially in urban areas blighted by poverty and unemployment. In tourist resorts, other foreigners are not above suspicion – never leave money or cameras in your room. Car crimes and break-ins are possible and purse-snatching and pickpocketing are not uncommon in crowded places such as the Grand Bazaar and İstiklal Caddesi in Istanbul. An especially common scam targeting single young men involves a local invite to a bar, where tourists are intimidated into paying extortionary bills. There are also instances of tourists being drugged and robbed.

So take the same precautions as you would at home – don't leave valuables or your bag visible in a car, use a handbag with a long strap slung diagonally over the shoulder and don't walk down dark streets on your own at night.

Make sure that your travel insurance covers you for both the European and Asian sides of Turkey.

Drugs

The film *Midnight Express* is always mentioned in this context, much to the annoyance of the Turks. But although the script may have been exaggerated, anyone found in possession of drugs can expect long-term imprisonment.

Military zones

These are normally clearly marked in several languages, often also by a sign with a picture of an armed soldier. You should keep clear (especially in a parked car which could be considered a car bomb), and also avoid photographing anything with a military content.

Political security

There have been terror attacks in southeastern Turkey, Ankara and Istanbul, much of it tracing back to Kurdish separatists though some perpetrated by Islamist groups, most notably ISIL. There have also been violent demonstrations in major cities, particularly in the far southeast; be sure to take current local advice before travelling in the region.

Tourist crime

Not all the many millions of Westerners who flood into Turkey each year are well behaved. The Turks take a very dim view of drunken tourists scaling statues of Atatürk, or being anything other than respectful towards locals, their national icons, religions or football teams.

Customs Regulations

You are allowed to bring into the country up to 600 cigarettes, 50 cigars, 250g pipe tobacco (500g if bought in Turkey), 1 litre of alcohol over 22 percent, 2 litres of alcohol under 22 percent, 1kg chocolate, coffee and tea.

Exiting into the EU, into Greece in particular, the duty-free limit for souvenirs is currently €430 – the value of purchases must be backed up by receipts. Within this allowance are 4 litres of wine, 200 cigarettes and one

In a Turkish bath.

litre of spirits (ie *rakı*). Carpets and leather jackets are especially likely to provoke Greek suspicions.

Exporting antiques

It is strictly forbidden to take antiques, including rugs and carpets, out of the country. Should you buy anything old or old-looking, be sure to have it validated by the seller, who should get a clearance certificate from the Department of Antiquities – often something handled by the directorate of the nearest museum. Respectable carpet dealers should be familiar with the procedure. Fossils, by the way, are considered antiquities.

E

Electricity

Voltage is 220–240 volts, 50Hz, out of two standard, continental-European round-pin sockets. Supply in rural areas (including many resorts) is highly variable (ie prone to blackouts) and unbuffered. Do not leave laptops, mobile phones or other portable devices charging in your room in your absence, as sudden, violent electrical storms are quite likely to zap them.

Embassies and Consulates

Turkish embassies/consulates abroad

UK

43 Belgrave Square, London SW1X 8PA
Tel: 020-7393 0202
http://london.emb.mfa.gov.tr
EIRE
8 Raglan Road, Ballsbridge, Dublin 4
Tel: 01 668 52 40
http://dublin.emb.mfa.gov.tr
US
2525 Massachusetts Avenue NW, Washington DC 20008
Tel: 202-612 6700
Consulates in New York, Boston, Houston, Los Angeles and Chicago; addresses given on website.
www.washington.emb.mfa.gov.tr

Foreign embassies and consulates in Turkey

Although all embassies are in Ankara, consulates in Istanbul may be able to handle visa and passport matters, eg if you require a visa for travelling to somewhere else. In popular tourist areas, you may find an honorary consul, a local person appointed to take on consular responsibilities.

Australia
MNG Building, Uğur Mumcu Cad 88, 7th Floor, Gaziosmanpaşa, Ankara
Tel: 0312-459 9500
Ritz Carlton Residences
Suzer Plaza, Asker Ocağı Cad 15, Elmadağ, Şişli, Istanbul
Tel: 0212-393 3300
Kolin Hotel
Boğazkent Mevkii, Level 2
Kepez, Çanakkale
Tel: 0286-218 1721
www.turkey.embassy.gov.au/anka/home.html
Canada
Cinnah Cad 58, Çankaya, Ankara
Tel: 0312-409 2700
Büyükdere Cad 209
Tekfen Tower, 16th floor
Dördüncü Levent
Tel: 0212-385 9700
www.canadainternational.gc.ca/turkey-turquie/offices-bureaux/embassy-ambassade.aspx?lang=eng
Ireland
MNG Building, Uğur Mumcu Cad 88, 1st Floor, Gaziosmanpaşa, Ankara
Tel: 0312-459 1000
Honorary consulates in Istanbul, Antalya and İzmir.
www.dfa.ie/irish-embassy/turkey/
New Zealand
Kızkulesi Sok 11, Gaziosmanpaşa, Ankara
Tel: 0312-446 3333
Honorary Consulate: İnönü Cad 48/3, Taksim, Istanbul Tel: 0212-244 0272

☉ Emergency Numbers

Ambulance (public) 112
Police 155
Fire 110
Forest fires 177
Turizm (Foreigners') Police
Istanbul, tel: 0212-527 4503
Ankara, tel: 0312-384 0606
Antalya, tel: 0242-243 1061
İzmir, tel: 0232-417 3785

www.nzembassy.com/turkey
South Africa
Filistin Sok 27, Gaziosmanpaşa,
Ankara
Tel: 0312-405 6861
www.southafrica.org.tr
UK
Şehit Ersan Cad 46/A, Çankaya,
Ankara
Tel: 0312-455 3344
Meşrutiyet Cad 34, Tepebaşı/Beyoğlu
Tel: 0212-334 6400
1442 Sok 49, Alsancak, İzmir
Tel: 0232-463 5151
Honorary consulates in Antalya,
Bodrum, Marmaris and Fethiye.
www.gov.uk/government/world/
organisations/british-embassy-ankara
US
Atatürk Bul 110, Kavaklıdere, Ankara
Tel: 0312-455 5555
Sariyer Caddesi 75, Poligon, Istanbul
Tel: 0212-335 9000
http://tr.usembassy.gov

Etiquette

Compared with Western Europe, Turkish society is formal, particularly in rural areas. It is therefore important to observe a few ground rules to avoid causing offence.

Your visit is governed by the rules of hospitality that form a substantial part of the psyche of Turkish society, and which mean that you are truly regarded as a guest and (mostly) to be accorded the utmost help. This will show itself in the extent to which people will offer endless cups of tea, personal hospitality, invite you to their home, all of which can be gracefully and tactfully refused if you wish, without giving offence.

Feet are regarded as unclean – so don't put them where someone might sit, or point them towards anyone. Should you be invited into a Turkish home, remove your shoes and leave them by the door.

On the beach

Beachwear is worn only on the beach, and heading inland bare-chested is considered extremely offensive. Topless sunbathing is frowned upon, although all too many tourists strip off at the first patch of sand. At some family resorts you will still see women entering the water fully clothed.

In mosques

Non-Muslims should not enter a mosque during prayer time, and not at all on Friday, the holy day. The *ezan* (call to prayer) issues from the minaret five times a day between dawn and about 90 minutes after sunset.

Both men and women should be modestly dressed. For women this means a longish skirt or trousers, and covered shoulders. For men, shorts are not acceptable. Before entering, remove your shoes. You can leave them on the special racks or carry them. Women should cover their heads, so you should always carry a scarf or hat. Off the beaten tourist track there may not be an attendant to supervise you, but do follow these guidelines to avoid giving offence.

Take care not to disturb, touch or walk in front of anyone who may be at prayer. The larger, more famous mosques are open throughout the day from the first prayer to the last one at night. Smaller ones may only open at prayer times; you may have to find a caretaker (*bekçi*) or wait for prayer time, and enter as the worshippers leave.

In Turkish Baths

The traditional Turkish bath (*hamam*) has its own etiquette. The sexes are segregated, either in different parts of the bath or by different times or days. Some tourist hamams allow mixed bathing, but you will pay more.

Contrary to popular belief, the vast majority of hamams offer a relaxing and invigorating experience which is nothing to be afraid of. Modesty is the order of the day; both men and women should keep their underpants on and cover themselves with a wrap (*peştamal*).

The easiest way to enjoy a Turkish bath is to go with someone who has been before and knows the ropes; otherwise just watch your neighbours and copy them.

You don't need to have anything with you, but you can of course take along your own wrap, towels, loofa mitt and toiletries, as buying the latter two on the spot can be expensive.

See also page 152 for more about hamams.

Privacy is sacrosanct

Family life in Turkey is very private, so public displays of affection, even hand-holding between husband and wife, are rarely seen in the streets outside the main cities. To avoid causing offence, it is wise to honour these traditions.

H

Health and Medical Care

Turkey is a pretty healthy country as long as you are sensible. If you do fall ill, the standard of health care in private facilities in the big cities is getting better all the time, but you should still have medical insurance to cover the costs. Most drugs are available without prescription from a pharmacy (*eczane*).

Health advice

In the UK, detailed health advice, tailored to individual needs, is available from MASTA (Medical Advice for Travellers Abroad). They have a web-based system and travel clinics throughout the UK: http://masta-travel-health.com.

Alternatively, you could try the Fleet Street Travel Clinic, tel: 020-7353 5678; www.fleetstreetclinic.com, which also administers jabs.

Health hazards

Traveller's diarrhoea is the main hazard, best avoided by paying attention to food and water hygiene. Drink only bottled water or water from a spring marked as potable, wash and/ or peel all fruit and vegetables, and ensure cooked food is piping hot. It's safest to eat freshly prepared local produce. Refrigeration – especially of cold mezes – can be poor, even in tourist resorts, so only eat fresh batches of these. Grilled meat or fish is usually safe if properly cooked through. Do *not* buy *midye dolması* (stuffed mussels) from street-sellers in summer – the mussels will have been unchilled for hours, and utterly toxic.

Some form of diarrhoea treatment and pre-packaged sachets are a useful addition to your first-aid kit. But should you succumb, it's advisable to resort to drugs only if you absolutely have to. The best treatment is to maintain fluid levels with plenty of non-alcoholic drinks or rehydration salts, eat very plain food and avoid dairy products. Even if fluids are repeatedly vomited, rehydration therapy will eventually work. If the diarrhoea lasts more than 48 hours, seek medical advice.

Sun and heat The other major hazards in summer are heatstroke and sunburn. The answer is pure common sense. Wear a hat and sunglasses, put on a wrap on the beach, use high-factor sunblock and after-sun cream, drink plenty of water and soft drinks, and cut down on alcohol intake. If you or a companion get an overwhelming headache, are dizzy or disoriented and cannot bring your body temperature down, put the patient in a cool bath and get someone to ring for a doctor. True heatstroke is a serious medical condition.

Stings and bites If you stand on a sea urchin, ray, weever fish or similar sea creature, or are bitten by any animal, it is vitally important to seek medical attention as soon as possible. Stings can produce a severe allergic reaction, while a bite may require vaccination against rabies. While waiting for the doctor, the best first aid is to encourage limited bleeding, wash the bite-wound thoroughly for several minutes, then bandage it (but do not suture). You should expect to undergo five injections of human diploid cell vaccine (HDCV), to be started within 24 hours, together with a single human rabies immunoglobulin (HRIG) jab.

Inoculations

As a rule, inoculations are not necessary, but it is always wise to be up to date with polio, tetanus and tuberculosis when travelling. Should you plan to visit eastern Anatolia, consider immunisation against typhoid.

Antimalarial tablets are recommended in summer in the Tigris and Euphrates basins, along the border with Syria and Iraq.

You may wish to consider immunisation against hepatitis A (spread through contaminated food and water). HIV and hepatitis B are prevalent and precautions should be taken.

Medical insurance

An insurance policy, including cover for medical evacuation, is essential, as medical costs in Turkey are high and EU reciprocal agreements do not apply.

If you already have a general annual travel policy, check that it will cover you on the Asian side of the country (not all companies consider Turkey "Europe").

Medical treatment

Pharmacies

These should be your first port of call for treating minor ailments. There is a rota system whereby one pharmacist in every district – the *nöbetçi* – stays open 24 hours for emergencies, and the address will be noted in pharmacists' windows.

Most standard drugs are available in Turkey without a prescription. Although self-treatment is not recommended, it is easy to replace routine medication at any pharmacy (*eczane*) should it be necessary. It is a good idea to show the pharmacist the empty container, to be sure that you are being given the right drug. Remember that generic drugs can be marketed under different names.

Doctors and dentists

Though doctors and dentists in the cities often speak English or German, and many have been trained abroad to a high standard, unless it is an emergency, it is better to wait until you return home for treatment. Most four- and five-star hotels have a doctor on call, speaking some English and/or German, in case of emergency.

Hospitals

Although there are a number of excellent private hospitals in the major cities, health care does not generally meet Western expectations of nursing and aftercare, though some hospitals are better than others, and are fine in an emergency. The further you go from the major cities, the more limited medical facilities become.

It is also vital to note that hospitals work on a pay-as-you-go basis, requiring payment on the spot in advance of any required treatment, including scans and X-rays. This has been known to happen even in extreme emergencies. It is one very good reason to keep some cash and a credit card on you at all times.

Ambulances

Certain services operate independently; others are attached to particular hospitals. The average Turkish ambulance is little better than a taxi, and in a minor emergency a taxi can be the best and quickest way to get to hospital.

Istanbul, for example, is relatively well provided with ambulances, but so bad is the traffic during the morning and evening rush hours that many drivers stubbornly refuse to give way to the emergency services. The following are worth ringing, however:

Medline is a private company that serves hospitals in Istanbul (tel: 444 1212). Their ambulances have emergency equipment, and a doctor and paramedic on board. www.medline.com.tr.

Emergency Hospitals

Ankara
Bayındır Hospital, Atatürk Blv 201, Kavaklıdere
Tel: 0312-428 0808
Memorial Ankara Hospital, Mevlana Blv 1422, Çankaya
Tel: 0549-639 3366
Çankaya Hospital, Çankaya
Tel: 0312-426 1450
Güven Hospital, Şimşek Sok 29, Kavaklıdere
Tel: 444 9494
Antalya
Akdeniz University Hospital
Tel: 0242-249 6000
InterHospital
Tel: 0242-311 1500
Bodrum
American Hospital
Marsmabedi Cad 33/35, Türkkuyusu
Tel: 444 4478
Istanbul
American Hospital, Güzelbahçe Sok 20, Nişantaşı
Tel: 444 3777
Florence Nightingale Hospital, Abide-i Hürriyet Cad 166, Şişli
Tel: 0212-375 6161
Hisar Hospital Intercontinental, Site Yolu Cad 7, Ümraniye
Tel: 0505-188 7804

A range of Turkish newspapers for sale.

Acıbadem International Hospital, Istanbul Cad 82, Yeşilköy
Tel: 0216-544 4664
İzmir
Başkent Üniversitesi Hospital, Caher Dudayev Bul 175, Karşıyaka
Tel: 0232-241 1000
EMOT Hospital, 1418 Sok 14, Kahramanlar
Tel: 0232-441 0121

I

Internet

Turks have a passion for new technology, and are very keen on the internet – it is probably one of the most wired-up (or rather, wire-less) societies in the world. Government offices, media, universities and even modest businesses have websites, and most Turkish youth are online around the clock. As disposable income is not yet sufficient to permit universal private computer ownership, internet cafés remain to be found, though as of 2019, a majority of Turks have smartphones. Wi-Fi zones are widespread, and even surprisingly modest *pansiyons* will have them in common areas, if not every room. Alternatively, local SIM cards are a worthy investment for those preferring constant online access.

L

LGBTQ Travellers

Turkish attitudes to gays, or to overtly gay behaviour, are conflicted.

On the one hand, they adulate their own amazingly exhuberant transvestite or transsexual singers; on the other, Turks can be publicly intolerant of gay couples – something which has unfortunately increased under AK rule.

Homosexual acts between adults over 18 are legal, and in Istanbul, Ankara, İzmir and coastal resorts such as Alanya, you'll find much greater tolerance and even gay bars and discos. Be circumspect in public and you shouldn't have any problems.

M

Maps

Decent maps are notoriously difficult to come by for Turkey. Except for those packaged together with commercial trekking guides to the Kaçkar mountains, Lycian Way and St Paul Trail (see www.trekkingin-turkey.com), there are no publicly available large-scale topographic maps, as these are seen as a threat to national security. Currently the best touring maps are the seven 1:500,000 sheets published by Kartographischer Verlag Reinhard Ryborsch in Frankfurt; these may be officially out of stock but can still be found from online dealers. Once in Turkey, the 1:400,000 *Adım Adım Türkiye Yol Atlası ve Rehberi* atlas produced by MepMedya is very accurate, and detailed enough for cycle-touring despite the lack of contour lines; available online (http://mepmedyashop.com) and at major bookshops in Istanbul. The best regional touring

maps are Sabri Aydal's 1:250,000 products for Cappadocia, Lycia, Pamphylia and Pisidia, available from bookshops and museums in those regions. *Insight Fleximaps* (Turkey 1:2,400,000) and Istanbul (1:12,500) are durable, laminated maps. Otherwise, the best source of Turkey maps online is US-based www.geospatial.com.

Media

Turkey enjoyed a media explosion beginning in the 1990s. Although more than 150 outlets were shut down following the 2016 coup, thousands remain active. Quantity does not necessarily mean quality, however. The radio waves are so crowded with channels that stations have to take turns; there are dozens of regular TV channels, while apartment buildings bristle with aerials and dishes as people tune in to the world's cable and satellite networks.

Television

From a single state-run TV channel at the beginning of the 1980s, Turkey now has over 24 main channels, the majority privately owned. You will find additional regional channels depending on where you are. Although entertainment programmes, soap operas, game shows and pop videos dominate the small screen, some channels also show foreign films (sometimes with subtitles) and international sports.

Through satellite and cable, dozens of foreign channels including BBC Entertainment, BBC Earth, MTV and CNN can be viewed. Visitors will usually find satellite or cable in the major hotels, although you should check before booking if this is important to you.
TRT Channel 2 broadcasts the news in English around the clock.

Radio

Until the early 1990s, only state-run stations were on air, and broadcasts were inclined to be more soporific than stimulating. Today, Istanbul alone has so many private stations playing Western pop and rock, with news broadcasts thrown in, that they jostle for frequency space, and it can be difficult to get a clear signal on the station you want.

Açık Radyo (FM 94.9) and Metro FM (97.2MHz) broadcast rock, jazz and soul.

TRT3 (FM 88.2, 94 or 99MHz) State-run station appealing to more sophisticated listeners, playing jazz, Latin and classical music. TRT3 also broadcasts news in English following the Turkish bulletin at 10am, 11am, noon, 1pm, 3pm, 4pm, 5pm, 6pm, 8pm, 9pm and 10pm.

BBC World Service can be received if you have a shortwave radio with a good aerial, but reception is not very clear.

Newspapers and magazines

In **Turkish** There are over a score of major Turkish newspapers, chasing a relatively small reading public and competing with radio, TV and the internet. The abrupt closures of several of the largest outlets in 2016 (including the bold, investigative *Radikal* and *Taraf* and Gülenist *Zaman*) made international headlines.

Hürriyet and *Sabah* are Turkey's bestselling national mainstream newspapers and leading public-opinion makers, though not necessarily espousing the highest-quality journalism. The embattled *Cumhuriyet* upholds Atatürk's secularist, democratic vision (despite half of its staff having been jailed in 2016).

You will also see Turkish editions of many international magazines, plus countless popular Turkish weeklies and monthlies. *Atlas* is a quality monthly travel title with English text summaries.

In **English** international newspapers and magazines can be found at news-stands and bookshops in tourist areas and hotels. Newspapers are usually a day or two late, and sold at many times the UK cover price.

A local English-language daily paper, the *Hürriyet Daily News* (www.hurriyetdailynews.com), provides coverage of local and international events. As well as listing cinemas showing English-language films, and the main satellite and TV channel programmes, it is useful for its classifieds, should you be looking for an apartment, local travel agent or Turkish lessons. Another, rather good online news portal in English is Gülen-linked *Turkish Minute* (www.turkishminute.

com), run by former staff of *Zaman* following its 2016 closure.

Cornucopia is a glossy, bimonthly English-language magazine featuring Turkish arts, history and culture from a rather elitist perspective. It is stocked at better Turkish bookshops selling foreign-language publications, or you can subscribe at www.cornucopia.net, which also has an excellent online bookshop and reviews archive.

Tourist guides

The Guide is a useful English-language city-guide magazine, published bimonthly in Istanbul (also at www.theguideistanbul.com), annually for Bodrum. It offers visitors practical information, arts news, and restaurant and shopping listings.

Time Out publishes a weekly Turkish listings magazine in Istanbul and a monthly English-language edition, also online at www.timeoutistanbul.com/en/.

Books

It can be hard to find foreign-language books outside Istanbul and Ankara, although many large hotel shops have a few, often uninspired, titles, usually in English, French or German. They can cost anything up to double their original price.

See page 402 for a list of books on Turkey.

Money

Currency

The currency is the Turkish lira (formerly TL), subdivided into 100 *kuruş*. At the time of writing, 1 Turkish lira was equivalent in value to 0.17 euros (US$0.19/£0.15). Coins come in denominations of 1, 5, 10, 25 and 50 *kuruş*, plus 1 Turkish lira; bills are denominated as 5, 10, 20, 50, 100 and 200 Turkish lira. Unlimited foreign currency and up to US$5,000 equivalent in can be imported, but you will always get a better exchange rate within Turkey.

Obtaining cash

Banks are plentiful in Turkey, but they are slow, and with the near-ubiquity of ATMs (see below) you can easily get through your whole stay without entering one. Travellers' cheques are a lot of hassle and not recommended. Given that the risk of theft is low, it is easier to use foreign currency, whether US

dollars, sterling or euros, which can be used directly for larger souvenir purchases. Most traders are happy to haggle in all three.

Credit and debit cards

Major credit cards are accepted by more and more shops, restaurants, hotels and petrol stations. Fewer outlets accept Amex, which can only be used with certain bank-linked countertop machines (particularly Garanti Bankası). Chip-and-PIN routine is now the norm (you may be asked to sign slips as well).

ATMs

There are 24-hour cash dispensers accepting credit cards and bank cards using your PIN, on every street corner; there are also many stand-alone machines in remoter resorts or on ferry docks, inside bus stations, etc.

The machines usually offer you a choice of six languages in which to conduct your transaction, but they issue only Turkish lira. If a machine starts being exceptionally slow or uncooperative, cancel the transaction, if possible, and find another machine; eaten cards or double-billed transactions because of mysterious "timing out" issues are not unknown.

Foreign-exchange offices

Foreign currency is in great demand in Turkey so you won't have to look very hard for a place to change foreign-currency notes. Sterling and euros can attract a better rate than less frequently traded currencies. Foreign-exchange offices *(döviz bürolar)* are usually much more efficient than banks, though they generally offer poorer rates. They are plentiful and open Mon–Sat 8.30/9am–7pm. No commission is charged for cash. Allow 15 minutes minimum for a bank transaction, including waiting in line; take a number from the dispensing machine and wait for your teller window *(gişe)* to come free.

Tipping

It is customary to tip a small amount to anyone who does you a small service: the hotel cleaner, porter, doorman who gets you a taxi and so on. Even in cinemas you give something to the person who shows you to your seat.

The only potential difficulty is arming yourself with plenty of small change *(bozuk para)* in advance. At the time of writing, anything between 2–5 lira would be in order.

In restaurants, round the bill up by 10 percent, unless service has been included.

Taxis are the exception: you don't tip taxi drivers and they do not expect it, though you can round the fare up to the nearest suitable figure as change can be a problem.

Credit Card Hotlines

The local numbers to ring if your card is lost or stolen during your stay in Turkey are:

Diners, Mastercard and Visa
Tel: 00 800 13 887 0903 or 00 800 13 535 0900.

It is probably simpler to ring the hotline in your own country – bring that number along.

Opening Hours

Private offices Generally Mon–Fri 9am–6pm.
Government offices 8.30am–noon, 1–5.30pm; may close earlier in winter.
Shops Most close on Sunday, but major stores open all week. The large shopping centres and smart clothing boutiques open later, at 10am, closing between 7pm and 10pm. Some supermarkets stay open until midnight. Small neighbourhood stores are generally open 8am–8.30/9pm; some even shut up for the night as late as 10pm.

☉ Public Holidays

1 January New Year's Day
23 April Independence and Children's Day
1 May Labour and Solidarity Day
19 May Atatürk's Birthday, and Youth and Sports Day
30 August Victory (at Dumlupınar) Day
6 October Liberation of Istanbul (Istanbul only)
29 October Republic Day
10 November Atatürk's Death Anniversary, observed at 9.05am

Banks Mon–Fri 8.30am–noon, 1.30–5pm for state banks, with private ones open right through the day; a few main branches also open Saturday morning. Several banks at Istanbul airport are open 24 hours a day.
Petrol stations Larger ones, especially along main roads, remain open 24 hours a day; others will close between 9 and 11pm.

Photography

Taking photographs is perfectly acceptable in almost any context; Turks are generally pleased to be included in photographs, and of course if on holiday themselves will be snapping away. It is polite, however, to ask first and to respect their wishes if they say no. Veiled women often prefer not to be photographed. Some people may ask for a copy; if you take their address or email, do send the pictures.

Museums sometimes charge for the use of cameras or videos; flash photography may not be allowed as it can supposedly damage paints and textiles.

Mosques usually allow discreet flash-free photography – be tactful.

Postal Services

A post office *(postane)* is marked by the letters **PTT,** and is usually open Mon–Sat 9am–12.30pm and 1.30–5pm (Sat 10am–4pm). Services at the larger PTTs include poste restante and metered phones (the latter often available a bit later than postal services, especially in tourist areas where they can be attended until midnight). There are also small PTT kiosks in tourist areas where you can get stamps, post letters and buy phonecards. Stamps are available only from PTT outlets.

PTT postboxes are yellow, marked PTT and *şehiriçi* (local), *yurtiçi* (domestic) and *yurtdışı* (international).

Airmail takes a week or so to reach the UK/US. Express post costs more, but is supposed to take no more than three days to arrive. If you are sending a parcel, the contents will be inspected, so don't seal it

beforehand. Rates within Turkey are very reasonable – a few lira to send a book or a small packet, for example.

Religious Festivals

Turkish religious holidays are linked to the Islamic lunar calendar and move back 11 or 12 days each year. Secular festivals may also move to coincide with weekends, and precise dates can change annually. Plenty of Islamic websites can inform you as to when the major festivals will fall in the Western calendar.

During these major holidays, shops and businesses are closed, though local shops will usually reopen on the second or third day.

Ramazan Anyone will tell you that the worst time to travel in Turkey is during the holy month of Ramazan (Ramadan elsewhere), when a majority of the population (even non-devout Muslims) pride themselves on fasting from dawn to dusk. This includes the intake of water and cigarettes, with the result that taxi drivers may put you out as the sunset approaches so they can stop to eat, many restaurants close all day or have very limited offerings, and many people are extremely irritable (a known phenomenon, called *Ramazan kafası* or 'Ramazan head').

Until 2017, Ramazan will fall in June/July, the heat (in the far southeast or south coast especially) and the long daylight hours accentuating the ordeal. The holiest point of Ramazan is **Kadir Gecesi** or The Night of Power, between the 27th and 28th day, when the Qur'an was said to have been revealed to Muhammad; mosques are full as it is believed that prayer is especially efficacious on this night.

Şeker Bayram The fast of Ramazan ends with a three-day celebration, 'Sugar Holiday', when everyone, especially children, is offered sweets wherever they go.

Kurban Bayram The Feast of the Sacrifice is a four-day holiday celebrating the substituting of a sacrificial ram for Abraham's son Ishmael. It involves the ritual throat-slitting of beasts, though no longer in public.

New Year Most Turks observe New Year's Eve and New Year's Day with family and friends, or take a holiday skiing or on the balmy south coast.

Miraç Kandili, currently occurring in June, celebrates the Prophet Muhammad's nocturnal journey to Jerusalem and the seven heavens on the winged horse Burak. Though not an official holiday, mosques are especially illuminated, as they are all during Ramazan.

Nevruz (Persian New Year, also Nowruz) is celebrated throughout eastern Turkey and elsewhere. Originally thought to be a Zoroastrian fire or spring equinox festival, it is now associated with Kurdish and Alevî traditions in Turkey.

Religious Services

Turkey is (still just) officially a secular state, although 99 percent of the population – according to official statistics – are Muslim. There are significant Jewish, Armenian and Greek Orthodox minorities, but these remain concentrated in Istanbul and İzmir.

However, due to its long history of mixed races and cultures, Turkey has hundreds of non-Muslim places of worship. Most are now places of historical interest but Istanbul, Ankara and İzmir still have some functioning churches and synagogues.

Attending a service can be a way of meeting people who live and work in the place you are visiting, and of experiencing the building in its intended setting.

S

Smoking

Smoking has long been banned on public transport, airports and terminals, while since July 2009 it has also been prohibited inside all public buildings, bars, clubs and restaurants, on pain of a sharp fine for proprietors. The rule, it is often defied, while many establishments get around it by making use of outside terraces which constitute a grey area – in the Aegean regions and Istanbul you may see people puffing away on hubble-bubbles there. Terraces are often part-enclosed with awnings and plastic wind-breaks, and heated in winter.

T

Tax

Taxes, chiefly VAT (KDV) at varying rates, are included in the prices of some goods and services, but you may see them itemised separately as a component of the price on a bill or receipt – particularly for car hire. If you think someone is trying to do you for it twice, look for a wall notice reading *Fiyatlaırmız KDV Dahildir* (Our Prices Include VAT).

Telephones

Public phones

Though an increasing share of visitors opt for SIM cards or using Skype when in a Wi-Fi zone, public phones can still be found in the streets or grouped in busy areas such as bus and railway stations and airports. Some post offices (PTTs) have metered phones for which you pay after your call, as do all TT (*Türk Telekom*) centres. Most public phones use phonecards (*telefon kartlartı*), which can be bought from PTTs or TTs, newsstands and vendors near groups of phone booths.

There are also credit-card phones at airports and in the lobbies of some five-star hotels in major cities. Never phone from your hotel room, other than the briefest of local calls to land lines, unless you want to be landed with a horrendous bill.

Useful national and international codes and operator services are posted in phone boxes. Instructions in card-phone boxes are in English, French and German as well as Turkish, and these days the phones may well ask you which language you would prefer when you pick up the receiver.

Mobiles

Almost all Turks have mobile phones. Most European mobiles will log on to one of the local networks, but you shouldn't use it for anything other than text messaging. Making or receiving calls is extortionately expensive, as Turkish networks are not subject to EU price caps for roaming – bills of £120 on return home are not uncommon. Do yourself a favour and purchase a local SIM card on a pay-as-you-go package

(the three local companies, with offices at big airports, are Türkcell, Vodaphone and Turk Telecom); they start from about 80 Turkish lira (and about 100TL in major airports), with some call time included, and will save you a lot of money. Your account will be blocked after 120 days unless you register your device, a process that involves a lot of form-filling and payment of 500 Turkish lira at a tax office (in Istanbul it is near the Şişhane metro stop).

Dialling codes

Country code
If dialling Turkey from abroad: 90

Common regional codes
You don't dial the area code if calling the area you are in. If calling from abroad, drop the initial 0.
Adana 0322
Ankara 0312
Alanya/Antalya 0242
Bodrum/Marmaris 0252
Bursa 0224
Çanakkale 0226
Cappadocia 0384
Çeşme 0232
Diyarbakır 0412
Edirne 0284
Erzurum 0442
Istanbul Asian side 0216
Istanbul European side 0212
(use these codes if calling from one side of the city to the other)
İzmir 0232
Kars 0474
Kayseri 0352
Konya 0332
Kuşadası 0256
Kütahya 0274
Pamukkale 0258
Samsun 0362
Selçuk 0232
Sinop 0368
Trabzon 0462
Van 0432

International codes
Australia 61
Canada 1
Ireland 353
New Zealand 64
UK 44
USA 1
Dial 00 and then the country code, followed by the number.

Useful Numbers
Directory enquiries (Istanbul) **118**
International operator **115**
International directory enquiries **115**

Toilets

You will probably find traditional Turkish squat toilet facilities disconcerting. There may well be a choice of Western-style and squat toilets. Arm yourself with a supply of paper (which goes in the bin, not the hole, as the drains can't cope with it). The spigot and small plastic cup is for good Muslims – who disdain toilet paper – to clean themselves afterwards. Western toilets will actually have a little squirter rigged up, which you work with a tap usually on the wall behind, below the tank.

You will find clean Western-style facilities in the more up-market hotels and restaurants, shopping malls and at all museums and archaeological sites. Public toilets in cities can be revolting; in rural places sometimes sparkling clean; those at motorway and road-side service stations, acceptable. Special baby-changing rooms are starting to appear.

You will usually be charged a fee of 1 Turkish lira per visit in public facilities, so keep a supply of small change available.

Tourist Information

Local tourist information offices

A government-run tourist information office, *Turizm Danışma Burosu*, is marked with a white oval sign featuring a coloured "i". They are usually open daily 9am–12.30pm & 1.30–5.30pm, at Istanbul airports until 9pm, and in summer those in busy resorts may also stay open into the evening.

Don't expect that much from them, however; there are a few outstanding ones (like the Sultanahmet office in Istanbul), but in many, especially in less-visited areas, staff may not speak even rudimentary English. Some have useful lists of accommodation but may have no facilities to make bookings. In some cities local associations have set up their own rival facilities which can be a great improvement. For instance, the Alanya Hotels Association (ALTID) has regulated prices and standards, organised beach lifeguards and extra security, and staffs its office with English-speakers.

Main tourist offices:
Istanbul – Sultanahmet Square
Tel: 0212-518 8754

Also at all airports, Sirkeci train station, Karaköy ferry port and Taksim.
Alanya – Damlataş Cad 1
Tel: 0242-523 1240
Ankara – Anafartalar Cad 67. Also at the train station and the airport.
Tel: 0312-310 8787
Antalya – Anafartalar Cad 31
Tel: 0242-247 7660
Bodrum – Barış Meyd 48
Tel: 0252-316 1091
İzmir – 1344 Sok 2, Pasaport
Tel: 0232-483 5117
Also at the airport.

Tourist offices

UK
4th Floor, 29–30 St James's Street, London SW1A 1HB
Tel: 020-7839 7778
www.gototurkey.co.uk
US
821 United Nations Plaza, New York, NY 10017
Tel: 212-687 2194
Also in Los Angeles and Washington DC
www.goturkeytourism.com

Websites

Turkey hotels:
www.boutiquesmallhotels.com
Charming small hotels across the country.
Istanbul hotels:
www.istanbulhotels.com
Useful accommodation website.
Travel advisories:
www.gov.uk/foreign-travel-advice/turkey
www.travel.state.gov
Regularly updated travel and general health advice from the UK Foreign and Commonwealth Office and US State Department.
Health for travellers:
www.cdc.gov/travel
Advice on health from a US government site.
General tourist information:
www.allaboutturkey.com
Incredibly informative site maintained by tourist guide Burak Sansal.
www.turkeytravelplanner.com
Tom Brosnahan, with five decades' experience in Turkey, runs this excellent, generally current site which includes an active discussion forum.
www.trekkinginturkey.com
Everything about major trekking areas and long-distance routes, including printed guides and maps for sale.

www.turkishtravelblog.com
Regional guides and travel tips from expat Natalie Sayin, gathered over a decade from all across Turkey.

Tour Operators and Travel Agents in Turkey

Unless you are planning to move around a lot, packages with local operators are often much more reasonably priced than booking independently.

Istanbul

Abelya Turizm
Perpa Ticaret Merkezi
A Blok, 11/1486
Şişli
Tel: 0212-320 9050
www.abelyatour.com
Good all-round agency offering city tours, remoter ones to Bursa and Cappadocia, and more unusual outings to beauty spots in Thrace and the nearby Black Sea coast (like İğneada and Ağva).
Arnika
Cumhuriyet Cad, Celal Öker Sok 4/1, Harbiye
Tel: 0212-225 0335
www.arnika.com.tr
Tours to Turkey's far east and southeast; prices do not include airfares.
Gençtur
İstiklâl Caddesi, Aznavur Pasajı 212, 8th Floor, Galatasaray
Tel: 0212-244 6230
http://genctur.com.tr/
Student travel agency offering discount cards and airfares.
Plan Tours
Cumhuriyet Cad 83/1, Elmadağ
Tel: 0212-234 7777
www.plantours.com
City sightseeing tours, ticketing, hotel reservations, car and yacht rentals, chauffeur-driven services, Bosphorus cruises, Jewish heritage and biblical tours.
Sunday Holiday
Abdülhakhamit Cad 82/2, Taksim
Tel: 0212-252 7613
www.sundayholiday.com.tr
City and Cappadocia tours, city packages, hotel bookings and car rental.
Viking Turizm
Mete Cad 18, Taksim
Tel: 444 8454 nationwide; head office 0212-334 2600
www.vikingturizm.com.tr
Mainly corporate travel and events/incentive-trip organisation.

Thrace and Marmara

Çanakkale
Kenan Çelik
Tel: 0532-738 6675
www.kcelik.com
This retired English professor offers by far the best custom tours of the Gallipoli battlefields, taking you to little-known sites; you must have your own car though.

Eceabat
Crowded House Tours
Zübeyde Hanım Meyd 28
Tel: 0286-814 1565
www.crowdedhousegallipoli.com
The best mainstream group tours of the Gallipoli battlefields, additionally offering excursions further afield.

Aegean Coast

Bodrum
Arya Yachting
Caferpaşa Cad 21/A
Tel: 0252-316 1580
www.arya.com.tr
Yachting or *gulet* excursions and tailor-made or themed inland tours.

İzmir
Rainbow Tours
İlhan Selçuk Sok 6/G, Narlıdere, İzmir
Tel: 0232-239 5196
www.rainbowtourturkey.com
Pilgrimage tours of Christian and Pauline sites in Turkey.

Dalyan
Kaunos Tours
Sarısu Sok 1/A, Ortaca, Muğla
Tel: 0252-284 2816
www.kaunostours.com
Outfitters for scuba, white-water rafting, canyoning, sea-kayaking, horse-riding and mountain biking; also car hire.

Marmaris
Alternatif Outdoor
Şirinyer Mahallesi, 133 Sok 10/1
Tel: 0252-417 2720
www.alternatifraft.com
Main local outfitters for sea-kayaking, river-rafting, canyoning, trekking; many other storefront agencies subcontract to them.

Mediterranean Coast

Antalya
Antalya Rafting
Perge Bulvarı 32/8, Meydankavağı Merkez
Tel: 0242-311 0495, 0553-936 5363
www.antalyarafting.com.tr
Not just rafting but jeep safaris, canyoning and rock-climbing.
Mithra Travel
Hesapçı Sok 70, Kaleiçi
Tel: 0242-248 7747
www.mithratravel.com
Sightseeing tours, self-guided trekking tours, mountain bike and car hire.

Fethiye and around

Before Lunch Cruises
The *gulet Ros*, quayside, near Fora Café
Tel: 0535-636 0076
www.beforelunch.com
Specialists in high-quality, 3-night/4-day cruises in the Gulf of Fethiye.
Seven Capes
Kınalı Mahallesi, Kaya Köyü
Tel: 0537-403 3779
www.sevencapes.com
Sea-kayaking trips along the nearby coast, as far as the eponymous Yedi Burunlar ('Seven Capes' in Turkish); also escorted one-week walks along the Carian Trail.
Sky Sports
Ölüdeniz-Fethiye
Under the Tonoz Hotel
Tel: 0252-617 0511
www.skysports-turkey.com
The most established of several outfitters here taking clients on tandem paraglides off nearby Baba Dağı.

Kaş

Amber Travel
Yeni Camii Cad 7/A
Tel: 0242-836 1630
www.ambertravel.com
Good for tailor-made, country-wide cultural itineraries and mountain-bike tours.
Kaş Diving
Hükümet Cad 10/1
Tel: 0242-836 4045
www.kas-diving.com
Professional and welcoming diving centre with over two decades of experience. They also arrange canyoning and paragliding through their trusted local partner, Sky Sports.
Dragoman
Uzunçarşı Cad 15
Tel: 0242-836 3614
Similar, and similar-quality, offerings as Kas Diving but also hiking, biking and cultural tours.

Cappadocia

Kapadokya Balloons Göreme
Nevşehir Yolu 14/A, Nevşehir
Tel: 0384-271 2442
www.kapadokyaballoons.com
Idyllic hot-air-balloon rides over Cappadocia's landscape.
Turkish Heritage Tours
Yavuz Sokak, 1 Göreme
Tel: 0384-271 2687
www.goreme.com
Excellent local day-tours with genial guides, and even cooking or 'belly-dancing' courses.
Middle Earth Travel
Kuran Kursu 12-12/A, Göreme
Tel: 0384-271 2559

A wide selection of postcards of Turkey.

Hot-air balloons preparing to take off in Cappadocia.

www.middleearthtravel.com
Hiking in Cappadocia and along the Lycian and St Paul's Trails, plus climbing on Mount Ararat and Kaçkar/Aladağlar treks. Local tours and sightseeing, too.

Red Valley
Cumhuriyet Meyd 4, Ürgüp
Tel: 0384-341 5061
www.redvalleytours.com
Well-regarded, full-day walking and sightseeing tours (four colour-coded ones) and cave exploration through the magical Cappadocian landscape. Also arranges balloon rides and local hotel stays.

Yuki Tour
Şehit Cem Bul Cad 38/A, Ürgüp
Tel: 0532-287 1663
www.yukitour.com
A wide range of well-run tours covering nation-wide highlights, including farflung destinations like the Black Sea coast and Eastern Turkey. Some tours begin in Trabzon or Diyarbakır.

The East

Diyarbakır
Bat-Air Turizm
İnönü Cad 9
Tel: 0412-223 5373
Standard walk-in agency for basic travel needs (air, train tickets).

Şanlıurfa
Harran Nemrut Tur
Inside the Aslan Guesthouse
Demokrasi Caddesi, 1351 Sok 10
Tel: 0414-215 1575, 0542-761 3065
Affordable, full-day minibus tours to Harran (including Şuayb and Soğmatar, Nemrut Dağı, Mardin and environs, plus Göbekli Tepe. Minimum three customers;

worth it as public transport is challenging.

Van
Alkans Tour Agency
Ordu Cad 20
Tel: 0530-349 2793
www.easternturkeytour.org
Excellent 10–14-day tours covering Eastern Turkey, from Trabzon to Gaziantep, along with 6-day treks to the summit of Mount Ararat.

Ayanis Turizm
Cumhüriyet Caddesi
Under the Belediye Sarayı
Tel: 0432-210 1515
www.ayanis.com.tr
One-day tours of Lake Van highlights or the İshak Paşa Sarayı, but also more unusual destinations like Ahlat cemetery and the Nemrut volcanic crater-lakes near Tatvan.

Travellers with Disabilities

Turkey has relatively few facilities for the disabled. Simply manoeuvring a wheelchair through the streets, for instance, presents a strenuous challenge. There are few toilet facilities for disabled people, and many mosques do not allow wheelchairs to enter. However, as with everything in Turkey, people are friendly, kind and helpful, and will do their best to assist you in getting into a museum or building.

Progress has certainly been made in recent years, particularly within Istanbul, where most touristic attractions are now accessible as well as the tramvay, funiculars and select ferries across the Bosphorus. The city's metro lines – as well as those of Ankara, Bursa and İzmir – are also now equipped to offer

wheelchair access, as are all major airports and newer hotels. The Turkish Tourist Office in London (www.gototurkey.co.uk) issues a guide to facilities for the disabled in Turkey.

For more detailed information, it is worth contacting your country's own disabled association before you travel:
UK
Disability Rights UK
www.disabilityrights.org
US
SATH (Society for Accessible Travel and Hospitality)
Tel: 212-447 7284
www.sath.org

Visas and Passports

Visa requirements and costs for entering Turkey vary substantially according to your nationality. All travellers need a passport valid for at least 60 days beyond your intended stay in the country.

As of October 28, 2018, tourist visas are no longer available via kiosks at ports of entry, so in the case that your nationality requires a visa you must obtain one beforehand (at least 48 hours before

⏲ Time Zone

Turkish Standard Time is 2 hours ahead of Greenwich Mean Time. In common with Europe, it advances by one hour in summer (end March to end Oct).

your flight) through the following, official website: www.evisa.gov.tr/en/. Any other sites purporting to sell them are fakes and scams. You apply, pay and download it to show the border officials. Immigration officials are supposed to accept 'soft' copies stored on your device or smart phone, but to be on the safe side print out a hard copy.

Citizens of the following countries require visas (a current, complete list will be found on the official website): UK (£20/€25), Canada (€50), Australia (€50), USA (US$30/€25), Belgium (€25), the Netherlands (€25), Norway (€25), South Africa (30 days only; free) and Ireland (€25) You will be issued with a multiple-entry tourist visa valid for 90 days (within 180) from a date you specify (prudently, slightly before you plan to enter the country).

Provided that they have a valid passport, nationals of many countries (including Denmark, France, Germany, Italy and New Zealand) do not need a visa for visits of up to three months. Your date of entry will be stamped into the passport free of charge.

If you overstay the length of your tourist visa, fines on exit are stiff – starting from €60 per day of over-stay. Some people reckon it better to accept voluntary deportation with the proviso of being banned from re-entry for 6 months.

Selfies in Istanbul.

Extending your stay

Under post-2012, quasi-Schengen regulations, non-resident foreigners are only allowed to stay in Turkey for 90 days, cumulative, in any 180-day period. If you have reason from the outset to believe you'll be in the country longer, it is best to contact your nearest embassy (or, simpler, the e-visa website) before entering the country for advice on the most appropriate alternative visa to a tourist one. It is effectively impossible to extend a tourist visa once in Turkey.

W

Weights and Measures

Metric, although land is still sold by the *dönüm* (1000 sq m).

Women Travellers

Turkish attitudes towards women are liberal in cosmopolitan cities and tourist areas, but more restrictive in provincial towns. Women in rural regions cover their heads with scarves as much as a means of protecting their hair from dust and dirt as for reasons of religious conservatism, although Islamic fundamentalism

has – as we discuss elsewhere – has made gains in recent years.

Travelling alone

The major cities in Turkey and tourist areas are liberal and Westernised, and are very safe compared with many other countries. Leering and suggestive comments may be irritatingly common, but physical attacks are rare. Women visitors should not be afraid to travel alone, or to go out in the evening, although provocative dress may create problems, and at night you might feel more relaxed with a companion.

In some situations, however, Turks do still segregate the sexes. On buses you are not expected to sit next to a male stranger. Restaurants often have a designated *aile salonu* (family room), and sometimes prefer a lone woman to sit there.

No Turkish woman, whether on her own or with a male partner, is welcome at a traditional coffee shop or tearoom (*kahvehane* or *çayhane*) – they are strictly male preserves, although foreign females are usually treated as honorary men if they want to go in.

Harassment

You should expect some Turkish men to chat you up, sometimes in an outrageously flamboyant fashion, but you can reduce harassment to a minimum by dressing respectably and looking as if you know where you are going. Turkish women get some degree of harassment too, but they cope by sticking together and mastering the firm brush-off. Unfortunately resort touts tend to be very good at manipulating foreign females.

If you are groped by a stranger, speak up loudly; the shame will usually be enough to scare him off and everyone nearby will make it a point of honour to rush to your defence.

What to wear

In the big cities you will still see a few young Turkish girls wearing whatever is the current fashion, be it shorts, miniskirts or Lycra, though given the current climate, subtle or otherwise pressure is being brought to bear on them. Foreigners are advised to dress fairly conservatively. Cover up your swimming costume or bikini when you leave the beach.

Atatürk's great language reform took place in 1928–29, when the Arabic script was replaced by a modified Roman alphabet, and the vocabulary saw many Persian and Arabic words yield to those of Turkish or French origin, with the intentions of simplifying the language, boosting literacy – and creating a barrier to enquiry into the Ottoman past. One legacy of the flowery elaborations of Ottoman speech is the way Turkish people exchange formal greetings: these pleasantries and politenesses follow a set routine in which both sides of the exchange follow formulaic patterns of questions with set answers.

Turkish is undoubtedly a difficult language for Europeans to learn. Although the grammar is consistent and logical, with few irregularities, and pronunciation follows phonetic spelling, both the vocabulary and grammatical structure are very different from any language that English-speakers may have tackled before. The vocabulary in particular is difficult to remember, especially over a short visit, though you may recognise a few words of French or English origin once you have deciphered the Turkish spelling.

It is probably most useful to try to master basic pronunciation, so you can say addresses and place names correctly, and read and use some set phrases. In most places it's rare that you won't be able to find someone speaking either English or another Western European language.

PRONUNCIATION

As spelling is phonetic, pronunciation is the easiest part of learning the language, once you have mastered the few different Turkish vowel and consonant sounds.

Letters are always pronounced in the same way. One tricky consonant is the "c", which is always pronounced

"j" as in "jump", so the Turkish word "*camii*" (mosque) is pronounced "jah-mi", and "*caddesi*" (road, street) is pronounced "jah-des-i". The soft "g" (ğ) is never voiced, but lengthens the preceding vowel. Also, look out for the dotless i, "I (ı)", which sounds like the vestigial vowel between the "b" and the "l" in "stable"; it is quite different from the dotted "İ (i)". Compare "*ızgara*" (grill, pronounced uhz-gara) with "*incir*" (fig, pronounced inn-jeer). Double consonants are both pronounced – there are no diphthongs. Each syllable in a word carries (approximately) equal stress, as do words in a phrase.

The basic rules of pronunciation are as follows:

c "j" as in jump
ç "ch" as in chill
s "s" as in sleep
ş "sh" as in sharp
g "g" as in good
ğ is silent, lengthens the previous vowel, and never begins a word
a "ah" as in father
e "e" as in let
i with a dot as in tin
ı without a dot is an "uh" sound, like the second "e" in ever
o is pronounced "o" as in toad
ö with diaeresis is similar to "ur" as in spurt, or German "oe" as in Goethe
u is pronounced like "oo" as in room
ü is like the "ew" in pew, or u-sound in French "*tu*" (impossible without pursing your lips).

USEFUL WORDS AND PHRASES

Days of the Week

Monday *Pazartesi*
Tuesday *Salı*
Wednesday *Çarşamba*
Thursday *Perşembe*

Friday *Cuma*
Saturday *Cumartesi*
Sunday *Pazar*

Months

January *Ocak*
February *Şubat*
March *Mart*
April *Nisan*
May *Mayıs*
June *Haziran*
July *Temmuz*
August *Ağustos*
September *Eylül*
October *Ekim*
November *Kasım*
December *Aralık*

Numbers

1 *bir*
2 *iki*
3 *üç*
4 *dört*
5 *beş*
6 *altı*
7 *yedi*
8 *sekiz*
9 *dokuz*
10 *on*
11 *on bir*
12 *on iki*
20 *yirmi*
21 *yirmi bir*
22 *yirmi iki*
30 *otuz*
40 *kırk*
50 *elli*
60 *altmış*
70 *yetmiş*
80 *seksen*
90 *doksan*
100 *yüz*
200 *iki yüz*
1,000 *bin*
2,000 *iki bin*
1,000,000 *bir milyon*
To make a complex number, add the components one by one eg, 5,650,000 = *beş milyon altı yüz elli bin*

(in Turkish spelling these would normally be run together).

GREETINGS

Hello *Merhaba*
Good morning (early) *Günaydın*
Good day *Iyi günler*
Good evening *Iyi aksamlar*
Goodnight *Iyi geceler*
Welcome! *Hoş geldiniz!*
Reply: *It is well we have found you! (ie,*
Happy to be here! *Hoş bulduk!*
Please, with pleasure, please go first (multipurpose, polite expression) *Buyurun*
Don't mention it *Rica ederim*
Pleased to meet you (literally, **I have become honoured**) *Çok memnun oldum*
How are you? *Nasılsınız?*
Thanks, I/we am/are fine *Teşekkürler, iyiyim/iyiyiz*
My name is… *Adım…*
I am English/Scottish/American/ Australian *Ben İngilizim/İskoçyalım/ Amerikalım/Avustralyalım*
We are sightseeing *Geziyoruz*
We'll see each other again ("see you") *Görüşürüz*
God willing *İnşallah*
Goodbye *Hoşça kalın or Allaha ısmarlardık*
Reply: "**Go happily**" *Güle güle* (only said by the person staying behind)
Leave me alone *Beni rahat bırakin*
Get lost *Çekil git*
I don't want any *Istemiyorum*

ESSENTIALS

Yes *Evet*
No *Hayır/yok*
OK *Tamam*
Please *Lütfen*
Thank you *Teşekkür ederim/sağol/ mersi*
You're welcome *Bir şey değil*
Excuse me/I beg your pardon (in a crowd) *Affedersiniz*
Excuse me *Pardon*
I don't speak Turkish *Türkçe bilmiyorum*

⊙ Money

Bank *Banka*
Credit card *Kredi kartı*
Exchange office *Döviz bürosu*
Exchange rate *Dövis kuru*
Traveller's cheque *Seyahat çeki*
ATM *Banka makinesi*

Do you speak English? *İngilizce biliyor musunuz?*
I don't understand/I haven't understood *Anlamıyorum/Anlamadım*
I don't know *Bilmiyorum*
Please write it down *Onu benim için heceleyebilir misiniz?*
Wait a moment! *Bir dakika!*
Slowly *Yavaş*
Enough *Yeter*
Where is it? *Nerede?*
Where is the…? *… Nerede?*
Where is the toilet? *Tuvalet nerede?*
What time is it? *Saatiniz var mı?*
At what time? *Saat kaça?*
Today *Bugün*
Tomorrow *Yarın*
Yesterday *Dün*
The day after tomorrow *Öbür gün*
Now *Şimdi*
Later *Sonra*
When? *Ne zaman*
Morning/in the morning *Sabah*
Afternoon/in the afternoon *Oğleden sonra*
Evening/in the evening *Akşam*
This evening *Bu akşam*
Here *Burada*
There *Şurada*
Over there *Orada*
Is there a foreign-language newspaper? *Yabancı gazete var mı?*
Is there a minibus? *Minibüs var mı?*
Is there a telephone? *Telefon var mı?*
Yes, there is *Evet, var*
No, there isn't *Hayır, yok*
There is no ticket *Bilet yok*

SIGHTSEEING

Directions

How do I get to Bodrum? *Bodrum'a nasıl giderim?*
How far is it to…? *…'a/'e ne kadar uzakdır?*
Near *Yakın*
Far *Uzak*
Left *Sol*
On the left/to the left *Solda/sol'a*
Right *Sağ*
On the right/to the right *Sağda/sağ'a*
Straight on *Doğru*
North *Kuzey*
South *Güney*
East *Doğu*
West *Batı*

Sights/Places

City *Şehir*
Village *Köy*
Forest *Orman*

Sea *Deniz*
Lake *Göl*
Farm *Çiftlik*
Church *Kilisesi*
Mosque *Cami*
Ruins *Harabeler, örenyeri*
Post office *Postane, PeTeTe (sounding out of the acronym)*
What time will it open/close? *Kaçta açılıcak/kapanacak?*

Travelling

Car *Araba*
Petrol/gas station *Benzin istasyonu*
Petrol/gas *Benzin (süper/normal)*
Diesel *Mazot*
Fill it up, please *Dolu, lütfen*
Flat tyre/puncture *Patlak lastik*
My car has broken down *Arabam arızalandı*
Bus station *Otogar*
Bus stop *Durak*
Bus *Otobüs*
Train station *Gar/İstasyon*
Train *Tren*
Taxi *Taksi*
Airport *Havalimanı/Havaalanı*
Aeroplane *Uçak*
Port/harbour *Liman*
Boat *Gemi*
Ferry *Feribot/Vapur*
Quay *İskele*
Ticket *Bilet*
Ticket office *Gişe*
Left luggage *Emanet*
Return ticket *Gidişdönüs bileti*
Can I reserve a seat? *Reservasyon yapabilir miyim?*

⊙ Common Signs

Giriş/Çıkış *Entrance/Exit*
Tehlike çıkışı *Emergency exit*
Giriş ücretsiz/ücretli *Free/paid admission*
Açık *Open*
Kapalı *Closed*
Varış *Arrivals*
Kalkış *Departures*
Askeri bölge *Military zone*
Sigara icilmez *No smoking*
Girmek yasaktır *No entry*
Fotoğraf çekmayınız *No photographs*
Lütfen ayakkabılarınızı çıkartınız *Please take off your shoes*
Bay *Men*
Bayan *Women*
Tuvalet/Umumi *Toilet*
Arızalı *Out of order*
İçme su, içibilir *Drinking water, potable*
İçilmez *Non-potable water*

⊙ Emergencies

Help! *İmdat!*
Fire *Yangın!*
Please call the police *Polis çağırın*
Please call an ambulance
Ambulans çağırın
Please call the fire brigade
İtfaiye çağırın
This is an emergency *Bu acıldır*
There has been an accident
Kaza oldu
I'd like an interpreter *Tercüman istiyorum*
I want to speak to someone from the British Consulate
İngiltere konsoloslugundan biri ile görüşmek istiyorum

What time does it leave? *Kaçta kalkıyor?*
Where does it leave from? *Nereden kalkıyor?*
How long does it take? *Ne kadar sürüyor?*
Which bus is it? *Hangi otobüsdir?*

HEALTH

Remember that in an emergency it can be quicker to get to hospital by taxi.
Clinic *Klinik/Sağlık Ocağı*
Dentist *Dişçi*
Doctor *Doktor*
Emergency service/room *Acil servis*
First aid *İlk yardım*
Hospital *Hastane*
Pharmacist *Eczacı*
Pharmacy *Eczane*
I am ill *Hastayım*
I have a fever *Ateşim var*
I have diarrhoea *İshallım*
I am diabetic *Şeker hastasıyım*
I'm allergic to... *Karşı ... alerjim var*
I have asthma *Astim hastasıyım*
I have a heart condition *Kalp hastasıyım*
I am pregnant *Gebeyim/Hamileyim*
It hurts here *Burası acıyor*
I have lost a filling *Dolgu düştü*
I need a prescription for... *İçin ... bir reçete istiyorum*

ACCOMMODATION

Hotel *Otel*
Pension/guesthouse *Pansiyon*
Single/double/triple *Tek/çift/üç kişilik*
Full board *Tam pansiyon*
Half board *Yarım pansiyon*

With a shower *Duşlu*
With a bathroom *Banyolu*
With a balcony *Balkonlu*
With a sea view *Deniz manzaralı*
With air conditioning *Klimalı*
Centrally heated *Kaloriferli*
Lift/elevator *Asansör*
Room service *Oda servisi*
Key *Anahtar*
Bed *Yatak*
Blanket *Battaniye*
Pillow *Yastık*
Shower *Duş*
Soap *Sabun*
Plug (sink) *Tıkaç*
Towel *Havlu*
Basin *Lavabo*
Toilet *Tuvalet*
Toilet paper *Tuvalet kağıdı*
Hot water *Sıcak su*
Cold water *Soğuk su*
Dining room *Yemek salonu*
I need/...is necessary *lazım/...gerek*
I have a reservation *Reservasyonım var*
Do you have a room available? *Boş odanız var mı?*
I'd like a room for one/three nights *Bir/üç gece için bir oda istiyorum*
I'm sorry, we are full *Maalesef doluyuz*
Is there wireless internet? *Kablosuz varmı?*
What's the password? *Şifre nedir?*

SHOPPING

Price *Fiyat*
Cheap *Ucuz*
Expensive *Pahalı*
No bargaining (sign) *Pazarlık edilmez*
Old *Eski*
New *Yeni*
Big *Büyük*
Bigger *Daha büyük*
Small *Küçük*
Smaller *Daha küçük*
Very nice/beautiful *Çok güzel*
This *Bu*
These *Bunlar*
That *Şu*
I would like... *Isterim...*
I don't want *Istemem*
There isn't any *Yok*
How much is it? *Ne kadar?*
How many? *Kaç tane?*
Do you take credit cards? *Kredi kartleri geçerlimi?*

EATING OUT

Table *Masa*

Cup *Fincan*
Glass *Bardak*
Wine glass *Kadeh*
Bottle *Şişe*
Plate *Tabak*
Fork *Çatal*
Knife *Bıçak*
Spoon *Kaşık*
Napkin *Peçete*
Salt *Tuz*
Black pepper *Kara biber*
Starters *Mezeler*
Soup *Çorba*
Fish *Balık*
Meat dishes *Et yemekleri*
Grills *Izgara*
Eggs *Yumurta*
Vegetarian dishes *Etsiz yemekleri*
Salads *Salatalar*
Fruit *Meyve*
Bread *Ekmek*
Peppery hot *Acı*
Non-spicy *Acısız*
Water *Su*
Mineral water *Maden suyu*
Fizzy water *Soda*
Beer *Bira*
Red/white wine *Kırmızı/beyaz sarap*
Fresh orange juice *Sıkma portakal suyu*
Coffee *Kahve*
Tea *Çay*
A table for two/four, please *İki/dört kişilik bir masa, lütfen*
Can we eat outside? *Dışarıda yiyebilir miyiz?*
Excuse me (to get service or attention) *Bakar mısınız?*
Menu *Menü*
I didn't order this *Ben bunu ısmarlamadım*

⊙ Road Signs

Dikkat *Beware/Caution*
Çekme bölgesi *Tow-away zone*
Yavaş *Slow*
Dur *Stop*
Araç giremez *No entry with vehicle*
Tek yön *One-way*
Çıkmaz sokak *Dead-end road*
Bozuk satıh *Poor road surface*
Düşük banket *Abrupt verge/shoulder*
Yol yapımı *Roadworks*
Yol kapalı *Road closed*
Yaya geçidi *Pedestrian crossing*
Şehir merkezi/Centrum *City centre*
Otopark ücretlidir *Fee-paying carpark*
Park yapmayınız *Do not park here*

Some more water/bread/wine, please *Biraz daha su/ekmek/şarap, rica ediyoruz*
I can eat... *Yiyorum...*
I cannot eat... *Yiyemiyorum...*
Can you bring the bill? *Hesabımız verirmisiniz?*
Service included/excluded *Servis dahil/hariç*

MENU DECODER

Kahvaltı/Breakfast

Beyaz peynir *White cheese*
Kaşar peyniri *Yellow hard cheese*
Domates *Tomatoes*
Zeytin *Olives*
Salatalık *Cucumber*
Reçel *Jam*
Bal *Honey*
Tereyağ *Butter*
Extra dishes which you may order for a more substantial breakfast:
Haşlanmış yumurta *Hard-boiled eggs*
Rafadan yumurta *Soft-boiled eggs*
Menemen *Scrambled-egg omelette with tomatoes, peppers, onion and cheese*
Sahanda yumurta *Fried eggs*
Sucuklu yumurta *Eggs fried with cured dry sausage*
Sade/peynirli/mantarlı omlet *Plain/ cheese/mushroom omelette*

Çorbalar/Soups

Haşlama *Mutton broth*
Tavuk çorbası/tavuk suyu *Chicken soup*
Düğün çorbası *'Wedding soup' (thickened with eggs and lemon)*
Ezogelin çorbası *Lentil soup with rice*
Mercimek çorbası *Lentil soup*
Domates çorbası *Tomato soup*
İşkembe çorbası *Tripe soup*
Paça çorbası *Lamb's feet soup*
Şehriye çorbası *Fine noodle soup*
Yayla çorbası *Yoghurt soup*
Tarhana çorbası *Soup made from a dried sourdough base*

Soguk mezeler/Cold starters

These are usually offered from a large tray of assorted dishes, or you can choose from a cold cabinet; there are dozens of variations.
Beyaz peynir *White cheese*
Zeytin *Olives*
Turşu *Pickled vegetables – Turkish pickles are sour and salty, sometimes spicy but never sweet*

⊙ For Vegetarians

I eat only fruit and vegetables **Yalnız meyve ve sebze yiyorum**
I cannot eat any meat at all **Hiç et yemiyorum**
I can eat fish **Balık yiyorum**

Beyin salatası *Raw lamb brains*
Patlıcan ezmesi *Aubergine purée*
Piyaz *White-bean salad with olive oil and lemon*
Barbunya pilaki *Marinated red kidney beans*
Antep esmesi *Spicy hot red paste or salad of chopped peppers and tomato*
Çerkez tavuğu *Shredded chicken in walnut sauce*
Haydari *Dip of chopped dill and garlic in thick yoghurt*
Cacık *Yoghurt, cucumber and herb dip*
Semizotu *Purslane in yoghurt*
Fava *Purée of beans*
Dolmalar *Any vegetable stuffed with rice mixed with dill, pine nuts and currants*
Yalancı yaprak dolması *Stuffed vine leaves without meat*
Mücver *Cougette/zucchini frittata*
Midye dolması *Stuffed mussels*
Biber dolması *Stuffed peppers*
Lakerda *Sliced salt-cured, then marinated, bonito*
Hamsi *Fresh anchovies preserved in oil*
Zeytinyağlı *Vegetables cooked with olive oil, served cold*
Deniz börülcesi *Marsh samphire, glasswort*
İmam bayıldı *Aubergine stuffed with tomato and onion, cooked with olive oil*

Sıcak mezeler/Hot starters

Sigara böreği *Crisp fried rolls of pastry with cheese or meat filling (can also be triangular: muska)*
Arnavut ciğeri *Albanian-style fried diced lamb's liver*
Kalamar tava *Deep-fried squid rings*
Midye tava *Deep-fried mussels*
Tarator *Nut and garlic sauce served with above, or with fried vegetables*
Paçanga böreği *Turnovers stuffed with pastırma (cured beef)*

Salata/Salads

Karışık *Mixed*
Çoban salatası *"Shepherd's salad" (chopped mixed tomato, cucumber, pepper, onion and parsley)*
Yeşil salata *Green salad*
Mevsim salatası *Seasonal salad*
Roka *Rocket/arugula*

Salatalık *Cucumber*
Domates *Tomatoes*
Marul *Lettuce*
Semizotu *Purslane*
Söğus *Sliced salad vegetables with no dressing*
Roka *Rocket*

Types of pide (Turkish pizza)

Kıymalı *topped with minced meat*
Sucuklu *topped with dry sausage*
Yumurtalı *topped with chopped egg*
Kuşbaşılı *topped with small meat chunks*

Et yemekleri/Meat dishes

Kebap *Kebab*
Döner *Sliced, layered lamb grilled on revolving spit*
Tavuk döner *As above, made with chicken*
Şiş kebap *Cubed meat grilled on skewer, eg kuzu şiş (lamb), tavuk şiş (chicken)*
Adana kebap *Minced lamb grilled on skewer; spicy*
Urfa kebap *As above; not spicy*
Bursa/İskender/yoğurtlu kebap *Dish of döner slices laid on pieces of bread with tomato sauce, melted butter and yoghurt with garlic*
Piliç *Roast chicken*
Pirzola *Cutlets*
Izgara *Grill/grilled – usually over charcoal*
Köfte *Meatballs*
Köfte ızgara *Grilled meatballs*
İnegöl köftesi *Mince rissoles laced with cheese*
Kiremitte kebap *Meat grilled on a ceramic plate*
Bıldırcın ızgara *Grilled quail*
Kuzu tandır/fırın *Lamb baked on the bone*
Hünkâr beğendili köfte *Meatballs with aubergine purée*
Kadınbudu köfte *"Ladies' thighs": meat and rice croquettes in gravy*
Karnıyarık *Aubergines split in half and filled with minced lamb mixed with pine nuts and currants*
Kavurma *Meat stir-fried or braised, cooked in its own fat and juices*
Çoban kavurma *Lamb fried with peppers, tomatoes and onions*
Dil *Tongue (usually beef)*
Saç kavurma *Wok-fried meat, vegetables and spices*
Etli kabak dolması *Courgettes (zucchini) stuffed with meat*
Etli nohut *Chickpea and lamb stew*
Etli kuru fasuliye *Haricot bean and lamb stew*

Taxi rank on İstiklâl Caddesi, Istanbul.

Kağıt kebabı *Lamb and vegetables cooked in paper or foil*
Güveç *Casserole*

Balık yemekleri/Fish dishes

Most fish is eaten plainly grilled or fried, and priced by weight. It will be less expensive if it is local and in season. Always ask the price – whether by weight *(kilosu)* or portion *(porsyon)* – before ordering.

Balık ızgara *Grilled fish*
Balık tavada *Fried fish*
Balık şiş *Cubed fish grilled on skewer*
Alabalık *Trout*
Levrek *Sea bass*
Lüfer *Bluefish*
Hamsi *Anchovies*
Sardalye *Sardines*
Karagöz *Two-banded bream*
Mercan *Pandora, red bream*
Çipura *Gilt-head bream*
Uskumru *Atlantic mackerel*
İstavrit *Horse mackerel*
Palamut *Small bonito*
Kalkan *Turbot*
Gümüş *Silverfish (like whitebait)*
Barbunya *Small red mullet*
Tekir *Large red mullet*
Kefal *Grey mullet*
Kılıç balığı *Swordfish*
Dil balığı *Sole*
İskaroz *Parrot fish*
Karides *Shrimp, prawns*
Karides güveç *Prawn casserole with peppers, tomato and melted cheese*
Hamsi pilav *Rice baked with anchovies*

Sebze/Vegetables

Ispanak *Spinach*
Bamya *Okra, lady's fingers*

Soğan *Onion*
Kusru fasulye *White haricots*
Mantar *Mushrooms*
Bezelye *Peas*

Tatlı/Desserts

Baklava *Layers of filo pastry with nuts and syrup*
Ekmek kadayıf *Bread pudding soaked in syrup*
Güllaç *Dessert made with layers of rice wafer, sugar and milk flavoured with rose water*
Tavuk göğsü *Milk pudding made with pounded chicken breast*
Kazandibi *Caramelised version of tavuk göğsü*
Dondurma *Turkish gelato*
Muhallebi *Cherry-pit flour or cornstarch, milk and rose-water blancmange*
Sütlaç *Rice pudding*
Aşure *"Noah's pudding" made with dried fruits, nuts, seeds and pulses*
Kabak tatlısı *Candied pumpkin*
Ayva tatlısı *Candied quince*
Kaymaklı *Either of the above with clotted cream*
Komposto *Poached fruit*
Krem caramel *Caramel custard, French crème caramel*
Pasta *Gâteau-style cake, patisserie*

Meyve/Fruits

Kavun *Honeydew melon*
Nar *Pomegranate*
Muz *Banana*
Kiraz *Sweet cherry*
Vişne *Sour cherry*
Şeftali *Peach*
Elma *Apple*
Armut *Pear*
Üzüm *Grape*

Soft or cold drinks

Su *Water*
Maden suyu *Mineral water*
Soda/gazoz *Sparkling water*
Ayran *Yoghurt whisked with cold water and salt*
Meyve suyu *Fruit juice*
Vişne suyu *Sour cherry juice*
Nar suyu *Pomegranate juice*
Karadut *Black mulberry juice*
Sıkma portakal suyu *Orange juice*
Şerbet *Sweetened, iced fruit juice drink*
Limonata *Lemon drink*
Şıra *Grape must*
Boza *Millet-based drink*
Buz *Ice*
Taze sıkılmış *Fresh squeezed*

Hot drinks

Çay *Tea*
Açık *Weak*
Demli *Dark, very brewed*
Bir bardak çay *Glass of tea*
Bir fincan kahve *Cup of coffee*
Ada çayı *"Island tea" made with dried wild sage*
Elma çayı *"Apple" tea made with chemical flavouring*
Kahve *Coffee*
Neskafe *Any instant coffee*
Sütlü *With milk*
Şeker *Sugar*
Türk kahvesi *Turkish coffee*
Az şekerli *With little sugar*
Orta şekerli *Medium sweet*
Çok şekerli *Cloyingly sweet*
Sade *Without sugar*
Süzme kahve *Filter coffee*
Sahlep *Hot, thick sweet winter drink made of powdered sahlep root, milk and cinnamon*

Alcoholic drinks

Bira *Beer*
Siyah *Dark (beer)*
Cintonik *Gin and tonic*
Votka *Vodka*
Yerli *Local, Turkish*
Şarap *Wine*
Şarap listesi *Wine list*
Kırmızı şarap *Red wine*
Beyaz şarap *White wine*
Roze şarap *Rosé*
Sek *Dry*
Antik *Aged*
Özel *Special*
Tatlı *Sweet*
Şişe *Bottle*
Yarım şişe *Half bottle*
Rakı *Turkish national aperitif, strongly aniseed-flavoured*

⊙ Alcohol

Turkish vintners include: Kavaklıdere, Doluca, Kayra, Sevilen (the four largest, with vineyards and cellars nationwide), Turasan, Narbağ and Peribacası, Sevilen, Suvla and Feyzi Kutman.
Turkish beers: Efes Pilsen, Efes Dark, Efes Lite (low alcohol), Efes Xtra (high alcohol), Gusta (a wheat beer), Tuborg, Carlsberg.
Spirits, especially rakı, are made in Turkey by a half-dozen private companies. Imports are still preferred (and charged for accordingly in bars).

FURTHER READING

There are plenty of books in English about all aspects of Turkey: such a complex country with so many layers of history and culture couldn't fail to generate a wealth of histories, memoirs, poetry, fiction, biographies and travel writing. Not much Turkish writing has been translated into English, however. Some good books in English have been written and issued by Turkish publishers, but are difficult to obtain outside Turkey.

ANCIENT HISTORY AND ARCHAEOLOGY

Ancient Turkey by Antonio Sagona and Paul Zimansky. A well-illustrated, thematic introduction to the development of mankind in Anatolia, from the Palaeolithic period through to important early civilisations such as the Hittites and Urartians.

Çatal Höyük, by James Mellaart. Mellaart was a tricky character, but also the first excavator of this site.

The Hittites, by O.R. Gurney. Classic history of the earliest Anatolian civilisation for non-specialists. Gurney practically invented Hittite studies single-handedly.

Troy and the Trojans, by Carl Blegen. Has marked its 50th anniversary, but still an essential introduction to Troy's first systematic excavator.

On the Surface: Çatalhöyük 1993–1995, by Ian Hodder. The resumption of excavations, predicted to last well into the 2020s.

Hattusha, The Capital of the Hittites, by Kurt Bittel. Expert site guide, from Hattuşa's main 20th-century excavator.

Schliemann of Troy: Treasure and Deceit, by David Traill. Schliemann's reputation as an archaeologist crumbles here, along with the walls of Troy, though the latter fare better in the end.

BYZANTINE, OTTOMAN AND REPUBLICAN HISTORY

Byzantium, three volumes: *The Early Centuries, The Apogee* and *The Decline and Fall*, by John Julius Norwich. Thorough, accessible, readable and entertaining account of the history of the empire up to the Ottoman conquest of 1453. TIme for only one volume? Get his *A Short History of Byzantium*, distilled from the preceding three.

Constantinople, City of the World's Desire, 1453–1924, by Philip Mansel. Outstandingly researched portrait of the imperial city. Scholarly and gripping, with a mass of information, anecdote and analysis.

Constantinople: The Last Great Siege, 1453, by Roger Crowley. Absolutely gripping account of the event, a worthy equal of the classic Runciman tome, by a Cambridge English graduate and former Istanbul resident.

The Decline of Medieval Hellenism in Asia Minor and the Process of Islamization from the Eleventh through the Fifteenth Century, by Speros Vryonis. Or, how the Byzantine Empire culturally became the Ottoman Empire.

The Fall of Constantinople, 1453, by Steven Runciman. Still the definitive account of the event, by the late, great British medieval historian.

Gallipoli, by Les Carlyon. The best of several extant studies of the campaign, so clearly written you don't even need a map to follow the narrative.

A History of the Ottoman Era, by Douglas A. Howard. Engaging, scholarly work with a plenitude of illustrations and fascinating anecdotes as well as a good dose of cultural and spiritual threads – a welcome complement to this political account of the entirety of the Ottoman era.

Istanbul: City of Majesty at the Crossroads of the World, by Thomas F. Madden. A biography of Turkey's unrivaled city, compressing thousands of years into an vivid, accessible account with a welcome dose of anecdote.

The Making of Modern Turkey, by Feroz Ahmad. Lively and unorthodox, full of wonderful anecdotes. His *Turkey: The Quest for Identity* updates matters to 2014, revising 2003 (and 1993) editions.

Osman's Dream, by Caroline Finkel. Meticulously researched history of the Ottoman Empire, broader in scope than Kinross's volume – and with more modern scholarship.

The Ottoman Centuries, by Lord Kinross. Highly readable, one-stop history that's still a good bet despite newer contenders.

The Ottomans, Dissolving Images, by Andrew Wheatcroft. Analysis of trends in Ottoman social life, and its perception by the West – amply demonstrated by period art, cartoons and photos.

On Secret Service East of Constantinople: The Plot to Bring Down the British Empire, by Peter Hopkirk. Brilliant account of Ottoman and German conspiracies to stir up Muslim holy war against Britain and Russia in India, Persia, Afghanistan and central Asia from 1914 onwards, by the author of *The Great Game*.

Turkey: A Modern History, by Erik J. Zürcher. The best single title for the post-1800 period (updated to 2016) – a revisionist demolition of sacred (republican) cows. Includes partisan, annotated bibliography.

MINORITIES AND ETHNIC ISSUES

From Empire to Republic: Turkish Nationalism and the Armenian Genocide, and *A Shameful Act: The Armenian Genocide and the Question of Turkish Responsibility*, by Taner Akçam. Unflinchingly, Akçam confronts the events of 1895 and 1915, showing how CUP ideology made them almost inevitable, and that the cover-up of the massacres – which only began in earnest during the 1930s – was both essential to Turkish republicanism and remains at the heart of Turkey's current problems.

A History of the Armenian Genocide, by Ronald Grigor Suny. Published a century after the horrific events of 1915, this clearly written and exhaustively researched account cuts through the manifold theories on how it all came about.

The Kurds: A Divided Nation in Search of a State, by Michael M. Gunter. The most up-to-date condensation of the modern Kurdish struggle; roughly one-third of this book is devoted to Turkey's Kurds.

The Lost Messiah: In Search of the Mystical Rabbi Sabbatai Sevi, by John Freely. Sevi's millennial, Kabbalistic, 17th-century movement in İzmir and Salonica produced the Dönme, a crypto-Judaic sect disproportionately prominent in modern Turkish history.

Rebel Land: Unraveling the Riddle of History in a Turkish Town, by Christopher de Bellaigue. Central republican authority confronts rural Kurdish society, Alevî and Sunni, after the Armenian deportations, in a remote east-Anatolian county town. An even-handed exploration reading like a thriller, from the days of Sultan Abdülhamid II to the second AK victory in 2007.

Secret Nation: The Hidden Armenians of Turkey, by Avedis Hadjian. Recounts over a century of struggle for the country's remaining Armenians, of which increasing numbers have begun to publicly emerge in the wake of the 2007 Hrant Dink killing.

The Thirty-Year Genocide: Turkey's Destruction of Its Christian Minorities, 1894–1924, by Benny Morris and Dror Ze'evi. Accounts for the near disappearance of Anatolia's Christian communities, previously comprising a fifth of the population.

Twice a Stranger: The Mass Expulsions That Forged Modern Greece and Turkey, by Bruce Clark. Compassionate study, with interviews of survivors, of the 1923 population exchanges, which both countries are still digesting three generations on.

CURRENT VIEWS AND ANALYSES

Frontline Turkey: The Conflict at the Heart of the Middle East, by Ezgi Basaran. Tracing the re-sparking of Kurdish tensions in the wake of the Arab Spring, Turkish journalist and former editor of *Radikal*

(among the prominent left-leaning outlets forcibly closed in 2016), argues for the centrality of the conflict in the current turmoil gripping the Middle East.

Sons of the Conquerors: The Rise of the Turkic World, by Hugh Pope. Essays on the Turkish, and Turkic, diaspora, from China to the US and various points in between.

The New Sultan: Erdogan and the Crisis of Modern Turkey, by Soner Cagaptay. A careful examination of Erdogan's controversial rise and steady consolidation of power, as well his vision for Turkey as a major power.

Turkey Unveiled, by Nicole and Hugh Pope. Readable, interlinked essays by two foreign correspondents who spent most of the 1980s and 1990s in the country. Sound assessment of most issues, despite their evident affection for the country, but a bit too much in thrall to Özal, whom they got to know pretty well.

Under the Shadow: Rage and Revolution in Modern Turkey, by Kaya Genç. Incisive overview of Turkey's current, polarized predicament, attempting to reflect both sides of the divide, from Gezi Park protesters and censored journalists to equally zealous AKP loyalists envisioning a conservative, Islamic future for Turkey.

LIVES AND LETTERS

Atatürk: The Biography of the Founder of Modern Turkey, by Andrew Mango. More focused on military events than Kinross's volume (see below), but authoritative.

Atatürk: The Rebirth of a Nation, by Lord Kinross. Still probably the best, most readable overview of the man and his times.

Beyond the Orchard, by Azize Ethem. Account of life in contemporary Turkey by a British woman who married a returned-from-exile Ottoman aristocrat and settled at Akyaka, near Marmaris, before it was a popular resort.

An English Consul in Turkey, Paul Rycaut at Smyrna 1667–78, by Sonia Anderson. Rycaut spent 17 years in Turkey, 11 as consul in Smyrna, whose contemporary English community of traders, industrialists and passers-through is vividly described in this biographical study.

Everyday Life in Ottoman Turkey, by Raphaela Lewis. Slightly deceptive title in that it concentrates on Istanbul, with a few sections on the provinces.

The Fisherman of Halicarnassus: the Man Who Made Bodrum Famous, by Roger Williams. Genial but rigorously fact-checked biography of Cevat Şakir Kabaağaçlı, stressing his philosophy (he has been widely hailed as Turkey's first ecologist), his equally colourful predecessors and peers, the first 'Blue Cruises' plus the history and folklore of the area. Turkish edition (by Bilgi Yayınevi) available if you forget to buy before departure.

The Imperial Harem of the Sultans, Daily Life at the Çırağan Palace during the 19th Century, by Leyla (Saz) Hanımefendi (trans Landon Thomas; Hil Yayınevi, Turkey). The only contemporary account of daily harem life at during the 19th-century reign of Abdülmecid, originally published in French in 1925, which gives a vivid portrait of this hidden world.

Istanbul: Memories of a City, by Orhan Pamuk. A literary journey through the city interwoven with a highly personal account of the childhood and family life of Turkey's Nobel laureate.

Mother Land, by Dmetri Kakmi. Coming of age and family secrets on bicommunal, 1960s Tenedos (Bozcaada), seen both from a boy's point of view and that of the adult Kakmi, returning to the island for some answers. Many twists in a tale that will irritate those who like to see things in black and white.

Portrait of a Turkish Family, by İrfan Orga. Vividly and movingly describes the author's family life and his growing up first as a child in Ottoman Turkey before World War I, then through the war and the years of Atatürk's reforms, before exile in Britain. His later **The Caravan Moves On** is a crisp snapshot of the Menderes era, and a realistic portrayal of a Taurus Mountains Yörük community, who have elsewhere had pages of idealistic nonsense written about them.

Dark Journey, his most recent release (found and published several decades after his death), is equally compelling, following the struggles of a poor widow through the early years of the Republic.

Talaat Pasha: Father of Modern Turkey, Architect of Genocide, by Hans-Lukas Kieser. The first English biography of the mastermind of the Armenian genocide. Published 2018.

Tales from the Expat Harem: Foreign Women in Modern Turkey, edited by Anastasia M. Ashman and Jennifer Eaton Gökmen. Heterogenous accounts of local life by 32 foreign women who have either travelled long-term or settled in Turkey.

The Turkish Embassy Letters, by Lady Mary Wortley Montagu. Collection of lively and intelligent letters, written in 1716 when the writer's husband had just been appointed ambassador. One of the most fascinating of early travel writers.

Under a Crescent Moon, by Daniel de Souza. Turkish society viewed through the prism of a foreigner's incarceration during the early 1980s; often blackly funny, and in its empathy the antithesis of Midnight Express.

ART AND ARCHITECTURE

Ancient Civilizations and Ruins of Turkey, by Ekrem Akurgal. Published in Turkey, sometimes sold (for inflated prices) at archaeological sites; comprehensive but beware dated scholarship.

Greco-Roman Cities of Aegean Turkey, by Henry Matthews. An engaging, highly readable overview of Turkey's most impressive Greco-Roman architecture, from ancient Troy to Halicarnassus, with up-to-date insights gleaned from the most recent archaeological work.

Byzantine Architecture, by Cyril Mango. Analysis of the most important churches, about a quarter of these falling within modern Turkey.

Early Christian and Byzantine Architecture, by Richard Krautheimer. Covers the entire empire and all periods, not just Anatolia; first published in 1965, still a standard work.

The Church of Hagia Sophia in Trebizond, by David Talbot Rice. The full story from the head of the team which restored its brilliant frescoes, now sadly removed from view by religious fanatics.

Eastern Turkey: An Archaeological and Architectural Survey, by T.A. Sinclair. Four massive, prohibitively priced volumes (consult a university

library), but it has absolutely every monument east of Cappadocia, with useful maps.

A History of Ottoman Architecture, by Godfrey Goodwin. Comprehensive and definitive, covering every kind of building all over Turkey. Goodwin's other great book is a monograph on Sinan, the greatest of the Ottoman architects.

Imperial Istanbul, by Jane Taylor. Includes all the Ottoman monuments of Bursa and Edirne as well. Very clearly written, but the 1998 edition (still available) has better maps than the 2007 reprint.

Istanbul Architecture, by Murat Gül and Trevor Howells. Excellent summary of all major, and many minor, Istanbul buildings, especially strong on the 19th to 21st centuries, a period neglected by most guides.

CARPETS

Kilim: The Complete Guide: History – Pattern – Technique – Identification, by Alastair Hull and José Luczyc-Wyhowska. Comprehensive illustrated survey of Turkish kilims.

⊙ Send us your thoughts

We do our best to ensure the information in our books is as accurate and up-to-date as possible. The books are updated on a regular basis using local contacts, who painstakingly add, amend and correct as required. However, some details (such as telephone numbers and opening times) are liable to change, and we are ultimately reliant on our readers to put us in the picture.

We welcome your feedback, especially your experience of using the book "on the road". Maybe you came across a great bar or new attraction we missed.

We will acknowledge all contributions, and we'll offer an Insight Guide to the best letters received.

Please write to us at:
Insight Guides
PO Box 7910
London SE1 1WE

Or email us at:
hello@insightguides.com

Kilims: Masterpieces from Turkey, by Yanni Petsopoulos and Belkis Balpınar. Less rigorous but more available than Petsopoulos' rare but definitive Kilims: Flat-Woven Tapestry Rugs (long o/p).

Oriental Rugs: Turkish. Volume 4 of this series, by Kurt Zipper and Claudia Fritzsche. Weaving techniques, symbols and rug categories, plus regional surveys of distinctive patterns – as of the 1980s; market pressures have changed things a bit since.

MODERN TRAVEL WRITING

The Bridge, by Geert Mak. The Galata Bridge and its often louche social milieu is the starting point for a brilliant, alternative summary of the city around it. Mak uses life around the Galata Bridge in Istanbul as a metaphor for the wider country.

Meander: East to West along a Turkish River, by Jeremy Seal. In which Mr. Seal follows the course of the present-day Büyük Menderes in a canoe, with disquisitions on history and vanishing village life en route. A better read than his vastly overrated and (from the title onwards) sophomoric A Fez of the Heart, travels around Turkey in search of a functional fez, the red felt hat banned in 1925.

From the Holy Mountain, A Journey in the Shadow of Byzantium, by William Dalrymple. Starting from Mount Athos in Greece, the author follows the trail of Eastern Christianity into the Middle East. Although only one section is devoted to eastern Turkey, Dalrymple's view of the status of living Christians and their monuments is justifiably pessimistic (though there has been improvement since the early-1990s vintage of the account).

Ottoman Odyssey: Travels through a Lost Empire, by Alev Scott. Through vivid encounters well beyond the borders of modern Turkey, an exiled British-Turkish journalist traces the social legacy of the Ottoman era, contrasting historical realities with present day myths and memories.

South from Ephesus: Travels Through Aegean Turkey, by Brian Sewell. Contrarian art critic's view (reprinted 2012) of pre-mass-tourism coastal Turkey of the 1970s and early 1980s. Both curmudgeonly – the original edition's subtitle was 'An

Escape from the Tyranny of Western Art' – and very funny in spots.

ANTHOLOGIES

Istanbul, A Traveller's Companion, selected and introduced by Laurence Kelly. A wonderful collection of extracts from 14 centuries of writing, arranged around landmark buildings to act as a background guide, which brings to life sites that visitors can still see.

Istanbul, Tales of the City, selected by John Miller. Pocket-sized eclectic collection of prose and poetry, including pieces by Simone de Beauvoir, Disraeli and Gore Vidal.

Living Poets of Turkey: An Anthology of Modern Poems, Translated with a Introduction, by Talat S. Halman (Milet Publishing, Turkey). As it says, and currently the easiest obtainable collection.

FICTION

The Aviary Gate, by Katie Hickman. Gripping historical romance set in the Topkapı Palace harem at the end of the 16th century.

Border, by Kapka Kassabova. Equal parts travelogue, history and memoir, Kassabova recounts tales of border guards, smugglers and refugees past and present in little visited Thrace, at the crossroads of Turkey, Greece and the author's native Bulgaria.

Gardens of Water, by Alan Drew. Family drama and the temptations of the West for the traditionally reared, set against a backdrop of the terrible 1999 earthquakes that devastated northwestern Turkey.

Mehmet My Hawk, by Yaşar Kemal. Until the advent of Orhan Pamuk, the best-known Turkish novelist in translation. This is just one, the most famous, of many novels, some set in and around İstanbul, some epics set in rural Anatolia.

The Rage of the Vulture, by Barry Unsworth. Historical novel by the best-selling author, set in the twilight years of the Ottoman Empire and focusing on Sultan Abdülhamid II.

The White Castle, The Black Book, The New Life, My Name if Red, Snow, The Museum of Innocence, Silent House, A Strangeness in My Mind, The Red-Haired Woman. Novels by Orhan Pamuk. Introspective, perceptive, sometimes over-complex best-sellers by much-lauded contemporary Turkish writer who won the Nobel Prize for Literature in 2006.

The Flea Palace, The Bastard of Istanbul, by Elif Shafak. The first is a sort of Turkish equivalent to Cairo-set The *Yacoubian Building*; the second raised hackles amongst nationalists with its tale of an Armenian-American girl in search of her roots sheltering with a Turkish family. *The Forty Rules of Love* depicts a dissatisfied western woman delving into the sources – and those forty rules, promulgated by the 13th-century mystics Mevlâna and Shams-i Tabriz, and their relationship. Her latest, *Three Daughters of Eve*, follows a Turkish woman in modern, terror-stricken Istanbul, whose memories force her to ponder deep societal rifts over matters of faith, secularism, poverty, wealth and feminism.

Without a Country, by Ayse Kulin. True, timely story tracing four generations of a Jewish family forced to flee Germany in the 1930s, its backdrop an ambitious sweep of modern Turkish history.

FOOD AND COOKING

Classic Turkish Cookery, by Ghillie and Jonathan Başan, introduced by Josceline Dimbleby. A beautifully illustrated book which places Turkish cooking in its geographical and cultural context; the recipes are a practical and authentic introduction to the best of Turkish dishes, gleaned from sources all over the country.

Timeless Tastes, Turkish Culinary Culture, project director Semahat Arsel. Published to celebrate the 40th anniversary (in 1996) of the Divan Hotel, long renowned for its kitchen and its patisserie. The book has several authors: experts on culinary art and history, and professional chefs who give their recipes. This history of Turkish cooking at the most elevated level is illustrated with Ottoman miniatures and engravings.

GUIDES

Aegean Turkey, Lycian Turkey, Turkey's Southern Shore, Turkey Beyond the Maeanders, by George E. Bean. Scholarly specialist guides to the archaeological sites of Turkey, compiled from Professor Bean's research. Mostly out of print, but the 1960s-vintage scholarship has aged relatively well.

Strolling through Istanbul, A Guide to the City, by Hilary Sumner-Boyd and John Freely. First written and published in the early 1970s and one of the first proper guides to the city, this book is still valuable, though it has outlived both of its authors.

The Heritage of Eastern Turkey, From Earliest Settlements to Islam, by Antonio Sagona. Illustrated guide to the archaeology and history of eastern Turkey, from the Neolithic to the Selçuk periods, by one who has spent many seasons excavating in the region.

OTHER INSIGHT GUIDES

There are other Insight Guides which highlight destinations in this region. *Insight Explore: Istanbul* offers a series of walking tours exploring various facets of the city. Insight Fleximaps *Istanbul* and *Turkey* are hard-wearing laminated maps with recommended sights and practical information.

CREDITS

PHOTO CREDITS

123RF 31R, 41, 131T, 174B, 211, 214T, 217, 281, 296, 300T, 300B, 301T, 316T, 332
akg-images 36, 54/55T, 54BL, 55BR, 55TR, 55ML, 360BL, 360/361T, 361TR
Alamy 7ML, 23, 29, 47, 51, 153TR, 159, 163B, 172, 173, 208BR, 209BR, 209BL, 233, 250BR, 250BL, 251BR, 251TR, 294, 297, 307, 323
Ancient Art & Architecture Collection 54/55B
AWL Images 122, 168, 318/319, 320
Bigstock 43, 219T, 315B
Bridgeman Art Library 130
Christie's Images 50
Corbis 18, 72, 74/75, 83, 137
Dreamstime 11B, 35, 39, 40, 134T, 135, 151, 161B, 161T, 165, 171B, 174T, 209ML, 249, 254, 259, 298, 311, 312, 314, 315T, 316B, 328T, 329B, 352B, 356T, 358B
Fotolia 147, 299T
Frank Noon/Apa Publications 1, 6BR, 6BL, 7TR, 7MR, 7BR, 7MR, 8T, 8B, 9TR, 9BL, 12/13, 19T, 20, 24/25, 26, 28, 30, 76, 77, 78, 81, 84, 86, 87, 88, 91L, 92, 93, 94, 95, 96, 98, 99, 100BR, 101ML, 101BR, 114/115T, 114BR, 114BL, 115BR, 116/117, 118/119, 123T, 123B, 131B, 142, 144T, 145, 150, 154/155, 156, 157T, 166, 177, 178, 179, 180, 185T, 185B, 186, 187T, 187B, 190T, 190B, 191, 192T,

192B, 193, 194, 195T, 196, 197, 198T, 198B, 201, 202, 204, 205, 206, 207, 213T, 213B, 214B, 216T, 218, 219B, 220T, 220B, 221, 222T, 223, 225, 227, 228T, 228B, 229, 230, 231T, 231B, 232, 234/235, 236, 237T, 237B, 239, 240, 241, 242, 243, 245B, 245T, 246T, 246B, 247, 248T, 248B, 251ML, 251BL, 252, 253, 256, 257T, 257B, 258T, 258B, 260, 261, 262, 263, 264T, 265, 266, 267B, 268, 269, 270T, 270B, 271, 272, 273, 274, 275, 276B, 276T, 277T, 277B, 279, 280, 285T, 285B, 286, 287B, 287T, 289, 290, 291B, 291T, 304, 305, 306B, 306T, 321T, 321B, 322, 325, 326, 327, 328B, 329T, 330/331, 333, 334T, 334B, 335B, 335T, 338/339, 340, 341B, 341T, 345B, 346T, 346B, 347T, 348T, 348B, 349T, 349B, 350T, 350B, 351, 352T, 353T, 353B, 354, 356B, 357, 358T, 359, 361BR, 361BL, 362, 363, 364, 365B, 365T, 366, 367, 368, 369, 370T, 370B, 371B, 371T, 372, 373, 374
Getty Images 45, 60, 62, 63, 65, 66, 67, 68, 69, 70, 82, 85, 90, 103, 184, 250/251T
iStock 7TL, 7BL, 10, 11T, 21, 22, 44, 71, 79, 80, 104, 105, 106, 110, 113, 115BL, 115TR, 120/121, 134B, 141, 152B, 152MR, 157B, 158, 163T, 167, 171T, 175, 176, 189, 195B, 199, 200, 203, 208/209T, 208BL, 210, 215, 216B,

222B, 224, 255, 264B, 267T, 278, 293, 295, 299B, 301B, 302T, 303, 308, 309, 313T, 317, 336BR, 336/337T, 336BL, 337BR, 337BL, 337TR, 337ML, 344, 345T, 347B, 355, 386, 402
Library of Congress 61
Marcus Wilson-Smith/Apa Publications 37
Mary Evans Picture Library 181, 361ML
Phil Wood/Apa Publications 360BR
Public domain 27T, 27B, 32, 42, 49, 52, 56, 57, 58, 59, 64
Rebecca Erol/Apa Publications 4, 6M, 9BR, 14/15, 16/17, 19B, 33, 34, 89, 91R, 97L, 97R, 100/101T, 100BL, 101BL, 101TR, 102, 107, 108, 109, 111, 112, 126, 127T, 127B, 128, 129, 133, 138B, 138T, 140, 143, 144B, 146, 149, 153BR, 153BL, 164, 376, 378, 379, 380, 381, 383, 389, 394, 396/397, 401
Robert Harding 284
Scala Archives 313B
SuperStock 38, 48, 53, 182/183, 282/283, 302B
TIPS Images 152/153T, 209TR
TopFoto 46
Werner Forman Archive 54BR
Werner Forman Archive/ Topkapi Saray Museum, Istanbul MS Hazine 841 31L

COVER CREDITS

Front cover: Goreme, Cappadocia *AWL Images*
Back cover: Urfa *Dreamstime*
Front flap: (from top) Turquoise Coast *iStock*; Safavid book *Rebecca Erol/Apa Publications*; Iznik tiles *Rebecca Erol/* *Apa Publications*; Istanbul *Rebecca Erol/Apa Publications*
Back flap: Kemer beach *Frank Noon/ Apa Publications*

INSIGHT GUIDE CREDITS

Distribution
UK, Ireland and Europe
Apa Publications (UK) Ltd;
sales@insightguides.com
United States and Canada
Ingram Publisher Services;
ips@ingramcontent.com
Australia and New Zealand
Woodslane; info@woodslane.com.au
Southeast Asia
Apa Publications (SN) Pte;
singaporeoffice@insightguides.com
Worldwide
Apa Publications (UK) Ltd;
sales@insightguides.com
Special Sales, Content Licensing and CoPublishing
Insight Guides can be purchased in bulk quantities at discounted prices. We can create special editions, personalised jackets and corporate imprints tailored to your needs.
sales@insightguides.com
www.insightguides.biz

Printed in China by CTPS

All Rights Reserved
© 2019 Apa Digital (CH) AG and
Apa Publications (UK) Ltd

First Edition 1988
Eighth Edition 2019

Every effort has been made to provide accurate information in this publication, but changes are inevitable. The publisher cannot be responsible for any resulting loss, inconvenience or injury. We would appreciate it if readers would call our attention to any errors or outdated information. We also welcome your suggestions; please contact us at: hello@insightguides.com

www.insightguides.com

Editor: Zara Sekhavati
Author: Marc Dubin, Terry Richardson
Updater: Anthon Jackson
Head of DTP and Pre-Press: Rebeka Davies
Managing Editor: Carine Tracanelli
Picture Editor: Tom Smyth
Cartography: original cartography Lovell Johns, updated by Carte

Legend

City maps

	Freeway/Highway/Motorway
	Divided Highway
	Main Roads
	Minor Roads
	Pedestrian Roads
	Steps
	Footpath
	Railway
	Funicular Railway
	Cable Car
	Tunnel
	City Wall
	Important Building
	Built Up Area
	Other Land
	Transport Hub
	Park
	Pedestrian Area
	Bus Station
	Tourist Information
	Main Post Office
	Cathedral/Church
	Mosque
	Synagogue
	Statue/Monument
	Beach
	Airport

Regional maps

	Freeway/Highway/Motorway (with junction)
	Freeway/Highway/Motorway (under construction)
	Divided Highway
	Main Road
	Secondary Road
	Minor Road
	Track
	Footpath
	International Boundary
	State/Province Boundary
	National Park/Reserve
	Marine Park
	Ferry Route
	Marshland/Swamp
	Glacier Salt Lake
	Airport/Airfield
	Ancient Site
	Border Control
	Cable Car
	Castle/Castle Ruins
	Cave
	Chateau/Stately Home
	Church/Church Ruins
	Crater
	Lighthouse
	Mountain Peak
	Place of Interest
	Viewpoint

CONTRIBUTORS

This new edition of *Insight Guide Turkey* was thoroughly updated by **Anthon Jackson**.
Anthon Jackson, a writer and photographer with a keen interest in the Middle East, first visited Turkey in 2008, returning many times since. As a writer he has contributed to a dozen travel guidebooks since 2011. Currently based in Denmark, he holds a Master of Arts in Arab and Islamic Studies.
This book is based on a previous edition written by Marc Dubin and Terry Richardson.

ABOUT INSIGHT GUIDES

Insight Guides have more than 45 years' experience of publishing high-quality, visual travel guides. We produce 400 full-colour titles, in both print and digital form, covering more than 200 destinations across the globe, in a variety of formats to meet your different needs.
Insight Guides are written by local authors, whose expertise is evident in the extensive historical and cultural background features. Each destination is carefully researched by regional experts to ensure our guides provide the very latest information. All the reviews in **Insight Guides** are independent; we strive to maintain an impartial view. Our reviews are carefully selected to guide you to the best places to eat, go out and shop, so you can be confident that when we say a place is special, we really mean it.

INDEX

MAIN REFERENCES ARE IN BOLD TYPE